THE
Federalists

A STUDY IN ADMINISTRATIVE HISTORY

—

by Leonard D. White

UNIVERSITY OF CHICAGO

THE MACMILLAN COMPANY
NEW YORK
1948

PRINTED IN THE UNITED STATES OF AMERICA

To

CHARLES EDWARD MERRIAM

*In token of
long friendship*

PREFACE

Early in 1790 James Madison wrote his friend, Thomas Jefferson, that the House of Representatives had sent a bill to the Senate for taking a census. "It contained a schedule for ascertaining the component classes of the Society, a kind of information extremely requisite to the Legislator, and much wanted for the science of Political Economy. . . . It was thrown out by the Senate as a waste of trouble and supplying materials for idle people to make a book." Fortunately the Senate reconsidered its decision and happily also it is still possible to "make a book" about the men who managed the affairs of the young Republic, the administrative problems they encountered, and the materials with which they had to work.

These men—Washington, Hamilton, Jefferson, Oliver Wolcott, Timothy Pickering, Albert Gallatin, John Adams, and many others—dealt with most of the administrative problems that presidents and department heads face today, although on a much smaller scale. In public reports, office memoranda, and private letters they gradually built up a philosophy of public management that is remarkably modern. Much hard thinking went on about the public business in the early days when precedents were in the making, thinking of which we have been long unaware.

This volume begins a systematic study of American ideas about public administration. My principal interest has been to explore the origin and growth of the opinions that Americans now possess about public management. These ideas can only be understood in the light of prevailing values and the events, personalities, and institutions from which they are largely derived. Although I have given some notice to the characteristics of society, the flow of events, and the quality of personalities, the emphasis has been placed on the practical problems of government and the formulation of ideas as these problems were surmounted; the background has already been well filled in by others.

The title, *The Federalists,* does not imply that the Jeffersonian Republicans, or Democrats, as they eventually became called, had no ideas about administration or made no contributions to it. They, as well as the Federalists, had views about the management of the public business, but on the national scene they had no opportunity to put them into effect before 1801. From 1789 to 1801 the Republicans gave shape to their philosophy of government and administration, opposed many of the administrative ideas of the Federalists, and at some important points forced the latter to give ground. It was nevertheless the Federalists who manned the ship of state and whose views about administration prevailed during these important twelve years.

A few of the leaders of this generation, notably Alexander Hamilton and Albert Gallatin, thought systematically about administration in the daily round of public business; others in high office operated on a consistent set of often unformulated rules in which was contained a working philosophy of administration—men such as Washington, Wolcott, and Pickering. These men, in what they said and did, had something to contribute to public management that is untouched by time and valid even on the scale of modern administration.

The materials used in the preparation of this study have been almost exclusively drawn from original sources. This was a necessity, since neither historian nor political scientist had preceded me in organizing this special field. Some helpful monographs have been cited in the text, and many others have been consulted, as well as a wide range of general historical works, biographies, and specialized articles. It did not seem necessary to append a bibliography of such materials, which are both easily available and largely irrelevant.

It is useful, however, to indicate the principal sources that contain the history of public administration during this period. They include in one group the *Statutes at Large,* the *Annals of Congress,* the *Executive Journal of the Senate,* the *American State Papers,* the decisions of the federal courts, the *Territorial Papers* edited by Carter, and the *Naval Documents related to the Quasi-War between the United States and France.* In another group are the invaluable collected letters and papers of the public men of the day—Washington, Hamilton, Jefferson, Madison, Adams, King, Ames, and others. Here also may be noted such works as Steiner, *Life and Correspondence of James McHenry,* and Gibbs, *Memoirs of the Administrations of Washington and Adams,* edited from the papers of Oliver Wolcott. A great need of American scholarship is the publication of the collected papers of other men important in the public life of the country.

Unpublished material in the archives is of primary importance for

the history of public administration. Some has been used in this enterprise, but much remains to be explored and organized. The principal
archival data consulted include the papers of Oliver Wolcott and
Timothy Pickering, the Domestic Letters of the State Department, the
Reports of Bureau Officers of the State Department, the Letters from
the Collectors, especially from Portsmouth, N. H., and Providence,
R. I., the Letter Books of the Postmaster General, and the Minute Book
of the federal district court for the first district of Pennsylvania. More
precise bibliographical references to these and other manuscript materials will be found in the text.

It is a pleasure to record here the assistance that I have received from
many sources. The Social Science Research Committee of the University
of Chicago has generously made grants without which it would have
been impossible to compensate for the many obstacles which academic
life perhaps inevitably throws in the way of research. Before its termination the Public Administration Committee of the Social Science
Research Council established a subcommittee on administrative history.
Its members were Solon J. Buck, Archivist of the United States; John
M. Gaus, Harvard University; Julius Goebel, Jr., Columbia University; James Hart, University of Virginia; Roy Nichols, University
of Pennsylvania; Lloyd M. Short, University of Minnesota; and the
present author. Spencer Parratt of Syracuse University also met with
the committee. The advice of these gentlemen was most helpful in the
formative stage of the study. My especial thanks are due to Mr. Buck,
who invited the committee to meet in the National Archives, and who
gave many clues to the great body of invaluable manuscripts over
which he presides. Some of my colleagues at the University of Chicago
also allowed me to form them into a committee for advice and consultation—Bessie L. Pierce, William T. Hutchinson, Floyd W. Reeves,
Max Rheinstein, Louis Wirth, and Jacob Viner. Their help, often
given at the round table in the Quadrangle Club, is deeply appreciated.
Charles E. Merriam undertook the task of reading the manuscript in
an early draft—a responsibility which one can only assign to a friend—
and both at this stage and elsewhere gave me invaluable guidance. The
entire manuscript was read by Don K. Price, associate director of Public Administration Clearing House, and parts were read by Louis
Brownlow and James Hart, each of whom made important suggestions.

My debt to libraries and archives is especially great. The University
of Chicago Library has been my chief reliance for the mass of pub-

lished material. For two summers I enjoyed the friendly hospitality of
the Baker Library at Dartmouth College—an admirable institution
providing excellent working facilities for visiting scholars. Unpublished
manuscript material has been drawn upon in the National Archives,
the Library of Congress, the Library of the Treasury Department, the
Library of the Post Office Department, the Massachusetts Historical
Society, and the Connecticut Historical Society. The cordial assistance
of the directors and staffs of these institutions is gratefully acknowledged.

In 1944 I was invited by Boston University to deliver the Gaspar C.
Bacon Lectures on the Constitution of the United States, and presented
the subject matter of three chapters of this book: George Washington
as an Administrator, the Hamilton-Jefferson Feud, and The Federalist
Ideal of Public Administration. These lectures were subsequently
printed in the *Boston University Law Review*.

My research associate, Jean Schneider, has lived with this book since
its inception. Her skill and diligence in discovering materials, her per-
ceptiveness in analysis, and her high standards of editorial revision
have been an invaluable asset. For the errors and inadequacies I assume
responsibility.

September 1, 1947.   L. D. W.

CONTENTS

xi

LIST OF TABLES

THE FEDERALISTS

Chapter One

THE COURSE OF GOVERNMENT, 1789–1801

O<small>N</small> O<small>CTOBER</small> 25, 1794, the President of the United States was returning from Bedford, Pennsylvania, to the seat of government. While crossing the Susquehanna River, his coach became lodged between two boulders in midstream, and there he was forced to sit in the rain until it could be extricated.[1] Such misfortunes were common annoyances of the time, and we may presume that Washington, a constant traveler, was philosophical in the face of this unwelcome delay. He may well have seized the occasion to reflect upon the great changes which had occurred since the spring day in Philadelphia in 1787 when he was chosen to preside over the work of the Constitutional Convention. He might have taken deep satisfaction in the accomplishments of these few years, despite his anxieties about the outcome of the expedition then on foot to subdue the rebellious whiskey distillers of western Pennsylvania.

The government of the Confederation had steadily run down until its movements had almost ceased. Washington could remember that when he entered New York late in April 1789, to become the first President under the new Constitution, he took over almost nothing from the dying Confederation. There *was,* indeed, a foreign office with John Jay and a couple of clerks to deal with correspondence from John Adams in London and Thomas Jefferson in Paris; there *was* a Treasury Board with an empty treasury; there *was* a "Secretary at War" with an authorized army of 840 men; there were a dozen clerks whose pay was in arrears, and an unknown but fearful burden of debt, almost no revenue, and a prostrate credit. But one could hardly perceive in the winter of 1789 a government of the Union.

A new government had to be created to hold together, if possible,

---

[1] Washington to the Secretary of the Treasury, Oct. 26, 1794, *The Writings of George Washington* (John C. Fitzpatrick, ed., 39 vols., Washington: Government Printing Office, 1931–44), XXXIV, 9; hereafter referred to as *Writings.*

nearly 4,000,000 people concentrated along the Atlantic seaboard, bordered on the north by the British possessions in Canada, on the south and west by Spanish holdings in the Floridas and Louisiana. This vast area, greater by far in extent than any of the European powers and containing resources the nature and value of which could not be guessed, was mostly in the hands of the Indians west of the Alleghenies —a wilderness which was already a powerful magnet to the restless, land-hungry, adventurous citizens of the east. By 1794 fifteen states had been erected within the more settled portions—one (Kentucky) across the mountains—and they were in charge of most matters which government had to undertake for citizens.

Washington could remember, now with a measure of relief, the doubt in many men's minds whether the new experiment would succeed. He knew in 1789 that he was putting his hand to a desperate venture. The Constitution had been adopted only by the narrowest margins and by the utmost effort in a number of states, especially the crucial state of New York. The back-country people were hostile to one more government which could add more taxes to those that they endured, and which might compel payment of their debts at face value to the rich people in the towns and cities. He could recall the dismay caused among all men of property when the farmers of western Massachusetts took up arms under Captain Daniel Shays to close the courts in which judgments on their debts were made against them. He knew the states were jealous of each other and of the general government. He knew that the country fell into three great geographical divisions, each of which seemed large enough to support its independence, and that feeling between the tobacco- and rice-growing south and the mercantile east ran high. Although he could not yet be fully confident that his fellow countrymen would support a central government to bind all into one, he could, in 1794, look back on five years of substantial progress toward this greatest of achievements.

As he balanced his resources in 1794 against those at his command in 1789, he could count great gains. The departments of state had been established and each was making its contribution to national unity. The Treasury had successfully organized the customs and internal revenue services and regular collections were flowing into the coffers of the general government; the credit of the country had been restored by the fiscal legislation of Congress and the operations of Alexander Hamilton; a diplomatic and consular service was stationed abroad; the army had been reorganized and strengthened, and the states quickly produced the 15,000 militiamen that Washington asked for in 1794; the Post Office was steadily extending its routes; federal laws and revenue collections were being enforced in federal courts through federal attorneys and marshals. The wraith of the Confederation had been supplanted by a vigorous new government.

With Washington and Hamilton, Jefferson, Knox, and Timothy Pickering guiding the ship of state from Philadelphia, the public business of the country had proceeded in all its details. Sebastian Bauman received and dispatched the mails in New York and made forward-looking suggestions to the general Post Office; bluff Benjamin Lincoln cleared ships and collected the customs in Boston; Arthur St. Clair struggled through the virgin forests of the Northwest Territory, erecting counties and lecturing the territorial judges; an elusive "villain" steadily robbed the mails between Boston and New York, baffling the Postmaster General and all his subordinates; Stephen Higginson in the north and John Habersham in the south bought supplies for the army and for the naval vessels under control of the War Department; Philip Freneau translated letters for Jefferson and abused the Federalists in the *National Gazette,* while John Fenno maintained the Federalist cause in the *Gazette of the United States.* Truly the machinery of government was in motion.

Washington would have realized, however, that the great administrative structure was still far from perfect; and he would have found no cause for satisfaction in some of the events which were much in his mind. He had already lost Jefferson from his official family; Hamilton he knew was determined to resign in the near future; Knox was leaving the War Department; a minority of Congress, with able leaders, were bitter against the Secretary of the Treasury, were jealous of the executive branch, and were ready to join in the criticism of himself which had already given him much distress. Party spirit and maneuvers, moreover, he saw rising on every side; and these party divisions seemed to him ominously connected with the divergence of interest and opinion between north and south. Weary with office, he had wanted to retire in 1793; but the uncertainty of the times confirmed his deep sense of duty to remain. The very errand, indeed, which took him to Bedford was his greatest anxiety, for the whole moral authority of the government was challenged by the stubborn refusal of the western farmers to pay their federal taxes.

Nor could he have been easy about the threats to peace pouring in across the Atlantic. There had been delay in working out the terms of the treaty of peace with the mother country and new sources of irritation were appearing, especially the impressment of American seamen and interference with American trade. War had broken out between England and France in 1793 and both countries were guilty of assaults on American rights. What was worse, the people had passionately lined up either for France, the traditional friend whose help had won independence, or for Great Britain, the old mother country now fighting a revolutionary movement which seemed to endanger the rights of property everywhere. The moral authority of the government was challenged in Pennsylvania, to be sure, but it was weakened more insidiously and dangerously by the echoes of distant events of Europe in America.

He would not have been as confident as were most Americans in 1790 and 1791 in the first flush of success. It was early in 1790 that he wrote Catherine Macaulay Graham, "That the Government, though not absolutely perfect, is one of the best in the world, I have little doubt. . . . It was indeed next to a Miracle that there should have been so much unanimity, in points of such importance, among such a number of Citizens, so widely scattered, and so different in their habits in many respects as the Americans were." [2] And in the same month the *Gazette of the United States* reported that "the great machine of government for this extensive empire" had been set in motion, and that the great concern now was to adjust "its various movements so as to produce the best good of the whole." [3] Two observers of widely different tastes agreed that the initial results were good. Stephen Higginson, a leading Boston merchant, wrote to the Secretary of War, Henry Knox, that "Habits of industry and frugality are taking place of those of luxury and dissipation, more generally and with more celerity than I expected. . . . there seems to be a general conviction, that the Union must be supported, as the alone Source of national Security; and that every burthen necessary to the Object must be cheerfully bourne. . . . in short the Government of the Union seems now to have a fair prospect." [4] And the Secretary of State, Thomas

---

[2] Jan. 9, 1790, *Writings*, XXX, 496–97.

[3] Jan. 27, 1790.

[4] April 7, 1790, "Letters of Stephen Higginson, 1783–1804," American Historical Association, *Annual Report, 1896*, I, 781–82.

Jefferson, declared, "In general, our affairs are proceeding in a train of unparalleled prosperity." [5]

By 1794 the affairs of the Republic had become far more involved, but still Washington knew that the "important people" stood solidly behind the new government. They had supported Hamilton in the great financial reforms which restored public credit. They had gained a modest degree of protection in the tariff of 1789 and important advantages in the coastwise trade and overseas commerce. They were to rally behind the treaty which Jay brought back from London in 1795, dissatisfied though they were with some of its terms. They spoke energetically and intelligently through their representatives in the House— Ames and Sedgwick of Massachusetts, Boudinot of New Jersey, Harper of South Carolina, Williamson of North Carolina; and in the Senate, Cabot of Massachusetts, Ellsworth of Connecticut, and King of New York.

Who were the "important people" for whom these leaders spoke and upon whom the President leaned for support? With exceptions, they were the landowners: the New England farmers; the New York patroons and holders of estates; the thrifty German farmers in eastern Pennsylvania; the plantation owners of the south. They were the shipowners and shipbuilders of New England and the middle coast. They were the great merchants and enterprisers "to the eastward," and in New York, Philadelphia, Baltimore, and other seaports—the Elias H. Derbys, the Robert Morrises, the Benjamin Stodderts, and the insurance brokers and lawyers associated with the "mercantile interest." They were the clergy, although the sun of their influence was setting. They were the officers of the Revolutionary Army and the socially minded, often ambitious officers of the state militia. They formed the backbone of the Federalist party, whose leaders sat in the high seats of government—in Congress, the courts, and the government offices—from 1789 to 1801. [6]

Washington and Hamilton had a clear understanding of what these people needed from the new government, and they set about to provide

---

[5] Jefferson to C. W. F. Dumas, May 13, 1791, *The Writings of Thomas Jefferson* (Andrew A. Lipscomb and Albert Ellery Bergh, eds., 20 vols., Washington: Thomas Jefferson Memorial Association, 1905), VIII, 197. This edition is hereafter referred to as the Memorial edition.

[6] Dixon Ryan Fox, *The Decline of Aristocracy in the Politics of New York* (New York: Columbia University, 1919), ch. i.

it. They were sensitive to the failures of the country since peace had come to it in 1783,[7] and were determined to wring from unpromising beginnings the future welfare of their country. *Peace* was essential, and Washington could remember with satisfaction his decision of 1793 to stand aside from the war between France and Britain. Could he have then foreseen Adams' success in avoiding war with France in 1798 he would have declared it a contribution to the foremost need of the country. *Confidence* was essential, and Washington could believe in 1794 that it had been largely won. Confidence in the money markets of Europe with respect to the solvency and stability of the new government was now assured. Confidence in the rights of property and contract as protected by the new Constitution seemed fully warranted. Confidence in the capacity of Americans to govern themselves on a national scale was being built up with unexpected speed. Confidence in the power of the government to secure obedience was being demonstrated in western Pennsylvania as Washington took the bumpy road from Bedford back to Philadelphia. *Support* was needed for the public economy and had been forthcoming in the restoration of credit, in aid to shipping and foreign commerce, and in the organization of the Bank of the United States. *Machinery of government* and vigorous administration were needed, and with the touch of Hamilton's genius and the steadiness of Washington, these great national assets had been won—as of 1794.

Such gains in public confidence confirmed the ideas of progress which were characteristic of the time: the concept of the indefinite perfectibility of man and his institutions, the belief that man could determine the main lines of his progress, and the opinion that institutions existed to further progress and that education was one of the principal means. It was still two years before Condorcet was to be translated into an American edition, but Washington, although not a philosopher, would have accepted Condorcet's premises that there were no bounds to the improvement of the human faculties.[8] Franklin had made this point of view familiar to Americans, and in high quarters and low, all would have exclaimed with the Reverend Samuel Still-

[7] For a sympathetic account of the government of the Confederation, see Merrill Jensen, *The Articles of Confederation* (Madison: University of Wisconsin Press, 1940).

[8] M. de Condorcet, *Outlines of an Historical View of the Progress of the Human Mind* (tr. from the French; Philadelphia, 1796), cited in Arthur Alphonse Ekirch, Jr., *The Idea of Progress in America, 1815–1860* (New York: Columbia University Press, 1944), p. 15.

Paine, asserted that while society was a blessing, "government, even in its best state, is but a necessary evil; in its worst state, an intolerable one." These radical views were anathema to the "important people," and Washington had little patience with them. They were, nevertheless, like the undeveloped state of communications, among the difficulties which an energetic government had to face.

Washington's contribution to the new government was principally political and administrative in nature. These were essential ingredients to the success of the new regime, but there were also great financial and economic tasks to be undertaken. Washington had contributed little personally to the solution of these problems, but he had given a free hand to his closest adviser, Alexander Hamilton. The President was not at home in this field and had taken no part in the congressional battles over assumption, funding, provision for payment of the debt, and creation of the Bank; when Jefferson reproached him on these matters, he merely replied that time would furnish the test of their wisdom. Time had given Washington satisfaction; he had told Congress more than once of the restoration of American credit, and in 1794 the way seemed clear to the regular reduction and eventual liquidation of the public debt.

Washington might well have reflected on a program to develop the estate of the American people as soon as the debt was out of the way. He had not yet invited Congress to do much. He would remember that Congress had not yet responded to the recommendations of his first annual address, in which he urged the promotion of manufactures to render the country independent of others, especially for military supplies; uniformity in currency, and weights and measures; the encouragement of invention; the development of post roads; and the promotion of science and literature. This was a relatively modest program, and as it turned out, was nearly the full measure of his recommendations for internal improvements. Washington would have thought, in 1794, of a national university, of premiums and aids to agriculture to encourage experiments and the diffusion of better methods of farming, of government establishments for the manufacture of military supplies, and of better roads and bridges. He would not have ventured much farther.

Hamilton, whose great contribution to the new government was principally administrative and economic, would have gone much farther, and at the invitation of Congress had already outlined a national program for economic development. Washington's political judgment restrained him from publicly espousing this program and much of it never reached the statute book. Its national implications were great, but preoccupation with affairs across the Atlantic set aside these domestic matters.

Such were the plans for the subject matter of administration. The more detailed aspects of the management and conduct of business also had made their appearance, and Washington could recount in memory the succession of problems which had come to his desk and the solutions which he, his department heads, and Congress had worked out. The method of communication with Congress on appointments and of consultation on treaties, the extent of congressional reliance on executive leadership in policy and its administration, the discovery of a dividing line between policy and administration, the extent of executive discretion in expenditures, the power of Congress to investigate expenditures and to call for the papers of the executive, an independent branch—all these stood at one level. At another were problems of the internal management of the departments and the control of the field services, the relations of one department to another, the best means of making government purchases, the standards for selection of officers and employees, and the methods of carrying on the complex fiscal operations of the government. These operating problems led Washington into much detail, and he had proved a ready master of them. At still another level was a group of arrangements with which Washington had less to do than Congress—the determination of the law of officers, the bounding of their discretion, the assurance of their responsibility for wrongful acts and at the same time their protection in the performance of duty.

In the middle of his second term the President was already looking forward to retirement, and thoughts of Mount Vernon must have mingled with those of his official cares. He had already determined to demonstrate to the world the supreme achievement of a democratic government—the peaceful and orderly change of the head of the state in accordance with the voice of the people, a change involving no interruption to the business of government. He could not foresee what deep emotion would be stirred in the hearts of his countrymen at the sight of this spectacle. John Adams later was to tell his wife, "A solemn scene it was, indeed; and it was made more affecting to me by the presence of the General, whose countenance was as serene and unclouded as the day. . . . In the chamber of the House of Representatives was a multitude as great as the space could contain, and I believe scarcely a dry eye but Washington's. . . . All agree that, taken altogether, it was the sublimest thing ever exhibited in America." [10] And Robert Goodloe Harper was to write his constituents that Washington "probably never appeared greater; and certainly his appearance never excited more sensibility or more admiration." [11]

But in 1794 Washington could not foresee these events, nor those of Adams' administration which he was to witness. He could not guess that he would have to send an ultimatum to Adams to secure his wishes in the organization of the Provisional Army in 1798; he could guess perhaps that Hamilton would continue a power but he could hardly imagine that Adams' Cabinet would defer to Hamilton, a private citizen practicing law in New York, rather than to their official superior; he could hardly believe that a President would indulge in an angry tirade to force one department head to resign and would summarily discharge another.

As he sat in his coach on October 25, 1794, he knew not these events beyond the horizon. He knew, however, that the experiment in self-government was well on its way. He knew the thirteen original states had organized stable governments under written constitutions and were conducting the civil affairs of their people in peace and order. He had helped to establish a general government with powers over a wide range of common interests, which had quickly earned respect and support. Prosperity had returned after the trying days of the Confederation. The first challenge to the authority of the new government, raised by the whiskey-distilling farmers of western Pennsylvania, was being met firmly and decisively, but with no spirit of vengeance.

Throughout the length and breadth of the United States a new system of public offices had been organized to carry on the business of the federal government. This business, to be sure, was yet limited in scope, but it was essential to the very existence of the great experiment. Upon its successful performance rested the fate of the new Republic. Nowhere in the history of the world had a republican government undertaken to organize so vast an area. Nowhere on such a

---

[10] Adams to Abigail Adams, March 5, 1797, *The Works of John Adams* (Charles Francis Adams, ed., 10 vols., Boston: Little, Brown and Company, 1850–56), I, 506–7.
[11] March 13, 1797, in *Papers of James A. Bayard, 1796–1815* (Elizabeth Donnan, ed.), American Historical Association, *Annual Report, 1913*, II, 29.

scale had any people tried to set up a system of government whose executive and administrative agencies were so directly responsible to popular assemblies. That stability, competence, impartiality, and integrity in the management of the public business could be achieved with such a degree of democratic control was unproved, and to a skeptical world seemed unlikely.

As the President made the slow and uncomfortable journey back to Philadelphia amidst the autumn colors of 1794, he could feel confidence in the prospect of success in this great governmental experiment of the New World. An English visitor had already written, "The government is the government *of* the people, and *for* the people." [12] With rising expectation the President could recall his charge to the nation in his first inaugural—". . . the preservation of the sacred fire of liberty and the destiny of the republican model of government are justly considered, perhaps, as *deeply,* as *finally,* staked on the experiment intrusted to the hands of the American people." It was an experiment in administration as well as an experiment in politics and the art of self-government.

---

[12] Thomas Cooper, *Some Information Respecting America* (London, 1794), p. 53.

Chapter Two

"AN EFFICIENT AND RESPONSABLE EXECUTIVE"

Early in 1790 President Washington wrote to one of his friends: "I always believed that an unequivocally free and equal Representation of the People in the Legislature, together with an efficient and responsable Executive, were the great Pillars on which the preservation of American Freedom must depend."[1]

The Constitutional Convention, over which Washington presided, had laid the foundation for the kind of executive that he believed essential. The Convention had established a strong executive branch, placed at its head a single magistrate, with powers and duties of his own, elected independently of Congress but responsible to it and to the people.

THE CONVENTION AND THE EXECUTIVE

The executive models before the Convention were the English kingship and cabinet council, the Committee of the States, and the chief magistrates of the thirteen "sovereign" states. The history which the Convention recalled was the history of colonial governors, and the very brief record of government under the Articles of Confederation and the respective states. The event which was seldom absent from memory was Shays' rebellion. The ruling consideration was not the revolutionary ardor of the 1770's but the sober necessity of order, commercial recovery, and fiscal rehabilitation. No one could be sure that the states would be saved from fatal commercial warfare, from ruinous fiscal devices, or from the devastating effects of mere distance. No one could assert with confidence that the three great regions—eastern, middle, and southern, each as great geographically as most European nations—would not go their own ways, leaving the West to its fate. No one

---

[1] Washington to Catherine Macaulay Graham, Jan. 9, 1790, *Writings*, XXX, 496.

could be certain that enough power would be lodged in a common government and organized with sufficient energy to permit the infant Republic effectively to meet its foreign and its domestic problems. "Our affairs," said John Jay in a moving passage, "seem to lead to some crisis, some revolution—something that I cannot foresee or conjecture. I am uneasy and apprehensive; more so than during the war." [2] The record of the times was not promising.

A strong executive was attained in the Convention only by the hardest and most persistent fighting. At the outset Edmund Randolph had proposed an executive of three, in order to represent the major geographical divisions and to put "the remote parts" on an equal footing with the center.[3] He was successfully opposed by James Wilson who "preferred a single magistrate, as giving most energy, despatch, and responsibility, to the office." In an executive of three equal members, Wilson saw "nothing but uncontrolled, continued, and violent animosities; which would not only interrupt the public administration, but diffuse their poison through the other branches of government, through the states, and at length through the people at large." [4]

To secure an independent executive branch was even more difficult than to secure a single magistrate at its head. Less than two weeks from final adjournment, with the issue still undecided, Wilson confessed that this matter was "in truth the most difficult of all on which we have had to decide." [5] Roger Sherman of Connecticut spoke for many when he declared that the executive magistracy was "nothing more than an institution for carrying the will of the legislature into effect; that the person or persons ought to be appointed by, and accountable to, the legislature only, which was the depository of the supreme will of the society." "An independence of the executive on the supreme legislature was, in his opinion, the very essence of tyranny, if there was any such thing." [6] To which Gouverneur Morris replied that

---

[2] Jay to George Washington, June 27, 1786, *The Correspondence and Public Papers of John Jay, 1763–1826* (Henry P. Johnston, ed., 4 vols., New York: G. P. Putnam's Sons, 1890–1893), III, 204.

[3] Jonathan Elliot, ed., *The Debates in the Several State Conventions on the Adoption of the Federal Constitution . . . together with the Journal of the Federal Convention* (2d ed., 4 vols., 1836; Vol. 5, Supplementary, 1845, Washington: Printed for the editor), V, 141, 149.

[4] *Ibid.*, V, 141, 150.

[5] *Ibid.*, V, 509.

[6] *Ibid.*, V, 140, 142.

if the executive were not independent, "usurpation and tyranny on the part of the legislature will be the consequence." [7] And James Madison declared, "Experience had proved a tendency in our government to throw all power into the legislative vortex. The executives of the states are in general little more than ciphers; the legislatures omnipotent. If no effectual check be devised for restraining the instability and encroachments of the latter, a revolution of some kind or other would be inevitable." [8]

The Convention did not propose, however, to set up an executive free of all responsibility to the legislature, although the extreme advocates of an independent executive, led by Charles Pinckney and Rufus King, fought for it. The President became responsible to the legislative branch by impeachment. With Randolph "the propriety of impeachments was a favorite principle," and Madison joined in supporting some provision to defend the community against "the incapacity, negligence, or perfidy of the chief magistrate." [9] On this point Randolph carried the day.

In addition, the Convention provided that the concurrence of the Senate was necessary to validate important appointments. Three major fields of policy and administration were thus subjected to the influence of the Senate: *the army,* by means of confirmation of all commissioned officers; *the foreign service,* by confirmation of ambassadors, ministers, and consuls; and *the civil service,* by confirmation of the more important civil appointments. By a last minute decision, however, Congress was authorized to vest the appointment of such inferior officers as they thought proper in the President alone, in the courts of law, or in the heads of departments.[10] The appointment of judges was also subject to senatorial confirmation.

Furthermore it was understood that the executive branch was bound by law. This fundamental obligation, a prescription drawn from the long course of English constitutional history, was implicit in the clause vesting the legislative power in Congress. Offices were established by

---

[7] *Ibid.,* V, 323.

[8] *Ibid.,* V, 327. The Convention rejected a proposal to create an executive council, and other proposals to make the Chief Executive to some degree dependent on the executives of the states.

[9] *Ibid.,* V, 341, 342.

[10] Max Farrand, ed., *The Records of the Federal Convention of 1787* (4 vols., New Haven: Yale University Press, 1911, 1937), II, 627. The initial vote on this modification was a tie, 5 to 5, but when put a second time was carried unanimously.

law, apart from a few mentioned in the Constitution—not by executive fiat. Another constitutional provision affecting the course of administration at every point was the requirement, growing out of colonial experience with royal governors, that no money could be drawn from the Treasury except as authorized by law. As a consequence, offices and employments could be created only with the consent of Congress and as underwritten by an appropriation, annually reconsidered. The power to declare war and make peace was vested in Congress, not in the executive; the power to make treaties was shared with the Senate; and the President was allowed to act as commander in chief of the state militia only when it was called into active duty.

Nevertheless, the President was endowed with the capacity of initiative, both in policy and in administration. Upon the President was conferred "the executive power"; he became commander in chief of the armed forces; he was to see that the laws of Congress were enforced; he nominated all important officials, military, judicial, and civil, including foreign representatives; he received foreign ambassadors and by implication conducted foreign relations; he was the legatee of whatever the Convention, Congress, and later generations would agree to read into the phrase, "the executive power."

On matters of policy the President had authority to "give to the Congress information of the state of the Union, and recommend to their consideration such measures as he shall judge necessary and expedient"—an authority which in both foreign and domestic policy gave him the right and opportunity to lead Congress as far as presidential personalities, congressional susceptibilities, and (eventually) party affiliations would permit.

In making these major decisions concerning the chief magistrate the Convention overrode the fears of its minority. Steering a novel course between the great powers of the English king and the feeble powers of most state executives, the Convention recommended a chief magistrate strong enough to lend energy and dispatch to the general government. With the irresolute plural executive of the Confederation drifting ineffectively at the head of government in the very city in which the Convention gathered, it was relatively easy to concentrate executive authority in one; but it required boldness and determination to recommend to the factious states and liberty-loving citizens a chief magistrate with power so vast that monarchy seemed to some only one step away.

Military command, foreign negotiations, the initiative in domestic policy, the direction of the departments of state, the appointment of the judiciary, the military, and high civil officials with the confirmation of the Senate, and of many inferior officers without it, the qualified veto over acts of Congress, the capacity for reelection—these powers and qualities of the chief magistrate demonstrated the intention of the majority of the Convention to concentrate executive authority in the interest of effective government. The Convention would perhaps not have concurred with Hamilton that "the true test of a good government is its aptitude and tendency to produce a good administration." [11] It intended, nevertheless, so far as the constitutional framework was concerned, to secure the foundation of effective administration, free from the possibility of interference by the states, and deriving authority from the people themselves.[12]

Although General Washington did not participate in the debates concerning the character and powers of the presidency, he listened attentively, we may assume, to all that was said.

THE ADMINISTRATIVE POWER

While the Constitutional Convention thus laid good foundations, much would depend on the attitude and decisions of Congress in the formative years. These, in turn, would depend on the character and personality of the President, as well as upon the powers vested in the legislative branch. Fortunately for the future of the executive agency, the first President commanded the widest respect and confidence, especially during the crucial years of 1790 and 1791. Members of Congress were the more ready to accept the essential implications of an independent executive when discretion was to be exercised at the outset by a man whose integrity and patriotism were beyond question. No member, no committee of Congress, no party sought to lay hands on the independence of the executive branch, although there were many differences of opinion concerning the exact boundaries of responsibility.

---

[11] *The Federalist* (Edward Gaylord Bourne, ed., New York: Tudor Publishing Co., 1937), No. 68.

[12] This study is not concerned with the extent and limitations of executive power as defined in the Constitution and decisions of the Supreme Court. This phase of executive power is dealt with in all works on constitutional law and in such studies as Edward S. Corwin, *The President: Office and Powers* (New York: New York University Press, 1940), and Norman J. Small, *Some Presidential Interpretations of the Presidency* (Baltimore: Johns Hopkins Press, 1932).

In these early years Congress took care to maintain the unity of the executive branch by vesting the great bulk of administrative authority in the President and by placing him in a position to direct the affairs of every subordinate officer.[13] The laws required all major and many minor decisions to be made by the President himself; his agency was involved at every turn.

(1) Certain general continuing powers were vested in his office. They included prescribing the duties of the heads of departments (Treasury excepted), and their obligation to act in accordance with his instructions—an over-all, inclusive grant of administrative power. All loan and debt transactions were made subject to his approval.[14] The direction of the armed forces, already placed in his hands by the Constitution, was specifically confirmed by statute. He nominated or appointed and removed officers. Finally, each use of the seal of the United States required his consent.

(2) A large number of specific continuing authorities were vested directly in the President by statute. He was required to sign patents

---

[13] This aspect of the matter is dealt with in the next chapter.

[14] The initial draft of the first bill authorizing a loan put the business in the hands of the Secretary of the Treasury. Madison secured an amendment to give the President both the power to effect the loan and to direct its application. *Annals of Congress,* II, 1584–85 (May 19, 1790).

The frequent citations to the *Annals* require explanation, due to confusion in their printing. Laurence F. Schmeckebier in *Government Publications and Their Use* (2d ed., Washington: Brookings Institution, 1939), pp. 119–20, makes the following statement. "The *Annals* comprise 42 volumes, covering the first 17 congresses and the 1st session of the 18th (1789–1824). Some volumes are for a single session, some for a portion of a session, a few for an entire congress, and some for portions of two sessions. The volumes are not numbered on the title pages, but numbers have been assigned and generally appear on the back titles. . . .

"This series is generally known as the *Annals of Congress,* following the half title. The full title is *The Debates and Proceedings in the Congress of the United States; with an Appendix, Containing Important State Papers and Public Documents and All the Laws of a Public Nature; with a Copious Index.* The series is occasionally cited as *History of Congress,* which is the running head on the pages. Volumes 1 and 2 for the 1st Congress are duplicated by another compilation with the same title page (as regards wording, but not typography) and imprint date (1834), but with the running page head 'Gales and Seaton's History of Debates in Congress.' The text in the two sets is apparently the same, but they are not printed from the same type, and after the first few pages the text breaks differently at the end of each page. . . . Why two sets with different make-up should have been published in the same year is somewhat of a mystery." Schmeckebier also notes that "The pages have two columns, and each column is numbered as if it were a page."

References in this book are to the edition with the running head "History of Congress." Use of dates in citations will facilitate access to either edition of the *Annals.*

for inventions. He had to approve each contract for building a lighthouse. He established and modified many administrative districts. He made regulations governing trade with the Indians. He prescribed rules for the distribution of prize money among officers and crew. These are merely examples of scores of such specific grants.

(3) Many *ad hoc* powers were also laid in his hands. Thus he was required to devise a form for a land patent, and a passport for vessels. He was authorized to lay an embargo, to make individual exceptions, and to revoke the embargo in his discretion. He was authorized to order aliens to leave the country, or to license them to remain; and in case they returned after deportation, to keep them in prison at his discretion. He approved a contract for the purchase of copper for the Mint, and was directed to collect information on the copper mines south of Lake Superior. He was authorized to erect two docks. He was directed to prohibit travel on the trace from Knoxville to Price's settlement if the Indians objected. These, too, are only examples of a host of *ad hoc* administrative authorities placed in the President's office. Congress vested duties large and small in the single office of Chief Executive rather than in the offices subordinate to him. Their execution he might delegate to one or another of his "assistants," but not his ultimate responsibility.

Embedded in these provisions was a congressional acceptance of the superior position of the President in relation to department heads. This understanding was first developed in 1789 in the debate over the removal power. It was restated in the course of debate in 1793 by John Steele who declared that "the Secretary is only a finger of his hand." [15] It was explored further by William Smith of South Carolina a couple of months later, when he argued (probably stating Hamilton's views):

Between the Chief Magistrate and his immediate agents either a general discretion or instruction must be presumed, because it is presumable he [i.e., the President] will do his duty, and punish where either a discretion has not been allowed, or instructions have not been given, or where those instructions have been contravened. . . .

To go further . . . the Secretary had, *virtute officii,* a legal authority to [act] . . . according to law, without instructions. . . .

---

[15] *Annals,* III, 794 (Jan. 5, 1793); in 1789 Sedgwick had said, "all officers concerned in Executive business . . . were the eyes and arms of the principal Magistrate, the instruments of execution." *Ibid.,* I, 613 (June 29, 1789).

He did not, however, intend that the doctrine here advanced should touch the question as to what official propriety might have required between the Chief Magistrate and the Secretary. It was the point of legality only which he meant to examine. In all Executive functions relating to the finances, the Secretary must be considered as the agent of the President, and the Legislature must take it for granted, where the contrary is not manifest, that the relation has been properly attended to. . . .[16]

The argument that a department head had, by virtue of his office, authority to act without instructions from the President was denied by Madison [17] and was not pressed at this time. It was clearly the intent of Congress to vest administrative authority in the Chief Executive rather than in lesser administrative agents. Practice, as will soon become apparent, confirmed the doctrine.[18]

THE POWER TO REMOVE

Within three weeks after the first inauguration a major crisis was brewing in Congress concerning the relation of the President to the heads of departments and by necessary implication to the whole system of administration. The issue arose in connection with the bill to create the Department of Foreign Affairs, which in its first draft specifically authorized the President to remove the Secretary without requiring the advice and consent of the Senate. This proposal, which was in harmony with the idea of presidential control of departmental affairs, was instantly challenged. For five days in June it completely absorbed the attention of the House and precipitated the first major constitutional debate. It revealed a difference of opinion concerning the nature of the presidency and of its relations to administration that was deeply significant.

The constitutional aspect of the problem has often been dealt with and will be dismissed briefly in order to concentrate attention on its administrative phase. Four major constitutional theses were put forward: (1) that the power to remove was an inherent part of the executive power conferred by the Constitution upon the President alone; (2) that the power to remove was incident to the power to appoint and must follow the constitutional requirement established for appointment, i.e., the advice and consent of the Senate were necessary for re-

---

[16] *Ibid.*, III, 915, 917 (March 1, 1793).

[17] *Ibid.*, III, 942.

[18] See especially ch. iii, pp. 32–36.

moval of officials whose appointment required Senate concurrence; (3) that the office of Secretary was established by law, and that Congress could consequently attach any conditions not forbidden by the Constitution, including the condition that the incumbent could be removed only with the consent of the Senate; (4) that the only method of removing the head of a department was by impeachment.

The fundamental *administrative* problem was whether the responsibility for the interpretation and execution of the laws and the supervision of administration should lie in the President alone or be divided between the President and the Senate. Although the central feature of the debate turned on the meaning of the Constitution, the practical consequences of the alternative decisions were explored and both sides argued as well from the standpoint of "expediency" as of constitutional necessities. Eventually by a safe although not too impressive majority in the House, the advocates of presidential responsibility for administration triumphed; but in the Senate only the casting vote of the Vice President saved the day.[19]

The most extreme view against presidential authority over department heads was proposed and stubbornly defended by William Smith of South Carolina, although he made only one convert to his position. He argued that the only method of dispossessing the head of a department was by impeachment. He considered apparently that these officials held by permanent tenure unless guilty of high crimes and misdemeanors. It would follow that the President would have little or no control over them and their work.[20]

Theodorick Bland of Virginia suggested more solid ground on which the opponents of presidential removal could stand. "A new President," he declared, "might, by turning out the great officers, bring about a change of the ministry, and throw the affairs of the Union into dis-

---

[19] Adams, *Works*, I, 449–50.

[20] *Annals*, I, 457 (June 16, 1789). This is the same William Smith who was to become a leading Federalist and a loyal follower of Hamilton. In 1797 he acknowledged his early error in a letter to James McHenry: "If you look into the Debates of Congress you will find this subject [removals] fully handled; I was on that occasion on the wrong & Madison on the right side. . . ." *Sewanee Review*, XIV (1906), 87. Smith also claimed that office was a species of property which should not be held at the mere will of the President. *Annals*, I, 458. In analogous vein, Judge Livermore of New Hampshire argued that the personal reputation of a Secretary would depend "on the single will of the President, who may ruin him on bare suspicion." This, said Livermore, contradicted all his notions of propriety; every person ought to have a hearing before he is punished. *Ibid.*, I, 479.

order: would not this, in fact, make the President a monarch, and give
him absolute power over all the great departments of Government?" [21]
Whether Bland was in effect subscribing to the concept of parliamentary responsibility and a titular Chief Executive we cannot be sure.
This interpretation is feasible, although improbable. In any event he
definitely opposed the absolute power of the President over department
heads. Elbridge Gerry concurred in this point of view,[22] and so apparently did James Jackson of Georgia. Jackson, indeed, urged that
the heads of departments enjoyed constitutional status and had rights
conferred by the Constitution.[23]

The danger to liberty which was implicit in a strong executive was
the steady undercurrent of the arguments of this group, nowhere
more cogently put than by John Page of Virginia.

The doctrine of energy in Government, as I said before, is the true doctrine of tyrants. . . . Energy of Government may be the destruction of
liberty; it should not, therefore, be too much cherished in a free country.
A spirit of independence should be cultivated. . . .
The liberty and security of our fellow-citizens is our great object, and
not the prompt execution of the laws. Indecision, delay, blunders, nay, vil-
lainous actions in the administration of Government, are trifles compared to
legalizing the full exertion of a tyrannical despotism. . . .[24]

Members of Congress who argued in the opposite sense were keenly
aware of the administrative consequences of senatorial confirmation
of removals. They buttressed their constitutional arguments with appeals to the need for effective unity, energy, and responsibility in the
execution of law. The basic position in favor of permitting the President to remove a department head without securing the consent of the
Senate was put by Madison in the first day of the debate in these
words:

It is one of the most prominent features of the Constitution, a principle
that pervades the whole system, that there should be the highest possible
degree of responsibility in all the Executive officers thereof; any thing, therefore, which tends to lessen this responsibility, is contrary to its spirit and

---

[21] *Ibid.,* I, 381 (May 19, 1789).
[22] *Ibid.,* I, 473 (June 16, 1789).
[23] *Ibid.,* I, 530 (June 18, 1789).
[24] *Ibid.,* I, 550-51.

intention, and, unless it is saddled upon us expressly by the letter of that work, I shall oppose the admission of it into any act of the Legislature. Now, if the heads of the Executive departments are subjected to removal by the President alone, we have in him security for the good behaviour of the officer. If he does not conform to the judgment of the President in doing the executive duties of his office, he can be displaced. This makes him responsible to the great Executive power, and makes the President responsible to the public for the conduct of the person he has nominated and appointed to aid him in the administration of his department. . . .[25]

And later he repeated the argument even more effectively:

Vest this power in the Senate jointly with the President, and you abolish at once that great principle of unity and responsibility in the Executive department, which was intended for the security of liberty and the public good. If the President should possess alone the power of removal from office, those who are employed in the execution of the law will be in their proper situation, and the chain of dependence be preserved; the lowest officers, the middle grade, and the highest, will depend, as they ought, on the President, and the President on the community. . . .[26]

Others emphasized this concept of the presidential office, especially Fisher Ames and John Laurance. The former replied to Gerry,

The Executive powers are delegated to the President, with a view to have a responsible officer to superintend, control, inspect, and check the officers necessarily employed in administering the laws. The only bond between him and those he employs, is the confidence he has in their integrity and talents; when that confidence ceases, the principal ought to have power to remove those whom he can no longer trust with safety. . . .

. . . more injury will arise from not removing improper officers than from displacing good ones. I believe experience has convinced us that it is an irksome business; and officers are more frequently continued in place after

---

[25] *Ibid.*, I, 379 (May 19, 1789).

[26] *Ibid.*, I, 499 (June 17, 1789). See also his very interesting comments in a letter to Randolph, May 31, 1789, in *Letters and Other Writings of James Madison* (4 vols., published by order of Congress, Philadelphia: J. B. Lippincott, 1865), I, 474–75; and in a letter to Randolph, June 17, 1789, in which he writes, "On the contrary construction . . . by degrees, the Executive power would slide into one branch of the Legislature; on the most favorable supposition it would be a two-headed monster." *Ibid.*, I, 477. This edition of the Madison letters will hereafter be cited as the Congressional edition.

they become unfit to perform their duties, than turned out while their talents and integrity are useful. . . .[27]

Laurance flatly asserted, "I contend, that every President ought to have those men about him in whom he can place the most confidence, provided the Senate approve his choice." [28]

The administrative incompetence which would result from any other solution was pointed out by more than one member of the House. Abraham Baldwin argued that if there should be a "resentment" between the President and the heads of departments, the one or the other ought to be removed. "They must not go on pulling different ways, for the public will receive most manifest injury." [29] Egbert Benson commented on the danger of "perpetual discord," and declared that without presidential authority to remove, "the administration of the Government [would] become impracticable." [30]

Elias Boudinot of New Jersey exposed the practical consequences of the proposal for senatorial approval of removals of department heads by pointing out that if the President should request concurrence in removal, the Senate would be bound to make an investigation of the facts.

Who, then, are the parties? The supreme Executive officer against his assistant; and the Senate are to sit as judges to determine whether sufficient cause of removal exists. . . . But suppose they shall decide in favor of the officer, what a situation is the President then in, surrounded by officers with whom, by his situation, he is compelled to act, but in whom he can have no confidence. . . .[31]

After several days of acute and thoughtful debate, the power of the President to remove the Secretary of Foreign Affairs without requiring the consent of the Senate was confirmed by the test vote of 30 to 18.[32]

---

[27] *Annals,* I, 474, 476 (June 16, 1789).
[28] *Ibid.,* I, 485 (June 17); Theodore Sedgwick, after insisting upon the need for an effective means of removal in case of insanity, a belated discovery of lack of talents, the development of vicious habits, a total neglect of office, an odious and unpopular policy, or an effort at personal aggrandizement, dramatically asked, ". . . is there no way suddenly to seize the worthless wretch, and hurl him from the pinnacle of power?" *Ibid.,* I, 460 (June 16).
[29] *Ibid.,* I, 559 (June 19).
[30] *Ibid.,* I, 507 (June 17).
[31] *Ibid.,* I, 468–69 (June 16).
[32] *Ibid.,* I, 580 (June 22).

The final vote was 31 to 19.[33] As a consequence, the administrative system was firmly anchored to the Chief Executive.

The true intent of the Constitution concerning the location of the power to remove an officer appointed with the consent of the Senate, interpreted in this debate and apparently conclusively settled, was reopened by the Tenure of Office Act (1867) and again by a displaced postmaster in 1926. The same basic constitutional differences of opinion arose.[34] The administrative consequences of senatorial participation in the removal power would have been the same in 1789 as in 1926; at any time they would have been fatal to unity, energy, and responsibility in the executive. The decision of 1789, therefore, to recognize that the power to remove lay with the Chief Executive was of crucial importance in the early formation of the presidential office.

Neither the Constitutional Convention nor the first Congress was hesitant in concentrating executive and administrative authority in the hands of a responsible President.

---

[33] *Ibid.*, I, 585.
[34] *Myers* vs. *United States*, 272 U.S. 52 (1926).

Chapter Three

WASHINGTON AND HIS ASSISTANTS

THE Constitutional Convention had displayed a notable lack of interest in the organization of the executive branch, apart from the office of the Chief Magistrate. It was assumed, and incidentally mentioned a couple of times, that there would be departments to handle the foreign affairs of the country, the army, and the fiscal business. There was no debate concerning the number, powers, responsibility, or duties of the heads of departments. They were barely recognized in the Constitution in the phrase authorizing the President to secure their opinions in writing.

From his inauguration on April 30, 1789, to mid-September Washington was a President without an organization other than that which carried over in an acting capacity from the Confederation period. Jay continued temporarily as Secretary of Foreign Affairs. Treasury business was transacted by the old Treasury Board until Hamilton took office on September 11. General Knox remained as Secretary of War and his new appointment to the same office took effect on September 12, 1789. Edmund Randolph was appointed Attorney General on September 26, and Samuel Osgood was reappointed Postmaster General. It was not until March 22, 1790, that Thomas Jefferson arrived in New York to become Secretary of State.[1]

The establishment of these departments and offices required the formation of detailed working relations between the President and the great state officials. These relations were highly important in themselves and also did much to determine the character of the presidency as an administrative office. Whether the actual exercise of the power to govern would remain where the Convention had placed it, or would settle in the hands of ministers on the British pattern, was the first problem to be determined by events.

---

[1] Washington postponed much business until the government was organized; for example, see *Writings*, XXX, 350.

26

VIEWS OF WASHINGTON, HAMILTON, AND ADAMS

Washington had not been in office a month before he defined his future relations to his department heads, none of whom had yet been appointed. In a letter to the French minister he said, "The impossibility that one man should be able to perform all the great business of the State, I take to have been the reason for instituting the great Departments, and appointing officers therein, to assist the supreme Magistrate in discharging the duties of his trust." [2] The President looked upon the Secretaries (they were often called ministers at the outset) as *assistants,* not as rivals or as substitutes.

All major decisions in matters of administration and many minor ones were made by the President. No department head, not even Hamilton, settled any matter of importance without consulting the President and securing his approval. All of them referred to the President numerous matters of detail as well as large and many small issues of administrative policy. Jefferson told William Short quite bluntly that "the nature of our government . . . renders it's heads [i.e., the President and Senate] too responsible to permit them to resign the direction of affairs to those under them. The public would not be satisfied with that kind of resignation, & be assured it does not exist. . . ." [3] Washington accepted full responsibility as a matter of course, and throughout the eight years of his service there is no indication of a tendency to consider department heads other than dependent agencies of the Chief Executive.[4]

---

[2] Washington to Comte de Moustier, May 25, 1789, *ibid.,* XXX, 334.

[3] Sept. 30, 1790, *The Works of Thomas Jefferson* (Federal edition, Paul Leicester Ford, ed., 12 vols., New York: G. P. Putnam's Sons, 1904–05), VI, 147. This edition is hereafter referred to as the Federal edition.

[4] Washington, however, took full advantage of their counsel and was deferential to their views. Writing to the Secretary of War on Saturday afternoon, Feb. 25, 1792, he said, "I have given the enclosed draft of a letter to Captain Brandt a careful perusal. Such additions as are made with a pencil *may* be adviseable; but, after you have given them an attentive consideration, they may *stand* or *fall* as you shall think best." *Writings,* XXXI, 484–85. Writing to Jefferson about British affairs on April 4, 1791, Washington concluded concerning different lines of action, "The option is therefore left to your judgment as events may make the one or the other the part of propriety." *Ibid.,* XXXI, 268. Again in January 1792, he wrote Jefferson, "Enclosed is the rough draught of a letter to G. M. [Gouverneur Morris]. I pray you to examine it and alter any word, or sentence you may think too strong; or the whole of it, retaining my object; from which I shall make a fair copy, and then take a press one; be not scrupulous therefore in making the alterations you judge necessary." *Ibid.,* XXXI, 467. And the next month, "The P—— has put one or two queries in the Margin of the Report *merely* for consideration." *Ibid.,* XXXI, 487.

In *The Federalist,* Alexander Hamilton had taken a position similar to that of Washington. His statement is so full of interest that it requires quotation in full.

The administration of government, in its largest sense, comprehends all the operations of the body politic, whether legislative, executive, or judiciary; but in its most usual, and perhaps its most precise signification, it is limited to executive details, and falls peculiarly within the province of the executive department. The actual conduct of foreign negotiations, the preparatory plans of finance, the application and disbursement of the public moneys in conformity to the general appropriations of the legislature, the arrangement of the army and navy, the directions of the operations of war,—these, and other matters of a like nature, constitute what seems to be most properly understood by the administration of government. The persons, therefore, to whose immediate management these different matters are committed, ought to be considered as the assistants or deputies of the chief magistrate, and on this account, they ought to derive their offices from his appointment, at least from his nomination, and ought to be subject to his superintendence. . . .[5]

This paragraph contains one of the earliest formal definitions of public administration. It also makes clear Hamilton's theoretical position concerning the subordinate status of department heads in relation to the President. It conforms to the view which he had expressed in the Convention a year before.[6]

Whether privately Hamilton looked toward the British cabinet system, in which ministers played an important and at times a dominant role in public policy with the support of a party majority in the House, is uncertain. His early relations with the House suggest the possibility.[7]

---

[5] *The Federalist,* No. 72.

[6] To be subject to the superintendence of the President did not, however, mean to Hamilton that all departmental business should be submitted to him. In a letter to McHenry he wrote, "I cannot adopt the opinion, *that every measure, in all its circumstances,* which may involve considerable expenditure, should be submitted through the Secretary of the appropriate department to the President for his approval, and that, without such approval, formally and explicitly announced, no act leading to its execution should take place. . . .

"A precise rule for distinguishing the different cases is impracticable; it must be matter of sound discretion and of fair confidence on all sides." *The Works of Alexander Hamilton* (2d ed., Henry Cabot Lodge, ed., 12 vols., New York: G. P. Putnam's Sons, 1903), VII, 172.

[7] Especially his cultivation of requests from the House directly to the Secretary for reports on public policy. This connection was fought by Jefferson and apparently was

A recent student of Hamilton, L. K. Caldwell, leans in the direction of this interpretation. "Essentially," he concludes, "Hamilton was advocating the centralized constitution of Great Britain with a representative parliament of broadest authority, but with the directive power of government safely lodged in a cabinet of zealous ministers acting in the name of a powerful, independent impartial chief executive. It was a system ideally suited to the freest play of Hamilton's executive talents. . . ."

In the *Federalist Papers* Hamilton did not comment on the probable role of parties in the future government of the country, but as Secretary of the Treasury he participated fully in the leadership of the Federalist party. Jefferson indeed thought Hamilton was in complete control of the party; he was certainly its ablest and most prominent leader and as such, on the British pattern, could have aspired to the premiership. His loyal acceptance of Washington's primacy and his theoretical view of the status of a department head precluded any attempt on his part in this direction. No other "minister" possessed the talents or public standing for such a role, unless it was Jefferson.

On a number of vital matters Jefferson differed fundamentally with the policy of President Washington. As long as he remained Secretary of State, however, he carried the President's policies into effect, as he claimed, "as sincerely as if they had been my own, tho' I ever considered them as inconsistent with the honor & interest of our country." [8] Jefferson's solution was resignation.

John Adams held the same general view of the position of department heads as Washington. "The worst evil that can happen in any government is a divided executive; and, as a plural executive must, from the nature of men, be forever divided, this is a demonstration that a plural executive is a great evil, and incompatible with liberty. That emulation in the human heart, which produces rivalries of men, cities, and nations, which produces almost all the good in human life, produces, also, almost all the evil. This is my philosophy of government." So wrote the second President of the United States to his Secretary of State, Timothy Pickering, in 1797. [9] It might have been pondered better by Pickering, in the light of the subsequent relationship between

---

disliked by Washington. The English cabinet system of the 1790's was of course much different from that which took shape after the Reform Act of 1832.

[8] Jefferson to Washington, Sept. 9, 1792, *Works* (Federal ed.), VII, 140.

[9] Oct. 31, 1797, Adams, *Works*, VIII, 560.

these two strong-willed men. With reference to Treasury powers over the stamp tax, Adams wrote to Oliver Wolcott, "But the office of the secretary of the treasury is, in that bill, premeditatedly set up as a rival to that of the President; and that policy will be pursued, if we are not on our guard, till we have a quintuple or a centuple executive directory, with all the Babylonish dialect which modern pedants most affect."[10]

THE PRESIDENT AND DEPARTMENTAL BUSINESS

In their respective *departmental* jurisdictions, Washington recognized the full responsibility of the heads of departments and offices. He searched diligently for men of stature as Secretaries. In 1794 he began looking for a successor to Knox in the War Department and wrote to C. C. Pinckney his specifications:

. . . as the Officer who is at the head of that department is a branch of the Executive, and called to its Councils upon interesting questions of National importance he ought to be a man, not only of competent skill in the science of War, but possessing a general knowledge of political subjects, of known attachment to the Government we have chosen, and of proved integrity. . . .[11]

His general rule of noninterference in departmental business he stated in a letter to the Alexandria collector of customs, ". . . it is not agreeable to me to go into the detail of business with any except the head of the Department to which it belongs, or thro' him with the immediate Agent."[12] In 1791 the President informed the Postmaster General, "that the general post Office being considered as a branch of the revenue department, it is his wish that in all matters of arrangement relative thereto, a communication may be had with the Secretary of the Treas-

---

[10] Oct. 20, 1797, *ibid.,* VIII, 555.

[11] Jan. 22, 1794, *Writings,* XXXIII, 249; cf. Wolcott's characterization of the office of Secretary of the Treasury in 1795: "The office of Secretary of the Treasury is justly viewed as of high consequence to the public; it will be found a very responsible situation, and no man can hold it without being opposed and attacked. Other qualifications than those which respect skill and capacity for the mere business of the treasury will be desirable. . . ." George Gibbs, *Memoirs of the Administrations of Washington and John Adams, edited from the papers of Oliver Wolcott, Secretary of the Treasury* (2 vols.; New York, 1846), I, 178.

[12] *Writings,* XXXII, 417–18.

ury. . . ." [13] The appointment of clerks he left to the Secretaries.[14] The appointment of such important officials as the Comptroller, the Postmaster General, and the Director of the Mint, however, he settled himself, after consultation with his advisers.

There remain records of only rare instances in which the rule was not scrupulously observed, and these were incidental in nature.[15] No Secretary could complain that he was not master in his own house. Of this the most famous demonstration is doubtless Washington's rebuff to the French minister who sought to deal directly with the President rather than through the Secretary of State. "I have, however, been taught to believe," wrote the President in his blandest style, "that there is, in most polished nations, a system established, with regard to the foreign as well as the other great Departments, which, from the utility, the necessity, and the reason of the thing, provides that business should be digested and prepared by the Heads of those departments." [16] Washington did not reach down into departmental operations, although much departmental business rose from subordinate levels to his desk.

TYPES OF OFFICIAL CONTACTS

The initiative in matters requiring the attention of the President was shared by him and his Secretaries. We find some instances in which Washington appeared as the prime mover, many more in which the Secretaries proposed action for the President's consideration or approval, and others in which a complex business was moved forward by a series of initiatives coming from both sides.

The office of President quickly became a busy one. By mid-summer 1789 Washington complained that he had no leisure to read or answer the dispatches that were pouring in upon him from all quarters.[17] A year later he again confided to his friend, David Stuart, that "These public meetings . . . with the references *to* and *from* the different

---

[13] *Ibid.*, XXXI, 349.

[14] *Ibid.*, XXX, 365.

[15] Examples include the President's request to the United States marshals, through his private secretary, Tobias Lear, of the "number of souls" disclosed by the first census (*ibid.*, XXXI, 313, n. 12, letters of July 13, 1791); a letter approving certain proceedings of the Director of the Mint, July 9, 1792 (*ibid.*, XXXII, 84–85); an order to the U. S. attorney for the Pennsylvania district to nol-pros an indictment, March 13, 1793 (*ibid.*, XXXII, 386).

[16] Washington to Comte de Moustier, May 25, 1789, *ibid.*, XXX, 334.

[17] Washington to David Stuart, July 26, 1789, *ibid.*, XXX, 361.

Departments of State . . . is as much, if not more, than I am able to undergo. . . ."[18] John Adams wrote his wife, "The business of all kinds, and writing particularly, out of the habit of which I have been so long, press upon me very severely. . . ."[19] And again he wrote Abigail, "To reconcile you to your fate, I have a great mind to give you a detail of mine. A peck of troubles in a large bundle of papers, often in a handwriting almost illegible, comes every day from the office of —, office of —, office of —, &c., &c., &c. Thousands of sea letters, Mediterranean passes, and commissions and patents to sign. . . ."[20] Both Washington and Adams had to struggle for the "exercise on horseback" which each enjoyed and relied upon to maintain health and energy. But neither quailed before the mass of business which, even in a relatively simple age, their relations with their heads of departments made it essential for them to transact.

Contacts between the President and his department heads were close and unremitting. In the official correspondence there remain hundreds of written communications and records of oral consultation. Washington invited Jefferson, Hamilton, and others to have breakfast with him to discuss matters which often he had transmitted to them on the previous day. He went to his Secretaries' offices to consult them. He was accustomed to send a file to any one of his Secretaries with the request that he come to the President's house on the following day at ten o'clock, or eleven o'clock, with a written or oral opinion. In due course of time these meetings with the heads of departments grew into the Cabinet. Characteristic examples of different types of presidential contacts with department heads appear in the following paragraphs.

(1) Often the exchange of letters with heads of departments conveyed Washington's *approval of plans or actions* which had been submitted to him in writing. Thus, addressing Hamilton on September 18, 1790, "The appointment of that gentleman to negotiate the Loans in Holland, and the Instructions you have given for his government, meet my approbation";[21] and on September 24, 1791, "I . . . have to inform you, that your proceedings with respect to the request of the Minister of France, meet my entire approbation."[22] To Jefferson,

---

[18] *Ibid.*, XXXI, 55 (June 15, 1790).
[19] *Letters of John Adams, addressed to his wife* (Charles Francis Adams, ed., 2 vols., Boston: Charles C. Little and James Brown, 1841), II, 246–47 (March 9, 1797).
[20] *Ibid.*, II, 257 (Dec. 13, 1798).
[21] *Writings*, XXXI, 118.
[22] *Ibid.*, XXXI, 374–75.

March 19, 1791, "The President concurs with the Secretary of State in opinion that. . . ." [23] And to the Secretary of War, April 1, 1791, "Your proceeding upon the intelligence therein contained (which I think truly alarming) meets my entire approbation. . . ." [24] There are instances, of course, in which Washington expressed doubt or disapproval—but of the latter relatively few.

(2) In some cases the letters from Washington conveyed *directions* concerning administrative operations. Thus he outlined the organization of the internal revenue service in a letter of March 15, 1791, to Hamilton, and directed him to "add such instructions to the respective officers, as shall be necessary for their government in the execution of their several offices, in conformity to the Law, and to the tenor of these presents." [25] Another example illustrates Washington's sense of unity of responsibility. "Who is Mr. Rosecrantz?" he asked the Secretary of War in 1792. "And under what authority has he attended the councils of the Indians at Buffalo Creek? Subordinate interferences must be absolutely interdicted, or counteraction of the measures of Governmt, perplexity and confusion will inevitably ensue. No person should presume to speak to the Indians on business of a public nature except those who derive their Authority and receive their instructions from the War Office for that purpose." [26]

(3) From time to time Washington requested his department heads to give *opinions on the constitutionality of acts of Congress*. It is of interest to observe that he consulted Hamilton and Jefferson on constitutional issues as regularly as he did the Attorney General. In the case of the constitutionality of the Bank of the United States, he called upon the Attorney General first, "in whose line it seemed more particularly to be"; [27] but when he received an adverse opinion he turned to Jefferson and then to Hamilton, who alone found the arguments to sustain the validity of his project.

(4) Very commonly Washington wrote his Secretaries for their *opinions on policy questions,* foreign and domestic alike. Thus, for example, we find him writing Jefferson on July 15, 1790, "Have you formed an opinion on the subject I submitted to you on Tuesday [i.e.,

---

[23] *Ibid.,* XXXI, 247.
[24] *Ibid.,* XXXI, 259.
[25] *Ibid.,* XXXI, 238–39.
[26] *Ibid.,* XXXII, 116–17.
[27] *Ibid.,* XXXI, 216.

concerning the seat of the federal government]"; [28] on January 4, 1791, "The P. begs to see Mr. Jefferson before he proceeds further in the Proclamation"; [29] on August 21, 1791, "When you have read the enclosed letters I will converse with you on the subject of them." [30] As the opposition to payment of the tax on distilled liquors mounted in the summer of 1792 in North Carolina, the President asked Hamilton whether "the Governor of that State ought to be written to on the subject." [31] When France asked for the payment of 3,000,000 livres in 1793, Washington desired "that the Secretary will, tomorrow morning, give the President his opinion on the practicability of complying with the Minister's request." [32] The stream of requests for advice was never-ending; and the deadline was usually abrupt.

(5) It is well known that Washington depended on his advisers to *prepare drafts of his public papers;* the evolution of the Farewell Address is a notable example.[33] He regularly circularized the department heads for ideas and material for his annual messages to Congress. In a very human passage in a private letter to Hamilton late in 1790 he wrote, "The article of your Notes which respect the loan in Holland I am somewhat at a loss to frame into a paragraph for the Speech, and therefore pray your assistance. I had got it as pr. the enclosed, but upon a revision, it does not appear right. Be so good therefore as to new model, and let me have it (if convenient to you) this afternoon. . . ." [34]

(6) With Jefferson and his successors in the State Department, particularly, there is a stream of letters designed to give *information*. Thus on June 19, 1790, Washington wrote the Secretary of State, "The enclosed Letters and documents from Mr. Gouvr. Morris are sent for the perusal of the Secretary of State. The private letters from the Marquis de la Fayette and Mr. Payne he also gives Mr. Jefferson a sight of; because there are some ideas in the latter which are new, and in the former general information respecting the Affairs of France. . . ." [35]

These examples must suffice to illuminate the daily interplay between

---

[28] *Ibid.,* XXXI, 69.

[29] *Ibid.,* XXXI, 191.

[30] *Ibid.,* XXXI, 343.

[31] *Ibid.,* XXXII, 137.

[32] *Ibid.,* XXXII, 336.

[33] Victor Hugo Paltsits, ed., *Washington's Farewell Address* (New York: New York Public Library, 1935).

[34] *Writings,* XXXI, 161.

[35] *Ibid.,* XXXI, 56.

the President and the heads of departments.[36] They are selected to illustrate the normal, rather than the crisis situations which developed from time to time.[37] They confirm William Blount's view of the officers of government, that "none of them eat the Bread of idleness."

The flow of business and the means of dealing with it during these early years fortunately were reported in detail by one of the principal participants, Thomas Jefferson. After he became President he sent a circular to the heads of departments describing the practice under both Washington and Adams. The essential portion follows:

Having been a member of the first administration under Gen Washington, I can state with exactness what our course then was. Letters of business came addressed sometimes to the President, but most frequently to the heads of departments. If addressed to himself, he referred them to the proper department to be acted on: if to one of the secretaries, the letter, if it required no answer, was communicated to the President, simply for his information. If an answer was requisite, the secretary of the department communicated the letter & his proposed answer to the President. Generally they were simply sent back after perusal, which signified his approbation. Sometimes he returned them with an informal note, suggesting an alteration or a query. If a doubt of any importance arose, he reserved it for conference. By this means, he was always in accurate possession of all facts and proceedings in every part of the Union, and to whatsoever department they related; he formed a central point for the different branches; preserved an unity of object and action among them; exercised that participation in the suggestion of affairs which his office made incumbent on him; and met himself the due responsibility for whatever was done. During Mr. Adams' administration, his long and habitual absences from the seat of government, rendered this kind of communication impracticable, removed him from any

---

[36] In the light of contemporary affairs it may be added that in June 1790, after his illness, Washington went on a three-day fishing trip, taking Jefferson and others with him. The *Pennsylvania Packet* of June 12, 1790, carried a dispatch as follows: "*New York*, June 10.—Yesterday afternoon the PRESIDENT of the United States returned from Sandy Hook and the fishing banks, where he had been for the benefit of the sea air, and to amuse himself in the delightful recreation of fishing. We are told he has had excellent sport, having himself caught a great number of sea-bass and black fish—the weather proved remarkably fine, which, together with the salubrity of the air and wholesome exercise, rendered this little voyage extremely agreeable, and cannot fail, we hope, of being very serviceable to a speedy and complete restoration of his health." Taken from William Spohn Baker, *Washington After the Revolution, 1784–1799* (Philadelphia: J. B. Lippincott, 1898), p. 183.

[37] For some of these crisis situations, see below: Hamilton–Jefferson feud, pp. 222 ff.; resignation of Randolph, pp. 170–71.

share in the transaction of affairs, and parcelled out the government, in fact, among four independent heads, drawing sometimes in opposite directions. That the former is preferable to the latter course, cannot be doubted. It gave, indeed, to the heads of departments the trouble of making up, once a day, a packet of all their communications for the perusal of the President; it commonly also retarded one day their despatches by mail. But in pressing cases, this injury was prevented by presenting that case singly for immediate attention; and it produced us in return the benefit of his sanction for every act we did. Whether any change of circumstances may render a change in this procedure necessary, a little experience will show us. But I cannot withhold recommending to heads of departments, that we should adopt this course for the present, leaving any necessary modifications of it to time and trial. . . .[38]

FEDERALIST DOCTRINE

The early dominance of the Chief Executive in the field of administration was due in part to the strength of Washington's public position; in part to the express requirements of the Constitution and of the laws, which specified the agency of the President for many types of public business; in part to the importance which even insignificant matters acquired as precedents; in part to the relatively small scale of public affairs, the convenience with which the President and heads of departments could meet and confer, and his capacity to deal with detail. It was also deeply affected by the personal characteristics of Washington as an administrator.

Only two department heads, Hamilton and Jefferson, had sufficient force of character or stock of ideas to permit any effective influence on Washington's practice in the exercise of his powers and in the determination of general policy. Washington did not well understand commerce and finance, and was inclined to follow Hamilton in these areas. He had his own views, however, on foreign policy and on major issues was his own foreign secretary. In military matters he was completely at home, and the incompetence of his third Secretary of War, James McHenry, forced him to take the lead in a field which was congenial to him.

When the Federalists turned over the government to Jefferson in 1801 they left behind them a clear and consistent pattern of executive relationships. They fully accepted the statement of the Constitution

---

[38] Nov. 6, 1801, Jefferson, *Works* (Federal ed.), IX, 310–12.

that the executive power was vested in the President. Their representatives in the legislative branch wrote this theory into the statutes conferring administrative authority. Their members in the executive branch put into practice what the Constitution and law enjoined. Washington made the decisions of executive policy, but on the basis of regular conference with department heads. The rise of the Cabinet as an organ of consultation and advice did not obscure the single responsibility of the President or the subordinate position of Cabinet members. Even after the Federalists had split into factions during Adams' administration, the leading figures on both sides agreed in maintaining the unity of executive power and the dominating position of the President. The power to govern was quietly but certainly taken over by the President. The heads of departments became his assistants. In the executive branch, according to Federalist orthodoxy, the President was undisputed master.

Chapter Four

THE DUTY TO CONSULT

As soon as Washington had appointed the heads of departments he established the practice of transacting business only after it had been considered and referred to him by one of the Secretaries or the Attorney General. Since he had postponed as much as possible during the spring and summer of 1789, and since everything had to be done to put the new government into motion, the pressure of work was extreme. Hamilton, Knox, and after March 1790, Jefferson were in and out of the President's house constantly on the affairs of their respective agencies.

EARLY PRECEDENTS

It was not long before matters of state came to Washington's desk for decision which concerned more than one department, or were of such importance that he was unwilling to rely merely on the advice of the Secretary who was most directly concerned.[1] He naturally turned to his other department heads or to advisers elsewhere for counsel. Before the departments had been organized he asked the opinions of Adams, Hamilton, Madison, and Jay on the advisability of a tour of the United States.[2] In October 1789, he consulted Hamilton, Knox, Madison, and Jay individually with regard to making an eastern tour;[3] and at the same time he discussed with Hamilton, Madison, and Jay the propriety of taking some informal means of sounding out the British government's intention of giving up the western posts and entering into a commercial treaty.[4] In February 1790 a question arose

---

[1] Early speculations about a privy council and the various attempts by the Constitutional Convention to establish one are fully summarized by Henry Barrett Learned, *The President's Cabinet* (New Haven: Yale University Press, 1912).

[2] Washington, *Writings*, XXX, 319–22.

[3] *The Diaries of George Washington, 1748–1799* (John C. Fitzpatrick, ed., 4 vols., Boston and New York: Houghton Mifflin, 1925), IV, 14, 15, 16, 17.

[4] *Ibid.*, IV, 16, 17.

in his mind concerning his power to negotiate with the Indian leader, McGillivray; he consulted Knox and asked him to get the opinions of Jay and Hamilton.[5] Two months later Knox made a report on the sale of certain lands by Georgia; Washington talked it over with Hamilton and then "placed it in the hands of the Secretary of State to consider."[6] In July 1790 he asked the opinion, individually, of the heads of departments, John Adams, and John Jay, concerning the state of British relations.[7] In August, Tobias Lear, his secretary, headed a document, "Quaeries to and opinions of the Vice President—the heads of the Departments and Chief Justice of the U.S." The President had asked only for separate opinions.[8]

On the constitutionality of the bill to establish the Bank of the United States, Washington first addressed the Attorney General, Edmund Randolph (February 1791), then Jefferson, and then Hamilton; they gave individual opinions and apparently did not meet with the President.[9]

In the spring of 1791 Washington was absent on his southern journey. From Mount Vernon he wrote the three Secretaries, "to express my wish, if any serious and important cases should arise during my absence, . . . that the Secretaries for the Departments of State, Treasury, and War may hold consultations thereon. . . ." If necessary the President undertook to return to Philadelphia, and in addition gave a power to the Secretaries to proceed: "Or should they determine that measures, relevant to the case, may be legally and properly pursued without the immediate agency of the President, I will approve and ratify the measures, which may be conformed to such determination."[10] This authority, although exceptional and limited to matters on which the direct agency of the President was not required by law, clearly provided for the possibility of *collective* action by the heads of the departments, and gave advance assurance of presidential validation. In accordance with this authority, a consultation was held on April 11, 1791, with reference to foreign loans, and on May 7 the President expressed his approval.[11]

---

[5] *Ibid.,* IV, 90.

[6] *Ibid.,* IV, 124–25, 126–27.

[7] *Ibid.,* IV, 139, 142.

[8] Washington, *Writings,* XXXI, 102, n. 78.

[9] *Ibid.,* XXXI, 216.

[10] April 4, 1791, *ibid.,* XXXI, 272–73.

[11] Washington to the Secretary of the Treasury, *ibid.,* XXXI, 285–86; to the Secretary of State, June 17, 1791, *ibid.,* XXXI, 299.

Washington's letters and memoranda disclose meetings with "the heads of the Great Departments" on November 26, 1791, and December 28, 1791, on foreign affairs and military matters respectively [12] and in 1792 at least three such meetings took place.[13] Others may have been held. These were genuinely Cabinet meetings. The crisis in foreign affairs which developed in 1793 brought about conferences with such frequency that by the end of the year the Cabinet as an institution for consultation and advice was firmly established. Many precedents, however, remained to be worked out, and Washington felt under no obligation to call together the heads of departments on all important matters. The day he returned to Philadelphia from his rendezvous with the troops advancing against the western Pennsylvania whiskey distillers he spent in conference "from eight to four" with Hamilton and Randolph, going over the negotiations with the rebellious excise taxpayers. William Bradford, the Attorney General, was away; Knox was not invited.[14]

The President occasionally directed the heads of departments to meet without him for collective consideration of some problem on which Washington wanted advice, even when he was at the seat of government.[15] Typically, however, the President met with his Secretaries, often on less than twenty-four hours' notice and frequently with a command to each to bring a written opinion on the subject under consideration. When the President was about to leave for Mount Vernon in June 1794, he gave a blanket authority to the Secretaries to act collectively during his absence. "In the interim, occurrences may happen, out of the common rotine [sic] which might suffer by delay. Where this is the case, and the matter is of importance, advise with the other

---

12 *Ibid.*, XXXI, 428, 453; also probably a similar meeting about Dec. 10, 1791, on the tariff. *Ibid.*, XXXI, 442.

13 See Learned, *op. cit.*, pp. 125–26 for an account of two of them; and Mary L. Hinsdale, *A History of the President's Cabinet* (Ann Arbor: George Wahr, 1911), pp. 12–13.

14 MS. in the National Archives, Domestic Letters of the State Department, VII, 177; hereafter referred to as State Dept., Domestic Letters.

15 For an example see Washington, *Writings*, XXXIII, 34 (July 29, 1793). Another case is noted by William Vans Murray in 1796: "Cabinet business is conducted by the Three conjointly—for instance Randolph was directed by the P. to address the B. minister in a memorial on the provision orders—& was desired to lay it before the other heads of Departt & the attorney Genl.—& they thought it too fiery & hostile for that season of our negociation & refused their consent." Bernard C. Steiner, *The Life and Correspondence of James McHenry* (Cleveland: Burrows Brothers, 1907), p. 166.

Secretaries and the Attorney General, and carry any unanimous opinion into effect, without suspending the execution for my decision thereon; but advise me thereof by Post."[16] This authority put the Secretaries *pro tanto* in the possession of presidential powers, but it was exceptional and did not indicate any general acquisition of independent power of collective action by the Cabinet.

It is important to grasp the fact, however, that *matters of administration* were almost entirely departmental in nature and those that came to the attention of the Chief Executive were settled between the President and the heads of departments individually. Occasionally an interdepartmental problem arose. The President decided such matters without recourse to Cabinet advice. For example, we may note Washington's decision to keep the Post Office in the Treasury, not to transfer it to the State Department. Rarely, an administrative matter was turned over to the Cabinet for consideration, such as the utilization of the collectors of customs as agents to enforce the Neutrality Proclamation of 1793.[17] This, however, had become involved in the Hamilton-Jefferson feud.

Although Washington uniformly asked for advice, he retained the power to decide all matters except (as already noted) when away from the seat of government. Cabinet opinions were not infrequently divided, Jefferson usually comprising the minority, occasionally joined by Randolph. Washington did not debate a case with his advisers, but listened to their arguments or read their written opinions and then decided the issue. The Cabinet, nevertheless, assumed considerable importance as a frequently convening advisory council, dealing with matters of high policy, especially in relation to the conduct of foreign affairs. The power of the President to require "opinions in writing" had grown into an institution.

THE CABINET UNDER JOHN ADAMS

When John Adams became President in 1797, the practice of Cabinet meetings was therefore well established.[18] Adams of course was cognizant of the custom. The new President retained Washington's Secre-

---

[16] Washington to the Secretaries of State, Treasury, and War, June 16, 1794, *Writings*, XXXIII, 403.

[17] See below, ch. xviii.

[18] According to Learned the first reference to the Cabinet (as "the great council of the nation") in Congress occurred on April 25, 1798, *Annals*, VIII, 1552, cited in Learned, *President's Cabinet*, p. 138. The term, cabinet, had been used earlier in the newspapers, *ibid*. See also Hinsdale, *op. cit.*, p. 15.

taries [19] and continued the practice of close consultation with them on all important matters of public business. His Cabinet first met two days after his inauguration, and frequently thereafter, even through the subsequent crises between him and the department heads. [20]

President Adams was as attached to his country house in Quincy as George Washington had been to Mount Vernon. [21] Washington had set the precedent of occasional absences from the seat of government to take a tour through New England and later through the south as well as to relax on his plantation on the Potomac. He was away during eight years at least 181 days. [22] He took much care to clear up business before he left, depended on the mails to permit him to continue to transact public affairs, and always held himself ready to return in case of emergency.

Washington's personal dominance permitted such absences without danger of loss of control. Adams followed the precedent, indeed amplified it, for he was gone 385 days in four years, sometimes several months at a time. [23] These absences were much longer than any which occurred

[19] Richard Hildreth states, "Wolcott certainly, and probably also the other cabinet officers, had tendered their resignations; but Adams had declined to accept them, and the cabinet remained as Washington left it." *The History of the United States of America* (6 vols., New York: Harper and Brothers, 1849–52), V, 45.

[20] The full account of Adams' relations to his department heads is reserved for later exposition in ch. xx.

[21] As Vice President he was restive away from his home. In 1796 he wrote his wife, "I will not sit here in summer, in all events. I would sooner resign my office. . . . Other gentlemen of the Senate and House are frequently asking leave of absence; but my attendance is perpetual, and will, if continued much longer, disorder my health, which hitherto has been very good. But I want my horse, my farm, my long walks, and, more than all, the bosom of my friend." Adams, *Works*, I, 490. Hamilton wrote him a somewhat sharp letter on September 9, 1792, asking him to return to Philadelphia. *Ibid.*, VIII, 514–15.

[22] James D. Richardson, *A Compilation of the Messages and Papers of the Presidents, 1789–1902* (10 vols., New York: Bureau of National Literature and Art, 1903), VII, 364.

[23] *Ibid.* Putting together the evidence available in contemporary letters, it appears that Adams left Philadelphia about July 27, 1797 (two weeks after the adjournment of Congress), and returned November 10, 1797 (three days before Congress reconvened). In 1798 he left the seat of government about July 25 and returned about November 20. Next spring Congress ended on March 3, 1799, and Adams was on his way to Quincy March 11, returning to Trenton on October 10 after repeated requests for his presence. Adams' reluctance to leave Quincy he put in these terms to Stoddert: "But you must be sensible that for me to spend two or three months at Trenton with unknown accommodations, cannot be very agreeable. Alone, and in private, I can put up with any thing; but in my public station, you know I cannot" (September 4, 1799, Adams, *Works*, IX, 19). In 1800 he left Philadelphia sometime before June 30, and returned to Washington on November 1, to begin business for the first time in the new "federal city."

during Washington's two terms of office. Nor was Adams careful to clear up departmental business before he departed from the seat of government; Gibbs states that he left in 1798 without notifying either Pickering or McHenry; and that in 1799 he left "precipitately." [24] Adams expected the department heads to communicate regularly with him on their respective affairs, and promised not to be away from his summer home in Quincy more than one day at a time. He certainly did not expect them to take advantage of Cabinet meetings in his absence to formulate policy or to make decisions. Adams' leadership of the Cabinet, however, was less firm than Washington's, and there developed a tendency toward independent collective action. In 1800 the Secretary of the Treasury asserted to James McHenry, "Mr. Stoddert, Mr. Dexter, and myself, govern this great nation." [25] During 1798 McHenry, seeking to protect himself against presidential wrath, began asking for Cabinet opinions to support his official acts during Adams' absence. This went on until the end of the year, when Wolcott suggested that written official opinions ought not to be called for except by the President.[26] McHenry was doubtless unaware of the implications of his action.

Despite mounting strains, the President continued a courteous and deferential attitude toward his Cabinet, and in the last months of his term dealt with a reconstituted Cabinet in the same vein. With rare but crucial exceptions, Adams took full advantage of the advice of the department heads. The exceptions were Adams' personal decisions in the spring of 1797 to reopen negotiations with France and in the fall of 1799 to send the second mission to France without further delay. Most of the Cabinet were outraged by this failure to consult and Picker-

[24] Gibbs, *Memoirs*, II, 90, 248.

[25] Oliver Wolcott to McHenry, July 18, 1800, *ibid.*, II, 382. Benjamin Stoddert was Secretary of the Navy; Samuel Dexter was then Secretary of War.

[26] Steiner; *McHenry*, p. 351, n. 2. Analogous cases had occurred under Washington's administration. On May 2, 1794, Edmund Randolph asked the Secretaries of Treasury and War whether any steps should be taken on a petition of John Leamy (State Dept., Domestic Letters, VI, 249). On December 9, 1794, he asked the opinion of the Secretaries of the Treasury and War and the Attorney General on a matter arising out of correspondence with the British minister (*ibid.*, VIII, 3); on December 11, 1794, he wrote a New York merchant indicating that he was consulting the heads of departments on his own responsibility (*ibid.*, VIII, 7); and on August 18, 1795, he wrote them asking whether they thought the President needed to take action on a letter from Governor Blount (*ibid.*, VIII, 377). It is doubtful whether McHenry was acquainted with these precedents which in any event are not to be understood as suggesting an independent source of executive action.

ing, at least, began to talk about another Federalist for President in 1801.

Adams asserted his authority in May 1800, removing Pickering and requiring McHenry to resign. The explosion raised the whole issue of the relative position of the President and the department heads, and sooner or later Adams, Hamilton, Wolcott, McHenry, and Pickering expressed their views on the problem. The precise issue was not the power of the President to remove (although even here some reservations appeared) but rather *the duty of the President to consult* before reaching a decision on matters of policy.

At the time Adams declined to make any public justification of his action, but in his *Letters to the Boston Patriot* in 1809 he put his position clearly. After referring to the British system in which, as he said, the ministers are everything, he continued,

Here, according to the practice, if not the Constitution, the ministers are responsible for nothing, the President for every thing. He is made to answer before the people, not only for every thing done by his ministers, but even for all the acts of the legislature. Witness the alien and sedition laws. In all great and essential measures he is bound by his honor and his conscience, by his oath to the Constitution, as well as his responsibility to the public opinion of the nation, to act his own mature and unbiased judgment, though unfortunately, it may be in direct contradiction to the advice of all his ministers. . . .[27]

Despite his growing hatred of Adams, Alexander Hamilton was obliged to take substantially the same position, although insisting that a President was under an obligation to consult his ministers. In his pamphlet on *The Public Conduct and Character of John Adams,* Hamilton put his views in these terms:

A President is not bound to conform to the advice of his ministers. He is even under no positive injunction to ask or require it. But the Constitution presumes that he will consult them; and the genius of our government and the public good recommend the practice.

As the President nominates his ministers, and may displace them when he pleases, it must be his own fault if he be not surrounded by men, who for ability and integrity deserve his confidence. And if his ministers are of this character, the consulting of them will always be likely to be useful to himself and to the state. . . .

[27] Adams, *Works,* IX, 270.

The stately system of not consulting ministers is likely to have a further disadvantage. It will tend to exclude from places of primary trust the men most fit to occupy them.[28]

Wolcott took the same position on the issue of consultation. In a letter to Hamilton, a year after the event, he said,

The peculiar indelicacy of his conduct [i.e., Adams'], consisted first, in encouraging an expectation that the mission would be suspended until a change of circumstances occurred; secondly, in availing himself of opinions so far only, as they could serve his own concealed views; and thirdly, in deciding contrary to what was expected, without hearing the arguments of the officers on a collateral point, which he well knew they deemed of great importance. It must be evident, that no man's character can be safe, when opinions can be required in a partial manner. Justice demanded either that the Secretaries should not be at all consulted, or that they should be permitted to record their sentiments respecting any points which in their judgment were connected with the general question of the mission.[29]

McHenry and Pickering took quite different ground. Although they were less specific, they seemed to imply that a President should not remove heads of departments for a difference of opinion, no matter how profound. "Mr. Adams," said McHenry, "affects to consider a President of the United States as every thing in government and the heads of departments little more than mere clerks. I cannot subscribe to this hypothesis. Do not the heads of departments like him hold a high and responsible station in government? In offering advice to a President, do they not perform an incumbent duty?"[30] Adams, he said, should "conciliate his ministers by a conduct, which does not reduce them, on great occasions, to ciphers in the government and, by this means, endeavor, at least, to restore mutual confidence and harmony of action."[31]

Pickering took the more extreme position that it was the duty of a department head to combat the President if he thought the President's policy was unsound. "I do not subscribe to all Mr. Stoddert's opinions on the duty of Heads of Departments. Particularly that of *implicit obedience,* or *resignation.* On the contrary, I should think it their duty

---

[28] *The Works of Alexander Hamilton* (J. C. Hamilton, ed., 7 vols., New York: John F. Trow, 1850–51), VII, 687–726 at 708.

[29] Oct. 2, 1800, Gibbs, *Memoirs,* II, 278.

[30] Steiner, *McHenry,* p. 418.

[31] *Ibid.,* p. 420.

to prevent, as far as practicable, the mischievous measures of a wrong-headed president." [32] This theory was also Pickering's practice. At what point, if any, Pickering thought it became the duty of a Cabinet member to resign was not clear.

Pickering's objective was not, however, to establish the Cabinet as an autonomous or competing center of administrative action. He had no design to set up the English cabinet system or to transfer the real authority to govern from the President to the heads of departments. He stood for the right of Secretaries to differ from the policy of their principal and still continue as members of his advisory council. Pickering insisted upon the duty of the President to consult on all important measures, and on the duty of department heads to exert themselves to mold the President's views into accordance with their own. But he went further, and declined to recognize that where deep differences of views on policy existed, unity and energy and responsibility in government required the resignation of subordinate assistants.

CABINET UNITY

Washington commenced his first administration with three Secretaries selected for their eminence in diplomacy, finance, and war and Indian affairs respectively; for due representation of the three great geographical divisions of the country; and, in two cases at least, for their capacity to advise intelligently on general political problems. Hamilton and Jefferson rapidly moved away from each other. Washington tried for over a year to hold together a body of advisers deeply divided among themselves. The effort failed and Jefferson resigned. [33] In 1795 the President wrote Pickering, then acting Secretary of State, "I shall not, whilst I have the honor to Administer the government, bring a man into any office, of consequence knowingly whose political tenets are adverse to the measures which the *general* government are pursuing; for this, in my opinion, would be a sort of political Suicide; that it wd. embarrass its movements is most certain." [34]

During the remainder of Washington's administration there was no disposition by heads of departments to depart from their obligation

---

[32] Pickering to McHenry, Feb. 13, 1811, *ibid.,* p. 568.
[33] See below, ch. xix.
[34] Sept. 27, 1795, Washington, *Writings,* XXXIV, 315.

to support the general policy of the government; Washington, indeed, dominated the group by reason of his personal qualities and public position.

The concept of unity among the President's intimate advisers that Washington espoused in 1795 was strongly and effectively supported in the House of Representatives by one of its leading Federalist members, Robert Goodloe Harper. In 1798, rebutting Republican criticism of a supposed "resolution . . . formed by the Executive to employ, in official stations, none but those who were known to approve the political system adopted by the Administration," he made a reasoned defense of just such a policy.

But what did this supposed determination, at which gentlemen expressed such alarm, amount to? Simply to this—that the Executive, in conducting those concerns of the Government wherewith it is exclusively charged, and for the management of which it is solely responsible, should employ such persons as subordinate agents, as were known to agree with him in opinion about the right mode of conducting them. Was this anything so extraordinary? Was it not practised by every man of common understanding in the management of his own private affairs? . . .

And shall the President of the United States, in conducting the affairs of this Union, neglect those plain and ordinary maxims of prudence, which every man observes in his private affairs? The Executive is charged with the foreign relations of the country, and with the whole execution of all its laws. The greatest differences of opinion that exist among us, arise from these relations. The Executive has adopted a certain system as to the manner in which they ought to be conducted. This system is disliked and opposed by one set of men, while another description approves and supports it. The whole question is, whether the subordinate agents, who are to execute this system under the orders of the President, shall be chosen from among those who like it, or those who think it radically wrong, and have never omitted any opportunity of attempting to change it? . . .

If the Executive, therefore, has a system in the conduct of those affairs wherewith it is charged, . . . it is its duty to use the most effectual means for carrying it into effect. One of the most efficacious of these means is, to make use of men who, otherwise qualified, believe the system to be right. Such men, consequently, and such alone, ought to be employed; and hence it follows, that for the Executive to neglect this, the determination to do which gentlemen charge against it as an impropriety and even a crime, would be at best an act of folly, if not the breach of a sacred obligation.[35]

---

[35] *Annals*, VII, 874–77 (Jan. 19, 1798).

The Secretary of the Navy, Benjamin Stoddert, took the same position concerning the status and duty of the head of a department. In a
letter to John Adams, written in 1809, he declared, "I did not hold, and
never had held myself at liberty to oppose a measure of yours, and
retain my office. . . ." [36] It was Stoddert and Harper, not Pickering or
McHenry, who forecast the future evolution of the Cabinet.[37]

Twelve years' experience under the Federalists, therefore, served to
establish the practice and habit of consultation between the President
and the heads of departments collectively, but without any implication
that the President was either bound to consult or to accept the advice
that he received. The powers of the executive branch remained in the
office of the President. So far as the conduct of administration in its
narrower sense is concerned, the Cabinet as a collective agency remained unimportant since departmental business continued to be transacted between the President and the head of each department separately. Neither under the Cabinet nor within the office of the Chief

---

[36] Adams, *Works,* IX, 270–71, n. 1.

[37] The idea of Cabinet members' independence was, however, zealously defended by
some, especially when Jefferson was about to take over the presidency. John Steele was
then Comptroller of the Treasury, and wrote his friend John Haywood, Treasurer of
North Carolina, about his prospects if he should accept a necessarily brief appointment
by Adams as Secretary of the Treasury. On December 16, 1800, Haywood replied,
". . . I should feel not only pain but mortification, as a Citizen of the United States,
were I to suppose for one moment, that we are ever to have a President capable of
acting on a scale so narrow and illiberal as to be led to discharge and oust from office
a meritorious and informed Officer merely because he may chance to have been opposed
to his election; or may hold political opinions differing from his own; this I think can
never happen, inasmuch as it would be a Conduct which every liberal and enlightened
mind must unceasingly condemn, and which every man who respected himself must
spurn and shudder at.— . . . Suppose all the Counsellors of a President of the same
political cast and taking precisely the same view of Governmental affairs; where then
would be that collision of opinion and of sentiment which in doubtful cases would
point & lead to safety and to truth?—I take it, a succeeding President is entitled to no
consideration whatever in the appointments made or about to be made by his Predecessor:—when he comes into office if he finds the Departments properly filled, he ought
to rejoice at it:—if he finds any one of them inadequately supported or improperly
filled, either with reference to character or the duties enjoined or expected by the
Country; then, and in such case, it undoubtedly becomes his duty to interfere and to
remedy the deficiency by another and a more judicious selection; but except in such
case only, I hold he has no right to complain or to be dissatisfied. . . ." *The Papers of
John Steele* (Henry M. Wagstaff, ed., 2 vols., Publications of the North Carolina
Historical Commission, 1924), I, 198, 200.

Executive did any agencies of overhead management appear; the business of government was carried on directly and immediately through the lines of the departmental organizations. The duty to consult was one exercised at the discretion of the President.

Chapter Five

THE EXECUTIVE IMPULSE

T<small>HE</small> American Constitution requires both branches of the legislative body and the Chief Executive to come to an agreement not only on major questions of policy but also on major matters of administration. Although the Constitution provided an executive branch coordinate with the legislative, it was not independent. A delicate balance between them was forced into existence by the powers vested in each and by the checks of one against the other. The kind of an administrative system the country would have was bound up with the working relations which had to be explored, point by point, between George Washington as President, the Senate, the House of Representatives, and Hamilton, Jefferson, and Knox as heads of departments. It required nearly the whole of Washington's two terms to work out the first pattern and the process was marked by much argument, much perplexity, and occasionally by high feelings on all sides. Many of the precedents which were standing when Adams took over the presidency remain substantially unchanged today. Their importance to the whole system of government, to the quality of the executive power, and especially to the administrative system was very great.

The framers of the Constitution were firm in their intention to provide an energetic executive. They were also firm in their determination not to leave open the possibility that it would degenerate into "a detestable monarchy" or an indigenous tyranny. They therefore made the executive responsible to Congress, especially through impeachment and through lawmaking and appropriating powers. But the Constitution could not contain an answer to the multitude of adjustments that were required when a coordinate authority in which was vested the entire executive power faced its opposite number fully vested with the legislative power. The metes and bounds of each, and the practices which were essential to harmonize one with the other, had to grow out of experience. Many problems of adjustment arose, both in the domestic and foreign fields.

They were complicated by the early rise of political parties. For a brief time Congress deliberated as a group of individual members. The controversy over the adoption of the Constitution quickly faded away and new divisions of opinion awaited new issues. They were soon discovered in Hamilton's plans for fiscal reform and for the development of manufactures. During 1790 the lines were forming and leaders coming forward: Hamilton, Ames, William Smith, and others for the Federalists; Jefferson, Madison, Giles, and others for the Republicans.[1] The search for a balance between the executive and legislative branches became itself a phase of the struggle for political power.[2]

There existed, nevertheless, a sense of competition and an urge for dominance between the two branches as such, separate and distinct from party conflict. This competition began, indeed, before parties had crystallized. Just after the new government was inaugurated John Adams declared that the legislative and executive powers were natural enemies,[3] and predicted the collapse of the system because too much authority was vested in the former and too little capacity for resistance in the latter.[4]

---

[1] Party terminology during the Federalist period was unsettled. The struggle over the adoption of the Constitution was the occasion for the formation of two groups generally known as the Federalists and the Anti-Federalists. This issue and the corresponding party division quickly disappeared. As new issues arose, the party name Federalist was resumed by the advocates of Hamilton's financial policies and the Jay Treaty. Their opponents, gradually organizing around Jefferson and Madison, came to be known as Republicans, a name that suggested their party enemies were in favor of a monarchy. They were also called Democratic-Republicans and toward the end of the Federalist period were sometimes called Democrats. In his inaugural address Jefferson used the term, Republican, in his well-known phrase, "We are all Republicans, we are all Federalists." Apart from quotations, this work will ordinarily employ the term, Republican, to refer to the followers of Jefferson while reserving the privilege of occasional use of an alternative.

[2] The second Congress, elected in 1790, contained a majority in each branch favorable to the administration. In the third Congress, the Republicans elected the Speaker and the House was in their hands, although closely divided; in the Senate the balance was so even that John Adams repeatedly settled important questions by his deciding vote. The Federalists increased their hold on the Senate in the elections of 1794 and managed to elect their candidate for Speaker in the fourth House of Representatives. Although party lines were not closely formed, the Federalists in general held control of both Houses under John Adams.

[3] Adams, Works, VI, 435.

[4] Ibid., VI, 432. On the subject matter of this and related chapters, see James Hart, The American Presidency in Action: 1789 (New York: Macmillan, 1948).

THE NATURE OF LEGISLATIVE AND EXECUTIVE POWER

The opportunity for mutual encroachment was ample, in part because no one could state where legislative power as such left off and executive power began. The Constitution vested these powers but did not define them. There was genuine doubt and much difference of opinion among members of Congress. There were no useful precedents. But as hard cases came to puzzle Congress, several members with a taste for generalization tried to draw the line. The first of these efforts which has come to our attention was made by an able Federalist member from Massachusetts, Theodore Sedgwick, in one of many debates on the responsibility for laying out post roads.

Sedgwick favored granting authority to designate post roads as an administrative act to the President and Postmaster General; the majority preferred the roads to be designated as a legislative act by Congress itself. Sedgwick said:

It was true . . . that it was impossible precisely to define a boundary line between the business of Legislative and Executive; but from his own experience, as a public man, and from reflection, he was induced to believe, that as a general rule, the establishment of principles was the peculiar province of the former, and the execution of them, that of the latter. He would, therefore, at least, generally, as much as possible, avoid going into detail. . . .[5]

Nearly a year later Madison tried to state some general distinctions. He drew a difference

between the deliberative functions of the House and the ministerial functions of the Executive powers. The deliberative functions, he conceived, should be first exercised before the ministerial began to act. . . . The fundamental principles of any measure, he was of opinion, should be decided in the House, perhaps even before a reference to a select committee. . . .

Mr. Madison saw some difficulty in drawing the exact line between subjects of legislative and ministerial deliberations, but still such a line most certainly existed. . . .[6]

---

[5] *Annals*, III, 239–40 (Dec. 7, 1791).
[6] *Ibid.*, III, 698–99, 700 (Nov. 19, 1792).

Madison failed to clarify the minds of his colleagues in the House. In 1794 William B. Giles of Virginia declared the purpose of resolutions introduced by him against the Treasury to be "to ascertain the boundaries of discretion and authority between the Legislature and the Treasury Department."[7] Giles feared the loss of legislative power to the executive branch and forecast the rise of administrative legislation.

A species of laws will grow out of an inattention to, and a consequent ignorance of, this subject [finance], which may be called the rules of office, the forms of the Treasury, the practical constructions of laws contravening the legal constructions. In all conflicts between this species of laws and the laws pronounced by the Constitutional tribunal, the advantage would be in favor of the Treasury system: because this would be the practical, that the theoretic system of legislation. . . .[8]

Neither Sedgwick, Madison, Giles, or any of their contemporaries made much progress in a general distinction between the inherent nature of the two powers which were vested respectively in the legislative and executive branches. In view of the inconclusive efforts of judges and scholars to define their exact boundaries in the century and a half which followed, this is not surprising. The answer had to be found in precedent, gradually accumulating, not in theory.[9]

The priority of the legislative power was nevertheless acknowledged on all sides, and the jealousy with which Congress guarded its position was amply illustrated during the Federalist era.

Washington clearly understood and carefully observed his obligation to act in accordance with law, and within the financial limitations of current appropriations. Writing to the Attorney General on February 11, 1790, he expressed succinctly his understanding of the rule of law: "For, as the Constitution of the United States, and the Laws made under it, must mark the line of my official conduct, I could not justify my taking a single step in any matter, which appeared to me to require their agency, without its being first obtained. . . ."[10] Instigated by

---

[7] *Ibid.*, IV, 464 (Feb. 24, 1794).

[8] *Ibid.*, IV, 465.

[9] Hamilton recognized the special interest of the Senate in current business and in 1789 advised Washington "that members of the Senate should . . . have a right of *individual* access on matters relative to the *public administration*," although denying such a right to members of the House. Hamilton, *Works* (Hamilton ed.), IV, 3.

[10] Washington, *Writings,* XXXI, 9.

Jefferson, Washington admonished Arthur St. Clair, Governor of the Northwest Territory, against executive regulations "which can, with propriety, only be established by Laws. . . . the utmost circumspection should be observed in the conduct of the Executive; for there are not wanting persons who would rejoice to find the slightest ground of clamour against public Characters. . . ." [11]

In a letter to the Secretary of State in 1796, Washington observed, "The want of funds to carry on commerce with the Indian tribes, agreeably to a late act of Congress, is an unanswerable objection to the appointment of agents *at this time,* for that purpose. . . ." [12] This care to observe statutory and financial limitations was underlined by the President's course of action in emergency expenditures to relieve impressed American seamen; he sent a special message to Congress explaining the expenditure, "in order that you may do thereon what you shall find to be right." [13] Nor did Washington seek to expand the scope of his powers. "The powers of the Executive of the U. States are more definite, and better understood perhaps than those of almost any other Country; and my aim has been, and will continue to be, neither to stretch, nor relax from them in any instance whatever, unless imperious circumstances shd. render the measure indispensible." [14]

EXECUTIVE LEADERSHIP

"It may be interesting for the President to consider . . . whether there ought not to be some Executive impulse," wrote Hamilton on March 8, 1794. "Many persons," he added, "look to the President for the suggestion of measures corresponding with the exigency of affairs." [15] Precedents were not slow in gathering to illustrate an "Executive impulse." The regard of Congress for its own powers and independence was also not slow in making its appearance.

In his official contacts with Congress Washington was deferential. His messages went no further than to suggest subjects for consideration, and in no case did they contain any indication concerning the

---

[11] Jan. 2, 1791, *ibid.,* XXXI, 190; Jefferson, *Works* (Federal ed.), VI, 166–67.

[12] Washington, *Writings,* XXXV, 149.

[13] *Ibid.,* XXXI, 477. In 1794 Washington called upon the governors of the several states to enforce the embargo by the militia where necessary; he was careful to explain in an immediate message to Congress that he conceived this power to be "incidental to an embargo." *Ibid.,* XXXIII, 306.

[14] *Ibid.,* XXXIII, 422.

[15] Hamilton, *Works* (Hamilton ed.), IV, 508.

policy which he thought Congress should pursue. "Motives of delicacy," he once wrote, "have uniformly restrained the P—— from introducing any topick which relates to Legislative matters to members of either house of Congress, lest it should be suspected that he wished to influence the question before it." He would not permit congressional committees to solicit his opinion, but intimated his willingness to express his views, "when *asked*," to a friend.[16]

Although Washington carefully maintained correct formal relations with Congress, he privately entertained grave misgivings concerning their mutual relationship. He was determined to protect the constitutional position of the office which he held and watched with suspicion any tendencies to diminish it. His rebuff at the hands of the Senate when he made his single effort at personal consultation did not encourage friendly intercourse or the rise of close institutional relations. His private attitude toward Congress is well reflected in an incident which occurred in March 1792.

The House had passed a resolution congratulating the French on their new constitution, a gesture which apparently upset the President. He sent for Jefferson, and complained, "That he apprehendd the legislature wd be endeavoring to invade the executive." An hour after receiving Jefferson's reassurances, he sent Tobias Lear to Jefferson for further advice on the unexpected initiative of the House. Jefferson told Lear,

That if expressing a sentiment were really an invasion of the Executive power, it was so faint a one, that it would be difficult to demonstrate it to the public, & to a public partial to the French revoln. & not disposed to consider the approbn of it from any quarter as improper. That the Senate indeed had given many indicns of their wish to invade the Executive power, the Represent. had done it in one case which was indeed mischievous and alarming, that of giving orders to the heads of the executive depmts without consulting the Pres. . . .[17]

With his customary caution, however, Washington carefully refrained from committing his views on his official relationships to writing.[18] We can only infer what they were from his actions, which were scrupu-

---

[16] Feb. 1792, Washington, *Writings,* XXXI, 493.

[17] Jefferson, *Works* (Federal ed.), I, 211–13.

[18] His rare comments on Congress are illustrated in a letter to Lafayette, Aug. 11, 1790: "Congress, after having been in session ever since last fall are to adjourn in two or three days. Though they have been much perplexed in their proceedings on some

lously correct in recognition of the coordinate position of Congress and
the primacy of law.

This formal deference, however, did not reflect the strong leadership
of Congress which was forthcoming in fact from Washington and his
department heads, notably Hamilton. The first Congress went through
its first session without any known suggestions from the President;
even the vitally important bill on the removal power did not stir the
President to exert his influence on congressional opinion so far as
presently available records indicate. The last weeks of the first session,
however, found Hamilton installed in the Treasury and Knox in the
War Department; early in the second session, Jefferson was in the
Department of State. Congress of its own volition immediately turned
to the executive branch for guidance and discovered in Hamilton a personality to whom such leadership was congenial.[19]

The House Committee on Ways and Means was discharged within
a week after Hamilton assumed his duties and its business was referred
to him for a report.[20] Within the next two years the House asked
Hamilton for advice leading to the great reports on public credit, on a
national bank, and on manufactures—documents which laid the foundations of Federalist economic policy. To Hamilton also is due the
report on the Mint, and, at the very close of his service, the second
report on public credit. Through Hamilton the Postmaster General
submitted a report and the draft of a post office bill which he had
prepared.[21] The Secretary of the Treasury became one of the most important forces in the first Congress and highly influential, although
under attack, during the second Congress. "Measures decided upon
by the executive were submitted to the legislature, and duly passed.
There was no disregard of the carefully planned policies of Washington and Hamilton. . . ."[22]

---

questions of a local and intricate nature; yet they have done a great deal of important
business, and will leave the public affairs in as satisfactory a state as could reasonably
have been expected." *Writings*, XXXI, 86; cf. *ibid.*, XXXI, 142.

[19] "Hamilton . . . grasped the truth at once . . . that not even the Constitution
of the United States could keep apart two such inseparable factors in government as
executive and legislature. His official position naturally brought him into close contact
with Congress, and enabled him to see that such a loosely organized body was simply
waiting for a commander." Ralph Volney Harlow, *The History of Legislative Methods
in the Period before 1825* (New Haven: Yale University Press, 1917), p. 140.

[20] *Annals*, I, 895 (Sept. 17, 1789).

[21] *Ibid.*, I, 1076–77 (Jan. 22, 1790).

[22] Harlow, *op. cit.*, p. 148.

Jefferson also took an active role with respect to those domestic affairs which were committed to the Department of State. After nearly a week's general conference with Washington upon assuming office, "it was concluded that the Secretary's information [be offered] to a Committee of Congress with whom he was to converse on the subject of the Provision to be made, that the salaries allowed to our Diplomatic characters was too low. . . ." [23] Jefferson drafted a bill "to promote the progress of the useful arts" which was introduced in the House in 1791 by Alexander White of Virginia.[24] In 1792 he corresponded with Representative Hugh Williamson of North Carolina in regard to the revision of the patent law, making alterations in Williamson's draft.[25]

Despite Washington's scrupulous principles he also occasionally brought his opinions to bear on Congress by informal as well as formal means. He personally wrote out his ideas on the militia, which he sent to Knox to be worked into the bill submitted to Congress on January 21, 1790.[26] In February 1790, Washington suggested to Edmund Randolph, the Attorney General, that he mention proposed amendments to the judiciary act "to such members of the Senate and House of Representatives as are acquainted with the subject." [27] In May 1790, the President himself conferred with Senators Carroll and Izard with the intent of leading the Senate to reverse the action of the House reducing the amount appropriated for the foreign service.[28] In 1792 he sent Jefferson to speak privately to the members of the House Committee investigating the St. Clair disaster.[29] These incidents were, however, exceptions to his standard rule.

To what extent Washington was involved in Hamilton's congressional activity is not clear. It is certain that Washington followed closely the work of Congress, since he asked for copies of each printed bill; [30] the measures which Hamilton pushed were approved by the President; it cannot be doubted that Washington knew the Secretary of the Treasury was in daily contact with his friends in both Houses.

[23] March 26, 1790, Washington, *Diaries*, IV, 110.
[24] Jefferson, *Works* (Federal ed.), VI, 189–93; *Annals*, II, 1937 (Feb. 7, 1791).
[25] Jefferson, *Works* (Federal ed.), VI, 458–59.
[26] Dec. 19, 1789, Washington, *Diaries*, IV, 60; Richardson, *Messages*, I, 71.
[27] Washington, *Writings*, XXXI, 9–10.
[28] May 7, 1790, *Diaries*, IV, 128. This is probably the first instance in which the executive sought to protect its proposals by repairing damage done in one House by action in the other.
[29] Jefferson, *Works* (Federal ed.), I, 215.
[30] Washington, *Writings*, XXXI, 207, n. 35.

Washington himself was temperamentally unsuited for this type of leadership and it may be presumed tacitly gave Hamilton his head.

Indeed, if Senator William Maclay of Pennsylvania can be accepted as a trustworthy observer, Hamilton dominated the whole legislative procedure of the House. "Nothing," he wrote, "is done without him." According to Maclay, Hamilton prepared "all matters," arranged for the membership of the committees to which business was referred, and in some cases attended committee hearings. At the time of the funding bill, Maclay wrote in his diary, "Mr. Hamilton . . . was here early to wait on the Speaker, and I believe spent most of his time in running from place to place among the members." [31] The story of the private dinner at which Hamilton, in the presence of Jefferson, arranged the legislative compromise which saved assumption and put the seat of the general government on the Potomac by switching the votes of two members of the House is told in Jefferson's *Anas*.[32]

Neither under Washington nor Adams did there develop in either branch of Congress a floor leader recognized to be the spokesman of the executive branch. From 1789 to 1795 Hamilton, as Secretary of the Treasury, performed the function of executive leadership, and certain Congressmen were understood to reflect his views on most matters— as, for example, William Smith of South Carolina in the House and Rufus King in the Senate. No one, however, spoke for the President, who, as already noted, generally declined to exert his influence for or against pending legislation. There was usually some member in the House in charge of the party forces, but he was looked upon as an assistant to the Speaker, not as a representative of the President.[33]

In the early years of his administration Washington maintained close personal relations with Madison. Madison wrote the President's reply to the House address responding to the first inaugural speech;[34] reviewed the draft of the special message of August 7, 1789, and others;[35] was appealed to by the President on August 9, 1789, for help in dealing with two House factions, one of which wanted oral

---

[31] Data from *Journal of William Maclay* (Edgar S. Maclay, ed., New York: D. Appleton, 1890) gathered by Harlow, *op. cit.*, pp. 141–43.

[32] Jefferson, *Works* (Federal ed.), I, 175–77.

[33] Harlow, *op. cit.*, p. 176. Under Jefferson the floor leader was "distinctly the lieutenant of the executive." *Ibid.*

[34] Washington, *Writings*, XXX, 310–11.

[35] *Ibid.*, XXX, 369–70.

communication of nominations: "What do you think I had best do?" [36] In September Madison was consulted on appointments: "I am very troublesome, but you must excuse me. Ascribe it to friendship and confidence. . . ." [37] He was sounded out on British relations on October 8, 1789; [38] on February 11, 1792, was invited to "a family dinner" to discuss the affairs of the "Federal district"; [39] and in 1793 was still advising on the troubled affairs of the new seat of government.[40] Madison, however, never became a spokesman for the administration.

After Hamilton resigned, executive leadership was less effective and tended to be dispersed among the department heads according to their respective jurisdictions. When John Adams became President this tendency was accelerated, with Hamilton in the background advising both the heads of departments and prominent Federalists in each House. Adams, like his predecessor, declined to exert direct influence upon the deliberations of the coordinate legislative branch.

THE PRESIDENT, CONGRESS, AND FOREIGN AFFAIRS

Considerable doubt concerning the relative position of the Senate and the President in making treaties was settled in the first instance during Washington's administration.[41] A majority in the House was at first sensitive about any action which might seem to encroach on presidential power in this field. The bill to provide funds for a treaty with the Creek Indians specified in its first draft the number of commissioners. Sedgwick moved to strike out the reference to the number of negotiators: "He thought it a dangerous doctrine to be established, that the House had any authority to interfere in the management of treaties." Although John Page argued that the House could specify how money could be spent, and that it had a concurrent jurisdiction in the formation of treaties, Sedgwick prevailed.[42] Executive freedom

---

[36] *Ibid.*, XXX, 375.

[37] *Ibid.*, XXX, 415.

[38] *Diaries*, IV, 17.

[39] *Writings*, XXXI, 479.

[40] *Ibid.*, XXXII, 379. Washington entertained Senators and Representatives at dinner on a planned schedule, but from accounts of these affairs it appears unlikely that Washington used them to sound out congressional opinion. See Maclay, *Journal*, pp. 137–38 for an account of a dinner with the President.

[41] This subject is dealt with analytically, with a wealth of historical illustration, in Quincy Wright, *The Control of American Foreign Relations* (New York: Macmillan, 1922).

[42] *Annals*, I, 690–91, 697 (Aug. 11, 1789); for the act see 1 Stat. 54 (Aug. 20, 1789).

to fix foreign service salaries within a specified maximum was granted.[43] A resolution favoring nonintercourse with Great Britain, offered as Jay was about to undertake his negotiations, was opposed as "an infringement on the right of the Executive to negotiate, and an indelicacy towards that department." [44]

One important question was whether the President alone made treaties (subject to ratification) or whether the making of the treaty itself was also a function in which the Senate participated as an executive council; in the latter case it would expect to be consulted at various stages—should negotiations be undertaken, under what limitations and conditions, what compromises were allowable for corresponding advantages, and so throughout the course of diplomatic bargaining.[45] Also at stake was the President's authority to issue a proclamation of neutrality without the advice and consent of the Senate. A third problem concerned the authority of the House of Representatives to exercise an independent judgment on the execution of a treaty in cases where funds were necessary.

Washington showed early deference to the Senate in the field of treaty making, but gradually withdrew to the position that the power of the Senate was engaged only after a treaty had been negotiated and signed. The executive-congressional balance was involved in the form of communication between the President and the Senate—whether written or oral. To a Senate delegation which visited the President in August 1789, Washington prescribed oral communication in case of treaties on the ground that "a variety of matters are contained, all of which not only require consideration, but some of them may undergo much discussion; to do which by written communications would be tedious without being satisfactory." [46]

Washington, however, was not endowed with the qualities which would make for success in verbal argument with Senators; his first and only appearance to ask for their advice was a resounding failure. Cantankerous Senator Maclay, fearing that "the President wishes to tread on the necks of the Senate," supported a motion to commit the President's request for the Senate's opinion—thus removing the Presi-

---

[43] *Annals,* I, 1081–92, *passim* (Jan. 26–27, 1790).

[44] *Ibid.,* IV, 600 (April 18, 1794).

[45] See quotation from King in Farrand, *Records of the Federal Convention,* III, 424–25.

[46] Washington, *Writings,* XXX, 373.

dent from the scene of the Senate's deliberations. "As I sat down," wrote Maclay, "the President of the United States started up in a violent fret. *'This defeats every purpose of my coming here'* were the first words that he said." [47] The chief result of the first conference, as Hayden notes, was that it was the last. [48]

While Washington did not again ask for the Senate's advice orally, he continued in the early years of his administration to keep the Senate closely informed about foreign negotiations. For example, he sometimes apprised the Senate of the terms of the proposed agreement and expressly requested it to reply whether or not it would consent. Or he submitted the names of the negotiators together with a statement of their instructions and declared he would accept the Senate's confirmation of his nominees as an indication of its intention to consent to the treaty formulated in pursuance of these instructions. He continued to inform the Senate of the progress of negotiations and to consult it even after ratifications had been exchanged. [49]

But the first great crisis in American foreign relations imposed a different pattern of relationships between the Senate and the President, the pattern which was to become traditional. By 1792 the country seemed to be drifting into war with Great Britain. A small group of leading Federalist Senators eventually suggested to Washington a special mission to the Court of St. James to make a last effort for a peaceful settlement, and upon Washington's acquiescence proposed John Jay as envoy extraordinary. The issues were delicate and complex and public opinion was at fever heat. These Federalist Senators, in the light of the existing situation, abandoned the initial practice of Senate consideration and approval of diplomatic instructions in favor of presidential direction of the whole negotiation. Rufus King, one of the group, wrote in his diary on April 16, 1794: "From the Difficulty of passing particular instructions in the Senate, it seems to me to be most suitable that the Pr. shd. instruct, and that the Treaty shd. be con-

---

[47] Aug. 22, 1789, Maclay, *Journal,* p. 131. In *Memoirs of John Quincy Adams* (Charles Francis Adams, ed., 12 vols., Philadelphia: J. B. Lippincott, 1874–77), VI, 427, Washington is reported as having said as he left the Senate chamber that "he would be damned if he ever went there again."

[48] Ralston Hayden, *The Senate and Treaties, 1789–1817* (New York: Macmillan, 1920), p. 104.

[49] Small, *Some Presidential Interpretations of the Presidency,* p. 69, and footnotes for references to Richardson, *Messages.*

cluded subject to the approbation of the Senate." [50] The opposition moved to require the President "to inform Senate of the whole business" before confirmation of Jay, but they were voted down. Thus, concludes Hayden, "the first great treaty under the Constitution had been negotiated by the President alone."

To this end more than one inherent element of the situation contributed. The initiation and conduct of negotiations inevitably involve a careful assessment of a complex situation, many aspects of which are known most intimately only by those who are in daily contact with affairs. The Senate, as a whole, could hardly become familiar with the details of the foreign scene—although a few individual members might. The conduct of negotiations in their formative stages calls for secrecy, and a numerous body guards secrets poorly. "The President," said Jefferson, "had no confidence in the secresy of the Senate." [51] The conduct of negotiations, moreover, requires give and take and progressive modification of demands and concessions. A numerous body, once committed, is unlikely to possess the flexibility requisite for negotiation, especially since the positions of the various members are known at least to their colleagues; they would have to be protected against the probability of subsequent charges of vacillation or complaisance to a foreign power.

The Federalist solution of presidential powers in the field of treaty making was, therefore, to confirm the leadership and sole direction of the President in all the stages of negotiation, leaving to the Senate the confirmation of foreign representatives (regular or extraordinary) and an independent judgment as to the ratification of a completed treaty.

Presidential authority in this area of public business was further strengthened by the Proclamation of Neutrality in 1793. This act was challenged as an encroachment on the powers of the Senate, committing the country to a foreign policy in the determination of which the Senate was entitled to be consulted, and also as an infringement

---

[50] *The Life and Correspondence of Rufus King* (Charles R. King, ed., 6 vols., New York: G. P. Putnam's Sons, 1894–1900), I, 521.

[51] Jefferson, *Works* (Federal ed.), I, 206–7 (March 11, 1792); 216 (April 9, 1792). This view was shared by Jefferson himself. Writing on Feb. 26, 1793, he said, "We all thought if the Senate should be consulted & consequently apprized of our line, it would become known to Hammond [the British minister], & we should lose all chance of saving anything more at the treaty than our Ultimatum." *Ibid.,* I, 258–59.

on the authority of the Congress, since it potentially committed the country to war, the declaration of which was vested in Congress. These views did not prevail; and another important precedent in favor of executive authority was thus established.

A third and hard-fought issue arose in connection with the execution of the Jay Treaty. In discussing the Algerine negotiations in 1792, Jefferson had advised Washington that it would be prudent to consult the House on the approval of the treaty, "especially in a case of money, as they held the purse strings & would be jealous of them," lest he be "left in the lurch." Washington first concurred in this advice, but shortly changed his mind, saying, according to Jefferson, that if the Representatives would not do what the Constitution called on them to do, the government would be at an end.[52]

In 1796 the House of Representatives was asked to appropriate funds to implement the Jay Treaty, whereupon its enemies called for the papers pertaining to the negotiation.[53] This request raised the issue, to what extent the House was entitled to participate in the treaty process through its undoubted power over appropriations. The immediate question concerned the corollary right to ask for the relevant papers. After consulting his Cabinet, and Hamilton privately, Washington refused to comply with the request for the Jay papers, asserting that it would create "a dangerous precedent," that the treaty-making power was vested exclusively in the President and Senate, that the intervention of the lower House had been specifically rejected by the Constitutional Convention, and that it was essential to the "due administration" of the government to preserve the boundaries fixed by the Constitution.[54] In a letter to Hamilton, Washington expressed freely his sentiments on this effort of the House to invade the treaty-making province: "From the first moment, and from the fullest conviction in my own mind, I had resolved to *resist the principle* wch. was evidently intended to be established by the call of the House of Representatives; and only deliberated on the manner, in which this could be done, with the least bad consequences." [55]

---

[52] Jefferson, *Works* (Federal ed.), I, 205–7 (March 11, 1792); I, 216–17 (April 9, 1792).

[53] *Annals,* V, 759–60 (March 24, 1796).

[54] Richardson, *Messages,* I, 194–96 (March 30, 1796).

[55] Washington, *Writings,* XXXV, 6; see also his letter to Charles Carroll, *ibid.,* XXXV, 29–31.

Although the House was rebuffed in its attempt to assert its influence over treaties by calling for papers,[56] it still remained in undisputed control of the purse strings and proceeded to assert the right to refuse appropriations in execution of a treaty which it deemed inexpedient. The resolution, the essential portion of which follows, was adopted 57 to 35:

when a Treaty stipulates regulations on any of the subjects submitted by the Constitution to the power of Congress, it must depend, for its execution, as to such stipulations, on a law or laws to be passed by Congress. And it is the Constitutional right and duty of the House of Representatives, in all such cases, to deliberate on the expediency or inexpediency of carrying such Treaty into effect, and to determine and act thereon, as, in their judgment, may be most conducive to the public good.[57]

Following this statement of principle the House by a narrow margin made the requested appropriation, leaving the problem for subsequent debate in later years.

In foreign affairs the central position of the President was more implicit than in the domestic field, and the course of events quickly confirmed the theory and practice of presidential initiative and leadership. The Senate receded from its early preference for consultation in the formative stages of negotiation in favor of an undisputed right to an independent judgment of a completed proposal. The House, rebuffed in its attempt to enter the field of foreign affairs by calling for papers concerning the Jay Treaty, asserted its constitutional right to exercise an independent judgment on appropriations required to implement a treaty. Responsibility for initiative and direction in foreign affairs, including the authority to issue proclamations of neutrality, had consequently become clearly vested in the President at the close of Washington's administration.

The second President, John Adams, was born and bred to diplomacy. The events of his administration were dominated by foreign policy and in the discharge of his functions in foreign affairs Adams clashed

---

[56] The House, however, asserted in a subsequent resolution that it was unnecessary for it to state the purpose underlying any call for papers relating to any of its constitutional functions. *Annals,* V, 771–72 (April 6, 1796).

[57] *Ibid.,* V, 771 (April 6); 782 (April 7, 1796).

with Congress on several occasions. His leadership in foreign affairs was not, however, successfully challenged.[58]

The place of the veto power in executive-legislative relations was discussed by Hamilton in *The Federalist* and by John Adams in private letters. The former insisted on the need of some kind of a veto to enable a President to protect the executive branch; the latter saw no good in a qualified veto and believed that the balance of power would be completely upset for lack of an absolute one. Jefferson also recognized that the veto power was designed, among other things, to protect the executive.[59]

Neither Washington nor Adams found it necessary to resort to the veto in order to protect the executive branch against encroachment. On matters of judgment concerning the expediency of measures, Washington was accustomed to yield to the views of Congress. In 1793 he wrote Edmund Pendleton,

You do me no more than Justice when you suppose that from motives of respect to the Legislature (and I might add from my interpretation of the Constitution) I give my Signature to many Bills with which my Judgment is at variance. . . . From the nature of the Constitution, I must approve all the parts of a Bill, or reject it in toto. To do the latter can only be Justified upon the clear and obvious ground of propriety; and I never had such confidence in my own faculty of judging as to be over tenacious of the opinions I may have imbibed in doubtful cases.[60]

The tonnage bill of 1789 was so contrary to Washington's "ideas of justice and policy" that he considered allowing it to become law without his signature, and finally signed it only because he was assured by some members that Congress would introduce new legislation to meet

---

[58] See below, ch. xx. The Republicans, however, were uneasy at the trend of executive influence. On May 13, 1798, Madison wrote to Jefferson, "The management of foreign relations appears to be the most susceptible of abuse of all the trusts committed to a Government, because they can be concealed or disclosed, or disclosed in such parts and at such times as will best suit particular views; and because the body of the people are less capable of judging, and are more under the influence of prejudices, on that branch of their affairs, than of any other." Madison, *Letters* (Congressional ed.), II, 140–41.

[59] Jefferson, *Works* (Federal ed.), VI, 204.

[60] Washington, *Writings*, XXXIII, 96.

his objections.[61] The first use of the veto power by Washington occurred in 1792, affecting an apportionment bill. Hamilton and Knox thought the bill constitutional; Jefferson thought it unconstitutional; Randolph was uncertain at first but eventually joined Jefferson.[62] Washington was much perturbed, noting that the vote on the bill was "perfectly geographical," and fearing that his veto would prove to the eastern interests that he was siding with a southern party. He called in Madison, who joined Jefferson and Randolph, and finally sent in a veto message.[63] ". . . both in and out of doors it gave pleasure to have at length an instance of the negative being exercised," wrote Jefferson.[64]

The only other occasion when Washington found "obvious grounds of impropriety" which would support a veto occurred in 1797 with reference to an army bill.[65] Adams vetoed no laws. The veto power, therefore, won formal recognition as a means of defending the executive against congressional encroachments, but no occasion arose to put it to use for this purpose.

Preoccupation with foreign affairs and the loss or threatened loss of party majority in the House of Representatives conspired to slow down the tendency toward strong executive leadership which was dominant during Washington's first term. Leading Federalists despaired of the future as they missed the sense of direction that had been forthcoming in the first few years. In a gloomy letter Fisher Ames declared that committees of Congress had become ministers and that nothing could be done by the executive. Nevertheless a pattern of executive leadership had been set, and under different forms was to become even more effective under Jefferson.

---

[61] *Ibid.,* XXX, 363. In a letter to Madison in August 1789, Washington asked Madison whether he should exercise the veto on a curious point. "Being clearly of opinion that there ought to be a difference in the wages of the members of the two branches of the Legislature would it be politic or prudent in the President when the Bill comes to him to send it back with his reasons for non-concurring?" *Ibid.,* XXX, 394. The issue could only have been one of opinion, and on a point where congressional preferences might seem conclusive.

[62] Hamilton, *Works* (Hamilton ed.), IV, 206–15.

[63] Richardson, *Messages,* I, 124 (April 5, 1792).

[64] Jefferson, *Works* (Federal ed.), I, 218. Hamilton had urged the veto of certain army pay resolutions in 1790. Hamilton, *Works* (Hamilton ed.), IV, 15–21.

[65] Richardson, *Messages,* I, 211–12 (Feb. 28, 1797).

Chapter Six

CONGRESS RESISTS

CONGRESS was quick to sense danger. Before any departments had been established or any Secretaries appointed James Jackson of Georgia raised the banner of congressional independence. "Are we, then," he asked, "to have all the officers the mere creatures of the President? This thirst of power will introduce a treasury branch into the House, and we shall have ministers obtrude upon us to govern and direct the measures of the Legislature, and to support the influence of their master." [1] Within a few years Jefferson was to tell Washington, "I could not but be uneasy when I saw that the Executive had swallowed up the legislative branch." [2]

THE POWER TO DIGEST AND PREPARE PLANS

The debate on the Treasury bill in June 1789, proposing to give the Secretary of the Treasury the duty "to digest and *report* plans for the improvement and management of the revenue, and the support of the public credit" revealed the fear of executive domination. [3] John Page of Virginia declared that this power would "create an undue influence within these walls" and would establish "a precedent which might be extended, until we admitted all the ministers of the Government on the floor, to explain and support the plans they have digested and reported: thus laying a foundation for an aristocracy or a detestable monarchy." [4] In the light of Madison's subsequent attitude, it is interesting to note that in 1789 he was at a loss to see any danger. "Inconsistent, unproductive, and expensive schemes, will be more injurious to our constituents than the undue influence which the well-digested plans of a well-informed officer can have. From a bad administration of the

---

[1] *Annals,* I, 487 (June 17, 1789).
[2] Oct. 1792, Jefferson, *Works* (Federal ed.), I, 236.
[3] Italics in quotations are author's.
[4] *Annals,* I, 592–93 (June 25, 1789); cf. remarks of Gerry, *ibid.,* I, 603.

Government, more detriment will arise than from any other source." [5]
The words "to digest and *report*" were nevertheless changed to read,
"to digest and *prepare*," and were written into the organic Treasury act.

That the House would be sensitive to excessive zeal by the heads of
departments was also suggested by its reception of the post office bill
which Hamilton laid before it on January 22, 1790. The clerk read the
Secretary's report and was about to read the attached bill when Thomas
Fitzsimons of Pennsylvania interrupted. He "thought there was a
degree of indelicacy, not to say impropriety, in permitting the heads
of departments to bring bills before the House. He thought it was sufficient for them to make reports of facts, with their opinions thereon,
and leave the rest to the discretion of the Legislature. It would certainly
be time enough for them to report bills when they were desired to do
it." The report was forthwith referred to a committee without a reading
of the bill. [6]

REFERENCES TO HEADS OF DEPARTMENTS

From the establishment of the Treasury Department in 1789, the
House of Representatives began to refer matters to the Secretary for a
report. From the beginning some members of the House feared the
consequent influence of the Department, or, more explicitly, of Alexander Hamilton. The history of such references to department heads
from 1790 to 1794 is one of the central threads of early legislative-
executive relations.

The first instance, already noted, occurred in 1789, when Hamilton
was asked to report on the public credit. [7] Shortly after Congress reconvened in January 1790, the House referred to the Treasury Department
the petition of an importer, Christopher Saddler, for relief from a forfeiture incurred for violation of the customs laws. Hamilton seized the
occasion to suggest the need of general legislation to cover cases of this
kind. [8] Michael Jenifer Stone of Maryland instantly objected to sending

---

[5] *Ibid.*, I, 604–5.

[6] *Ibid.*, I, 1076–77.

[7] *Ibid.*, I, 904 (Sept. 21, 1789).

[8] *American State Papers: Documents, Legislative and Executive of the Congress of
the United States* (38 vols., in 10 classes, Washington: Gales and Seaton, 1832–61),
Finance, I, 37. In May 1790, the House showed signs of a willingness to curb Hamilton.
The twelfth section of the bill to provide for the public debt originally authorized
Hamilton to appoint the requisite number of clerks to the loan commissioner in each
of the states. Hugh Williamson induced the House to strike out this provision. The
loan commissioners appointed their own clerks. *Annals*, II, 1587 (May 24, 1790).

this suggestion to a committee of the House: "he thought it was not referred to him [i. e., Hamilton] to report on the necessity of establishing a commission for the final determination on applications of this kind." [9] Stone's objection was overruled, and references to all three Secretaries flowed henceforth from the House in a steady stream. The practice was conducive to confirming Hamilton's leadership in the House, and his opponents determined to break it.

On December 7, 1790, William B. Giles of Virginia took the seat which he was to occupy until after Hamilton had left the Treasury and from which he was to cause Hamilton so much trouble. Almost exactly a year later the House received a petition from the inhabitants of Northumberland County, Pennsylvania, praying for the repeal of the duties on distilled spirits. It was moved to refer the petition to the Secretary of the Treasury. Giles objected: "He thought the subject cognizable by the House only." [10] The issue was fully joined.[11]

On January 2, 1792, Jefferson entertained some members of the House at dinner. "We got on the subject of References by the legislature to the heads of Deptmts, considering their mischief in every direction." Two days later an initial attack on a proposed reference to the Secretary of the Treasury was launched, without success. On January 19 a second attempt was made to block a reference to Hamilton, whose friends again prevailed. The issue came to a head on March 7 and 8, when a new request for a report from the Treasury carried only by the narrow margin of four votes, 31 to 27.[12] The subject came up again for discussion in November 1792.

The issue was not misunderstood on either side.[13] Hamilton wrote to his friend, Edward Carrington,

Mr. Madison nevertheless opposed a reference to me to report ways and means for the Western expedition, and combated, on principle, the propriety of such references.

He well knew that if he had prevailed a certain consequence was my resignation; . . .

---

[9] *Ibid.*, I, 1067 (Jan. 19, 1790).

[10] *Ibid.*, III, 299 (Dec. 30, 1791); Findley agreed with Giles.

[11] For the struggle between Hamilton and Jefferson, see below, ch. xix.

[12] Jefferson, *Works* (Federal ed.), I, 198–99; *Annals,* III, 452 (March 8, 1792).

[13] Jefferson privately avowed the end in view: "They endeavored a few days ago to take away one means of influence by condemning references to the heads of department." Jefferson to Thomas Pinckney, Dec. 3, 1792, *Works* (Federal ed.), VII, 191.

. . . Mr. Madison, laying aside his wonted caution, boldly led his troops, as he imagined, to a certain victory. He was disappointed. Though late, I became apprised of the danger. Measures of counteraction were adopted, and when the question was called Mr. Madison was confounded to find characters voting against him whom he counted upon as certain. . . .[14]

And Jefferson wrote in his diary,

An animated debate took place on the tendency of references to the heads of deptmts; and it seemed that a great majority would be against it. the house adjourned. Treasury greatly alarmed, & much industry supposed to be used before next morning when it was brought on again & debated thro' the day, & on the question the Treasury carried it by 31. to 27. but deeply wounded. . . . On the whole it shewed that treasury influence was tottering.[15]

The principle which Madison, Giles, and their supporters were defending was the independence of Congress in its legislative business. It was stated baldly by John F. Mercer of Maryland early in 1792. "I have long remarked in this House," he exclaimed, "that the Executive, or rather the Treasury Department, was really *the efficient Legislature of the country*, so far as relates to the revenue, which is the vital principle of Government." [16] The reference of such matters as personal claims to the proper department for a report was agreed to by all.[17] But reference of matters of legislation and especially of finance stood, in Republican eyes, on a wholly different footing. "The laws," said Abraham Baldwin of Georgia, "should be framed by the Legislature." The Treasury Act, he continued, was "couched in such general lan-

---

[14] May 26, 1792, Hamilton, *Works* (Lodge ed.), IX, 521–22.

[15] Jefferson, *Works* (Federal ed.), I, 198–99. What some of Jefferson's more outspoken friends in the House thought of Hamilton's leadership may be glimpsed in the following excerpt from a speech by William Findley of western Pennsylvania. "He said the exercise of the power assumed by the Secretary, was inconsistent with that public confidence upon which the Government alone was founded; that it was inconsistent with public safety and a Government of laws; that the Secretary seemed to take the whole Government upon his shoulders, and to consider all the great interests thereof to be committed to his providence. His reports spoke the language of a Frederick of Prussia, or some other despotic Prince, who had all the political powers vested in himself—not the language of a dependent Secretary, under a free and well-ordered Government." *Annals,* III, 922–23 (March 1, 1793).

[16] *Ibid.,* III, 351 (Jan. 27, 1792).

[17] Cf. remark by Findley, *ibid.,* III, 451 (March 8, 1792).

guage as to afford a latitude for the introduction of new systems, such as were never expected by the Legislature. . . . Both modes of originating laws have been tried; but that system which originated in the House . . . had sat well on the feelings of the people, whose interests and wishes, joys and sorrows, must be better known to their Representatives than it is possible for any Executive officer to be acquainted with, in so extensive a country." [18]

The importance of a House active in matters of finance and the danger of legislative lassitude or indifference were argued by Republican William Findley.

Let the House fix its own principles, judge for themselves of the proper sources of revenue, and of the uses to which it ought to be applied; and capacity and information will grow out of the investigation. If the members differ in opinion, as may be expected, they will propose different systems; and, by comparison and discussion, they will become the better acquainted with the subject. . . . But with respect to the general interests of the community, the knowledge of which must grow out of a representation of all the local interests, this can only be found among the members of this House; and, if the representation was more numerous and more equal, that kind of information would be still more perfect. . . .[19]

So far as the initiation of finance bills was concerned, Mercer flatly declared, "He conceived the power of the House to originate plans of finance . . . as incommunicable." [20]

He was reluctantly willing to have the President propose plans but in no case the heads of departments, "the inferior organs of the Executive power." But if the President proposed, said Mercer, "I want no opinions resulting from him. If they are to influence me, they are wrong; if not to influence, they are useless. . . . Some say the Secretary's Reports are like Smith's Treatise on the Wealth of Nations. We do not come here to go to school, or hear lectures from the Secretaries on finance or any other subject." [21]

Madison had shifted his ground since 1789 and now fought against Hamilton's influence in the House. In the March (1792) debate he

[18] *Ibid.*, III, 703, 705 (Nov. 20, 1792).
[19] *Ibid.*, III, 448 (March 8, 1792).
[20] *Ibid.*, III, 696 (Nov. 19, 1792).
[21] *Ibid.*, III, 707 (Nov. 20, 1792).

apparently remained silent; in November, according to the reporter, he closed the debate with "a few powerful observations."

He insisted that a reference to the Secretary of the Treasury on subjects of loans, taxes, and provision for loans, &c., was, in fact, a delegation of the authority of the Legislature, although it would admit of much sophistical argument to the contrary. . . . he peremptorily denied that the plans of that officer came into the House in either an equitable or unbiassed manner. . . . [They] were accompanied by a force of reasoning not on both sides, but on one only. . . . it was evident the Secretary's plans were not introduced in such manner as to leave the House the freedom of exercising their own understandings in a proper constitutional manner.[22]

The Federalists' position in favor of reliance upon the information, initiative, and plans of the executive had been consistently stated from the beginning.[23] They denied that Congress suffered any loss of authority or influence by requesting plans from the executive heads; to the contrary they asserted that this was a normal and proper procedure. They pointed to the practice of other countries, and to the improvement of finance in their own. They insisted that Congress, a numerous body, could not effectively bring order into the complicated mass of data which was involved in fiscal affairs, although they warmly supported the capacity of Congress to decide on the virtue of plans presented to it and to work out alternatives. Elias Boudinot gave the best exposition of this point of view in 1789.

It has been said, that the members coming from the different parts of the Union are the most proper persons to give information. I deny the principle. . . . We are called from the pursuit of our different occupations, and come without the least preparation to bring forward a subject that requires a great degree of assiduous application to understand; add to this the locality of our ideas, which is too commonly the case, and we shall appear not very fit to answer the end of our appointment. . . . If we had the subject digested and prepared, we should determine with ease on its fitness, its combination, and its principles, and might supply omissions or defects without hazard; and this in half the time we could frame a system, if left to reduce the chaos into order.[24]

---

22 *Ibid.*, III, 722 (Nov. 21, 1792).

23 See especially the speeches of Boudinot, June 25, 1789 (*ibid.*, I, 599–600); Sedgwick, March 8, 1792 (*ibid.*, III, 437–39); and Ames, Nov. 21, 1792 (*ibid.*, III, 715–722).

24 *Ibid.*, I, 600 (June 25, 1789); see also reference to Ames, *ibid.*

In an able speech in 1792 Fisher Ames concluded:

common sense will decide instantly that the knowledge of our financial affairs, and of the means of improving them, is to be obtained the most accurately from the officer whose duty it is made, by our own law, to understand them; who is appointed and commissioned for that very purpose; and to whom every day's practice in his office must afford some additional information of official details, as well as of the operation of the laws. . . .[25]

On every occasion that the issue came to a vote until 1794 the Federalists were able to prevail, but by narrow margins. On March 26, 1794, for the first time, the House declined to ask the Secretary of the Treasury for his recommendation for additional revenue and turned instead to its own committee. The report in the *Annals* is far from complete,[26] but Madison has left a record in a letter to Jefferson: "the question whether the ways and means should be referred to the Secretary of the Treasury, as heretofore, or to a Committee, lately came on, and decided the sense of the House to be regenerated on that point. . . . the point was carried by 49 against 46." [27] The effect upon Hamilton was noted by a contemporary, William B. Grove, a Federalist member of the House committee to which the matter was referred. Writing to his friend, John Steele, on April 2, 1794, he said, "I am one of 15—a committee on this subject—to report ways & means—We have done nothing final yet, we had a meeting yesterday, & had Secy. H. before us, he appeared cursedly mortifyed." [28] The retirement of Hamilton in January 1795 markedly lessened the tension between the Treasury and the House. His successor, Oliver Wolcott, was not a man to push plans upon Congress.[29]

Suspicious Republicans continued to splutter from time to time.[30]

---

[25] *Ibid.,* III, 716 (Nov. 21, 1792).

[26] *Ibid.,* IV, 531.

[27] March 31, 1794, Madison, *Letters* (Congressional ed.), II, 9–10.

[28] John Steele, *Papers,* I, 114.

[29] Some special cases require brief notice. On Jan. 20, 1790, the House declined to submit to the Treasury a report of one of its committees (*Annals,* I, 1067–72); on Nov. 1, 1791, the House refused to submit a section of the President's address to the Secretary of the Treasury, as derogatory to the Chief Executive (*ibid.,* III, 151); on Jan. 12, 1795, there was an excited objection to a letter from the Secretary of War which was construed as taking the side of the Senate in a controversy with the House and which caused a new outburst of jealousy toward the executive (*ibid.,* IV, 1072–80).

[30] For example, see *ibid.,* IV, 1120; V, 243, remarks of Giles.

The trend settled in the direction of asking for departmental reports on past transactions and on routine matters rather than on future policy.[31] The House sought leadership within its own ranks, first through greater reliance on select committees and the Committee of the Whole, and later, under Albert Gallatin's influence, through a standing Ways and Means Committee.[32] Congress tended to drift as executive leadership became less vigorous and as the relatively undisciplined members resisted their own leadership as well as that of the President and the heads of departments.

The precedents of 1792 nevertheless stood.[33] Congress never forsook the right to turn to the executive departments for information and for plans concerning future programs. Less advantage was taken of this procedure after 1794, but the possibility of executive leadership by responding to congressional requests remained unimpaired.

One of the last, almost defiant acts of the Federalists, was to require the Secretary of the Treasury "to digest, prepare and lay before Congress at the commencement of every session, a report on the subject of finance, containing estimates of the public revenue and public expenditures, and plans for improving or increasing the revenues." [34] Theodore Sedgwick wrote to Rufus King, "Besides the bankrupt bill, we have passed one more of great importance. It makes it the *Duty* of the Secry. of the Treasury, at the commencement of a session, to report to the Legislature on all the subjects of revenue & finance. This will give splendor to the officer and respectability to the executive Department of Govt." [35]

---

[31] But not exclusively; see, for example, *ibid.*, V, 856; and Gallatin's remarks, *ibid.*, VI, 2274.

[32] Henry Adams, *The Life of Albert Gallatin* (Philadelphia: J. B. Lippincott, 1880), p. 157; *Annals*, V, 159 (Dec. 21, 1795).

[33] After the great debate of November 1792, the House modified the form of many requests by directing them to the President rather than to the heads of departments, but practice was not uniform (*ibid.*, III, 735, Dec. 4, 1792). For example, on April 4, 1796, the Secretary of the Treasury was directed to prepare and report a plan for direct taxes, specifying objects and mode of collection (*ibid.*, V, 856); on May 20, 1796, to prepare "a mode for collecting a tax on snuff" (*ibid.*, V, 1417); and on May 23, to report a plan for customs districts on the Mississippi (*ibid.*, V, 1428).

[34] 2 Stat. 79 (May 10, 1800).

[35] May 11, 1800, King, *Correspondence*, III, 236. The House of Representatives had an early lesson in its far-reaching control over administration through the power to refuse funds. The Mint had miserably failed to coin an adequate supply of hard

ATTENDANCE OF HEADS OF DEPARTMENTS IN CONGRESS

A related problem concerned the personal attendance of the heads of departments in Congress, an arrangement which would obviously build up the influence of Secretaries and the executive branch in the legislative body. The matter first arose when Hamilton informed the House of Representatives on January 9, 1790, that he had prepared the plan for the support of the public credit called for by the House and was ready to report. Elbridge Gerry promptly moved that the report be submitted in writing. The brief debate that ensued turned principally on the convenience of the House in best grasping a complex subject and on protection to the Secretary of the Treasury against misunderstanding his plan. Fisher Ames was for submission in writing, to secure "a degree of permanency favorable to the responsibility of the officer, while, at the same time, they would be less liable to be misunderstood." This seemed to be the general opinion, but George Clymer expressed doubts concerning the propriety "of receiving oral communications from the Head of such an important Department." The House voted to receive the report in writing, doubtless contrary to Hamilton's desire.[36]

In November 1792, it was proposed to request Hamilton and Knox to appear before the House in connection with the discussion of the committee report on the St. Clair military defeat, "to the end that they may attend the House, and furnish such information as may be conducive to the due investigation" of the case. Opposition was led by Madison and other Republicans, while the motion was supported by the Federalists and, oddly, by the unpredictable Gerry who in 1790 had moved to exclude Hamilton from presenting the report on public credit. Republican apprehension was voiced by Abraham Venable who urged "the impropriety of any of the Heads of Departments coming forward, and attempting in any way to influence the deliberations of the Legislature." Page bluntly said that their attendance would clog the freedom of inquiry and debate. Madison, this time successful, asserted that the call upon the Secretaries would "introduce a precedent

---

money and in 1796 dissatisfaction in and out of Congress ran high. It was proposed to abolish the Mint by the simple expedient of withholding appropriations. The Mint was saved, by a vote of 40 in favor of no future appropriation against 45 in favor of a grant; but the precedent was a significant one. *Annals,* V, 264.

[36] *Ibid.,* I, 1043–45 (Jan. 9, 1790).

which would lead to perplexing and embarrassing consequences." No further attempt was made to permit the heads of departments to appear face to face with Congress. [37] Henry Knox, whose department was under fire, asked for an opportunity to be heard, and was allowed to appear before a House committee but not before the House.[38]

Good Federalists continued to insist on the propriety of calling department heads to the House, although they took no advantage of the principle they sustained. In 1794 William Smith declared the House could "admit the Secretary of State, if they consider it as expedient"; [39] and Jonathan Dayton, later Speaker, concurred: "The House had a right to call Heads of Departments to give their opinions on any particular subject, if they thought proper." [40]

Thus long before the end of Washington's second term Congress had recovered from its initial willing reliance on executive leadership and from its respectful deference to the Chief Executive. A sign of the times was the refusal of the House to adjourn in 1796 to attend the President's reception (an annual affair since 1790) on the occasion of his birthday.[41] The Republicans had won control of the third House of Representatives and were an active minority in the fourth. The Senate was less restive but quickly began to concern itself with the President's nominations, and exercised its power to resist by occasional refusal to confirm appointments. The House showed a marked jealousy of executive management of legislative business, although it did not abandon the practice of leaning upon the departments for reports, for information, and even for plans. Personal contacts between the Secretaries and leading Federalist Congressmen remained close and uninterrupted. Events kept the two branches of government in mesh although their respective ambitions tended at times to throw them out of gear.

[37] *Ibid.*, III, 679–84 (Nov. 13, 1792).

[38] *Ibid.*, III, 685–89 (Nov. 14, 1792). Another possibility of House resistance to executive influence lay in its capacity to direct official acts in detail through the close itemization of appropriations. This possibility was not overlooked, but for convenience in exposition, it is dealt with in a subsequent chapter, xxvi.

[39] *Annals*, IV, 885 (Nov. 17, 1794).

[40] *Ibid.*, IV, 886.

[41] Washington, *Writings*, XXXIV, 477, n. 38; *Annals*, V, 355.

Chapter Seven

CONGRESS REACHES OUT

I<small>N THESE</small> early years Congress was not merely engaged in defensive action to protect its own field of responsibility from executive invasion. It was also exploiting its share in the conduct of administration. Three aspects of these claims call for exploration in the light of the events of the 1790's: the authority to make particular administrative decisions, as in laying out post roads; the power to investigate official acts and to call for official papers; and participation (beyond mere confirmation) in appointments.

LEGISLATION EMBODYING SPECIFIC ADMINISTRATIVE DECISIONS

Early legislation contained many examples of laws which in effect made particular administrative decisions. Frequently claims were settled by special appropriations, sometimes after an inquiry by a committee, sometimes after an executive report. But claims for remission of customs penalties were regularly determined by the Treasury. Congress itself decided upon the ports of entry and delivery rather than delegating this duty to the President or the Treasury, but it allowed the President to establish excise districts. On at least one occasion Congress intervened to direct the collector of the customs at Philadelphia in the performance of his duties.[1] Congress specified what lighthouses were to be built, but resisted the efforts of some southern members to dip into what came later to be known as the pork barrel. One member was willing for Congress to act as a vendue master in the sale of public land.[2]

The greatest struggle over this type of direct participation in the public business came in the battle on post roads. The issue was whether

---

[1] 1 Stat. 373 (June 4, 1794).
[2] *Annals,* I, 1068 (Jan. 20, 1790).

to vest the power to designate post roads in the President and the Post-master General, or to reserve it for Congress. With great persistence the Federalists tried on five successive occasions to vest the power in the executive but without success.

Early in 1790 the House struck out a clause in a pending post office bill empowering the President to establish post offices and post roads.[3] Later in the debate Theodore Sedgwick proposed to authorize the Post-master General, with the approval of the President, to establish post roads. He was defeated "by a great majority."[4] The bill went to the Senate with a long list of post roads in its first and second sections, and was duly returned by the Senate with a provision authorizing the President and the Postmaster General to designate these roads. The debate on concurrence, which the House refused, throws much light on this angle of legislative-presidential relations.[5]

Against concurrence it was argued that this would be the delegation of legislative power in one of its most important aspects. The revenue would center in the hands of the executive and might be converted into "an engine destructive to the liberties of the United States." The delegation was unconstitutional since the power to establish post roads was expressly reserved to Congress. It would be an embarrassing burden to the President, and could be better performed by the representatives of the people.[6]

In favor of executive decision it was said that the roads proposed by the House would be a great burden on the revenue; that conditions changed continually and to keep abreast of them would be a "perpetual source" of legislation; that precedent under the late Congress favored the Postmaster General; that all responsibility would be dissipated if divided into "sixty-five parts";[7] and that executive decision was completely constitutional.

---

[3] *Ibid.*, II, 1527 (April 13, 1790).

[4] *Ibid.*, II, 1641 (June 16, 1790).

[5] *Ibid.*, II, 1676–77 (July 8, 1790).

[6] At another stage in the debate John Page asked pointedly, "In Virginia, for instance, cannot the ten Representatives say, with more certainty, what post roads would be proper in that State than any one man?" *Ibid.*, III, 233 (Dec. 6, 1791).

[7] The Federalist *Gazette of the United States* entered the fray (July 24, 1790): ". . . the situation of the Post-Office bill is truly critical.—The House of Representatives are strenuous to have sixty Post-Masters' General.—The Senate are averse to more than ONE. . . . If sixty Post Masters' General are sixty times better than one, the amendment of the Senate . . . is a most abominable unpopular amendment."

The two Houses could not agree and the bill was lost, only to be taken up again in the next Congress. A new effort was promptly made to have the House delegate its power to the President, but to no end.[8] A final drive was staged by the Federalists late in 1791; some new arguments were made but the conclusion remained the same. Alexander White now claimed that in his opinion the House had a right to send a person to lay out the post roads, agreeably to their directions.[9] This interpretation of the extent of legislative power passed unnoticed, but fear of executive power in establishing post roads was expressed by more than one. Thus Samuel Livermore said, "If the post office were to be regulated by the will of a single person, the dissemination of intelligence might be impeded, and the people kept entirely in the dark with respect to the transactions of Government." [10] Even John Vining saw potential trouble: "to a good President it would be a burden; to a bad President, a dangerous power of establishing offices and roads in those places only where his interest would be promoted, and removing others of long standing, in order to harass those he might suppose inimical to his ambitious views." [11]

The House was not to be shaken from its determination to lay out the post roads. The important act of 1792 in its first section specified each post road, but authorized the Postmaster General (not the President) to enter into contracts for extending the line of posts, without causing any diminution of the post office revenue.[12] In the successive revisions of the post office act through 1801 no change was made in derogation of congressional responsibility to designate post roads and to authorize their discontinuance.[13] While in general Congress tended to legislate on broad matters of policy, it did nevertheless insist on dealing with some matters which would now be recognized as falling in the proper field of administrative discretion.

[8] *Annals*, II, 1887–90 (Jan. 31, 1791).

[9] *Ibid.*, III, 237 (Dec. 7, 1791). White also insinuated that "such advances towards Monarchy, if not checked in season, . . . would tend to unhinge the present Government." *Ibid.*, III, 233.

[10] *Ibid.*, III, 230 (Dec. 6, 1791).

[11] *Ibid.*, III, 235 (Dec. 6, 1791).

[12] 1 Stat. 232 (Feb. 20, 1792).

[13] Competition between enterprising towns for the post road is illustrated in the struggle between Exeter and Portsmouth, N. H. One Granite State Representative, Nicholas Gilman, supported the claims of Exeter; another, Samuel Livermore, those of Portsmouth in a congressional debate. *Annals*, III, 356–62. (Feb. 2, 1792)

THE POWER TO INVESTIGATE AND TO CALL FOR PAPERS

One of the means by which a legislative body maintains supervision of the executive is through investigations of official agencies. The Constitution was silent on this point, but practice, based on English precedent, quickly filled the gap.[14]

The matter came up for discussion in 1790 in response to a request by Robert Morris for an investigation of his accounts as Superintendent of Finance during the Confederation. Elbridge Gerry and others spoke against a congressional committee and in favor of an executive inquiry. "The President of the United States," said Gerry, "is the only competent authority to take cognizance of the conduct of officers in the Executive Department; if we pursue the proposed plan of appointing committees, we destroy the responsibility of Executive officers, and divest the House of a great and essential privilege, that of impeaching our Executive officers for mal-administration."[15] But Madison and others argued for a House committee, which was duly appointed.

The second case, the House investigation in 1792 of the defeat of General St. Clair, involved more formality and established precedents. William Giles proposed to request the President to institute an inquiry, but the final decision was in favor of a committee "to inquire into the causes of the failure of the late expedition under Major General St. Clair; and that the said committee be empowered to call for such persons, papers, and records, as may be necessary to assist their inquiries."[16] The ground on which the investigation stood was put by Hugh Williamson: an inquiry into the expenditure of all public money was the indispensable duty of the House.

This was the first time the House had instituted a formal investigation into the conduct of officers under the control of the executive, and Washington called a Cabinet meeting to deliberate on the request for papers which the committee had promptly made on General Knox. An account of the meeting is preserved in Jefferson's *Anas*.

The commee had written to Knox for the original letters, instns, &c. The President he had called us to consult, merely because it was the first

---

[14] On this topic, see Marshall Edward Dimock, *Congressional Investigating Committees* (Baltimore: Johns Hopkins Press, 1929).

[15] *Annals*, II, 1464 (March 19, 1790).

[16] *Ibid.*, III, 490–94 (March 7, 1792). The presidential inquiry was defeated 21 to 35.

example, & he wished that so far as it shd become a precedent, it should be rightly conducted. He neither acknowledged nor denied, nor even doubted the propriety of what the house were doing, for he had not thought upon it, nor was acquainted with subjects of this kind. He could readily conceive there might be papers of so secret a nature as that they ought not to be given up. —We were not prepared & wished time to think & enquire.

Apr. 2. Met again at P's on same subject. We had all considered and were of one mind 1. that the house was an inquest, & therefore might institute inquiries. 2. that they might call for papers generally. 3. that the Executive ought to communicate such papers as the public good would permit, & ought to refuse those the disclosure of which would injure the public. Consequently were to exercise a discretion. 4. that neither the commee nor House had a right to call on the head of a deptmt, who & whose papers were under the Presidt. alone, but that the commee shd instruct their chairman to move the house to address the President. . . . Hamilt. agrd with us in all these points except as to the powr of the house to call on heads of departmts. He observed that as to his departmt the act constituting it had made it subject to Congress in some points, but he thot himself not so far subject as to be obliged to produce all papers they might call for. They might demand secrets of a very mischievous nature. . . . Finally agreed to speak separation [sic] to the members of the commee & bring them by persuasion into the right channel. It was agreed in this case that there was not a paper which might not be properly produced, that copies only should be sent, with an assurance that if they should desire it, a clerk should attend with the originals to be verified by themselves. . . .[17]

The next great inquiry was on Hamilton's authorization to make certain foreign loans and his application of the proceeds.[18] The charges of exceeding his discretionary power, contained in the Giles resolutions of February 1793, were disposed of by debate. In 1794, however, a further investigation of the Treasury took place by the Baldwin Committee.[19] The power of the House to investigate the expenditure of funds was thereby fully established.[20]

---

[17] Jefferson, *Works* (Federal ed.), I, 214–15.

[18] *Annals*, III, 835 (Jan. 23, 1793); see below, ch. xxviii.

[19] *Annals*, IV, 463, 466 (Feb. 24, 1794).

[20] See above, ch. v, for an account of the call for papers by the House of Representatives in connection with the Jay Treaty. Calls upon department heads for information also became a congressional weapon, annoying Hamilton and causing him much labor. *American State Papers: Finance*, I, 274; Gibbs, *Memoirs*, I, 127, 129. Ebenezer Hazard probably reflected good Federalist views when he wrote Jeremy Belknap, "Taking advantage of Congressional prerogative, a fool can ask more questions in a day than

CONGRESSIONAL INFLUENCE UPON APPOINTMENTS

The clause conferring upon the Senate the power to confirm the nominations of the President to other than inferior officers was warmly disputed when the terms of the Constitution were under consideration. In the Convention itself, some thought the consequences would be evil, fearing that the President might "secure the complaisance" of the Senate by patronage deals and that the single responsibility of the President for the conduct of the executive branch would be diminished. Others believed that an unchecked authority to appoint would prove a dangerous concentration of power, and that the judgment of men from different parts of the Union should be brought into play.

Alexander Hamilton miscalculated the progress of events in this area. He defended the power to confirm as a check on favoritism and a source of stability. Moreover he thought the Senate would seldom exercise their prerogative, since to do so "might cast a kind of stigma upon the individual rejected, and might have the appearance of a reflection upon the judgment of the chief magistrate. . . ." He denied that the President could secure the obedience of the Senate by bargains on appointments—a "forced and improbable" supposition.[21]

John Adams came much nearer the mark. In his letter to Roger Sherman, he argued that the negative of the Senate upon appointments lessened the responsibility of the executive, interested a branch of the legislature in the management of the executive, divided the attention of the people, and would excite the ambition of the Senate. In a far-seeing analysis, he wrote:

A senator of great influence will be naturally ambitious and desirous of increasing his influence. Will he not be under a temptation to use his in-fluence with the president as well as his brother senators, to appoint persons to office in the several states, who will exert themselves in elections, to get

---

a wise man can answer in a month; and yet, should such an one be sent to Congress, every head of a department lies at his mercy. Answer him according to his folly, he grows angry, runs to tell Congress, and, to be sure, the officer must be dismissed, to put the gentleman in good humour again. I would almost as soon be a Virginia negro as a public officer under such a master. A knave can do at least as much mischief as a fool. . . ." *Belknap Papers: Correspondence between Jeremy Belknap and Ebenezer Hazard,* Part II, Collections of the Massachusetts Historical Society, 5th Series, Vol. III (1877), p. 323.

[21] *The Federalist,* No. 76.

out his enemies or opposers, both in senate and house of representatives, and to get in his friends, perhaps his instruments? . . . Will he not naturally be tempted to make use of his whole patronage, his whole influence, in advising to appointments . . . to increase his interest and promote his views? . . .[22]

Washington expressed no theoretical views on senatorial confirmation, but took good care to preserve both his and the Senate's freedom of action. In August 1789 he was waited upon by a Senate committee to find out how he wished to handle appointments. He expressed his preference for written communications, saying:

it could be no pleasing thing I conceive, for the President, on the one hand to be present and hear the propriety of his nominations questioned; nor for the Senate on the other hand to be under the smallest restraint from his presence from the fullest and freest inquiry into the Character of the Person nominated. The President in a situation like this would be reduced to one of two things: either to be a silent witness of the decision by Ballot, if there are objections to the nomination; or in justification thereof (if he should think it right) to support it by argument. Neither of which might be agreeable; and the latter improper; for as the President has a right to nominate without assigning his reasons, so has the Senate a right to dissent without giving theirs.[23]

Senators and to a lesser extent Representatives promptly began to interest themselves in appointments. By the end of Adams' administration the convention had become well established that Congressmen were normally consulted concerning nominations to federal office. While members of Congress were turned to at the outset principally as good sources of information, it is not in accord with the evidence to conclude with Carl R. Fish that their influence under Washington was "simply that of men with special opportunities for information." [24]

From an early date it was the custom in the Post Office, indeed, to defer to the representatives of the people. There is an illuminating entry in the diary of Richard Smith, a member of the Continental

---

[22] July 1789, Adams, *Works,* VI, 432–36 at 433–34. The complete letter should be consulted by students of this topic.

[23] Washington, *Writings,* XXX, 374, 377–79.

[24] Carl Russell Fish, *The Civil Service and the Patronage* (Cambridge: Harvard University Press, 1904), p. 24.

Congress in 1775: "*Tuesday 19 Sept*ʳ [1775] . . . Dʳ Franklin the PostMaster General desired the Delegates of New Jersey to nominate Deputy PostMasters throughout that Colony which we did accordingly." [25]

The support of Senators was promptly solicited upon the inauguration of the new government.[26] Congressmen began to fulfill Adams' predictions as Washington and his advisers collected information about candidates for office. On August 12, 1789, Representative Jeremiah Wadsworth of Connecticut wrote to Oliver Wolcott, offering him the support of the state delegation if he would apply to the President for an office in the Treasury. Wolcott sent his application to the President through Wadsworth's hands, and was eventually appointed Auditor.[27] In his diary under date of February 5, 1790, Washington wrote, "Received from Doctr. Williamson, of North Carolina, a list of names he thought would be proper to fill the Revenue offices in that State. Submitted the same to the Senators of that State for their inspection and alteration." [28] In June 1790, Jefferson consulted members of the North Carolina delegation on candidates for district judge and attorney and gave Washington notes of their opinions.[29] In November 1790, Hamilton consulted with the North Carolina representatives on behalf of Washington.[30] On December 2, 1790, he reported to the President the recommendations of Representative Nicholas Gilman of New Hampshire, and suggested that the President might wish to await "the arrival of the eastern members" before making an appointment.[31] In 1791 we find Representatives Gerry and Ames intervening in the Boston postmastership at the instance of the incumbent postmaster who was about to be displaced.[32] At the same time Senator Butler of South Carolina was calling on the Postmaster General with reference to the

[25] "Diary of Richard Smith in the Continental Congress, 1775–1776," *American Historical Review*, I (1896), 288–310, 493–516, at p. 291.

[26] For example, note correspondence between Christopher Gore of Massachusetts and Senator Rufus King of New York in King, *Correspondence*, I, 357, 365, 366, 367, 368.

[27] Gibbs, *Memoirs*, I, 19.

[28] Washington, *Diaries*, IV, 85.

[29] Gaillard Hunt, "Office-Seeking During Washington's Administration," *Am. Hist. Rev.*, I (1896), 273–74.

[30] Hamilton to Washington, Hamilton, *Works* (Hamilton ed.), IV, 82.

[31] Hamilton to Washington, *ibid.*, IV, 84–86.

[32] Timothy Pickering to Rev. John Clarke, Dec. 1, 1791, MS. in Massachusetts Historical Society, Pickering Papers, VI, 48.

Charleston office.[33] In 1792 Washington asked Jefferson to inquire of Senator Monroe of Virginia if there could be any opposition to a person under consideration; he told Jefferson "he would not appoint one in whom he could foresee any material opposition." [34] In 1794 the Georgia delegation offered a nomination for the vacant post of Attorney General.[35]

The deference which was uniformly paid to Washington and the independence which he taught all to expect in his appointments left Congressmen with the expectation of being consulted and the opportunity to express their views, but, as clearly appeared in Washington's letter to James Monroe (who had objected to the appointment of Hamilton as special envoy) nothing more. In a somewhat frigid communication he informed Monroe,

> I request, if you are possessed of any facts or information, which would disqualify Colo. Hamilton for the mission to which you refer, that you would be so obliging as to communicate them to me in writing. . . .
> as I *alone* am responsible for a proper nomination, it certainly behoves me to name such an one as in my judgment combines the requisites for a mission so peculiarly interesting to the *peace* and happiness of this country. . . .[36]

John Adams was less successful in repelling congressional influence on appointments. He made relatively few civil appointments, but where called upon to nominate to the Senate, he apparently received preliminary advice from the respective state delegations.

Two examples will illustrate the importance of congressional endorsement. In a letter to Benjamin Adams in 1799, President Adams wrote, "Our kinsman must apply to the senators and representatives of his own State for recommendations. . . . If I were to nominate him without previous recommendations from the senators and representatives from your State, the Senate would probably negative him. . . . The Samuel Adams appointed a custom-house officer, was named by the senators and representatives of New Hampshire. I know him

---

[33] Timothy Pickering to John Gardner, Dec. 27, 1791, *ibid.*, VI, 50.

[34] Jefferson to Monroe, April 11, 1792, Jefferson, *Works* (Federal ed.), VI, 474.

[35] Randolph to James Jackson and others, Jan. 24, 1794, State Dept., Domestic Letters, VI, 41.

[36] April 9, 1794, Washington, *Writings*, XXXIII, 320–21.

not." [37] An exchange of correspondence between James and Andrew Bayard in 1801 is equally revealing. James A. Bayard, a member of the House from Delaware, waited on the President to secure the nomination of his cousin, Samuel Bayard, as circuit judge in New York. Immediately after the conference he wrote Andrew (Samuel's brother), "the President assured me that unless the N York Delegation should press upon him some man whom with propriety he could not resist, Samuel should be appointed." [38] But two weeks later he had to report the failure of his mission. "Benson of N York has succeeded as Circuit Judge in place of your Brother Samuel. His character and the weight of an unanimous recommendation from the N York Delegation turned the scale." [39]

President Adams relied upon the Secretary of the Treasury to select persons to be nominated by him as land-tax commissioners (1798) but the initial recommendations apparently came from or through members of Congress. Jonathan Dayton of New Jersey wrote Oliver Wolcott, "Knowing that it is not requested nor expected of the Members of one State to recommend Commissioners for another under the valuation law, it is with reluctance that I comply with the request of several gentlemen of Pennsylvania to name to you Mr Isaac Snowden Junr of Philadelphia for that office. . . ." [40]

In 1798 and 1799 Adams had to issue many commissions to officers in the Provisional Army. Party spirit ran high, and congressional influence was powerful. Washington, as Lieutenant General and Commander in Chief, was forced to complain to the War Department in bitter terms. In October 1798, he observed,

The applications are made, *chiefly* through members of Congress. These, oftentimes to get *rid* of them; oftener still perhaps, for local and Electioneering purposes, and to please and gratify their party, more than from any real merit in the applicant, are handed in, backed by a sollicitude to succed, in order to strengthen their interest. Possibly, no injustice would be done, if I was to proceed a step further and give it as an opinion, that most of the candidates brought forward by the opposition members, possess sentiments

---

[37] April 22, 1799, Adams, *Works*, VIII, 636.

[38] *Papers of James A. Bayard* (E. Donnan, ed.), pp. 123–24.

[39] *Ibid.*, p. 131.

[40] Sept. 4, 1798, MS. in the Connecticut Historical Society, Oliver Wolcott Papers, VI, 67.

similar to their own, and might poison the army by disseminating them, if they were appointed. . . .[41]

In March 1799, Washington wrote much more forcibly. After referring to the care with which he and two major generals had examined applications for commissions and decided upon their recommendations, he asked, "and what has followed? Why any member of Congress who had a friend to serve, or a prejudice to endulge, could set them at naught." [42] Citing the merits of Caleb Gibbs which led to his inclusion in Washington's list, he continued, "yet, the Veto of a Member of Congress (I presume) was *more respected,* and sufficient to set him aside." [43]

The evidence at hand thus makes it clear that Congressmen quickly became interested in appointments to federal office. Members of both Houses carried on correspondence with the President and the heads of departments in favor of their friends or constituents. State delegations comprising both Senators and Representatives acted as a group in important cases. The rule of senatorial courtesy had not fully taken shape, but the special concern of members with appointments in their own states was recognized to the usual exclusion of members from other states. And John Adams admitted that his nominations would probably fail in the Senate without the previous recommendation of the State delegations.[44]

Washington was instinctively unwilling to challenge the Senate with unpopular nominations, and Adams apparently clearly understood that it was necessary, as he had predicted, to yield to congressional ambition.

[41] Washington to McHenry, Oct. 21, 1798, *Writings,* XXXVI, 504–5.

[42] Washington to McHenry, March 25, 1799, *ibid.,* XXXVII, 157–64 at 160–61.

[43] *Ibid.,* XXXVII, 161.

[44] To what extent occasional refusal of the Senate to concur in the President's nominations was due to the failure to secure consent of the appropriate Senator or delegation is uncertain. Washington experienced two such rebuffs, apart from some military appointments. With respect to the first, Benjamin Fishbourn, Miss Lucy M. Salmon declared, "The Senators from Georgia had expressed a preference for another person, and for that reason the nomination was rejected." (*History of the Appointing Power of the President,* Am. Hist. Assoc., *Papers,* Vol. I, No. 5 [1886], p. 26, n. 3.) The other case, John Rutledge, clearly involved different considerations. Several instances of Senate refusal to confirm military appointments under John Adams rest on obscure grounds, except that of his son-in-law, William S. Smith.

Chapter Eight

FEDERALIST AND REPUBLICAN THEORIES OF THE EXECUTIVE POWER

Not all Federalists and not all Republicans agreed with the views of their fellow partisans at every point, but two substantially different concepts of the executive power and its relationship to Congress clearly emerged during the administrations of Washington and Adams. Hamilton was the leading theorist of the Federalists, Jefferson of the Republicans, but in Congress and without, others made their own contributions to the institutions of the new regime. The character of the American executive and of the administrative system was largely shaped by their opposing views and practices.[1]

Both Federalists and Republicans recognized that government rested upon consent and that power could only be exerted with the support of the citizens. Elbridge Gerry truly said, "The energy of your Government depends upon the approbation of the people."[2] Stephen Higginson told Oliver Wolcott in 1798 that the government "should have two or three able men in their service, to inform the people of the expediency or necessity of the measures adopted. . . . A popular government like ours, dependent upon the support and confidence of the people, cannot have a fair chance, unless constant and convincing displays of the wisdom and rectitude of public measures are regularly made for their instruction; and to depend upon volunteer exertions to make such displays, is to render the public tranquillity, if not safety, very precarious."[3] But "public relations" did not become a function of government although party newspapers were resorted to by both sides.

---

[1] Lynton K. Caldwell, *The Administrative Theories of Hamilton and Jefferson* (Chicago: University of Chicago Press, 1944), *passim*.

[2] *Annals*, I, 314 (May 9, 1789).

[3] Gibbs, *Memoirs*, II, 178.

The Federalists emphasized the necessity for power in government and for energy in the executive branch. The Republicans emphasized the liberties of the citizen and the primacy of representative assemblies. The latter accused their opponents of sympathy for monarchy and hostility to republican institutions, but these charges, largely unfounded, had little to do with administration. Hamilton, above all his contemporaries (except Ames), insisted on the necessity for executive leadership of an otherwise drifting legislature; Jefferson thought the people's representatives would readily find their way if left alone to educate each other by free discussion and compromise. Jefferson, as well as Hamilton, took a liberal view of executive power in extreme emergencies; Hamilton, with Jefferson, believed that official discretion should be reduced to a minimum in the ranks of subordinate officers. By 1792 Jefferson thought the executive power had swallowed up the legislative branch; in 1796 Hamilton thought the legislative branch had so curtailed executive power that an able man could find no useful place in the government.

In the Constitutional Convention Hamilton had gone far toward the model of the British monarchy, adapted to republican forms. "The English model," he declared, "was the only good one on this subject," [4] and toward it he would go as far as republican principles would permit in order to secure stability and permanency. He consequently proposed to vest the supreme executive authority in a "Governour" to be selected by electors chosen by the people, to serve during good behavior, and to be vested with an absolute veto, the execution of laws, the conduct of war "when authorized or begun," the conclusion of treaties with the consent of the Senate, the sole appointment of the heads of departments (the Senate to concur in others), and the power to pardon. [5]

An elective monarchy Hamilton recognized was not within the range of practical politics, and in *The Federalist* he set himself to defend the executive power as it was organized by the Convention. It is in *The Federalist* that we find the most systematic presentation of Hamilton's thought on the executive branch. Its three major aspects were independence, power, and responsibility.

Hamilton emphasized at every point the necessity of organizing an executive which in its own sphere could act independently of the

---

[4] Farrand, *Records of the Federal Convention*, I, 289.
[5] *Ibid.*, I, 292.

legislative branch.[6] He approved the device of the electoral college which avoided the selection of the President by Congress and which based the office firmly on the people themselves. He recognized that the executive was necessarily and rightly bound by law, as by the Constitution, but within the four corners of the law he desired freedom of executive action. "It is one thing," he declared, "to be subordinate to the laws, and another to be dependent on the legislative body."[7] He argued for the qualified negative, although he would have preferred an absolute veto. "Without the one or the other, the former [i.e., the President] would be absolutely unable to defend himself against the depredations of the latter."[8] The treaty power he believed to be neither specifically legislative nor executive in nature, and consequently asserted that the double responsibility fixed in the Constitution was "one of the best digested and most unexceptionable parts of the plan."[9] He recognized that the President might "secure the complaisance of the Senate to his views" through the influence of appointments, but minimized the probable danger.[10] He believed that the consent of the Senate was necessary for removal as well as for appointment, and his views on this point proved embarrassing to Madison in the subsequent debate on the removal power.[11] In short, while Hamilton accepted the primacy of law and the legislative checks on executive power written into the Constitution, he was an unshaken advocate of an executive authority able to act independently within its own field.

Reflecting both his views on good government and his own personality, Hamilton stood for an energetic executive. He asserted in *The Federalist:*

. . . Energy in the Executive is a leading character in the definition of good government.

. . . A feeble Executive implies a feeble execution of the government. A feeble execution is but another phrase for a bad execution; . . .

---

[6] *The Federalist,* No. 68.

[7] *Ibid.,* No. 71.

[8] *Ibid.,* No. 73; "The primary inducement to conferring the power in question upon the Executive," he added, "is, to enable him to defend himself. . . ."

[9] *Ibid.,* No. 75.

[10] *Ibid.,* No. 76.

[11] *Ibid.,* No. 77.

. . . all men of sense will agree in the necessity of an energetic Executive, . . .

The ingredients which constitute energy in the Executive are, first, unity; secondly, duration; thirdly, an adequate provision for its support; fourthly, competent powers.

The ingredients which constitute safety in the republican sense are, first, a due dependence on the people, secondly, a due responsibility.[12]

Federalists generally joined with Hamilton in a dislike of official boards, believing them weak and irresponsible. Washington held that "wherever, and whenever one person is found adequate to the discharge of a duty by close application thereto it is worse executed by two persons, and scarcely done at all if three or more are employed therein. . . ."[13] Jeremiah Wadsworth of Connecticut declared that "a Board of Treasury is the worst of all institutions,"[14] in the fight to prevent Gerry from pushing such a plan through the House. At the early age of twenty-three, Hamilton's views were set on this point.

A single man, in each department of the administration, would be greatly preferable. It would give us a chance of more knowledge, more activity, more responsibility, and, of course, more zeal and attention. Boards partake of a part of the inconveniences of larger assemblies. Their decisions are slower, their energy less, their responsibility more diffused. They will not have the same abilities and knowledge as an administration by single men. Men of the first pretensions will not so readily engage in them; because they will be less conspicuous, of less importance, have less opportunity of distinguishing themselves. The members of Boards will take less pains to inform themselves and arrive to eminence, because they have fewer motives to do it. All these reasons conspire to give a preference to the plan of vesting the great executive departments of the State in the hands of individuals. . . .[15]

While Hamilton desired a strong executive, he also desired one which was responsible. His insistence on unity in the executive branch was due in part to his belief that "the sole and undivided responsibility

---

[12] *Ibid.*, No. 70.
[13] Washington, *Writings*, XXXII, 160.
[14] *Annals*, I, 389; for Gerry's attitude, see *ibid.*, I, 384–89 (May 20, 1789).
[15] Hamilton, *Works* (Hamilton ed.), I, 154–55 (Sept. 3, 1780).

of one man will naturally beget a livelier sense of duty and a more exact regard to reputation." [16] He may have favored that type of responsibility which was slowly crystallizing into the British cabinet system; but his description of the proper relations between the President and the heads of departments, already noted, points in another direction. He did not foresee the type of party responsibility which soon emerged.[17] The enforcement of formal responsibility of the President and other executive officers through impeachment he accepted, and readily acknowledged the authority of Congress to investigate the executive departments.

Hamilton believed that the administration must supply leadership to the legislative branch. His own forceful contributions to Congress merely reflected what he thought a normal situation. He construed Article II of the Constitution as bestowing plenary executive power upon the President, and sought to reduce the powers of Congress in the field of foreign affairs to the constitutional minimum.

His emphasis on executive leadership was not merely the counterpart of his own imperious personality. He believed the American economy should be directed away from too exclusive a reliance on agriculture into a balanced agricultural-industrial economy. Such an economy required national action and effective leadership on a national scale. In such leadership he saw the principal instrument of emerging economic policy.

John Adams was also an uncompromising friend of the executive, on theoretical as well as practical grounds. His theoretical position he set out in 1789, especially in an exchange of letters with Roger Sherman, from which the following quotations are taken.

The duration of our president is neither perpetual nor for life; it is only for four years; but his power during those four years is much greater than that of an avoyer, a consul, a podestà, a doge, a stadtholder; nay, than a king of Poland; nay, than a king of Sparta. I know of no first magistrate

---

16 *The Federalist,* No. 76.

17 The place of political parties in government perplexed the Federalist leaders. Washington was alarmed at the consequences of their conflict; Hamilton thought they would be no asset to the public service; Sedgwick "descanted on the pernicious consequences which might result from the collision of parties." *Annals,* III, 278 (Dec. 22, 1791). Harper, on the other hand, made a very able statement, pointing out the inevitability of parties and asserting that their general effects were beneficial. *Ibid.,* VII, 874 (Jan. 19, 1798).

in any republican government, excepting England and Neuchatel, who possesses a constitutional dignity, authority, and power comparable to his. . . .

That these powers are necessary, I readily admit. . . . But it is equally certain, I think, that they ought to have been still greater, or much less. The limitations upon them in the cases of war, treaties, and appointments to office, and especially the limitation on the president's independence as a branch of the legislative, will be the destruction of this constitution, and involve us in anarchy, if not amended. . . . In our constitution the sovereignty,—that is, the legislative power,—is divided into three branches. The house and senate are equal, but the third branch, though essential, is not equal. The president must pass judgment upon every law; but in some cases his judgment may be overruled. These cases will be such as attack his constitutional power; it is, therefore, certain he has not equal power to defend himself, or the constitution, or the judicial power, as the senate and house have.

Power naturally grows. Why? Because human passions are insatiable. But that power alone can grow which already is too great; that which is unchecked; that which has no equal power to control it. The legislative power, in our constitution, is greater than the executive; it will, therefore, encroach, because both aristocratical and democratical passions are insatiable. The legislative power will increase, the executive will diminish. . . .[18]

In a letter to Thomas Jefferson, Adams declared,

I would, therefore, have given more power to the president, and less to the senate. The nomination and appointment to all offices, I would have given to the president, assisted only by a privy council of his own creation; but not a vote or voice would I have given to the senate or any senator unless he were of the privy council. . . .[19]

The more extreme Federalist view of legislative-executive relations was that held and eloquently expressed by Fisher Ames of Massachusetts. At the close of Washington's administration he wrote a confidential letter to Alexander Hamilton about the situation in the government.

---

[18] July 18, 1789, Adams, *Works,* VI, 430–31. In a subsequent letter to Sherman, Adams wrote, "Nay, I go further, and say, that from the constitution of human nature, and the constant course of human affairs, it is certain that our constitution will be subverted, if not amended, and that in a very short time, merely for want of a decisive negative in the executive." *Ibid.,* VI, 432.

[19] Dec. 6, 1787, *ibid.,* VIII, 464.

Our proceedings smell of anarchy. . . .

. . . Our whole system is little removed from simple democracy. What we call *the government* is a phantom, as long as the democrats prevail in the House. The heads of departments are head clerks. Instead of being the ministry, the organs of the executive power, and imparting a kind of momentum to the operation of the laws, they are precluded of late even from communicating with the House, by reports. In other countries, they may speak as well as act. We allow them to do neither. We forbid even the use of a speaking-trumpet; or, more properly, as the Constitution has ordained that they shall be dumb, we forbid them to explain themselves by signs. Two evils, obvious to you, result from all this. The efficiency of the government is reduced to its minimum—the proneness of a popular body to usurpation is already advancing to its maximum; committees already are the ministers; and while the House indulges a jealousy of encroachment on its functions, which are properly deliberative, it does not perceive that these are impaired and nullified by the monopoly as well as the perversion of information, by these very committees. . . .[20]

To Jefferson and his friends these ideas smelled of monarchy and the subversion of the popular assembly. Most of them feared executive power and would curb it within narrow limits. The more extreme Republicans, indeed, had a concept of executive organization which would quickly have resulted in administrative anarchy. They looked upon heads of departments as independent of the President, and upon representatives abroad as free to pursue their own policy, not that of the President. They fought executive discretion and would have specified so far as possible the exact use of every appropriation. They viewed the executive as a ministerial agency, intended merely to carry out the will of Congress.

"The executive," said Tom Paine, "is not invested with the power of deliberating whether it shall act or not; it has no discretionary authority in the case; for it can *act no other thing* than what the laws decree, and it is *obliged* to act conformably thereto; and in this view of the case, the executive is made up of all the official departments that execute the laws, of which that which is called the judiciary is the chief." Paine added two guides drawn from reason and experience. "The one is, never to invest any individual with extraordinary power; for besides his being tempted to misuse it, it will excite contention and

---

[20] Jan. 26, 1797, Hamilton, *Works* (Hamilton ed.), VI, 198–203 at 200–201.

commotion in the nation for the office. Secondly, never to invest power long in the hands of any number of individuals. The inconveniences that may be supposed to accompany frequent changes are less to be feared than the danger that arises from long continuance." [21]

The extremists, who were laboring in the cause of liberty as they saw it, were few in number. The Republican concept of executive power was more thoughtfully developed by Jefferson, Madison, and Gallatin. These men recognized the necessity for a strong executive, but they emphasized the primacy of the legislative branch and its freedom from executive domination. They were largely governed by fear of monarchy and of encroachment on civil liberty. Jefferson put the ground of their opposition to the Federalists as follows:

Here then was the real ground of the opposition which was made to the course of administration. It's object was to preserve the legislature pure and independant of the Executive, to restrain the administration to republican forms and principles, and not permit the constitution to be construed into a monarchy, and to be warped in practice into all the principles and pollutions of their favorite English model. . . .[22]

When Jefferson embarked in the new government he determined "to intermeddle not at all with the legislature," and in 1792 told Washington that he had broken his rule only once, as the dupe of the Secretary of the Treasury in the matter of the funding legislation. "As I never had the desire to influence the members, so neither had I any other means than my friendships, which I valued too highly to risk by usurpations on their freedom of judgment, & the conscientious pursuit of their own sense of duty." [23] Jefferson charged Hamilton with the complete breakdown of the independence of the House by means which he darkly hinted were corrupt—patronage, speculative opportunities in public securities, favors at the Bank of the United States and the like. ". . . the whole action of the legislature was now under the direction of the treasury." [24] This encroachment disturbed Jefferson deeply. To Washington he declared, "if the equilibrium of the three great bodies Legislative, Executive, and judiciary could be preserved,

---

[21] *Life and Writings of Thomas Paine* (Independence edition, Daniel Edwin Wheeler, ed., 10 vols., New York: Vincent Parke, 1908), IX, 274–75, 275–76.

[22] *Anas,* Jefferson, *Works* (Federal ed.), I, 178.

[23] Sept. 9, 1792, *ibid.,* VII, 137–38.

[24] *Ibid.,* I, 172–79.

if the Legislature could be kept independant, I should never fear the
result of such a government. . . ."[25]

At the same time Jefferson was conscious of the necessity for executive power. In a well-known passage Hamilton observed,

But it is not true, as is alleged, that he [Jefferson] is an enemy to the
power of the Executive, or that he is for confounding all the powers in the
House of Representatives. It is a fact which I have frequently mentioned,
that, while we were in the administration together, he was generally for a
large construction of the Executive authority and not backward to act upon
it in cases which coincided with his views. . . .[26]

Subsequently, as President, Jefferson amply confirmed Hamilton's
judgment.

---

[25] *Ibid.*, I, 236.
[26] Hamilton to James A. Bayard, Jan. 16, 1801, Hamilton, *Works* (Lodge ed.), X, 413.

Chapter Nine

GEORGE WASHINGTON AS AN ADMINISTRATOR

W<small>HEN</small> Washington took the oath of office as President of the United States, the character and quality of the presidency were defined merely by the appropriate sentences of the Constitution. When he issued his Farewell Address in September 1796, the impact of events and the personality of Washington on the office had given it living form and substance. The character of Washington was one of the most significant single influences which gave identity to the presidency as an administrative, as well as a ceremonial, political, and military office, and it is accordingly appropriate to round out an account of its formation with an analysis of the qualities of mind and of the understanding of administration which he brought to his task.

The character of Washington, combined with his long public service, was one that inspired confidence in the new general government. Confidence was the greatest single asset that any man could have brought to the new enterprise. Again and again in the early debates on the presidency, acknowledgment was made of the universal respect in which Washington was held. "The President," said James Madison in 1793, "was the last man in the world to whom any measure whatever of a deceptive tendency could be credibly attributed." [1]

The simplicity and the dignity of Washington's personality have often been touched upon. The words of a contemporary English visitor

---

[1] *Annals,* III, 943 (March 1, 1793). Adams' fulsome praise in the Senate, April 21, 1789, may be discounted (Adams, *Works,* VIII, 486–87). See Madison's comparison of Washington and Adams in *The Writings of James Madison* (Gaillard Hunt, ed., 9 vols., New York: G. P. Putnam's Sons, 1900–1910), VI, 310, Madison to Jefferson, Feb. 1798.

to the President, Thomas Twining, speak eloquently of the impact which Washington must have had upon his time.

13th May.—At one o'clock to-day I called at General Washington's with the picture and letter I had for him. He lived in a small red brick house on the left side of High Street, not much higher up than Fourth Street. There was nothing in the exterior of the house that denoted the rank of its possessor. Next door was a hair-dresser. Having stated my object to a servant who came to the door, I was conducted up a neat but rather narrow staircase, carpeted in the middle, and was shown into a middling-sized well-furnished drawing-room on the left of the passage. Nearly opposite the door was the fireplace, with a wood-fire in it. The floor was carpeted. On the left of the fireplace was a sofa, which sloped across the room. There were no pictures on the walls, no ornaments on the chimney-piece. Two windows on the right of the entrance looked into the street. There was nobody in the room, but in a minute Mrs. Washington came in, when I repeated the object of my calling, and put into her hands the letter for General Washington, and his miniature. She said she would deliver them to the President, and, inviting me to sit down, retired for that purpose. She soon returned, and said the President would come presently. Mrs. Washington was a middle-sized lady, rather stout; her manner extremely kind and unaffected. She sat down on the sofa, and invited me to sit by her. I spoke of the pleasant days I had passed at Washington, and of the attentions I had received from her granddaughter, Mrs. Law.

While engaged in this conversation, but with my thoughts turned to the expected arrival of the General, the door opened, and Mrs. Washington and myself rising, she said, "The President," and introduced me to him. Never did I feel more interest than at this moment, when I saw the tall, upright, venerable figure of this great man advancing towards me to take me by the hand. There was a seriousness in his manner which seemed to contribute to the impressive dignity of his person, without diminishing the confidence and ease which the benevolence of his countenance and the kindness of his address inspired. There are persons in whose appearance one looks in vain for the qualities they are known to possess, but the appearance of General Washington harmonized in a singular manner with the dignity and modesty of his public life. So completely did he *look* the great and good man he really was, that I felt rather respect than awe in his presence, and experienced neither the surprise nor disappointment with which a personal introduction to distinguished individuals is often accompanied. . . .

The General's age was rather more than sixty-four. In person he was tall, well-proportioned, and upright. His hair was powdered and tied behind.

Although his deportment was that of a general, the expression of his features had rather the calm dignity of a legislator than the severity of a soldier. . . .[2]

While during the later years of his administration Washington was the subject of much criticism and abuse, mostly factional in origin, the deep veneration in which he was held expressed itself publicly on the last day of his second term as he turned over the reins of government to his successor. "He came unattended and on foot, with the modest appearance of a private citizen. No sooner was his person seen, than a burst of applause such as I had never before known, and which it would be as impossible for me to describe, as my own sensations produced by it, saluted the venerable Hero and Patriot. . . ."[3]

WASHINGTON'S GENERAL IDEAS ON ADMINISTRATION

The vast importance of good administration of the new system was never out of Washington's mind; frequently he revealed his concern for the effective conduct of national affairs. Writing on January 21, 1790, to Thomas Jefferson to persuade him to become Secretary of State, he said, "I consider the successful Administration of the general Government as an object of almost infinite consequence to the present and future happiness of the Citizens of the United States."[4]

In all his early actions as President, Washington was acutely aware that he was setting precedents and creating a system. "Many things which appear of little importance in themselves and at the beginning," he stated, "may have great and durable consequences from their having been established at the commencement of a new general government. It will be much easier to commence the administration, upon a well adjusted system, built on tenable grounds, than to correct errors or alter inconveniences after they shall have been confirmed by habit."[5]

Washington never wrote out a systematic view of the functions and

---

[2] May 13, 1795, Thomas Twining, *Travels in America 100 Years Ago* (New York: Harper and Brothers, 1902), pp. 128–30, 132–33. Twining had visited Washington, the future seat of government, mentioned in the above quotation. For Jefferson's analysis of Washington's character, see Jefferson, *Works* (Federal ed.), XI, 375–77.

[3] Rufus King, *Correspondence*, II, 159; see also for another eyewitness account Robert G. Harper's Letter to his Constituents, March 13, 1797, Am. Hist. Assoc., *Annual Report, 1913,* II, 29–30.

[4] Washington, *Writings*, XXX, 510.

[5] May 10, 1789, *ibid.,* XXX, 321.

appropriate qualities of a chief executive.[6] "With me," he said, "it has always been a maxim, rather to let my designs appear from my works than by my expressions."[7] But that he had a firm grasp of the means of conducting affairs which he put to daily use cannot be doubted by anyone who reads his letters and his public papers. Washington was an able administrator. With a sure and almost intuitive understanding he established in eight years an office with settled relationships to Congress, to the departments of state, and to a public which had to be taught that the head of a state could be powerful without escaping control. In his daily administrative tasks he was systematic, orderly, energetic, solicitous of the opinions of others but independent in his own judgment, insistent upon facts and deliberation but decisive, intent upon general goals and the consistency of particular actions with them. Less inventive than Hamilton, he was not brilliant but steady; he balanced different courses of conduct against each other in the recesses of his mind rather than in argumentation with his associates; always sensitive to public opinion, no criticism could swerve him from the decisions which his intelligence and conscience dictated.

In response to hostile petitions against the Jay Treaty, he uniformly replied,

In every act of my administration, I have sought the happiness of my fellow-citizens. My system for the attainment of this object has uniformly been to overlook all personal, local and partial considerations: to contemplate the United States, as one great whole. . . .
While I feel the most lively gratitude for the many instances of approba-

---

[6] In 1792 he described the character of a "judicious and skilful superintendant [of the Federal City]. . . . One in whom is united knowledge of Men and things, industry, integrity, impartiality, and firmness." *Ibid.,* XXXII, 223.

[7] Dec. 21, 1797, *ibid.,* XXXVI, 113. Norman J. Small comments as follows: "Whether Washington, like his successors, was in possession of any definite opinions as to the powers of the Presidency at the date of his entry into that office, or whether he formulated any theory as to the Chief Magistracy during his subsequent years in the service cannot be conclusively determined. . . .

. . . Being essentially a man of deed and not of contemplation, a man for whom facts and not abstractions had any attraction, he was preoccupied with the problem of putting into successful operation the product of the Philadelphia Convention." (*Some Presidential Interpretations of the Presidency,* p. 13.) Vernon Louis Parrington thought so little of Washington's contribution to the thought of his time that he did not include him in his *Main Currents in American Thought* (3 vols., New York: Harcourt, Brace, 1927–30).

tion from my country; I can no otherwise deserve it, than by obeying the dictates of my conscience. . . .[8]

His principal success was to plant in the minds of the American people the model of a government which commanded respect by reason of its integrity, energy, and competence.

In his first inaugural address, Washington observed that he was "unpracticed in the duties of civil administration." [9] His competent performance in administration grew out of two separate aspects of his experience—his life as a plantation manager and his life as a military commander. The former is not to be despised; the number of persons whom Washington supervised directly at Mount Vernon was greater than the number required to carry on the functions of any of the departments of state in New York or Philadelphia (omitting their embryonic field services); and the lessons which he learned in plantation management he applied to public affairs. In his instructions to his manager at Mount Vernon he once wrote,

there is much more in what is called head work, that is in the manner of conducting business, than is generally imagined. For take two Managers and give to each the same number of labourers, and let these labourers be equal in all respects. Let both these Managers rise equally early, go equally late to rest, be equally active, sober and industrious, and yet, in the course of the year, one of them, without pushing the hands that are under him more than the other, shall have performed infinitely more work. To what is this owing? Why, simply to contrivance resulting from that forethought and arrangement which will guard against the misapplication of labour, and doing it unseasonably. . . .[10]

---

[8] Letter to the Boston Selectmen, July 28, 1795, *Writings*, XXXIV, 252–53.

[9] At the end of his first term, when contemplating retirement, Washington told Madison that "he had from the beginning found himself deficient in many of the essential qualifications, owing to his inexperience in the forms of public business, his unfitness to judge of legal questions, and questions arising out of the Constitution; that others more conversant in such matters would be better able to execute the trust; that he found himself also in the decline of life, his health becoming sensibly more infirm, & perhaps his faculties also; that the fatigues & disagreeableness of his situation were in fact scarcely tolerable to him. . . ." (Madison, *Writings*, Hunt ed., VI, 108, n). Washington suffered from a bad memory, to which he referred as early as 1789 (Washington, *Writings*, XXX, 456); it became progressively worse.

[10] Jan. 1, 1789, *ibid.*, XXX, 175–76, n. 4; cf. *ibid.*, XXXIII, 389; and especially *ibid.*, XXXVII, 460.

As a military commander Washington encountered a wide range of administrative problems, not the least of which were his relations to the Congress. Not until he assumed command of the Continental Army in Cambridge in 1775 had he directly encountered important public management responsibilities. During the hard years which followed he learned much by experience, but what he learned was consonant with the underlying common-sense dictates which plantation management since 1759 had already confirmed.

While Washington never committed to paper an organized philosophy of government or of administration, his working rules stand out with remarkable clarity. He attached great importance to system and plan; he insisted upon energetic handling of public affairs, promptly and decisively; he based his actions solidly upon facts; he understood the necessity of freedom from detail although he was not too successful in avoiding it; and he set much store upon the dignity of the presidential office, not to gratify a personal sense of station but to lend prestige to the infant general government. These rules, implicit in what Washington did rather than in what he said, are examined in the following pages.

SYSTEM AND PLAN

"System," wrote Washington, "to all things is the soul of business. To deliberate maturely, and execute promptly is the way to conduct it to advantage." [11] Addressing Benjamin Stoddert in 1792 on the duties of the Commissioners in conducting the affairs of the Federal City, he advised,

there is in my judgmt. but one line of conduct proper for these Gentlemen to pursue, and that is to take a comprehensive view of the trust reposed in them, the general expectation of the community at large, and the means to effect it. form their plans agreeably thereto upon sound and just principles and to see that they are carried into effect by whomsoever they shall employ in the Execution thereof, without regard to any local concern or interest whatsoever. . . . [12]

Toward the end of his life he put into a sentence the essence of his greatness as an administrator: ". . . for the more combined, and distant

---

[11] *Ibid.*, XXXVI, 113.
[12] *Ibid.*, XXXII, 224.

things are seen, the more likely they are to be turned to advantage." [13]
Perspective on distant goals and the combination of many things to
their achievement, patience meanwhile, were close to the heart of
Washington's character.

These maxims were illustrated in Washington's working habits.[14]
After taking office and before the new government was organized, he
read extensively among the papers of the Confederation period and
digested them for future reference. On June 8, 1789, he requested the
acting heads of the former departments for "a clear account" in writing
of their respective agencies.[15] From time to time he requested a statement of those duties which required the "agency" of the presidency,
to be sure that he omitted no task imposed upon him. Before leaving
New York or Philadelphia he regularly asked each Secretary to review
any pending business which might require his attention.[16] Well before
each session of Congress, he requested his secretary, Tobias Lear, and
the department heads, as well as Madison and others, to organize material and present ideas for his messages. When Jefferson finally arrived
to become Secretary of State, Washington spent the greater part of a
week in almost unbroken conference with him. Washington was, in
short, an exceptionally orderly chief magistrate, and in his daily routine
kept within the framework of general plans. But planning in the sense
of forming a national economy either in the Hamiltonian or Jeffersonian pattern was not among his preoccupations.

ENERGY

Energy and firmness were cardinal virtues in Washington's sense
of administration. While awaiting inauguration as President he observed with indignation the incompetence of the Confederation authorities. On April 10, 1789, he wrote to the Acting Secretary of War,

the stupor, or listlessness with which our public measures seem to be per-
vaded, is, to me, matter of deep regret. Indeed it has so strange an appearance that I cannot but wonder how men who sollicit public confidence or

---

[13] Washington to James Anderson, Dec. 21, 1797, *ibid.*, XXXVI, 113.
[14] Paul Leland Haworth declares in his *George Washington: Country Gentleman*
(Indianapolis: Bobbs-Merrill, 1925), p. 76, that Washington was the most methodical
man that ever lived.
[15] Washington, *Writings*, XXX, 344.
[16] For example, *ibid.*, XXXI, 91–92.

who are even prevailed upon to accept of it can reconcile such conduct with their own feelings of propriety.

The delay is inauspicious to say the best of it, and the World must condemn it.[17]

He expected the heads of departments to give close attention to business and reminded them of this duty. ". . . let me, in a friendly way, impress the following maxims," he said, "upon the Executive Officers. In all important matters, to deliberate maturely, but to execute promptly and vigorously. And not to put things off until the Morrow which can be done, and require to be done to day. Without an adherence to these rules, business never will be *well* done, or done in an easy manner; but will always be in arrear, with one thing treading upon the heels of another." [18] In dealing with his department heads, Washington was prompt and decisive. He cleared quickly the business they brought to him, and pushed them for expedition in the discharge of their duties.

Washington was greatly annoyed by the failure of some officials to attend to their duties and not infrequently wrote sharp letters to them. On July 2, 1792, for example, he caused Lear to write Woodbury Langdon, one of the commissioners for settling accounts between the United States and the individual states,

I am commanded by the President of the United States to inform you, that it is indispensably necessary you should without delay repair to the seat of Government to prosecute jointly with your colleagues the business of your office as Commissioner. . . . I am further instructed by the President to say, that if any circumstances in your situation should be incompatible with your immediate and steady attendance, it is proper you should resign the Office. . . .[19]

---

[17] *Ibid.*, XXX, 280.

[18] *Ibid.*, XXXV, 138. In a letter to the Secretary of War written at Mount Vernon, Sept. 24, 1792, Washington referred to "some remissness on the part of the Contractors at Pittsburgh. This ought not to be suffered in the smallest degree; for one neglect or omission, is too apt to beget another, to the discontentment of the Troops and injury of the Service; whereas a rigid exaction in every case checks a departure on their part from the Contract in any; and no indulgence is ever allowed by them to the public." *Ibid.*, XXXII, 162.

[19] *Ibid.*, XXXII, 82–83. Cf. his remark to the Commissioners of the District of Columbia, "Coaxing a man to stay in Office, or to do his duty while he is in it, is not the way to accomplish the object." *Ibid.*, XXXV, 111.

The decisiveness with which Washington met the challenge of the disorderly distillers of whiskey in western Pennsylvania is one of the most dramatic examples of his energy and firmness. The episode is dealt with elsewhere; but the tone and temper of the Chief Executive in this crisis of law enforcement are revealed in his correspondence. "When . . . lenient and temporizing means have been used, and serve only to increase the disorder; longer forbearance would become unjustifiable remissness, and a neglect of that duty which is enjoined on the President." [20] And again, "neither the Military nor Civil government shall be trampled upon with impunity whilst I have the honor to be at the head of them." [21] Washington himself left Philadelphia and journeyed to Bedford as commander in chief to be certain that the militia was well organized and the expedition was properly directed. Nor did he fail to provide a compelling argument to the rebellious distillers; no less than 15,000 militia were assembled from Pennsylvania and neighboring states.

FACTS

In reaching decisions Washington required all available facts. Throughout his official correspondence there is repeated insistence upon facts rather than opinions. On September 14, 1791, he wrote Governor Clinton of New York with reference to British occupancy of the western posts; while recognizing the gravity of the situation he declined to take action other than to dispatch a "gentleman to the spot," so that his eventual decision could be based "upon the ground of well authenticated facts." [22] Commenting on General Wayne's plan for an Indian campaign, he noted that "The latter will be *right,* or *wrong,* according to the actual State of things at *those places* at the time it is proposed to make them, (to be ascertained from indubitable information). . . ." [23] Replying to a letter recommending a young Alexandrian as an ensign because a number of young country-born men would enlist under him, he answered, let him "ascertain *that* fact, and then apply with the list of them." [24]

---

[20] Sept. 17, 1792, *ibid.,* XXXII, 154.
[21] Sept. 24, 1792, *ibid.,* XXXII, 161.
[22] *Ibid.,* XXXI, 370.
[23] *Ibid.,* XXXII, 145.
[24] *Ibid.,* XXXII, 161.

Toward the end of his administration he wrote to Pickering, referring to a forthcoming statement on relations with France:

I have no doubt that you have taken care, and will continue to be assured,
of your facts; for as this business will certainly come before the public, not
only the facts, but the candour also, the expression, and force of every word,
will be examined with the most scrutinizing eye, and compared with everything that will admit of a different construction, and if there is the least
ground for it, we shall be charged with unfairness, and an intention to
impose on, and to mislead the public judgment.

Hence, and from a desire that the statement may be full, fair, calm and
argumentative; without asperity, or anything more irritating in the comments, than the narration of facts, which expose unfounded charges and
assertions, do themselves produce, I have wished that this letter to Mr.
Pinckney may be revised over, and over again. . . .[25]

AVOIDANCE OF DETAIL

Washington was more clear in principle about the necessity of avoiding detail than he was successful in practice. The interchange of correspondence between Hamilton, Jefferson, Knox, and the President reveals a mass of business which the heads of departments thought it
essential to clear with the Chief Executive, and which Washington
continued to accept throughout his two terms. Appointments, great
and small, were of direct concern to Washington, and no collector of
customs, captain of a cutter, keeper of a lighthouse, or surveyor of
revenue was appointed except after specific consideration by the President. In signing contracts for the construction of a lighthouse the President took time to enjoin economy in the selection of materials. Leaves
of absence of important officials were requested from and approved by
the President himself.

General Uriah Forrest remarked to McHenry, "You know Genl.
Washington is in all respects singularly attentive to any thing, and
perhaps the Federal City (being rather a Hobby Horse of his) more
than anything else had his attention. . . ."[26] This was partly on
account of the feuds and quarrels which developed there, partly by
reason of his intense interest in the new capital. Thus on August 29,
1791, we find Washington writing to Jefferson, "Ought there to be

---

[25] Jan. 4, 1797, *ibid.*, XXXV, 351–52.
[26] *Publications of the Southern History Association*, X (1906), 33.

any wood houses in the town? . . . Ought not Stoups, and projections of every sort and kind into the Streets, to be prohibited *absolutely*?"[27] On July 23, 1794, he wrote the Commissioners of the District of Columbia, "I wish, however, you had declared that so much of the stone walls, on which the railing in the Street is to be placed, as shall appear above the pavement (or surface of the ground before it is paved) should be of freestone hewed."[28] His repeated efforts to relieve himself of the details of laying out the Federal City by pointing out the proper duties of the Commissioners and of the superintendent were unavailing.

In military administration Washington grasped completely the importance of thrusting detail into other hands. Few better statements of the concept of a military staff as an aid to a commander have been made than that contained in a letter of Washington's to the Secretary of War on July 29, 1798, the main purpose of which was to protect himself against demands for appointment as his aide.

Of the propriety of remaining *perfectly* free from all engagements respecting my Aids, I am more and more convinced as the applications encrease and the little knowledge displayed of the qualifications which the Aids of the Commander in Chief ought to possess, is discovered by the Applicants. The variegated, and important duties of the Aids of a Commander in Chief, or, the Commander of a seperate Army, require experienced Officers, men of judgment, and men of business, *ready pens* to execute them properly and with dispatch. A great deal more is required of them than attending him at a Parade, or delivering verbal orders here and there; or copying a written one. They ought if I may be allowed to use the expression, to possess the Soul of the General; and from a *single* Idea given to them, to convey his meaning in the clearest and fullest manner. This, young men unacquainted with the Service and diffident, would not do; be their abilities what they may. . . .[29]

DIGNITY

In his own personality Washington was reserved and aloof; an easy congeniality did not come naturally to him. His personality coincided with his considered view concerning the public importance of surround-

---

[27] Washington, *Writings,* XXXI, 352.
[28] *Ibid.,* XXXIII, 440–41.
[29] *Ibid.,* XXXVI, 374–75.

ing the office of the Chief Executive with an impressive dignity.[30] The salary of the office, fixed by the first Congress at $25,000 a year, a figure far in excess of any other official salary and probably equaled by few of his American contemporaries, was an early proof of the general desire to form an office of great prestige. Washington's own choice of title was "His High Mightiness, the President of the United States and Protector of their Liberties"; fortunately a less "high toned" formalism was devised.[31] In his public appearances on official occasions, Washington rode in a coach drawn by four horses, sometimes six, followed by his official family in other coaches. At the outset, "to preserve the dignity and respect that was due to the first Magistrate," he decided to give invitations to dinner only "to official characters and strangers of distinction," and to receive no invitations.[32] His encounter with the gouty John Hancock, then governor of Massachusetts, at the time of his eastern trip is well known; he declined to call on Hancock until the governor had first paid his respects to the President of the United States.

One aspect of presidential formality which Washington did not enjoy, and for which he was criticized in Republican circles, was his weekly levee.[33] The levees were held every Tuesday between three and four o'clock in the afternoon. Visitors were introduced by Tobias Lear

---

[30] John Adams shared this attitude toward the external show of public office. "Neither dignity nor authority," he once wrote, "can be supported in human minds, collected into nations or any great numbers, without a splendor and majesty in some degree proportioned to them," *Works*, VIII, 493.

[31] Max Farrand, *The Framing of the Constitution of the United States* (New Haven: Yale University Press, 1913), p. 163. For the House debate on the presidential title, *Annals*, I, 318–24 (May 11, 1789).

[32] One of Washington's duties was to entertain Indian chiefs on formal occasions. John Adams noted on Dec. 4, 1796, that "The President dined four sets of Indians on four several days the last week." *Letters of John Adams, addressed to his wife*, II, 231. An early precedent (which curiously connected the first President with Franklin D. Roosevelt) occurred when Washington declined to attend the funeral ceremonies of Mrs. Isaac Roosevelt. Different accounts have been preserved of the atmosphere of Washington's dinners. Senator Maclay found them very formal, stiff, and almost oppressive (*Journal*, pp. 137–38, 206); but Jacob Hiltzheimer in his diary repeatedly commented upon Washington's ease; "an unassuming, easy and sociable man" (p. 171); "exceedingly affable to all" (p. 213). *Extracts from the Diary of Jacob Hiltzheimer of Philadelphia, 1765–1798* (Jacob Cox Parsons, ed., Philadelphia: Wm. F. Fell, 1893).

[33] Maclay, *Journal*, p. 351, Dec. 14, 1790: "This was levee day, and I accordingly dressed and did the needful. . . . The practice, however, considered as a feature of royalty, is certainly anti-republican."

or by some gentleman acquainted with the President. Washington dressed for the part

in black velvet; his hair in full dress, powdered and gathered behind in a large silk bag; yellow gloves on his hands; holding a cocked hat with cockade in it, and the edges adorned with a black feather about an inch deep. He wore knee and shoe buckles; and a long sword, with a finely wrought and polished steel hilt, which appeared at the left hip; the coat worn over the sword, so that the hilt, and the part below the folds of the coat behind, were in view. The scabbard was white polished leather.

He stood always in front of the fire-place, with his face towards the door of entrance. . . . He received his visitor with a dignified bow, while his hands were so disposed of as to indicate, that the salutation was not to be accompanied with shaking hands. This ceremony never occurred in these visits, even with his most near friends, that no distinction might be made.

As visitors came in, they formed a circle around the room. At a quarter past three, the door was closed, and the circle was formed for that day. He then began on the right, and spoke to each visitor, calling him by name, and exchanging a few words with him. When he had completed his circuit, he resumed his first position, and the visitors approached him in succession, bowed and retired. By four o'clock this ceremony was over.[34]

While Washington was reserved in personality he had no fondness for display, and on repeated occasions urged the avoidance of public notice or excessive ceremony. In this respect he differed from John Adams, whose pretension aroused much adverse criticism; Patrick Henry commented that it squinted toward monarchy. At the other extreme stood Jefferson who according to dubious tradition hitched his saddle horse before the capital as he walked in for his first inauguration. Hamilton, as might have been expected, insisted upon regard for the dignity of the presidential office, an attribute which, despite Republican abuse, had been well established at the conclusion of Washington's service as Chief Executive.

THE PRESIDENT AND PUBLIC OPINION

Washington was alert to the importance of a favorable public opinion in support of the new government and of the particular administrative

---

[34] William Sullivan, *The Public Men of the Revolution* (Philadelphia: Carey and Hart, 1847), p. 120.

decisions which were taken from time to time. From his correspondence it is clear that he took pains to ascertain what people were thinking and saying; that his decisions were affected, although not governed, by probable public reaction; and that on rare occasions he was prepared to influence public opinion.

At his invitation, a number of friends from different parts of the country, often not in public life, became informal reporters of public opinion to the President. On July 26, 1789, he wrote David Stuart of Virginia, "I should like to be informed, through so good a medium of the public opinion of both men and measures, and of none more than myself; not so much of what may be thought commendable parts, if any, of my conduct, as of those which are conceived to be of a different complexion." [35] On many occasions he directed his secretary, Tobias Lear, to sound out public opinion, especially on appointments.[36] On February 9, 1792, he wrote Jefferson with respect to a resident of Georgetown newly arrived in Philadelphia to "contrive to get him to his house," and "learn the sentiments of the people of that place, Carrolsburg &ca., with respect to the dispute between the Comrs. and Majr. L', and generally of the State of the business." [37]

To assess the state of opinion about the yeasty Pennsylvania whiskey distillers became a matter of prime importance; and it is not surprising to find Washington writing on August 10, 1794, to Burges Ball, "What (under the rose I ask it) is said, or thought, as far as it has appeared to you, of the conduct of the People in the Western Counties of this State (Pennsylvania) towards the excise Officers? and does there seem to be a disposition among those with whom you converse, to bring them to a Sense of their duty, and obedience to law, by coercion. . . ?" [38]

Washington's *major* decisions of policy and administration were affected to a very slight extent by what he learned of public opinion. The hostility to the Jay Treaty did not swerve him. On lesser matters, however, he weighed the opinion of the community carefully and in some instances it was a decisive factor. Writing to Comte de Rochambeau in the summer of 1790 he said, "In a government which depends

---

[35] Washington, *Writings*, XXX, 360; see also *ibid.*, XXXI, 28–30 for an example of this correspondence.

[36] *Ibid.*, XXXI, 296.

[37] *Ibid.*, XXXI, 477–78.

[38] *Ibid.*, XXXIII, 463.

so much in its first stages on public opinion, much circumspection is still necessary for those who are engaged in its administration." [39]

Washington entertained a progressively unfavorable opinion of the value of newspapers, and was privately deeply wounded by their intemperate attacks upon his policy. As early as the spring of 1790 he wrote David Stuart, "It is to be lamented that the Editors of the different Gazettes in the Union, do not more generally, and more correctly (instead of stuffing their papers with scurrility, and nonsensical declamation, which few would read if they were apprised of the contents) publish the debates in Congress on all great national questions. . . ." [40]

In the autumn of 1791 Philip Freneau began publication of the *National Gazette,* which rapidly became the major instrument of opposition to the Federalist policy and program. In August 1792 Washington privately referred to its attacks upon almost every measure of the government and expressed his concern.[41] In October he wrote Gouverneur Morris: "From the complexion of some of our Newspapers Foreigners would be led to believe that inveterate political dissensions existed among us, and that we are on the very verge of disunion; but the fact is otherwise. . . ." [42]

Although Freneau's *National Gazette* expired in the fall of 1793 Republican editors continued their abuse, to Washington's constant discomfort. In a letter to Jefferson he revealed his anger at the hostile press.

Perceiving, and probably, hearing, that no abuse in the Gazettes would induce me to take notice of anonymous publications, against me; those who were disposed to do me *such friendly Offices,* have embraced without restraint every opportunity to weaken the confidence of the People; and, by having the *whole* game in their hands, they have scrupled not to publish things that do not, as well as those which do exist; and to mutilate the latter, so as to make them subserve the purposes which they have in view.

Later in the same letter he referred to the abuse by his critics as couched "in such exaggerated and indecent terms as could scarcely be applied to a Nero; a notorious defaulter; or even to a common pickpocket." [43]

---

[39] *Ibid.,* XXXI, 83–84.
[40] *Ibid.,* XXXI, 30.
[41] *Ibid.,* XXXII, 136.
[42] *Ibid.,* XXXII, 189.
[43] July 6, 1796, *ibid.,* XXXV, 119, 120.

In public, however, Washington maintained a resolute and unbroken silence.

There is little evidence that Washington attempted to "manage" opinion, although Federalist and Republican leaders alike were alert to the importance both of the press and the post office in this respect. The distribution of large contracts for shipbuilding in different parts of the country was undoubtedly determined in part by the desire to secure a favorable public reaction. Two early examples were the construction of revenue cutters in 1790, and of frigates in 1794. In the first instance, Hamilton wrote the President, "To avoid dissatisfaction, it may appear best to build them in different ports of the Union," and specified where ten could be built from New Hampshire to Savannah; Washington endorsed this plan.[44] In the second instance the President directed frigates to be built at Baltimore and at Norfolk: "The wealth, and populousness of the two states will not only warrant, but require this change, if there is an equality in other respects."[45]

At times Washington took steps to influence public opinion. On January 16, 1792, he directed the Secretary of War to publish a statement on the Indian War, adding, "When the Community are called upon for considerable exertions to relieve a part which is suffering under the hand of an enemy, it is desirable to manifest that due pains have been taken by those entrusted with the administration of their affairs to avoid the evil."[46] In the early effort to enforce the tax on distilled spirits, he instructed the Attorney General to attend in person the Circuit Court at York, "for the further purpose, also, of giving to this measure of Government a more solemn and serious aspect."[47] Writing Jefferson concerning suggestions for rephrasing of his fourth annual message in 1792, he remarked, "For while so many unpleasant things are announced as the Speech contains, it cannot be amiss to accompany them with communications of a more agreeable nature."[48] In discussing the recall of Monroe from Paris, Washington wrote Pickering, the Secretary of State, "As the measure, when known, will excite much speculation, and set all the envenomed pens to work; it

---

[44] Sept. 10, 1790, Hamilton, *Works* (Hamilton ed.), IV, 46–47; Washington, *Writings,* XXXI, 118 (Sept. 20, 1790).

[45] Washington to the Secretary of War, April 16, 1794, *ibid.,* XXXIII, 333.

[46] *Ibid.,* XXXI, 459.

[47] Oct. 1, 1792, *ibid.,* XXXII, 171–72.

[48] *Ibid.,* XXXII, 200.

is worthy of consideration what part, and how much of the causes which have produced this event, should be spoken of *unofficially* by the officers of Government." [49]

So far as interference in the course of elections is concerned, Washington pursued a policy of complete nonintervention. In the elections of 1792 Colonel John F. Mercer of Maryland [50] asserted that Washington had told his nephew, Bushrod, that Mercer was the best representative "that now goes or ever did go to that Body from this State." Washington immediately commissioned an intermediary to deny this assertion, and shortly thereafter wrote directly to Colonel Mercer:

I was not a little displeased to find . . . that my name had been freely used by you or your friends, for electioneering purposes, when I had never associated your name and the Election together; and when there had been the most scrupulous and pointed caution observed on my part, not to express a sentiment respecting the fitness, or unfitness of any Candidate for representation. . . . Conceiving that the exercise of an influence (if I really possessed any) however remote, would be highly improper. . . . [51]

On broader grounds Washington conceived his principal duty to be to weld together a numerous body of states, scattered over an area immense under the conditions of the eighteenth century, diverse in many of their interests and conflicting in some, jealous and suspicious of each other and tending to fall into three principal sections, or even two. The great trends of opinion which he saw crystallizing around the southern and northern interests consequently disturbed him deeply. Less than a year after his inauguration his correspondent, David Stuart, had written Washington about "A spirit of jealousy which may become dangerous to the Union, towards the Eastern States." [52]

Washington replied,

Was it not always believed that there are some points which peculiarly interest the eastern States? and did any One, who reads human nature, and

---

[49] *Ibid.,* XXXV, 174.

[50] John F. Mercer, of a distinguished Virginia family, was a Virginia delegate to the Constitutional Congress from 1782–85. After his marriage in 1785, he moved to Maryland, and was a representative to Congress from that state, 1792–94. He served as governor of Maryland from 1801–3.

[51] Washington, *Writings,* XXXII, 165.

[52] *Ibid.,* XXXI, 28, n. 54.

more especially the character of the eastern people conceive that they would not pursue them steadily by a combination of their force? Are there not other points which equally concern the southern States? If these States are less tenacious of their interest, or, if whilst the eastern move in a solid phalanx to effect their views, the southern are always divided, which of the two is most to be blamed? That there is a diversity of interests in the Union none has denied. That this is the case also in every State is equally certain. And that it even extends to the Counties of individual States can be as readily proved . . .

. . . to accommodate differences, temper and mutual forbearance are requisite. Common danger brought the States into confederacy, and on their union our safety and importance depend. . . .[53]

On matters great and small, therefore, Washington recognized that he must measure his public acts against the tone and temper of public opinion. His personal fortunes counted for nothing in the outcome, but his task of consolidating the new general government counted for everything. While Hamilton sought to conciliate the mercantile and professional "persons of property," Washington with a broader perspective was seeking to cultivate a favorable opinion in the far-flung sections of the Union and among all groups and interests so far as possible. Here, again, Washington preferred to let his deeds speak rather than his promises.[54]

The contribution of Washington's personality and sense of administration to the office of presidency as an administrative agency was thus of great significance. He possessed a deep-seated understanding of the importance of good administration both as a means of consolidating popular support for the general government, and as an essential source of strength of the government itself. He understood good administration to be characterized by integrity, system, energy, reliance on facts, relative freedom from detail, and due responsibility

---

[53] *Ibid.,* XXXI, 28–29.

[54] Brooks Adams' estimate of Washington as an administrator is contained in the following passage: "The original union and the original administrative system of the government was, as far as so complex an organism might be, the product of Washington's single mind and of his commanding personality," in Henry Adams, *The Degradation of the Democratic Dogma* (New York: Macmillan, 1919), p. 108.

to Congress. These understandings came partly from his experience as a plantation manager and as a military commander, but they also reflected the habitual cast of Washington's mind. He was as an administrator what he was as a man.

Chapter Ten

THE TREASURY

THE development of the presidency during Washington's administration and the accumulation of experience under John Adams gave the country the pivot around which government business turned. While substantially all administrative authority was placed in presidential hands by Congress (in marked contrast to the dispersion of power in the states), agencies were required which would be capable of receiving administrative tasks by delegation and of performing them under not more than general presidential direction. These agencies Congress promptly provided in its first session.

In organizing the administrative system Congress had a free hand. The Constitution recognized administration principally by its incidental reference to the power of the President to require opinions in writing from the heads of departments. Time and experience were both lacking to permit Congress to undertake more than broad outlines. The organic statutes creating the three departments, State, Treasury, and War, the office of Attorney General, and in 1798, a fourth department, the Navy, were brief, simple, and general in their terms. Only in the Treasury Department did Congress work out the essential elements of internal organization.

By 1801, experience had done much to settle the relationships of department heads to the President and to their subordinates, had added some vivid chapters to interagency contacts, and had solidified routines.[1]

The largest department by far during the decade and the one in which the greatest expansion and development occurred was the Treasury. The State Department remained small in compass, despite its duties respecting home affairs. The War Department was intermediate,

---

[1] For earlier American experience, see Jennings B. Sanders, *Evolution of Executive Departments of the Continental Congress, 1774–1789* (Chapel Hill: University of North Carolina Press, 1935).

and was overshadowed by Hamilton both during and subsequent to his official career. Although important in Indian affairs and in the ever-impending foreign crises, it was handicapped by poor administration and inadequate leadership. The Attorney General remained throughout merely the person serving as the government's legal adviser who received a retaining fee and meanwhile carried on his private practice. The dominating organization was the Treasury, and not simply by reason of Hamilton's driving temperament for, as he remarked in 1792, "Most of the important measures of every government are connected with the treasury."[2]

The central position of the Treasury was illustrated not only by its functions, size, and leadership but also by its relation to some of the most vital issues and problems of the decade, notably the embargo and foreign trade regulation and the Whiskey Rebellion. These events are discussed elsewhere. Here we note that the Treasury collectors and naval officers were on the front line in the effort to enforce the Proclamation of Neutrality of 1793, the brief embargo of 1794 and the subsequent shipping regulations, when war seemed imminent; and it was the attacks on Treasury excise officers in western Pennsylvania which produced the first major challenge to the legal and administrative authority of the federal government.

The Treasury was important not merely on account of the intrinsic quality of the duties it performed, but also because it was the one department that had an extensive field service located in every large town and every section of the country. The importance of the Treasury, finally, was derived from the character of its constituency. Through the customs service, it dealt with the whole mercantile, fishing, and shipowning interests; through the Bank, it touched the principal financial and professional groups; through the excise officers and the land agents, it affected thousands of "small people" throughout the country; through the Purveyor of Public Supplies, it dealt with the large contractors; through the Post Office, it reached the newspapers, and the public at large.

---

[2] Hamilton to Carrington, May 26, 1792, Hamilton, *Works* (Lodge ed.), IX, 531. Jefferson in 1792 reported Washington as holding a different view: "He said that he considered the Treasury department as a much more limited one [i.e., than State] going only to the single object of revenue, while that of the Secretary of State embracing nearly all the objects of administration, was much more important. . . ." Jefferson, *Works* (Federal ed.), I, 195–96.

Jefferson looked upon this aggregation of patronage and power with undisguised alarm, believing that the first Secretary of the Treasury intended to corrupt democrats and pave the way for an American monarchy.

ORGANIZATION

The organic act establishing the Treasury Department followed a unique pattern.[3] The control of the President was noticed only in the words recognizing his constitutional power of removal. In contrast, a type of responsibility to Congress was clearly provided in the clause requiring the Secretary "to make report, and give information to either branch of the legislature, in person or in writing (as he may be required), respecting all matters referred to him by the Senate or House of Representatives, or which shall appertain to his office." A further relationship appeared in the Secretary's duty to "digest and prepare" plans for the improvement and management of the revenue, and for the support of the public credit, and in his duty to "prepare and report" estimates of revenue and expenditure. The Treasurer, too, was required to make an annual report to Congress. Nowhere, as in the legislation creating the State and War Departments, did the statute specifically give the President power to assign additional duties to the Secretary or to direct him in the performance of his duties. The statute strongly suggests that Congress at first believed the Treasury Department should be closely associated with it, certainly occupying a status dif-

---

[3] 1 Stat. 65 (Sept. 2, 1789). Whether Hamilton was influential in drafting the Treasury bill is an intriguing problem. In the absence of direct evidence, the writer believes that he did in fact largely determine the form of the Treasury Act. His son records that after the meeting of the new Congress in 1789, Hamilton's law work was much interrupted by daily conferences with leading members and with the President, who had early announced to Hamilton his intention of appointing him as Secretary of the Treasury. John C. Hamilton, *History of the Republic of the United States of America* (3d ed., 7 vols., Philadelphia: J. B. Lippincott, 1868), IV, 29. Knowing that he was to administer the Department, it is inconceivable that Hamilton would sit by idly while its powers and relationships were being debated by his friends (including at that time Madison). Many years later (1819) President James Monroe told his Cabinet that the Treasury Act was drawn by Hamilton. See John Quincy Adams, *Memoirs,* IV, 217. Henry B. Learned, *President's Cabinet,* p. 109, discounts this observation as also does Ralph V. Harlow, *History of Legislative Methods,* p. 134. The section concerning the Secretary's relation to Congress in any event is in strict accord with views which Hamilton expressed some years earlier. Hamilton to James Duane, Sept. 3, 1780, Hamilton, *Works* (Lodge ed.), I, 219–21.

ferent from that of State and War. But the act of September 11, 1789, establishing salaries promptly recognized the Secretary of the Treasury as an "Executive officer." [4]

Congress fixed in detail the internal structure of this Department, creating the several offices of Secretary of the Treasury, Comptroller, Auditor, Treasurer, Register, and an Assistant to the Secretary—later the Commissioner of the Revenue. The respective duties of each officer were specified in setting up the fundamentals of the central fiscal system.[5]

The distribution of duties within the Treasury took separate account of the day-by-day routine and of the larger problems of fiscal policy and general direction. The latter fell into the hands of the Secretary; the former, with some exceptions, fell into the hands of the principal Treasury officers. The formulation of financial policy, discussions with the President and members of Congress, the preparation of revenue measures, the drafting of public reports, the timing and specific authorization of financial operations, the disposition of public funds in banks and elsewhere were matters to which Hamilton and Wolcott gave personal attention. The routine of current business (except the work of the Comptroller) went on under the general supervision of the Secretary.

The Auditor made the first examination of accounts and stated balances on all claims. These were final settlements unless appeal was taken to the Comptroller, who acted in a semijudicial capacity and whose decisions on settlements were not subject to review by the Secretary of the Treasury. The Treasurer kept the record of funds received and disbursed and was in possession of all money paid in to the Treasury. The Register was in custody of records and participated in validating various financial documents.[6]

The basic internal structure of the Treasury Department stood intact throughout the whole Federalist period, despite several hostile investigations by Congress. The officials who provided continuity from 1789 to 1800 were Oliver Wolcott, the first Auditor, and Joseph Nourse, Register.

---

[4] 1 Stat. 67.

[5] The fiscal system is dealt with below, chs. xxvi–xxix.

[6] See description of duties of the Treasury officers (1794), *American State Papers: Finance,* I, 285.

FUNCTIONS

From 1789 to 1801 there was a steady expansion of Treasury functions and activities. Even before the Treasury Department was organized, three statutes had been approved vesting administrative duties in it: the collection act, setting up the customs service; the lighthouse act; and the act for registering and clearing vessels.[7] The subsequent organic act of September 2, 1789,[8] gave the following additional powers:

1. To digest and prepare plans for the improvement and management of the revenue and for the support of the public credit
2. To prepare and report estimates of the public revenue, and the public expenditures
3. To superintend the collection of the revenue
4. To decide on the forms of keeping and stating accounts and making returns
5. To grant all warrants for monies to be issued from the treasury
6. To execute such services in the sale of public lands as may be required by law
7. To report in person or in writing on matters referred by Congress, or pertaining to the office
8. To perform all such services relative to the finances as shall be directed
9. To superintend the adjustment and preservation of the public accounts
10. To direct prosecutions for delinquencies of officers of the revenue
11. To receive, keep, and disburse the monies of the United States.

This already extensive list of duties was increased from time to time. In 1790 the act providing payment for the debt authorized a loan of $12,000,000, the handling of which Washington naturally delegated to the Treasury; and for this purpose loan commissioners were set up in each state, acting under Treasury direction.[9] The land surveys already initiated by the geographer, Thomas Hutchins, were turned over to the Treasury by resolution of August 12, 1790,[10] and the office of Surveyor General was created in 1796.[11] In 1790 the collectors of cus-

---

[7] 1 Stat. 29; 1 Stat. 53; and 1 Stat. 55 respectively.
[8] 1 Stat. 65.
[9] 1 Stat. 138; loan commissioners, *ibid.*, sec. 6.
[10] 1 Stat. 187.
[11] 1 Stat. 464.

toms were directed to pay military pensions. [12] The Bank of the United States Act of 1791 vested power in the Secretary of the Treasury to receive reports from the Bank at periods specified by him and to examine its general accounts. [13] In 1792 the Treasury was given authority to purchase army supplies, validating and extending an activity which Hamilton had already been exercising without specific warrant of law. [14] The power to purchase was further extended in 1795, but was withdrawn (for army and navy supplies) in 1798. [15] In 1792 also was constituted the Sinking Fund Commission to purchase portions of the public debt; the Secretary of the Treasury was a member, and indeed the leading member of the Commission. [16] In 1793 the collectors became active in the enforcement of the Proclamation of Neutrality and in 1794, the embargo. [17] In 1796 they were required to assist in the enforcement of state quarantine laws. [18] Finally we note that in 1798 medical care for sick and disabled seamen was instituted by the general government.[19] The medical services were supported principally by deductions from seamen's wages (after 1799 from those of navy officers, seamen, and marines also) [20] to the amount of twenty cents for each month's service. Masters paid these sums to the collectors to provide for temporary relief and maintenance in hospitals or other proper institutions. Full responsibility for the service was vested in the President, who delegated his duties to the Treasury Department; the collectors of customs appear to have become directors of the hospitals ex officio.[21] The first marine hospital to be operated by the government was at Norfolk, purchased in 1800. Others were soon opened at Boston, Newport, and Charleston. Here was the beginning of the Marine Hospital Service, which eventually was to become the United States Public Health Service.

---

[12] Laurence F. Schmeckebier, *The Customs Service* (Baltimore: Johns Hopkins Press, 1924), p. 7.

[13] 1 Stat. 191, sec. 7, XVI.

[14] 1 Stat. 279.

[15] 1 Stat. 419; 1 Stat. 610; see below, pp. 362-63.

[16] 1 Stat. 281.

[17] 1 Stat. 369.

[18] 1 Stat. 474.

[19] 1 Stat. 605.

[20] 1 Stat. 729.

[21] Laurence F. Schmeckebier, *The Public Health Service* (Baltimore: Johns Hopkins Press, 1923), p. 3.

As duties multiplied, changes were made in Treasury organization. They illustrated the process of specialization which was gradually emerging as Hamilton found the burden of Treasury management required delegation. At Hamilton's suggestion in 1792, the supervision of the collection of duties on impost and tonnage was delegated to the Comptroller of the Treasury under the Secretary's direction,[22] and of the collection of other revenues to the Commissioner of the Revenue, Tench Coxe;[23] in the same year the supervision of lighthouses was also delegated to the Commissioner of the Revenue;[24] the superintendence of shipping was turned over to the Comptroller of the Treasury in 1793;[25] in 1794 the immediate direction of the excise on spirits was in the hands of the Commissioner of the Revenue;[26] the purchase of supplies was delegated to the Purveyor of Public Supplies, Tench Francis, in 1795;[27] the survey of public lands was delegated to the Surveyor General, Rufus Putnam, in 1796;[28] the Post Office from the beginning was directed by the Postmaster General under only the nominal supervision of the Treasury Department.

EMPLOYEES

To perform its varied and far-flung activities the Treasury required a considerable number of officials and employees. It is possible to make a close estimate for the central office in 1789 and the years immediately following. The total number on the Treasury pay roll for the central office on December 31, 1789, including the six chief officers, three principal clerks, twenty-eight clerks, and two messengers and office keepers, was thirty-nine.[29] By the end of the calendar year 1790 the number had grown to 70,[30] and by the end of the calendar year 1792 to 90.[31]

---

[22] 1 Stat. 279, sec. 6; Hamilton, *Works* (Hamilton ed.), III, 571.

[23] 1 Stat. 279, sec. 6.

[24] Lloyd Milton Short, *The Development of National Administrative Organization in the United States* (Baltimore: Johns Hopkins Press, 1923), p. 150.

[25] Hamilton, *Works* (Hamilton ed.), III, 573.

[26] *American State Papers: Finance*, I, 285.

[27] 1 Stat. 419.

[28] 1 Stat. 464.

[29] *American State Papers: Finance*, I, 34.

[30] *Ibid.*, I, 83–84.

[31] *Annals*, III, 1290; a statement showing persons holding civil office or employments for one year ending October 1, 1792, submitted to Congress gives a count of 81 full-time officers and employees, plus 26 part time. See *American State Papers: Miscellaneous*, I, 57–58.

Detailed figures for later years have not been obtained (except for 1801), but the office continued to expand with increasing business. On the scale of eighteenth-century affairs, this was a respectable establishment in itself, taking no note of the much more numerous subordinate field service. Oliver Wolcott, senior, wrote to his son (then Auditor) in 1790, "The superintending a business which requires fifteen clerks to execute, must be extremely arduous." [32]

By 1801 the Treasury far overtopped any other administrative agency, indeed it included over one half of the total civilian government personnel. In the departmental service, as it moved from Philadelphia to the "capital city," there were 78 officials and employees; in the field service, 1,615. The principal branches of the field service in 1801 included external revenues, about 1,100, and internal revenues, about 500. If to these are added the deputy postmasters, who had a formal Treasury connection, the field service would be expanded by approximately 880. [33]

LEADERSHIP: HAMILTON AND WOLCOTT

Among these officials and employees two men stood out, Alexander Hamilton and Oliver Wolcott. The latter was one of the first important top career men in government service. In succession Auditor, Comptroller, and Secretary of the Treasury, Wolcott claimed for his grandfather a colonial governor of Connecticut; for his father a signer of the Declaration of Independence and a governor of the state of Connecticut; for his uncle a speaker of the House of Representatives and a judge of the Supreme Court of Connecticut. He early displayed a taste for accounts, becoming a clerk in the office of the Committee of the Pay-Table in his native state, subsequently a member of the Committee and, upon its replacement in 1788 by the office of Comptroller of Public Accounts, the first incumbent of that post. With Oliver Ellsworth, a future United States Senator from Connecticut and Justice of the Supreme Court of the United States, he served as a commissioner to settle the accounts of the state with the United States.

At the age of twenty-nine Wolcott was urged by the Connecticut delegation in Congress to seek an appointment in the new Treasury Department. Offered the position of Auditor, he first declined: "The

---

[32] Gibbs, *Memoirs*, I, 45.
[33] *American State Papers: Miscellaneous*, I, 260–319.

office of Auditor will not answer the ideas of an appointment which
I had contemplated as proper for me." [34] Hamilton succeeded in over-
coming his reluctance. He found "a chaos of old accounts" [35] and
at the end of a few months declared his office "the most burdensome
under the government, but," he added, "I shall execute it in the best
manner which I can." [36] His success was such that in 1791 Hamilton
recommended him to the vacant office of Comptroller.

This gentleman's conduct in the station he now fills has been that of an
excellent officer. It has not only been good, but distinguished. It has combined all the requisites which can be desired: moderation with firmness,
liberality with exactness, indefatigable industry with an accurate and sound
discernment, a thorough knowledge of business, and a remarkable spirit of
order and arrangement. . . .[37]

Wolcott was appointed and settled with satisfaction into a hard-
working routine. "I . . . am contented with my situation," he wrote
in June 1792; and in December 1792, he declared, "I am *not* ambitious.
The office I hold is as good as an office can be. It is suited to my
talents, and I wish for nothing more." [38] When Hamilton resigned
in 1795 Wolcott wrote his father, "I shall take no measures for putting
myself in the way of this appointment; if it is offered to me I shall
accept it. . . ." So far as persuading and informing officials, or exercising the talents of a politician were concerned, he declared, "I shall
be understood, if I am appointed, to have no responsibility." [39]

He was a capable Secretary of the Treasury from 1795 to 1800, but

---

[34] Wolcott to Jeremiah Wadsworth, Sept. 10, 1789, Gibbs, *op. cit.*, I, 21. Earlier,
August 15, he had written to Wadsworth, "Those offices which relate to a treasury, and
are merely mechanical, are in my opinion very undesirable. If the duties are not properly discharged, they produce ruin and disgrace; if they are discharged well, intense
application is necessary, and success will only acquire the reputation of an honest,
plodding fellow of little genius or ability." *Ibid.*, I, 19. However, he decided to accept
the post of Auditor, since "in this city [New York] there are more chances than in
Connecticut." *Ibid.*, I, 22.

[35] *Ibid.*, I, 24.

[36] May 22, 1790, *ibid.*, I, 47.

[37] Hamilton, *Works* (Lodge ed.), IX, 479. These and other complimentary remarks
in Hamilton's letter to Washington must be read in light of the fact that Hamilton
feared Tench Coxe might be the President's choice; see ch. xix.

[38] Gibbs, *op. cit.*, I, 79, 85.

[39] *Ibid.*, I, 178.

on matters of fiscal policy he depended almost entirely on Hamilton. By degrees he was drawn into the factional disputes between the Adams and Hamiltonian wings of the Federalist party, and as an ardent admirer of Hamilton he occupied a very anomalous position in Adams' Cabinet.[40] His qualifications as an official were well stated by a contemporary friend, Joseph Hopkinson. "His devotion to the business and duties of his office were severe and unremitting. He possessed, in a high degree, a very rare qualification—the capacity for continued hard work, and was in everything systematic and orderly."[41] Rufus King, then in the Senate, confided to Christopher Gore, that Wolcott was "a good man—possesses firmness, industry, integrity, and sound Talents with a disposition to emulate his Predecessor's Example."[42] Another Federalist, Representative William Vans Murray, described Wolcott as "a very worthy man & quite equal to his duty."[43] Gibbs's own evaluation is balanced and accurate.

He had not, it is true, the brilliant qualities of genius, but he had a comprehensive and well regulated mind, a judgment matured and reliable, strong practical good sense and native shrewdness. . . . although not deficient in originality or boldness, he had no favorite schemes to engraft on that which was perfect in itself; he had no desire to obtain a shining reputation, and little ambition, other than to fill honorably an honorable station.[44]

Retiring as Secretary of the Treasury in 1800 with only a few hundred dollars and a small farm in Connecticut, Wolcott formed a lucrative business connection with the aid of Alexander Hamilton. His adherence to Federalist doctrine grew less pronounced, and in 1816 he was elected governor of Connecticut in opposition to the candidate of his former party. He was reelected annually until 1827 when he closed a public career of distinction, both in administration and in political leadership.

Alexander Hamilton was the greatest administrative genius of his

---

40 See Wolcott to Hamilton, Sept. 3, 1800, *ibid.*, II, 416–18.

41 *Ibid.*, I, 163.

42 King, *Correspondence*, II, 5.

43 Steiner, *McHenry*, p. 167.

44 Gibbs, *op. cit.*, I, 173–74. Wolcott was apparently a good supervisor; a clerk retiring from the Comptroller's Office addressed him in parting as "a gentleman, Sir, of your acknowledged Candor and benevolence." Wolcott Papers, XI, 34.

generation in America, and one of the great administrators of all time.[45] Endowed with restless energy and a high ambition, he was in the center of events from the outbreak of the Revolutionary War to his resignation as Secretary of the Treasury in 1795. He had the full stature of a statesman, with a remarkable grasp of national interest and a masterly concept of planned economic development under the broad direction of government. His interest in foreign policy was as keen as in domestic affairs; indeed the two were inseparable in Hamilton's all-inclusive grasp of what he hoped would be the national destiny. Military leadership, with its vast possibilities for dynamic action, had an unending attraction for him; he was Washington's aide at the age of twenty, accompanied the militia against the Whiskey Rebellion while Secretary of the Treasury, and insisted upon the post of second in command under Washington in the formation of the Provisional Army in 1798. He was a fiscal genius, bold, original, and constructive in the arrangements which restored American credit abroad and at home.

In every field to which he turned Hamilton dominated his associates. His enormous energy, his quick perception, his extraordinary capacity for analysis and clear expression, his willingness to take responsibility, his desire to be always at the point where great events were in the making conspired to make him inevitably a force in the public life of his age.

 To Hamilton is due the one outstanding administrative achievement of the Federalist period, an achievement which stood far above the normal capacity of a scattered rural eighteenth-century population unaccustomed to large affairs—the organization and management of the fiscal service of the federal government. As an administrator Hamilton was characterized by a passion for order, system, punctuality, accuracy, and energy. From him came the impulse to action, the insistence on prompt and complete discharge of duties, and the central support needed by collectors to convince still incredulous importers and shipmasters that the law would be enforced. He reserved initiative for himself, and for himself the ultimate official discretion. The less discretion in his agents, the better; but in every administrative system

---

[45] An excellent biography, although Hamiltonian in its orientation, is Frederick Scott Oliver, *Alexander Hamilton* (New York: G. P. Putnam's Sons, 1921); a recent biography is Nathan Schachner, *Alexander Hamilton* (New York: D. Appleton-Century, 1946).

some freedom must exist to temper the rigid operation of the machine. In keeping for himself the remission of fines and forfeitures for violation of the revenue laws, Hamilton reserved in his own hands the ultimate means of maintaining standards.

Both as an administrator and as a statesman, especially as a statesman, Hamilton suffered from the defects of his virtues. He was impatient, he could not endure competition, he meddled in everything. He went far in managing the War Department, whose nominal head, General Knox, was no match for him. He opposed his views on foreign policy to those of Jefferson, and the State Department had to write its dispatches in the tenor Hamilton dictated. He gave advice on constitutional problems which overbore the opinions of the Attorney General. He stirred up opposition in the House which eventually brought his official career to an end. His reactions were strong, almost violent. He crossed Jefferson, he openly assailed John Adams, and for years he fought Aaron Burr in New York. He tended to view men and matters in terms of black or white.

Despite these tragic consequences of his dynamic brilliancy, Hamilton was the administrative architect of the new government, balanced by Washington's common-sense judgments on official relationships. In the *Federalist Papers* Hamilton set out the first systematic exposition of public administration, a contribution which stood alone for generations. In his public life, he displayed a capacity for organization, system, and leadership which after a century and a half is hardly equaled. In providing a firm administrative establishment at the point where it was most needed, Hamilton performed a public service of outstanding importance.

Chapter Eleven

THE DEPARTMENT OF STATE

Aｌｔｈｏｕｇｈ the importance of foreign relations gave the Department of State a high place in the government, as an administrative organism it remained a relative pigmy throughout the Federalist period. The task imposed upon the Secretary of State in his central office was negligible, amounting at the utmost to the direction of the work of a half dozen clerks. The conduct of foreign negotiations was a matter so delicate and so concentrated that it fell to the personal attention of the Secretary of State. Nowhere in the Department was there a single person other than the Secretary who had experience or training in foreign affairs. Nothing beyond the necessary paper work and routine could consequently be delegated. To none of the four Secretaries who held office from 1790 to 1801 did it apparently occur to share with an experienced associate the tasks of deliberation, consultation, and consideration of policy. The product of the State Department was not organizational but individual. Furthermore, no formal specialization took place within the Department corresponding to that already noted for the Treasury, although particular clerks took care of special subject matters such as patents.

The major administrative problem of the State Department was to keep in adequate contact with its "field staff," i.e., the American representatives stationed abroad. In 1792 the number was still very small—ministers or chargés d'affaires at Paris, London, Lisbon, The Hague, and Madrid. By 1801 the number of diplomatic representatives had not changed, but a substantial consular force had been organized including a consul general at Algiers, 47 consuls, 4 vice consuls, and 11 commercial agents.[1] By 1796 James Monroe had so lost touch with

---

[1] *American State Papers: Miscellaneous*, I, 306–308. There were occasional special agents as well—not always openly avowed. "We want," wrote Jefferson to Madison, "an intelligent prudent native, who will go to reside at N. Orleans as a secret corre-

the policy of the government that Washington was forced to recall him from Paris; and William Carmichael at Madrid had been so indifferent to his correspondence that over two years elapsed without direct word from him to Philadelphia. With a truly remarkable forbearance, the Secretary of State wrote his agent in March 1791, "Your letter of May 6. 1789. is still the last we have received, & that is now near two years old. . . . A full explanation of the causes of this suspension of all information from you, is expected in answer to my letter of Aug. 6. It will be waited for yet a reasonable time, & in the mean while a final opinion suspended." [2]

The universal problem of maintaining a fresh sense of American interests among a body of diplomats stationed for many years abroad was not lost to Jefferson. He wrote frankly to his friend and former secretary, William Short, that it would be well for him to return, holding out the prospect of a seat in the Senate, and declared,

I think it possible that it will be established into a maxim of the new government to discontinue its foreign servants after a certain time of absence from their own country, because they lose in time that sufficient degree of intimacy with it's circumstances which alone can enable them to know & pursue it's interests. Seven years have been talked of. . . .[3]

The difficulties of communication were extreme in the conduct of the business of the Department of State, but they were part of a general problem, discussion of which is reserved for a later section.[4] Here it is sufficient to note that when Jefferson returned from England in 1789, sailing from Cowes to Norfolk, he congratulated himself on completing the journey in twenty-nine days "tho' a committee of American captains at Cowes had [de]termined we must expect a nine weeks passage." [5] A reply to a foreign dispatch could hardly be expected within a period of three months. In such circumstances instructions had to be general, confidence had to be complete, and the discretion

---

spondent, for 1000 D. a year. He might do a little business, merely to cover his real office. Do point out such a one. Virginia ought to offer more loungers equal to this & ready for it, than any other state." Jefferson, *Works* (Federal ed.), VII, 346 (May 27, 1793).

[2] *Ibid.*, VI, 221–22.

[3] Sept. 30, 1790, *ibid.*, VI, 148.

[4] See below, ch. xxxviii.

[5] Jefferson, *Works* (Federal ed.), VI, 20.

of the minister had to be wide. Strict instructions were likely to be a liability, as John Adams told Congress in 1782.

There is no man more impressed with the obligation of obedience to instructions; but, in ordinary cases, the principal is so near the deputy as to be able to attend to the whole progress of the business, and to be informed of every new fact and every sudden thought. Ambassadors in Europe can send expresses to their Courts, and give and receive intelligence in a few days with the utmost certainty. In such cases there is no room for mistake, misunderstanding, or surprise. But, in our case, it is very different. We are at an immense distance. Despatches are liable to foul play, and vessels are subject to accidents. New scenes open, the time presses, various nations are in suspense, and necessity forces us to act. . . .

I cannot think that a construction so literal and severe was ever intended to be put upon it; and, therefore, I see no way of doing my duty to congress, but to interpret the instruction, as we do all general precepts and maxims, by such restrictions and limitations, as reason, necessity, and the nature of things demand.

It may sometimes be known to a deputy, that an instruction from his principal was given upon information of mistaken facts. What is he to do? When he knows, that if the truth had been known, his principal would have given a directly contrary order, is he to follow that which issued upon mistake? When he knows, or has only good reason to believe, that, if his principal were on the spot, and fully informed of the present state of facts, he would give contrary directions, is he bound by such as were given before? It cannot be denied that instructions are binding, that it is a duty to obey them, and that a departure from them cannot be justified; but I think it cannot be denied, on the other hand, that, in our peculiar situation, cases may happen, in which it might become our duty to depend upon being excused (or, if you will, pardoned) for presuming, that if congress were upon the spot, they would judge as we do.[6]

ORGANIZATION

In the act creating the Department of State,[7] Congress placed full control of the Secretary of State in the President, four times repeating his subordination to the Chief Executive. Jefferson testified to his situation in a letter to Short, who was seeking a new diplomatic appointment. "One circumstance only in your letters must be corrected," wrote Jefferson, "that is, your idea of my influence in the foreign

---

[6] Adams, *Works,* VIII, 11–12.
[7] 1 Stat. 28 (July 27, 1789).

affairs. . . . your destination does not depend on me." [8] In an unde-
livered letter to the British minister, Jefferson observed truly, "in my
quality of Secretary of State to the United States, I cannot receive
any communication on the part of foreign ministers but for the purpose of laying it before the President, and of taking his orders upon
it." [9] Nor did Congress retain any specific means of exerting its authority over the business of the Department; for example, it required no
annual or special reports. Only two offices were created: that of Secretary and chief clerk. The great debate on the power of the President
to remove the Secretary has been reviewed earlier; there was little
discussion of other aspects of the bill.

The conduct of foreign negotiations and the selection of American
ministers remained under the close personal supervision and direction of both Washington and Adams.[10] The successive Secretaries of
State, Jefferson, Randolph, Pickering, and Marshall, were Secretaries
in a peculiarly apt sense of the term. Jefferson entertained deep convictions concerning the sound course of foreign policy, but he was repeatedly overruled by the President after Cabinet discussions, and on
some crucial occasions was obliged to sign dispatches whose import he
vigorously fought and never accepted. Randolph had no important
personal views on foreign policy. Pickering differed with Adams but
was pushed aside by the President. Marshall served for too brief a
period to impress his views of diplomatic policy upon the administration.

The selection of ministers and other diplomatic agents was made
by Washington after careful consideration of all the circumstances of
each case. He regularly conferred with a small circle, principally of
Federalist leaders, and was not infrequently disappointed by declinations. It does not appear that he relied especially on his Secretaries
of State for recommendations. The Jay mission was proposed by a
small group of Federalist Senators. On the special missions to France
Adams consulted neither Pickering nor anyone else. The issues involved in diplomatic appointments were far broader than departmental. Adams received private dispatches from his son, John Quincy

---

[8] Jefferson, *Works* (Federal ed.), VI, 147–48.

[9] *Ibid.*, VII, 245, n. 1. (Feb. 16, 1793).

[10] The principal secondary reference to the history of the Department of State is
Gaillard Hunt, *The Department of State of the United States* (New Haven: Yale University Press, 1914).

Adams, covering the affairs of all Europe, as well as the public dispatches to the Department. In domestic affairs, however, business was conducted with more freedom but still, as in all departments, under the scrutiny of the President on many matters, large and small.

FUNCTIONS

The description of departmental powers contained in the organic act of July 27, 1789, was simple. The duties of the Department of State included:

1. Correspondence, commissions, and instructions to ministers and consuls
2. Negotiations with public ministers from foreign states or princes
3. Memorials or other applications from foreign ministers or other foreigners
4. Such other matters respecting foreign affairs as the President assigned.

These remained the broad boundaries of its foreign responsibilities throughout the period. Its domestic duties were varied and tended to expand.

John Vining of Delaware, endowed with a deep sense of good administration, tried to persuade Congress to establish a fourth major agency, the Home Department. Included in a list of fifteen heads of subject matter for which he would thus provide were duties later conferred in large part on the State Department, i.e., to report plans for the improvement of manufactures, agriculture, and commerce; to manage patents and copyrights; to obtain a geographical account of the several states, report on post roads, and receive the census; to correspond with the states, procure their acts, and report on such as were contrary to the laws of the United States.[11] This important and on the whole coherent mass of duties certainly was the stuff out of which an active department could have been made; but Congress rejected the proposal by a "considerable majority." It was influenced by a desire to hold the new government to an acceptable economy and by the opinion that these tasks could be distributed among the three departments already created. Jefferson was correct in principle when he wrote William Short that "the whole domestic administration (war and finance excepted)" was placed in the Department of State.[12]

---

[11] *Annals,* I, 666 (July 26, 1789).

[12] *Works* (Federal ed.), VI, 26. The original designation of the department as Foreign Affairs was changed in September 1789 to State.

In accordance with this decision, Congress promptly vested in the State Department the custody and publication of the laws, and their distribution to the states; the custody of the seal of the United States; and the preparation and authentication of commissions issued by the President. Only the special warrant of the Chief Executive, however, could cause the seal to be affixed to any document.[13] From time to time additional domestic duties were assigned to the Department, the nature of which will be apparent from the following list:

1. The taking of the census, 1 Stat. 101 (March 1, 1790), and 2 Stat. 11 (February 28, 1800)
2. The grant of patents, 1 Stat. 109 (April 10, 1790), and 1 Stat. 318 (February 21, 1793)
3. The grant of copyrights, 1 Stat. 124 (May 31, 1790)
4. Supervision of the Mint, 1 Stat. 246 (April 2, 1792) and executive direction thereof
5. Recording land patents, 1 Stat. 464, sec. 7 (May 18, 1796)
6. Protection of American seamen, 1 Stat. 477 (May 28, 1796) and executive direction thereof
7. Grant of ship passports, 1 Stat. 489 (June 1, 1796)

In part the duties conferred were ministerial in nature, as in the custody and printing of the laws, the custody of the seal, the preparation and delivery of commissions, the countersignature and recording of land sales.

Other aspects of domestic affairs, however, were of considerable importance. The federal marshals and attorneys received their instructions from the Department of State and the federal judges corresponded with this office on matters of judicial business.[14] Petitions for pardons were received by the Department and recommendations prepared, in conjunction with the Attorney General, for the President's consideration.[15] The supervision of the territories fell to the Department although there is evidence that it was not vigorously carried on.[16] The Secretary maintained a lively correspondence with the governors of the states on diverse matters ranging from the ratification of con-

---

[13] 1 Stat. 68 (Sept. 15, 1789).
[14] Hunt, *op. cit.*, pp. 128–29.
[15] *Ibid.*, pp. 130–31.
[16] *Ibid.*, p. 131.

stitutional amendments and the conduct of foreign ships in American
waters to the sending of copies of laws for use of state officers.

AID TO SEAMEN

The relief and repatriation of impressed or stranded seamen were
constant problems of the State Department during the 1790's. The Department was only moderately successful in solving them. As early as
1792 American consuls were enjoined to prevent suffering by mariners
and seamen in foreign ports in cases of shipwreck, sickness, or captivity.
The consuls were allowed to pay each of them a per diem not exceeding twelve cents, an amount that was the source of much complaint.[17]
Masters of American ships were required to transport these mariners
and seamen back to the United States—for their labor *en voyage*.[18]

The release of impressed American seamen was also an irritating
and thankless task.[19] Decisive action on the part of the American
government to stop impressment was impossible and the authorities
were driven to various expedients to limit the practice so far as possible
and to secure release of those who were seized. The first device was
to provide identification papers, known as "protection"; this plan was
eventually incorporated in the act of 1796 for the relief of American
seamen. It was of little or no use.[20] The certificates of citizenship were
given out by various categories of public officers from notaries public
to collectors, governors, and the Secretaries of Departments; they were
readily forged and issued under conditions which permitted grave
doubt as to their authenticity; but after the act of 1796 the British

---

[17] Note, for example, Pickering to the Secretary of the Treasury, Sept. 22, 1797,
commenting on "the very insufficient allowance of *twelve cents a day*," and asking the
Secretary how he could make a further allowance to secure seamen from suffering.
Pickering Papers, VII, 216.

[18] 1 Stat. 254, sec. 7 (April 14, 1792).

[19] A valuable study on this subject, combining an interest in legal and administrative
phases is James Fulton Zimmerman, *Impressment of American Seamen* (New York:
Columbia University, 1925).

[20] 1 Stat. 477, sec. 4 (May 28, 1796). Rufus King later asserted that seamen would
have been better off if this part of the law had not been enacted; Zimmerman concurs
in this view, *op. cit.*, p. 61. Jefferson had early seen the extreme hazard of securing
freedom from impressment by requiring certificates of citizenship; see his letter of June
11, 1792, in *American State Papers: Foreign Relations*, III, 574, and in general the
extracts on impressments, *ibid.*, III, 573–83. Further data on impressments are available
in *ibid.*, I and II; note especially the account of a private citizen, John B. Cutting, amounting to over $7,600 advanced to distressed seamen in *ibid.*, I, 131–32.

government felt justified in seizing any American who lacked such a certificate. Since many sailors returned to an American port infrequently, they were not always able to secure "protection." Furthermore, there was carelessness on the part of both masters and men, as well as on the part of the collectors.[21]

The other principal recourse was to secure the early release of Americans. Good results were obtained at the outset in direct negotiations between United States consuls in British harbors and special port officers known as "regulating captains." The business was gradually taken over by London, and eventually had to be transacted between the American minister and the British Foreign Secretary. To assist the American minister the act of 1796 authorized the appointment of two agents to help secure the release of impressed seamen, one working in London, one in the West Indies.[22]

Although at the time of the Jay Treaty there was consideration of the desirability of turning over to the courts the disposition of cases of this sort the conduct of these transactions remained in the diplomatic sphere.[23] The American agent in the West Indies, however, dealt directly with admirals, captains, and colonial governors, with some of whom he was eminently successful. Crusty Admiral Parker, however, yielded not even to a writ of habeas corpus, but only to the Admiralty Board. Diplomatic representation was the ultimate resort.[24]

EMPLOYEES

To perform its varied duties, foreign and domestic, the Department maintained a very modest central staff. At the close of the Confederation period there were in the office besides the Secretary, John Jay, only two clerks, "or just enough, as may be inferred from a report of this date, for one of them to be in the office while the other went to luncheon."[25] The quarters consisted of two rooms, one used as a

---

[21] Zimmerman, *op. cit.,* p. 67; the author suggests that the reliability of notaries' acts in this period was not great.

[22] 1 Stat. 477, sec. 1.

[23] Zimmerman, *op. cit.,* p. 46.

[24] In the Pickering Papers there is correspondence concerning the charter of a ship to proceed on a government mission to the West Indies to pick up stranded seamen.

[25] Jay Caesar Guggenheimer, "The Development of the Executive Departments, 1775–1789," *Essays in the Constitutional History of the United States in the Formative Period, 1775–1789* (J. Franklin Jameson, ed., Boston and New York: Houghton, Mifflin, 1889), pp. 116–85, at p. 165.

parlor, the other as a workshop. Jay's estimate for 1789 provided for an undersecretary (in reality a chief clerk), two clerks, an interpreter, a doorkeeper and messenger, and a sum of $150 for translation at the current rate of two shillings per hundred words.[26] By 1792 the establishment had expanded by the addition of two more clerks;[27] but in 1800, under Marshall, it still included only one chief clerk, seven clerks, and a messenger.[28] It was not surprising that Jefferson, facing the accumulation of business upon his arrival in New York, wrote his son-in-law, "When this shall be got thro' I may be able to judge whether the ordinary business of my department will leave me any leisure. I fear there will be little." [29]

PATENTS

Considered in its primary aspect, the conduct of foreign affairs, the administration of the State Department was little more than directing an office of correspondence and performing the ceremonies of international intercourse. These operations are of so little significance, administratively, that the central business of the Department has perforce been passed over in comparative silence. However, the domestic business of the Department as the Home Office warrants attention, especially in the disposition of matters affecting patents and the Mint.

In its capacity as the Home Office the Department of State was the principal agency concerned with patenting inventions. The first legislation established a board comprising the Secretary of State, the Secretary of War, and the Attorney General, any two of whom could act to grant a patent.[30] In 1793 this authority was conferred upon the Secretary of State alone, after examination of the application by the Attorney General.[31] Great care was taken to safeguard the process. By the act of 1790 the patent had to be *examined* by the Attorney General, *sealed* by the direction of the President, and *recorded* by the

---

[26] Hunt, *op. cit.*, p. 80.

[27] *American State Papers: Miscellaneous*, I, 57.

[28] *Hunt, op. cit.*, p. 191.

[29] Jefferson to Thomas M. Randolph, March 28, 1790, *Works* (Federal ed.), VI, 37.

[30] 1 Stat. 109 (April 10, 1790). Requests for patents were sent directly to Congress in 1789 but were laid on the table. Two of these were the petitions of Alexander Lewis and of John Fitch for patents on the application of steam power to navigation. *Annals*, I, 233, 335 (May 4, 13, 1789).

[31] 1 Stat. 318 (Feb. 21, 1793).

Secretary of State before being delivered to the patentee. The first patent was issued to Francis Bailey on January 29, 1791, for a type punch to prevent counterfeiting.[32]

Henry Remsen, for some years a chief clerk in the State Department, has left an interesting record of patent procedure under Jefferson.

Patent business—the board of arts meet the last Saturday in each month. Wm. Crosby is to notify the members thereof the preceding day. When they meet all applications recd since the former meeting to be read and to lie a month under consideration. The Board does not even decide on them then, unless they are accompanied with specifications, drafts or models properly prepared. No models to be delivered to the persons depositing them, after the patents are issued, without the orders of the Secy of State. And no patents already made out or which may be made out to be delivered unless the claimants produce models, drafts & specifications. The specifications to be executed according to the usual form—If by an Attorney—see Specification enclosed in patent No.—but if by the claimant himself, see Specification enclosed in patent No.—. Should you be in doubt as to the want of explicitness in the specifications, drafts or models, Mr. Jefferson will remove it on application. When a patent is granted label the model, as I have done, or the models, as sometimes two models of the same thing are deposited.[33]

The personal nature of the Secretary's responsibility for determining the utility of inventions shines forth in one of Jefferson's letters to Dr. James Hutchinson, professor of chemistry at the University of Pennsylvania. "Congress having referred to me a Petition from a person of the name of Isaacs, setting forth that he has discovered an easy method of rendering sea water potable, I have had a cask of sea water procured, and the Petitioner has erected a small apparatus in my Office, in order to exhibit his process. Monday morning 10. o'clock is fixed on as the time for doing it. It would give me great satisfaction to be assisted on the occasion by your chemical knowledge." [34] The experiment was not convincing.[35]

The embarrassments of the patent business far exceeded its volume.

---

[32] Washington, *Writings*, XXXI, 353, n. 74.

[33] MS. in the National Archives, Department of State, Reports of Bureau Officers, vol. 1A, 1790–1834.

[34] State Department, Domestic Letters, March 12, 1791, IV, 213–14.

[35] *Ibid.*, IV, 309.

The entire work of what became the Patent Office was performed by a single clerk and all the records from 1790 to 1802 did not fill over a dozen pigeonholes.[36] The difficulties experienced by Jefferson, however, quickly became intolerable. In a letter to Hugh Williamson, then in Congress, Jefferson prayed to be relieved from the duty of granting patents,

> as being, of everything that ever was imposed on him, that which cuts up his time into the most useless fragments and gives him from time to time the most poignant mortification. The subjects are such as would require a great deal of time to understand & do justice by them, and not having that time to bestow on them, he has been oppressed beyond measure by the circumstances under which he has been obliged to give undue & uninformed opinions on rights often valuable, & always deemed so by the authors.[37]

A proposal to authorize special referees to make final determinations in disputed claims for a patent had been debated in the House of Representatives in 1790. The plan was objected to by members who argued that a citizen was entitled to a jury trial on review of such an administrative decision. Others retorted that juries were not competent to form a judgment and that justice would be far more probable from referees, "who are men of science."[38] One wishes that the debate had been reported more fully. The proposal did not become a part of the act of 1790.

The second patent act, however, although abolishing the ex officio board,[39] established arbitration procedure in the case of "interfering applications." Each of two claimants appointed a member of an arbitration board and the Secretary of State, the third member; if several claimants were involved, they either agreed upon the board, or the Secretary appointed all three members. The decision of the board was final, thus relieving the Secretary of State of the vexatious cases.

Patents were apparently signed by the President personally. There

---

[36] George W. Evans, "The Birth and Growth of the Patent Office," *Records of the Columbia Historical Society*, XXII (1919), 105–24 at p. 108.

[37] April 1, 1792, Jefferson, *Works* (Federal ed.), VI, 459; see also an earlier letter to Williamson on the same subject, Nov. 13, 1791, *ibid.*, VI, 328.

[38] *Annals*, II, 1413 (March 4, 1790).

[39] In a study based on the early files it is said that the board members were charged by inventors as being "by education and interest hostile to the industrial classes." Evans, *op. cit.*, p. 108.

is something paternal in the spectacle of George Washington signing a patent brought to him by the Attorney General of the United States guaranteeing to Samuel Morey of New Hampshire his rights to an invention to turn a spit.[40]

Inventors were not above seeking what advantage might lie in personal introductions to high executive officials. Thus we find Edmund Randolph writing to Senator Ralph Izard of South Carolina on February 18, 1794, in reply to a letter from the Senator on a pending patent.[41] And Eli Whitney, on his way "to Philadelphia, to lodge a model and receive a patent for a machine, which he has invented for cleansing cotton from its seeds," went armed with a letter from Elizur Goodrich, a connection of Oliver Wolcott.[42]

THE MINT

The State Department was responsible for the management of the Mint, although its possession was sought by the Treasury. The indecision of Congress concerning the proper location of the Mint appears from its action on January 15, 1790, requesting from the Secretary of State (not yet at the seat of government) a plan for a uniform system of coinage, weights and measures.[43] Before his report was rendered, the House directed the Secretary of the Treasury to prepare a plan for a Mint.[44]

Jefferson consequently omitted any reference to the Mint in his report on coinage which was submitted on July 13, 1790—after clearing it with Hamilton.[45] Hamilton reported on January 28, 1791—after clearing his recommendations with Jefferson.[46] He did not ask Congress to assign the Mint to Treasury, although he set out in detail the internal organization of the proposed establishment. Both reports were before the members when, by resolution at the close of the first Congress, a Mint was authorized, and the President directed to take

---

[40] MS. in the Library of Congress, Journal of the Proceedings of the President, January 1793–February 1797, p. 31 (Jan. 30, 1793). On Aug. 30, 1791, he signed fifteen patents. Washington, *Writings*, XXXI, 352, n. 74.

[41] State Dept., Domestic Letters, VI, 66.

[42] Gibbs, *Memoirs*, I, 128 (Feb. 25, 1794).

[43] *Annals*, I, 1058.

[44] *Ibid.*, II, 1530 (April 15, 1790).

[45] *American State Papers: Miscellaneous*, I, 13; Hamilton, *Works* (Hamilton ed.), IV, 23.

[46] *American State Papers: Finance*, I, 91; Hamilton, *Works* (Hamilton ed.), IV, 96.

preliminary steps.[47] It was not until April 2, 1792, that the Mint was fully established by law.[48]

The ultimate authority for the Mint was placed by law in the hands of the President himself. The immediate management was confided to the Director, but his acts were in most particulars made "subject to the approbation of the President of the United States." Congress definitely refrained from assigning the Mint either to Jefferson or Hamilton, a decision which was doubtless affected by the antagonism now apparent between them.

Jefferson, however, assuming that the Mint belonged to the State Department, had already taken the initiative with respect to its affairs, doubtless with Washington's knowledge. As early as April 23, 1790, Jefferson had written to a French correspondent to secure the services of a mintmaster; [49] and on January 5, 1792, he asked William Short to retain skilled workmen for the new establishment.[50] On the very day that Washington signed the act Jefferson submitted names to Washington for the Mint officers, and the first Director, David Rittenhouse, was Jefferson's choice. The Mint was assigned to the State Department and Jefferson became the accepted channel of communication between Rittenhouse and the President.[51]

The record of the Mint was disappointing, even to its friends.[52] Difficulties of every sort dogged its progress. On December 30, 1793, Jefferson told Congress that the coinage of precious metals was prevented because it required a bond so high ($10,000) from the chief

---

[47] 1 Stat. 225 (March 3, 1791).

[48] 1 Stat. 246. There are sentences in Hamilton's letter to Carrington, May 26, 1792, which reveal conflict with Jefferson over the Mint, "On the mint business I was opposed from the same quarters [i.e., Jefferson and Madison] and with still less success." Hamilton, *Works* (Lodge ed.), IX, 530. And in another passage Hamilton writes, "Mr. Jefferson proposes that the unit of weight and the unit in the coins shall be the same, and . . . my propositions are to preserve the dollar as a unit. . . ." Hamilton accused Madison of an intrigue to hoodwink Washington into an unsuspecting approval of Jefferson's plan. *Ibid.*, IX, 523.

[49] Jefferson, *Writings* (Memorial ed.), VIII, 23–24.

[50] *Ibid.*, VIII, 283; see also letter to Thomas Pinckney, June 14, 1792, *ibid.*, VIII, 375–77.

[51] Washington to Jefferson, July 9, 1792, Washington, *Writings*, XXXII, 86; Jefferson to Washington, Dec. 30, 1793, *American State Papers: Finance*, I, 270.

[52] The debate over placing the President's head on coins was the first of many controversies over the Mint and is of interest now only as an indication of Republican jealousy of monarchial institutions.

coiner and assayer that the officers could not secure it.[53] Inspired by a mistaken idea of economy, the lots on which the first buildings were erected were so small "as greatly to . . . delay the business." The owner of a neighboring lot possessed a right of way through the grounds of the Mint and the small sum of money necessary to prevent this "improper intrusion" was not forthcoming.[54] Technical problems were almost beyond the capacity of the mechanics of the time, and breakdowns were frequent.[55]

Complaint about the lack of coins mounted and in 1794 Rittenhouse was asked to explain. He admitted that expenses to date had been "only preparatory towards carrying on the business of the establishment," and said he awaited the completion of a more powerful press.[56] Elias Boudinot meanwhile carried on a private inquiry. Going to the Bank of the United States, he was told he could secure no cents there because the Bank could not get them from the Mint. Repairing to the Mint he was told that cents were not coined faster because the officers of the Mint did not know where to get them vented. He reported this to the House, where other members "adverted to the prodigious inconvenience which is felt all over the Union for want of copper coin." [57]

Shortly thereafter Rittenhouse retired and after a brief interval Boudinot became Director. Trouble did not cease. Just as Boudinot was ready "for a vigorous and systematic renewal of the coinage" the assayer died of an "apoplectic fit." The patience of Congress had nearly run out. The Speaker of the House, Jonathan Dayton, declared that the Mint had failed to answer expectations: "An impression is made on the public mind that it has been conducted with negligence." [58] Only by a narrow margin, and only with the benefit of considerations not relevant to the Mint did it escape. The vote was 40 to terminate it, 45 against.[59]

Boudinot failed, as well as Rittenhouse, to attain an output which appeased Congress. When in 1800 the question of removing the Mint to Washington was raised, a Senate committee recommended the end

---

[53] *American State Papers: Finance*, I, 270–71.
[54] *Ibid.*, I, 357.
[55] *Ibid.*, I, 353.
[56] *Ibid.*, I, 317.
[57] *Annals*, IV, 971 (Dec. 9, 1794).
[58] *Ibid.*, V, 255 (Jan. 19, 1796).
[59] *Ibid.*, V, 264 (Jan. 20, 1796).

of the Mint and the coinage of money by contract.[60] A compromise saved the Mint, but Congress declined to spend any money to move it to Washington. It remains to this day in Philadelphia.

One reason for the administrative failure of the Mint was its assignment to the State Department. The main preoccupation of this Department was necessarily with foreign affairs, and as the years unfolded, they absorbed the whole attention of the Secretary of State. No one in the office of the Secretary was responsible for the Mint and it received little, if any, attention. Territorial matters suffered from the same neglect; even under the conscientious Pickering, correspondence with territorial officers was pushed aside by the more urgent foreign problems.

Another difficulty arose from the almost complete lack of persons with the necessary experience or skill to transform metal into coins. Early attempts to secure technically competent artisans from abroad were only partially successful. Boudinot hesitated to accept the directorship of the Mint from "want of Chimical Knowledge" but yielded to the "earnest desire of the President." He later confided to a friend, "The Business is curious and opens up many sources of knowledge and contemplation that I was before a stranger to." [61] The business was as unknown in America as it was curious to Boudinot.

David Rittenhouse, the first Director of the Mint, was one of the country's most distinguished scientists, a mathematician, astronomer, and instrument maker who was eventually honored by election to the Royal Society of London. An active patriot, he had served the Committee of Safety and the state of Pennsylvania in various capacities. His scientific endowments were superior to his administrative skill and he was handicapped by poor health. Hamilton was obliged to tell the President after nearly three years of Rittenhouse's administration that the Mint had done comparatively nothing. He added, "And I am led to fear that as long as it continues under its present management the public expectation will be disappointed. The director, though a most respectable and excellent man, can hardly be expected on several accounts to give that close and undivided attention to it, which in its first stages is indispensable." [62]

---

[60] *American State Papers: Finance*, I, 632.
[61] *The Life, Public Services, Addresses, and Letters of Elias Boudinot* (Jane J. Boudinot, ed., 2 vols., Boston and New York: Houghton, Mifflin, 1896), II, 107, 109.
[62] Jan. 31, 1795, Hamilton, *Works* (Hamilton ed.), V. 70.

Adams' characterization bears less on his administrative skill: "Rittenhouse was a virtuous and amiable man; an exquisite mechanician, master of the astronomy known in his time, an expert mathematician, a patient calculator of numbers. . . . In politics, Rittenhouse was a good, simple, ignorant, well-meaning, Franklinian, democrat, totally ignorant of the world. . . ." [63] Jefferson, a life-long friend, as early as 1778 sought to dissuade Rittenhouse from diverting his energies to public affairs. ". . . nobody can conceive that nature ever intended to throw away a Newton upon the occupations of a crown." [64] With Hamilton's assistance, nature's ends were served.

THOMAS JEFFERSON

The first Secretary of State, Thomas Jefferson, holds a high place in the affections of Americans. His greatness is due not to his administrative skill but to his philosophy of government, his belief in man, his deeply ingrained democracy, and his insistence on the importance of the community in the balance between general and local concerns. Among the men of action of his day he was looked upon with a certain disdain, but his influence upon the century and a half of American life following the fall of the Federalists outweighs that of most of the men of deeds of his day. Robert Goodloe Harper's estimate of the man was therefore both correct and mistaken. Harper believed him "greatly deficient in most of those qualities which fit a man for the first station in a Government. . . . from his public conduct, I take him to be of a weak wavering indecisive character; deliberating when he ought to act, and frequently acting . . . without steadiness judgment or perseverance; . . . always pursuing certain visionary theories of the closet, which experience constantly contradicts. . . . I might think him fit to be a professor in a College, President of a Philosophical Society, or even Secretary of State; but certainly not the first magistrate of a great nation." [65]

The "certain visionary theories of the closet" remain an enduring American possession impressively recorded in the Jefferson Memorial on the banks of the Potomac, and Harper is forgotten except to the

---

[63] Adams to Jefferson, March 14, 1814, Adams, *Works*, X, 90.
[64] Jefferson to Rittenhouse, July 19, 1778. Jefferson, *Works* (Federal ed.), II, 345.
[65] Harper, Letter to his Constituents, Jan. 5, 1797. Am. Hist. Assoc., *Annual Report, 1913*, II, 25.

professional historian. But Jefferson himself corroborated Harper's judgment that he was not by nature or preference interested in the business of administration. His duties as head of the State Department he called "hateful labors"; [66] he was "worn down with drudgery"; [67] he was an "utter stranger" to the files and documents of his Department. He was so indifferent to the needs of the attorneys of the United States, over whose work he nominally presided, that he never thought of sending them copies of the statutes which they were to enforce.[68] He was sufficiently impractical so that he proposed to leave the enforcement of the Neutrality Proclamation to the grand juries—although this was a conclusion shrewdly tempered to his dislike of the Proclamation itself.

Liberty, freedom, self-government were the great passions of Jefferson's life; and it is perhaps not to be expected that such a man could be as great a master of the art of administration as he was of the art of politics and of life.

[66] Edwin Morris Betts, *Thomas Jefferson's Garden Book, 1766–1824* (Philadelphia: American Philosophical Society, 1944), p. 176.

[67] Jefferson to Humphreys, March 22, 1793, Jefferson, *Writings* (Memorial ed.), IX, 51.

[68] State Dept., Domestic Letters, VI, 182.

Chapter Twelve

WAR: "A DIFFICULT AND UNPOPULAR DEPARTMENT"

In this work no effort will be made to deal with military history, or the principles and practice of army organization and management. The component parts of the army established by Congress from 1789 to 1801, the organization of the militia, the gradual construction of naval vessels under army direction leading to the foundation of the Navy Department in 1798, the internal management of army and navy by professional military and naval officers, all comprise an important but specialized field of public affairs into which we shall not enter.[1] This study is concerned only with some phases of civilian administration in the War Department.

POWERS AND DUTIES

The Department of War, established on August 7, 1789, was initially vested with powers concerning land and naval forces, ships and supplies, military commissions, the grant of land for military service during the Revolution, the management of Indian affairs, and "such other matters respecting military or naval affairs, as the President . . . shall assign."[2] Subsequent legislation to 1801 did not add to these duties and activities.

Excluding the laws establishing and reorganizing the army of the United States, organizing the militia, and providing for the building of naval vessels, the principal supplementary legislation affecting the internal administration of the War Department to 1801 included, (1) the establishment of the office of paymaster in 1792,[3] (2) the purchase

[1] See James Ripley Jacobs, *The Beginning of the U. S. Army, 1783–1812* (Princeton, N. J.: Princeton University Press, 1947).

[2] 1 Stat. 49.

[3] 1 Stat. 279, sec. 3.

of military equipment by the Treasury in the same act,[4] (3) the creation of the office of superintendent of military stores in 1794,[5] (4) the provision of arsenals,[6] and (5) the various experiments in controlling trade with the Indians.[7] The last topic is dealt with elsewhere.

Inspection of this legislation suggests its secondary character. It also suggests that the War Department remained a highly homogeneous, single-function agency concerned almost exclusively with the maintenance and use of the armed forces. The principal exception was regulation of trading and other peaceful relations with the Indians. This duty was largely supervisory;[8] Indian treaties were negotiated by special commissioners, and the trading houses and Indian agents were far removed from the seat of government. So also the task of issuing military land warrants was simple and slight—one clerk was enough to carry it out.[9]

The War Department had relatively little to do with the militia of the various states. An effort to secure national inspection of the militia failed.[10] The jealousy of the states which prevented national standards of uniformity and inspection kept the War Department at a distance, except when the militia was actually called into action. The armed forces directly at the disposal of the Department numbered at most only about 5,000.

ORGANIZATION AND PERSONNEL

Throughout the Federalist period the civilian side of War Department organization and operation remained on a modest scale. Henry Knox became the first Secretary on September 12, 1789. At the outset, the Department consisted of himself and one clerk.[11] Shortly after James McHenry became Secretary of War in 1796, he was visited by a former French officer who had fought with Lafayette in the Revolutionary War. His description of his visit to the War Department is refreshingly illuminating.

---

[4] 1 Stat. 279, sec. 5.

[5] 1 Stat. 352, sec. 3.

[6] 1 Stat. 352, secs. 1, 2.

[7] 1 Stat. 137; 1 Stat. 452; 1 Stat. 469.

[8] L. M. Short, *Development of National Administrative Organization*, p. 125.

[9] *Ibid.*, p. 124.

[10] See below, ch. xxxi.

[11] Oliver Lyman Spaulding, *The United States Army in War and Peace* (New York: G. P. Putnam's Sons, 1937), p. 118.

The Government officials were as simple in their manners as ever. I had occasion to call upon Mr. McHenry, the Secretary of War. It was about eleven o'clock in the morning when I called. There was no sentinel at the door, all the rooms, the walls of which were covered with maps, were open, and in the midst of the solitude I found two clerks each sitting at his own table, engaged in writing. At last I met a servant, or rather *the* servant, for there was but one in the house, and asked for the Secretary. He replied that his master was absent for the moment, having gone to the barber's to be shaved. Mr. McHenry's name figured in the State Budget for $2,000, a salary quite sufficient in a country where the Secretary of War goes in the morning to his neighbor, the barber, at the corner, to get shaved. I was as much surprised to find all the business of the War Office transacted by two clerks, as I was to hear that the Secretary had gone to the barber's.[12]

By 1801 the Department had a small central establishment and a considerable civilian staff in the field. In the central office, in addition to the Secretary and the accountant, there were 14 clerks and 2 messengers; the clerks were largely engaged in bookkeeping. The civilian establishment included 11 agents and clerks in the quartermaster's department; two armories (one at Springfield, Massachusetts, the other at Harpers Ferry, Virginia) with officials numbering 7; a superintendent of military stores with a civilian staff of 12; the paymaster general and inspector's office with a staff of 6; two agents for fortifications (Boston and Newport, Rhode Island); and in the Indian department, a superintendent, 4 agents, 2 factors, 8 interpreters, and 5 clerks. These officials and employees totalled about 80.[13]

MANAGEMENT OF SUPPLY

The administrative record of the War Department under the Federalists was poor. Henry Knox was an executive of not more than ordinary talents, and James McHenry was an administrative failure. Hamilton had great influence with each of these Secretaries, but he was unable to overcome the stolid resistance of Knox or the cheerful incompetence of McHenry.[14] Pickering remained in the Department for too brief a period to have much effect upon it.

---

[12] U. S. War Department, *The Work of the War Department of the United States* (Washington: Government Printing Office, 1924), p. 10.

[13] *American State Papers: Miscellaneous,* I, 304, 312–14. This compilation does not include laborers in the armories and probably others.

[14] In 1794 when Knox was absent from Philadelphia, Hamilton handled War Department business for the Secretary, apparently by an informal agreement. In the

Evidence of serious mismanagement in the War Department was suggested before the Court of Inquiry which examined the causes of General Harmar's defeat by the Miami Indians in the fall of 1790.[15] Gross mismanagement was fully revealed in the report of the House Committee on the defeat of St. Clair by the Indians in November 1791, especially in the quartermaster's and contractors' departments.[16] The report placed the Secretary of War in a very unfavorable light and his explanations to a subsequent committee were far from satisfactory.[17] Washington was deeply concerned but took no action to find a new Secretary.

A summary of the evidence before the House Committee which investigated the causes of the defeat of General St. Clair will suggest the disrepair in which the Department found itself. The act for protecting the frontiers was approved by Washington on March 3, 1791, and on the following day he appointed Arthur St. Clair as major general and commander in chief of the expedition against the Indians. On March 6, 1791, the Secretary of War entered into a contract with William Duer to supply the troops en route to Fort Pitt, for which service Duer posted a bond for $4,000, with no security.[18] On March 23, 1791, Duer received an advance of $15,000 on this contract, and on a previous contract for the same services various advances were made on and after March 22. He put no funds in the hands of his agents, however, up to May 9, 1791—the date of rendezvous at Carlisle, Pennsylvania. The agents had to furnish supplies on credit. Throughout the next month repeated complaints were made to the Secretary of War from the field "of fatal mismanagements and neglects, in the quartermaster's and military stores department."

A quartermaster general was also appointed for the expedition in March 1791, but failed to arrive at Fort Pitt until June 10 where he tarried until the exasperated commander in chief issued him written instructions to come to camp without delay. These orders the quartermaster general neither answered nor obeyed, and finally arrived at

autumn of 1794 Hamilton marched with the militia against the Whiskey Rebellion. When in 1798 Hamilton became inspector general of the Provisional Army under Washington, he instantly became the initiating and dynamic center of activity, and on more than one occasion displayed his irritation at McHenry's incompetence.

[15] *American State Papers: Military Affairs* I, 20–36.

[16] *Ibid.*, I, 36–39.

[17] *Ibid.*, I, 40.

[18] A corresponding contract of October 1790, subsequently transferred to Duer, required a bond of $100,000.

camp on September 10. The person sent forward by the quartermaster to handle supplies was "totally incompetent for the business." Ten days before the surprise attack by the Indians, the army, well in the wilderness, had not more than three days' supply of flour.

Upon the disbandment of the expedition the privates were discharged without pay or settlement, other than three dollars and a note of discharge, specifying the time of their service and bearing endorsement that *some* advances had been made on account, without stating the amount. This was done deliberately to prevent the transfer of the note, apparently without any concern for the resulting problem of eventual settlement. The money for the pay of the levies did not leave Philadelphia until December 4, 1791, and arrived at Fort Washington on January 3, 1792, after the last of the soldiers were known to be entitled to their discharges. The War Department offered two excuses: one, the want of a paymaster for the army and the consequent difficulties of transmitting money at so great a distance; the other, that the army was *supposed* ("according to plan") to be at that time at the Miami village, "so far advanced in the wilderness, as not to admit the practicability of discharging the levies." The House Committee found that the causes for the failure of the expedition were three: lack of time during the summer to organize the army for the expedition; the want of discipline and training in the troops; and "delays consequent upon the gross and various mismanagements and neglects in the Quartermaster's and contractors' departments." [19]

The breakdown of the army supply services was notorious and Hamilton promptly stepped into the breach. The House inquiry was authorized on March 27, 1792. In April a bill was introduced into the Senate by a committee comprising three of Hamilton's close friends, Rufus King, Caleb Strong, and Oliver Ellsworth, authorizing the Treasury Department to take over the army supply services.[20] It became law on May 8, 1792,[21] the same date on which the House Committee on the St. Clair affair released its report.

Knox was unresponsive to Hamilton's initial overtures for the transfer of army purchases to Treasury in accordance with this act. In July 1792 Hamilton was finally forced to turn to the President for help. The Secretary of the Treasury wrote Washington:

[19] *American State Papers: Military Affairs,* I, 36–39 (May 8, 1792).
[20] *Annals,* III, 116, 120.
[21] 1 Stat. 279.

I have long had it at heart that some good system of regulations for the forwarding supplies to the army, issuing them there and accounting for them to the department of war, should be established. On conversing with the Secretary at War, I do not find that any such now exists: nor have the intimations I have taken the liberty to give on the subject, though perfectly well received, hitherto produced the desired effect. The utility of the thing does not seem to be as strongly impressed on the mind of the Secretary at War as it is on mine.

It has occurred to me that if you should think fit to call by letter upon the Secretary of the Treasury and the Secretary at War to report to you the *system and regulations under which the procuring, issuing and accounting for supplies to the army is conducted,* it would produce what appears to be now wanting. I submit the idea accordingly.[22]

Shortly afterward the President wrote both Secretaries for such a report. His letter to Knox is a little masterpiece, so drafted as to conceal any other agency than that of the commander in chief.[23] The request apparently precipitated action, since on August 10, 1792, Hamilton sent Washington a letter setting out the arrangements to which the Secretary of War had agreed, effective on September first.[24]

CIVIL–MILITARY RELATIONS

Despite congressional and public jealousy of a standing army, Washington and Adams chose military men rather than civilians to serve as Secretaries of War. Washington, however, had no uncertainty about the subordination of the military to the civil authority. Writing to Governor Henry Lee, in command of the militia at the time of the Whiskey Rebellion, he remarked,

There is but one point on which I think it proper to add a special recommendation. It is this, that every officer and soldier will constantly bear in mind that he comes to support the laws and that it would be peculiarly unbecoming in him to be in any way the infractor of them; that the essential principles of a free government confine the provinces of the Military to these two objects: 1st: to combat and subdue all who may be found in arms in opposition to the National will and authority; 2dly to aid and support the civil Magistrate in bringing offenders to justice. The dispensation of

---

22 July 22, 1792, Hamilton, *Works* (Hamilton ed.), IV, 226.
23 Washington, *Writings,* XXXII, 102, 103–4.
24 Hamilton, *Works* (Hamilton ed.), IV, 242–44. For a general treatment of the problem of government purchasing and contracts, see below, ch. xxix.

this justice belongs to the civil Magistrate and let it ever be our pride and our glory to leave the sacred deposit there unviolated. . . .[25]

He repeated these injunctions in 1795 to Major General Daniel Morgan:

Still it may be proper constantly and strongly to impress upon the Army that they are mere agents of Civil power: that out of Camp, they have no other authority, than other citizens [,] that offences against the laws are to be examined, not by a military officer, but by a Magistrate; that they are not exempt from arrests and indictments for violations of the law; that officers ought to be careful, not to give orders, which may lead the agents into infractions of the law; that no compulsion be used towards the inhabitants in the traffic, carried on between them and the army: that disputes be avoided, as much as possible, and be adjusted as quickly as may be, without urging them to an extreme: and that the whole country is not to be considered as within the limits of the camp.[26]

Military interference in congressional elections was the object of a sharp note from Washington in 1793. Receiving complaints from a member of the Executive Council of Virginia against a Captain Preston, he expressed his "pointed disapprobation of all such interferences of the military with the civil power." [27]

In the western territories there was much conflict between the military and civil authorities. Stress and strain developed principally over divided responsibility for dealing with the Indians, and the heads of military detachments often showed scant courtesy to requests for aid by civilian officials. Despite the fact that Indian traders were under the jurisdiction of the War Department, its agents were sabotaged by the army officers.

Benjamin Hawkins, Senator from North Carolina from 1790 to 1795, and general superintendent of all the tribes south of the Ohio River from 1796, was witness to these conflicts. An Indian trader at Fort Wilkinson, Price, was apparently driven from his quarters, a victim of the "violence, outrage and unprecedented conduct of the officers of the garrison." Hawkins was appealed to for counsel and wrote, "If the military gentlemen have determined at all events to remove Mr. Price, that determination is an insult to the President of the United

---

[25] Oct. 20, 1794, Washington, *Writings,* XXXIV, 6.
[26] March 27, 1795, *ibid.,* XXXIV, 159–60.
[27] Journal of the Proceedings of the President, May 1, 1793, pp. 104–5.

States." ". . . it must be known whether they or the President of the United States has a right to judge." Meanwhile he advised that until the Secretary of War could give directions, all intercourse between the military and civil agents be cut off and that the commanding general in the territory protect the trader against the local commander.[28]

Despite these distant, and often petty clashes, the subordination of the military to the civil authority was the undoubted policy and rule, and the military fully accepted the position which constitutional theory and British tradition assigned to them.

LEADERSHIP

The administrative ineptitude of the War Department can be traced in considerable measure to the character of two of its Secretaries, Henry Knox and James McHenry. Henry Knox, the son of a shipmaster, was born in Boston in 1750. At the age of twelve the death of his father left him the sole support of his mother and his education abruptly stopped. Military life fascinated him and in 1772 he became second in command of the Boston Grenadier Corps. Although his wife was the daughter of the royal Secretary of Massachusetts, Knox promptly withdrew from Boston and in 1775 joined the Revolutionary Army, in which he became colonel in charge of artillery. He participated effectively in the subsequent major campaigns, Boston, New York, New Jersey, and Yorktown, earning Washington's special commendation. In 1785 he became Secretary of War and served in this capacity until December 31, 1794. His personality fitted him better for military than for civil affairs. His sanguine disposition, his huge bulk (three hundred pounds), his tendency toward forceful and profane language, his courage and absorption in military movements combined to make him a successful general. In civil affairs, he was often beyond his depth and when asked by Washington to give his opinions on Cabinet matters he was perforce guided less by his education or experience and more by the fact that he was a "furious Federalist." In fact he regularly followed Hamilton, thus earning the contempt of Jefferson.[29]

---

[28] *Letters of Benjamin Hawkins, 1796–1806* (Savannah: Georgia Historical Society, 1916), pp. 305–7.

[29] "Knox subscribed at once to H's opn that we ought to declare the treaty void, acknoleging at the same time, like a fool as he is, that he knew nothing about it." Jefferson, *Anas*, April 18, 1793, Jefferson, *Works* (Federal ed.), I, 268.

Knox had a hospitable temperament and entertained far beyond his means, already strained by the gambling debts of a domineering wife. To recoup his fortunes, he became engaged as early as 1791 in extensive land speculation in Maine with William Duer. In consequence he was burdened with further debts and many vexatious law suits.

His generosity led him to aid his many friends. To Benjamin Lincoln, a comrade-in-arms, he wrote, "Although I do not conceive the office of Collector to the Port of Boston adequate to the merits of my friend, yet, as it is the best thing that can be offered at present, I sincerely congratulate you on the appointment." [30] Dr. Hugh Williamson, former congressman from North Carolina, passed a severe judgment in 1796; "Knox, as you know, was considered to be a Man who went on a most expensive Scale. The follies of a gambling wife were passed to the Debit of her Husband, in Addition to his own—no great Stock of Talents." [31] Knox had talents for military command, but in civil administration his capacity was modest.

After a brief interlude in which Timothy Pickering held the office of Secretary of War, he was succeeded by James McHenry, a warmhearted Irishman who arrived in Philadelphia from County Antrim in 1771 at the age of eighteen and set out to make his fortune. His temperament was not that of a successful businessman and it fell to his father and brother John, who followed James to America, to build up a considerable estate in an importing business in Baltimore. He turned to medicine, studied in Philadelphia under Benjamin Rush, and served during the Revolution as an army surgeon and as secretary to Washington.

At the close of the war he entered politics. He sat in Congress from 1783 to 1786, was a member of the Constitutional Convention, and subsequently was a member of the Maryland Assembly and Senate, "a stout Federalist." He was recommended in 1783 by Washington as a "Man of Letters and Abilities, of great integrity, sobriety and prudence. In a word, a Man of strict honor . . . of an amiable temper; very obliging, and of polished manners." [32]

His sense of official honor was high. Before taking office as Secretary

---

[30] Francis S. Drake, *Life and Correspondence of Henry Knox* (Boston: Samuel G. Drake, 1873), p. 103. For aid to his friend, Henry Jackson, see *ibid.*, p. 108.

[31] Steiner, *McHenry*, pp. 164-65.

[32] Washington, *Writings*, XXVI, 349.

of War, he broke off two mercantile partnerships, one at a loss of about £3,000, the other worth about £1,000 annually.[33] He was not Washington's first, but his fourth choice to succeed Pickering. His lack of success as an administrator can best be told in the words of his friends.

While Washington was searching for a proper person to appoint he asked Hamilton's advice. He replied in part, "*McHenry,* you know. He would give no strength to the administration, but he would not disgrace the office; his views are good; perhaps his health, &c., would prevent his accepting." [34] After three years' experience Hamilton wrote again to Washington, "my friend McHenry is wholly insufficient for his place, with the additional misfortune, of not having the least suspicion of the fact. . . . [His insufficiency] is so great as to leave no probability that the business of the War Department can make any tolerable progress in his hands." [35]

Washington had reached the same conclusion. "Your opinion . . . ," he wrote Hamilton, "accords with mine. . . . I early discovered after he entered upon the Duties of his Office that his talents were unequal to great exertions, or deep resources. In truth they were not expected; for the fact is, it was a Hobson's choice." [36]

McHenry's administrative failure was due to a common cause, inability to delegate details and to keep a firm hand on essentials. Hamilton plainly told him of his weakness.

I observe you plunged in a vast mass of details. I know from experience, that it is impossible for any man, whatever be his talents or diligence, to wade through such a mass, without neglecting the most material things, and attaching to his operations a feebleness and sloth of execution. It is essential to the success of the minister of a great department, that he subdivide the objects of his care, distribute them among competent assistants, and content himself with a general but vigilant superintendence. This course is particularly necessary when an unforeseen emergency has suddenly accumulated a number of new objects to be provided for and executed.[37]

Washington renewed this good advice [38] and Hamilton repeated

[33] Steiner, *op. cit.,* p. 168.
[34] Hamilton, *Works* (Hamilton ed.), VI, 63.
[35] *Ibid.,* VI, 333.
[36] Washington, *Writings,* XXXVI, 394.
[37] Hamilton, *Works* (Hamilton ed.), V, 139 (July 30, 1798).
[38] Washington, *Writings,* XXXVII, 163–64 (March 25, 1799).

it,[39] but to no avail. McHenry could not alter his habits. Wolcott made a judicious if generous estimate of the man as an administrator in a letter to Fisher Ames: ". . . he is a man of honour and entirely trustworthy; he is also a man of sense, and delivers correct opinions when required, but he is not skilled in the details of Executive business and he is at the head of a difficult and unpopular department." [40]

---

[39] Steiner, *op. cit.*, pp. 390–91 (June 14, 1799); and *ibid.*, pp. 397–98 (July 10, 1799). McHenry offered to resign on September 6, 1798, but Adams declined to accept the offer. *Ibid.*, pp. 338–39.

[40] *Ibid.*, p. 422 (Dec. 29, 1799).

Chapter Thirteen

THE NAVY DEPARTMENT

The American Navy was born amidst fierce contention between Federalists and Republicans.[1] The Republicans fought the reestablishment of a naval armament even under the War Department, believing that ships of war were an endless expense which would ruin the prospects of getting rid of the debt, that a navy was useless since our remoteness from Europe made an attack on our shores impossible, and that a navy constituted a danger to liberty. Debating the bill to provide six ships to protect American commerce against the Algerine corsairs, Abraham Clark of New Jersey objected in the House "to the establishment of a fleet, because, when once it had been commenced, there would be no end of it. We must then have a Secretary of the Navy, and a swarm of other people in office, at a monstrous expense." [2]

The political struggles between the navy-minded Federalists, led by John Adams and the eastern mercantile and shipping interests, and their opponents do not concern us. Nor are the failures of the American Navy during the Revolutionary War or the brilliant exploits of Truxtun, Preble, and other commanders, in the punishment of the Algerines and in the naval quasi-war with France in 1798 and 1799 relevant to a history of administration. The less dramatic but essential business of creating an organization that could find ships, equip them, recruit officers and crews, and maintain them as an effective fighting force at sea is the subject matter of naval administration.

The Navy Department almost falls outside the Federalist era, since it was not established until 1798. The naval vessels of the Revolutionary

---

[1] This party struggle is recorded in the very able study by Harold and Margaret Sprout, *The Rise of American Naval Power, 1776–1918* (Princeton: Princeton University Press, 1939), ch. iv.

[2] *Annals*, IV, 434 (Feb. 6, 1794).

War had been disposed of, and the first Congress was making an empty gift when in 1789 it placed the charge of naval matters in the hands of the War Department. The first public ships of the new general government, the revenue cutters, in fact came under the jurisdiction of the Treasury. Not until 1794 did Congress consider the need of public armed vessels to protect American commerce on the high seas. The act of 1794 providing for a naval armament of six ships was pushed through only with the aid of a rider providing that their construction should cease if peace were made with Algeria.[3]

Word of peace came in 1796 when the ships were still on the ways. Washington asked Congress what to do with the partly finished vessels, and precipitated another sharp conflict that ended in a compromise allowing three of them to be completed.[4] Work was slowly proceeding when in 1798 affairs with France grew worse and a naval war impended. The Federalists took the occasion to establish the Navy Department.

This was the first debate on a "new" department since 1789. The arguments on both sides turned on strictly administrative considerations, although the underlying difference of opinion was between the "big-navy" and "no-navy" men. The issue was, why should the supervision of naval vessels, hitherto in the War Department, require the establishment of a separate agency, or, in more general terms, what is the justification for a department?

The Federalists had answers. Harper declared that the only point was whether the creation of a department would "effect with more speed and economy the marine defence now existing, as well as that contemplated?"[5] He answered the question in the affirmative. Otis and others argued that the combined business was too much for any man, and that a separate department would secure the services of a specialist. ". . . it was a thing impossible for one man to undertake the business of the War and Navy Departments. As well might a merchant be set to do the business of a lawyer; a lawyer that of a physician; a carpenter that of a bricklayer; or a bricklayer that of a carpenter."[6]

The Republicans had replies. Gallatin opposed a department, partly because the army and navy were not large enough to require separate

---

[3] 1 Stat. 350 (March 27, 1794).
[4] 1 Stat. 453 (April 20, 1796).
[5] *Annals,* VIII, 1550 (April 25, 1798).
[6] *Ibid.,* VIII, 1548.

establishments, partly on account of the increased expense.[7] Robert Williams was against splitting the War Department: "whenever this rule of dividing business shall be adopted, we shall get men of inferior talents to do it."[8] Edward Livingston ridiculed the idea of the need of a specialist in shipbuilding or maritime affairs as the head of the Navy. "Could it be said that the Secretary of War had a perfect knowledge of everything under his direction, except what related to the navy? Certainly not. To be so, he must not only be a perfect engineer, but be acquainted with the construction of arms. To carry this idea to its full extent, it would not only be necessary to have separate departments, but also a great variety of subdivisions; they must have, he supposed, commissioners of gun-barrels and of ramrods."[9] Livingston argued also that a shipbuilder Secretary of the Navy would not be fit to be one of the great council of the nation. By an uncomfortably close margin for the Federalists (47 to 41), the bill went through the House and eventually became law.

The organic act creating the department, like its predecessors, was brief and simple. An "executive department" was established, the Department of the Navy; its chief officer was the Secretary, whose duty was "to execute such orders as he shall receive from the President of the United States" concerning the procurement of naval stores, the construction, equipment, and employment of vessels of war, and other naval matters.[10]

William Smith, now minister at Lisbon, wrote McHenry with regard to these developments. "I find you are at length likely to have some Symptoms of a Navy—& that there is to be a Navy Department, but I don't learn which way your propensity inclines, whether to the Army or Navy; as you are to be subdivided into two parts, I wish to know with which part the Soul remains, with the Navy part or the Army part? are you to be Mars or Neptune? are you to wield the Truncheon or the Trident? God prosper you in whatever capacity; you have an arduous task & sad Devils to deal with. . . ."[11] McHenry had no occasion to choose. After receiving a declination from George

---

[7] Ibid., VIII, 1545.
[8] Ibid., VIII, 1550.
[9] Ibid., VIII, 1553.
[10] 1 Stat. 553 (April 30, 1798).
[11] June 23, 1798, Sewanee Review, XIV (1906), 96.

Cabot of Massachusetts, Adams appointed as first Secretary of the Navy a successful Baltimore merchant, Benjamin Stoddert.

As an administrative agency, the central office of the Navy, like that of War, was on a very small scale. The Secretary's office comprised the chief clerk, four or five subordinate clerks, and a messenger, with a pay roll, in 1800, of $9,152. The Secretary's salary of $4,500 absorbed nearly half of this sum. The office of the accountant of the Navy was established in the summer of 1798.[12] It employed six or seven clerks.

The only professional civilian officer in the Department was Joshua Humphreys, principal naval constructor of the United States. He, like the navy storekeeper, was stationed in Philadelphia, although outside the Secretary's office—a section of the "field service" in the headquarters' city. He was the chief technical adviser of the Secretary of the Navy and according to Paullin, "a man of marked ability and skill in his profession." [13]

In a report early in 1801 Stoddert observed that the business of the Navy Department embraced too many objects for the superintendence of one person and recommended the establishment of a board of three or five navy officers to superintend, "in subordination to the Head of the Department," the more technical part of the work.[14]

The principal administrative mission of the Navy Department under Stoddert was to build a navy. This in turn was essentially a task of assembling materials, organizing yards and letting contracts, supervising and energizing the actual construction, and buying guns, equipment, and stores.[15] Urgency was the order of the day, and Stoddert put a naval force on the high seas in quick order. At the close of 1797 three ships were in service; at the close of 1798, twenty; and at the close of 1799, thirty-three.[16] This record contrasted favorably with that of the War Department which in 1794 had been directed to construct six armed ships. The three which were eventually completed—

---

[12] 1 Stat. 610 (July 16, 1798).

[13] Charles Oscar Paullin, "Early Naval Administration under the Constitution," U. S. Naval Institute, *Proceedings,* XXXII (1906), 1001–30 at 1016–17.

[14] *Annals,* X, 1432 (Jan. 12, 1801).

[15] A rich assembly of documents on the administrative operations of the Navy Department, as well as on the movements and activities of ships, is available in *Naval Documents related to the Quasi-War between the United States and France* prepared by the Office of Naval Records and Library, U. S. Navy Department (7 vols., Washington: Government Printing Office, 1935–38).

[16] Paullin, *op. cit.,* p. 1021.

the *Constitution,* the *United States,* and the *Constellation*—were launched in 1797. So great had been the delay that a House Committee made an investigation. The War Department was charged with "enormous expenses and unaccountable delays."[17] It was at Secretary of War McHenry's suggestion that his Department was relieved of further responsibility for naval affairs.

The building and equipping of armed ships was a large assignment, even for a country which had an enviable record in ship construction. As in the case of the revenue cutters in 1790, full political advantage was taken of the situation by building them in different parts of the country. Stoddert laid solid foundations in establishing six navy yards. "The navy-yards are the manufactories, repair-shops, and storehouses of the navy; the Navy Department, in one of its most important functions, is the central office that superintends the activities of the navy-yards."[18] When Congress appropriated funds in 1799 for six 74-gun ships, Stoddert and Adams determined to purchase permanent building grounds, despite lack of specific legislative authority—"a masterpiece of loose construction."[19] Within two years, grounds for navy yards had been purchased at Washington, Norfolk, Portsmouth, Philadelphia, New York, and Charlestown, Massachusetts. Plans for docks had not been brought to fruition when naval expansion was halted by the succession to power of Thomas Jefferson.

The basic administrative organization of a navy yard had been established in 1794. It consisted of a superintendent, naval constructor, navy agent, and clerk of the yard. The superintendent had general charge and the naval constructor immediate charge of the building of the vessel. The navy agent bought all materials except those purchased by the Treasury, and was paymaster for the artisans and laborers. The clerk received, issued, and accounted for public property in the yard.[20]

One of the ablest and most colorful of the navy agents was Stephen Higginson, Boston merchant, Federalist, and friend of Oliver Wolcott. Higginson became a general adviser to the leading figures in the administration. His views on the new navy were characteristic of the

---

[17] March 8, 1798, *American State Papers: Naval Affairs,* I, 33. The average cost of the three ships was $305,420. Paullin, *op. cit.,* p. 1009.

[18] *Ibid.,* p. 1024.

[19] A House report (April 27, 1802) charged the Navy Department with spending $199,030.92 without legal authority. *American State Papers: Naval Affairs,* I, 103.

[20] Paullin, *op. cit.,* pp. 1007–8.

energy and forthrightness of the man. To Wolcott he wrote, "it is a primary object to select proper characters for the Navy; such as have right habits, principles and feelings; capable of being trained to proper discipline. Upon this depends the reputation and utility of our Navy; but no aid can be derived to this purpose from any characters I ever knew in our Navy last war." [21] In a similar vein he wrote to Timothy Pickering,

the more I reflect upon the Subject the more I see the necessity of caution in our naval appointments, or else the public ships will become the receptacles, and the public money the Support of those only, who for want of principle, of capacity, of reputation or of energy are incapable of getting their living in the common pursuits of life. . . .

There is but one way that I see to check or avoid the Evil, and that is to appoint the Capts upon the evidence of particular and special recommendation or a personal knowledge of the reverse, and let them select their under Officers being responsible for their good conduct.—it is [not] to be presumed that the President can appoint to offices of this kind from his own knowledge of the characters, in general, and no dependence can be put upon common general recommendations. . . . [22]

The construction of naval vessels raised at once the question whether they should be built by contract or directly under government management. The decision was taken for public construction, although eventually some were built on contract and some by patriotic citizens who in at least one case advanced the money (at six per cent), built and equipped the ship under official direction, and turned it over ready for sea. [23] An interesting early example of government enterprise also was set on foot—the purchase of two islands (Grover and Blackbeard) off the Georgia coast, in order to secure a growth of live oak for ship timbers. [24]

---

[21] July 13, 1798, Gibbs, *Memoirs*, II, 72.

[22] June 9, 1798, "Letters of Stephen Higginson," Am. Hist. Assoc., *Annual Report, 1896*, I, 806–7.

[23] John J. Currier, *History of Newburyport, Mass., 1764–1905*, I (1906), 111; "Letters of Benjamin Stoddert, First Secretary of the Navy, to Nicholas Johnson of Newburyport, 1798–1799," *Essex Institute Historical Collections*, LXXIV (1938), 350–60. These letters provide interesting detail of business transactions between the Secretary and a naval agent.

[24] 1 Stat. 622 (Feb. 25, 1799). This statute deserves to rank as an early example of legislative planning for future needs. It directed the President "to cause the proper measures to be taken to have the same preserved for the future uses of the navy."

Benjamin Stoddert (1751–1813) was brought up to commerce.[25] At the age of twenty-six he became a captain in a Pennsylvania regiment, fought for two years, and then served for two years as secretary to the Board of War. Later as a Georgetown merchant he supplied goods to Washington's nephews, and in the early days of planning for the Federal City bought land privately in strategic places, at Washington's request, for subsequent cession to the government. He was no office seeker. While deciding whether to accept Adams' offer of appointment as Secretary of the Navy he wrote to Francis Lowndes, "I hate office—have no desire for fancied or real importance and wish to spend my life in retirement and ease without bustle of any kind. Yet it seems cowardly at such a time as this to refuse an important and highly responsible position." [26]

One element of his genuine success was his modesty and willingness to seek advice. Stephen Higginson was one of his consultants, as well as a navy agent. To him Stoddert wrote, "I am but new to my office & shall stand in need of all the aid I can obtain from enlightened and patriotic men like yourself in all parts of the Union." [27] And a month later he asked for Higginson's "candid opinion. . . . It was unfortunate that, in conferring the appointment of the Secretary of the Navy upon me, the President could not also confer the knowledge necessary for the Secretary of the Navy to possess to make him most useful to his country." [28]

Professional navy opinion does not agree with Stoddert's self-deprecation. Captain Knox writes, "great credit is due Secretary Stoddert for his able direction of the Navy under difficult circumstances." [29] And Paullin declares him "a worthy and efficient administrator." [30] On larger matters relating to the duties of a Secretary to his principal, Stoddert had a sense of the requirements of good administration which,

---

[25] *Dictionary of American Biography* (Allen Johnson and Dumas Malone, eds., 21 vols., New York: C. Scribner's Sons, 1928–44), XVIII, 62–63.

[26] May 26, 1798, Harriot Stoddert Turner, "Memoirs of Benjamin Stoddert," Columbia Historical Society, *Records,* XX (1917), 141–66 at 152.

[27] June 22, 1798, Thomas Wentworth Higginson, *Life and Times of Stephen Higginson* (Boston and New York: Houghton, Mifflin, 1907), p. 198.

[28] *Ibid.,* p. 207.

[29] Dudley W. Knox, *A History of the United States Navy* (New York: G. P. Putnam's Sons, 1936), p. 46.

[30] Paullin, *op. cit.,* p. 1016.

as we have seen, exceeded that of his Cabinet colleagues. Hard-working, conscientious, and experienced in the management of affairs, he succeeded in his task—the building, arming, equipping, and maintenance at sea of a reborn American Navy.

Chapter Fourteen

THE ATTORNEY GENERAL—"A SORT OF MONGREL"

THE office of Attorney General occupied a unique position in the official constellation.[1] It did not possess the status and dignity of a department, although after 1792 its incumbent regularly attended Cabinet meetings. The Attorney General was thought of rather as the legal adviser of the President and department heads, and as an agent to whom Congress might turn for information and advice. But the government was merely one of his clients, paying an annual retainer of $1,500,[2] one half of the salary assigned to the heads of departments. In accordance with the custom of that time, the Attorney General was not only allowed, but expected to pursue his private legal work.

Washington referred to this freedom to carry on a private practice in his letter offering Edmund Randolph the appointment as first Attorney General, September 28, 1789, "the Salary of this office appears to have been fixed, at what it is, from a belief that the Station would confer pre-eminence on its possessor, and procure for him a decided preference of Professional employment."[3] When Washington offered the post (in vain) to John Marshall in 1795, he held out "the prospect of a lucrative practice in this city."[4]

In a letter written in 1790 Randolph complained of his anomalous situation. "I am a sort of mongrel between the State and the U.S.; called an officer of some rank under the latter, and yet thrust out to

---

[1] The principal secondary historical work on the Attorney General is Homer Cummings and Carl McFarland, *Federal Justice: Chapters in the History of Justice and the Federal Executive* (New York: Macmillan, 1937)—an excellent work.

[2] Before Randolph was appointed Attorney General, the government resorted to the New York bar for legal advice. *Ibid.*, p. 20, n. 3.

[3] Washington, *Writings*, XXX, 419.

[4] Aug. 26, 1795, *ibid.*, XXXIV, 288.

get a livelihood in the former,—perhaps in a petty mayor's or county court. I cannot say much on this head without pain, which, could I have foreseen it, would have kept me at home to encounter my pecuniary difficulties there, rather than add to them here." [5] Randolph engaged in a varied private practice, one of his most outstanding exploits being to convince the Supreme Court, in *Chisholm* vs. *Georgia,* that a citizen could sue a state in the Supreme Court of the United States.[6] It required a constitutional amendment to undo this interpretation of the Constitution.[7]

The anomalous character of the office of Attorney General was perhaps in part responsible for the neglect of its duties by Charles Lee, its third incumbent (1795–1801).[8] Lee had been in office a little less than a year when Washington was forced to discipline him for lack of attention to his official business. The President wrote:

This letter is for your eye only. It is written for the purpose of expressing my regret for your continued absence from the Seat of Government. Rely upon it, it is productive of unpleasant remarks, in which I must be involved. It will, indeed is, considered as making a Sinecure of the Office. To suppose there is no particular occasion for the Law Officer of the government at the Seat of it during the recess of Congress is incorrect; many cases have presented themselves since the adjournment, requiring the opinion and advice of the Attorney General (besides other duties marked out by the Laws). Some points have called for your aid since I have been here, and will occur without an hours previous notice in times like the present. Let me entreat you therefore to come on without delay, and to be assured of the esteem and friendship of Your Affect.[9]

Lee's absence from the seat of government was still causing trouble in 1797. Pickering needed to recover papers sent Lee by John Davis, the federal attorney for Massachusetts. But Lee was away: "He is gone to Virginia, and his house is locked up," wrote Pickering to Davis! [10]

---

[5] Moncure Daniel Conway, *Omitted Chapters of History Disclosed in the Life and Papers of Edmund Randolph* (New York: G. P. Putnam's Sons, 1888), p. 135.

[6] 2 Dallas 419 (1793).

[7] Eleventh Amendment.

[8] The second incumbent, William Bradford, died after a brief tenure during the yellow fever epidemic in 1795.

[9] Washington to Lee, Nov. 14, 1796, *Writings,* XXXV, 277–78.

[10] Sept. 12, 1797, Pickering Papers, VII, 172.

The duties imposed upon the Attorney General by the Judiciary Act were simple and closely contained. Upon request of the President, or of heads of departments, he was directed to give opinions on matters of law. That was all. He was not placed in supervisory charge of the attorneys of the United States, whose offices were created by the same act.[11] He had no establishment, not even a single clerk. His private law office was the seat of his official duties. He was directed to appear only in cases before the Supreme Court, leaving the district attorneys in full possession of cases involving the interests of the United States in the district courts. He was assigned no duties in connection with the operation of the courts. He received no reports and was in a curious way disconnected from the actual conduct of the business of government. He was, in short, a legal adviser, not an administrator.

Soon, however, this unique status began to change. In 1790 the Attorney General became a member of the board which granted patents, along with the Secretary of State and the Secretary of War.[12] This duty lasted only until 1793,[13] but meanwhile the Attorney General became a member of the Sinking Fund Commission with Hamilton, Jefferson, and others.[14] In 1797 he was authorized to supervise the work of the agent appearing in behalf of the United States before the commissioners to determine British claims, largely a legal problem, and to appoint such additional agents as this business might make necessary. For these services he received an additional stipend of $600 a year.[15] Beginning in 1792 Randolph was regularly invited to Cabinet meetings and became involved in the struggle between Hamilton and Jefferson as well as in important issues of foreign and domestic policy.

Randolph's duties as legal counsel steadily increased, especially in the field of international law. On great matters of state involving problems of constitutional law Washington required opinions from Hamilton, Jefferson, and Knox as well as the Attorney General—for example on the constitutionality of the bank act and the first apportionment act. While Knox was seriously out of his depth, Hamilton and Jefferson

---

[11] 1 Stat. 73, sec. 35 (Sept. 24, 1789).
[12] 1 Stat. 109 (April 10, 1790).
[13] 1 Stat. 318 (Feb. 21, 1793).
[14] 1 Stat. 281 (May 8, 1792).
[15] 1 Stat. 523 (June 30, 1797).

contributed state papers of greatest importance, indeed, overshadowing the opinions of Randolph. But on lesser matters the Attorney General wrote a steadily accumulating series of opinions on affairs domestic and foreign, as well as responding to many requests from Congress for opinions on private claims against the United States.[16]

At an early date Randolph sought to establish his office, rather than that of the Secretary of State, as the central authority to supervise the district attorneys. Writing to Washington December 26, 1791, he referred to defects in his office, and continued,

Many instances have occurred in which the heads of the Departments have requested that suits should be prosecuted in different States under my direction. It has been always my inclination to conform to their wishes; but the want of a fixed relation between the attorneys of the districts and the Attorney General, has rendered it impossible for me to take charge of matters on which I was not authorized to give instructions.

From the same source it may frequently arise that the United States may be deeply affected by various proceedings in the inferior courts, which no appeal can rectify. The peculiar duty of the Attorney General calls upon him to watch over these cases; and being, in the eye of the world, responsible for the final issue, to offer his advice at the earliest stage of any business; and indeed, until repeated adjudications shall have settled a clear line of partition between the federal and State courts, his best exertions cannot be too often repeated, to oppose the danger of a schism. For this purpose the attorneys of the district ought, I conceive, to be under an obligation to transmit to him a state of every case in which the harmony of the two judiciaries may be hazarded, and to communicate to him those topics on

---

[16] Cummings and McFarland, *op. cit.,* pp. 22, 24. One of Randolph's most delicate tasks arose in late 1793 when Genêt formally demanded that the Attorney General prosecute Chief Justice Jay and Senator King for alleged libel, sending a copy of the letter to Jefferson for consideration of the President. Jefferson's instruction to Randolph, written for Washington, was a masterpiece of caution. ". . . the President, never doubting your readiness on all occasions to perform the functions of your office, yet thinks it incumbent on him to recommend it specially on the present occasion, as it concerns a public character peculiarly entitled to the protection of the laws. On the other hand, as our citizens ought not to be vexed with groundless prosecutions, duty to them requires it to be added, that if you judge the prosecution in question to be of that nature, you consider this recommendation as not extending to it; it's only object being to engage you to proceed in this case according to the duties of your office, the laws of the land & the privileges of the parties concerned." Dec. 18, 1793, Jefferson, *Works* (Federal ed.), VIII, 119. The suit was not pressed.

which the subjects of foreign nations may complain in the administration of justice.[17]

Randolph noted also the desirability of granting him authority to secure information from the district attorneys in order to enable the President to recommend to Congress improvements in the administration of justice;[18] and concluded by suggesting "the reasonableness of allowing him a transcribing clerk." Washington transmitted this request to Congress (without an endorsement) but Randolph failed to secure either a clerk or the supervision of the district attorneys. Implicit in Randolph's program was a centrally organized federal agency for the enforcement of federal law. It was a proposal far in advance of its time, and despite a favorable committee report to the House, no action was taken.[19]

The duties of the Attorney General with reference to the business of the lower federal courts were explored and severely restricted by the Supreme Court in *Hayburn's Case*.[20] The circuit court denied Hayburn, an invalid veteran, the right to petition it for approval of his application for a pension, on the ground that the business was not judicial and could not therefore be performed by a judge.[21] Randolph asked the Supreme Court for a mandamus to require the circuit court to act upon the petition. The Chief Justice inquired whether this was a part of the Attorney General's powers. "The issue was whether it was a part of the duty of the Attorney General of the United States 'to superintend the decisions of the inferior courts, and if to him they appeared improper, to move the supreme court for a revision.'"[22] The Supreme Court was equally divided; the result was in effect a decision that it was not the duty of the Attorney General "to superintend the decisions of the inferior courts."

An interesting administrative episode revolved around Jefferson's attempt to deprive Randolph of the sole responsibility for giving opinions on questions of law—one phase of the greater struggle in which

---

[17] *American State Papers: Miscellaneous*, I, 46.

[18] Randolph had already been asked by Congress to report on the administration of justice (*Annals*, II, 1719, Aug. 5, 1790) and had made a substantial report, *American State Papers: Miscellaneous*, I, 21–36.

[19] *Annals*, III, 329–30.

[20] 2 Dallas 409 (1792).

[21] April 12, 1792; the refusal was reported to Congress the next day in the form of a memorial from Hayburn, *Annals*, III, 556.

[22] See Cummings and McFarland, *op. cit.*, pp. 27–28 for a brief account.

Jefferson was engaged with Hamilton. The Supreme Court had declined to give its opinion on a series of legal problems on which Washington had requested advice, on the ground that the judicial function did not extend to this service.[23] The government was, therefore, driven back to its legal counsel, the Attorney General. Jefferson then proposed to set up a board to give such advice, to which Randolph countered by insisting that such an agency should be attached to his office. To Madison, Jefferson wrote, "In plain language, this would be to make him the sole arbiter of the line of conduct for the U. S. towards foreign nations." [24]

Jefferson was thoroughly dissatisfied with what he believed to be a lack of principle in Randolph. In an entry of August 23, 1793, in the *Anas*, Jefferson noted Randolph's attitude on a proposed letter to Genêt: "R. half for it, half against it, according to custom." [25] About two weeks earlier he had written to Madison, "I can by this confidential conveyance speak more freely of R. He is the poorest cameleon I ever saw having no colour of his own, & reflecting that nearest him." [26] Two years later he repeated his unfavorable estimate in a letter to William Giles: "The fact is that he [Randolph] has generally given his principles to the one party & his practice to the other. . . . Whether his conduct is to be ascribed to a superior view of things, an adherence to right without regard to party, as he pretends, or to an anxiety to trim between both, those who know his character and capacity will decide." [27]

Disregarding Jefferson's strictures for the moment, Randolph appears as a personality possessing charm and dignity, well versed in the law and accustomed to participation in public affairs, but plagued throughout much of his official career by indebtedness arising from land specu-

---

[23] Jefferson sent the President's request to the judges of the Supreme Court July 18, 1793, Jefferson *Works* (Federal ed.), VII, 451–52; see Jay, *Correspondence*, III, 488–89 for the Justices' reply of Aug. 8.

[24] Conway, *op. cit.*, pp. 186, 191; cited in Cummings and McFarland, *op. cit.*, p. 40.

[25] Jefferson, *Works* (Federal ed.), I, 321.

[26] Aug. 11, 1793, Samuel Flagg Bemis, ed., *The American Secretaries of State and Their Diplomacy* (10 vols., New York: A. A. Knopf, 1927–29), II, 100. This important letter does not appear in either the Federal or Memorial editions of Jefferson's papers. Excerpts from it may be found in Conway, *op. cit.*, pp. 190–91, and J. C. Hamilton, *History of the Republic*, V, 341–45.

[27] Dec. 31, 1795, Jefferson, *Works* (Federal ed.), VIII, 202–3. For a defense of Randolph against Jefferson's charges, see Conway, *op. cit.*, pp. 193 ff. For an account of the long family and personal connection between the two men, see *ibid.*, pp. 187–88.

lation and imprudent management of his affairs.[28] His career had been a brilliant one: aide-de-camp of Washington, member of the Virginia Convention of 1776 which recommended independence to the Continental Congress, first attorney general of the state of Virginia, mayor of Williamsburg, delegate to the Continental Congress, governor of Virginia in 1786, a member of the Annapolis Convention, and a leading delegate from Virginia to the Constitutional Convention. His deep-seated capacity for vacillation was revealed in his refusal to sign the Constitution in 1787, and his subsequent support of it, however reluctant, in the Virginia Convention in 1788.

Randolph left the office of Attorney General on January 2, 1794, to become Secretary of State. The circumstances of his enforced resignation from this office on August 19, 1795, remain shrouded in uncertainty. An intercepted dispatch from the French minister, Fauchet, gave ground for believing that Randolph had approached Fauchet for money with the implication that the foreign policy of the United States would consequently be more friendly to France.

The President was hastily summoned from Mount Vernon, reaching Philadelphia on August 11, 1795. For a week, in the midst of which he signed the Jay Treaty, he gave no intimation to Randolph of the impending storm, even entertaining Randolph at dinner. On August 19, in the presence of Pickering, Wolcott, and Bradford (then Attorney General), Washington drew from his pocket Fauchet's letter, gave it to Randolph, and asked for an explanation. Randolph read it through, expressed a wish to examine it more at leisure, withdrew, and instantly sent in his resignation.

Although there was no direct evidence of guilt, Washington was satisfied that Randolph's conduct was seriously at fault. Randolph's subsequent *Vindication*[29] stirred the President to profound anger.

---

[28] He was obliged to borrow money from Hamilton (along with John Adams and several members of Congress) when he reached New York (J. C. Hamilton, *op. cit.,* IV, 48); and when he left Philadelphia he had to borrow £2,000 from his brother-in-law (Bemis, *op. cit.,* II, 156). In 1793 Washington had extracted from Jefferson an account of Randolph's financial distress. Jefferson recorded in his *Anas,* "I knew that the embarrassments in his private affairs had obliged him to use expedts which had injured him with the merchts & shopkeepers & affected his character of independance; that these embarrassments were serious, & not likely to cease soon." *Works* (Federal ed.), I, 314. The sequel of Randolph's financial troubles is noted in Bemis, *op. cit.,* II, 156–58.

[29] Edmund Randolph, *A Vindication of Mr. Randolph's Resignation* (Philadelphia: Samuel H. Smith, 1795).

He sent for Pickering and with mounting wrath referred to his promise to the dying Peyton Randolph, an uncle who had adopted Edmund, to be as a father to the young orphan, his repeated assistance to Randolph throughout his career, and his discovery that Randolph had been "conducting an intrigue with the ambassador of a foreign government to promote the designs of that government, which were to overthrow the administration of which he, Randolph, was a trusted member, receiving from that ambassador money to aid in accomplishing that object; soliciting from him more for the same purpose."[30] According to Pickering's biographer, he finally threw the *Vindication* down, "and gave way to a terrific burst of denunciation."[31] Jefferson, however, held that the *Vindication* cleared Randolph of the charge of bribery, but did not give "high ideas of his wisdom or steadiness";[32] and on another occasion Jefferson said, "even those who did not know him will acquit him of the charge of bribery; those who knew him had done it from the first."[33] Hamilton confessed that he "never had confidence in Mr. Randolph" and thought there were very suspicious circumstances in his relations with Fauchet.[34] He considered Randolph's *Vindication* as "a confession of guilt."[35] Reviewing the evidence in 1927, D. R. Anderson concluded, "Randolph may have been voluble, imprudent, indecisive and unstable, but he was not dishonest, and there is no evidence that he betrayed his government or was more free in his discussions with foreign ministers than was unfortunately the custom of the day."[36]

[30] Octavius Pickering and Charles W. Upham, *The Life of Timothy Pickering* (4 vols., Boston: Little, Brown, 1867–73), III, 225–27. Volume I was written by Timothy Pickering's son, Octavius; after his death the work was completed by Mr. Upham. Hereafter cited as Upham, *Timothy Pickering*.

[31] *Ibid.*, III, 227. The disappointment to Washington must have been keen, for in 1789 the President had written Madison, "Mr. Randolph . . . I would prefer to any person I am acquainted of not superior abilities, from habits of intimacy with him." Washington, *Writings*, XXX, 414. Washington is reported to have said, "A damneder scoundrel God Almighty never permitted to disgrace humanity." J. C. Hamilton, *op. cit.*, VI, 309, n.; F. S. Oliver, *Alexander Hamilton*, p. 346.

[32] Jefferson to Monroe, March 2, 1796, Jefferson, *Works* (Federal ed.), VIII, 221.

[33] Jefferson to Giles, Dec. 31, 1795, *ibid.*, VIII, 201–2.

[34] Hamilton, *Works* (Hamilton ed.), VI, 48 (Oct. 16, 1795).

[35] *Ibid.*, VI, 79 (Dec. 24, 1795). Wolcott considered Randolph "a lost and desperate man" who had been unfaithful to the government and who had made treasonable or corrupt overtures to the French minister. Gibbs, *Memoirs*, I, 256.

[36] In Bemis, *op. cit.*, II, 149 ff., especially at 156. Cummings and McFarland treat Randolph's resignation with such circumspection as to leave the impression they believed Randolph guilty; see *op. cit.*, pp. 45–46. John T. Morse, Jr. reached the conclusion

Throughout the period under review, and indeed until 1818, the office of Attorney General retained the unique character which was impressed upon it at the outset; a law office to which the President and heads of departments could turn for legal advice (in consideration of an annual retaining fee of $1,500), and to which also any private citizen could repair for counsel. Randolph's efforts to build the office into even an embryonic department of law enforcement failed, and the district attorneys remained under the jurisdiction of the Secretary of State. As an administrative agency, the office was insignificant; but since its incumbent early won a place in the Cabinet, the Attorney General played a role of substantial importance in the general policy of the Federalist era.

---

that "the attorney general was a clear-headed, dispassionate adviser, of an excellent shrewdness in matters of international law, and . . . much more often right than either of the extremists between whom he stood." *Thomas Jefferson* (Boston and New York: Houghton, Mifflin, 1883), p. 134.

Chapter Fifteen

THE GENERAL POST OFFICE

COLONIAL EXPERIENCE

THE first recorded attempt to give postal service in the colonies was made by the Massachusetts General Court in 1639. "For preventing the miscarriage of letters. . . . It is ordered that notice bee given, that Richard Fairbanks, his house in Boston, is the place appointed for all letters, which are brought from beyond the Seas, or are to be sent thither . . . provided that no man shall bee compelled to bring his letters thither except hee please." [1] It was not until 1692 that an effective colonial postal system was established, the Crown granting a patent to Thomas Neale for this purpose. Neale found the venture unprofitable and in 1710 a new start was made by act of Parliament setting up one chief letter office in New York and other chief offices in each American colony, and establishing uniform rates for like distances.

From September 1773 to June 1774, a postal agent from London, Hugh Finlay, made a tour of inspection of the colonial offices from Maine to Georgia. His journal is a fascinating, even if uncomplimentary, account of the postal service at the close of Benjamin Franklin's administration as a royal Deputy Postmaster; [2] we may believe that the conditions he discovered continued without marked improvement into the period of independence.

---

[1] Quoted in Mary E. Woolley, "The Early History of the Colonial Post-Office," *Papers from the Historical Seminary of Brown University* (J. Franklin Jameson, ed., Providence, R. I., 1894), pp. 1–33, at p. 4. This is one of the principal works on early post office history.

[2] *Journal kept by Hugh Finlay, Surveyor of the Post Roads on the Continent of North America* (Brooklyn: Frank H. Norton, 1867); see also Ruth Lapham Butler, *Doctor Franklin: Postmaster General* (Garden City, N. Y.: Doubleday Doran, 1928).

In New London, Connecticut, Finlay found the ideal deputy: "Visited John S. Miller, the Deputy, he keeps his office in a room hir'd on purpose in the very centre of the town. He is a young man who talks sensibly of Post Office matters, and who seems to be a Post Master in his heart." [3] And in Newbury, Massachusetts, he "Examined the books, they were in form and up to this day: he has no office, but receives and delivers letters in his shop, he is a bookseller. He seems to be a stayed, sober man." [4]

These were the bright spots of Finlay's travels. In Falmouth [Maine], he found the deputy ready to resign.

He further represents that the employment is very troublesome to him, and of no manner of advantage, nay that it is a loss to him, for he cannot withstand the earnest solicitations of indigent people who have letters by the post, he delivers them, and never receives payment.

Every person who looks for a letter or a news paper freely enters his house, be it post day or not; he cannot afford to set apart a room in his house as an office; he is continually disturb'd in his family. . . .[5]

In Charles Town, South Carolina, which had a new deputy, Finlay "found the Books, accounts, papers and every thing relative to the former management in the greatest confusion, so as to render it impossible from them, to learn the true state of the offices in this district." [6] In all parts of the colonies he found the post riders pocketing the charges for carrying way letters (that is, from and to intermediate points), of which they made no record, as well as carrying letters secretly at their own rates. These perquisites counted heavily in the post riders' emoluments; in New Haven, according to Finlay, "The riders have told Mr. Kilby that the Devil might ride for them if these

---

[3] Finlay, *Journal*, p. 34.

[4] *Ibid.*, p. 22. It is interesting to note the principal occupations of the deputy postmasters in so far as Finlay recorded them. Three were customs officers, one each a bookseller, a printer, a teacher of writing, a keeper of a "very small shop," a warehouse owner, a "compting house" owner, and one "the first merchant in the place." The southern deputies were apparently men of more substance than their fellow deputies in New England.

[5] *Ibid.*, p. 16; Finlay records, "they [the deputies] one and all said, we have much trouble with the post, we cannot set apart an office, we receive the letters into our houses to oblige the Publick, and as for the Commission it is such a trifle it is not worth accepting. . . ." *Ibid.*, p. 76.

[6] *Ibid.*, p. 51.

way letters and packets were to be taken from them." [7] "In short," he concluded, "I find that it is the constant practice of all the riders between New York and Boston to defraud the Revenue as much as they can in pocketing the postage of all way letters." [8] These well-settled customs were not ended by the Declaration of Independence or the adoption of the Constitution.

Franklin's unceremonious discharge in 1774 was the signal for wide-spread boycott of the royal mail and for the spontaneous appearance of an independent postal system known as the "Constitutional Post." He was elected Postmaster General by the Continental Congress to direct a new postal system authorized on July 26, 1775. In 1782 Congress passed ordinances that furnished the foundation for postal operations until 1792.[9]

POLITICAL AND ADMINISTRATIVE IMPLICATIONS

The important political objects to be served by a widespread postal service were appreciated long before the post office was reaching the smaller or more remote centers of population. Rufus Putnam, honest and diligent public servant despite his difficulty with the English language, recognized them in a letter to the Postmaster General written from distant Marietta in the depths of the Northwest Territory.

I hope northing I have said or any other circumstance will opperate as a Discouragement sufficient to prevent the sending a Mail by this rout. for if it is considered in a Political light only, the information by this means obtained of the measures of government on the one hand & State of the people on the other, the knowledge diffused among the people by News-papers, by corrispondence between frinds and other communic[a]tions with these remote parts of the American Empire may be of infinite consequence to the government. Northing can be more fatal to a republican government then Ignorence among its Citizens, as they will be made the easy dupes of Designing men & insted of supporting the laws, the reason and policy of

---

[7] *Ibid.*, p. 40; see also comments from Savannah, p. 55; from Saybrook (Conn.), p. 38.

[8] *Ibid.*, p. 45.

[9] Wesley Everett Rich, *The History of the United States Post Office to the Year 1829* (Cambridge: Harvard University Press, 1924). For students of administration this is the most valuable secondary study. See also an unpublished doctoral dissertation, University of Chicago, by Ross Allan McReynolds, "History of the United States Post Office, 1607–1931" (1935).

which they are ignorent, they will flock in thousands after a Demagouge.
. . .[10]

Congressmen were naturally alert to these implications. In 1790 John Steele wrote a friend in North Carolina, "We have passed a bill in the House of Repvs. to establish a posteroad from Petersburg to Halifax . . . and Augusta—This would be throwing political information into the heart of the three Southern states. . . ."[11] An unidentified representative remarked in 1791, "wherever the newspapers had extended, or even the correspondence of the members, no opposition has been made to the laws; whereas, the contrary was experienced in those parts to which the information had not penetrated."[12] In his fourth annual message Washington asked Congress to facilitate "the circulation of political intelligence and information." Little wonder that Congress was so jealous of the power to establish post roads![13]

That there were important administrative consequences of a good postal service was also recognized. In 1789 Tench Coxe, then an applicant for the Postmaster General's office, wrote Madison, "In regard to the office I do not consider it a mere regulation of mails, and distribution of letters. But it is intimately blended with the connexion of the members of the union and particularly of the Atlantic and western territory. It may be made to aid considerably the advancement of internal commerce and territorial improvement, and expedite the sudden operations of the Executive department."[14]

THE GENERAL POST OFFICE

The organic postal act of 1792 specified there should be "one Postmaster General."[15] He was authorized to appoint an assistant, and

---

[10] Aug. 30, 1794, *The Memoirs of Rufus Putnam* (Rowena Buell, comp., Boston and New York: Houghton, Mifflin, 1903), p. 394.

[11] Steele to Joseph Winston, July 20, 1790, Steele, *Papers,* I, 71. The bill was defeated later.

[12] *Annals,* III, 253 (Dec. 16, 1791).

[13] See *ibid.,* II, 1680 (July 10, 1790) for Elbridge Gerry's alarm over a simple proposal in which he saw a hated "Court Press and Court Gazette."

[14] Harold Hutcheson, *Tench Coxe: A Study in American Economic Development* (Baltimore: Johns Hopkins Press, 1938), p. 19.

[15] The Postmasters General during this period were Ebenezer Hazard (1782–89); Samuel Osgood (1789–91); Timothy Pickering (1791–95); Joseph Habersham (1795–1801).

deputy postmasters; to determine how often to carry the mail and whether by "stage carriages" or horses; to prescribe regulations for the deputy postmasters and "to superintend the business of the department." [16] These provisions were the foundation of the General Post Office, as the central organization quickly was called.

The office of the Postmaster General remained a very modest one, despite the growth of business. Pickering performed all the business of the agency in 1792 with the aid of an assistant and one clerk in two rooms of his dwelling house.[17] The number of clerks was increased to four in 1794,[18] and in 1800 when the office was removed to Washington it consisted of the Postmaster General, his assistant, a chief clerk, five clerks, and a messenger.[19]

Pickering's successor, Joseph Habersham, described his duties and those of his staff in some detail in 1799.[20] With respect to his own office, he was somewhat on the defensive. "It has often been imagined," he wrote, "that the duties of the Postmaster General were very trifling and simple, even so much so, that some have considered it rather a sinecure, than an office of business." The personal duties of the Postmaster General, he said, were "to superintend the business generally; to direct the principal arrangements for carrying the mail; to establish post offices; appoint Postmasters; inform them in questions relating to the law and their duty; and attend to the exterior correspondence of the office." The exterior correspondence included "a multitude of letters" written by those interested in the regular conveyance of the mail; "many letters" on the malconduct of those who contracted to carry the mail; and a "multitude of letters" on subjects relating to the Post Office from individuals in all parts of the Union. "It is a fact," declared Habersham, "that the establishment of new offices, and the appointment of new Postmasters, with attending to complaints, receiving resignations, and making due inquiries for that purpose, is almost sufficient to engross the attention of one person."

The assistant to the Postmaster kept the accounts and dealt with stoppages of the mail or thefts. The solicitor made contracts and sued delinquent postmasters. The first clerk examined accounts, another

---

[16] 1 Stat. 232, sec. 3 (Feb. 20, 1792).
[17] Upham, *Timothy Pickering*, III, 3.
[18] 1 Stat. 354, sec. 8.
[19] *American State Papers: Finance*, I, 813.
[20] *American State Papers: Post Office*, pp. 17–21.

clerk dealt with dead letters, and others worked on books. Specialization had thus begun to make itself felt; Habersham declared it required from two to three quarters to break in a new clerk on his duties. The office was understaffed. Habersham admitted that "all the smaller duties have not been properly performed" since 1789, due to lack of help.

The bulk of current business transacted by the General Post Office consisted of the designation of post offices, the appointment of deputy postmasters, making contracts for carrying the mail, receiving periodic reports from the deputies, and keeping the accounts. The Letter Books of the Postmaster General [21] are full of correspondence dealing with these subjects. The office was one of general superintendence; its operations extended along 1,875 miles of post road at 75 post offices in 1790; in 1800 along 20,817 miles of post roads at 903 offices.[22] Samuel Osgood thought in 1790 that it might be advisable to "blend" the General Post Office with a city office so that the business would be better understood, but this mixture of the general and particular never took place.[23]

THE DEPUTY POSTMASTERS

The affairs of the post office were conducted by the deputy postmasters and by the contractors for carrying the mail. Few post offices were attractive outside the large towns, and one of the great problems during the 1790's was to find and keep reasonably competent postmasters. Osgood described the desirable qualifications: "My only object was to find a Character that would serve the public faithfully, and be acceptable in the place where he was to execute the duties of his Office." [24]

Pickering, too, was much influenced by character and ability to give service to the public. "Besides the requisite care and attention, an *obliging disposition* seems peculiarly necessary," he said. "I mention this, because in detail the business seems to be piddling; all its emolu-

---

[21] The Postmasters General Letter Books in the Library of the Post Office Department, Washington, D.C., contain the original manuscript copies of outgoing letters of the General Post Office from 1789. They have been carefully preserved. The letters are copied chronologically and bound in large volumes designated A, AA, B, BB, etc., through EE which ends the Federalist period in 1801. They are hereafter cited as Letter Book A, etc.

[22] *American State Papers: Post Office,* p. 66.

[23] *Ibid.,* p. 7.

[24] Osgood to William Smith, June 8, 1790, Letter Book A, p. 135.

ments arising from trifles; altho' in the whole it is important. Each trifle therefore demands a *patient attention*." [25]

But good selections were hard to make. In 1795 shortly after Joseph Habersham had succeeded Pickering, he wrote Noah Webster, "I am convinced that improper persons have been appointed Postmasters at the smaller offices & from the observations I have made it cannot well be avoided as in making these appointments they must be given to those who will accept of them.—In the small offices the Profits are trifling & persons will not hold them who are well qualified. . . . I do not think Tavern keepers are proper persons to be postmasters. . . ." [26]

The Postmasters General from 1789 to 1801 tried conscientiously to find proper persons. They sought advice from members of Congress, from leading merchants and local residents, from retiring postmasters and others. In appointing Thomas Wright Bacot to the important office at Charleston, South Carolina, Pickering wrote, "The warm recommendation of my nephews—the perfect concurrence of M[r] Izard [Senator from South Carolina] with their opinion of your merit, and the very respectable testimony of the Merchants of the first eminence in Charlestown in your favor, determine me to offer you the post office in that city." [27] The recommendations of merchants were highly regarded. ". . . the *general* accomodation of the public, especially of the mercantile interest, is my sole object," wrote Pickering to Congressman Fitzsimons of Pennsylvania.[28] To Samuel Blanchard, his selection for Boston, Pickering wrote, "In choosing a place for your office, you will be governed by the convenience of the mercantile interest, by which chiefly the office is supported. I hope you will find a place where your family can be under the same roof." [29]

Although Congressmen were sometimes consulted on appointments of deputy postmasters and sometimes came forward with recommendations,[30] there is little evidence that political affiliation was important

---

[25] Pickering Papers, VI, 43.

[26] Aug. 7, 1795, Letter Book BB, pp. 245–46. Mail had been left for twenty days in a tavern at Georgetown and was then accidentally discovered by a waiter, Letter Book A, pp. 88–89.

[27] Nov. 28, 1791, Letter Book A, p. 332.

[28] Nov. 28, 1791, Pickering Papers, VI, 42.

[29] Nov. 28, 1791, *ibid.,* VI, 43. The rule of local residence was generally recognized and enforced, Pickering to Bowman, Oct. 10, 1791, *ibid.,* VI, 33.

[30] For example, letter to Hugh Williamson of North Carolina, Oct. 27, 1789 (Letter Book A, p. 9); correspondence with Alexander White of Virginia (Letter Book AA, p. 126); reference to Murray of Maryland (Letter Book A, p. 398); Pickering to two

in making selections. Most offices were not objects of interest; appointments were made by the Postmaster General, not by the President; deputy postmasters were considered inferior officers for whom the consent of the Senate was not required. When Timothy Pickering became Postmaster General it was apparently taken for granted that all appointments by his predecessor expired,[31] but by the end of the decade the rule of continuing tenure had become established.

The Postmaster General soon resorted to many of the usual means of enforcing discipline and maintaining proper standards, but their application was often far from effective. Instructions were drafted for the guidance of postmasters in their daily routine, and were printed at an early date. Quarterly reports of financial operations and balances were required. In case of delay, which was not uncommon, correspondence was opened up with the delinquent deputy. There was no regular inspection, but the assistant postmaster general became a sort of roving inspector when occasion permitted. One of Osgood's first acts under the new government was to send the assistant postmaster general, Jonathan Burrall, "to the southward in order that he may, on the spot examine into the Character of the Deputies."[32] In June 1790 the postmaster at Baltimore died, and Osgood sent down Jonathan's brother, Charles Burrall, to secure the payment of monies due and to note "all irregularities that may occur to you."[33] Later Habersham told Congress it was one of the duties of the assistant "occasionally to travel the post road."

All postmasters were required to give bond with satisfactory sureties. No records have come to attention of an actual suit on bond, although some probably occurred; but there are a number of threats by the Postmaster General to go to the courts. In the last analysis, he was personally liable for delinquent accounts, as was emphatically stated by Pickering well after he had left the office. Writing to a delinquent deputy he called for an end of "repeated promises" unfulfilled: *I am personally* liable for a part of those arrears, which have been accumu-

---

appointees, Feb. 11, 1792—"At the request and on the recommendation of Mʳ Bourne, your representative in Congress, I have appointed you Postmaster. . . ." (Letter Book A, p. 406).

[31] Letter Book A, p. 267.

[32] Letter Book A (Oct. 5, 1789).

[33] Letter Book A, p. 141; in 1795 a special "undercover" agent was authorized, Habersham asking a correspondent to hire "a shrewd and reserved person" to discover who opened certain letters, Letter Book BB, p. 252.

lating *by my indulgence."* [34] Habersham complained of the difficulty of suing deputy postmasters.

Beyond threats and suits the ultimate means of control was removal. This was an infrequent occurrence, despite many complaints to— and by—the Postmaster General. Failure to make quarterly remittances and refusal to honor drafts upon their funds by the General Post Office were the most common occasions for "displacement." Thus Pickering removed John Singer, postmaster at Trenton, "for very improper conduct, concurring with his blameable delinquency in respect to remittances." [35] The postmaster at Savannah, Georgia, was removed in 1795: "his living in one house & keeping the office in another was the cause of frequent disappointment to those who wanted their letters . . ."; his deputy gave "general dissatisfaction"; and he declined to pay a draft from the General Post Office. Pickering thought he was a "very honest man" who had suffered "by giving credit for postage." [36]

How tender was the official conscience in making removals may be surmised from Pickering's letter to Mascott William, postmaster at Salem, Massachusetts.

You cannot be uninformed of the prevailing wishes of the merchants in Salem to have a person appointed to succeed you in the P Office. The *merchants* support the Department: because all correspondence yielding postage is chiefly amongst them. The merchants therefore must be accomodated. I have been unwilling to deprive you of the support you derived from the P Office, in your advanced period of Life, while you could possibly give tolerable Satisfaction to the persons having most intercourse with your office and have therefore passed by some representations on the Subject. But your age and infirmities by disabling you from executing the office satisfactorily, have given rise to fresh and extended representations of the necessity of providing a Substitute. This, I candidly tell you would have led me to do it, had I continued in the Department; and it will doubtless be done by my successor. And I mention it to you that you may be prepared for the change.[37]

Would that we knew more of these humble but essential servants of the public. Few of them remain as other than names. Sebastian

---

[34] Letter Book BB, p. 153.
[35] Letter Book A, pp. 430, 436, 446.
[36] Letter Book BB, pp. 211, 222, 346.
[37] Feb. 6, 1795, Letter Book BB, p. 101.

Bauman of New York was one of the more prominent postmasters. Born in Germany, his father was an official in the court of Maria Theresa.[38] He was educated at Heidelberg and was an engineer in the Austrian service, but, killing a fellow officer in a duel, he was forced to flee the country and arrived in New York about 1760. He was a professional soldier, joining the English army as an officer and becoming a captain in the Revolutionary Army in 1776. He rose to be a lieutenant colonel and a friend of Washington, as well as an intimate friend of Hamilton, whom he taught the art of artillery. His active interest in military affairs continued throughout his life.

In 1786 he was appointed postmaster of New York City and was reappointed under the new government. He was never contented with his position, complaining about the lack of adequate salary,[39] and was once criticized by Pickering for laxness in his office.[40] In 1795 Bauman wrote Pickering as he was about to leave the office of Postmaster General: ". . . *I have lost a friend* . . . The Post office in new york is now my living (I wish it were otherwise) for it is a living of the most unpleasing kind to a man of Sensibility; Because the best endeavours, punctuality, and utmost exertions both early & late, avail but little if compared to the many ill conceptions a Post office is susceptible to in a large City." [41] Bauman, nevertheless, leaves the impression of a capable, diligent, and ingenious official; one whose heart probably was always with the military, but who was faithful to his civil duties.

CONTRACTS AND CONTRACTORS

Deputy postmasters held office, by an administrative understanding, on a continuing basis. Contractors for carrying the mail were obliged to renew their arrangements annually.[42] Until 1792 there was no legal requirement to advertise contracts or to make the awards to the lowest responsible bidders, but practice tended in this direction. Whether to advertise or not, and whether to prefer the lowest bidder were early matters of concern, and sometimes of vexation to the Postmaster General.

---

[38] Frederic Gregory Mather, *The Refugees of 1776 from Long Island to Connecticut* (Albany: J. B. Lyon, 1913), p. 661.

[39] In 1791 his earnings were $1,495.49. *American State Papers: Post Office,* p. 13.

[40] Letter Book AA, p. 149.

[41] Pickering Papers, XLI, 144 (Jan. 12, 1795).

[42] Habersham to Henry Hook, July 14, 1795, Letter Book BB, p. 219.

In his report of 1790 to Congress, Samuel Osgood commented on the necessity of discretion in awarding contracts.

The advertising for proposals for carrying the mail places the Postmaster General in a disagreeable predicament: for many poor people make proposals at so low a rate that it is obvious the business cannot be done as it ought to be, and consequently there cannot be a strict adherence to the lowest proposals. Discretion must be used, and the contract must be given to him who will most probably perform the duty with punctuality. . . .[43]

Joseph Habersham's rule was, "The lowest proposal made by an honest sober man who is competent to the business should be accepted, unless the price be too extravagant. . . . Should the lowest proposal be much too high it is to be rejected & the road advertised anew." [44] That the refusal of the lowest bid was a ticklish business was much in Osgood's mind; having preferred a higher bid from Philadelphia to Baltimore, he wrote the Philadelphia deputy postmaster, "I have no doubt I shall be very much abused by Mr Page & his Party. . . . I rest assured that you & your friends will support me in this Business." [45]

In 1791 Timothy Pickering took the bold step of not advertising for bids. "The present Contractors and their Agents having had the experience of a year, will doubtless conduct the business with more propriety and regularity than new hands," he wrote to one of them; adding, "The old Contractors . . . can well afford to reduce the terms below those of their first Contracts." [46] The contractor, John Hoomes, declined to bid on what Pickering called these "liberal principles," as well he might considering that he held a monopoly of stagecoach traffic in Virginia, across whose roads all southern mail had to pass.[47] The Post Office Act of 1792 required the future advertising of bids.

Preference was given in principle to a few large contractors as against a number of smaller ones. Osgood reported in 1790 that there were then about twenty different contracts for carrying the mail which put the business into confusion: "every contractor consults his own

[43] Jan. 20, 1790, *American State Papers: Post Office,* p. 6.

[44] Habersham to Doctor Samuel Green, July 1, 1795, Letter Book BB, p. 208.

[45] Osgood to Robert Patton, Nov. 8, 1790, Letter Book A, pp. 194–95; to safeguard himself he reported the matter to Washington, Letter Book A, pp. 198–99.

[46] Pickering to John Hoomes, Oct. 24, 1791, Letter Book A, pp. 290–91.

[47] Letter Book A, p. 296.

interest as to the days and hours of arrival and departure of the mail, without having a due regard to the necessary connexion of the Post Office." [48] In the fall of the same year, he offered Hoomes a chance to bid for the whole carriage of the mails from Alexandria to Savannah, including cross roads. [49] This was on too large a scale even for the enterprising Hoomes. [50]

Control of the contractors to ensure punctual delivery of the mails was difficult, especially in the more remote sections. The necessity of securing a renewal of the contract every year was of course a spur to good performance, but not an adequate one. Penalties were imposed for unexplained delay in reaching destinations. [51] The postmasters at the two extremes of every route were required to keep registers of arrivals and departures, which were sent to the General Post Office monthly. These records furnished the basis for assessing penalties, but many were the excuses, and as Habersham complained in 1799, "At the unproductive offices . . . little attention is paid to this duty; and, as the compensation they receive is of no consideration, they cannot be compelled to do it promptly." [52] Pickering told contractors to dismiss unsatisfactory stage drivers. [53]

The performance of the stages between Philadelphia and Baltimore finally became so unsatisfactory that Habersham established a line of government stages, "an early experiment in public ownership." As such it was the subject of inquiry by a Republican Congress in 1802, and was terminated after about a decade. [54]

The contractors had their own troubles with stage drivers and post riders. Colonel Hoomes, on the southern mails, employed "Black Boys"

---

[48] *American State Papers: Post Office*, p. 6.

[49] Letter Book A, pp. 173–75 (Sept. 21, 1790).

[50] Letter Book A, p. 177. The names of all contractors and post riders for 1790 with a brief statement of the terms of each contract may be found in *American State Papers: Post Office*, pp. 9–12.

[51] For example, Gabriel P. Vanhorne suffered a deduction of $25 for lateness in carriage of the mails between Baltimore and Alexandria in October 1790 (Letter Book A, pp. 189–90). In 1795 Sumpler had fines deducted from his pay for lateness in delivery from Charleston to Columbia, but as Habersham said, "this cannot compensate the public for the injury they may have sustained." Letter Book BB, pp. 391–93.

[52] *American State Papers: Post Office*, p. 20.

[53] Pickering to Messrs. Staver and Greenleaf, May 5, 1792, Letter Book A, p. 466. "I have repeated complaints from different persons of the insufficiency of one of your stage drivers. . . . I must therefore desire you to discharge the driver referred to."

[54] *American State Papers: Post Office*, pp. 21–22.

on the cross roads, but against the preference of the Department. "Colo
Hoomes," wrote the assistant postmaster general, "is at liberty to
employ what Riders he pleases, but he incurs a heavy penalty if
they neglect their duty. I do not much like his employing Black
Boys. . . ."[55] The post rider went through Princeton on a summer
Saturday in 1795, stopped at a public house at the lower end of town
and refused to bring up the mail, going on to Brunswick with it, and,
we may suspect, with a foggy mind.[56] Major Erkuries Beatty, living on
a large farm near Princeton, wrote his brother John, then a member
of Congress, a revealing letter.

Dear Brother,
    I waited with considerable impatience almost all last Saturday morning
at Bridgetown for the arrival of the post, had to go home at last without
getting your Letter which was brought to me in the evening by a private
Gentleman, indeed if old Timothy knew how the mail is conducted in this
Country, I guess he would kick up a rumpus, for sometimes, it is lost &
picked up by Waggoners, which I do not wonder at for it is but a few days
ago that the man passed here carrying the mail, was so drunk he could
scarcely sit on his horse—By post, is in so much disrepute here, that the
people in general entrusts their Letters &c, by the Stage. . . .[57]

One of the leading contractors in the north was Levi Pease, principal
proprietor of the stage line from Hartford to Boston in 1783 and
principal figure in the first line from Boston to New York in 1784—
an enterprising blacksmith who had carried dispatches during the
Revolutionary War and who confounded the prediction of the chief
hackney coachman in Boston that the public would perhaps support
a stage from Boston to Hartford sometime, "but not in your day or
mine."[58] In 1786 Pease won the first contract for carrying the mail
between New York and Boston. Brissot de Warville, who traveled this
line in 1788, entered in his diary at Worcester, "The Tavern, where we
had a good American dinner, is a charming house of wood, well orna-

---

[55] Letter Book A, p. 219.
[56] Letter Book BB, p. 266.
[57] Dec. 29, 1794, Joseph M. Beatty, Jr. "Letters of the Four Beatty Brothers of the
Continental Army, 1774–1794," *Pennsylvania Magazine of History and Biography, XLIV*
(1920), 260–61.
[58] See the carefully documented study by Oliver W. Holmes, "Levi Pease, The Father
of New England Stage-Coaching," *Journal of Economic and Business History,* III (1931),
241–63.

mented. It is kept by Mr. Pease, one of the proprietors of the Boston stage. He has much merit for his activity and industry; but it is to be hoped he will change the present plan, so far as it respects his horses; they are overdone with the length and difficulty of the courses, which ruins them in a short time, besides retarding very much the progress." [59]

In 1789 Pease was underbid but saved his contract by a personal appearance before the Postmaster General who reported to Washington, "Mr. Pease informs me that he has been at great trouble and expense in establishing the Stages, and I believe it to be true; and further that he is the only person that will keep up a good line of Stages between this [New York] and Boston." [60] His lines extended throughout New England during the 1790's and in 1799 Habersham called on him to establish the government stages between Philadelphia and Baltimore. In 1810 Pease sold his stagecoach interests and retired to his New England farm—in the words of the *Massachusetts Spy,* "a kind of Father of the New England Roads." [61]

[59] Quoted in *ibid.,* p. 249.
[60] *Ibid.,* p. 252.
[61] *Ibid.,* pp. 260, 262.

Chapter Sixteen

TROUBLE ON THE POST ROAD

Nature conspired with the backwardness of man in the art of administration to make the management of the post office a frustrating experience. In 1789 the merchants of Philadelphia protested; Osgood admitted the inconveniences and declared, "I . . . am not without hope that I shall be able to remedy them in a great Measure. . . ." [1] In 1792 Pickering had to tell the Boston deputy postmaster, "Everything you have done respecting this letter is erroneous." [2] In 1795 Habersham asked a southern postmaster for "your most pointed attention" to frequent "failures of regularity" in the mails.[3]

The chronic complaints of the period bore on delay in carrying the mails, their insecurity against tampering by curious agents of the post office and by bold robbers who defied the death penalty, and the laxness and indifference of deputies and contractors, progressively more marked as the miles stretched away from Philadelphia.

SECURITY

The competing demands of speed and security in carrying the mails were frequently discussed but neither objective was reached. The advantages of stagecoaches and of post riders for quick delivery were widely debated in the light of their respective claims to safety.

To secure the mails en route, letters were placed in bags which were put in locked portmanteaus; only the postmasters had keys. At every post office on the line, however, the portmanteaus had to be opened, and there was occasional negligence in permitting them to lie about. Some complaints of lost mail turned out to be due to the carelessness

---

[1] Letter Book A, p. 12.
[2] Letter Book AA, pp. 138–39.
[3] Letter Book BB, pp. 383–84.

of patrons. Smith and Gorham sent money from Boston southward, which, as Jonathan Hastings later reported to Pickering, "their careless boy put . . . into the London Bag";[4] off to London it went while the alarm spread along the post road.

Pickering sternly reprimanded Hastings for his failure to examine the ship bag. In an even more astonishing case, a letter had been committed to a friend, who put the envelope with its enclosed money on a window sill whence it was blown into the street, picked up by a Negro, and given to a man who opened it and returned it to the post office.[5]

In 1792 an enterprising "villain" began to rob the mails leaving Boston. Several such cases were reported to Pickering, causing him "great pain."[6] "They bring the department into disrepute," he complained, "and will injure the public Revenue, by destroying the confidence of Merchants. . . ."[7] "I am mortified as well as grieved for the loss of your money. My thoughts have been occupied to contrive some means of discovery: but none satisfactory have occurred."[8] The robber was finally apprehended by reason of "his own Imprudence and Folly."[9] By 1795 the Post Office Department dared not trust the mail to dispatch its own remittances. On August 10, the chief clerk instructed a postmaster, "In future you will please not to remit any more money by the Mail as it is attended with too much risque."[10] And shortly afterward he wrote another concerning quarterly balances, "The distance is too great to remit hard Money by the mail. . . ."[11]

The protection of the mail was a problem that constantly vexed the Postmasters General, and with respect to which they became distinctly defensive. "The mails pass thro' many hands. Some may be unfaithful, though pains are taken to procure upright men. It is not easy to fix suspicion on any individual. To suspect & dismiss without proof, would be deemed unjust & tyrannical. . . . I cannot caution letter writers to be more careful, by a public advertisement, for that would be to give the signal for Robbing the Mails."[12] The possibility of

---

[4] Letter Book **AA**, p. 161, Oct. 12, 1792.
[5] Letter Book **AA**, pp. 160–61.
[6] Letter Book **AA**, p. 63.
[7] Letter Book **AA**, p. 97.
[8] Letter Book **AA**, p. 139.
[9] Letter Book BB, pp. 398–400.
[10] Letter Book BB, p. 250.
[11] Letter Book BB, p. 244.
[12] Aug. 11, 1792, Letter Book **AA**, p. 63.

public notice of these deficiencies, indeed, became an obsession. Habersham complained to a merchant who had advised the local postmaster that a letter contained money: "From this very circumstance the Robbery may have happened. . . . in the mean time by making it a matter of public investigation you will probably defeat every attempt that will be made for that purpose.—You would not I am sure endeavour to destroy the necessary confidence in the post by making your loss a matter of notoriety—where it is more than probable that it has arisen from the unguarded manner in which you put your letter in the Office. . . ." [13]

HANDLING THE MAIL

The Letter Books of the Postmaster General are sufficiently explicit to give us an idea how the mail was handled in these early days. The mail closed at each office a half hour before the arrival of the stage or post rider. It was then the task of the postmaster to make up packets of letters, if any, for each of the offices along the line. Immediately upon arrival, the stage driver or rider brought into the office the large, locked portmanteau in which was contained oiled bags with letters therein. The postmaster, who possessed a key, unlocked the portmanteau, removed letters for his office, enclosed those to be taken away, locked the portmanteau and returned it to the driver.[14] From ten to fifteen minutes were allowed to complete the task.[15] Every postmaster thus had access to all the mail moving along his route. The mail from Baltimore to Salem, Massachusetts, passed through "near 30 post offices" and the hands of many carriers.[16]

An innovating deputy proposed to Habersham that each post office have a bag. The Postmaster General agreed this would make the conveyance safer, but declared the scheme "certainly impracticable." And in those days it probably was.

Postmasters were expected to ascertain and collect the postage due, to mark the amount on the envelope, with the name of the originating

---

[13] Letter Book BB, pp. 398–400; Washington wrote a correspondent in 1796, "letters for sometime past have been opened, to come at Bank and Post notes." *Writings,* XXXIV, 417.

[14] Letter Book BB, p. 227; in 1791 it was necessary to send to Europe for a supply of locks. Letter Book A, pp. 250–51.

[15] Letter Book AA, p. 144.

[16] Letter Book AA, p. 139.

office.[17] Gradually stamps and stamp pads were supplied for the latter purpose. "They are so useful," said Pickering in 1792, "I wish every office were furnished with them." [18] Pickering thought a sign over the post office unnecessary, but authorized expenditure to put the words, Post Office, "on a board." [19] In general, offices were kept in the home of the deputy, but office rent was not allowed. ". . . and yet," said the Postmaster General, "in *some* cases it is evidently reasonable." [20]

Hours of attendance were not fixed but left to the good nature of the deputy. In 1792 Pickering was asked to prescribe hours. He replied, "the Postmasters generally . . . are commonly in the way to serve such as call upon them; and being disposed to accomodate their fellow Citizens restrain them to no fixed hours.—Yet where the business is inconsiderable, *constant* attendance is not to be expected." [21] To a deputy, Samuel Freeman, he wrote that where there was much business, the mail should be kept open until nine or half past nine in the evening; [22] and to another he said, "you need not rise out of Bed to receive letters" after nine o'clock.[23]

To the persons engaged in the post office, progress by 1792 in procedures and equipment seemed a cause of satisfaction. The mail was moving more rapidly, new lines were pushing out, the volume of business was expanding, although slowly, routines were well established, equipment was improving. The chief clerk in the General Post Office privately expressed his satisfaction and his aspirations—"I am very much pleased that the large Portmanteaux are found so convenient: If we had only *horses* and *carriages* the property of the Department, we should . . . be complete." [24]

STANDARDS OF PERFORMANCE

Despite much conscientious work, the standards of performance of the post office remained unsatisfactory and subject to continued

---

[17] Letter writing had not become a widely practised art. "On the average each person in the country, for the period of five years ending with 1799, sent but 1$\frac{4}{10}$ missives by the mails." Massachusetts Bureau of Statistics of Labor, *Annual Report,* XVI (1885), 170.

[18] Letter Book A, p. 367.

[19] Letter Book AA, pp. 98–99.

[20] Letter Book A, pp. 469–70.

[21] Letter Book AA, p. 16; apparently post office clerks in the larger offices worked about six hours a day, usually from nine to three. Letter Book BB, pp. 58–59.

[22] Letter Book AA, p. 239.

[23] Letter Book BB, p. 280.   [24] Letter Book AA, pp. 50–51.

criticism by high officials. Not even the letters of the President were free from the curious eyes of the deputy postmasters and riders; throughout the eight years of his administration Washington complained about the infidelity of the service. On October 3, 1789, he sent dispatches from New York to Governor Randolph of Virginia which failed to arrive until November 30. "The detention of these letters," wrote the President, "is a matter of some importance . . . and I wish exceedingly to know where they were detained, and whether it was owing to the inattention of any Post Master through whose hands they must have passed, or to a worse cause." [25] While on his southern trip in 1791 he commented to Hamilton, "the letters, which will have to pass through *many* hands, may find *some* who are not deficient in curiosity." [26] In 1796, writing again to Hamilton, he said, "About the middle of last Week I wrote to you; and that it might escape the eye of the Inquisitive (for some of my letters have lately been pried into) I took the liberty of putting it under a cover to Mr. Jay." [27]

Washington was not alone in experiencing trouble with the post office. In 1798 Jefferson wrote to his friend John Taylor, "But I owe you a political letter. Yet the infidelities of the post office and the circumstances of the times are against my writing freely & fully. . . ." [28] And just after Jefferson's inauguration, his friend, Elbridge Gerry, wrote him,

the seals of the letters which I have received for a number of years have been so often & so manifestly violated as to have destroyed my confidence in such institutions; which in most if not in all countries, are mere political traps. among such a number of officers, as are in the department of a post office, it would be an extraordinary case, if every one was proof against the corrupt arts of faction; & one prostituted officer on each line, is sufficient to betray all the secrets of the chief magistrate; conveyed thro' this channel.[29]

---

[25] Washington to Beverley Randolph, Dec. 14, 1789, Washington, *Writings,* XXX, 477–78.

[26] June 13, 1791, *ibid.,* XXXI, 294. Cf. John Steele, May 22, 1790, "The distance is so great, the people so inquisitive for news, that it is a very common practice to break up letters by the way." Steele, *Papers,* I, 60.

[27] Sept. 1, 1796, Washington, *Writings,* XXXV, 198–99.

[28] Nov. 26, 1798, Jefferson, *Works* (Federal ed.), VIII, 480.

[29] *Some Letters of Elbridge Gerry of Massachusetts, 1784–1804* (Worthington Chauncey Ford, ed., Brooklyn, N.Y.: Historical Printing Club, 1896), p. 22.

Lesser figures may have been less disturbed.

The standards of performance of the postal service were low, quite apart from the insatiable curiosity of postal employees and their occasional subornation by faction. In a Treasury circular of March 30, 1790, Hamilton advised the collectors to forward drafts "under the eye of some disinterested person, who, in case they should miscarry, can give evidence of their having been sent on."[30] Mails were slow and frequently delayed, due not only to the wretched roads but also to the lack of attention of the post riders.[31] Washington was forced to call down the postmaster at Alexandria, in terms which revealed gross carelessness at this office.

Sir: The letters enclosed, were sent up to your Office yesterday afternoon, and were returned to me. It is not the first, nor second time I have been served in this manner; but it may be considered as evidence of the inattention with which the duties of your Office are discharged.[32]

On September 30, 1793, Genêt sent a letter to the Secretary of State in Virginia "which," said Jefferson later, "from some unaccountable delay of the post never came to me in Virginia, tho' I remained there till Oct. 25. (and received there three subsequent mails), and it never reached me in Philadelphia till Dec. 2."[33] On September 13, 1799, the Secretary of the Navy sent an important letter to President Adams at Quincy, Massachusetts. It finally reached Adams after it had been sent by the Philadelphia post office "to the southward," eventually being put in the northern mail.[34]

The root of the troubles of the post office was weak administration, especially lax supervision of the deputy postmasters and carriers. "Most of the present postmasters," declared Elias Boudinot in 1791, "are men of reputable characters."[35] They were left too much to themselves, in

---

[30] Hamilton, *Works* (Hamilton ed.), III, 547.

[31] The northern mails were more reliable than the southern, Letter Book A, pp. 92–93.

[32] Aug. 4, 1798, Washington, *Writings,* XXXVI, 386. In July 1795, Washington sent a letter to Hamilton from Mount Vernon; the postmaster at Alexandria put this and other outgoing letters of the President into the bag of incoming mail addressed to him, and they all came back to Mount Vernon. *Ibid.,* XXXIV, 267–68.

[33] Jefferson to Washington, Dec. 11, 1793, Jefferson, *Works* (Federal ed.), VIII, 94.

[34] Adams to Stoddert, Sept. 21, 1799, Adams, *Works,* IX, 33. Madison complained of delay in January 1801, Madison, *Writings* (Hunt ed.), VI, 410.

[35] *Annals,* III, 295 (Dec. 28, 1791).

marked contrast to the collectors of customs and surveyors of internal revenue. Their emoluments were low and provided no inducement for energetic characters to come forward. Congress set the maximum at $1,800 derived from fees which usually provided a far smaller sum.[36]

POSTMASTERS GENERAL

Ebenezer Hazard was Postmaster General when Washington took office; he was replaced because the President was irritated by his return to post riders in lieu of stages in 1788, which Washington construed as a plot to limit the circulation of "intelligence" about the new Constitution (i.e., newspapers); and because he had allowed deputy postmasters to fall into arrears. Hazard could have been excused on the latter point since he had to do all the work himself; he had once hired a clerk but his salary was insufficient to stand the expense.[37] The charge of plotting against the Constitution was unfounded. Disappointed in subsequent applications for office, he went to Philadelphia in 1791, acquired a fortune in business and insurance,[38] and following a scholarly taste that he shared with his eminent friend, Jeremy Belknap, published a two-volume work on American history.[39]

Hazard declared that Samuel Osgood, his successor (1789), was the most suitable of several competitors, including Tench Coxe, Richard Bache (Franklin's son-in-law), and Colonel William Smith (John Adams' son-in-law). Osgood had been a member of the Board of the Treasury. He resigned his office as Postmaster General in 1791, being unwilling to move from New York to Philadelphia. Subsequently he left the Federalist party and became supervisor, then naval officer, of the port of New York under Jefferson.

Two men held the office of Postmaster General throughout most of the Federalist period, Timothy Pickering of Massachusetts and Joseph Habersham of Georgia. Joseph Habersham was a person of little color although a competent man of affairs who managed post office business with energy and integrity. He was born in Georgia, educated in England, active in the revolutionary movement, and a colonel in the Revo-

---

[36] 1 Stat. 232, sec. 23.

[37] *Belknap Papers, passim.*

[38] Marquis James, *Biography of a Business, 1792–1942: Insurance Company of North America* (Indianapolis, New York: Bobbs-Merrill, 1942), chs. i–iv.

[39] *Historical Collections: consisting of State Papers and other Authentic Documents. . . .* (2 vols., Philadelphia: T. Dobson, 1792–94).

lutionary Army. Although taking part in the public affairs of his native state, he was first of all a businessman and planter, following the footsteps of a successful father. In 1791 Washington asked Knox to ascertain "the rate of abilities possessed by Colo. (Joseph) Habersham: to what they would most usefully apply: whether he is a man of arrangement, of Industry, &ca. . . ." [40] The report was apparently satisfactory, for Washington appointed him Postmaster General in 1795, where he served until November 1801.

The administrative career of Timothy Pickering has been obscured by his reputation as a rigid and uncomprising Federalist who was willing, if necessary, to sacrifice the Union to maintain the hegemony of New England. He was, nevertheless, one of the most prominent officials of his day. The same qualities of mind and character made their impress upon both his political and administrative careers. The essential facts about his childhood were limited means, frugality, honesty, industry, and order; they went far to form the man. [41] The dominant characteristics of his mature personality were independence, combativeness, and courage, all harnessed to a strong and unswerving devotion to duty.

Pickering had an ardent taste for public office. With only occasional and brief intervals he held office, civil or military, for fifty years, from 1772 to 1821, beginning as selectman and assessor of Salem, Massachusetts, rising to become in succession Postmaster General, Secretary of War, and Secretary of State, and concluding his public life when an old man as chairman of the school committee of his native town. [42]

---

[40] July 22, 1791, Washington, *Writings*, XXXVII, 574.
[41] Henry Cabot Lodge, "Timothy Pickering," *Atlantic Monthly*, XLI (1878), 739–54.
[42] Offices Held by Timothy Pickering, 1772–1821.

Office	Date Appointed
Selectman and Assessor, Salem, Mass.	July 8, 1772
Town Clerk, Salem	1772
Committee of Correspondence, Salem	1774
Register of Deeds, Essex County	1774
Justice of the Peace	1775
Justice of the Superior Court of Common Pleas, Essex County	1775
Justice of the Maritime Court, Counties of Suffolk, Essex, and Middlesex	1775
Representative, General Court of Mass.	1776
Adjutant General, Revolutionary Army	1777
Member, Board of War	1777
Quartermaster General	1780

In 1774 Pickering sent a printed circular to the freeholders of Essex County proposing himself as register of deeds; in 1777 he resigned several county offices to become adjutant general under Washington, turning them over to his brother John with the understanding that when he came back from the wars, John would give back his brother's holdings. By 1783 he wrote that he had had "enough of public offices to be tired of them," but in 1784 he sought the office of Secretary of War, in 1785 the post of Treasurer of the United States. Later he wrote his brother, "If God spares my life till my sons grow up, I shall endeavor to put them to employments by which they may support themselves independently of any public offices; for that alone can give and insure an independence of spirit and that dignity of mind, which, while it renders the individual happy, does honor to human nature." [43] But soon he asked Hamilton for the opportunity to serve as his assistant; and later while in office he took much pains to secure places for his sons and relatives.

As an administrator Pickering was conscientious and hard working, driving himself without relaxation. ". . . he will be found an able and respectable officer," wrote Wolcott to his father in 1795. "You will hear of no complaints of profusion and extravagance. . . ." [44] Indeed Pickering allowed himself too few clerks to keep his work always in hand—and he had no subordinate in either of his Cabinet posts other than clerks. Files sometimes were lost or misplaced, and on one occasion

---

(*Continued*)

Office	Date Appointed
Prothonotary, Register, Orphan's Court, Court of General Quarter Sessions, Recorder, Luzerne County, Pa.	1787
Member, State Constitutional Convention, Pa.	1787
Commissioner to Negotiate Indian Treaties	1790 and later
Postmaster General	1791
Secretary of War	1795
Secretary of State	1795
Chief Justice, Court of Common Pleas, Newburyport, Mass.	1802
U. S. Senator from Massachusetts	1805
Representative in Congress from Essex District	1812
Member, Board of War for Mass.	1812
Member, Executive Council of Mass.	1817
Chairman, School Committee of Salem	1821

[43] Upham, *Timothy Pickering*, II, 440.
[44] Gibbs, *Memoirs*, I, 177.

Washington was much irritated: "The business . . . has been *shamefully* neglected. . . ."[45]

Like Washington, Pickering never wavered before a mass of detail. His correspondence is full of attention to the smallest matters. He selected the newspapers for the publication of the federal laws.[46] He attended to the disposition of a horse used by a dispatch rider to Pittsburgh.[47] He objected to requiring notarization of certain ship papers: "It is probable the plan was devised by a notary."[48] He followed up on the casting of cannon for the frigate Crescent at Cecil Furnace.[49] He issued orders for the relief of distressed seamen:

Be pleased to procure for John Allen an American seaman in the Hospital one pair of blue cloth trowsers—one pair of warm drawers, one neck handkerchief, two pair of strong woollen stockings, one pair of strong shoes, and a wooden leg, and present the bill to me for payment.[50]

Pickering had a strong sense of personal and official honesty, combined with courage. We can believe that he had a righteous sense of duty well performed in exposing Randolph to Washington. Finding that his chief clerk and passport clerk had received gifts for issuing a passport, Pickering dismissed them summarily. He was a man "of the sternest uprightness of character and most inflexible determination. One more honest and honorable never breathed; his very faults sprung from the strength and truth of his feelings."[51]

He was not an innovator. In 1792 Jefferson proposed a plan to speed up the mails, but Pickering rejected it as causing too great expense.[52] In the same year Sebastian Bauman, postmaster at New York, suggested a plan to register important letters. Pickering promptly and decisively turned down the proposal.

In Child's and Swaine's paper of yesterday I observe your advertisement proposing that all letters of consequence should be registered in the post-

---

[45] Washington to Lear, Feb. 15, 1796, *Writings*, XXXIV, 465.

[46] Pickering to John Morton, June 17, 1797, Pickering Papers, VI, 366.

[47] Pickering to Major Isaac Craig, July 15, 1797, *ibid.*, VI, 425.

[48] Pickering to the Comptroller of the Treasury, Aug. 21, 1797, *ibid.*, VII, 109.

[49] Pickering to Dacosta, Oct. 7, 1797, *ibid.*, VII, 274.

[50] Pickering to Francis Higgins, steward of the Pennsylvania Hospital, Dec. 4, 1798, *ibid.*, X, 4.

[51] Gibbs, *op. cit.*, I, 177.

[52] Jefferson, *Works* (Federal ed.), VI, 409.

office in which they are lodged for transmission by post. This mode, you add, would give persons who send letters of value "additional security." —How this should happen I know not, unless you would make yourself responsible, which surely you do not mean, seeing that such letters may pass thro' the hand of scores of people before they reach the places of their destination.

Your advertisement is a notification to persons disposed to plunder, that the mails are now become objects worthy of their attention: on this account I was sorry to see it.

Unless you have reasons for proposing the measure which do not occur to me, I should advise a discontinuance of the advertisement.[53]

His contemporaries often described Pickering as "a plain man." He was both plain and proud. Being invited as Secretary of State to dine with the British minister, he replied,

Congress do not allow persons holding *executive* offices under the United States (unless they possess private fortunes) to have any convivial intercourse with foreign ministers; and scarcely admit of it with the most intimate of their fellow citizens.—It is deemed honor enough for executive officers to toil without interruption for their country, and indulgence enough to live on mutton, mush and cold water.[54]

To Madame de Freire, wife of the minister from Portugal, he wrote, declining a dinner invitation, "I am, if you please, *too proud* to contract further obligations of this sort which I am *too poor* to discharge." [55]

Dismissed by Adams in 1800 for political insubordination, Pickering set out for western Pennsylvania to carve a farm out of the wilderness. "Though ashamed to beg," he declared at the age of fifty-five, "he was able and willing to dig." It was this pride and independence which caused Elbridge Gerry (a bitter enemy) to write Jefferson at the time, "But that tool & scapegoat of faction after having done more mischief than ever before was affected by a man of such mean & rude abilities, has retired to the woods, the proper situation for savage manners." [56]

Pickering, like Washington, never worked out any systematic views

---

[53] Pickering to Bauman, August 8, 1792, Pickering Papers, VI, 67.
[54] *Ibid.*, VIII, 204.
[55] *Ibid.*, VIII, 254.
[56] Gerry, *Letters,* p. 12.

of administration. He was guided by a strong sense of devotion to duty and by common sense; his mind was not creative; he was rather an energetic executor of a given system. His contribution to administration was in the realm of the ethics of honesty and integrity rather than in the art of management as such.

Chapter Seventeen

INTERNAL DEPARTMENTAL CONTROL

T HE business of all governments is largely transacted elsewhere than in the capital city. The major decisions of administrative policy are made there; but their application and realization take place in the many local offices where citizens and officials deal with each other. Field services were so essential for the convenience of government and people alike that they began to take shape at once; indeed, the customs service was authorized before the Treasury Department was created.

The essential administrative problems involved in a field service are to maintain energy and consistency in its operations and to ensure procedure in accordance with law. On both counts it is vital to maintain close relations between the center, where policy is formed, and the circumference. A field service is always a subordinate agency; but at the same time it is not a robot, for it must possess some discretion. Congress never disputed the need of having agents stationed at appropriate places for the transaction of public business and on the whole (apart from customs) left to the executive branch their geographical disposition.

Officials in the field services then as now far outnumbered those in the central establishment, but none were promoted to the principal offices in Philadelphia. Appointments to the high positions were made almost invariably from among persons of national consequence rather than from the "career men" in the field. The number of such positions was of course very small. Field appointments were made from residents of the state or community.

FIELD SERVICES

Congress established the customs service on July 31, 1789, marking out the collection districts and ports of entry. In each important port of entry were established three customs officers, the collector, naval officer, and surveyor; in the smaller ports one or both of the latter officers might be omitted. Their duties were specified in considerable detail; the collector assessed customs and tonnage dues and employed "proper persons" as weighers, gaugers, measurers, and inspectors, as well as seamen to man boats in the revenue service; the naval officer counter-signed all orders of the collector, received copies of manifests, and in general acted as a check upon the collector; the surveyor, who super-intended the weighers and measurers, was under the joint control of the collector and naval officer.[1] The customs service, which also became responsible by delegation for the lighthouses, immediately took its place as the most important field organization of the time.

The attorneys of the United States and the marshals were established by the Judiciary Act of September 24, 1789. The same Congress "adopted" the postal service, already organized under authority of the Continental Congress. By the close of the first session of the first Con-gress, therefore, five different field services had been authorized: cus-toms, lighthouses, district attorneys, marshals, and post offices. Others quickly followed.

In 1790 the President was authorized to build and man not over ten cutters for the better protection of the customs; they were placed under the direction of the collectors, but eventually developed into the Coast Guard. In 1790 also, Congress made its first appropriation for the diplomatic service. The consular service was authorized in 1792.

In 1791 the internal revenue offices were organized, originally for the collection of the tax on distilled spirits. Congress specified the principal officers: one supervisor to each district (i.e., a state in 1791), one or more inspectors in the discretion of the President for each sub-division ("survey"), and such offices of inspection and revenue agents to have charge of distilleries as the supervisors should deem necessary (amended in 1792 to require at least one office in each county).[2] This network of offices, together with customs, made the Treasury a rela-tive giant among the departments.

While new functions were assigned to the revenue officers from time to time, no additional field services were set up until 1798 when an organization (relatively short-lived) was created to assess and collect the tax on lands, buildings, and slaves. A wholly independent set of offices was established to *assess* these subjects of taxation, but the

---

[1] 1 Stat. 29, sec. 5.
[2] 1 Stat. 199, secs. 4, 7, 18; 1 Stat. 267, sec. 2.

collection was undertaken by the supervisors of internal revenue created in 1791.

An office for dealing with Indian affairs had been established by the Ordinance of 1786 and was continued by the new government in 1790. The Ordinance of 1786 created two superintendents of Indian affairs, one for the northern and one for the southern Indians. They were directed to obey all instructions received from the Secretary at War, who became "unquestionably the directing head of Indian affairs."[3] The Ordinance of 1787 creating the Northwest Territory and subsequent territorial government acts made the governors ex officio superintendents of Indian affairs.

TABLE I

FIELD ESTABLISHMENTS, 1789–1800

Establishment	Date of Organization under the New Government
1. Customs service	1789
2. Lighthouses	1789
3. Attorneys of the United States	1789
4. Marshals	1789
5. Post offices	1789
6. Revenue cutter service	1790
7. Indian superintendents	1790
8. Commissioners of Loans	1790
9. Internal revenue service	1791
10. Surveyor General	1796
11. Land tax service	1798
12. Land offices	1800

The task of surveying and selling lands was slow in getting under way. An act of 1796 made provision for a Surveyor General (whose office became "headquarters") and for surveyors; a field office for the sale of lands in section lots was located at Pittsburgh. In 1800 Congress expanded the establishment by creating the new field offices of register of the land office, four of which were set up in the Northwest Terri-

[3] George Dewey Harmon, *Sixty Years of Indian Affairs: Political, Economic, and Diplomatic, 1789–1850* (Chapel Hill: University of North Carolina Press, 1941), p. 5.

tory; associated with the register were two subordinate officers, the receiver of public monies for the sale of land, and the superintendent of public sales. The close of the Federalist period, therefore, saw the foundations well laid for future expansion.

Omitting reference to the territorial governments and excluding particular institutions and stations such as the hospitals for seamen and the various arsenals and military establishments, we may indicate the scope of the field offices in 1800 by the preceding list.

HEADQUARTERS CONTROL

Clearly the problem of central control of a widely dispersed force loomed largest in the Treasury Department. The foreign service provided a special case that in some instances proved troublesome enough but for which the remedy was to lie in improvements in communication rather than in forms of control. The postal service was widely dispersed, but its duties rarely endangered property or personal interests. It is not surprising, therefore, to discover that the most extensive forms of central direction and control of the field services developed in the Treasury.

The general pattern of relationship in the several departments was the same. It rested basically on the authority vested in the head of the department to "superintend" the affairs of the organization and on the power of the President and department heads to remove their subordinates. The former was expressly stated in the organic legislation, the latter was implied in the Constitution and endorsed by Congress. Both were buttressed by various devices which will fall under review in this section. Their net consequence was to ensure the dominance of the central office and to tie together the whole administrative machine in a closely knit web of duties and responsibilities.

The means of control fell into two categories, one designed to bear on the field agent as such, the other intended to control his action in particular cases. Both were exemplified in early practice. The first included the power to remove, to sue to compel performance of duty, and to sue for an accounting.

Power to remove. The authority to remove brought the whole hierarchy of officials at once within the disciplinary sphere of the President and department heads. The removal power was used sparingly by the Federalist leaders, but it was used frequently enough to preserve its vigor as a means of maintaining central authority.

Suit to compel performance. The suit (by government) against an official in case of failure to discharge his duties (not to make good loss of money or property) is an interesting example of eighteenth-century reliance on judicial rather than administrative methods of ensuring faithful execution of the law. The first collection act required every collector, naval officer, and surveyor to give bond with sureties approved by the Comptroller of the Treasury "conditioned for the true and faithful discharge of the duties of his office according to law"; and the Comptroller was authorized to put bonds in suit "upon any breach of the condition thereof." [4] These provisions were carried through the Federalist period and reenacted in 1799.[5] Various particular offenses were noted in the collection acts subjecting customs officers to forfeitures; each of these penalties presumably was collectible through the process of judicial suit on the bond. A parallel provision in the post office law, requiring the Postmaster General to sue on the bond of a postmaster for failure to render his accounts, was given energy by charging the sums due, after three months, to the Postmaster General himself.[6]

Suit to recover. In 1795 Congress made provision for the recovery of money from "persons accountable." Failure to respond to an order from the Comptroller to render accounts and vouchers to the Auditor authorized the Comptroller to sue for an accounting, the party sued to stand costs in any event.[7] Two years later Congress directed the Comptroller to sue any person accountable who neglected or refused to pay the balance due on his account, including (as a penalty) his commissions.[8] These cases involved money due the government.

The second group of procedures for supervising field agents was designed to control particular acts or decisions, and normally did not imply any disciplinary action. These procedures were by far the more important and comprised the normal mode of control of field agents. From 1789 to 1801 they included principally general superintendence

---

[4] 1 Stat. 29, sec. 28 (July 31, 1789); the Treasury Act of September 2, 1789, also gave the Comptroller authority to prosecute for all delinquencies of officers of the revenue, 1 Stat. 65, sec. 3.

[5] 1 Stat. 704, sec. 1.

[6] 1 Stat. 232, sec. 24 (Feb. 20, 1792); repeated and extended in 1 Stat. 733, secs. 22–23 (March 2, 1799).

[7] 1 Stat. 441 (March 3, 1795).

[8] 1 Stat. 512 (March 3, 1797).

and management, instructions and orders, rulings, and review of particular cases on appeal. The three latter types were most highly developed in the Treasury Department.

Authority to superintend. The basic authority of the central office over field agents was derived from brief provisions of the organic acts establishing the departments. The Treasury Act of 1789 declared, "it shall be the duty of the Secretary of the Treasury . . . to superintend the collection of the revenue"; [9] the Postmaster General was empowered "to superintend the business of the department, in all the duties that are, or may be assigned to it." [10] These general grants of administrative power tended to flow down (sometimes by statutory direction) to the second or third levels of administration. Thus an act of 1792 declared that the Commissioner of the Revenue "shall be charged with superintending, under the direction of the head of the department, the collection of the other revenues [i.e., other than duties on impost and tonnage] of the United States." [11] In 1794 occurred a standard phraseology repeated thereafter: "The duties . . . shall be received, collected, accounted for, and paid under and subject to the superintendence, control and direction of the department of the treasury, according to the authorities and duties of the respective officers thereof." [12]

The extent of the power of superintendence was challenged by some customs collectors, who alleged that their oath of office required them to execute their offices *according to law,* and thus obliged them to follow the law as they understood it, not as it might be explained to them by Alexander Hamilton. This assertion provided the occasion for one of Hamilton's able letters on administration, from which the following passages are excerpted:

. . . it becomes advisable to state the ideas which are entertained at the Treasury respecting the nature of the power of the head of the Department, "to superintend the collection of the revenue," and the obligation incident to it on the part of the officers immediately charged with that collection. . . .

The power of *superintending* the collection of the revenue, as incident to the duty of doing it, comprises, in my opinion, among a variety of particulars not necessary to be specified, the right of *settling,* for the govern-

---

[9] 1 Stat. 65, sec. 2 (Sept. 2, 1789).
[10] 1 Stat. 232, sec. 3 (Feb. 20, 1792).
[11] 1 Stat. 279, sec. 6 (May 8, 1792).
[12] 1 Stat. 376, sec. 4 (June 5, 1794).

ment of the officers employed in the collection of the several branches of
the revenue, the *construction* of the laws relating to the revenue, in all
cases of doubt.

This right is fairly implied in the force of the terms "to superintend,"
and is essential to uniformity and system in the execution of the laws.

It is evident that, without it, the most incongruous practices upon the
same laws might obtain in different districts of the United States. . . .

It is true that a remedy, in a large proportion of the cases, might be obtained from the courts of justice; but the vexatious course of tedious law-
suits to decide whether the practice of one officer or of another was the
most legal, would be a mode of redress very unsatisfactory to suffering
parties, and very ill suited, as an ordinary expedient, to the exigencies and
convenience of trade.

A reference has been made to the oath of office, prescribed by the first
collection law for the officers of customs.

They are by that law severally required to swear or affirm, that they will
execute and perform all the duties of their respective offices *according to law;*
whence it seems to have been inferred, that they are bound each to pursue
his own opinion of the meaning of the law.

But it is conceived that an officer of the customs executes his duty according to law, when, in the cases mentioned, he conforms his conduct to
the construction which is given to the law by that officer, who, by law, is
constituted the general superintendent of the collection of the revenue. The
power to superintend must imply a right to judge and direct; of course an
obligation to observe the directions which are given, on the part of those
to whom they are addressed. . . .[13]

Instructions. Implicit in the power to superintend, and explicit in a
variety of statutory directions to field officers lay the power of the head
of a department to issue instructions.[14] In the field of foreign relations
the instruction was the basic form of direction and control; it laid
down general policy to guide the minister and descended into such
detail as circumstances required or permitted. The territorial governors,
far removed from Philadelphia, likewise received formal instructions
for their guidance. The practice was well established in the Treasury

---

[13] July 20, 1792, Hamilton, *Works* (Hamilton ed.), III, 557–59.
[14] By way of example, the statutory duty of collectors in the first and subsequent
collection acts to keep accounts in such form *as may be directed;* to submit their books
to inspection of such persons *as may be appointed;* to pay to the order of the *authorized*
officer all monies collected; and corresponding directions issued to the internal revenue
officers in 1791.

and Post Office; in the latter case by explicit statutory language.[15]

The preparation of forms and procedures to be used in the course of business immediately engaged Hamilton's attention at the Treasury; they became the transmission belt of Treasury business,[16] and were eventually written into the collection act of 1799.[17] The first Secretary of the Treasury was his own procedures analyst; his instructions to the collectors are a model of their kind, and exemplify his genius for administration in its more detailed aspects. He indicated with the utmost clarity what he expected and took pains to explain the reasons underlying the instruction. In an early circular he directed the collectors to communicate the "imperfections and inconveniences" of the revenue system as they appeared in actual operation—warning them at the same time that "the complaints of the merchants will not always be infallible indications of defects." The enforcement of the Neutrality Proclamation of 1793 gave rise to one of his best known instructions, including a carefully prepared schedule of rules covering the cases most likely to be met with and concluding by referring to the President's expectation that the instructions would be executed "with the greatest vigilance, care, activity and impartiality." [18]

The power to issue instructions was normally vested only in the President or in the heads of departments. The assessment of the tax on lands, dwellings, and slaves presented so varied a problem that Congress conveyed this power to the boards of commissioners established in each state. They were authorized both to make regulations, binding on each commissioner and assessor, and to frame instructions informing the assessors of their duties.[19] By way of contrast, the regulations governing trade with the Indians were made by the President.

Rulings. An instruction purports to set out a general rule or course of action; it may or may not arise from a particular case. A ruling arises from a particular incident, stated by a subordinate officer to his superior. Many requests for rulings came welling up from harassed collectors, firmly establishing a form of central control which has always remained important. Some characteristic examples, to which

---

[15] 1 Stat. 232, sec. 3 (Feb. 20, 1792); 1 Stat. 733, sec. 1 (March 2, 1799).

[16] For examples see Hamilton, *Works* (Hamilton ed.), III, 539 ff.

[17] 1 Stat. 627, *passim.*

[18] Instructions to Collectors, Aug. 4, 1793, Hamilton, *Works* (Hamilton ed.), III, 574–77.

[19] 1 Stat. 580, sec. 8 (July 9, 1798).

Hamilton responded in carefully prepared communications, follow: [20] whether a vessel is liable to pay tonnage at each entry; whether American produce exported and returned for lack of a foreign market is liable to pay duty; whether the tonnage of a foreign vessel could be taken from its register; whether an inspector put on board a vessel in one district to go to another superintends the landing of goods in the second district.

Review. Another device for maintaining central control over field action lies in the possibility of review of a decision taken and completed by a subordinate agency. This jurisdiction tends to be semijudicial in form. It developed in the Treasury Department in connection with the tax on carriages. The classification of carriages for taxation was the duty of the collector of internal revenue. Before him an owner could enter a claim for exemption or remission, which usually would involve a plea for a lower classification. The decision was made by the supervisor of revenue, the next highest officer. The law, however, permitted a further appeal to the Secretary of the Treasury, thus setting up an administrative review at two levels above the officer making the original determination.[21]

Administration at headquarters. The logical conclusion of this series of controls is reached when the decision on a matter originating locally is taken out of the hands of the field agents and vested directly in the central office. Several instances of this sort appeared in the fiscal legislation.

The allowance of a drawback on imports subsequently exported depended upon satisfactory proof of the actual disposition of the goods abroad. Congress specified the form of this proof in the excise law of 1791.[22] Where the normal form was not available, the exporter was allowed to offer other evidence, whose sufficiency, if the value of the drawback was under $100, was determined by the collector; otherwise by the Comptroller of the Treasury. An analogous case appeared in the collection act of 1799; a collector was entitled to refuse payment of a debenture (an instrument stating amounts of duties paid on imports for which a drawback was claimed, payable at a future date) if he was satisfied that an error had arisen or fraud committed, up to a

---

[20] *Works* (Hamilton ed.), III, 543 ff.
[21] 1 Stat. 478, secs. 8–9 (May 28, 1796).
[22] 1 Stat. 199, sec. 57 (March 3, 1791).

debenture value of $100; for larger sums the case was transmitted for original decision to the Comptroller.[23] An act of 1795 made similar provisions for the cancellation of an exporter's bonds upon proof of foreign delivery of goods on which a drawback was claimed.[24] The complicated procedures governing drawbacks do not require examination to understand the point that is here relevant, that is, the outright transference of some determinations directly to the central office.[25]

The power to suspend the enforcement of an act was never put within the discretion of field officials, although we may surmise that they found occasion for a good deal of leeway off-the-record. In one of Hamilton's letters there is clear evidence of administrative discretion in postponing the effective operation of a law for whose execution Congress had set a specific date. The letter, to the collector at Baltimore, reads, "Ample time having been given to the commanders of vessels trading to foreign ports, it is my desire that the 9th section of the collection law *may hereafter be enforced*." [26] The date of the law to which he refers is August 4, 1790, effective after October 1, 1790; [27] the date of Hamilton's letter is February 6, 1792. The shipmasters had benefited by more than fifteen months' administrative grace.

The net consequence of the operation of these controls was to hold a tight rein on some field agents and a very loose rein on others. "The Officers [of customs]," said Stephen Higginson to the Secretary of the Treasury, "will do nothing . . . without your directions." [28] In the Treasury, duties were carefully defined by instructions from headquarters, rulings were made on particular cases in response to requests, reports were required at frequent intervals, delinquency was punished without delay or hesitation, and managerial functions, such as con-

---

[23] 1 Stat. 627, sec. 80 (March 2, 1799).

[24] 1 Stat. 420, sec. 9 (Feb. 26, 1795); extension of time before putting such bonds in suit was also handled centrally by the Comptroller, 1 Stat. 627, sec. 32.

[25] The remission of fines and forfeitures was put in the hands of the Secretary of the Treasury in the last instance. This authority is not included as a means of controlling the determinations of field agents but is viewed rather as an act of grace toward careless citizens; the assumption is that the penalties were correctly imposed in the first instance and would continue to be imposed under like circumstances.

[26] Hamilton to Otho H. Williams, *Works* (Hamilton ed.), III, 554; italics are author's.

[27] 1 Stat. 145.

[28] April 21, 1793, "Letters of Stephen Higginson," Am. Hist. Assoc., *Annual Report, 1896*, I, 787.

tracting for supplies and equipment, were closely guarded. At the opposite extreme stood the foreign service, both diplomatic and consular, far removed in space and time from Philadelphia, guided by instructions which events might rapidly outmode and controlled chiefly by the power of recall.

Chapter Eighteen

INTERDEPARTMENTAL RELATIONS

IN AN era when the departments numbered only three, when their duties were relatively "plain and simple," and when personal contact between Secretaries and the Chief Executive was frequent, it might be supposed that the relations between departments would be equally "plain and simple." In fact the problem of coordinating the operations of different agencies at points where they touched or overlapped arose at once.

The structure of the federal system was not at fault. The lines of responsibility to the Chief Executive were clearly established and during Washington's administration were unchallenged. Responsibility within the departments to the Secretaries was equally undoubted. Administrative work was carefully assigned to one of the three departments, the principal exception being the operation of the sinking fund, a joint responsibility of a board comprising the Secretaries of Treasury and State and the Attorney General. As he left the Treasury, Hamilton noted the accepted rule in a letter to Washington.

These observations proceed on the supposition that the President has adopted in principle and practice, the plan of distributing all the particular branches of the public service, except that of the law, among the three great departments; a plan which is believed to be founded on good reasons.[1]

The rule did not touch the problem of coordination. No department, however closely contained, lived in a world of its own. Often two or more had a legitimate interest in a given field of administration, and one sometimes performed services for others. The necessity of coordinating and harmonizing activities was implicit in even as simple an administrative structure as that of 1790 to 1800.

The lines of demarcation between departments were drawn only

---

[1] Jan. 31, 1795, Hamilton, *Works* (Hamilton ed.), V, 72.

by the broad descriptions of the duties of each in laws that left un-answered many problems of jurisdiction—for example, should the Post Office be assigned to Treasury as a revenue-producing agency or to State, as the recognized home of domestic affairs? Should corre-spondence with American diplomats abroad concerning foreign loans be carried on by Treasury or by State? Should correspondence with territorial governors about Indians be dealt with by State or by War? Should the enforcement of an embargo fall to State or to Treasury?

These questions were answerable only by experience within the departments and by presidential direction. On the whole, with the exception of procurement, the provision of services by one department for others gave rise to no perplexing problems. The adjustment of overlapping interests in a single area of public affairs was more diffi-cult, especially in the field of foreign relations. Conflict between State and Treasury at this point brought out some carefully considered state-ments of policy.

INTERDEPARTMENTAL SERVICES

There were several cases in which one agency provided service for another or others, in the capacity that may be called auxiliary. The most notable example was the Attorney General, whose duty it was to give legal advice to other departments upon their request. Another example was the Post Office, which was the principal medium of com-munication between the central and field offices of the federal govern-ment, and between the states and Philadelphia. While there were constant complaints about the service in general, there was no con-certed effort to improve it. The departments suffered in official silence.

The purchase of army supplies by the Treasury represented a more formal type of interdepartmental service. Initiated by Hamilton in 1792, it was abandoned in 1798 because it divided responsibility for War Department business. The Treasury also developed the account-ing system for other departments, as well as for itself; there is no evidence of objection by the departments. On the other hand, the initial examination of claims and bills against the departments by the Treasury was resisted and eventually a departmental accountant was set up in War and in Navy.

At the very moment of their conflict over neutrality enforcement,[2]

---

[2] Jefferson to Randolph, May 8, 1793, Jefferson, *Works* (Federal ed.), VII, 315–19.

the two department heads of State and Treasury agreed to employ the collectors of customs as the means of distributing passports to American vessels engaged in foreign trade. Jefferson politely requested Treasury to assist him [3] and Hamilton promptly consented: "It will be equally agreeable to me, that they be transmitted either directly from your office, or through this department. If you prefer the latter, which I shall with pleasure facilitate," etc.[4] There was equal readiness by State to accommodate Treasury with respect to foreign loans through the agency of William Short and others. Short, as an American diplomat, was to correspond with Jefferson; but in fact Hamilton wrote him directly on foreign loans, apparently with Jefferson's knowledge and consent.

The duties imposed upon the Secretary of State in 1796 to register land grants made by the Treasury were purely ministerial and gave rise to no dissension. At a lower level of organization a widespread problem of coordination existed in principle between the district attorneys, whose duty it was generally to prosecute for crimes and offenses against federal laws,[5] and other law enforcement officers, especially customs and excise, whose duty it was to prosecute for violation of the customs laws. The Department of State was the central office to which the district attorneys looked for instructions and general supervision, while the customs officers were of course attached to the Treasury. No instance has come to our attention of correspondence between the Treasury Department and the district attorneys on legal business of concern to the Treasury. Apparently there was no intrusion upon the authority of the Department of State.[6]

CONFLICT IN FOREIGN AFFAIRS

It was Jefferson's misfortune not to arrive at the seat of government until March 22, 1790, a full six months after Hamilton had taken office. In this interval Hamilton had not only gone far in organizing the Treasury and setting up its far-flung field service, he had also—*faute de mieux*—taken the initiative in the foreign field. To the United

---

[3] Jefferson to Hamilton, May 8, 1793, *ibid.,* VII, 319–20.

[4] Hamilton to Jefferson, May 9, 1793, Hamilton, *Works* (Hamilton ed.), IV, 394.

[5] 1 Stat. 73, sec. 35 (Sept. 24, 1789).

[6] There is a letter in which Washington asks Hamilton if the district attorneys should not be written to, in connection with the enforcement of the Neutrality Act, May 7, 1793, Washington, *Writings,* XXXII, 451.

States, Great Britain had sent an unaccredited agent, Major George Beckwith, who arrived in October 1789. Beckwith and Hamilton immediately engaged in conversations with Washington's knowledge and approval. The contact was also made known to Jefferson upon his appearance in New York. Until George Hammond arrived in October 1791 as the regularly accredited British minister, Beckwith kept in close touch with Hamilton.[7] With the establishment of regular diplomatic agents, it might be presumed that negotiations and contacts would have been consolidated into the Department of State; but this was not to happen. Hammond clearly understood the French bias of Jefferson and the British sympathies of Hamilton. In 1793 Hammond wrote to London that "he preferred to make most of his communications privately to Hamilton and to have relations with Jefferson only when absolutely necessary."[8]

This invasion of his special province was of course not concealed from so astute a person as Jefferson. As early as the spring of 1792 (five months after Hammond's arrival) Jefferson was smarting under Hamilton's aggressiveness. "It was observable," he wrote on March 11, 1792, "that whenever at any of our consultns anything was proposed as to Gr. Br. Hamilton had constantly ready something which Mr. Hammond had communicated to him, which suited the subject, and proved the intimacy of their communications: insomuch that I believe he communicated to Hammond all our views & knew from him in return the views of the British Court."[9] There can be no doubt that Jefferson's negotiations with Hammond were weakened by Hamilton's private exchange of opinions with the British minister. Hamilton did not hesitate to rewrite Jefferson's dispatches, as matters of foreign policy came up for Cabinet discussion. The tone of diplomatic exchanges between the United States and both Great Britain and France

---

[7] Samuel Flagg Bemis, *Jay's Treaty* (New York: Macmillan 1923), pp. 44, 75. Beckwith had had no contact with Jefferson until he called on the Secretary of State when about to leave. Jefferson, *Works* (Federal ed.), I, 191.

[8] Bemis, *op. cit.*, p. 104.

[9] Jefferson, *Works* (Federal ed.), I, 209. The warmth of Jefferson's outraged feelings was revealed to the President in the letter of September 9, 1792: "Yet the Secretary of the treasury, by his cabals with members of the legislature, & by high-toned declamation on other occasions, has forced down his own system [of foreign policy], which was exactly the reverse [i.e., of Jefferson's]. He undertook, of his own authority, the conferences with the ministers of those two nations, & was, on every consultation, provided with some report of a conversation with the one or the other of them, adapted to his views." *Ibid.*, VII, 140.

was set more nearly by Hamilton than by the Secretary of State.[10]

Hamilton recognized the delicacy of his situation in the field of foreign affairs. Long after Jefferson had resigned, Hamilton told Washington his view of the instructions Jefferson had written for Jay on his mission to Great Britain.

The truth, unfortunately, is, that it is in general a crude mass, which will do no credit to the administration. This was my impression of it at the time; but the delicacy of attempting too much reformation in the work of another head of department, the hurry of the moment, and a great confidence in the person to be sent, prevented my attempting that reformation.[11]

The clash of opinion between Jefferson and Hamilton concerning American foreign policy came to a head in early 1793 when news of war between France and Britain reached the United States. Hamilton had already assured Hammond of his intent to hold the United States to a neutral course; this view coincided with Washington's. A Cabinet meeting was held on April 19, 1793. "Jefferson opposed neutrality on principle, and was defeated. He urged delay, and was again defeated. He then argued the matter on constitutional grounds. The President had no powers, without the consent of Congress, to take such a step as was contemplated." [12] Jefferson was unable to carry the day except in matters of phraseology; here he succeeded in having the word, neutrality, omitted from the text. He affixed his signature to the Proclamation of Neutrality on April 22, 1793. Hamilton, helped greatly by Genêt's tactless course, had triumphed in Jefferson's own domain.

The method of enforcement of the Proclamation of Neutrality, a strictly administrative problem, further strained the relations between the two Secretaries. Hamilton immediately prepared a circular letter to the collectors of customs instructing them (in Jefferson's paraphrase) "to superintend their neighborhood, watch for all acts of our citizens

---

[10] For examples see the exchange between Hamilton and Jefferson on a note to Hammond recorded in Hamilton, *Works* (Hamilton ed.), IV, 141, 144, and 240; and for Jefferson's sensitivity on this point see Jefferson, *Works* (Federal ed.), I, 317.

[11] March 28, 1796, Hamilton, *Works* (Hamilton ed.), VI, 97. Hamilton himself had worked on a draft of an instruction, with Senators King, Ellsworth, and Cabot. See Hayden, *The Senate and Treaties*, p. 72. Hamilton submitted his views privately to Jay in a long letter dated May 6, 1794, *Works* (Hamilton ed.), IV, 551-55.

[12] Oliver, *Alexander Hamilton*, p. 331.

contrary to laws of neutrality or tending to infringe those laws, & inform him of it; & particularly to see if vessels should be building pierced for guns."[13] The next day (May 5, 1793) Washington wrote Hamilton that he wanted to speak to him about the circular,[14] and on the following day the President showed it to Jefferson. Washington then returned the circular to Hamilton for further consultation with Randolph and Jefferson,[15] and wrote Hamilton a note indicating his disposition not to take measures which might check shipbuilding and further to refrain from adopting measures that were not "indispensably necessary."[16]

The animus in the situation appears in a letter from Jefferson to Randolph, May 8, 1793. In this communication Jefferson raised objections to the whole proposal.

. . . the Collectors of the customs are to be made an established corps of spies or informers against their fellow citizens, whose actions they are to watch in secret, inform against in secret to the Secretary of the Treasury, who is to communicate it to the President. . . . This will at least furnish the collector with a convenient weapon to keep down a rival, draw a cloud over an inconvenient censor, or satisfy mere malice & private enmity.[17]

The object of this new institution is to be to prevent infractions of the laws of neutrality, & preserve our peace with foreign nations. Acts involving war, or proceedings which respect foreign nations, seem to belong either to the department of war, or to that which is charged with the affairs of foreign nations. But I cannot possibly conceive how the superintendance of the laws of neutrality, or the preservation of our peace with foreign nations can be ascribed to the department of the treasury, which I suppose to comprehend merely matters of revenue. It would be to add a new & a large field to a department already amply provided with business, patronage, & influence. . . .[18]

---

[13] Hamilton to Washington, May 4, 1793, Hamilton, *Works* (Hamilton ed.), IV, 392; Jefferson's summary is in Jefferson, *Works* (Federal ed.), I, 269; the text of the circular in its original form has not been located.

[14] Hamilton, *Works* (Hamilton ed.), IV, 392; Washington, *Writings*, XXXII, 447.

[15] Jefferson, *Works* (Federal ed.), I, 269.

[16] May 7, 1793, Washington, *Writings*, XXXII, 451.

[17] The collectors were heavily Federalist.

[18] Jefferson, *Works* (Federal ed.), VII, 316–17. Randolph naively sought out Hamilton at once and asked him "whether his correspondence has at any time been directed to the prying into the conduct of individuals or even an inspection over the legislatures." Hamilton of course denied the charge. M. D. Conway, *Edmund Randolph*, p. 204.

As an alternative means of enforcing neutrality Jefferson proposed to rely on the grand juries, "the constitutional inquisitors & informers of the country." And then in a postscript he added a characteristic Jeffersonian suggestion: "P.S. I understood Col? H. yesterday that he should confer with the President on the subject of our deliberation. As that is not exactly the channel thro' which I would wish my objections to be represented, should the President mention the subject to you I will thank you to communicate to him this note, or it's substance." [19]

Washington neatly solved the dispute by directing the Attorney General (not the Secretary of State, the normal channel) to instruct the district attorneys to require from the collectors of the several ports information of all infractions of neutrality; [20] and by implication to report directly to him, not to either Secretary. Hamilton's circular was not approved—at this time.

The enforcement of neutrality rapidly became a major problem as the French boldly sought to use American ports for their purposes, and the most effective means of action was clearly not a grand jury. The governors of the states were requested to seize any offending vessels and generally to guard against violations of neutrality.[21] On July 8, 1793, the three Cabinet members met in Washington's absence to consider a letter from Governor Mifflin of Pennsylvania, calling their attention to the brigantine, *Little Sarah,* outfitted and armed in the port of Philadelphia, then lying in the river between the city and Mud Island and perhaps ready to sail. The Governor asked for instructions. Hamilton and Knox advised immediate measures to set up a battery on Mud Island and if necessary to use coercion to prevent her sailing until the President could be consulted. Jefferson dissented.[22]

Governor Mifflin immediately asked for the loan of four cannon to mount on Mud Island, and the whole problem was reviewed with the President at a Cabinet meeting on July 15. The President was greatly disturbed; he had assumed that the governors would detect violations "in embryo & stop them when no force was requisite or a

[19] Jefferson, *Works* (Federal ed.), VII, 318–19.

[20] Washington, *Writings,* XXXII, 455, n. 35, transcribing the text from the Journal of the Proceedings of the President.

[21] See reference to this action, Jefferson to U. S. attorney for New York, June 12, 1793, Jefferson, *Works* (Federal ed.), VII, 380–82.

[22] *Ibid.,* VII, 437–38, and *ibid.,* I, 282–88.

very small party of militia wd. suffice"; he doubted whether he had power to establish permanent guards; and he was opposed to dispersing cannon "all over the U. S." According to Jefferson's account, the President delayed his decision until Jefferson had withdrawn, but after reprimanding Knox for putting the loan of cannon in motion, Washington finally agreed.[23]

The dangers involved in reliance upon the governors, evidenced to Washington in this episode, brought him back to Hamilton's initial proposal. On July 29, 1793, Washington asked the Cabinet to consider the expediency of directing the customs officers to supervise the observation of the Neutrality Proclamation. "Unless this, or some other *effectual* mode is adopted to check this evil in the first stage of its growth, the Executive of the U States will be incessantly harassed with complaints on this head, and probably when it may be difficult to afford a remedy." [24] On August 4, instructions were issued to the collectors of customs, three months after Hamilton had originally suggested this course of action.[25] The Treasury triumphed again in what Jefferson chose to consider the domain of foreign affairs.

Jefferson may well have felt annoyed, if not outraged, by Hamilton's activities in foreign problems. As a former minister to the King of France, dealing intimately with the course of diplomatic affairs of Europe and America, he ranked high among Americans entitled to speak on foreign policy with authority. Hamilton had never been to Europe, was personally unacquainted with the European courts, was without experience in diplomacy—and was head of a department concerned with revenue. But foreign policy involved the kind of question on which Washington insisted upon the opinions of his Cabinet in preference to advice of the Secretary of State alone. Jefferson suffered from the fact that his departmental problems as a matter of course came up for collective deliberation; Hamilton's usually could be settled by conference with the President alone. Furthermore, Hamilton's fiscal policy depended for its success upon peace; and he could therefore claim a competence to discuss foreign policy from the standpoint of his admitted fiscal responsibilities. Despite these considera-

---

[23] *Ibid.,* I, 291–93.

[24] Washington, *Writings,* XXXIII, 34.

[25] Hamilton, *Works* (Hamilton ed.), III, 574–77; the instructions were revised from the first draft.

tions, Jefferson believed that Hamilton was invading his prerogatives, and eventually told the President as much.

VIEWS OF JEFFERSON, HAMILTON, AND RANDOLPH

Jefferson, as Secretary of State, asserted his devotion to the rule of noninterference of one department with another. In defense of his conduct in his relations with Hamilton, he wrote to Washington:

When I embarked in the government, it was with a determination to intermeddle not at all with the legislature, & as little as possible with my co-departments. . . . The second part of my resolution has been religiously observed with the war department; & as to that of the Treasury, has never been farther swerved from than by the mere enunciation of my sentiments in conversation, and chiefly among those who, expressing the same sentiments, drew mine from me. If it has been supposed that I have ever intrigued among the members of the legislature to defeat the plans of the Secretary of the Treasury, it is contrary to all truth. . . .[26]

Hamilton suggested a different guide to departmental relations, the *rule of common concert* in view of common responsibility to the President. Jefferson recorded Hamilton's concept in his *Anas* at the point where he entered his recollections of the assumption controversy.

He [i.e., Hamilton] observed that the members of the administration ought to act in concert, that tho' this question was not of my department, yet a common duty should make it a common concern; that the President was the center on which all administrative questions ultimately rested, and that all of us should rally around him, and support with joint efforts measures approved by him. . . .[27]

This was in 1790. In October 1792, Hamilton stated fully his view of the proper relationship of one department head to another and to the President. Despite its length, the passage must be quoted *in extenso*.

---

[26] Sept. 9, 1792, Jefferson, *Works* (Federal ed.), VII, 137–38. Hamilton, of course, was convinced that Jefferson was the real leader of the congressional group opposed to him. In 1792 Hamilton wrote his friend Carrington, "a gentleman in the administration, in one department [i.e., Jefferson], ought not to have taken sides against another, in another department [i.e., Hamilton]," *Works* (Lodge ed.), IX, 529.

[27] Jefferson, *Works* (Federal ed.), I, 175.

The position must be reprobated that a man who had accepted an office in the Executive Department, should be held to throw the weight of his character into the scale, to support a measure which in his conscience *he disapproved, and in his station had opposed*—or, that the members of the administration should form together *a close and secret* combination, into whose measures the profane eye of the public should in no instance pry. But there is a very obvious medium between *aiding* or *countenancing,* and *intriguing* and *machinating* against a measure; between opposing it in the discharge of an official duty, or volunteering an opposition to it in the discharge of no duty; between entering into a close and secret combination with the other members of an administration, and being the active leader of an opposition to its measures.

The true line of propriety appears to me to be the following: A member of the administration, in one department, ought only to *aid* those measures of another which he approves—where he disapproves, if called upon to *act officially,* he ought to manifest his disapprobation, and avow his opposition, but out of an official line he ought not to interfere *as long as he thinks fit to continue a part of the administration.* When the measure in question has become a law of the land, especially with a direct sanction of the chief magistrate, it is peculiarly his duty to acquiesce. A contrary conduct is inconsistent with his relations as an officer of the government, and with a due respect as such for the decisions of the Legislature, and of the head of the executive department. The line here delineated, is drawn from obvious and very important considerations. The success of every government —its capacity to combine the exertion of public strength with the preservation of personal right and private security, qualities which define the perfection of a government, must always naturally depend on the energy of the executive department. This energy again must materially depend on the union and mutual deference which subsists between the members of that department, and the conformity of their conduct with the views of the executive chief.

Difference of opinion between men engaged in any common pursuit, is a natural appendage of human nature. When only exerted *in the discharge of a duty,* with delicacy and temper, among liberal and sensible men, it can create no animosity; but when it produces officious interferences, dictated by no call of duty—when it volunteers a display of itself in a quarter where there is no responsibility, to the obstruction and embarrassment of one who is charged with an immediate and direct responsibility, it must necessarily beget ill-humor and discord between the parties. Applied to the members of the executive administration of any government, it must necessarily tend to occasion, more or less, distracted councils, to foster factions in the community, and practically to weaken the government.

Moreover, the heads of the several executive departments are justly to be viewed as auxiliaries to the executive chief. Opposition to any measure of his, by either of those heads of departments, except in the shape of frank, firm, and independent advice to himself, is evidently contrary to the relations which subsist between the parties. And it cannot well be controverted that a measure becomes his, so as to involve the duty of acquiescence on the part of the members of his administration, as well by its having received his sanction in the form of a law, as by its having previously received his approbation.[28]

To much of this Jefferson would have agreed. Indeed he observed more than once that he had loyally carried out policies as a member of the government which he deeply disapproved, the President's policy having taken a direction different from his own.[29] He denied, as we have seen, Hamilton's charge that he interfered with the Treasury. He never developed as fully as Hamilton, however, his concept of the proper relationship of one department to another.

On January 2, 1794, Edmund Randolph stepped into Jefferson's post in the State Department. He had been a firsthand witness of the progressive deterioration of relations between Treasury and State, and took immediate steps to prevent a repetition. To keep interdepartmental relations clear and wholesome he wrote the following letter to his two colleagues in Treasury and War.

I have just taken the oath of Office, which reminds me that I am brought into a nearer relation to your department than hitherto. While official men are under no less an obligation than others, to live in harmony; there are too many opportunities for misconception and misrepresentations to interrupt it. I have therefore prescribed this rule for myself: that if any thing, supposed to be done in the other departments, shall create dissatisfaction in my mind, I will check any opinion, until I can obtain an explanation, which I will ask without reserve. By these means I shall avoid the uneasiness of suspicion; and I take the liberty of requesting, that the same line of conduct be pursued with respect to myself.[30]

These were the principal efforts to state general rules or procedures to govern the relations of one department to another. Both Hamilton's

---

concept of concerted action on matters which had received presidential approval and Jefferson's formula of departmental self-sufficiency had their place, but neither was destined to secure a degree of acceptance sufficient to prevent in later years a long history of interdepartmental disputes and feuds.

Chapter Nineteen

THE HAMILTON–JEFFERSON FEUD

O<small>N</small> S<small>EPTEMBER</small> 11, 1789, Alexander Hamilton took the oath of office as first Secretary of the Treasury. On March 22, 1790, Thomas Jefferson entered upon his duties as Secretary of State. By the summer of 1792, open warfare had broken out between these powerful members of the Cabinet. On August 23, 1792, President Washington wrote to Jefferson, and three days later to Hamilton, begging each of them for mutual forbearance lest their bitter quarrels "tare the Machine asunder" and disrupt the Union of the States. His appeal was in vain; Jefferson resigned his office December 31, 1793, and Hamilton, who had already told the President of his desire to resign, finally left office on January 31, 1795.

The great issues of policy, domestic and foreign, which occasioned this historic quarrel are well known. Jefferson cherished the ideal of an agricultural society; Hamilton a balanced economy calling for substantial development of manufactures, banking, corporations, and cities. Jefferson had an ardent faith in the masses; Hamilton had little. Jefferson favored little government and that mostly in the states and their smallest subdivisions; Hamilton needed a national government capable of energetic direction of the public economy to produce the balanced system he believed essential. Jefferson stood in principle for the predominance of popular legislative bodies; Hamilton expounded the theory and practice of executive leadership. In foreign affairs, Jefferson was attached to France and to the beneficent influence which he saw in the French Revolution, while Hamilton admired English institutions, feared the consequences of the Revolution, and believed that the interests of the United States required above all the maintenance of good relations with Great Britain. These conflicts of policy in matters both domestic and foreign were fundamental, and fatal to effective collaboration.[1]

The administrative phases of the great duel between Hamilton and Jefferson are less well known. When Jefferson and Hamilton met in New York in March 1790, they were comparative strangers. They had seen each other briefly during their service in the Continental Congress in 1783, but Jefferson had been out of the country for five years as the American minister in Paris, while Hamilton had been in the midst of the struggle to frame a constitution and to secure its adoption. Neither could have had a clear perception of the ideas of the other as, with Washington, they faced the problems of the future.

Jefferson's welcome in New York was friendly. He wrote, "The President received me cordially, and my Colleagues & the circle of principal citizens, apparently, with welcome."[2] There was a round of dinners and the new Secretary of State felt at home. Hamilton later recorded his early opinion of Jefferson as one of very great esteem, and Washington could have had no concern as to the ability and willingness of his principal advisers to cooperate effectively.

The first substantial break over public policy occurred in February 1791, when Jefferson declared Hamilton's plan to establish the Bank of the United States beyond the power of Congress to enact.[3] Hamilton's success in convincing Washington of the constitutionality of the bank bill persuaded Jefferson that Hamilton had to be watched and controlled.[4] Jefferson's fear of Hamilton's dominance was well founded.

---

[1] The most complete exposition of the conflict presented by Hamilton is found in his letter to Col. Edward Carrington, May 26, 1792, in John C. Hamilton, *History of the Republic of the United States,* IV, 520–40, and reprinted in Hamilton, *Works* (Lodge ed.), IX, 513–35; Jefferson presented his analysis of the break most fully in his letter to Washington of September 9, 1792, in Jefferson, *Works* (Federal ed.), VII, 137–49.

[2] *Ibid.,* I, 171.

[3] Jefferson, in his *Anas,* would lead us to believe that he lost confidence in Hamilton during the spring and summer of 1790 in the great struggle over assumption and the location of the Federal City. He alleged that Hamilton duped him: "I was most ignorantly & innocently made to hold the candle" (*ibid.,* I, 174). There can be no doubt that he bitterly regretted his part in securing approval of assumption as the price of locating the Federal City on the banks of the Potomac; he later wrote Washington, "of all the errors, of my political life, this has occasioned me the deepest regret" (*ibid.,* VII, 137). But in 1790 his contemporary letters indicate a recognition of its necessity to harmonize the warring states, and an absence of hostility to the measure. See *ibid.,* VI, 47, 53, 76–77, 79–80, 83–84.

[4] Hamilton has recorded that he did not finally become convinced of a combination against him until the session of Congress which began in October 1791. J. C. Hamilton, *op. cit.,* IV, 524.

Hamilton recognized no limits to the extension of his official activity and influence. The War Department fell into his orbit; and foreign policy had such an essential connection with his fiscal and domestic plans that he threw himself into diplomatic negotiations with the same attention he gave to financial operations. Hamilton's friendly biographers as well as his critics acknowledge this trait. Oliver wrote:

it is none the less true, not only that he threw the net of his department as widely as possible over the waters, but that his activity extended and his influence predominated far outside the limits of his own office. Every important proposal brought forward by his colleagues was minuted and reviewed by Hamilton, and it may be added that a large number, if not the majority, of these proposals were offered at his instigation, and were drawn upon lines which he had already sketched out. From the beginning to the end of his official career the cabinet was literally overwhelmed by his wide interest and untiring industry; and although in a short time his insistence provoked a violent resentment in certain quarters, in the main issues his policy prevailed, and the government submitted to the force of his will, whether the various ministers liked it or not.[5]

Hamilton's active intervention in the field of foreign affairs, a field peculiarly Jefferson's, set off an administrative feud that was to dominate the scene from 1791 to 1793.[6] The story of Jefferson's attempts at defense, his attack on Hamilton, Hamilton's counterattack, Washington's intervention, and the ultimate solution by the road of resignation makes a fascinating, if not a happy tale.

JEFFERSON AND THE TREASURY

Beginning in the spring of 1791 and continuing through 1792 one line of attack after another was opened on the Treasury to reduce Hamilton's influence. None succeeded, but their cumulative effect was to destroy Hamilton's capacity to move forward. The first assault was on the departmental level, Jefferson seeking to place his friends in the Treasury Department or to break up the Department itself.

Coxe vs. Wolcott. So far as has been ascertained, Jefferson's first move against Hamilton occurred on April 17, 1791. Nicholas Eveleigh, the Comptroller of the Treasury, died on April 16. Jefferson sought to

---

[5] Frederick S. Oliver, *Alexander Hamilton,* pp. 213–14.
[6] See previous chapter.

secure the appointment of his successor. Neither Jefferson nor Hamilton wasted a moment.

On April 17 Jefferson wrote the President, who was then on his southern trip, enclosing an application from Tench Coxe, Assistant to the Secretary of the Treasury.[7] On the same day, Hamilton wrote Washington recommending Wolcott, then Auditor, and went out of his way to observe that, "I am influenced by information that other characters will be brought to your view by weighty advocates."[8] Immediately on his return to Mount Vernon, Washington acknowledged Hamilton's letter and authorized him to inform Wolcott of the President's intention to appoint the latter as Comptroller.[9]

Jefferson took a bold step in undertaking, without consultation with Hamilton, to forward the appointment of Coxe to the second position in the Treasury Department. He apparently was assured of Coxe's personal loyalty at this early date, although the tie was not generally known until later.[10] Jefferson, however, exposed himself to an almost certain rebuff from the President, whose decision would naturally be governed primarily by the advice of the head of the department concerned. Jefferson also laid bare to Hamilton his intrigue to place his own man in the center of Hamilton's department—a challenge which the Secretary of the Treasury was not likely to overlook.

Pickering vs. Paine. A second occasion of the same sort occurred in the summer of 1791 when Samuel Osgood resigned as Postmaster General. Jefferson and Randolph tried to persuade Washington to appoint Thomas Paine, who was then in France. They knew well what they were doing—as Randolph observed, "It seemed to be a fair opportunity for a declaration of certain sentiments."[11] Washington's action in appointing the unyielding Federalist, Timothy Pickering (on Hamilton's recommendation), was a clear enough answer.[12]

---

[7] Jefferson, *Works* (Federal ed.), VI, 246–47.

[8] Hamilton, *Works* (Lodge ed.), IX, 479–82.

[9] June 13, 1791, Washington, *Writings*, XXXI, 292–93.

[10] In 1795 Hamilton again defeated the appointment of Coxe to the office of Comptroller. Hamilton to Washington, Feb. 12, 1795, Hamilton, *Works* (Hamilton ed.), V, 77–78.

[11] Randolph to Madison, July 21, 1791, J. C. Hamilton, *History,* IV, 515.

[12] J. C. Hamilton probably reflects the conservative opinion of 1791 when he wrote in his *History, loc. cit.,* "Should he [i.e., Paine] be intrusted with the patronage of the Post Office department, pervading the whole country, this channel for the dissemination of insurrectionary opinions would be entirely under Jefferson's command; for, both as to politics and religion, Paine and Jefferson had similar views."

Transfer of the Post Office. Failing in this attempt, Jefferson made a bolder effort in 1792. On February 20, the President approved an act of Congress putting the Post Office on a permanent basis. Jefferson seized the occasion to attempt to persuade the President to transfer the Post Office from Hamilton's domain to his. In two meetings with the President on February 28 and 29 he presented a plan "for doubling the velocity" of the posts. The record of the conversations is revealing of the administrative and political rivalry of Hamilton and Jefferson.[13]

I . . . observed . . . that I had hitherto never spoke to him on the subject of the post office, not knowing whether it was considered as a revenue law, or a law for the general accommodation of the citizens; that the law just passed seemed to have removed the doubt, by declaring that the whole profits of the office should be applied to extending the posts & that even the past profits should be refunded by the treasury for the same purpose: that I therefore conceived it was now in the department of the Secretary of State: that I thought it would be advantageous so to declare it for another reason, to wit, that the department of treasury possessed already such an influence as to swallow up the whole Executive powers, and that even the future Presidents (not supported by the weight of character which himself possessed) would not be able to make head against this department. That in urging this measure I had certainly no personal interest, since, if I was supposed to have any appetite for power, yet as my career would certainly be exactly as short as his own, the intervening time was too short to be an object. My real wish was to avail the public of every occasion during the residue of the President's period, to place things on a safe footing. . . .

Jefferson's request for the Post Office was one to which Washington could not have acceded without disrupting his Cabinet and he naturally followed the rule of not disturbing status quo. There is no record of any formal reply to Jefferson's proposal; it was quietly shelved and perhaps never came to Hamilton's attention. The only response of which there remains a record is an indirect one over six months later when Washington acceded to Jefferson's desire to place the Mint in the State Department. The President added in his letter: "The Post

---

[13] Jefferson's account of his conversations with the President are in the *Anas,* Jefferson, *Works* (Federal ed.), I, 192–98; his plan for postal reform, *ibid.,* VI, 382–83.

Office (as a branch of Revenue) was annexed to the Treasury in the time of Mr. Osgood; and when Colő. Pickering was appointed thereto, he was informed . . . that he was to consider it in that light. . . ." [14]

Jefferson retired from the State Department in possession of the Mint but not of the Post Office. A curious turn was given to his effort to capture the Post Office when Hamilton proposed, a year and a month later when he resigned as Secretary of the Treasury, to exchange it for the Mint. By this time a convinced Federalist was in the State Department; but Hamilton also recognized what Jefferson had privately urged upon Washington earlier, that the Post Office was becoming something other than a revenue office. [15]

Control of the Mint. Whether to assign the Mint to the Treasury as a subordinate fiscal unit, or to the Department of State as the general agency for home affairs was another debatable issue. Congress apparently was undecided; the President turned it over to Jefferson. Washington's letter to Jefferson suggests the opportunistic quality of his decision: "If from relationship, or usage in similar cases . . . the Mint does not appertain to the Department of the Treasury I am more inclined to add it to that of State than to multiply the duties of the other." [16]

In view of the nature of the work of the Mint, Hamilton could hardly have failed to see in this decision a defeat. He suggested in 1795 that the Mint properly belonged in the Treasury, as a "most material link in the money system of the country," but Washington did not disturb the existing arrangement. On this point Jefferson was victor. [17]

Division of the Treasury Department. How far Jefferson was prepared to go to reduce the power of the Treasury Department is revealed by his proposal to Madison in August 1793. Jefferson had already submitted his resignation, and had been told by Washington that

[14] Washington to Jefferson, Oct. 20, 1792, Washington, *Writings,* XXXII, 187.

[15] Hamilton to Washington, Jan. 31, 1795, Hamilton, *Works* (Hamilton ed.), V, 70–72.

[16] Oct. 20, 1792, Washington, *Writings,* XXXII, 187.

[17] A minor but perhaps revealing episode may be added. On June 21, 1791, Hamilton asked Jefferson to require some foreign officer to transmit occasionally a report on foreign currency and rates of exchange. Apparently Jefferson neglected the request, since on Dec. 26, 1792, Hamilton renewed it. See Hamilton, *Works* (Hamilton ed.), IV, 162, 332–33. On March 20, 1793, Washington directed the Secretary of State to secure samples of foreign coins in accordance with the terms of the act regulating them. See Washington, *Writings,* XXXII, 395.

Hamilton also intended to retire.[18] Jefferson now suggested to Madison splitting the Treasury. "It would be the moment for dividing the Treasury between two equal chiefs of the customs and Internal Taxes, if the Senate were not so unsound." [19] Federalist predominance in the upper House precluded success in this direction. In fact, at every point that Jefferson tried to break down the internal cohesion of the Treasury Department, he failed. Meanwhile he was deeply engaged in another series of moves against Hamilton through the House of Representatives—seeking to end the practice of referring matters to heads of departments and to keep Secretaries from the floor of the House; [20] and setting on foot, with Giles and Madison, a hostile investigation of Hamilton's management of funds.[21] The temper of the skirmish is disclosed in Madison's private letter to Jefferson early in 1794 referring to the charges against the Secretary of the Treasury, "His trial is not yet concluded." [22]

Jefferson's Conversations with the President. In private conversations and letters throughout 1792 Jefferson pursued his campaign against Hamilton directly with the President, attacking his fiscal policy and the integrity of some of his supporters in Congress. The record of these meetings is supplied by Jefferson himself. On February 28 and 29, 1792, he had long conferences with Washington in which he protested against the power of the Treasury. He complained about the issuance of paper money by the Bank, more than hinted at corruption among members of the House, and especially warned Washington against subsidies for manufactures, as proposed in Hamilton's Report on Manufactures.[23] In May 1792 he wrote a long letter to the President at Mount Vernon, in which appears the most complete exposition of his charges. He asserted that an artificial debt had been created beyond the power of the country ever to pay, that the excise tax was odious, that the interest rate on government obligations was excessive, that the meager stock of coins would soon be exported, to be replaced by paper money, and that there was a "corrupt squadron" in Congress. He alleged that Hamilton sought to establish a monarchy, and spoke

---

[18] Jefferson, *Works* (Federal ed.), I, 310.
[19] J. C. Hamilton, *History,* V, 341 (Aug. 11, 1793).
[20] See above, ch. vi.
[21] See below, ch. xxviii.
[22] Madison, *Letters* (Congressional ed.), II, 10.
[23] Jefferson, *Works* (Federal ed.), I, 192–98.

darkly about the danger of southern secession.[24] In July he repeated these charges in a private conversation with the President.[25]

In midsummer 1792 Jefferson induced Colonel George Mason of Virginia to lay before Washington similar criticisms of the fiscal policy of the government. The President immediately communicated their substance to Hamilton in a letter of his own, referring to the criticisms as coming from "sensible and moderate men." [26] Hamilton responded with a detailed defense, point by point,[27] and nothing further was heard of them. He was not, however, unaware of the source from which they came.

Later in 1792 Jefferson privately accused Hamilton of having monarchy in contemplation, through the means of a "corps of interested persons who should be steadily at the orders of the Treasury." Washington insisted there were hardly ten men of consequence who supported monarchy, defended the government's fiscal policy, and scouted the existence of a "corrupt squadron" in Congress. At the same time he begged Jefferson not to retire, since he "thought it important to preserve the check of my opinions in the administration in order to keep things in their proper channel & prevent them from going too far." [28]

Attack in the Press. The persistence of Jefferson in seeking to destroy an adversary whose policy he believed fatal was not exhausted by his efforts to divide the Treasury, to weaken Hamilton in the House, or to undermine his standing with the President. He also turned to the press. With his knowledge and approval, Madison arranged to bring Philip Freneau to Philadelphia to start a newspaper.[29] Jefferson appointed Freneau to the position of translating clerk in the State Department and in October 1791, the *National Gazette* made its first appearance. It soon became the vehicle for attacks upon the policy of the government, upon Hamilton, and eventually upon Washington. These attacks were often bitter in their character and deeply irritated Washington.

As early as August 1792, the President referred in a private letter to

---

[24] Jefferson to Washington, May 23, 1792, *ibid.,* VI, 487–95.

[25] *Ibid.,* I, 227–31.

[26] July 29, 1792, Washington, *Writings,* XXXII, 95–100.

[27] Hamilton, *Works* (Lodge ed.), II, 426 ff.

[28] Oct. 1, 1792, Jefferson, *Works* (Federal ed.), I, 233–37.

[29] Lewis Leary, *That Rascal Freneau* (New Brunswick, N. J.: Rutgers University Press, 1941), pp. 186–92.

"the Seeds of discontent, distrust, and irritations which are so plenti-
fully sown. . . ." [30] On May 23, 1793, he could no longer forbear complaining openly to Jefferson, according to whose account "he said he
despised all their attacks on him personally, but that there never had
been an act of the government, not meaning in the Executive line
only, but in any line which that paper had not abused. . . . He was
evidently sore & warm, and I took his intention to be that I should
interpose in some way with Freneau, perhaps withdraw his appointment of translating clerk to my office. But," Jefferson added, "I will
not do it." [31] In short, Jefferson was untiring in his attempts to defeat
Hamilton and to drive him from the government. Until the summer
of 1792 the President chose to ignore their quarrels; but Hamilton was
less restrained in carrying the attack to his opponent.

HAMILTON COUNTERATTACKS

During 1790 and 1791 Hamilton was driving forward his program
of fiscal reconstruction, defending himself in Congress through his
friends in the two Houses, and in Cabinet discussions dominating
both domestic and foreign policy, on the whole supported by the
independent judgment of Washington. It was not until the summer
of 1792 that he openly fought Jefferson in the *Gazette of the United
States.* He was not, however, unaware of what he called "malicious
intrigues to stab me in the dark." [32]

Before noting the papers in the *Gazette,* it is in order to point out
an earlier move by Hamilton to block Jefferson's effort to secure his
designation (as Secretary of State) as successor to the presidency in
case of death or disability of both the President and Vice President.
Debate on the bill to define the succession to the presidency first took
place in the House on January 10 and 13, 1791, with inconclusive
results. The Federalist leaders proposed the Chief Justice of the
Supreme Court; Madison and others stood for the Secretary of State. [33]
The discussion was resumed by the next Congress; the Senate passed
a bill devolving the succession upon the President of the Senate, pro
tempore, and then the Speaker of the House. Jefferson's friends again

[30] Washington, *Writings,* XXXII, 136.
[31] Jefferson, *Works* (Federal ed.), I, 274.
[32] Hamilton to Jay, Dec. 18, 1792, Hamilton, *Works* (Lodge ed.), X, 29–30.
[33] *Annals,* II, 1853–56, 1862–65.

fought for the Secretary of State. By the close margin of 27 to 24 the Federalists prevailed, although the vote can hardly yet be called a party division.[34] The debate was renewed on February 9 and 10, 1792, and this time the House acted in favor of the Secretary of State.[35] But the Senate refused to budge from its preference and on February 21 the House receded.[36] Jefferson lost.

Hamilton's share in Jefferson's defeat was subsequently avowed by him in his letter to Edward Carrington. "You know," he wrote, "how much it was a point to establish the Secretary of State, as the officer who was to administer the Government in defect of the President and Vice-President. Here, I acknowledge, though I took far less part than was supposed, I ran counter to Mr. Jefferson's wishes; but if I had had no other reason for it, I had already experienced opposition from him, which rendered it a measure of self-defence." [37] Jefferson was doubtless fully aware of the opposition of the Secretary of the Treasury.

In the face of the attacks by Freneau in the *National Gazette* Hamilton was less restrained than Washington. In a series of letters to the *Gazette of the United States* beginning in July and ending in December 1792,[38] he charged Jefferson with initial opposition to the Constitution, with opposition to almost all the important measures of the administration, especially the provisions concerning the debt, public credit, and the Bank of the United States, with a desire to depress the national authority, with a willingness to pay French debts at the expense of the Dutch, with the clandestine circulation of "foul and pestilent whispers," and with exhibiting a "caballing, self-sufficient, and refractory temper," as well as with the sponsorship of Freneau. Hamilton asserted openly that his objective was to expose "a public officer who is too little scrupled to embarrass and disparage the government of which he is a member. . . ." [39] The country was treated to the extraordinary spectacle of the Secretary of the Treasury openly attacking the Secretary of State in the newspapers, while a translating clerk in the Department of State castigated the Secretary of the Treasury.

---

[34] *Ibid.*, III, 280–82, 302.
[35] *Ibid.*, III, 403.
[36] *Ibid.*, III, 417; the vote to recede was 31 to 24; the act is printed in 1 Stat. 239.
[37] Hamilton, *Works* (Lodge ed.), IV, 530–31.
[38] *Ibid.*, VII, 229–303.
[39] *Ibid.*, VII, 242.

THE PRESIDENT INTERVENES

For the most part Washington had ignored the controversy in his official family, but this unseemly publicity forced him to take cognizance of the deep rift which had developed. From the relative peace of Mount Vernon he wrote Jefferson on August 23, 1792:

How unfortunate, and how much it is to be regretted then, that whilst we are encompassed on all sides with avowed enemies and insidious friends, that internal dissensions should be harrowing and tearing our vitals. The last, to me, is the most serious, the most alarming, and the most afflicting of the two. And without more charity for the opinions and acts of one another in Governmental matters, or some more infalible criterion by which the truth of speculative opinions, before they have undergone the test of experience, are to be forejudged than has yet fallen to the lot of fallibility, I believe it will be difficult, if not impracticable, to manage the Reins of Government or to keep the parts of it together: for if, instead of laying our shoulders to the machine after measures are decided on, one pulls this way and another that, before the utility of the thing is fairly tried, it must, inevitably, be torn asunder. And, in my opinion the fairest prospect of happiness and prosperity that ever was presented to man, will be lost, perhaps for ever!

My earnest wish, and my fondest hope therefore is, that instead of wounding suspicions, and irritable charges, there may be liberal allowances, mutual forbearances, and temporising yieldings on *all sides*. Under the exercise of these, matters will go on smoothly, and, if possible, more prosperously. Without them every thing must rub; the Wheels of Government will clog; our enemies will triumph, and by throwing their weight into the disaffected Scale, may accomplish the ruin of the goodly fabric we have been erecting.[40]

Three days later he followed this appeal with a similar letter to Hamilton,[41] and on September 9, both Secretaries responded at length, in terms which must have caused Washington to despair of reconciliation. While Hamilton offered to embrace any opportunity to heal or terminate the differences which existed, he declared that he was "the deeply injured party," declined to recede for the present from

---

[40] Washington, *Writings,* XXXII, 130–31.
[41] Aug. 26, 1792, *ibid.,* XXXII, 132–34.

the "retaliations which have fallen upon certain public characters," and asserted that he had been "an object of uniform opposition from Mr. Jefferson . . . [and] the frequent subject of the most unkind whispers and insinuations. . . ." He declared Jefferson was bent upon his subversion and the subversion of the government.[42]

In a lengthy reply Jefferson acknowledged that he utterly disapproved of the system of the Secretary of the Treasury, which he believed was calculated to undermine the republic by corrupting the legislative branch and making it docile to the Treasury. He asserted, with truth, that Hamilton had forced acceptance of his views concerning France and England which, Jefferson said, were not only "exactly the reverse" of his own but "inconsistent with the honor & interest of our country." He pointedly asked "which of us has . . . stepped farthest into the controul of the department of the other?" He did not conceal that he knew Hamilton was the author of the papers in the *Gazette of the United States,* and defended himself against Hamilton's charges, denying especially that he influenced, "directly or indirectly," the opinions expressed in Freneau's *National Gazette.* He allowed, however, that he took for granted that Freneau would give "free place to pieces written against the aristocratical & monarchical principles," although he urged Washington to believe that he did not expect "any criticisms on the proceedings of government." As to his course of action, he took note of his intention to retire after the fall elections (1792) and meanwhile to refrain from newspaper controversy until he became a private citizen.[43]

Despite this unpromising exchange of letters Washington persisted in his efforts to restore unity among his advisers. Jefferson recorded on February 7, 1793, that the President informed him privately that he had proposed a "coalescence" and that Hamilton had expressed his willingness.[44] When the President and Jefferson met on October 1, 1792, at the breakfast table of Mount Vernon, Washington sought to mediate between his Cabinet members. Jefferson was obdurate in his accusations and Washington finished the conversation with "another exhortation" against Jefferson's threatened retirement.[45] After

---

[42] Hamilton, *Works* (Lodge ed.), VII, 303–6.

[43] Jefferson, *Works* (Federal ed.), VII, 136–49.

[44] *Ibid.,* I, 251; no record of the proposal remains among the papers of either Washington or Hamilton.

[45] *Ibid.,* I, 233–37.

reaching Philadelphia he sent Washington letters to clear up his record concerning the Constitution. In reply Washington expressed his "sincere esteem and regard for you both," and asked plaintively why "shd. either of you be so tenacious of your opinions," and repeated his ardent "wish that some line could be marked out by which both of you could walk." [46]

No such line could be found.

RESIGNATIONS

How difficult Washington's task was can be appreciated by the views which Hamilton and Jefferson held of each other. Both left considered judgments, as well as less considered criticisms. Jefferson summed up his final estimate of Hamilton in these words.

Hamilton was indeed a singular character. Of acute understanding, disinterested, honest, and honorable in all· private transactions, amiable in society, and duly valuing virtue in private life, yet so bewitched & perverted by the British example, as to be under thoro' conviction that corruption was essential to the government of a nation. . . .[47]

Hamilton's mature views about Jefferson are contained in letters written at the height of the contested election of 1800, when no one could be certain whether Burr or Jefferson would become President.[48] He wrote Gouverneur Morris, "If there be a man in the world I ought to hate, it is Jefferson." [49] To James A. Bayard he wrote a long estimate of the character of his political enemy.

Perhaps, myself the first, at some expense of popularity, to unfold the true character of Jefferson, it is too late for me to become his apologist. Nor can I have any disposition to do it.

---

[46] Oct. 18, 1792, Washington, *Writings*, XXXII, 185–86.

[47] Jefferson, *Works* (Federal ed.), I, 180.

[48] In 1792 he wrote C. C. Pinckney these words about his rival. "That gentleman [Jefferson], whom I once *very much esteemed,* but who does not permit me to retain that sentiment for him, is certainly a man of sublimated and paradoxical imagination, entertaining and propagating opinions inconsistent with dignified and orderly government." Hamilton, *Works* (Hamilton ed.), V, 533.

[49] *Ibid.,* VI, 499.

I admit that his politics are tinctured with fanaticism; that he is too much in earnest in his democracy; that he has been a mischievous enemy to the principal measures of our past administration; that he is crafty and per-severing in his objects; that he is not scrupulous about the means of success, nor very mindful of truth, and that he is a contemptible hypocrite. But, it is not true, as is alleged, that he is an enemy to the power of the Executive, or that he is for confounding all the powers in the House of Representatives. It is a fact, which I have frequently mentioned, that, while we were in the administration together, he was generally for a large construction of the Executive authority, and not backward to act upon it in cases which coin-cided with his views. Let it be added, that in his theoretic ideas, he has considered as improper the participations of the Senate in the Executive authority. I have more than once made the reflection, that viewing himself as the reversioner, he was solicitous to come into the possession of a good estate. Nor is it true, that Jefferson is zealot enough to do any thing in pursuance of his principles, which will contravene his popularity or his interest. He is as likely as any man I know, to temporize; to calculate what will be likely to promote his own reputation and advantage, and the prob-able result of such a temper is the preservation of systems, though originally opposed, which being once established, could not be overturned without danger to the person who did it. To my mind, a true estimate of Mr. Jefferson's character warrants the expectation of a temporizing, rather than a violent system. That Jefferson has manifested a culpable predilection for France, is certainly true; but I think it a question, whether it did not pro-ceed quite as much from her *popularity* among us as from sentiment; and in proportion as that popularity is diminished, his zeal will cool. Add to this, that there is no fair reason to suppose him capable of being corrupted, which is a security that he will not go beyond certain limits. . . .[50]

The denouement was not long delayed. The newspaper battle came to an end at the close of 1792; the assault on Hamilton in the House of Representatives opened at once and came to a head in the decisive vote on the Giles resolutions in February 1793. On April 19, 1793, was reached the crucial decision on foreign policy in favor of neutral-ity between France and Great Britain—a defeat for Jefferson in his own field. Hamilton, pursuing Washington's policy, practically took over the Department of State so far as its major moves were concerned. On July 31, 1793, Jefferson handed in his resignation, and in Septem-

[50] *Ibid.*, VI, 419–20 (Jan. 16, 1800).

ber left for Monticello, returning for a few weeks in the autumn.[51]
His resignation became effective on December 31, 1793. On New
Year's eve he must have brooded over an unhappy sequence of frustra-
tion and defeat.

---

[51] The terms on which Jefferson stayed through the autumn of 1793 are set out in
his letter to Madison: "The arrangement on which I had consented to remain another
quarter was that the President was to be absent three weeks, and after that I was to be
absent 6. weeks. This got me rid of 9. weeks of the 13. and the remaining 4. Congress
would be setting. My view in this was precisely to avoid being at any more councils as
much as possible, that I might not be committed in anything further." Sept. 15, 1793,
Works (Federal ed.), VIII, 48.

Chapter Twenty

THE HAMILTON–ADAMS CONFLICT

JOHN ADAMS became the second President of the United States on March 4, 1797, after a long career in the public service as diplomat and Vice President. Since 1789 he had been in a position to know intimately the course of domestic and foreign policy, as well as the personal, political, and institutional disputes that had developed during Washington's administration. As a leading Federalist he had observed the conflict between Jefferson and Hamilton, and it must be assumed knew well the dominant position of the latter in the councils of their common party. He probably knew less than we do today of the stream of correspondence which after February 1795 continued to connect Hamilton with public affairs.

The controversies within Adams' Cabinet, its disruption in 1800, and Adams' defeat by Jefferson were precipitated in large measure by Hamilton's determination to guide the policy of the government, although not one of its members. Adams' position was shaken, but the outcome was a resounding affirmation of the authority of the President as chief executive and of the subordination of the department heads to his leadership and direction. Adams confirmed the character of the presidency as the Constitutional Convention had outlined it and as Washington had already formed it—but only after events which stirred grave doubts concerning its future.

HAMILTON AND THE CABINET

The cross currents that developed in Adams' Cabinet can only be understood by recognizing Hamilton's relation to the government subsequent to his retirement as Secretary of the Treasury at the end of January 1795. His interest in public affairs and his concern for sound policy, domestic and foreign, were no less as a private lawyer in New York than they had been as Secretary of the Treasury in Philadelphia.[1] He remained the dynamic center of the Federalist party to whom President Washington, members of the Cabinet, ministers stationed abroad, Senators and Representatives alike turned for advice. In the midst of a successful professional career, he kept his hands on the business of state.

This extraordinary activity was to continue into Adams' administration, when it progressively developed an impossible administrative situation within the Cabinet. Following his resignation from the Treasury, Hamilton remained in Philadelphia a fortnight, in frequent consultation with the President.[2] He then withdrew to New York, and not until the following summer did the correspondence between him and Washington begin—at the President's initiative.[3] It remained lively throughout the remainder of Washington's term. The tenor of the communications between the President and his former Secretary of the Treasury is well revealed in a quotation from one of Washington's letters: "Altho' you are not in the Administration, a thing I sincerely regret, I must, nevertheless, (knowing how intimately acquainted you are with all the concerns of this country) request the favor of you. . . ."[4]

Hamilton also maintained a steady correspondence with members of the Cabinet, who sent their hard problems to New York for solution. In reply to Oliver Wolcott, Hamilton wrote a long letter on April 10, 1795, on fiscal matters, proposing in detail provisions for meeting payments on the public debt, and concluding, "Write me as freely as you please."[5] Wolcott embraced this invitation, asking guidance from his former chief on most matters of fiscal importance. Thus on June 18, 1795, he propounded seven questions concerning payment of the domestic debt; Hamilton answered in part on June 22, but on July 28

---

[1] His son remarked, "his interest in public affairs was predominant. He felt that he belonged to the nation." John C. Hamilton, *History of the Republic of the United States*, VI, 253.

[2] *Ibid.*, VI, 213.

[3] There is an unusually revealing passage in a letter from Hamilton to Wolcott, April 10, 1795: "I send a letter to the Attorney-General which you will read, seal, and deliver. You will easily divine my reason for addressing it to him. *The President ought to view this matter as it is, but I do not write to him because I do not wish to appear officious.*" Italics author's. Hamilton, *Works* (Hamilton ed.), V, 630.

[4] Aug. 31, 1795, Washington, *Writings*, XXXIV, 296.

[5] Hamilton, *Works* (Hamilton ed.), V, 626–30.

Wolcott had to write again, "Will you reply briefly to a few questions I lately stated? I care not how briefly. Your ideas upon a system projected essentially by you, will enable me to proceed with less hesitation." [6] In short Hamilton contributed on fiscal policy at every important juncture.

In foreign affairs the ratification of the Jay Treaty, the demand of the House of Representatives for the papers relevant to the treaty, British seizures of American vessels, the increasing hostility of France, and the prospect of a French war filled the two years from 1795 to 1797 with disturbing problems. Wolcott became Hamilton's chief means of exerting his influence in Cabinet discussions in this field.[7] Randolph did not correspond with Hamilton except rarely, but there is some evidence that Hamilton got his views before the Secretary of State through an intermediary.[8] On every major issue of foreign policy Washington and one or more Cabinet members asked for Hamilton's advice.

Beyond the field of finance and foreign affairs Hamilton's opinion was requested on a variety of topics. Thus in November 1795, Timothy Pickering, then acting Secretary of State as well as Secretary of War, asked Hamilton's aid in selecting a Secretary of War. ". . . will you have the goodness to express your mind? Will you consider the whole list? Will you indulge me with your sentiments on all the subjects of this letter?" [9] In December 1795, Senator Rufus King asked Hamilton's opinion on the confirmation of John Rutledge to the Supreme Court.[10] In April 1796, Hamilton wrote King on congressional strategy in the event the House refused to implement the Jay Treaty.[11] In June he wrote James McHenry to advise Pickering to dismiss an American consul in France who had become *persona non grata*.[12] In December Wolcott asked Hamilton to become an intermediary with the Bank of New York.[13]

---

[6] *Ibid.,* VI, 7, 9, 24.

[7] Wolcott to Hamilton, July 20, 1795, *ibid.,* VI, 20: "I have received your several letters, dated June 22d, 26th, 30th, and the 2d current."

[8] William Bradford to Hamilton, May 21, 1795, *ibid.,* VI, 1, "I showed your letter to the Secretary of State. . . ."

[9] Nov. 17, 1795, *ibid.,* VI, 68–69.

[10] Hamilton to King, Dec. 14, 1795, *ibid.,* VI, 76–77.

[11] April 15, 1796, *ibid.,* VI, 103–5.

[12] June 1, 1796, *ibid.,* VI, 127–28.

[13] Dec. 8, 1796, *ibid.,* VI, 176.

When John Adams became President he continued Washington's
Cabinet. Two members had been Hamilton's subordinates; the third
was a close friend who early formed the habit of relying heavily
upon the superior talents of his mentor. The Attorney General, Charles
Lee, was a man of only moderate ability and force. The first Secretary
of the Navy, Benjamin Stoddert, taking office in 1798, was an Adams
man. Apart from Lee and Stoddert, the Cabinet members had formed
the well-established habit of consulting on public affairs with Hamilton; and the issue arose whether this habit would continue.

That it could continue with the knowledge of Adams was unlikely.
He had a strong sense of personal dignity, coupled with a quick sensitivity to injury and a hasty temper. Moreover he had been elected by
only three votes—a Pyrrhic victory which rankled for a long time.
Furthermore he doubted the loyalty of some leading members of the
Federalist party whom he believed had been in favor of the election
of Thomas Pinckney in 1796. While his relations with Hamilton had
not been marred by friction, he had heard that Hamilton preferred
Pinckney; and a suspicion of rivalry in settling the policy of his government would have been an immediate occasion for a rupture. Adams
distrusted the strong pro-British inclination of Hamilton, which, opposed to Jefferson's friendship for France, he feared would disrupt the
country. Indeed at the very outset of his administration he imagined
Hamilton would be his rival in 1800 as the presidential candidate of
the Federalist party.[14]

Despite these risks, the dependence of Wolcott, Pickering, and
McHenry upon the advice of Hamilton increased after March 4, 1797,
rather than diminished.[15] Hamilton himself tended to become more

---

[14] *Letters of John Adams Addressed to his Wife,* March 17, 1797, II, 252. The cycle
of Adams' views on Hamilton appears in three excerpts from letters: (1) Adams to
John Trumbull, Jan. 23, 1791 (Adams, *Works,* IX, 573), "The Secretary of the Treas-
ury is all that you think him. There is no office in the government better filled." (2)
Adams' Diary, Aug. 11, 1796 (*ibid.,* III, 423). "He said they wanted Hamilton for
Vice-President. I was wholly silent." (3) Wolcott to Fisher Ames, Dec. 29, 1799 (Gibbs,
Memoirs, II, 315), "his resentments against General Hamilton are excessive."

[15] The steady stream of correspondence between Hamilton and the department heads
in Adams' time is printed in volume six of the John C. Hamilton edition of the *Works
of Alexander Hamilton.* By way of example, Hamilton wrote to Pickering on March
22, 1797, to offer a detailed plan of action on the French crisis (*ibid.,* VI, 213); to
Wolcott on March 30 on the same subject (*ibid.,* VI, 218); on April 5 to Wolcott to
advise him to bend his feelings to a "pliancy to circumstances" (*ibid.,* VI, 229); on
April 13 to object to the Treasury policy of detaining armed vessels (*ibid.,* VI, 238);

imperious, as he faced Adams instead of Washington. The Cabinet members fell out of sympathy with Adams' policy, as did a substantial wing of Federalist leaders. All turned to Hamilton for guidance, and gradually there emerged an extraordinary situation in which the control of public policy became the prize of a struggle between a New York lawyer and a President who apparently was not fully aware of the activity of his rival.

The situation was rendered more serious by reason of Adams' long absences from the seat of government to which reference has already been made. Although he believed he could manage the affairs of the United States as well in Quincy, Massachusetts, as in Philadelphia, there resulted a loss of leadership and executive impulse.

Adams was, to be sure, prompt in answering communications from his Secretaries; mail went back and forth on every post; and while four days were required each way, usually a minimum of nine days for a round trip, this delay was not considered unusual in the last years of the eighteenth century. In 1799 he wrote from Quincy:

"The people elected me to administer the government," it is true, and I do administer it here at Quincy, as really as I could do at Philadelphia. The Secretaries of State, Treasury, War, Navy, and the Attorney-General, transmit me daily by the post all the business of consequence, and nothing is done without my advice and direction, when I am here, more than when I am in the same city with them. The post goes very rapidly, and I answer by the return of it, so that nothing suffers or is lost.[16]

It was only a month earlier that Wolcott had written to Hamilton, "We have no President here, and the appearances of languor and indecision are discouraging to the friends of government." [17]

Three episodes revealed the administrative disharmony that developed from 1797 to 1800—all concerned with our relations with France: the dispatch of the first mission to Paris in 1797 in an effort to seek an accommodation; the determination of Hamilton's military

---

to Wolcott on April 22 on the nomination for the New York collectorship, Gaillard Hunt, "Office-Seeking during the Administration of John Adams," *Am. Hist. Rev.*, II (1897), 245. On June 9, 1798, Pickering wrote Hamilton, "I wish you were in a situation not only 'to see all the cards,' but to play them. With all my soul I would give you my *hand*, and engage in any other *game*, in which I might best co-operate on the same side, *to win the stakes*." *Works* (Hamilton ed.), VI, 307.

[16] Adams to Uriah Forrest, May 13, 1799, Adams, *Works*, VIII, 645–46.

[17] April 1, 1799, Hamilton, *Works* (Hamilton ed.), VI, 406.

rank in the army which was organized in 1798 when the mission failed; and the nomination of William Vans Murray and the dispatch of the second mission to France in 1799.

THE FIRST MISSION TO FRANCE

Washington had recalled the minister plenipotentiary at Paris, James Monroe, in August 1796 and Charles Cotesworth Pinckney had been sent in his place. Pinckney arrived in December 1796, was refused recognition, and eventually was required to withdraw from the country. The news of his hostile reception reached Philadelphia in the early winter of 1797. Hamilton began to consider the next step and on January 22, 1797, wrote Washington favoring an extraordinary mission "under some shape or other." [18] The impending inauguration of Adams turned Hamilton's attention to the means of guiding the new President's decision. The resulting correspondence illustrates well Hamilton's methods. In February he wrote Theodore Sedgwick, a Federalist Senator and a close friend who had access to Adams, "Were I Mr. Adams, then I believe I should begin my Presidency by naming an extraordinary commission to the French republic." [19] Shortly after the inauguration he wrote Pickering to urge such a commission to include Pinckney (still abroad), Cabot, and either Madison or Jefferson. [20] In this letter occurs a significant sentence: "The share I have had in the public administration added to my interest as a citizen, make me extremely anxious that at this delicate crisis a course of conduct exactly proper may be adopted." [21]

Meanwhile Adams had been reaching the same conclusion. Whether

---

[18] *Ibid.,* VI, 194.

[19] Feb. 26, 1797, *ibid.,* VI, 209.

[20] March 22, 1797, *ibid.,* VI, 213–15.

[21] Correspondence between Hamilton and Wolcott produced this illuminating letter from Wolcott to his mentor: "To you I will say, but in the most perfect confidence, that the President had determined on instituting a commission, *but it would not have been composed as you now propose.* I believe no one of the heads of departments knows of the decision except myself. I had attributed it to Mr. Ames, from a casual expression, and I own, that by means of my most sincere and urgent expostulations— nay, supplications—it was postponed. . . .

You know that I am accustomed to respect your opinions; and I am not so ignorant of the extent of your influence upon the friends of government, as not to be sensible, that if you are known to favor the sending of a commission, so the thing must and will be. . . ." March 31, 1797, *ibid.,* VI, 221, 224.

he formed his plan as a result of Sedgwick's intervention, arising from Hamilton's prompting, is not possible to determine.[22] On May 31, 1797, Adams nominated C. C. Pinckney, Francis Dana, and John Marshall as envoys extraordinary and ministers plenipotentiary. On June 6, Hamilton wrote Wolcott, "I like very well the course of Executive conduct in regard to the controversy with France." [23] In his edition of the *Works of John Adams,* Charles Francis Adams comments, "But for this accidental coincidence in the views of the President and Mr. Hamilton, it is not unlikely that the breach would have commenced at this moment, so little did the ministers feel under any obligation to sympathise with the responsible head of the administration." [24] Hamilton certainly was intent on securing a "course of conduct exactly proper," and spared no pains to bring the members of the Cabinet and Federalists in Congress to accept his views.

THE ISSUE OF HAMILTON'S MILITARY RANK

The failure of the mission to France undertaken by Pinckney, Marshall, and Gerry (who had replaced Dana) so strained relations that cautious observers like John Jay fully expected war between France and the United States to break out as soon as French hostilities with Great Britain ceased. Congress authorized a provisional army on May 28, 1798, and on June 22 empowered the President to appoint commissioned officers for an army of 10,000 men.[25] On the same day Adams wrote Washington, "We must have your name," and on July 2, without further consultation, nominated him as lieutenant general and commander in chief. The Senate immediately confirmed the nomination and the Secretary of War was dispatched to Mount Vernon to de-

---

[22] Adams fully trusted the loyalty of his Cabinet at this time. The suspicious Gerry had written him that Hamilton was conspiring against him; Adams replied that, "Pickering and all his colleagues are as much attached to me as I desire. I have no jealousies from that quarter," and cleared Hamilton of any intrigue. Adams, *Works,* VIII, 520–25, at 523 (Feb. 1797).

[23] Hamilton, *Works* (Hamilton ed.), VI, 253.

[24] Adams, *Works,* VIII, 542, n.

[25] Adams was not convinced of the necessity of a large army. "The Army was none of my Work. I only advised a few Companies of Artillery to garrison our most exposed forts. . . . Hamilton's Project of an Army of fifty thousand Men, ten thousand of them to be horse, appeared to me proper only for Bedlam." Adams to Benjamin Rush, Aug. 23, 1805, Alexander Biddle, ed., *Old Family Letters,* Series A (Philadelphia: J. B. Lippincott, 1892), p. 76.

liver the commission and to consult on the arrangements for organizing the army.

Well before these events, Hamilton had determined to become
second in command under Washington or, if the latter should decline,
commander in chief. As early as May 19, 1798, he had written Washington, "in the event of an open rupture with France, the public
voice will again call you to command the armies of your country";
to which Washington replied, asking whether in this case he could
count on Hamilton's aid.[26] Hamilton took immediate advantage of
the opening to state that if he were invited to a station proportionate
to the sacrifice he would make, he would be willing to enter the army,
and named the post of inspector general as the one he would accept.
He added, significantly, that he took it for granted, "that your choice
would regulate the Executive." [27]

Equally early it was evident that Adams had no intention of appointing Hamilton to any such high command. The matter was broached
to him without delay by Pickering and the response was so unpromising that on June 6, 1798, Pickering privately wrote Washington,
"From the conversation that I and others have had with the President,
there appears to us to be a disinclination to appoint Colo. Hamilton in
what we think is his proper station, and that alone in which we
suppose he will serve: the *Second* to You; and *Chief* in your absence. . . ." [28]

Washington had given Adams explicit and repeated notice of his
willingness to serve as commander in chief only if he could have
"coadjutors" in whom he had "entire confidence." He fully recognized
the President's final authority to nominate, but also insisted upon the
President's nominating to the general staff only persons who had
Washington's previous approval.[29] At the first moment he sent to
Adams his suggestions for general staff officers, transmitting them
personally by McHenry. At the head of the list were three major
generals in the order of Hamilton (as inspector general), C. C.
Pinckney, and Henry Knox or alternatively Henry Lee.

---

[26] Hamilton, *Works* (Hamilton ed.), VI, 289–93.

[27] June 2, 1798, *ibid.,* VI, 293–94. Hamilton apparently never addressed Adams on
the question of his appointment or his rank, if appointed.

[28] Washington, *Writings,* XXXVI, 324, n. 96.

[29] Washington to McHenry, July 4, 1798, *ibid.,* XXXVI, 304–12; Washington to
Adams, July 4, *ibid.,* XXXVI, 312–15; Washington to McHenry, July 5, *ibid.,* XXXVI,
318–20; McHenry to Adams, July 12, Adams, *Works,* VIII, 574, n. 1.

In a letter to Washington full of hurt feelings and breathing indignation, General Knox absolutely refused to serve under Hamilton [30] and proceeded to visit Adams at his country home in Quincy. Unfortunately no record of what was doubtless a stormy interview has been preserved. On August 14, 1798, however, Adams wrote McHenry that in his opinion Knox was legally entitled to seniority, and that Pinckney preceded Hamilton thus placing him third. That Adams was emotionally stirred is apparent from one sentence in an otherwise dispassionate letter: "You may depend upon it, the five New England States will not patiently submit to the humiliation that has been meditated for them." [31]

There followed during the next six weeks an agitated exchange of letters among those concerned, leaving Adams adamant, Hamilton immovable, and Washington on the point of resignation. The top command of the Provisional Army seemed about to disintegrate before it was even fully formed.

The Cabinet determined to make one final effort to persuade the absent President to consent to Washington's recommendations. Pickering, Wolcott, and Stoddert agreed to make a "respectful representation" to Adams,[32] but eventually they agreed to have Wolcott alone take the lead. The Secretary of the Treasury wrote a temperate letter recapitulating the events of the long-drawn-out controversy, and emphasizing the desirability of acceding to Washington's wishes.[33]

This letter apparently shook Adams from his earlier determination to date Knox's commission one day earlier than Pinckney's, and two days earlier than Hamilton's—thus fixing beyond recall their relative rank. On September 30, probably the day he received Wolcott's letter, he sent a "curt note" to McHenry—"Sir: Inclosed are the Commissions for the three Generals Signed and all dated on the Same Day." [34] This "settlement" settled nothing and Adams gave no suggestion to

---

[30] Washington to Knox, July 16, 1798, Washington, *Writings*, XXXVI, 345–47; Knox to Washington, July 29, *ibid.*, XXXVI, 347–49, n. 15; Washington to Knox, Aug. 9, *ibid.*, XXXVI, 396–401.

[31] Adams, *Works*, VIII, 580.

[32] McHenry to Hamilton, Sept. 10, 1798, Hamilton, *Works* (Hamilton ed.), VI, 356.

[33] Wolcott to Adams, Sept. 17, 1798, Gibbs, *op. cit.*, II, 93–99. Adams apparently never replied to this letter, but prepared a rough draft which is printed in his *Works*, VIII, 601–4, n.

[34] Steiner, *McHenry*, p. 341.

the Secretary of War as to what he believed would be the consequences of his abrupt decision.

Meanwhile Washington also was taking steps to end what had become for him an intolerable situation. On September 25, 1798, he dispatched a strong letter to the President, restating the conditions on which he had agreed to accept the nomination as commander in chief, complaining that these conditions had not been observed, and concluding by asking point-blank, "to be informed whether your determination to reverse the order of the three Major Generals is final, and whether you mean to appoint another Adjutant General without my concurrence." [35] Adams was not given an explicit intimation of Washington's intention to resign, but the tone of the letter was sufficiently uncompromising to permit deductions to be drawn.

This demand from the first President of the United States upon his successor forced a full capitulation. Fortunately a bridge still remained over which Adams could cross without too obvious a loss of position, but whether he intended to withdraw over it on September 30 when he signed the commissions is uncertain, despite his later assurances.

In any event, Adams' reply of October 9 to Washington gave all necessary assurances. Explaining that he dated the commissions on the same day, hoping that an amicable adjustment would take place, he continued, "But, if these hopes should be disappointed and controversies should arise, they will, of course, be submitted to you as Commander-in-chief, and if, after all, any one should be so obstinate as to appeal to me from the judgment of the Commander-in-chief, I was determined to confirm that judgment." [36] Thus the struggle between Hamilton and Adams came to an end—in a defeat for Adams which could only have been accepted as a humiliating experience by a high-tempered and strong-willed President. The defeat was not forgotten.[37]

While this episode throws light on Hamilton's character—in which ambition, an unquenchable passion to take part in great events, and

---

[35] Washington, *Writings*, XXXVI, 453–62.

[36] Adams, *Works*, VIII, 600–1.

[37] Adams sent this dry comment to Stoddert: "There are two principles which produce a tenaciousness of rank. One is a sense of honor and consciousness of dignity, which cannot bear disgrace or degradation; the other is a selfish vanity and aspiring ambition, which is desirous of rising at any rate, and leaping over the heads of all others who are higher." July 23, 1799, *ibid.*, VIII, 671.

a deep devotion to public ends were inextricably confused—and on Adams' stubborn determination not to play Hamilton's game, it is chiefly significant because it illustrates how a struggle for political and military leadership disrupted the normal official obligations of Cabinet officers to their superior, the President. Pickering, Wolcott, and McHenry, all were driven into an equivocal position, caught between their duty to carry out the directions of the President (about which there could be no doubt) and their personal and political loyalty to the principal personality of the Federalist party, who disputed the correctness of the President's judgment—in a case involving his own military ambitions.

THE SECOND FRENCH MISSION

The effort to improve relations with France which was undertaken by Pinckney, Gerry, and Marshall had come to a fruitless end in March 1798. In May the X.Y.Z. papers were made public and a great wave of indignation swept the country, epitomized by President Adams' ringing declaration to Congress on June 21, 1798, that he would never send another minister to France without assurances that he would be received as the representative "of a great, free, powerful, and independent nation." [38] Preparations were made for war with France.

Congress reconvened in December 1798. In his annual message Adams held out the possibility of resumption of negotiations while urging continued preparation for war.[39] Meanwhile the French government made known its willingness to receive an American minister on Adams' terms. On February 18, 1799, without previous consultation with the Secretary of State or the Cabinet, he nominated William Vans Murray, then minister at The Hague, as minister plenipotentiary to the French Republic.

The reception of this nomination was governed by political views. The Jeffersonians were jubilant; the Federalists were outraged. Sedgwick wrote Hamilton the news. Hamilton, too, was upset but quickly collected himself and advised Sedgwick what course to take.

The step announced in your letter just received, in all its circumstances, would astonish, if any thing from that quarter could astonish.

---

[38] Richardson, *Messages,* I, 266.
[39] *Ibid.,* I, 273.

But as it has happened, my present impression is, that the measure must go into effect with the additional idea of a Commission of Three.

The mode must be accommodated with the President. *Murray* is certainly not strong enough for so immensely important a mission.[40]

This letter left New York on Thursday, February 21, 1799, and presumably was delivered on Saturday. That evening the committee of Senators to whom the nomination had been referred waited upon the President to propose Hamilton's line of action. Adams declined to receive them as a committee, and as individual senators only with the understanding that the conference should not be mentioned in the committee report or taken as a precedent.[41] He insisted upon a decision by the Senate but intimated that if Murray were rejected he would then appoint a commission of three. The Federalists thereupon agreed to reject Murray; Adams got wind of this decision and sent word privately to Sedgwick to postpone the committee report. On Monday, February 25, he sent to the Senate the names of Oliver Ellsworth, Patrick Henry, and Murray as a commission to treat with France, in lieu of Murray. They were confirmed on February 27, 1799.

Many years later Adams explained his decision to nominate Murray in terms which revealed the breach that had developed between the Cabinet and the President.

In the case now in question I perfectly knew the sentiments of all my ministers. I knew every argument they could allege, and moreover, I knew the secret motives that governed them better than they did themselves. . . .

I knew that if I called the heads of departments together and asked their advice, three of them would very laconically protest against the measure. The other two would be loath to dissent from their brethren, and would more modestly and mildly concur with them. The consequence would be, that the whole would be instantaneously communicated to A, B, C, D, E, F, &c., in the Senate, and G, H, I, &c., in the House of Representatives; the public and the presses would have it at once, and a clamor raised and a prejudice propagated against the measure, that would probably excite the Senate to put their negative on the whole plan. If I

---

[40] Hamilton, *Works* (Hamilton ed.), VI, 397.
[41] There are two accounts of this meeting, a contemporary one by Sedgwick (*ibid.,* VI, 399–400) and a later one by Pickering (Upham, *Timothy Pickering,* III, 439–42).

had called the heads of department together, and asked their advice, I knew from past experience that their answers would have been flat negatives. . . .[42]

After further attempts by Pickering, Wolcott, and McHenry to postpone the sailing of the second mission, the President made a peremptory decision to dispatch the envoys forthwith. This decision blasted hopes for more delay, and enraged that wing of the Federalist party which had been disregarded in the nomination of Murray the preceding February.[43] Adams did not consult his Cabinet to secure their views on the expediency of launching the mission at this juncture because he knew that three Secretaries believed the mission "impolitic and unwise," to use McHenry's words,[44] and because his mind was "made up" and "unchangeable," to quote Adams.[45] The Secretaries, nevertheless, were perturbed because they had no opportunity to express their views; and the gap between them and the President was substantially widened.[46]

Hamilton was apparently not active in the attempt to delay the departure of the envoys. He thought a mistake had been made, and wrote Washington, "all my calculations lead me to regret the measure. I hope that it may not in its consequences involve the United States in a war on the side of France with her enemies."[47]

---

[42] Adams, *Works*, IX, 270–71, *Letters to the Boston Patriot*, No. X (1809).

[43] Pickering to George Cabot, Oct. 24, 1799, "the great question of the mission to France has been finally decided by the *President alone*. . . . an angel from heaven would have produced no change. In most matters, we are consulted, and our ideas often adopted; but on this all-important question, from first to last, we have been absolutely excluded." Henry Cabot Lodge, *Life and Letters of George Cabot* (Boston: Little, Brown, 1877), p. 249.

[44] McHenry to Washington, Nov. 10, 1799, Gibbs, *op. cit.*, II, 282.

[45] Pickering to Washington, Oct. 24, 1799, *ibid.*, II, 280.

[46] Members of the Cabinet were fully cognizant of the political repercussions of reopening negotiations. McHenry expressed himself in these words: "the mission, which, as far as my information extends, is become an apple of discord to the federalists, that may so operate upon the ensuing election of President, as to put in jeopardy the fruits of all their past labours, by consigning to men, devoted to French innovations and demoralizing principles, the reins of government." McHenry to Washington, Nov. 10, 1799, *ibid.*, II, 282. And Wolcott in these terms: "It is certain that the federal party will be paralyzed: nor do I perceive how the present system of measures can be maintained. . . . and the administration of John Adams, so much extolled, will end by the transfer of the powers of the government to the rival party." *Ibid.*, II, 286–87.

[47] Oct. 21, 1799, Hamilton, *Works* (Hamilton ed.), VI, 414.

THE COLLAPSE OF ADAMS' CABINET

After the envoys to France were on their way, outward appearances of cordiality were maintained between the President and the three members of the Cabinet who had opposed the mission, Pickering, McHenry, and Wolcott. On November 10, 1799, McHenry wrote Washington a survey of the situation, readily acknowledging the Cabinet opposition to Adams, recognizing Adams' irritation, and forecasting the probability that Adams would remove some of his Cabinet advisers.[48] In spite of Adams' calm, there was, in Wolcott's words, "a sensation of unhappiness" among the officers of government.[49] The tension was finally broken in May 1800, when Adams asked for the resignation of McHenry, and summarily removed Pickering.

Adams had been told on more than one occasion that McHenry was unsuited for his post but had paid no attention. While McHenry might well have been removed for incompetence, he was invited to resign for other reasons. The President sent for him on May 5, and after clearing a minor appointment, accused him of one fault after another. He apparently fell into a rage; McHenry reported shortly afterward that he "became indecorous, and at times, outrageous." The President complained that Washington had saddled him with three Secretaries, that McHenry had refused to appoint an Adams' elector (in the electoral college of 1796) to be a captain in the Provisional Army, that he had "biased" Washington to prefer Hamilton over Knox, that he had eulogized Washington and had attempted to praise Hamilton in a report to Congress, that he had advised suspending the mission to France; and ended by demanding his resignation.[50] McHenry resigned the next morning.[51] Five days later Adams turned to Pickering.

Pickering had crossed Adams more than once. In October 1798, he published a letter on Gerry's role in the X.Y.Z. affair, concerning which Gerry immediately complained to the President; Adams asked

---

[48] Steiner, *op. cit.*, p. 419.

[49] Wolcott to Fisher Ames, Dec. 29, 1799, Gibbs, *op. cit.*, II, 315.

[50] McHenry to John McHenry, May 20, 1800, *ibid.*, II, 348. Charles Francis Adams admitted that "Mr. Adams was neither so considerate nor so dignified in his case as he was in that of Mr. Pickering." Adams, *Works,* IX, 53, n.

[51] Shortly afterward, Adams, repenting of his violence, took occasion to tell Wolcott that he had confidence in McHenry's integrity, was pleased that McHenry was affluent and not distressed by loss of office, and would consider appointing McHenry to any suitable office. Gibbs, *op. cit.*, II, 410–11.

Pickering to publish Gerry's remonstrance. "It will satisfy him, and do no harm to any one." Pickering flatly refused and threatened to display, not Gerry's "pusillanimity, weakness, and meanness alone, but his *duplicity* and *treachery*." Adams thereupon advised Gerry to keep quiet; but when he came to write his own report on the French negotiations, he declined to follow Pickering's version of Gerry's conduct.[52]

Much more dangerous was Pickering's interference when Adams nominated his son-in-law, William S. Smith, as adjutant general above two officers listed by Washington as entitled to prior consideration. Pickering (then Secretary of State) believed that Colonel Smith's military talents were unequal to the office, that Smith's business conduct had been questionable, and that Adams would damage his position by such a family preference. He consequently went to the Senate and talked with "not more than half a dozen" Federalist Senators, urging rejection of the nomination. The Senate refused to confirm. Pickering wrote Jay shortly afterward that he was aware the step "was a delicate one," and that he would have preferred to state his objections to the President had not the peremptory tone of Adams' preference for Smith prevented.[53] Many years later he recalled that he expected his action would come to the President's ears and that he would be removed from office.[54]

Pickering, as we have seen, opposed the President in determining Hamilton's military rank, and in sending the second mission to France. The extent of this opposition was not fully known by Adams, but the fact of disagreement was not concealed. There was, therefore, ample ground for Adams to desire a Secretary of State in whom he could have greater confidence. He had reached the conclusion to make a change before Congress convened on December 2, 1799, but delayed action to avoid "a turbulent session." [55]

Apparently not trusting his temper again, after his outburst against McHenry, Adams wrote Pickering on May 10, 1800, "As I perceive a necessity of introducing a change in the administration of the office of State, I think it proper to make this communication of it to the present Secretary of State, that he may have an opportunity of resign-

---

[52] Adams, *Works*, VIII, 610, 614, 616, 617, 621–23.

[53] Upham, *op. cit.*, III, 464–66.

[54] Timothy Pickering, *A Review of the Correspondence between the Hon. John Adams . . . and . . . Wm. Cunningham . . .* (Salem: Cushing and Appleton, 1824), p. 147.

[55] Stoddert to Adams, Oct. 27, 1811, Adams, *Works*, X, 5.

ing, if he chooses." [56] Pickering did not choose to resign. Adams abruptly removed him on May 12, 1800: "Divers causes and considerations, essential to the administration of the government, in my judgment, requiring a change in the department of State, you are hereby discharged from any further service as Secretary of State." [57]

The political causes and implications of these Cabinet changes fall outside the scope of this study.[58] The administrative considerations were fully adequate to support Adams' decision. There was a deep difference of opinion on important matters of public policy between Adams and three members of his Cabinet. There was a lack of candor in the efforts of these Cabinet members to defeat the President's purpose. There was an improper readiness on their part to follow the will of Alexander Hamilton, their party and personal leader, rather than that of the President, their official chief. The mutual confidence which the Constitution presumed and which Congress had confirmed in validating the removal power of the President had disappeared. As Adams said earlier, he knew the remedy, although he long delayed its application. Timothy Pickering enjoyed the privilege of being the first Cabinet officer to be removed by a President.

---

[56] Ibid., IX, 53.

[57] Ibid., IX, 55.

[58] Adams has been accused of sacrificing McHenry and Pickering in order to ensure his own reelection by an understanding with the Republicans. While Adams ardently desired a second term, the evidence for this interpretation is not impressive, and there were adequate administrative reasons for requiring their resignations. Replying to a letter from a Massachusetts correspondent who asked the reasons for discharging Pickering, "for the sake of counteracting injurious impressions," Adams wrote, "it would be altogether improper for me to enter into any conversation or correspondence relative to the changes in administration. If a President of the United States has not authority enough to change his own secretaries, he is no longer fit for his office." Ibid., IX, 79 and footnote.

Chapter Twenty-one

"FITNESS OF CHARACTER"—
PUBLIC SERVICE IDEALS

THE success of the Federalists in establishing a strong executive, a single center of administrative impulse, departments of state with their appropriate duties, and field services was a major contribution to the life of the young Republic. Their success in developing firm relationships between the legislative and executive branches, in restraining the aggressions of one agency upon another, and in maintaining intact the unity of the administrative system was distinctly less. These continuing problems need not, however, obscure the high achievement of creating from nothing an extensive organization to serve the general interest and of working out procedures for the daily conduct of public business.

Despite its compactness and simplicity from the point of view of a later age, the administrative machine seemed vast and complex to the citizens of 1800. It was far greater than any they were familiar with either in the states or in business. It called for the exercise of all that was then known of the administrative art.

Like more mature and complicated systems, this one depended on certain fundamentals for success. Manpower was the chief requirement. Adequate financial support, discretion in the use of funds, and proper accounting for their application ranked high. Smooth working procedures in the management of supplies and in the relations between headquarters and field were important. Proper legal authority in official hands and responsibility to courts for its use were essential. These and other matters comprise the content of the following chapters —a subject matter necessarily more technical in its nature than that which has preceded but in its own context not without interest or

253

significance. These humbler matters and lesser men were also among the indispensables to the success of the new enterprise.

THE APPOINTING POWER

The Constitution departed radically from the Articles of Confederation in defining the appointing power. Its framers were practically unanimous in agreeing to terminate the provision in the Articles by which "the United States, in Congress assembled, shall have authority . . . to appoint such . . . civil officers as may be necessary for managing the general affairs of the United States under their direction." [1] The practice of intriguing with members of Congress for appointments had already begun, and corresponding intrigues in the states were the subject of adverse comment. After considerable discussion of the advisability of an executive council, the Constitutional Convention finally agreed to vest the appointing power in the President, by and with the consent of the Senate, or in the case of inferior officers, in the President alone, the heads of departments, or the courts, as Congress should prescribe.

The term, inferior officers, tended to be closely restricted, and their appointment was usually placed in the hands of the Chief Executive. It has been estimated that Washington nominated over 350 civil officials, not including the Supreme Court justices and heads of departments.[2] The original collection act of 1789 authorized the collectors to employ proper persons as weighers, gaugers, measurers, and inspectors, but in 1799, the approval of the Secretary of the Treasury was required for these minor customs officers.[3] Deputy postmasters were appointed by the Postmaster General.

An exceptional but interesting authority "to examine all candidates for employment or promotion in the hospital department" for the military forces was established in 1799. The duty of serving as a board for this purpose was put upon the three senior medical officers present,[4] probably the first example of an examining board in the administrative history of the United States.

---

[1] Art. IX

[2] Hunt, "Office-Seeking during Washington's Administration," *Am. Hist. Rev.*, I (1896), 272, n. 2.

[3] 1 Stat. 29, sec. 5 (July 31, 1789); 1 Stat. 627, sec. 21 (March 2, 1799).

[4] 1 Stat. 721, sec. 9 (March 2, 1799).

Contrary to practice in the states, federal officials were appointed, not elected.[5] There was not a single elective executive officer except the President and Vice President. In consequence the whole federal service depended directly or indirectly upon the President. Not even the most ardent Republican in Congress raised his voice for popular election of federal executive officers.

The new civil service grew substantially in size between 1789 and 1801. By 1792 it was in full working order. There were then about 780 employees (excluding the deputy postmasters), of whom approximately 660 were employed in the Treasury Department.[6] In 1801 the number of employees (excluding about 880 deputy postmasters) was 2,120, of whom about 1,615 were employed in the Treasury field service.[7] Within a decade, therefore, the number of positions in the new government had increased nearly threefold.

Positions were created by Congress only in response to need, and reluctantly. As Randolph declared to an office seeker, "Clerkships cannot be constituted, but on public considerations."[8] To create an office in order to satisfy a claimant would have been an abhorrent practice to Federalists and Republicans alike.

Officials and employees fell into three broad categories. At the top was a handful of immediate representatives of the authority and dignity of the government: heads of departments, territorial governors and officials, Indian commissioners and superintendents, and ministers at foreign posts. A second group comprised an important class of officials responsible for the operation of the administrative machine along the lines of established policy. This group included the principal Treasury officials (Comptroller, Auditor, Commissioner of the Revenue, Treasurer, and Register), the chief clerks, the Director and Treasurer of the Mint, the Purveyor, the accountants in the War and Navy Departments, the War Department paymaster, the loan commissioners, the collectors of customs, the surveyors of revenue, the receivers

---

[5] Cf. remarks on the state systems by a good Federalist, William Vans Murray: "Look at the immense body of public functionaries, who in this country are elected immediately by the people, or by their electors. . . . Including every description of Legislators, Councils, Governors, Courts, Jurors, and Sheriffs, there are above twelve thousand. . . . These all act in the States, counties, townships, and hundreds. . . ." *Annals,* IV, 907 (Nov. 25, 1794).

[6] *American State Papers: Miscellaneous,* I, 57–68.

[7] *Ibid.,* I, 260–319.

[8] State Dept., Domestic Letters, VI, 80.

and registers of the land offices, and the district attorneys. The third group, relatively numerous, comprised a wide variety of subordinate personnel, such as clerks, deputy postmasters, customs and excise employees, marshals, surveyors, Indian agents, officers and seamen on the cutters, lighthouse keepers, "door keepers" (messengers), and others.

Of the three thousand federal employees in 1801, only about 150 were in the departmental service, the remainder in the field. Every state had a substantial quota of federal agents. The following table shows the distribution by states of the principal classes of officials and employees: the customs service, internal revenue, postmasters, attorneys, and marshals.[9]

TABLE II

NUMBER OF SPECIFIED FEDERAL OFFICIALS
IN THE RESPECTIVE STATES, 1801

State	Number
New Hampshire	77
Massachusetts	529
Vermont	48
Rhode Island	76
Connecticut	157
New York	214
New Jersey	72
Pennsylvania	153
Delaware	35
Maryland	189
Virginia	376
North Carolina	261
South Carolina	128
Georgia	92
Kentucky	32
Tennessee	28

The distribution by states of clerks and others employed in the central offices cannot be ascertained, but so far as the principal officers, including the judges, were concerned, both Washington and Adams took

---

[9] Table derived from *American State Papers: Miscellaneous*, I, 260–304.

good care to secure a wide representation. All parts of the country contributed to the new public service, and all sections became acquainted with it.

Tenure of office was not prescribed either by the Constitution or, with a few exceptions, by statute. It was understood to be at the pleasure of the appointing agency, apart from the judges, and almost universally permanence in lower offices was taken for granted. Jefferson would have agreed with Federalist Senator George Read of Delaware. "Some pretend an opinion," he wrote, "that a rotation in office is a salutary thing in republican governments; but this has always appeared to me an insincere reason urged by those who use it; . . . when a fit character hath been selected for office, either by the people or by their executive authority, and he discovers such fitness by an able discharge of duty for a time, such person hath a reasonable claim to an after-continuance in office, and I consider it as conducing to the interest of the community for whom such officer acts, by means of the improved knowledge of the duties of office which he acquires."[10]

This doctrine was formally put to work in the post office in 1799, when tenure "until they are otherwise removed" was written into the law for the Postmaster General, deputy postmasters, contractors, and other employees.[11]

Rufus King was not the only one who believed that "the people would be alarmed at an unnecessary creation of New Corps which must increase the expence as well as influence of the Government."[12] The Jeffersonian Republicans waged an unending war on the "Macedonian phalanxes" and at the close of twelve years the Federalists were obliged to admit that they had not fully met their goals in setting the character of the new public service.

WASHINGTON'S PERSONNEL POLICY

Washington's standards for appointment were extraordinarily high, far above the levels which had been developed in Great Britain or France, and far above what his contemporaries and successors were able to maintain in the United States. He was deeply impressed with

---

[10] William Thompson Read, *Life and Correspondence of George Read* (Philadelphia: J. B. Lippincott, 1870), p. 543.

[11] 1 Stat. 733, sec. 31 (March 2, 1799).

[12] Farrand, *Records of the Federal Convention,* II, 539.

the importance of securing "the first characters" to serve the new government, and at the same time aware of the vexations which were sure to arise from this Pandora's box which perforce he had to open. Writing to Samuel Vaughan shortly before leaving Mount Vernon, he observed:

It is the nature of Republicans, who are nearly in a state of equality, to be extremely jealous as to the disposal of all honorary or lucrative appointments. Perfectly convinced I am, that, if injudicious or unpopular measures should be taken by the Executive under the New Government with regards to appointments, the Government itself would be in the utmost danger of being utterly subverted by those measures. . . .[13]

And less than a week after his inauguration he wrote his friend, Edward Rutledge, "I anticipate that one of the most difficult and delicate parts of the duty of my Office will be that which relates to nominations for appointments."[14]

The President took timely measures to protect himself as best he might against the office seekers. He adopted the firm policy of making no commitments—a rule which he repeated again and again in his correspondence. He received no applicants personally.[15] He seldom replied to any applications for office by letter or verbally, "lest something might be drawn from a civil answer, that was not intended."[16] John Adams commented, "No man, I believe, has influence with the President. He seeks information from all quarters, and judges more independently than any man I ever knew."[17]

Washington's rules of selection shone in statesmanlike splendor. The dominating standard was the rule of fitness. In November 1789, he said, "In every nomination to office I have endeavored, as far as my own knowledge extended, or information could be obtained, to make fitness of character my primary object."[18] Such expressions recur frequently in his letters.

---

[13] March 21, 1789, Washington, *Writings*, XXX, 237–41 at 240. This letter contains one of the earliest and one of the most complete expositions of Washington's guiding rules.

[14] May 5, 1789, *ibid.*, XXX, 309.

[15] *Ibid.*, XXX, 329.

[16] Washington to Edmund Pendleton, March 17, 1794, *ibid.*, XXXIII, 298.

[17] Adams to Silvanus Bourn, Aug. 30, 1789, Adams, *Works*, IX, 561.

[18] Washington, *Writings*, XXX, 469.

Fitness of character is, however, a term subject to variable interpretations and it is necessary to look farther to ascertain the more specific guides that Washington relied upon. Fitness did not mean to him technical competence (except in legal and a very few scientific appointments),[19] nor can it be said that in Washington's time technical competence was recognized generally as a prerequisite for selection. A review of the President's letters and other material leads to the conclusion that, apart from personal integrity, standing in the community was one of the principal ingredients of fitness. In his judicial appointments Washington referred to his "solicitude for drawing the first characters of the Union into the Judiciary,"[20] and in his form letter to the associate justices of the Supreme Court notifying them of their nomination, he declared, "I have thought it my duty to nominate . . . such men as I conceived would give dignity and lustre to our National Character. . . ."[21]

In his dignified defense of the nomination of Benjamin Fishbourn, who had been rejected by the Senate (the first such case), Washington made much of the fact that Fishbourn had been repeatedly elected or appointed to offices in his own state and community.[22] In adopting the rule of good standing in the public eye the President was deliberately seeking to consolidate the position and prestige of the new government among the people in all parts of the country.

Another element of fitness was the place of residence of the candidate, the object being to secure a favorable geographical distribution, and local residence for the lesser posts. The first Cabinet contained representatives of Massachusetts, New York, and Virginia. The first Supreme Court contained judges from Massachusetts, New York, Penn-

---

[19] Thus, he notified his nephew, Bushrod Washington, later a member of the Supreme Court, "your standing at the bar would not justify my nomination of you as Attorney to the Federal district Court . . ." *ibid.*, XXX, 366. Note also the requirement of mathematical competence for surveyor general (combined with political correctness), Washington to Marshall, July 15, 1796, *ibid.*, XXXV, 139–41; and of experience in business for deputy paymaster and storekeeper in the War Department, *ibid.*, XXXV, 159–60 (1796).

[20] Washington to Madison, Sept. 25(?), 1789, *ibid.*, XXX, 414; see also his letter to Pendleton, Sept. 28, 1789, *ibid.*, XXX, 419–20.

[21] Sept. 30, 1789, *ibid.*, XXX, 424–25; and also to the district judges, Sept. 30, 1789, *ibid.*, XXX, 425. Pickering described the desirable qualifications of a federal judge to be "discernment, law-knowledge & integrity." Pickering to Governor Fenner, Sept. 20, 1796, Pickering Papers, VI, 227.

[22] Richardson, *Messages*, I, 58–59 (Aug. 6, 1789).

sylvania, Virginia, Maryland, and South Carolina.[23] Appointments in the field service were naturally and regularly drawn from the state and locality in which the officials were to serve; [24] local jealousy would have tolerated nothing less. The residence rule was explicitly stated by Timothy Pickering in 1791, as one dating "from time immemorial."

In respect to appointments to public offices, the principle by which the person appointing should be governed, seems to be obvious. An office of general nature, equally affecting all the states in the union, may be filled by a citizen of the *United States*. An office which in its execution is confined to a particular state, ought to be exercised by a citizen of that state. In like manner an office which especially regards a county or a town, should be held by an inhabitant of such county or town—if it afford a person qualified to execute it. This principle has evidently governed the President of the U. States in his appointments. 'Tis a principle recognized in the new constitution of Pennsylvania. 'Tis a principle which from time immemorial has governed appointments in the province & state of Massachusetts, where, of consequence, a departure from the principle would be peculiarly offensive.[25]

Washington gave some preference to former holders of state offices, especially in the customs service. Reporting a conversation with the President, Richard Henry Lee noted his approval of the principle that state officers in similar lines who had behaved well deserved preference in the service of the United States.[26] Many applications were put on this ground and some figures given by Carl R. Fish indicate that the rule was frequently followed.[27]

A number of special cases throw further light on Washington's policy. In one of his celebrated letters he declined to allow military service in the Revolutionary War as a claim for favorable considera-

[23] "In the appointments to the great offices of the government, my aim has been to combine geographical situations, and sometimes other considerations, with abilities; and fitness of *known* characters." Washington to Carrington, Oct. 9, 1795, Washington, *Writings*, XXXIV, 331.

[24] In favor of John Vining for supervisor of revenue in Delaware, Washington mentions "his living near the centre of the State, amidst the Stills, and where the most discontent is said to be." Washington to Hamilton, Sept. 16, 1791, *ibid.*, XXXI, 372.

[25] Pickering to Bowman, Oct. 10, 1791, Pickering Papers, VI, 33.

[26] Richard Henry Lee to Charles Lee, June 7, 1789, *The Letters of Richard Henry Lee* (James Curtis Ballagh, ed., 2 vols., New York: Macmillan, 1912–14), II, 490.

[27] Fish, *Civil Service and the Patronage*, ch. i.

tion by veterans' dependents. Writing to the widow of Brigadier General Wooster, he said:

Sympathizing with you, as I do, in the great misfortunes, which have befallen your family in consequence of the War; my feelings as an individual would forcibly prompt me to do every thing in my power to repair those misfortunes. But as a public man, acting only with a reference to the public good, I must be allowed to decide upon all points of my duty without consulting my private inclinations and wishes. I must be permitted, with the best lights I can obtain, and upon a general view of characters and circumstances, to nominate such persons alone to offices, as, in my judgment, shall be the best qualified to discharge the functions of the departments to which they shall be appointed.[28]

In army appointments in 1791, however, he asked for preference to veterans "in all other respects equal"[29]—no violation of the rule of fitness. There are also occasional indications of Washington's desire to assist veterans or their distressed families,[30] but the rule he followed was established in the letter to Mary Wooster.

At the same time it was natural and inevitable that the active supporters of the Revolution would expect and secure recognition. The *Gazette of the United States* expressed this opinion in restrained terms on July 15, 1789. "The appointment to offices of trust and profit will soon commence; and there can be no doubt but that those will have the preference, who have most distinguished themselves in the cause of freedom." Revolutionary Army officers did receive civil appointments from their old commander in chief—Henry Knox and James McHenry as Secretaries of War, Benjamin Lincoln as collector of the port at Boston, Sebastian Bauman as postmaster in New York, and many others. They were appointed, however, not as military pensioners but as men fit by public character and talents for their respective offices—although in some cases their talents proved modest.

The financial needs of applicants were not overlooked by Washington, although they were never a controlling factor.[31] The justice and

---

[28] Washington to Mary Wooster, May 21, 1789, *Writings*, XXX, 327–28.

[29] Washington to Darke, April 4, 1791, *ibid.*, XXXI, 270.

[30] For example, Washington to Howard, Aug. 25, 1793, *ibid.*, XXXIII, 67; to McHenry, *ibid.*, XXXIII, 72–73.

[31] For example, *ibid.*, XXX, 468–69, 472–74 (Griffin case); *ibid.*, XXXI, 496–97 (Richard Morris).

propriety of preferring citizens to aliens were pointed out to a French-
man who applied for office.[32] But aliens were appointed abroad as
U. S. consuls, without salary.[33] For the army post of adjutant general,
the President required the candidate to be "a man of liberal education
and correct in his writing"; Colonel Posey was disqualified in consequence.[34]

Three circumstances served to bar applicants from nomination by
Washington: family relationship, indolence, and drink. Before entering upon his duties he declared "so far as I know my own heart, I
would not be in the remotest degree influenced, in making nominations, by motives arising from the ties of amity or blood. . . ."[35]
While casting about for a successor to Randolph as Secretary of State,
he wrote Hamilton reviewing a number of personalities; referring to
Colonel Innis he remarked, "his extreme indolence renders his abilities
(great as they are said to be) of little use."[36] Addiction to drink was
looked upon with strong disapprobation in both civil and military
personnel. Corresponding with Hamilton on an appointment as lighthouse keeper, the President said, "If the person recommended by Colo.
Parker is intemperate in drinking . . . this would be an insuperable
objection, let his pretensions and promises of reformation be what
they may."[37] To Henry Knox he wrote after General Harmar's
defeat, "I expected *little* from the moment I heard he was a *drunk-
ard*."[38] His policy with respect to drinking among army officers he
expressed to Knox in 1792: "So long as the vice of drunkenness exists
in the Army so long I hope, Ejections of those Officers who are found
guilty of it will continue; for that and gaming will debilitate and
render unfit for active service any Army whatsoever."[39]

---

[32] Tobias Lear to Jorré, Nov. 15, 1791, *ibid.*, XXXI, 418; Adams had "an invincible
aversion to the appointment of foreigners." Adams, *Works*, IX, 65–66, 77.

[33] Washington, *Writings*, XXXI, 496.

[34] *Ibid.*, XXXII, 160–61.

[35] Washington to Vaughan, March 21, 1789, *ibid.*, XXX, 238.

[36] Oct. 29, 1795, *ibid.*, XXXIV, 349; see also Hamilton's report on General Hand
who was next in line for an appointment as supervisor of revenue, "he has been so
materially defective in the execution of his present office as to forbid an assurance that
the superior one would be executed by him with due attention and exertion." Hamilton
to Washington, June 14, 1794, Hamilton, *Works* (Hamilton ed.), IV, 567.

[37] Oct. 1, 1792, Washington, *Writings*, XXXII, 174.

[38] Nov. 19, 1790, *ibid.*, XXXI, 156.

[39] Aug. 1, 1792, *ibid.*, XXXII, 105. Washington also objected to making any nominations from among members of Congress. Washington to Hamilton, Oct. 29, 1795,
ibid., XXXIV, 348.

Senators and representatives were among Washington's sources of information about prospective nominees. Hamilton, Jefferson, and a number of private citizens also gathered data for the President.[40] He himself made direct personal inquiries when feasible. En route between Mount Vernon and Philadelphia in September 1791, he stopped in Wilmington, Delaware; "Whilst I was in Wilmington waiting breakfast today," he wrote Hamilton, "I made the best enquiry time and circumstances would permit, for some fit character to fill the office lately held by Doctr. Latimer. . . . Doctor Latimer, whom I afterwards called upon, at New port, for the purpose of enquiry, also speaks well of Barratt." [41] Writing from Mount Vernon in 1792 to Hamilton, he said, "The Collector was not at Baltimore when I passed through that place; but from the Naval Officer I learnt. . . ." [42] We may imagine the feelings of the naval officer when thus unexpectedly called upon by the President of the United States.

THE CONTROLLING PERSONNEL

For the top positions Washington sought statesmen who would command the confidence of the country. In his first departmental appointments he was fortunate in securing Hamilton, who represented the northern commercial interests, Jefferson, who stood for the southern agricultural interests, and Knox, "from the eastward"—a well-known military figure and a symbol of the Revolutionary Army. Randolph, the Attorney General, was both a prominent Virginian and a defender of the states.

The departure of Jefferson on December 31, 1793, was repaired by moving Randolph from the office of Attorney General to that of State and by appointing William Bradford of Pennsylvania to the chief law office. Randolph's sudden resignation under charges on August 19, 1795, precipitated a long search for new advisers to the President; indeed, with Knox's resignation on December 31, 1794, Hamilton's retirement on January 31, 1795, and Bradford's death on August 23,

---

[40] Hamilton was Washington's principal reliance. For a good example of his services in this connection see a letter to Washington of June 14, 1794, with reference to the office of supervisor of revenue of Pennsylvania in Hamilton, *Works* (Hamilton ed.), IV, 566–68; a letter of Sept. 29, 1790, with reference to captains of cutters, *ibid.*, IV, 72–73; a letter of Dec. 2, 1790, with reference to New Hampshire characters, *ibid.*, IV, 84–86.

[41] Washington, *Writings,* XXXI, 371.

[42] *Ibid.*, XXXII, 106.

1795, Washington was forced completely to reconstruct his Cabinet in the course of this year.

The Cabinet changes required in 1795 revealed a strong reluctance on the part of leading men to serve in high federal posts. Wolcott succeeded Hamilton and served until near the close of Adams' term. Colonel Pickering, formerly Postmaster General, succeeded Knox in the War Department, and in the summer of 1795 was made acting Secretary of State while Washington surveyed the scene. He offered the State Department first to William Patterson of New Jersey, who declined to exchange his judicial post for one political.[43] He then turned to Thomas Johnson, whom he had earlier hoped to bring into his administration, but without success.[44] Then he appealed to Charles Cotesworth Pinckney: "Equally unnecessary is it, to observe to you, that the affairs of this country are in a violent paroxysm; and that it is the duty of its old and uniform friends to assist in piloting the Vessel, in which we are all embarked, between the rocks of Sylla and charibdas. . . ."[45] Pinckney declined. With some hesitation Washington next invited Patrick Henry to become Secretary of State, but the great orator of the Revolution refused to accept official honors.[46] After vainly sounding out Rufus King through Hamilton, the President finally, almost in despair, appointed the acting Secretary, Timothy Pickering, a staunch Federalist but a man whose qualifications for this post hardly matched the President's specifications.

This appointment made necessary a new Secretary of War. Early in 1794 Washington had already approached C. C. Pinckney for this post, but without success.[47] He also sounded out Colonel Carrington, but Carrington declined to be considered.[48] He then made a formal offer to John Eager Howard, one-time governor of Maryland, who declined.[49] Finally, he secured the consent of James McHenry of Maryland, who served through most of Adams' administration. Washing-

---

[43] Washington to Carrington, Oct. 9, 1795, *ibid.*, XXXIV, 331.

[44] Washington to Johnson, Aug. 24, 1795, *ibid.*, XXXIV, 284–85.

[45] Aug. 24, 1795, *ibid.*, XXXIV, 285; either there is an error in the date of the letter to Pinckney or Washington thought Johnson might decline and by the same post offered the State Department to both men.

[46] Oct. 9, 1795, *ibid.*, XXXIV, 334–35. Jefferson alleged that the offer was not made until there was a moral certainty that Henry would not accept and then only to draw him over to the Federalists. March 2, 1796, Jefferson, *Works* (Federal ed.), VIII, 222.

[47] Jan. 22, 1794, Washington, *Writings,* XXXIII, 248–49.

[48] Washington to Hamilton, Oct. 29, 1795, *ibid.*, XXXIV, 349.

[49] Nov. 19, 1795, *ibid.*, XXXIV, 365–66.

ton's first choice for Attorney General to succeed Bradford, John Marshall, refused the office, and the President had to be content with the former collector of Alexandria, Charles Lee.[50] It is no wonder that Washington became impatient. "In short," he wrote Hamilton, "what with the non-acceptance of some; the known dereliction of those who are most fit; the exceptional drawbacks from others; and a wish (if it were practicable) to make a geographical distribution of the *great* officers of the Administration, I find the selection of proper characters an arduous duty." [51] These replacements lowered the level of personal capacity in the Cabinet,[52] but at the same time they greatly lessened internal dissension in the President's official family and the tension between the legislative and executive branches.

The foreign service began with some able men. To London went Thomas Pinckney and Rufus King; to Paris, Gouverneur Morris and James Monroe; to the Netherlands, William Short, John Quincy Adams, and William Vans Murray; to Lisbon, David Humphreys and William L. Smith; and to Madrid, Short, Pinckney, and Humphreys from other diplomatic assignments. These were extraordinarily talented men to discover in a country with limited diplomatic experience.

The judicial appointments gave Washington considerable trouble. Among his offers to the Supreme Court bench in 1789, one of the five associate justices declined (R. H. Harrison), and one resigned in 1791 (John Rutledge). To fill the latter vacancy Washington wrote one of the most unusual letters of his official career, offering a seat on the Supreme Court jointly, in the same letter, to C. C. Pinckney and Edward Rutledge, and asking them to decide which would accept.[53] Both declined. Among the first nominations to the district judges, Edmund Pendleton and Thomas Johnson declined.[54]

The vice-presidency was filled by election. John Adams was tired of his station as early as 1791. To John Trumbull he wrote, "I find the office I hold, though laborious, so wholly insignificant, and . . . so stupidly pinched and betrayed, that I wish myself again at the bar, old as I am." [55] Two years later he wrote to his wife, "my country has in

---

[50] Washington to Marshall, Aug. 26, 1795, *ibid.*, XXXIV, 287–88.

[51] Oct. 29, 1795, *ibid.*, XXXIV, 349.

[52] W. V. Murray to McHenry, Jan. 1, 1795, "We certainly are retrograding as to characters." Steiner, *McHenry*, p. 158.

[53] May 24, 1791, Washington, *Writings*, XXXI, 290–91.

[54] *Ibid.*, XXX, 470, 472.

[55] Jan. 23, 1791, Adams, *Works*, IX, 573.

its wisdom contrived for me the most insignificant office that ever the invention of man contrived or his imagination conceived." [56] In 1794 he wrote again to Abigail, declaring he was "wearied to death with *ennui*" and sighing for his rocks, his habitation, and his wife.[57] He waited out eight years and was rewarded with the presidency. Jefferson waited out four, mended his fences, and became President in 1801.

---

[56] *Ibid.*, I, 460.
[57] *Ibid.*, I, 465.

Chapter Twenty-two

IDEALS AND PRACTICE

THE high standards set by Washington were also those of John Adams. To Mercy Warren he wrote, "I should belie the whole course of my public and private conduct and all the maxims of my life, if I should ever consider public authority entrusted to me to be made subservient to my private views, or those of my Family or Friends." [1] In a letter to his Secretary of War, he laid down standards equally applicable to the civil or military branches.

Merit I consider, however, as the only true scale of graduation in the army. Services and rank in the last war, or in any other war, are only to be taken into consideration as presumptive evidence of merit, and may at any time be set aside by contrary proof. Services and rank in civil life, and in time of peace, I think, ought not to be forgotten or neglected, for they are often of more utility and consequence to the public than military services. The officers, I think, ought not to be flattered with any positive assurance of rising in succession. The right, authority, and duty of government to depart from the line of succession, in clear cases of unusual merit, of extraordinary services, or uncommon talent, ought always to be asserted and maintained, and constantly to be held up to the view of the army. [2]

In the *Federal Gazette* "Timoleon" offered equally lofty guides to executive action. "In the distribution of offices in republican governments," he wrote, "the following circumstances should be attended to." They were knowledge, integrity, and industry; an irreproachable private character; the married state ("a single man by a very little labor may always maintain himself"); conduct in previous business, but with tolerance to one who had been unfortunate, without im-

---

[1] May 29, 1789, *Warren-Adams Letters* (2 vols., Massachusetts Historical Society, Collections, Vols. LXXII, LXXIII, 1917–25), II, 314.

[2] May 7, 1799, Adams, *Works,* VIII, 640–41.

prudence. "In the distribution of offices," said Timoleon, "rulers should *look* out for the most suitable men. . . . Modest men will not apply for them, and imprudent men do not deserve them." [3]

To these observations a writer in the *American Museum* responded by another list of qualifications. They were: integrity; a good reputation; religion and sincere piety; sufficient abilities; gravity, wisdom, and sound judgment; decision, close attention, and perseverance; a "great command of his passions" and steady attendance. The writer of this essay, while flying near to perfection in his description of public officers, had something further to say of enduring interest.

Good government manifestly depends much more on the goodness of the men who fill the public offices, than on the goodness of the form of government, constitution, or even laws of the state; for the errors of all these, under the administration of good men, will be mended or made tolerable, either by the authority of the legislature, or favourable construction; but weak and wicked men will pervert the best laws to the purposes of favour or oppression—And one principal thing which makes one form of government better than another, is, that there is a greater and a more natural chance of the appointment of suitable men to public offices in the one than in the other. . . .[4]

The success of the Federalists in maintaining these noble ideals was on the whole substantial. Practice, however, was not always perfect. The contrast between ideals and performance reveals the pull and tug of conflicting influences. Partisanship and family relations could not be wholly overlooked even by the founding fathers.

OFFICE SEEKING UNDER THE FEDERALISTS

Despite Timoleon's plea to government to *look* for talent, most posts (excluding the highest) were filled by selection from among persons who looked for office. The applications were numerous and "respectable." They were addressed directly to the President, or were sent to the several heads of departments, to such officials as the Comptroller of the Treasury, and to members of both Houses.[5] They ranged

---

[3] Reprinted in the *Gazette of the United States,* May 2, 1789.

[4] Reprinted in *ibid.,* May 6, 1789.

[5] An application to Judge Iredell brought the reply that since he had been on the bench he had rigidly adhered to the rule of not soliciting office for others. Griffith J. McRee, *Life and Correspondence of James Iredell* (2 vols., New York: D. Appleton, 1857–58), II, 426.

all the way from an interest in the federal bench, in a diplomatic appointment, or the governorship of a western territory to the place of superintendent of a dockyard or an under officer of a revenue cutter. They came from great and small.[6] Even the redoubtable merchant, Stephen Higginson, at a low point in his commercial affairs, wrote the Vice President (John Adams), "I have decided to offer myself a Candidate for some new office, which I presume must soon be instituted in the Revenue. if it be decently respectable, and tolerably productive, I should gladly embrace it. . . . That of Inspector . . . would meet my Views."[7]

The character of the claims put forward by applicants throws light on popular attitudes toward office under the new government. Nearly three-fourths of a group examined by Gaillard Hunt based their requests wholly upon fitness.[8] Military service was often referred to but seldom as the sole consideration. Another substantial group requested the same office that had been held under the Confederation. A number asked appointments to repair fortunes lost in the Revolutionary cause or to relieve distress. Finally there were claims resting in part on political opinions—few at first but gradually increasing in number.

Many of the early applications displayed an apprehensive modesty. John Hamilton wrote to his Congressman, John Steele, "my friends have urged me to sollicit for the office of federal attorney for this District—the task imposed upon me of begging an appointment is of all others the most disagreable & with much pain & disquietude of Mind I have struggled thro' an address to the President.—"[9] Others were more assured in presenting their talents to the public. A letter to Steele in 1798 tells something of the effect Washington's policy in appointments had produced. "I had formed an opinion that such places [surveyor of revenue] were most generally filled with men of

---

[6] President Sullivan of New Hampshire asked Secretary Knox for his "favorable influence in behalf of James Wheelock Esq[r] Brother to the now presid[t] of Dartmouth Colledge & Son to the late Presid[t] of that university, he has received a Liberal Education, is a good Accountant, is faithful and Industrious; his reputation is high, his address & behaviour is pleasing; he wishes the place of an assistant in some of the offices about the seat of Federal Government. . . ." *Letters and Papers of Major-General John Sullivan* (Otis G. Hammond, ed., 3 vols., Concord: New Hampshire Historical Society, 1930–39), III, 604–5.

[7] "Letters of Stephen Higginson," Am. Hist. Assoc., *Annual Report, 1896*, I, 774, 782.

[8] Hunt, "Office-Seeking during Washington's Administration," *Am. Hist. Rev.*, I, 275.

[9] John Steele, *Papers*, I, 56.

merit who had in some way rendered their country services. . . ." [10]

The competition for appointment as Treasurer of the Mint in the autumn of 1797 provides a good case study in office seeking and in tests of qualification and disqualification. Pickering advised Adams on the applications received, which numbered over a dozen within three weeks from the death of the incumbent. That of Dr. David Jackson was set aside—he was in easy circumstances, a warm Democrat, and strongly opposed to the measures of the government. Jonathan Williams was said to have "lived splendidly" in France and to have failed—"and few bankrupts are free from stain." Huger, thought Pickering, had abilities "in the lowest grade," was sometimes disabled by gout and too much inclined to drink; Dr. Conover had married the daughter of the Philadelphia lawyer, Lewis, but Lewis was said to be much displeased with the match; John Caldwell was a brother-in-law of the Secretary of War; Reverend Mr. Armstrong of Trenton had been disappointed in an expected patrimony, had a large family, but was prepared to add to his prospective income as Treasurer of the Mint by supplying in the Philadelphia pulpits. Dr. Benjamin Rush was the leading candidate—"We both know the Doctor's ingenuity, extensive learning and agreeable qualities. . . . The Dr's friends wish he possessed more stability: I seriously wish it; for he has talents that might be politically very useful. . . ." [11] Rush was eventually appointed.

Selections from a private letter of the Comptroller to the Secretary of the Treasury in the mid-nineties bring out other considerations. The Comptroller, John Steele, was pushing the claims of a southerner, Colonel Orr, for an army contract. He wrote that Orr was a native of the United States, able to give security "above all exception," and of the "most respectable connections"—a nephew of Colonel Grayson of Virginia and nearly allied by marriage to Bushrod Washington. Steele added, "It is important I think to the character of our Govt that it should be supposed that men from different parts of the United States might enter the lists of competition for things of this kind with equal prospects of success. . . . The prejudices that exist agt southern men generally as men of business are . . . inapplicable to him, and his

[10] *Ibid.*, I, 164.

[11] Pickering to Adams, Sept. 5, 1797, Pickering Papers, VII, 158; and Sept. 9, 1797, *ibid.*, VII, 167; Pickering to Richard Peters, Sept. 28, 1797, *ibid.*, VII, 237–38.

political opinions are like those of all honest men at the present juncture." [12]

The highest offices sometimes went begging, for various reasons; but the middle and smaller offices and positions were objects of attention on the part of many. Office seeking was more decorous in the early years than it later became, but the pressure upon those who could nominate or appoint was considerable from the outset. There were more claimants than could be fed from the available loaves and fishes. Progressively, but on the whole moderately, considerations supplementary to fitness of character became effective.

PARTISANSHIP AND APPOINTMENTS

During the first year or two of Washington's administration the question of loyalty to the new government was important and, while never specifically stated as a *sine qua non*, was nevertheless a matter of concern. The evidence is found principally in letters other than those of the President, who, so far as we have ascertained, almost never referred to this matter in writing.[13] Hamilton, however, from time to time assured the President of the loyalty of applicants,[14] and care was taken to avoid the appointment of former Tories or persons whose loyalty to the new Constitution could be questioned.

This test, however, rapidly receded as the new government established itself. For a few years political parties were still inchoate, although there was much controversy over particular issues. By the election of 1792, however, Hamilton's opponents offered organized political resistance and in the years immediately following the Republican and Federalist parties took form.[15] In the presidential elec-

---

[12] Wolcott Papers, XXII, 31 (undated).

[13] But note Washington to McHenry, Nov. 30, 1789, in which the President comments on William Paca, an applicant for district judge in Maryland: "his sentiments have not been altogether in favor of the General Government, and a little adverse on the score of Paper emissions etc." Washington, *Writings*, XXX, 471. Cf. Adams to Walton, Sept. 25, 1789, Adams, *Works*, VIII, 495.

[14] For example, with respect to Keith Spence, "a man of education and abilities, well known and respected—a firm friend to the Revolution and to the National Government. . . ." Hamilton to Washington, Dec. 2, 1790, Hamilton, *Works* (Hamilton ed.), IV, 85.

[15] See Samuel Eliot Morison, *The Life and Letters of Harrison Gray Otis, Federalist, 1765–1848* (2 vols., Boston and New York: Houghton, Mifflin, 1913); O. G. Libby, "Political Factions in Washington's Administrations," *Quarterly Journal of the University of North Dakota*, III (1913), 291–318.

tion of 1796 the two groups faced each other with reasonably clear, competing policies.

The violence of party dispute was unexampled. Morison describes these years as "one of the most intense periods of party feeling that the country has ever passed through. . . . Members of the two parties studiously avoided each other on the street and in society: there were Republican taverns and Federalist taverns; Republican salons, and Federalist salons." [16] In 1796 Adams wrote his wife, "I have no very ardent desire to be the butt of party malevolence. Having tasted of that cup, I find it bitter, nauseous, and unwholesome." [17] Combative Timothy Pickering declared in 1796, "If angels were to administer the principal offices of government, they would not escape reproaches from the present unprincipled slanderers of public men and their measures." [18]

Political conformity as a test for office had begun to play a part by 1792, although still a relatively modest one. [19] The earliest evidence which has been noted is in a letter of Timothy Pickering, then Postmaster General. Writing to an applicant for the office at Marblehead, Massachusetts, he said,

Candour will not suffer me to stop here. Were the office much more valuable, I should not think it expedient for you to receive it. On account of the "political sentiments" you refer to, it would subject *me* to *censure,* and *you* perhaps to *persecution.* As a *private* man, I should defy reproach for my attachment to an *upright* fellow citizen, of whatever opinions in politics or religion. As vested with a *public trust,* I think myself bound to discharge it, in this article, by introducing to public beneficial situations honest men *who have claims on the public* for their services in effecting the

---

[16] Morison, *op. cit.,* I, 61–62.

[17] Adams, *Works,* I, 485.

[18] Pickering to John Clarke, July 22, 1796, Pickering Papers, VI, 207.

[19] The first mention of party affiliation in the House of Representatives occurred on March 8, 1792, when Page of Virginia exclaimed, "I thank God, although I am a Republican. . ." *Annals,* III, 443. A month later he said, "I speak like the representative of plain dealing, honest Republicans." *Ibid.,* III, 567 (April 20, 1792). An unsuccessful attempt to forbid inspectors of revenue from interfering either directly or indirectly in elections reflected concern over the influence of revenue officers in elections. British precedent was called upon, but the proposal was defeated 37 to 21. *Ibid.,* II, 1876–78 (Jan. 21, 1791).

establishment of a government of which I am an executive officer,—or against whom, in this respect, no exception can be taken.[20]

Washington's eventual requirement of political conformity in high office has already been mentioned. He did not, however, intend to bar all but professed Federalists. He was concerned with *offices of consequence;* and even here his policy excluded only those whose political tenets were *adverse* to the President's *program*.

The narrow margin of Federalist success in the elections of 1796 and the bitter difference of opinion on foreign policy hardened the Federalists under Adams against their political opponents. Adams himself said, "Washington appointed a multitude of democrats and jacobins of the deepest die. I have been more cautious in this respect." John Adams, however, never committed himself to a party monopoly of office, despite the high feelings of the public during his administration. He wrote Oliver Wolcott:

Neither Mr. Parker nor any other person ever had authority from me to say, that any man's political creed would be an insuperable bar to promotion. No such rule has ever been adopted. Political principles and discretion will aways be considered, with all other qualifications, and well weighed, in all appointments. But no such monopolizing, and contracted, and illiberal system, as that alleged to have been expressed by Mr. Parker, was ever adopted by me.[21]

Direct reference to party attitude nevertheless became more common and less concealed. In 1795 Noah Webster told Oliver Wolcott that the New York collector of customs was "a most inveterate & avowed enemy of the Govt" and went on to ask, "If men, who are loading the govt with curses, & denouncing our Chief Magistrate, as a tyrant . . . are to be raised to opulence and nabobship, . . . who are the friends that will maintain that govt?" [22] Pickering wrote Adams with respect to a candidate for Treasurer of the Mint, "I take Colo Nichols to

---

[20] Pickering to Thomas Robie, March 31, 1792, Pickering Papers, VI, 63; Upham, *Timothy Pickering,* III, 11.

[21] Oct. 4, 1800, Adams, *Works,* IX, 87. That Mrs. Adams set an early precedent for subsequent first ladies of the land appears from a letter dated July 25, 1797, to an unidentified correspondent: "I have the pleasure to inform you that your request is complied with. I did not fail on my arrival here [Philadelphia], to communicate to the president a conversation which your Mamma had with me just before I left Home: there has been no opening untill *the removal* of Mr. Jarvis." Mass. Hist. Soc. *Proceedings,* LXII (1928), 24.

[22] Wolcott Papers, VI, 72.

be a very worthy man, & a steady supporter of the Government."[23]
The district attorney for Tennessee resigned in 1798; in searching for
a successor, Pickering wrote that it was "important that a man well
attached to the General Government" should be appointed.[24] By the
end of 1798 we find Pickering looking into the political views of marshals, who from the beginning had a four-year term. Are there "any
considerations, personal or political," he asked, "which ought to determine the President to appoint another" in place of a marshal whose
term had expired?[25] In 1800 Adams told Gerry that an applicant for
office "is represented to me as a Jacobin, who was very busy in a late
election in the town of Roxbury, on the wrong side. His pretensions,
however, shall be considered with all others impartially. . . ."[26]

The organization of the Provisional Army in 1798 was a strictly
partisan affair. The Federalists distrusted the loyalty of their opponents
as well as their party views, and determined to take no chances with
unreliable supporters of France; Washington was in full agreement.
In the summer of 1798 he wrote McHenry, "The State of Maryland is
highly Federal, both in its collective and Individual character, and I
see no office of any Importance allotted to a Member of it."[27] In
September he wrote without reserve: "you could as soon scrub the
blackamore white, as to change the principles of a profest Democrat;
. . . he will leave nothing unattempted to overturn the Government
of this Country."[28] Adams was also writing the Secretary of War to
beware of commissioning officers who at the late election spoke "in a
manner highly disorganizing and inflammatory."[29] The Federalist
press boasted that the officers "have it in charge not to inlist any man
into the service of the United States, who, within a certain period of
time, has had the audacity to mount the French cockade."[30]

---

[23] Sept. 12, 1797, Pickering Papers, VII, 180.
[24] Feb. 16, 1798, ibid., VIII, 140.
[25] Pickering to Yellott, Dec. 12, 1798, ibid., X, 42.
[26] Adams, Works, IX, 577.
[27] Washington, Writings, XXXVI, 385.
[28] Washington to McHenry, ibid., XXXVI, 474; cf. ibid., XXXVI, 366, in which
Washington says of an applicant for a commission, "sound is his Politic's."
[29] Adams to McHenry, Aug. 18 and Sept. 13, 1798, Adams, Works, VIII, 582, and
n. 2; 594–95.
[30] Centinel, Aug. 18, 1798, quoted in Manning Julian Dauer, Jr., "The Basis of the
Support for John Adams in the Federalist Party," unpublished doctoral dissertation,
University of Illinos (1933), p. 222. William Hindman, Federalist Representative from
Maryland, wrote McHenry on June 1, 1799, "I have laid it down as an undeviating

McHenry's attitude was expressed in a letter to William Darke of Virginia, who had offered a company commanded by John Oferall. McHenry asked for information as to Oferall's principles, and when Darke indignantly asked "who has the right to question the patriotism of a Virginian," wrote a long defense from which the following excerpt is taken.

In the present crisis of our affairs, and state of party in the country, it was, and is deemed important not to accept companies composed of disaffected persons who may for improper motives, be desirous to intrude themselves into the army, under the pretense of patriotic associations; and to guard against it, certificates have been, and are required, from prominent and known characters, or those whose virtues, talents, and usefulness, have given them a weight and respectability in the community, setting forth the principles of the associates, those of the officers elect, especially, and that the company have complied with the conditions prescribed by law. . . .[31]

By the winter of 1799 the discrimination against the Republicans had gone so far that Hamilton protested to McHenry.

I regret, also, that the objection against anti-federalism has been carried so far as to exclude several of the characters proposed by us. We were very attentive to the importance of appointing friends of the government to military stations; but we thought it well to relax the rule in favor of particular merit in a few instances, and especially in reference to the inferior grades. It does not seem advisable to exclude all hope, and to give to appointments too absolute a party feature. . . .[32]

Maxim not to recommend any, but those whose Principles I had strong Reason to believe were decidedly favourable to our Government, many opposition Characters have unfortunately & unavoidably obtained Appointments, this You could not prevent, as it was not in your Power to have a certain Knowledge of every Applicant, & Many have been represented as proper by Gentlemen on whom You had Reliance." *Publications of the Southern History Association*, X (1906), 152.

[31] *Gazette of the United States*, Feb. 27, 1799. I owe this correspondence to Dauer, *ibid*. Stephen Higginson warned Pickering against accepting the services of General William Hull of Massachusetts, "it is a well known fact, that Hull and many of his Officers are of the most inveterate grade of Jacobins in this State." Am. Hist. Assoc., *Annual Report, 1896*, I, 816.

[32] Hamilton to McHenry, Feb. 6, 1799, Hamilton, *Works* (Hamilton ed.), V, 210. Hamilton, however, had been guilty of party preferences; on June 1, 1798, he wrote McHenry, "A Capt *Hacker* formerly of our Navy is desirous of being employed. One or two good men have recommended him to me. It seems however—that he has been heretofore rather Democratic—I barely wish that his pretensions may be fairly but carefully considered & that he may have just chance as he merits." *Naval Documents related to the Quasi-War between the United States and France*, I, 102.

The evidence clearly indicates that party opinions had become an important test for officeholding under Washington so far as high positions were concerned and under Adams for lesser ones as well.[33] Gaillard Hunt was justified in concluding: "There cannot be any doubt that Adams endeavored to obtain worthy men for the appointments he made, but if he did not wholly proscribe members of the Republican party he at least showed such a preference for Federalists that few who were not members of that party received any favors at his hands." [34] And as William A. Robinson noted, from a contemporary Massachusetts orator, "The Federalists in this state have long considered the possession of office as a vested right." [35]

The contest between senators and governors for the control of federal patronage broke out in New Hampshire. James McHenry wrote the Granite State Senators, Livermore and Langdon, for nominations of officers for the Provisional Army and requested them to consult Governor John T. Gilman and others. Gilman sat down to an indignant letter to the Secretary of War:

it is a fact that my feelings were severely wounded by that letter, copy of which I received from Mr. Livermore.

. . . If my ideas of the letter are right, I may with Messers Peabody & Cass and in common with other characters throughout the state who may be consulted, recommend persons to Messers Langdon & Livermore, and perhaps after this is done no one of their names will ever be forwarded to you. . . .

Considering the station in which my fellow citizens have placed me— the exertions I have made in support of our Federal Government . . . an attempt on my part to cooperate in this business in the way in which I understood it, would be a greater deduction from self-respect than any other public act of my life. . . .

To make matters worse for Gilman, Senator Langdon was a Republican and not on speaking terms with the Governor. Hamilton had apprised Washington of a Langdon and a Gilman party in New

---

[33] Pickering was also distributing public printing on a partisan basis, where feasible. Pickering to James Morrison, April 4, 1799, Pickering Papers, X, 564.

[34] Hunt, "Office-Seeking during the Administration of John Adams," Am. Hist. Rev., II, 254. Cf. Fish, Civil Service and the Patronage, pp. 20–21.

[35] Jeffersonian Democracy in New England (New Haven: Yale University Press, 1916), p. 110.

Hampshire as early as 1790.[36] McHenry had sent corresponding letters to the senators of several other states, and it must be presumed that he carelessly overlooked Langdon's relations with Gilman.[37]

McHenry later wrote a thoughtful and dispassionate letter on the growing tendency to find places for partisans. Its prophetic terms deserve to be recalled.

During the whole of the administration of General Washington, appointments to office, were invariably made, not with a view to the extension of executive influence or future elections, but upon the ground of the fitness and qualifications of the persons for the offices to be filled, and a regard to an equitable distribution of them among the several states.

This rule was not followed with the same punctilious observance by Mr. Adams. He thought it an essential part of the art of governing to apply the influence of rewards, through the medium of appointments to offices, to future elections.

This new principle in our government (if I may so express myself) is calculated to excite serious apprehensions. And I fear that the present President, in practicing upon it, will go further than did his predecessor. But this is not the worst of it. I fear above all things, the operation of this principle upon the conduct of the needy man of talents, who believes in no religion, the ambitious rich man without virtue or honesty, and your political adventurers and office hunters of every description. All of these (and they are a numerous and increasing brood belonging to both parties) either see, or will see, that the direct road to public employment, to the Presidency itself, is in and through elections, and that whoever can influence elections (no matter by what means) gains everything.

It is in the very nature of this principle to make good men bad, to compel them to resort to improper practices by like practice, and to call up, and keep in perpetual activity, all the evil spirits of the nation. And as no President can gratify more than a small portion of these perturbed beings under our government, in its present form, may it not, in a little time, render everything that ought to be stable, fluctuating and insecure, and fill all offices, even to the first and highest, with the most profligate, needy, desperate and unprincipled men in the community?[38]

---

[36] Hamilton, *Works* (Hamilton ed.), IV. 85.

[37] Governor Gilman's letter of May 22, 1799, is printed in full in the *Granite Monthly*, XXXVIII (1906), 123–24.

[38] Steiner, *McHenry*, pp. 502–3. Cf. Hamilton's observation: "And it will rarely happen that the advancement of the public service will be the primary object either of party victories or of party negotiations." *The Federalist*, No. 76.

None of the leading Federalists, however, sought to make room for party adherents by removing officials and employees whose political reliability had become uncertain. But they were not averse to finding places for their family connections.

NEPOTISM

The Federalists governed the United States in an era when nepotism was rampant in the two countries they knew best, Great Britain and France. In their colonial governments they had seen enough of favors to relatives to drill them thoroughly in one of the normal prerogatives of officeholding in the eighteenth century. In the new general government Washington set a high standard, but it was too austere for many of his associates to follow. Public jealousy of officials and the "high tone" of many leading Federalists, however, held down the practice of appointing relatives to public office. Some examples will illustrate the situation during the 1790's.

Washington early pronounced himself against favoritism of all kinds in making appointments, especially to his family connections.[39] His restraint was applauded by Tench Coxe, who wrote in 1794, "*a native citizen of the United States, transferred from private life to that station, has not, during so long a term, appointed a single relation to any office of honour or emolument.*"[40]

John Adams was no less sure of his principles, but he was possessed of an ambitious son-in-law, Colonel William S. Smith. His son, John Quincy Adams, stood on his own feet; the father did nothing and needed to do nothing for him. In a letter to his mother before the election of 1796, the young Adams made it clear that he would never give his father trouble "by solicitation for office of any kind."[41] Colonel William S. Smith was a horse of another color. He served successfully in the army during the Revolutionary War, and was appointed Secretary of the Legation at London by the Congress of the Confederation. He there married Adams' daughter Abigail, and provided the household circle in which Adams relaxed. Adams developed a strong attachment, mingled with sharp disappointment, toward his son-in-law. Returning to the United States, Smith engaged in various business

---

[39] Washington, *Writings*, XXX, 366.

[40] Tench Coxe, *A View of the United States of America* (Philadelphia: W. Hall, etc., 1794), p. 319.

[41] Adams, *Works*, VIII, 529, n.

enterprises in which lack of success was darkened by the suspicion of low business practices. He also held administrative positions under Washington, whose aide he had been; in 1789, marshal of New York State; in 1791, supervisor of the revenue for the New York district; and subsequently surveyor of the Port of New York.[42]

After Adams became President he appointed Smith colonel of a New York regiment. In the formation of the Provisional Army in 1798, Washington, as commander in chief, proposed Smith as brigadier or adjutant general. Adams properly sent in the nomination as adjutant general with others. Timothy Pickering, as we have seen, betook himself to the Senate where he persuaded his Federalist friends to vote against confirmation.[43] Colonel Smith was able to muster only two or three votes.[44] Adams was deeply wounded.[45]

In December 1798, Smith was proposed by the general officers of the Provisional Army, alternately with one other officer, to be appointed lieutenant colonel commandant. "This event," said Adams, "has embarrassed me. I know not what to do." He then spoke frankly to his son-in-law.

Upon this occasion I must be plain with you. Your pride and ostentation, which I myself have seen with inexpressible grief for many years, have excited among your neighbors so much envy and resentment, that, if they have to allege against you any instance of dishonorable and dishonest conduct, as it is pretended they have, you may depend upon it, it will never be forgiven or forgotten. He whose vanity has been indulged and displayed to the humiliation and mortification of others, may depend on meeting their revenge whenever they shall find an opportunity for it. They are now taking vengeance on you with a witness.

If I were to nominate you to any thing more than a regiment, according to reports and spirit that prevail, I have no doubt you would be again negatived by the Senate. If I nominate you to a regiment, I still fear it will not pass. It is a great misfortune to the public that the office I hold should be disgraced by a nomination of my son-in-law, which the Senate of the United States think themselves obliged to negative. If the disgrace should

---

[42] *Dictionary of American Biography*, XVII, 368–69; for a colorful but uncritical biography, see Katherine Metcalf Roof, *Colonel William Smith and Lady* (Boston: Houghton Mifflin, 1929).

[43] William S. Smith's vindication of himself may be found in a letter to McHenry, Dec. 20, 1798, *Publications of the Southern History Association*, XI (1907), 38–43.

[44] See above, ch. xx; Upham, *Timothy Pickering*, III, 464.

[45] Rufus King, *Correspondence*, II, 430–31; III, 264; "his resentment appeared implacable."

be repeated, it will be a serious thing to the public, as well as to me, and you, and our children.[46]

Despite these strictures, Adams made the nomination, the Senate confirmed it, and Smith entered upon active duty. He still remained a problem to his father-in-law. On May 22, 1799, the President inferentially accused him of meddling in army affairs, and concluded a sharp letter with these words, "I will not interfere with the discipline and order of the army, because you are my son-in-law." [47]

Colonel Smith nevertheless continued to seek military preferment. In 1800 he asked his father-in-law to appoint him commandant of a regiment of artillerists and engineers. Adams asked Hamilton's opinion and McHenry's; the former thought the appointment correct but liable to cause criticism. Adams replied that he expected criticism in everything relating to Colonel Smith, but added, "I see no reason or justice in excluding him from all service, while his comrades are all ambassadors or generals, merely because he married my daughter." [48]

Adams also nominated another son-in-law, Joshua Johnson, as superintendent of the Stamp Office. Pickering was disgusted, believing Johnson's business record in London was not beyond question. The Senate divided equally and Jefferson cast the deciding vote for Johnson "from the respect he had for the President's discernment." Adams was again deeply chagrined.[49] The cases of Colonel Smith and Johnson were, after all, exceptional. John Adams was no man to push his relatives.

Especially interesting are the favors of Timothy Pickering, a public servant of undoubted probity who vehemently denied the use of influence in behalf of his relatives but whose record can be squared with his declarations only by supposing complete, though honorable, self-deception. Pickering, it will be remembered, held high office continuously from 1791 to 1800. In July 1797, his eldest son John, then twenty, went off to Lisbon as secretary to the United States Minister, William Smith. Of this appointment the Secretary of State wrote, "I thought upon the whole that tho' a couple of years would perhaps be spent abroad, which would for the same space of time delay his appear-

---

[46] Dec. 19, 1798, Adams, *Works*, VIII, 617–18.
[47] *Ibid.*, VIII, 652.
[48] *Ibid.*, IX, 61, 63; Hamilton, *Works* (Hamilton ed.), V, 430–31.
[49] King, *Correspondence*, III, 248.

ing at the bar, yet he would see the world, learn several living lan-
guages, and lay a broader foundation of liberal knowledge; and on
his return resume his studies with a mind enlarged, and finally engage
in practice with superior advantage." [50] In January 1799 Pickering
wrote Rufus King, Minister at London, asking him to appoint John
his secretary in view of the pending resignation of Dandridge: "it
would gratify *him,* be incomparably more useful than a longer residence at Lisbon, and at the same time procure to *you* as diligent, as
able and as faithful a secretary as you would any where find. . . . I
suppose it possible that he may spend a little time every week in the
study of the Common Law, and in term-time visit Westminster
Hall." [51] Not hearing from King he renewed the "proposition" on May
4 and on May 6. In a letter which crossed these, King informed the
Secretary of State that although there would be no vacancy he would
welcome John "as a member of his family." [52] Pickering also had
another plan on foot for his eldest; he "intended that John should
have gone with Mr Smith to Constantinople," but that mission was
suspended and John went to London.

Another son, Timothy, discovered "a predilection for a military
life." The father preferred "the public service in the Navy. . . . An
education in our navy will give you a *profession.* . . . A good naval
officer . . . will never want employment in *mercantile navigation,*"
and concluded his paternal advice with these words: "I inclose your
commission as a midshipman. . . ." [53]

A nephew, Samuel Williams, was United States consul at Hamburg,
subsequently at London, and in 1797 was appointed United States
agent in London to prosecute claims of American citizens for British
spoliations. This post permitted service as private agent to Americans,
on commission. [54] Writing to Samuel, Pickering declared, "your
brother Timothy having informed me that the change would be agreeable to you, I of course presented to the President the recommendation,
and your appointment followed." [55]

"Brother Timothy" was a Boston merchant. Early in 1798 Pickering

[50] Pickering to David Humphreys, July 18, 1797, Pickering Papers, XXXVII, 216.
[51] Jan. 20, 1799, *ibid.,* X, 251.
[52] Pickering to King, *ibid.,* XI, 16, 37; King to Pickering, *ibid.,* XXIV, 175.
[53] Pickering to Timothy Pickering, Jr., June 17, 1799, *ibid.,* XI, 294.
[54] Pickering to Samuel Williams, Jan. 11, 1798, *ibid.,* VIII, 44–45.
[55] Dec. 16, 1797, *ibid.,* X, 77.

placed part of the insurance on the frigate *Crescent* (amounting to $40,000) with him.[56] Then Pickering recommended Timothy to secure provisions for the Purveyor. Lest the full significance of the transaction be overlooked, the Secretary of State added, "I assure myself that you will undertake the business, and that it will be done with that diligence, propriety & economy which shall satisfy the Purveyor and present you to the public as a fit agent for more extended employment in the same line should there be occasion—which is much to be apprehended."[57]

Another nephew, Timothy Newman, took to the sea and became captain of the frigate *Crescent*. "The appointment of Captain Newman to the command of the frigate was determined on by the Secy of War. Captain Newman several times spoke & wrote to me; but being a relation, I chose to leave the choice to the Secy of War upon such information as he should obtain."[58] In 1799 Newman became a master commandant in the navy.[59]

For the appointment of his cousin, William Wingate, as postmaster at Haverhill, Massachusetts, Pickering seems not to have been directly involved. Wingate was such a sorry specimen that no one would have wished to claim any responsibility. He first applied for the office at Boston, but Pickering, then Postmaster General, rejected the application: "I am persuaded I should incur not a little reproach were I to introduce a *Stranger* to fill it; and the reproach would be the more pointed, if that *stranger* to Boston were *my near relation*."[60] In 1794 the assistant postmaster general appointed Wingate postmaster in Haverhill at the instance of Pickering's brother while Timothy Pickering was absent on Indian affairs.[61] In 1797, when William's sins had become apparent, Pickering wrote Ichabod Tucker:

My assistant did not know his character. I never thought well enough of him to have given him any office. . . . until the postmaster general [Habersham] lately mentioned it, I did not know that William Wingate

---

[56] Pickering to Timothy Williams, Jan. 25, 1798, *ibid.,* VIII, 83–84; also *ibid.,* VIII, 88, 112, 138.

[57] Pickering to Timothy Williams, Jan. 30, 1798, *ibid.,* VIII, 95.

[58] Pickering to Col. Thompson, Oct. 5, 1797, *ibid.,* VII, 263.

[59] Pickering to Timothy Williams, July 8, 1799, *ibid.,* XI, 401.

[60] Pickering to William Wingate, Oct. 10, 1791, *ibid.,* VI, 35.

[61] Pickering to his sister, Mrs. Sargeant, Sept. 22, 1797, *ibid.,* VII, 213.

had ever held the office—or if I ever knew it, I had no recollection of it. If I were capable of helping a scoundrel to an office he should not be one of my own relations.[62]

Pickering's aid to his nephew, Timothy Williams, occasioned some sarcastic remarks on the part of the previous supplier of beef and pork to the Purveyor. Pickering made an indignant, if unconvincing, defense of his patronage to his relatives.

No conduct in my life . . . will countenance your insinuations. . . .

I will now detail to you the simple facts. When Mr Francis was about to purchase provisions for the Constitution frigate, he called upon me and said that he was not satisfied with your agency: that he had a quantity of beef and pork to procure; & wished me to recommend a suitable person to do the business. I told him that my nephew T. Williams would procure these articles with as much dispatch and economy as any man, and I could answer for his fidelity. . . .

I will add, sir, that the circumstances of being a relation, has never induced my recommendation of a single individual to a public office.[63]

Pickering had plenty of precedent for his family devotion. Henry Knox, Secretary of War, appointed his brother, William Knox, a clerk in the War Department office where he remained until he died, insane, in 1797.[64] Alexander Hamilton, while engaged deeply against Adams, did not hesitate to ask McHenry for a captain's commission in the Provisional Army in 1798 for his nephew, Philip Church.[65] He also asked the Secretary of the Navy "as a personal favor" for a commission for his cousin, Captain Robert Hamilton.[66] The President courteously assented to both requests.[67] McHenry, while Secretary of War, pushed the candidacy of his brother-in-law, John Caldwell, for Treasurer of the Mint.[68] McHenry's nephew was secretary to William Vans Murray, United States Minister at The Hague.[69] Elias Boudinot, Director of

[62] Oct. 10, 1797, *ibid.,* VII, 289.

[63] Pickering to Henry Jackson, June 22, 1798, *ibid.,* VIII, 587.

[64] Francis S. Drake, *Henry Knox,* p. 9.

[65] Hamilton, *Works* (Hamilton ed.), V, 138.

[66] Aug. 7, 1798, *ibid.,* VI, 336.

[67] Adams, *Works,* VIII, 608.

[68] Steiner, *op. cit.,* pp. 260–61, n.; Pickering Papers, VII, 168.

[69] *Ibid.,* X, 157.

the Mint, recommended his nephew, Isaac Cox Barnet, for consul at Brest [70] and his relative by marriage, Dr. Benjamin Rush, as Treasurer of the Mint.[71] And Rush proposed his brother for the post of associate justice of the Supreme Court.[72] The brother of Senator George Cabot of Massachusetts, Samuel Cabot, was commercial agent of the United States in London.[73]

Oliver Wolcott, while Auditor, sought to secure the appointment of his brother, Frederick, as inspector of revenue, his health permitting; [74] and later asked Habersham to appoint Frederick as postmaster at Litchfield.[75] Chauncey Goodrich, brother-in-law of Oliver Wolcott, wrote the latter respecting an appointment for his brother Elizur as collector of customs at New Haven, an office which he held until removed by Jefferson.[76] Jonathan Dayton, Speaker of the House, asked Wolcott for the appointment of his business partner "to the agency in the port of New York"; [77] Rufus King took his brother to London as his secretary.[78] Other cases could be cited, but these are sufficient to indicate that concern for one's relatives by blood or marriage was not unknown in top Federalist circles. The number was, nevertheless, comparatively small, and the relatively good record of the Federalists for their day and age need not be obscured by such examples. Washington would have disapproved the actions of his assistants.

REMOVAL FROM OFFICE

Congress recognized the power of the President alone to remove officials even where the appointment required the consent of the Senate. During the Federalist period the necessity for removing officials seldom arose, but there were enough cases to establish precedents. For the most part removals were occasioned for serious delinquency or for failure to account for public funds; but in Adams' administration there were a few instances in which political opinions were probably among

---

[70] Ibid., XXXVII, 19.
[71] Ibid., VII, 158, 236.
[72] Ibid., IX, 288.
[73] Ibid., VI, 185.
[74] Wolcott Papers, XVII, 16.
[75] Ibid., VI, 94.
[76] Ibid., V, 65.
[77] Ibid., VI, 66.
[78] King, Correspondence, II, 200.

the reasons for dismissal. Federalists and Republicans agreed that removals should be made only for cause.[79]

The number of removals is not easy to determine. There are no col-lected records with respect to inferior officers, but there is good evi-dence in cases requiring Senate confirmation of successors.[80]

Removals of civil officials (other than inferior officers) by Wash-ington numbered seventeen. This figure includes the recall of three foreign ministers, Monroe, Carmichael, and Thomas Pinckney (at his request), and the removal of two consuls, eight collectors, and four surveyors of internal revenue. In addition six military officers were separated from the service. The number of replacements of civil offi-cers (other than inferior ones) by Adams, including failure to reap-point in two cases, was twenty-one. Among these were the Secretary of State, Timothy Pickering, one minister and four consular officers, one marshal, seven collectors, five surveyors, one supervisor, and one commissioner of court. Adams also removed six army officers.[81] Even in the light of the modest size of the public service of this period, these numbers are extremely small and reflect the high standard of integrity which generally prevailed among federal officeholders.

The vexatious task of removing officials was approached gingerly. Shortly after Pickering became Postmaster General he wrote his predecessor for advice with reference to the Boston postmaster. ". . . when a person has long held an office, & especially if he has a family to support: tho' men of discernment, and even a whole people, may wish for his removal; yet their compassion surmounts every con-sideration of public advantage and individual convenience. What in such cases, is the duty of those who have the power of making a bene-ficial exchange?"[82] The same solicitude marked Hamilton's treatment

---

[79] James Sullivan, Republican of Massachusetts, declared, "To remove men from office, for their having their own opinions, is a species of tyranny of which we have loudly complained. To withhold offices from men who are satisfied with their country's constitution, because they do not love the present administration, when they are *better* qualified than others, would be no less than a militation with the principles of a free government." Thomas C. Amory, *Life of James Sullivan* (2 vols., Boston: Phillips, Sampson, 1859), II, 94.

[80] Carl Russell Fish, "Removal of Officials by the Presidents of the United States," Am. Hist. Assoc., *Annual Report, 1899,* I, 65–86. The list officially compiled in 1840 and published as House Document No. 132, 26th Cong., 1st sess., March 13, 1840, is incomplete so far as Washington's administration is concerned.

[81] Fish, "Removal of Officials . . . ," *op. cit.,* pp. 69–70.

[82] Pickering to Samuel Osgood, Nov. 30, 1791, Pickering Papers, VI, 44.

of the commissioner of loans for New York, who was kept on for a considerable time despite a paralytic stroke. Finally Hamilton advised the President, "with extreme regret and reluctance," that a change was essential.[83] Jefferson thought it unjust to turn out those who had behaved well, "merely to put others in." [84]

The case of diplomatic officers was on a somewhat different footing, as Pickering explained to Monroe after his recall from Paris. ". . . the President of the United States may be possessed of facts and information which would not only justify but require the recall of a foreign minister, or the dismission of an officer at home, although they should not furnish ground for a legal investigation." [85]

In the Treasury Department the cause of removals of subordinate officials was usually neglect or delinquency in the handling of funds. Thus Hudson Muse, collector of the district of Tappahannock, and Abraham Archer of Yorktown, were dismissed for failure to pay Treasury drafts drawn upon money in their possession. There was no charge of dishonesty, but of negligence. "Punctuality in this respect," wrote Hamilton to Washington, "is too indispensable not to be made the invariable condition of continuance in office." [86] The marshal of Georgia, Oliver Bowen, was indicted in 1799 for taking illegal fees, and subsequently discharged.[87]

The case of the chief clerk and the passport clerk in the State Department tells a good deal of the temper of the times. In the *Aurora* of January 24, 1798, the Secretary of State, Pickering, was charged with "a shameful breach of the laws" by asking a gratuity of five dollars from a Scotch merchant who desired a passport—for which no fee was permitted. Pickering was furious. "The Jacobinic scoundrels," he wrote the next day, "feasted on the imaginary discovery of *guilt* and *baseness*. . . . They will find, however, the fruitlessness of their malice; in attacking me, the vipers bite a file." He immediately cleared himself

---

[83] Hamilton to Washington, Jan. 12, 1795, Hamilton, *Works* (Hamilton ed.), V, 63.

[84] Jefferson, *Works* (Federal ed.), VI, 45.

[85] July 17, 1797, Pickering Papers, XXXVII, 215.

[86] June 16, 1794, Hamilton, *Works* (Hamilton ed.), IV, 568–69; see also Washington, *Writings,* XXXII, 162–63. For other cases see *Journal of the Executive Proceedings of the Senate of the United States of America* (3 vols., Washington: Duff Green, 1828); hereafter cited as *Senate Executive Journal.* For Gray, surveyor and inspector at Alexandria, *ibid.,* I, 270; for Sylvanus Walker, inspector, third district of So. Carolina, *ibid.,* I, 208.

[87] Pickering to Judge Patterson, Oct. 18, 1799, Pickering Papers, XII, 196.

by an affidavit from the merchant, and then called in his clerks. The episode can best be told in his own words.

I called in two of my clerks, in succession, & handed them the paper to read: the second at once acknowledged that *he* had taken the five dollars—but thought no harm, the payment being a *free gift*. I told him the act was glaringly improper, and that he must quit my office. He pleaded his innocence of intention,—and that he had never done an immoral act.—Persisting in my first sentiment, he said *he did not stand alone*. This alarmed me still more; for I saw it would affect my chief clerk, with whom I had always left blank passports to be filled up as people called, to prevent disappointment or delay. I am therefore constrained to dismiss both. I have consulted all my colleagues, & they concur with me in the necessity of this painful step: painful, because the Clerks sustained fair characters, had been long in the office, would have been recommended for their fidelity to any employment, were careful, steady, industrious, and the chief clerk, from his long and accurate acquaintance with the books, papers & business of the office was eminently useful.[88]

Removal for political reasons was unknown during the eight years of Washington's service as President. After Adams became President he was urged at times to replace officials for party reasons and a few changes were made in which party differences played a part. Two cases involved Joseph Whipple, collector at Portsmouth, and William Gardner, commissioner of loans for New Hampshire, of whom a correspondent wrote to the Secretary of the Treasury, "Their political conduct has been disrespectful to the Government and offensive to good men in the extreme." [89]

With respect to Gardner, Wolcott sent a carefully worded statement to Hamilton.

Of the motives which occasioned the dismission of Mr Gardiner,[90] I must speak with reserve, as they are known more particularly to President Adams, than to myself. Of this I am however certain, that there was good

---

[88] The two clerks were Taylor and Blackwell. Pickering to the Reverend John Clarke, Jan. 26, 1798, *ibid.*, VIII, 85–87; *ibid.*, XXXVII, 264. The letter to Clarke may be found in Upham, *Timothy Pickering,* III, 308.

[89] Hunt, "Office-Seeking during the Administration of John Adams," *Am. Hist. Rev.,* II, 255.

[90] Wolcott mispelled Gardner's name.

evidence, that M! Gardiner when applied to, for interest on the Funded Stock, was in the habit of answering to the following effect—*I have rec'd funds for the payment of interest to the end of the last quarter—but I doubt whether I shall be able to pay any interest in future—the Government is plunging the Country into expences which I know are insupportable.* Such language . . . undoubtedly furnished just cause for dismission.[91]

The consequence of the removal of Gardner and Whipple was promptly reported by Stephen Higginson. ". . . the removal of Whipple &c at Portsm? has a good Effect, it has produced a change in the manner of a number in the public Service, who were very Jacobinical; & very free with their Tongues upon french affairs.—" [92]

These removals were later defended by Adams in a letter to Benjamin Lincoln. "When I came into office, it was my determination to make as few removals as possible—not one from personal motives, not one from party considerations. This resolution I have invariably observed." He explained these cases on the ground of "infidelity to a trust" and "gross misconduct in office" and added that "the daily language of several officers at Portsmouth, were so evincive of aversion, if not hostility, to the national Constitution and government, that I could not avoid making some changes." Gallatin, however, declared these men were turned out of office for their political opinions.[93]

The principal cases of removal of highly placed public officials, excluding the recall of diplomats, were three: Edmund Randolph, Secretary of State; Tench Coxe, Commissioner of Revenue; and Timothy Pickering, Secretary of State. The resignation of Randolph as Secretary of State in 1795, under charges, was in effect a removal; it has been discussed at an earlier point. The dismissal of Pickering from the same office in 1800 has also been noticed.

The discharge of Tench Coxe as Commissioner of Revenue involved more than one consideration. Born in 1755, he studied at the College of Philadelphia (now the University of Pennsylvania) and at an early age entered the mercantile house of his father. Uncertain as to where he would cast his lot during the Revolution, he was once condemned as a traitor, but succeeded in clearing his record and joined the Pennsylvania militia. He was active in civic affairs in Philadelphia, a mem-

---

[91] Oct. 10, 1801, Wolcott Papers, XXI, 15.
[92] Higginson to Wolcott, July 28, 1798, *ibid.*, VI, 44.
[93] Adams to Lincoln, March 10, 1800, Adams, *Works*, IX, 47; *Annals*, IX, 2971.

ber of the Annapolis Convention and of the Continental Congress, 1788–89. Hamilton appointed him assistant to the Secretary of the Treasury in 1790, and in 1792 he became Commissioner of the Revenue, in direct charge of customs, excise, and lighthouses under the Secretary of the Treasury.

By 1791 Coxe had apparently shifted his political allegiance from Hamilton to Jefferson. Coxe indeed later declared that he had favored Jefferson in the debate over the succession to the presidency in January 1791, and had then incurred the "irremovable unfriendliness and indeed hostility" of Hamilton.[94] In 1795 Hamilton warned Washington against Coxe, who by that time was firmly attached to the Republican group. ". . . there is real danger that Mr. Coxe would first perplex and embarrass, and afterwards misrepresent and calumniate." [95] Wolcott retained Coxe after Hamilton retired but the Federalists considered him a "commissioned traitor." [96] In December 1797, Adams removed him from office. In the unpublished Pickering Papers there is a lengthy report to the President, apparently prepared by the Secretary of State and other members of the Cabinet, which sets out the grounds for removal. The memorandum suggested that the Secretary of the Treasury had no confidence in the Commissioner of the Revenue and stated that "their sentiments towards each other (occasioned by the improper conduct of the latter) are utterly incompatible with that harmonious conduct and co-operation in offices so closely connected, which the public interests indispensably require." [97]

Senator Cabot hailed the removal. "I rejoice to hear that you have finally expelled a traitor from the Treasury, who never deserved to have been trusted. The toleration of such a fellow in office after his duplicity was known indicates truly a weakness in the government. . . ." [98] Coxe asked for a congressional inquiry but to no avail.[99] When his friend Jefferson became President, his fortunes rose

---

[94] Hunt, "Office-Seeking during the Administration of John Adams," *Am. Hist. Rev.,* II, 260.

[95] Feb. 12, 1795, Hamilton, *Works* (Hamilton ed.), V, 77–78. Shortly afterward, Aug. 5, 1795, Hamilton wrote to Wolcott of Coxe, "That man is too cunning to be wise. I have been so much in the habit of seeing him mistaken that I hold his opinion cheap." Wolcott Papers, VII, 8.

[96] Cabot to Wolcott, May 31, 1797, H. C. Lodge, *George Cabot,* p. 140.

[97] Pickering Papers, VII, 550–59. Probable date, Dec. 18, 1797.

[98] Cabot to Wolcott, Jan. 19, 1798, Lodge, *op. cit.,* p. 148. Wolcott's own relations to John Adams bear a curious resemblance to those of the unfortunate Coxe to Wolcott.

[99] *Annals,* VII, 775 (Dec. 27, 1797).

again. Gallatin told Jefferson that Coxe had applied for seven different offices by June 1801;[100] in January 1803 he was appointed supervisor of revenue for Pennsylvania and in November he became Purveyor of Public Supplies, an office which he held until its abolishment in 1812.

Carl R. Fish considered the discharge of Coxe as the first removal for party reasons.[101] Gaillard Hunt held that it was "the most important removal from office for political reasons by Adams."[102] It was one of a mere handful, at most; the "multitude of Jacobins" whom Adams said he took over from his predecessor were left undisturbed in their offices.

---

[100] Harold Hutcheson, *Tench Coxe*, p. 42, n. 152.

[101] *Civil Service and the Patronage*, p. 19.

[102] "Office-Seeking during the Administration of John Adams," *Am. Hist. Rev.*, II, 256.

Chapter Twenty-three

THE RULE OF PARSIMONY

Stinginess

THE compensation of civil servants is a universal problem of public administration, partly fiscal, partly managerial, partly political. Pay policy in the 1790's was strictly pragmatic, but underlying practice were some general ideas and some deep-seated prejudices—or convictions. Attitudes and practice alike throw much light on the daily presuppositions of eighteenth century administration.

No one disagreed in principle with Washington's dignified remarks on official salaries. In his annual message of 1796 the President said:

> The compensations to the Officers of the United States, in various instances, and in none more than in respect to the most important stations, appear to call for Legislative revision. The consequences of a defective provision, are of serious import to the Government. If private wealth, is to supply the defect of public retribution, it will greatly contract the sphere within which, the selection of Characters for Office, is to be made, and will proportionally diminish the probability of a choice of Men, able, as well as upright: Besides that it would be repugnant to the vital principles of our Government, virtually to exclude from public trusts, talents and virtue, unless accompanied by wealth.[1]

This recommendation was put in terms likely to appeal to Republicans, since Federalists were already convinced of the soundness of liberal pay scales. Republicans, however, were not persuaded, and the parties took up positions for combat.

FEDERALIST AND REPUBLICAN ATTITUDES ON PUBLIC PAY SCALES

Public opinion in the 1790's was typically unfavorable to generous treatment of government officials and employees. The country was only

---

[1] Washington, *Writings,* XXXV, 317–18.

slowly recovering from the depressed conditions of the 1780's. The bulk of the population was rural and its money income was extremely modest. High salaries smacked of monarchy and corruption; democracy and purity meant a minimum of public expense, and salaries and wages in conformity with republican simplicity.

Federalists and Republicans fought each other continually on the salary question. Fisher Ames put tersely what the Federalists believed correct doctrine. "He did not think the least possible sum for which an office could be executed was the wisest or best to be adopted. The true rule was, that such a sum should be paid for service as was sufficient to command men of talents to perform it. Anything below this was parsimonious and unwise."[2] Oliver Wolcott echoed these sentiments. "Good abilities command high prices at market."[3] And the staunch Federalist Senator from Massachusetts, George Cabot, declared in 1797, "If Congress should be disposed to do all that they ought, I trust they will rescue us from the continued disgrace of starving our public officers."[4] It was a maxim of the Federalists to give liberal compensations, said Robert G. Harper. "Nothing is more true, than that men of talents and character will not long leave their homes and devote their time to the public service, unless they are at least supported decently; and that if we wish for able and faithful services we must pay their price. This the federal government has never done."[5]

To Jeffersonian Democrats and the plain people, these ideas seemed ill suited to a republican society. In 1790 the North Carolina House of Commons passed resolutions against "the monstrous salaries given to the public officers" in the new government. Petitions from certain inhabitants of New Jersey came to the House of Representatives in 1796, complaining that, "A militia-man, returning from service to his family, has only ten cents per day; a member of Congress has thirty cents per

[2] *Annals*, VI, 2001 (Jan. 27, 1797). Cf. Robert Morris' comment during the Revolution: "If Congress mean to succeed in this contest, they must pay good executive men to do their business as it ought to be done, and not lavish millions away by their own mismanagement." Ellis Paxson Oberholtzer, *Robert Morris: Patriot and Financier* (New York: Macmillan, 1903), p. 34.

[3] Gibbs, *Memoirs*, I, 68.

[4] Henry C. Lodge, *George Cabot*, p. 139.

[5] *Select Works of Robert Goodloe Harper* . . . (Baltimore: O. H. Neilson, 1814), p. 334.

mile. This they regard as an aristocratical distinction." [6] Opposition to more attractive scales of pay was unremitting. Jefferson declared with satisfaction, "Our public œconomy also is such as to offer drudgery and subsistence only to those entrusted with its administration, a wise & necessary precaution against the degeneracy of the public servants." [7] In 1794 Madison wrote Jefferson from Philadelphia, "The people all over the State are signing with avidity a remonstrance against the high salaries of the Govt." [8] Robert Rutherford of Virginia "was for keeping things in their due simplicity, and by no means to add to salaries. He could not think of giving the honey from the hive, the marrow from the bones of the people. He was for holding tight the purse-strings of six or seven millions of respectable people; he could not think of lavishing the precious article of money, however his caution might displease the gentleman from Massachusetts." [9] Public opinion, except among the Federalist leaders, favored economy if not parsimony in the payment of public officials. The artisans, mechanics, farmers, and seamen of the time, working out-of-doors for a modest livelihood, were not likely to look with equanimity upon handsome livings to clerks who merely wrote in books.

PAY SCALES

Principal officers. Congress set the salaries of the principal officials of the general government. Only one was impressive, and in the light of payments made to royal heads of states in 1789, it was modest enough—the President was allowed $25,000 per annum for salary and expenses. The figure was a compromise between $20,000 and

---

[6] *Annals,* V, 267 (Jan. 26, 1796). Jeremy Belknap wrote to Ebenezer Hazard, Sept. 3, 1789, "I have just seen a letter from a gentleman in Connecticut, who says the salary of the door-keeper of Congress is equal to that of the Chief Justice of Connecticut. Great complaint of high salaries!" *Belknap Papers,* II, 164.

[7] Jefferson to de Meusnier, April 29, 1795, Jefferson, *Works* (Federal ed.), VIII, 174.

[8] Dec. 21, 1794, Madison, *Writings* (Hunt ed.), VI, 229.

[9] *Annals,* VI, 2006 (Jan. 27, 1797). The Republicans were divided upon the matter of *congressional* salaries. Thomas Claiborne tried to reduce the six dollars per diem but John Page asked pointedly, "What true Republican could wish to exclude from a seat in Congress a physician, lawyer, merchant, farmer, or any other person possessed of such well-known abilities and virtues as to attract the attention and respect of a district which might wish to intrust its interests to him as a Representative? Or, rather, who ought not to desire that, as all offices are open to all, that the son of the poorest citizen might be enabled, if qualified, to fill a seat here or elsewhere, to do it without sacrificing his private interest?" *Ibid.,* IV, 1142 (Jan. 27, 1795).

$30,000; John Vining of Delaware spoke the general sentiment when he said on the floor of the House:

there are cases in which generosity is the best economy, and no loss is ever sustained by a decent support of the Magistrate. A certain appearance of parade and external dignity is necessary to be supported. Did I, said he, represent a larger State, I would speak with more confidence on the subject. We are haunted by the ghost of poverty; we are stunned with the clamor of complaint throughout the State. . . . But our calculations ought not to be confined to the present moment alone. . . . We should remember that the present time is the season for organizing the Government. . . .[10]

The salaries of department heads were fixed at $3,500 for Treasury and State, $3,000 for War. The Attorney General was allowed $1,500. Only three other officials received $2,000 or over: the Comptroller of the Treasury, the Treasurer, and the Governor of the Northwestern Territory. Ministers and foreign representatives of lesser rank did better. Gouverneur Morris in Paris and Thomas Pinckney in London each received an annual compensation of $9,000 and a single allowance of $9,000 for "outfit." The residents at Lisbon and The Hague and the chargé d'affaires at Madrid were given $4,500. Consuls lived on their fees.

When Oliver Wolcott was invited by Hamilton in 1789 to serve as Auditor, he had to consider whether he could live on his official stipend of $1,500 per annum. His friend, Oliver Ellsworth, in reassuring him on this point, gave us an invaluable glimpse into the expenditures of high officials in New York at that time. He wrote:

You may wish to know what would be the probable expense of your living in this place.

---

[10] *Ibid.,* I, 645 (July 16, 1789). Before his inauguration John Adams was complaining to his wife: ". . . our prospects . . . appear every day worse and worse. House rent at twenty-seven hundred dollars a year, fifteen hundred dollars for a carriage, one thousand for one pair of horses, all the glasses, ornaments, kitchen furniture, the best chairs, settees, plateaus, &c., all to purchase, all the china, delph or wedgewood, glass and crockery of every sort to purchase, and not a farthing probably will the House of Representatives allow, though the Senate have voted a small addition. All the linen besides. I shall not pretend to keep more than one pair of horses for a carriage, and one for a saddle. Secretaries, servants, wood, charities which are demanded as rights, and the million dittoes present such a prospect as is enough to disgust any one. Yet not one word must we say." *Letters of John Adams, Addressed to His Wife,* II, 242–43.

House and stable would be about $200 00
Wood per cord, (best,) 4 00
   "   "   "   (oak,) 2 50
Hay, per ton, ... 8 00
Marketing higher than at Hartford, 25 per cent.

It would not be expected that your office should subject you to more expense of company, or a different style of living, than you would choose. It is my opinion that you could live within 1000 dollars, as your family now is, and that you might expect, on some future occasion, such further advancement as your talents and services will entitle you to. I wish to see you transplanted into the national government for its sake and your own. . . .[11]

Judges were paid on the scale set for department heads. The Chief Justice of the Supreme Court received $4,000, his colleagues $3,500 each. The salaries of the district judges varied from $800 (Delaware) to $1,800 (South Carolina).[12] It was indeed an austere level of democratic simplicity that Congress imposed upon the leading figures in the judicial and administrative circles of the new general government.

TABLE III

SALARIES OF UNITED STATES OFFICIALS, 1799

Officer	Salary
Secretary of State	$5,000
Secretary of the Treasury	5,000
Secretary of War	4,500
Secretary of the Navy	4,500
Attorney General	3,000
Comptroller of the Treasury	3,500
Treasurer	3,000
Auditor	3,000
Commissioner of the Revenue	3,000
Register	2,400
Accountant of the War Department	2,000
Accountant of the Navy Department	2,000
Postmaster General	3,000
Assistant Postmaster General	1,700

[11] Gibbs, op. cit., I, 22.
[12] 1 Stat. 72 (Sept. 23, 1789).

Despite efforts on the part of the Federalists to pay top officials more generously, and despite the increase in the cost of living after 1795, it was not until 1799 that a new level of compensation was approved by Congress. These salaries are shown in the preceding table.[13]

Many federal officials were employed with the understanding that they would supplement their income by private pursuits. In 1796 Pickering (then Secretary of State) frankly declared that "it may be doubted whether any very competent person for surveyor general can be found, who will not improve the opportunity presented by his station, of making or advancing his fortune in lands over the Ohio. If Congress intended to exclude the Surveyor General from any land [purchases], his pay should have been so increased as to induce a proper character to submit to the restriction. The defect of compensation was a principal reason of Mr DeWitt's declining the office."[14] In 1797 he wrote Zephaniah Swift offering him the position of judge in the Northwest Territory. "The salary," he said, "I am aware, presents no allurement: but knowing that you were interested in the lands reserved or ceded to Connecticut, within that territory; and thinking it possible that a coincidence of private with public considerations might persuade you to go to that country, I ask (with the privity of the President) whether the office of judge in the Territory will be agreeable to you?"[15] And in corresponding with the prospective chief justice of the Mississippi Territory, he admitted that the salary ($800) was quite inadequate, but added, "You will doubtless duly appreciate the cheapness of good lands in the Natchez country, and the ease with which a family may be maintained. . . ."[16]

Many, if not most, of the fee officers devoted only part of their time to their public duties. Postmasters and marshals required additional income from private pursuits. In only the larger offices could the postmasters live on their official income. Even in Charleston, South Carolina, it was difficult to find an incumbent "unless it can be made to coincide with . . . other employments."[17] The subordinate officers

---

[13] Data from 1 Stat. 729 (March 2, 1799). Of this act Sedgwick wrote King that compared with what ought to have been done it was a paltry measure. Rufus King, *Correspondence,* II, 583.

[14] Pickering to Washington, July 19, 1796, Pickering Papers, VI, 203.

[15] *Ibid.,* VII, 525.

[16] *Ibid.,* IX, 89.

[17] *Ibid.,* VI, 64.

of the internal revenue service were on a part-time basis.[18] Collectors in the small ports had time enough to carry on private enterprises and doubtless many of them did; in larger ports the duties of office required full-time attention. No law or regulation has been discovered establishing a rule on eligibility to part-time private employment.

The public service was not, however, allowed to suffer from divided loyalty. When Henry W. De Saussure had under advisement an appointment as Director of the Mint, he inquired whether he could continue the practice of law. Randolph replied that while there was no incompatibility in the nature of the work, the time necessary for the one might interfere with the other. "If therefore the business of the Mint should meet an obstacle from the prosecution of that profession, it will be expected, either that private occupations will absolutely yield to public office, or that the officer would retire from his public station." [19]

Clerks and subordinates. The titles of clerk, principal clerk, and chief clerk were recognized in the earliest legislation of Congress. The act fixing executive salaries in 1789 established $500 as the maximum for clerks.[20] In 1795 Congress authorized department heads to vary compensations "as the services to be performed shall in their judgment require," but observing a ceiling of $1,000 for principal clerks and without exceeding the total appropriation for salaries.[21] In 1797 Pickering paid the four clerks in the State Department $990, $950, $650, and $500 respectively.[22] Most clerks in 1800 received between $700 and $800, but a few exceeded $1,000 up to $1,400.

The Treasury organization of 1789 established three principal clerks. Their duty was to supervise the work in each of the Treasury offices. In the office of the Comptroller the principal clerk rated a salary of $800, in the others, $600. The title of chief clerk was established in the State and War Departments, the former receiving $800, the latter initially $600. The distinction between principal and chief was

---

[18] *American State Papers: Finance,* I, 578.

[19] State Dept., Domestic Letters, VIII, 323.

[20] 1 Stat. 67.

[21] 1 Stat. 443; a valuable document prepared under the direction of Ismar Baruch, *History of Position Classification and Salary Standardization in the Federal Service, 1789–1938* (mimeo., Farm Credit Administration, 1939) deals principally with a later period.

[22] Pickering to Committee of Ways and Means, Jan. 17, 1798, Pickering Papers, VIII, 70–71.

less in salary than in status; the latter being the head of the clerical staff of the whole department, the former presiding over a single office such as that of the Register. These salaries rose during the decade: in 1801 State paid $1,750; Treasury, $1,800; War, $1,840; and Navy, $1,700.[23]

Eighteenth century clerks were as dissatisfied with their emoluments as their twentieth century successors. In 1793 the chief clerks petitioned for an increase of pay, without success;[24] in 1794 the War Department clerks were rebuffed in their struggle for better pay;[25] appeals for extraordinary expenses of clerks during the epidemic of 1793 were denied.[26]

Fee officers. By far the larger number of federal officials were compensated by fees for services rendered. Nearly the whole of the field service was paid on this basis, including the collectors, naval officers, and surveyors; the supervisors and inspectors of revenue; the attorneys and marshals; the deputy postmasters; and the consuls.

To a country impoverished and lacking a proper supply of circulating medium and means of moving funds readily from place to place, the fee system was a godsend. Officials were compensated if there was a demand for their services; otherwise the government expended nothing. They were paid on the spot, by those whom the law required to deal with them. There was no problem of collection—the self-interest of the official was sufficient. Public posting of the schedule of fees and stern laws against taking excessive amounts were relied upon to protect the public. English precedent and contemporary convenience spread the system far and wide.

Its inherent dangers were foreseen, nevertheless. In 1793 Fitzsimons of Pennsylvania declared that public officers should be compensated for their services without receiving fees, "when it is considered how difficult it is to guard against abuses and frauds."[27] There was considerable complaint against excessive fees notwithstanding the strict provisions of the laws.

How well did the fee-takers fare? Although there was hardship in

[23] *American State Papers: Miscellaneous,* I, 304.
[24] *Annals,* IV, 152 (Dec. 31, 1793).
[25] *Ibid.,* IV, 225 (Jan. 15, 1794).
[26] *Ibid.,* IV, 498 (March 11, 1794) and 522 (March 17, 1794).
[27] *Ibid.,* III, 877 (Feb. 16, 1793).

some small offices,[28] high incomes were frequent in the large ones. Indeed, some collectors earned more than the Secretary of the Treasury. In 1792 the collector of Boston received net $4,223.72; New York, $4,609.04; and Philadelphia, $4,397.72. Salem earned just over $1,000 for its collector, Norfolk nearly $2,500.[29] By 1801 these figures had risen substantially; Philadelphia—then the biggest port—produced collector's fees to the amount of $8,452.17,[30] exceeding the salary of the Secretary of the Treasury by more than $3,400.

The story was different in the small ports where business was light and complaints heavy. The collector of Portsmouth, New Hampshire, reported to Hamilton in February 1790, that his income was $257; he continued, ". . . the public business has required my constant and arduous service with the assistance of a Clerk a considerable part of the time & would not admit of any attention to my private affairs." [31] In 1792 he reported his earnings as $546.88 and calculated their actual value to the government at not less than $1,000; "an unwillingness to relinquish an office that I am not averse to, hath induced me again to mention this matter to you." [32]

The supervisors of revenue, collecting the excise tax on stills and distilled liquor, did poorly. Their fees were not fixed by Congress directly. The President was authorized to make such allowances out of their collections as he deemed reasonable and proper up to a maximum for all revenue officers in a district of seven per cent of the whole product of their duties, and up to an over-all maximum of $45,000.[33] The most lucrative supervisor's office in 1792 was that of Massachusetts, which produced an income of $1,209.10; only three others topped $1,000 and New York was worth only $102.54.[34]

The postmasters also were forced to rely on fees from their local patronage. In the big towns they prospered, but in the others they

---

[28] Such as the case of the So. Carolina collector of the carriage tax who had to ride forty miles for a fifty-cent fee. *Ibid.,* VII, 1068–69.

[29] *American State Papers: Miscellaneous,* I, 60–61.

[30] *Ibid.,* I, 271.

[31] Feb. 18, 1790, Letters from the Collector, Portsmouth, N. H., Sept. 22, 1789–March 19, 1833. Copies of letters from a number of ports of entry are preserved in the National Archives. The Portsmouth set is unnumbered, and letters are identified in the letter book only by date.

[32] Oct. 17, 1792, *ibid.*

[33] 1 Stat. 199, sec. 58 (March 3, 1791).

[34] *American State Papers: Miscellaneous,* I, 67.

earned only modest amounts. The fees of the postmasters were fixed by the Postmaster General, who was authorized by the act of 1782 (continued in force after 1789) to allow such commissions "as he shall think their respective services may merit," but not over twenty per cent of their revenue.[35] The post office act of 1792 for a time set a maximum of $1,800 to any postmaster.[36] Taking the commissions for 1800, the office at Philadelphia led the list with a figure of $4,625.57; New York was at Philadelphia's heels with $4,567.45; Baltimore ranked third, with fees of $3,235.45, all larger than the allowance to the Postmaster General. But there were other towns like Annapolis, which returned $298.06; Princeton, New Jersey, $367.49; and Gloucester, Massachusetts, the fisherman's town, $125.17. Many more gave the local postmaster a mere $25 to $100 a year.[37]

The marshals were miserably rewarded by their fees, and it is not surprising to find them seeking other employment. In 1792 the marshal of North Carolina took in $606.47; he was the most active one. In Massachusetts the marshal earned $289.00; in Maryland, $253.72; and in New York he found his services could produce an income of only $48.63.[38] We may surmise that this was an exceptionally peaceful year in the old Dutch colony. In 1795 Hamilton described the office of marshal as "a troublesome and unprofitable place." [39]

ADEQUACY

"Men," declared the *Gazette of the United States,* "must be rewarded for doing their duty—the imperfections of humanity require the spur of interest: 'If you expect work well done, you must pay well.' " [40] Were public officials and employees well recompensed in the light of the standards of the 1790's or were they the victims of public parsimony?

Oliver Wolcott could not have thought himself overpaid when he set up housekeeping in Philadelphia in 1790. "I have been to Philadelphia," he wrote his father, "to procure a house, and have succeeded, though with some difficulty. I am to pay the excessive rent of one

---

[35] *Journals of the Continental Congress, 1774–1789* (34 vols., Washington: Govt. Printing Office, 1904–37), XXIII, 670.
[36] 1 Stat. 232, sec. 23.
[37] *American State Papers: Miscellaneous,* I, 289–99.
[38] *Ibid.,* I, 59–60.
[39] Hamilton to Washington, Jan. 14, 1795, Hamilton, *Works* (Hamilton ed.), V, 64.
[40] Feb. 16, 1791.

hundred pounds, which if known would probably divert some of the envy which my old acquaintances feel on account of the 'high salary' which is given me." [41] His salary, as Auditor, was $1,500 a year.

There was much contemporary evidence that many salaries were low. John Adams said in 1796 that "the expenses of living at the seat of government are so exorbitant, so far beyond all proportion to the salaries, and the sure reward of integrity in the discharge of public functions is such obloquy, contempt, and insult, that no man of any feeling is willing to renounce his home, forsake his property and profession for the sake of removing to Philadelphia, where he is almost sure of disgrace and ruin." [42] A year earlier William Smith charged in the House that Jefferson, Knox, and Hamilton had all resigned "chiefly for one reason, the smallness of the salary." [43] This was certainly less than the whole truth.

Nevertheless the charge had some foundation. Hamilton secured much more in the practice of law than as Secretary of the Treasury, and Wolcott put himself in a comfortable financial situation only after he entered business. Stoddert and Habersham had enjoyed private incomes superior to their official salaries, and McHenry suffered loss when he became Secretary of War. On the other hand Pickering and Knox, Benjamin Lincoln and Sebastian Bauman earned no more, perhaps less, in their respective private capacities. It is not possible to determine the extent to which prevailing salaries were important in the flood of declinations that Washington encountered in 1795; they were probably one of several considerations. But the fact remains that men high in public station during the Federalist period were not attracted to office, or led to abandon it, because of inadequate salaries.

The regular full-time clerks in the departmental offices were paid at about the commercial rate in the early 1790's but somewhat lower after 1796 when the higher cost of living had produced an improvement in the countinghouses. It was at this time that Wolcott complained he could not retain able clerks.[44]

The Federalists were unable to provide compensation for officials and employees on the scale they thought proper. Their theory clashed with that of the Republicans and they were forced to compromise.

---

[41] Gibbs, *op. cit.*, I, 57.
[42] Adams, *Works*, I, 483.
[43] *Annals*, IV, 1141.
[44] Gibbs, *op. cit.*, I, 255.

Behind theory were some stubborn facts. Urban commercial standards of life and income opposed those of rural America on the floor of the House of Representatives, and complete victory went to neither side. The tiny civil service was dissatisfied, and for different reasons so were the Republicans. Federalist doctrine, clearly stated and consistently pursued, could be revived when the hour was propitious—but the hour was long delayed.

Chapter Twenty-four

SOME CIVIL SERVANTS

THE eighteenth century civil service differed in many respects from that of a later period. Its temper and outlook were influenced by the class distinctions of the mother country; its working habits were those of a relatively leisurely era; its tools were of the simplest kind.

The interests and ambitions of men were, however, modern enough. The civil service had no such diversity of talents as would one day be required but the variety and richness of personality it contained make it a very human and indeed a fascinating study.

Most civil servants were engaged in finance, record keeping, and the ordinary type of clerical operations, chiefly plain copying. The professional side of the service was modest indeed, comprising the judges, the district attorneys and an occasional legal counsel elsewhere, and a small number of physicians and surgeons in the army, navy, and marine hospitals. Add a few surveyors in the western wilderness, a few engineers in the army and a naval constructor, and the roll of professionally trained officials is complete. Science—other than the professions—was absent. Statisticians were unknown and professional economists could not be found on the North American continent, much less in the departments of state. It was not an age of experts.

THE COLLECTORS

In the public economy of the decade 1790–1800, the collectors were important figures. Their annual earnings in the larger ports were highly respectable. There they presided over substantial business offices: the number of employees at the Boston customhouse was 57; at New York, the same; at Philadelphia, 50; at Baltimore, 67; at Charleston, 47.[1]

---

[1] These figures are derived from *American State Papers: Miscellaneous,* I, 263–78.

In his appointments to the office of collector, Washington was partial to former members of the Revolutionary Army. In twenty cases where the evidence is available, sixteen had served in a military capacity—some in high rank. Collectors, naval officers, and surveyors held office at pleasure, but changes came almost entirely by resignation or death of the incumbent. Jefferson retained some prominent collectors who had served under the Federalists.

Although the collectors in the smaller ports were unlikely to have more than a local reputation, in the big towns they were men of importance, known sometimes beyond their community and state throughout the country. Bluff General Benjamin Lincoln, collector of the port of Boston from 1789 until he retired in 1809, belonged to the one-time famous New England Lincoln family which produced an impressive line of public figures. His official career began in 1757 at the age of twenty-four, as town clerk of Hingham, Massachusetts; he became justice of the peace, a member of the provincial legislature and of the Provincial Congress, and in the Revolutionary Army attained the rank of brigadier general before he was captured by General Clinton. After exchange by the British, he served as Secretary of War from 1781 to 1783, and was acting as lieutenant governor of Massachusetts in 1789 when he applied for a federal position, telling Washington that he had lost much of his property and that his emoluments as lieutenant governor were "insufficient." According to Christopher Gore, his appointment as collector "renewed his youth and happiness." [2] Lincoln became a valued correspondent of Hamilton and an active figure in the Federalist party. He was a friend of John Adams, who proposed in 1798 that he become second in command of the Provisional Army instead of Hamilton: to which the indignant Pickering retorted that Lincoln was usually asleep. [3]

Benjamin Goodhue charged him with "unpardonable neglect" of the Baker Island light off Salem and asked Oliver Wolcott to put it under the care of the Salem collector. [4] The old general became involved in financial trouble in 1798. Wolcott had to insist upon the payment of balances due and finally, losing confidence in Lincoln's discretion and judgment, asked Stephen Higginson privately whether

[2] Gore to Rufus King, King, *Correspondence,* I, 366.
[3] Pickering Papers, IX, 311–12.
[4] Wolcott Papers, XI, 58.

Lincoln ought not to be removed.[5] No action was taken, however, and he served until his voluntary retirement in 1809.

A different type was represented by John Lamb, collector of the port of New York. The son of Anthony Lamb, sentenced by an English court to be deported to America as an accomplice of the notorious burglar, Jack Sheppard (who died on the gallows), he became a prosperous wine merchant. After passage of the Stamp Act, he became a leader of the Sons of Liberty, "was active in haranguing the populace, corresponded with patriots in other colonies, and continued to be an irrepressible agitator during the next decade." After the battle of Concord and Lexington, Lamb and Isaac Sears seized the customhouse (a prophetic act). Subsequently he became an artillery captain, was wounded, captured, and exchanged, and in 1783 was brevetted a brigadier general. In 1784 he was appointed collector of customs of the port of New York by the state legislature, of which he was a member. During his incumbency of the same office under Washington, a large shortage occurred due to the guilt of one of his deputies, a former criminal. Lamb was held responsible, resigned, sold his lands to cover the lost funds, and in 1800 died in poverty.[6]

Jeremiah Olney was the collector at Providence, Rhode Island, from 1789 through the administrations of Washington, Adams, and Jefferson. He was a scion of the New England family established in 1635 by Thomas Olney, one of the founders of the Baptist Church in America; and one of the thirteen original proprietors of Providence, Rhode Island.[7] He was a colonel in the 1st Rhode Island regiment during the Revolutionary War, was commended by Washington, and in 1798 was rated by him as among the preferred officers for the Provisional Army.[8] He was president of the Rhode Island Society of the Cincinnati. His brother Stephen, a captain in the Revolutionary Army, represented North Providence for twenty years in the state legislature.

Olney was a strict and conscientious customs officer, literal in his interpretations and consequently often at odds with importers and shipmasters. The brig *Happy Return* left for Dublin, was stranded and

---

[5] Nov. 21, 1798, *ibid.*, Vol. XLIII.

[6] *Dictionary of American Biography*, X, 555–56; see also Isaac Q. Leake, *Memoir of the Life and Times of General John Lamb* (Albany: Joel Munsell, 1850).

[7] *Appleton's Cyclopaedia of American Biography* (James Grant Wilson and John Fiske, eds., 6 vols., New York: D. Appleton, 1887–89), IV, 578.

[8] Washington, *Writings*, XXXVI, 333.

abandoned. Her rigging, sails, cables, and anchors were taken off, however, and returned to Providence, whereupon the diligent Olney demanded bond of the owners for the payment of duties; "the Gentlemen thinking it unreasonable and unjust that they should be obliged to pay duties on them," refused to obey his injunction.[9]

The sloop *Nancy,* bound from Providence to Alexandria, was allowed by Olney to depart without a permit and manifest. On its arrival Collector Charles Lee promptly seized the cargo for failure to possess a manifest and was upheld by Hamilton. The unfortunate Olney was roundly berated by the innocent master and owners, and was put to much trouble to secure the eventual release of the *Nancy's* cargo of cheese, lime, and tow cloth.[10]

Nothing daunted, Olney seized upon a half barrel of oranges, two barrels of limes, one case of pickles, and thirty coconuts which had been allowed to pass without duty by General Jedediah Huntington, collector at New London, Connecticut, into which port the ships *Vigilant* and *Hope* had been forced by storms on their way to Providence. The articles were not imported for sale, but Olney held them for instructions from the Secretary of the Treasury; it was clear from his letters that he held a poor opinion of the diligence and capacity of his neighboring colleague, Huntington.[11]

That Olney had to watch against deliberate flouting of the navigation and tariff acts was beyond doubt. The firm of Brown and Francis of Providence was especially independent; by deliberate misrepresentation they sent off the ship *Warren* to Calcutta in November 1790, without clearance—although Olney attended at his office after church, on Thanksgiving day, to accommodate the master.[12] In November 1791, the master of the sloop *Clementina* sought to excuse his arrival at Newport with neither manifest nor permit by pleading that he forgot to call for these papers.[13]

Olney's greatest troubles arose from "a merchant of considerable eminence" in Providence, Welcome Arnold. The collector first offended

---

[9] July 19, 1790. Letters from the Collector at Providence, R. I. (2 vols., Vol. I, June 25, 1790–Dec. 5, 1809; Vol. II, Jan. 2, 1810–Nov. 5, 1832), Vol. I MS. in the archives of the Treasury Department. References are from letters written by the collector to the Secretary of the Treasury.

[10] Sept. 8; Oct. 1; Oct. 4, 1790, *ibid.*

[11] Jan. 17, 1791, *ibid.*

[12] Nov. 29, 1790, *ibid.*

[13] Nov. 3, 1791, *ibid.*

Arnold early in 1791 by putting in suit an overdue bond.[14] On the afternoon of November 6, 1792, the ship *Neptune,* owned by Arnold and loaded with goods from Surinam, in the name of Dexter, docked at Providence. Olney refused to accept bond from Arnold and Dexter as security for entry, charging that Arnold was the real owner, that the transfer of ownership to Dexter was fraudulent, and that Arnold, being then in default on a bond, could not offer further security under the law. The case eventually reached the Supreme Court of the United States which affirmed the decision of the Rhode Island superior court in favor of Arnold.[15]

If we can judge from the letters of Olney, the life of a collector in a lesser port was not an easy one. He was subject to pressure from the mercantile interests for favorable application of the navigation acts and customs dues; and in a small community where mercantile interests were dominant, the social pressure might well have been severe. Thus Olney begged for directions on a point disputed by the merchants, "that I may not be further censured as having made a demand not warranted by law." [16] In putting in a claim in 1791 for increased compensation, he informed Hamilton:

Officers of the Customs, who faithfully discharge their duties to the public, have ever, in this Country, met with the censure and ill-will of the generality of the merchants and those concerned in navigation. The Law will, at times, bear hard upon them all; and if the Collectors do not then favor them more than consists with a due execution thereof, they are almost sure to lose the esteem of those who were their friends, and to gain the enmity of those who before wished them well. This consideration forcibly points out the expediency of placing those officers in an independent situation, in respect to their emoluments; lest from the smallness of their income, they should be privately tempted to wink at breaches of the law, by which the revenue would be defrauded, and the Nation lose infinitely more than would be sufficient to afford its officers an handsome support, and set them above temptation. . . . But while I hold it [my office], I mean unproductive as it is, to continue a strict and impartial discharge of the trust reposed in me, regardless of my own Popularity and the consequent loss of Friends.[17]

[14] June 21, 1791; July 29, 1791, *ibid.*
[15] *Olney* vs. *Arnold,* 3 Dallas 308 (1796).
[16] July 19, 1790, Letters from the Collector at Providence, R. I., Vol. 1.
[17] Jan. 6, 1791, *ibid.*

Shortly afterward, he wrote that he had been repeatedly censured by the merchants for his strictness in executing the revenue laws.[18] Toward the close of 1791, we find him again asking Hamilton's approval of his conduct, since "some interested men . . . have clamoured loudly against me" and he needed consolation "in order to heal my wounded feelings." [19] Olney's own record of pettifogging insistence upon more than the letter of the law leaves the reader with some sympathy for the vexed merchants—and the harassed Secretary of the Treasury.

TWO TREASURY OFFICIALS

John Steele was one of a number of members of both Houses of Congress who exchanged the hazards of political life for the security of an administrative position. Born in North Carolina in 1764, he was too young for military service in the Revolutionary Army but he was active in state politics, representing his borough of Salisbury in the Assembly at the age of twenty-three. He was a member of the two state conventions that considered the ratification of the Constitution and in April 1790 took his seat in the House of Representatives. Although diligent in the interests of his southern constituents he was defeated in the elections of 1792 and retired from Philadelphia in March 1793. He corresponded with Tench Coxe about a Treasury appointment; Coxe asked him whether he had been accustomed to accounts, whether he had read or practiced law, whether he had any particular office in mind, and "particularly who in the present list of Senators and Representatives of North Carolina" Coxe could consult.[20] Steele was appointed Comptroller of the Treasury in 1796 and held office until September 30, 1802. Returning to North Carolina he again became active in politics, serving several terms in the lower house of the state legislature. While Comptroller, he complained about his salary, admitting at the same time that should an officer express dissatisfaction, "the remedy is in every one's mouth let him resign and others of equal merit will be found ready to fill the vacancy. This is certainly true in part. . . ." [21] Wolcott put his character in brief but

---

[18] Jan. 17, 1791, *ibid*.
[19] Oct. 11, 1791, *ibid*.
[20] John Steele, *Papers*, I, 101–2.
[21] Wolcott Papers, XXII, 51.

illuminating terms—"An honest Man, but of a Proud, Jealous, & irritable temper." [22]

Joseph Nourse was one of the first career men in the general government. Born in London in 1754, he emigrated to Virginia and in 1776 joined the Revolutionary Army as military secretary to General Charles Lee. He was clerk and paymaster of the Board of War from 1777 to 1781, and after a brief service as assistant auditor general, he became Register of the Treasury in 1781. Reappointed in 1789 to the same post by Washington, he served without a break until he retired in 1829— nearly fifty years! His second passion was the American Bible Society, of which he was a vice president for twenty-five years. [23]

THE CLERKS

The special symbol of public agencies, the government clerk, [24] promptly appeared on the scene in 1789, promptly proved his value, and promptly began to ask for more pay. The chief clerks in State and War were designated by law to take charge of their departments in case of a vacancy in the office of Secretary. They were supervisory-managerial officials, with only a very small number of immediate subordinates, to be sure, but with considerable responsibility for keeping papers in order and for expediting business.

Henry Remsen, chief clerk of the Department of State, was one of the best known of this group. During the Confederation he had been commissioner to count and destroy paper money, assistant to the auditor in the adjustment of accounts and claims, interpreter of Low Dutch to Congress, undersecretary of Congress, and chief clerk of the Department of State under John Jay. He had, as he wrote on May 11, 1789, "been uniformly attached to the American cause and . . . lost nearly all of his property." [25] Jefferson carried him over into the new government. William Barton, principal clerk in the office of Com-

---

[22] *Ibid.*, XXII, 20.

[23] *Appleton's Cyclopaedia of American Biography*, IV, 540.

[24] While the public service was practically a male monopoly, it is of passing interest to note that a woman, Miss Mary R. Goddard, was postmistress at Baltimore in 1789–90; and that an attempt to displace her for failure to render her accounts "has made some noise and has brought an attack . . . in the Philadelphia Paper—" Postmaster General, Letter Book A, p. 31, Nov. 24, 1789.

[25] Gaillard Hunt, *Calendar of Applications and Recommendations for Office during the Presidency of George Washington* (Washington: Govt. Printing Office, 1901), p. 106.

missioner of Revenue, was brother-in-law of David Rittenhouse and familiar with such prominent men as Hamilton, Tench Coxe, Madison, and Boudinot. In 1789 he had been "recommended indefinitely" by Rittenhouse: "His education and principles are such as to make him useful." [26]

Remsen's resignation in 1792 caused a temporary flurry in the State Department office. William Barton from Treasury applied for the place; Jacob Blackwell and George Taylor, clerks in the office, had strong claims to preference. Jefferson appointed Taylor, discovering that if he brought in an outsider (i.e., Barton) all his clerks would resign. "This," said Jefferson, "would be to me an irreparable loss, because the two seniors have been very long in the office, are perfectly intimate with all the papers & proceedings for years back, to all of which I am an utter stranger, & to which consequently they serve me as an index." [27] As between Blackwell and Taylor, Jefferson decided on humanitarian grounds. He informed Blackwell, "He [i.e., Taylor] is a married man, with a family; yourself single. There can be no doubt but that 500. dollars place a single man as much at his ease as 800. to a married one." [28] Blackwell carried on, nevertheless, and both men served until 1798 when, as already noted, they were summarily dismissed by Pickering for taking passport gratuities.

In a miniature civil service such as that of the federal government from 1789 to 1801 the opportunities for promotion were few enough. Yet the spur of hope for a better position was recognized clearly by Hamilton who wrote Washington concerning the advancement of Oliver Wolcott from Auditor to Comptroller, "The expectation of promotion in civil as in military life is a great stimulus to virtuous exertion, while examples of unrewarded exertion, supported by talent and qualification, are proportionable discouragements. Where they do not produce resignations they leave men dissatisfied, and a dissatisfied man seldom does his duty well." [29]

The appointment of clerks was left to the heads of departments; [30] Hamilton delegated to the principal Treasury officials the selection of

---

[26] *Ibid.*, p. 8.

[27] Jefferson to Barton, April 1, 1792, Jefferson, *Works* (Federal ed.), VI, 458.

[28] April 1, 1792, *ibid.*, VI, 457.

[29] Hamilton, *Works* (Lodge ed.), IX, 480.

[30] Washington, *Writings,* XXX, 447, 490; XXXII, 43–44; XXXIII, 118.

clerks for their respective offices.[31] He had seventeen in his own office in 1792; the Comptroller, nine; the Auditor, nineteen; the Register, twenty-four plus fourteen who served part of the year; but the Treasurer required only two. The War Department had seven in the Secretary's office, seven in the pay office; the office for settling accounts with the states had five regulars and eleven working part time.[32] These were the large clerical staffs.

The duties of clerks were varied. In the Treasury they were concerned with keeping books and accounts. In every office they did a mass of writing and copying, all of which was, of course, by hand. In the Mint they acted as writers, bookkeepers, paymasters, weighers, comptrollers, and purchasing agents—and also did "such out-of-doors business" as was required by the Director. They numbered three! The customary hours were six per day.[33] Appointment was without term and was understood to be permanent.[34]

The public service has often been charged on the one hand with being the refuge of the unsuccessful, and on the other of being the training ground (at public expense) of future enterprisers. While neither charge could be sustained against the public service of the 1790's, both had their prototypes. Senator George Cabot recommended to Wolcott one Stephen Sewall of Marblehead, who, at the age of about fifty, had spent his whole life in keeping merchants' books. With a numerous family to support, Cabot suggested that an appointment as clerk in the Treasury at $500 a year would be an act of great humanity "and probably will be useful to the public." [35] Joseph Chambers became a clerk in the Comptroller's office "with a view to qualify himself for public business by acquiring a familiar knowledge of the forms and principles of accounting at the Treasy." He was a successful auditing clerk but later undertook trading ventures in the southwest.[36]

---

[31] Hamilton, *Works* (Lodge ed.), VII, 390.

[32] *American State Papers: Miscellaneous*, I, 57–59; chief clerks are not included in these figures.

[33] Pickering Papers, VIII, 71.

[34] Cf. the testimony of Jefferson: "When I came into office I found the clerkships all filled by gentlemen who had been in them several years, and who to the title of possession added that of irreproachable conduct. I have therefore not had a single appointment to make." Jefferson to Monroe, Jan. 18, 1791, Jefferson, *Works* (Federal ed.), VI, 174.

[35] Wolcott Papers, XVIII, 1.

[36] Steele, *Papers,* I, 247.

Apparently some of the Treasury clerks became involved in the political conflict of the times. After Wolcott resigned he anticipated persecution and wrote Cabot that "the Engines for effecting these purposes are prepared and the operations have commenced—Some of the Clerks in the Offices either of the Auditor Comptroller, or Register, will continue to furnish Extracts from the files & records, which will be published and misrepresented in Duanes paper." [37] A clerk named Campbell was supposed in 1801 to be furnishing records against Pickering. [38]

In the small clerical offices of the time there was an intimacy which has long since vanished. When Wolcott retired in 1800 he received a number of letters from clerks in the Treasury offices. The formality of the following example does not hide the warmth of its feeling.

As an individual in the Department of the Treasury since its first establishment, and for nearly eight years previous thereto, employed in different offices under the late government, I hope Sir, I may be permitted, without the imputation of vanity, to express the extreme regret I feel, in the approach of that period, which by depriving the public of your important services, at the same time, sensibly affects all those, who under an official superintendence, have so long experienced your indulgence, and friendly disposition. [39]

To John Steele a fond father wrote concerning his son Henry who set out from Spring Hill, North Carolina, to the city and a government post.

I have directed him to look up to you as a Father, and be Guided by you in all matters both with respect to his Business, his morals and even his amusements which you were so good as to promise me you would super-intend. Henry has always behaved well in every employment he has been in yet, and I hope he will Continue so to do. But he has now arrived or soon will, at the most Critical period of a mans life, when the passions are too powerful for reason, but I hope, with your advice and example, and

---

[37] Wolcott Papers, VI, 91.

[38] Ibid., XXI, 15. Clerks were a trustworthy lot, as a rule, but Samuel Lewis, a clerk in the War Department, was imprisoned for unaccounted balances due the government, Annals, X, 519.

[39] Joshua Dawson to Wolcott, Dec. 24, 1800, Wolcott Papers, XV, 153.

the assistance of divine providence he will Steer Clear of any Scandalous or Immoral Conduct that might be a Stain on his Character.[40]

A secondary but colorful figure who flitted in and out of a government clerkship was John P. Ripley, graduate of Dartmouth College in 1791 and grandson of its first president, Eleazar Wheelock. Ripley was an irresponsible romantic, forever escaping reality in bold dreams at the expense of his friends and relatives.[41] After a year as an assistant teacher at Phillips Exeter he became a clerk in Wolcott's office. Already in debt, he was forced to borrow further from Judge Thomas McKean to recoup from the ravages of the smallpox. To pay this obligation he borrowed from Wolcott, but shortly sailed from Boston, as he wrote his mother, "to arms—in the best service in Europe, the Russian. . . . the encouragement for *adventuring* foreigners the most flattering in the world." To Wolcott he wrote at the same moment that he was off "to try the sweep of the sword," meanwhile assuring him of his intention to pay his debt. From London he went to Amsterdam where he borrowed 1,500 Dutch florins on a draft drawn on his uncle, President John Wheelock of Dartmouth College, who declined to honor the draft when it turned up in Hanover some months later. Ripley had now decided to join the Polish army in the cause of liberty but was arrested by the Austrians while en route to army headquarters. After a brief detention he abandoned the sword and in 1797 turned up again in Philadelphia as a clerk in Timothy Pickering's office. Disappointed in his application for a consular appointment (Wolcott said to Pickering, "Ripley will not do") and overcome by a desire for revenge, he reported matters to the Spanish minister relating to Blount's activities which appeared to implicate the Secretary of State.[42] In 1798 he was in jail. His adventures over, he began the practice of law in Philadelphia upon his release, and died there in 1816 at the age of forty-one.

The birth of ambition for the life of a clerk was charmingly revealed in correspondence between Pickering and a young friend, Abraham

[40] Steele, *Papers*, I, 185.

[41] This paragraph is based on a paper by Edgar L. Erickson, "The European Adventure of an Eighteenth Century American," *Pennsylvania History*, III (1936), 259–66; a collection of Ripley's letters in the Dartmouth College Library; and a letter from Ripley to Wolcott, Wolcott Papers, XIII, 33.

[42] His deposition in the Blount case appears in Francis Wharton, *State Trials of the United States during the Administrations of Washington and Adams* (Philadelphia: Carey and Hart, 1849), pp. 243–44.

Bradley of Wilkes-Barre, Pennsylvania. An impecunious schoolmaster, Bradley married in haste. Returning on foot from Philadelphia, where he had visited the Postmaster General, he wrote his patron:

If Mr Wetmore resigns I suppose you will appoint Mr Burrall assistant; if you should, & you think I am competent to discharge the duties of a clerk, you would do me a very great kindness in giving me the place. When I was in the city I enquired & computed the various expences of house hire, food & cloathing & found that the salary would leave one or two hundred dollars after paying all that were necessary. My wife in the country does all our washing, cooking, tailoring & hairdressing, besides spinning & knitting stockings: was she in the city her duty would be much easier if she had no assistance, for spinning & bakeing would be entirely out of the way; & she would have better utensils for performing the other parts. I had tho'ts of proposing the subject to you when I was in the city, but you had done me so many kindnesses, & it looked so much like begging of offices I thot to try to live without rather than ask. But when I was on my journey I began to consider what things were necessary & how I should procure them if I turned farmer: that I must build something of a house, a barn, fences [—] that there were oxen & ploughs, a cart, shed, hoes axes &c &c. to be procured, & that I had not wherewithal to procure one article I began to think it was only asking for employment, which every one was bound modestly to do rather than suffer. If any person wishes the place who is better qualified for it than it is probable I should be after a month or two's service, I have nothing to say. I must ask pardon for the hurry & confusion of this letter. I came but 34 miles yesterday, & I must either get home or lodge in the swamp tomorrow night. My respects to Mrs Pickering & Miss Betsy.[43]

The young Bradley was unsuccessful in this appeal but in 1799 achieved his goal. He became a clerk and subsequently assistant postmaster general.

Getting and keeping good clerks was apparently a problem in the 1790's, due in part to the relatively small supply. In 1795 Wolcott complained of the mass of business and the scarcity "of that class of men in the public service, who understand details, and endeavor to keep things in order."[44] In July 1795, he reported to Hamilton, "I have suffered an irreparable loss by the appointment of Mr. Kane, to

[43] Aug. 26, 1792, Pickering Papers, XLI, 80.
[44] Wolcott to Hamilton, Oct. 6, 1795, Hamilton, *Works* (Hamilton ed.), VI, 43.

be assistant cashier of the bank." [45] Wolcott pointed out in 1798 that "more than ordinary skill in clerkship" was needed in the office of internal revenue collector and told Congress that the delay in the settlement of accounts was due to "want of skill in clerkship." [46]

Good penmanship was one of the marks of a competent clerk. Pickering wrote to an applicant, "As to a clerkship, altho' your letters are tolerably correct, yet several words are misspelt; and if your composition were perfectly correct, your handwriting is not good enough for a public office. Do not therefore entertain the smallest hope of being introduced to one—I cannot recommend you." [47] A literary reputation was an asset in seeking a clerkship. The minor poet, Joseph Dennie, was received by Pickering in the State Department, apparently without a handwriting test but with an admonition about work: "If with his genius and taste, he can in a sufficient degree relinquish the pursuits of literature, and submit to the drudgery of business, it will give me much pleasure to have been in any degree instrumental in availing the public of his talents." [48]

Dennie found his time much occupied with his official work and literary connections. "Private and confidential Secretary to the Secy. of State is my designation," he wrote to his parents, "and my official duty demands the indispensable attendance of six hours daily in the ordinary routine of business. . . . I have a large and airy office to myself, and pleasantly situated in the centre of this City. . . . I am well accommodated with lodgings at the house of William Meredith, Esq., a lawyer of distinction and unsullied reputation here. His family is small and correct. I have convenient apartments, and the comfortable aid of a servant man. . . . I am treated here with much attention and respect, and, known as a professed man of letters and as *Commis* of the Bureau, I have a ready passport into good company."

---

[45] Gibbs, *Memoirs,* I, 219.

[46] *American State Papers: Finance,* I, 578.

[47] Pickering to Toppan Webster, Oct. 25, 1797, Pickering Papers, VII, 364.

[48] Pickering to Lewis R. Morris, April 29, 1799, *ibid.,* X, 644. Hamilton's recommendation of Thomas Marshall to a clerkship in the Treasury Department smacks little of his usual regard for high standards. Marshall was a mechanic by trade, skilled in machine weaving. He emigrated to America in 1791 and served as superintendent of the cotton mill of the Society for Useful Manufactures, one of Hamilton's many interests. When the Society collapsed he went off to Philadelphia with a letter of recommendation from Hamilton to Wolcott. Joseph Stancliffe Davis, *Essays in the Earlier History of American Corporations* (2 vols., Cambridge: Harvard University Press, 1917), I, 496–97.

Dennie told his parents that he had dined and talked much at the table of Sir R. Liston, the British minister, and often repaired to the houses of "our officers." Furthermore he frequently resorted "to the President's, a good man but somewhat obstinate, and, growing old, a sort of political dimness has ensued. . . ."[49] Dennie was strongly pro-British in sentiment.

Pickering thought little of his value as a clerk. Writing after his removal to his successor, John Marshall, Pickering said, "But I cannot, because I ought not, conceal from you, that Mr. Dennie's habits and literary turn—I should rather say, his insatiable appetite for knowledge, useful as well as ornamental, render his service as a clerk less productive than the labours of many dull men."[50]

The only "clerk" whose name is remembered today was Philip M. Freneau, poet, editor, and mariner. Graduating from the College of New Jersey (Princeton) in 1771 with James Madison, he early displayed talent in poetic composition and during the Revolution (when not suffering on a British prison ship) wrote such stirring poems that he became known as "the poet of the American Revolution." For several years after 1784 he was master of a brig sailing the Atlantic and the Caribbean. In 1789 he became editor of the *New York Daily Advertiser* and in 1791 translating clerk in the Department of State. Here he contributed the letters to the *National Gazette* which so irritated Washington.[51] Leaving the Department with Jefferson, he returned to editing and writing. His biographer declares, "Unquestionably he was the most significant poetic figure in America before Bryant."[52] But Freneau was hardly the typical government clerk—a man of imagination and of various talents, a warm democrat and supporter of France who came to Philadelphia to help his friends Madison and Jefferson protect American democracy and the French "alliance."

[49] Harold Milton Ellis, *Joseph Dennie and His Circle,* University of Texas, Studies in English, No. 3 (1915), pp. 114–16, 117, 118, 120.

[50] *Ibid.,* p. 130.

[51] Jefferson accused a clerk in the Treasury, William Irvine, of writing pieces under the pen name, Veritas, as a part of the Federalist political game. *Works* (Federal ed.), I, 279.

[52] *Dictionary of American Biography,* VII, 27–28.

Chapter Twenty-five

NOTES ON PRESTIGE

W<small>ASHINGTON</small> deliberately set out to win esteem for the new government by appointing prominent citizens to office. After twelve years of unremitting search for proper "characters" the public service had acquired a standing that was in part cultivated and in part the consequence of many influences bearing on it.

The officeholding class as such was not in high repute among Americans at the end of the eighteenth century. Government and public officials still suffered from lingering connotations of British oppression, nepotism, and corruption. Officeholders as a group competed with old social classes of great prestige, notably the clergy, the merchants, and the southern gentlemen planters. In an era of vast opportunity for private enterprise, bold and active men were attracted to buying and selling, land speculation, shipbuilding and the carrying trade. Within the field of government, although some able men held important offices, those who sought preferment tended to go into politics, not administration. On this subject Robert Goodloe Harper made a pointed declaration in the House.

In some countries, indeed, office conferred power, and was therefore sought by ambitious men as a means of obtaining power. Office there gave patronage, authority, and influence, and was therefore eagerly pursued. But in this country, he said, the case was different. Offices here gave a scanty maintenance, much labor, and no patronage or influence, and, therefore, ambitious politicians did not desire them. That House was the place for such men to appear. There and there alone they had a conspicuous theatre for the display of their talents; there and there alone could they acquire fame, popularity, and political importance; there and there alone could they make a strong impression on the country and the Government, give weight to their own opinions, and force their own system into activity. There, of course, they would desire to remain and not to undertake offices, which, though respectable, were not brilliant, imposed much labor, but conferred neither splendor nor authority.[1]

The general government was new, untried, and at the outset of uncertain stability or duration. It had and could have none of the traditions which surrounded the institutions of the old states—Massachusetts, Connecticut, New York, Pennsylvania, Maryland, Virginia. "In other countries," said Fisher Ames, "where their Governments had been of long standing, persons were trained up with a view to public employments; but in this country this had not been the case, and, therefore, the President found the circle from which to select proper characters for office was very confined." [2]

The writings of many of the leading figures in public life from 1789 to 1801 suggest a strong distaste for office and a low estimate of its standing. These statements, however, must be taken with reservations; they were made by men who in fact gave most of their lives to government service, who in some cases were seekers for office, and who, like their modern counterparts, occasionally thought in moments of distress or weariness that they would like to be far from official cares. Some, like Washington, continued public life reluctantly; [3] and others, like Hamilton, could do much better for themselves elsewhere.

Hamilton's attitude, privately declared two years after he retired from the Treasury, is exceptionally interesting. He wrote to a relative in Scotland:

Public office in this country has few attractions. The pecuniary emolument is so inconsiderable as to amount to a sacrifice to any man who can employ his time with advantage in any liberal profession. The opportunity of doing good, from the jealousy of power and the spirit of faction, is too small in any station to warrant a long continuance of private sacrifices. The enterprise of party had so far succeeded as materially to weaken the necessary influence and energy of the executive authority, and so far diminish the power of doing good in that department, as greatly to take away the motives which a virtuous man might have for making sacrifices. The prospect was even bad for gratifying in future the love of fame, if that passion was to be the spring of action.[4]

---

[1] Annals, VII, 874 (Jan. 19, 1798).

[2] Ibid., VI, 2004 (Jan. 27, 1797).

[3] In a moment of temper, Washington once referred to himself as the "slave" of the people. Washington to Henry Lee, July 21, 1793, Washington, Writings, XXXIII, 23.

[4] Hamilton to ——— Hamilton, May 2, 1797, Hamilton, Works (Lodge ed.), X, 259.

Hamilton's successor, Oliver Wolcott, received a letter from his father, the governor of Connecticut, which stated his own estimate of high federal offices.

The inadequate support which the most important officers of the government receive, their high responsibility, severe services, the malignity which they have to encounter from the envy and venal influence of some, and the stupid pride and ignorance of others, must be very discouraging to men to continue in services in which they are conscious that the public derive every attainable benefit from their greatest exertions and most able and faithful conduct.[5]

Jefferson, just established as Secretary of State, wrote Francis Willis:

The happiest moments of my life have been the few which I have past at home in the bosom of my family. Emploiment any where else is a mere [*illegible*] of time; it is burning the candle of life in perfect waste for the individual himself. I have no complaint against any body. I have had more of the confidence of my country than my share. I only say that public emploiment contributes neither to advantage nor happiness. It is but honorable exile from one's family & affairs. . . .[6]

We may mark that although Jefferson conceived office as an exile, it was an *honorable* one. John Adams left the presidency looking forward to the labors of agriculture and the amusements of literature, "in both of which I have always taken more delight than in any public office, of whatever rank." [7]

Timothy Pickering, although an inveterate office seeker and holder, often complained about the handicaps of public life and praised the pursuits of the farmer. Shortly before he became Postmaster General, and while an applicant for several offices, he wrote his wife in this gloomy vein: "There is nothing I would more earnestly pray for in respect to my sons, than that they might engage in such private pursuits as to preclude even the wish for a public employment." [8] After years of officeholding, while Secretary of State, he wrote the American

---

[5] July 4, 1796, Gibbs, *Memoirs*, I, 371–72.
[6] April 13, 1790, Jefferson, *Works* (Federal ed.), VI, 46.
[7] Adams, *Works*, IX, 94.
[8] Upham, *Timothy Pickering*, II, 440.

minister at Lisbon, "above all I cannot bear the idea of a dependence on *public employment* for the means of living." [9]

And yet the leading Federalists held on, some with genuine reluctance, some with momentary nostalgia for farm and fireside, some with genuine satisfaction in their public place. The sense of public obligation was admirably put by William Vans Murray in urging McHenry to accept appointment as Secretary of War.

Depend on this, that men long known to the public *must* accept these high offices or the Govt. dwindles into insignificance—and what public duty is there wh. to a certain degree does not demand some sacrifice of predetermined schemes of life & personal quiet? Vanity & ambition I know you will say will always supply candidates enough. I know that, & that is the reason why such *candidates* shd. not be accepted. [10]

The call to public service in these formative years was sufficiently compelling to bring to office some of the ablest men of the generation —not merely Washington, Hamilton, and Jefferson, but John Adams and his son, Wolcott, Steele, Pickering, King, Benjamin Hawkins, Tench Coxe, Higginson and Stoddert, John Marshall and C. C. Pinckney. Seldom has the country been served by more gifted men in posts official and diplomatic. The first precedents of officeholding in high place were honorable ones.

Attitudes were much different among those who were eligible to the lesser offices. Here there was a craving for public position, even when the income was painfully small. [11] Washington received many requests for appointments; so did Hamilton, Jefferson, Pickering, and others in high position. On more than one occasion, Washington had his first news of the death of an officeholder through an application from a would-be successor. [12]

The nature of the competition for clerical jobs appears in a letter of William Hindman written when the first Secretary of the Navy was about to take office (1798): "Our Friend Stoddart reach'd here Yester Afternoon, & will wait upon the President this Morning, being

9 Pickering Papers, XI, 376.

10 Steiner, *James McHenry*, p. 166.

11 Edward Channing, *A History of the United States* (6 vols., New York: Macmillan, 1905–25; supplementary vol., general index, compiled by Eva G. Moore, 1932), IV, 48 ff.

12 For an example, see Washington, *Writings*, XXXIII, 436.

anxious to be geered & enter upon the Duties of his Office; the applicants for Clerkship are numerous, & some of the first Characters in
the United States." [13] The directors of the Bank in Philadelphia in 1800
gave an unwitting testimonial to the integrity and competence of the
Treasury clerks; they needed an agent in Washington, "an active, intelligent, and confidential character," and asked Wolcott to permit
one of his clerks, Jones, to act in this capacity.[14]

With more complete information it might be possible to compare
the prestige of officeholding in the state and federal governments.
Woodrow Wilson commented on the superior status of the former.
"It was hard, in filling even the greater offices, to find men of eminence
who were willing to leave the service of their States or the security
and ease of private life to try the untrodden paths of federal government. The States were old and secure—so men thought—the federal
government was new and an experiment." [15] John Jay allowed New
York to vote for him as governor in 1792 while he still held the position
of Chief Justice of the Supreme Court. Charles Carroll of Carrollton
resigned his seat in the United States Senate to sit in the Maryland
State Legislature.[16] On the other hand John Collins, governor of Rhode
Island from 1786 to May 5, 1790, asked Washington for the post of
collector of the Newport district on May 24, 1790.[17] Many federal
officeholders had had previous state experience. This type of evidence
is inconclusive, but for some years the public life of the states probably
outweighed that of the general government in the minds of the politically active.

One further comment is in order. Despite Harper's remarks on the
superior attractiveness of political life, there were members of both
Houses who deliberately chose administrative office and were prepared
to sacrifice their legislative seats to attain it. Senator Tristram Dalton
of Massachusetts was ready to resign in 1790 to become Postmaster
General.[18] William Smith of South Carolina asked Wolcott to help

---

[13] Steiner, *op. cit.,* p. 303.

[14] Gibbs, *op. cit.,* II, 387.

[15] Woodrow Wilson, *George Washington* (New York: Harper and Brothers, 1896),
p. 280.

[16] Washington, *Writings,* XXXII, 254.

[17] Hunt, "Office-seeking during Washington's Administration," *Am. Hist. Rev.,* I
(1896), 279.

[18] King, *Correspondence,* I, 392.

him to a diplomatic post in 1795, and again in 1796.[19] Benjamin Goodhue was willing to exchange his seat in the House for the position of
supervisor of revenue.[20] Senator Watson of New York expected to
resign in 1800 because his legislative duties interfered with his work
as naval agent in his state.[21]

To different men, different values; and in various regions, various
traditions. The tradition of public service was high in Virginia, New
York, Connecticut, and Massachusetts. In Virginia the obligation to
participate in public affairs came from the background of the English
country gentlemen, whose manner of life was reproduced on the
spacious plantations of the Rappahannock and the James. In New
England it arose from the Puritan code of duty and the practice of
self-government in the congregations and the town meetings. These
influences were of course also important in other colonies and states.
Such were some of the foundations upon which was built a prestige
value of the public service of the new government that could be looked
upon with satisfaction by its creators.

---

[19] Wolcott Papers, VIII, 86, 88.
[20] *Ibid.*, XI, 55, 56.
[21] King, *Correspondence*, III, 207.

Chapter Twenty-six

APPROPRIATIONS: EXECUTIVE FREEDOM OR LEGISLATIVE RESTRAINT

AT NO point was suspicion of government more definitely written into law and practice than in the management of federal finance. The utmost care was taken to ensure that public funds would be legally expended, to prevent either misapplication or embezzlement, and to guarantee that the immediate representatives of the people would bear the responsibility for determining how much money should be provided, the sources from which it should be derived, and the purposes to which it should be applied. A system was devised which stood up under repeated investigations before 1800 and which in its essential features still remains in operation—a monument to the administrative and fiscal genius of Alexander Hamilton.

Long experience in the colonies suggested that Congress would be jealous of the public purse and events well confirmed this expectation. The Constitution had settled the fiscal primacy of Congress in the clause providing that, "No money shall be drawn from the treasury, but in consequence of appropriations made by law."

The development of appropriation procedure was marked by conflict between the executive and legislative branches, a part of the struggle which has already been described. The Republicans in Congress sought to control the expenditure of funds and to curtail the discretion of the heads of departments. The executive branch resisted through its Federalist friends in the House and Senate, seeking to hold a degree of freedom of action which it believed necessary in the interest of efficient management. The problem is a very modern as well as an ancient source of perplexity.

The initial step in the appropriation procedure, the preparation of estimates, fell quickly into executive hands.

ESTIMATES

Early in the first session, the House constituted a Committee on Ways and Means with Elbridge Gerry as chairman to "prepare and report" an estimate of supplies for the remainder of 1789.[1] In July he presented sketchy figures showing a probable cost of current operations, excluding the establishment of revenue officers, of about $600,000, and interest and arrearages making a total of nearly $8,300,000.[2] No action was taken. Shortly after Hamilton's appointment as Secretary of the Treasury, the Committee on Ways and Means was discharged and its business turned over to him. He was directed "to report to this House an estimate of the sums requisite to be appropriated."[3] Four days later Hamilton submitted estimates which were immediately referred to a special committee of three for the purpose of drafting an appropriation bill; eight days later, on September 29, 1789, the first appropriation act for the support of government was signed by the President.[4] The preparation of estimates was not undertaken again by Congress during the Federalist period. The initiative in planning expenditures for *authorized* activities remained in the departments.

The estimates for 1790 could be based on slightly better foundations than those for 1789. They were closely itemized. For several succeeding years they were also itemized but in 1796 the requests for funds no longer contained such detail.[5]

There is almost no evidence that either Washington or Adams went over the estimates before the Secretary of the Treasury submitted them to the House of Representatives. By 1799 some fiscal competition between the War and Navy Departments had apparently developed and Adams told James McHenry quite plainly that he could and would, if necessary, decide between them. His ironical letter to McHenry tells the story.

As it is an excellent principle for every man in public life to magnify his office, and make it honorable, I admire the dexterity with which you dignify yours, by representing an army, and means adequate to its support, as the first thing necessary to make the nation respected. Genius in a general is oftener an instrument of divine vengeance than a guardian angel. Stoddert, I warrant you, instead of representing the navy as the fourth and last article necessary for national respectability, would have felt the importance of his office enough to have stated a navy as the first and most indispensable. It

---

[1] *Annals*, I, 231–32 (April 29, 1789).
[2] *American State Papers: Finance*, I, 11–13.
[3] *Annals*, I, 894–95 (Sept. 17).
[4] *Ibid.*, I, 904–5 (Sept. 21); 1 Stat. 95.
[5] *American State Papers: Finance*, I, 359.

would not be necessary for me to decide the controversy between you; if it should be, I should be at no loss. My answer would be ready.[6]

The Treasury Department, not the President, immediately became the agency for the transmission of estimates to Congress. There is scanty evidence to determine to what extent it assumed responsibility for review and revision. The law authorized the Treasury to prepare and report estimates of revenue and expenditures, but did not specify the duty of revising figures that were supplied by the departments. The function of review was nevertheless undertaken. The following letter of the Secretary of the Treasury to the Secretary of War indicates that budget making in the modern sense of the term began early in the federal administrative practice.

The requests contained in your letter of the 15 of April have been complied with.

There are two points arising out of the Estimate of the Qr Master General, which you transmitted, to which I beg to call your attention.

One Item of Expenditure in the estimate is 450 Pack-Horses. It has been noticed to me by the Accounting Officers of the Treasury, that there appear to have been already expended in the purchase of this article a large sum by the present Qr Masters' Department—And it is recollected that a very considerable number of horses were purchased and paid for, for the use of the Campaign under General St Clair, a great part of which survived the Campaign and it is understood were put out to be recruited for future service.

This renders it desireable that Inquiry should be made what ultimately became of these horses—what are the calculations of the quantity of transportation for which so extensive a provision of pack-horses is intended.

I submit also to your consideration whether under the prospects of the Campaign the provision need be made at once to the extent contemplated or may be made successively so always as to be in measure for ulterior operations—The maintenance of a superfluous number of Packhorses, when not required for Service, has an objectionable side on the score of expence. Whether the procuring them much sooner than they will be wanted may not have other inconveniences is for you to determine.

In making these suggestions, I certainly do not mean to throw any impediment in the way of timely preparation. This is a primary idea. But if expence can be saved by a delay in providing not injurious, it is of course to be desired.

---

[6] Adams, *Works,* VIII, 662.

Another item in the estimate of the Qr Master General is 12000 dollars for *pay* of his Department to the 1st of July.

This sum appears considerable especially as separate sums are estimated for Horse Masters Waggon Masters and Drivers—No light on this head can be obtained from any accounts heretofore rendered at the Treasury. I understood you that none was possessed by your Department.

Hence the necessity of an inquiry into the circumstances.[7]

For the most part, however, the figures submitted by the respective agencies were merely brought together in a single file by Joseph Nourse, the Register, and transmitted to the clerk of the House. There was no budget document, no balance of income and outgo, no budget message from the President, and no executive recommendations on general fiscal policy. As more revenue was needed from time to time the Treasury recommended new taxes, such as the various excises, or increases in the customs rates. In the modern sense of the term, it can hardly be said that "a budget" existed in the 1790's—but most of the essential procedures had been adopted by the Treasury, within limits.

APPROPRIATIONS

Although varying somewhat the *estimates* were presented in substantial detail throughout the Federalist period. The form of the appropriation act varied, the degree of itemization fluctuating with the Republican-Federalist balance in the House. The Federalists stood steadily for general grants and wide discretion; the Republicans for their opposites.[8]

The appropriation act of 1789 was written in the most general terms. It prescribed simply:

That there be appropriated for the service of the present year, to be paid out of the monies which arise, either from the requisitions heretofore made upon the several states, or from the duties on impost and tonnage, the following sums, viz. A sum not exceeding two hundred and sixteen thousand dollars for defraying the expenses of the civil list, under the late and present government; a sum not exceeding one hundred and thirty-seven thousand dollars for defraying the expenses of the department of war; a sum not

---

[7] April 18, 1793, Wolcott Papers, XXII, 65.

[8] A valuable monograph on the subject of this section is Lucius Wilmerding, Jr., *The Spending Power* (New Haven: Yale University Press, 1943); see especially chs. i–ii.

exceeding one hundred and ninety thousand dollars for discharging the warrants issued by the late board of treasury, and remaining unsatisfied; and a sum not exceeding ninety-six thousand dollars for paying the pensions to invalids.[9]

Four lump sums for the civil list, War Department, outstanding warrants, and veterans' pensions, with no itemization and no reference to Hamilton's estimates, left full discretion to the executive branch in the expenditure of $639,000 for the remaining months of 1789.

The form of the principal appropriation act for 1790 was the same as for 1789 except that Congress tied its grants to the estimates by adding at the end of the three lump sums for the civil list, War Department, and pensions, the phrase, *"as estimated in the statements accompanying the aforesaid report,"* i.e., the departmental estimates.[10] The appropriation act followed closely the amounts requested by the departments. Appropriations for 1791 again took the form of lump sums, with a number of special acts for particular purposes which were usually initiated by a message from the President.[11] No disposition to question executive leadership or fiscal discretion appeared.

The debates on the grants for 1792, however, revealed an emerging sense of House responsibility for appropriations. Estimates had nearly doubled since 1791 and differences of opinion on policy had crystallized. Josiah Parker of Virginia rose "to provoke an inquiry into the expenditure of money" and expressed his hope that "a habit would follow to look into the expenditure of all public appropriations."[12] William B. Giles, who was to play a leading part in future scenes of the fiscal drama, declared, "He was against allowing an unnecessary latitude in appropriations." Gerry and Madison, while resisting the attack on the pending appropriations, took occasion to urge the desirability of more effective House control over public expenditures.[13] The form of the appropriation act was modified; after granting the traditional lump sums, instead of the customary phrase "as estimated by the Secretary

---

[9] 1 Stat. 95 (Sept. 29, 1789).

[10] 1 Stat. 104 (March 26, 1790).

[11] For example, an appropriation of $20,000 to carry out the treaty with Morocco (1 Stat. 214); and of $312,686.20 for raising an additional regiment (1 Stat. 222, sec. 15).

[12] *Annals,* III, 221, 222 (Dec. 2, 1791).

[13] *Ibid.,* III, 224–27.

of the Treasury," this and subsequent acts used the language, *"that is to say,"* and then specified the destination of the funds.[14]

The appropriation for 1793 raised sharply the whole problem of itemization. An over-all estimate of $50,000 for War Department contingencies was attacked and the President was requested to produce a statement of the items. This was forthcoming from the Secretary of War[15] and the House passed a bill which "specified all the items of each sum granted to the support of the War Department." The Senate subsequently amended it to one aggregate sum for all War Department purposes, thus flatly nullifying the attempt of the House to itemize the contingency and other funds. A major debate arose in the House, which unfortunately is only summarized by the reporter. It was objected that the Senate's action "leaves too much discretionary power in the hands of the Head of the Department"; the amount involved was nearly a million dollars. By the narrow margin of one vote the House insisted on its version[16] and the Senate yielded. The appropriation act of 1793 consequently specified the principal objects for the War Department, but still in considerable sums and with ample latitude for official discretion within their boundaries.[17]

Beginning with 1794 Congress passed two general appropriation acts, one for "the support of Government," one for the support of the military establishment.[18] No further change in the form of the appropriation acts developed during 1795 or 1796.

Republican interest in closer congressional control of finance had not, however, diminished, and now fell under the capable leadership of Albert Gallatin, a member of the House from 1795 to 1801 and leader of the Republican party after Madison and Giles withdrew in

---

[14] 1 Stat. 226.

[15] *Annals,* III, 735, 742.

[16] *Ibid.,* III, 889–90 (Feb. 22, 1793).

[17] 1 Stat. 325 at 328. For example, for five hundred rifles, $6,000; for defraying the expenses of the Indian department, $50,000; for the pay of troops authorized by law, $304,308; for forage, $34,856; for the defensive protection of the frontiers, $50,000.

[18] 1 Stat. 342 and 346. One reason for segregating the War Department bill apparently was to expedite the passage of the civil list bill so that Congressmen could receive their salaries. Madison said that members had been reduced to the most serious difficulties by the delays in the payment of their salaries, and Nicholas added that it was not fair to suppose that every gentleman in the House came to town with enough money in his pocket to meet his expenses. Another reason was to secure ample time to consider military expenditures, free from any pressure to vote the civil list. *Annals,* IV, 168; V, 263.

1797 and 1798 respectively. Gallatin has left his own statement of his objectives in this field. "But I was specially jealous of Executive encroachments, and to keep that branch within the strict limits of Constitution and of law, allowing no more discretion than what appeared strictly necessary, was my constant effort." [19]

In 1797 Gallatin proposed "that each appropriation should be specific; that it might not be supposed to be in the power of the Treasury Department to appropriate to one object money which had been specifically appropriated for any other object. . . . they knew . . . that so far as related to the Military Department, the items had been totally mixed. . . . Such construction of the law . . . totally defeated the object of appropriation. . . ." [20] The language of the act "for the support of Government" for 1797 was rewritten to insert a phrase requested by Gallatin, i.e., *"the following sums be respectively appropriated,"* in lieu of the former text, "there be appropriated a sum not exceeding ———." [21] A corresponding change was introduced in making appropriations for the military and naval establishments, but the objects indicated were still very general in nature—much more general than in the "act for the support of Government." [22]

This phraseology marked the culmination of the Republican drive for control of Federalist discretion in the executive branch during the period under review. The military and naval bill of 1798 reverted to the usual language, abandoning Gallatin's substitute.[23] Gallatin's phraseology was retained in the act "for the support of Government" in 1798 [24] and in 1799 [25] but was dropped entirely in 1800.[26] The form of the last Federalist appropriation acts was comparable to that of 1792.

The War and Navy Departments proved particularly resistant to any attempt to fasten itemized appropriations upon them. Despite the

---

[19] Henry Adams, *Life of Albert Gallatin,* p. 157.

[20] *Annals,* VI, 2040 (Jan. 31, 1797).

[21] 1 Stat. 498 (March 3, 1797).

[22] 1 Stat. 508 (March 3, 1797). The trend alarmed Wolcott, who wrote Hamilton in 1798, "the management of the Treasury becomes more and more difficult. The Legislature will not pass laws in gross. Their appropriations are minute. Gallatin, to whom they yield, is evidently intending to break down this department, by charging it with an impracticable detail." Hamilton, *Works* (Hamilton ed.), VI, 279.

[23] 1 Stat. 563 (June 12, 1798).

[24] 1 Stat. 542 (March 19, 1798).

[25] 1 Stat. 717 (March 2, 1799).

[26] 2 Stat. 62 (May 7, 1800).

various experiments in legislative language, the Treasury frankly admitted in 1797 that it was the custom "not to consider each appropriation as specific, but the whole as a general grant of money." [27] In 1802 a House report reviewed previous practice and Gallatin (then Secretary of the Treasury) found that the sums appropriated to the army and navy had been "indiscriminately applicable to every distinct object of expenditure embraced under those two general heads." [28] Gallatin's success in limiting executive discretion during the Federalist period was not marked; as he himself observed, he was a member of the opposition. He rightly claimed, however, "a powerful influence on the spirit and leading principles of subsequent Administrations" in his drive to restrict executive power by specific appropriations.

The future Secretary of the Treasury had fortunately an apt sense of administrative needs. Although he believed that Congress could enforce true economy only by making specific appropriations, he knew their dangers and limitations. "Even these," he said, "must be made with due knowledge of the subject, since, if carried too far by too many subdivisions, they became injurious, if not impracticable. This subject has ever been a bone of contention between the legislative and executive branches in every representative government, and it is in reality the only proper and efficient legislative check on executive prodigality." [29]

The consequences of an itemized appropriation act upon the conduct of government are subtle and far-reaching. The discretion of administrative officers is progressively limited, the flexibility of management reduced, and the responsibility for management *pro tanto* transferred to the appropriating body. At the same time, the representatives of the people are more certain that their money is used for the purposes authorized. These objectives were not lost to view by the disputants of the 1790's.

The issue came to a head in connection with the effort to drive Hamilton from the Treasury.

William B. Giles introduced resolutions of censure in February 1793, the first of which went straight to the matter of official discretion: "*Resolved,* That it is essential to the due administration of the Govern-

---

[27] *Annals,* VI, 2322 (Feb. 27, 1797).
[28] *American State Papers: Finance,* I, 755.
[29] Adams, *Gallatin,* pp. 156–57.

ment of the United States, that laws making specific appropriations of money should be strictly observed by the administrator of the finances thereof." [30] The ensuing debate revealed that even Hamilton's critics were not prepared to deny some exceptions to the rule of strict compliance might exist. The strongest case for executive conformity was put by William Findley, who declared:

The application of appropriations is the most sacred and important trust the Legislature can confer. If they may be made to bend to the will or projecting policy of a Financier, there is an end of all security and confidence. . . . where the money is appropriated solely to a special purpose, as in the case of the loans, he who executes the law has no degree of power over the appropriation. . . .

But Findley admitted almost in the same breath that

an Executive officer, pressed by some urgent and unexpected necessity, may be induced to depart from the authorized path of duty, and have great merit in so doing. . . . But in such emergency, the officer so acting will embrace the earliest opportunity to explain the matter and obtain a justification. . . . [31]

Madison, while attacking Hamilton's course of action, nevertheless agreed that in the use of funds "there might perhaps be a difference of opinion." [32]

He would not deny that there might be emergencies, in the course of human affairs, of so extraordinary and pressing a nature, as to absolve the Executive from an inflexible conformity to the injunctions of the law. It was, nevertheless, as essential to remember, as it was obvious to remark, that in all such cases, the necessity should be palpable; that the Executive sanction should flow from the supreme source; and that the first opportunity should be seized for communicating to the Legislature the measures pursued, with the reasons explaining the necessity of them. This early communication was equally enforced by prudence and by duty. It was the best evidence of the motives for assuming the extraordinary power; it was a respect manifestly due to the Legislative authority; and it was more partic-

---

[30] *Annals,* III, 900 (Feb. 28, 1793).
[31] *Ibid.,* III, 920–21, 922 (March 1, 1793).
[32] *Ibid.,* III, 938 (March 1, 1793).

ularly indispensable, as that alone would enable the Legislature, by a provident amendment of the law, to accommodate it to like emergencies in future.[33]

The Federalists stoutly defended executive discretion. Murray observed with respect to the abstract propositions of the first Giles resolution, "Were they agreed to by the House, it would be under provisions and restrictions. They could not have the implicit force of axioms, but at most must be yielded to as wholesome maxims, the application of which must be frequently modified by a certain degree of discretion." [34] The principal argument was made by William Smith, Hamilton's close supporter; his position was put in the two following passages:

Though the position contained in the first resolution, as a general rule, was not to be denied; yet it must be admitted, that there may be cases of a sufficient urgency to justify a departure from it, and to make it the duty of the Legislature to indemnify an officer; as if an adherence would in particular cases, and under particular circumstances, prove ruinous to the public credit, or prevent the taking measures essential to the public safety, against invasion or insurrection. In cases of that nature, and which cannot be foreseen by the Legislature nor guarded against, a discretionary authority must be deemed to reside in the President, or some other Executive officer, to be exercised for the public good. . . .[35]

With respect to discretion, Mr. S. observed that . . . in all Governments a discretionary latitude was implied in Executive officers, where that discretion resulted from the nature of the office, or was in pursuance of general authority delegated by law. This principle was so obvious that it required no illustration; were it contradicted, he would appeal to the conduct of the Secretary of State, who, though directed to report to the House on the commercial intercourse with foreign nations, had, in the exercise of a warrantable discretion, judiciously withheld his Report. . . .[36]

---

[33] *Ibid.,* III, 941. The Republicans perhaps were not aware that Jefferson had already committed himself in principle to Hamilton's position. On June 11, 1792, he instructed Pinckney, our minister at London, to give his "most active exertions and protection" to impressed seamen; this, said Jefferson, will require considerable expense, for which no law has yet provided. ". . . we think it fairer to take the risk of it on the Executive than to leave it on your shoulders." He asked Pinckney for vouchers of his expenses "to be communicated to the legislature." Jefferson, *Works* (Federal ed.), VII, 106.

[34] *Annals,* III, 903 (Feb. 28, 1793).

[35] *Ibid.,* III, 901 (Feb. 28, 1793).

[36] *Ibid.,* III, 911 (March 1, 1793).

Hamilton boldly stated his own conception of his responsibility to exercise a discretionary judgment in the interest of the public welfare.

If . . . a doubt had occurred about the strict regularity of what was contemplated as a possible resort, a mind sufficiently alive to the public interest, and sufficiently firm in the pursuit of it, would have dismissed that doubt, as an obstacle, suggested by a pusillanimous caution, to the exercise of those higher motives, which ought ever to govern a man, invested with a great public trust. It would have occurred, that there was reasonable ground to rely, that the necessity of the case, and the magnitude of the occasion, would ensure a justification, and that, if the contrary should happen, there remained still the consolation of having sacrificed personal interest and tranquillity, no matter to what extent, to an important public interest, and of having avoided the humiliation which would have been justly due to an opposite and to a feeble conduct.[37]

That this opinion was not the outcome of an immediate necessity for justification was amply confirmed by a corresponding statement to McHenry, made in 1799.

The disbursements, finally, must no doubt be regulated by the laws of appropriation; but provisory measures will often be unavoidable, and confidence must sometimes be reposed in an after legislative sanction and provision.

This has been the course in times past, and it must always be the case. A different plan will arrest and disorder all the wheels of public service. The theory of no system can be invariably pursued with liberal [literal?] strictness.

I commit myself without hesitation to the consequences of this opinion, because, as far as I am concerned, I would rather be responsible on proper occasions for formal deviations, than for a feeble, insufficient, and unprosperous course of public business, proceeding from an over-scrupulous adherence to general rules; and I have no doubt that a different spirit will ever be found in experience injurious equally to the interests of the state

[37] *American State Papers: Finance*, I, 204 (Feb. 13, 1793). When Oliver Wolcott became Secretary of the Treasury, his father (doubtless in view of Hamilton's experience) wrote to caution him against departure from rules. "In conducting a national fiscal department, it is . . . in certain public exigencies and upon unforeseen events for the officer [i.e., Secretary of the Treasury] to exercise some discretionary powers. . . .

"But the exercise of such discretion is ever attended with much risque, and it will be peculiarly so under our government. . . . In this view therefore, I think that an officer should never depart from established rules unless the necessity was most urgent, important and apparent." Gibbs, *Memoirs*, I, 180.

and to the reputation and success of the persons whom it may govern. . . . [38]

The substantial majorities by which the House rejected the Giles resolutions confirmed the theory of administrative discretion which Hamilton espoused, although this action did not prevent later efforts to fasten the restrictions of a detailed annual appropriation upon the executive departments.

What was the "reasonable discretion" to allow an executive department in the management of its funds; where administrative freedom should yield to legislative restraint—these remained unsolved problems.

---

[38] Nov. 12, 1799, Hamilton, *Works* (Lodge ed.), VII, 172–73.

Chapter Twenty-seven

GETTING AND SPENDING

THE Constitution had cured one of the radical defects of the Articles of Confederation by authorizing Congress to levy taxes directly upon persons and things, in lieu of depending upon requisitions on the states. Congress immediately took advantage of this power; its second enactment was a law to lay a duty on imports.[1] Customs duties remained the principal source of national income throughout the Federalist period, but in 1791 an excise tax was laid upon spirits distilled in the United States.[2] It was productive of some income but more discontent. The expectation that the post office revenue would be an important source of funds was not realized.

SOURCES OF REVENUE AND MEANS OF COLLECTION

Increasing expenditures led to new excise taxes in 1794 on snuff and refined sugar,[3] on pleasure carriages,[4] on licenses for selling wines and foreign distilled liquors,[5] and on property sold at auction.[6] In 1797 a duty on stamped paper, perilously reminiscent of George III, was established,[7] and in 1798 a direct tax was laid on land, dwelling houses, and slaves.[8] These successive excises were attacked day in and day out by the Republicans.

The only other important income, excepting foreign and domestic

---

[1] 1 Stat. 24 (July 4, 1789).
[2] 1 Stat. 199 (March 3, 1791).
[3] 1 Stat. 384 (June 5, 1794).
[4] 1 Stat. 373 (June 5, 1794).
[5] 1 Stat. 376 (June 5, 1794).
[6] 1 Stat. 397 (June 9, 1794).
[7] 1 Stat. 527 (July 6, 1797).
[8] 1 Stat. 580 (July 9, 1798).

loans, arose from the sale of public lands. Much was hoped for and little realized from this vast potential resource. The receipts from these principal revenues, other than loans, are shown in the following table.[9]

TABLE IV

PAYMENTS TO GOVERNMENT, 1789-1799

Duties on merchandise and tonnage	$50,321,525.77
Internal revenues (excises)	3,632,768.93
Postage	280,808.84
Sale of public lands	100,339.84
Fines, penalties, and forfeitures	17,078.81

To collect these revenues a large administrative corps was required. It included, for customs and tonnage, the collectors, naval officers, and surveyors, with their subordinate personnel; for the excise taxes, the supervisors of the revenue, inspectors of surveys, collectors of the revenue, and their subordinates; the deputy postmasters; the land agents; and the marshals for fines and forfeitures. In 1800 the principal groups numbered as follows: collectors, 82; naval officers, 13; surveyors, 55; supervisors, 16; inspectors, 22; collectors of the revenue, 321; auxiliary officers, 100.[10]

The sums collected by these various officers came into the Treasury by diverse channels. For nearly two years a large part never passed out of the hands of the collecting agents, since Hamilton ordered customs officers and deputy postmasters to pay the bills of government directly to such creditors as were in their vicinity. Balances were transmitted periodically by the collectors and supervisors, deputy postmasters and marshals, to the appropriate department and thence to the Treasury. The risks of transmission of "hard money" or notes were considerable and as soon as the Bank of the United States was organized, it and its branches became the convenient fiscal agent of the government, receiving deposits and making payments. Hamilton

---

[9] *American State Papers: Finance,* I, 665.

[10] For customs personnel, *American State Papers: Miscellaneous,* I, 261–80; for excise personnel, *American State Papers: Finance,* I, 719.

later declared the Bank "an absolutely indispensable engine in the management of the finances."[11]

The organic act creating the Treasury Department outlined the basic features of the disbursing system, making it the duty of the Secretary of the Treasury to grant all warrants for monies to be issued from the Treasury, of the Comptroller to countersign them, of the Register to record them, and of the Treasurer to receive and keep the monies of the United States and to disburse them in accordance with the Secretary's warrants.[12]

The duties of the Treasurer and of the Register were ministerial in nature; those of the Comptroller were discretionary as to the legality of warrants but not as to their expediency. This distinction was stated by Hamilton in 1795.

The Secretary and Comptroller, in granting warrants upon the Treasury, are both answerable for their legality. In this respect, the Comptroller is a check upon the Secretary. With regard to the expediency of an advance, in my opinion, the right of judging is exclusively with the head of the department. The Comptroller has no voice in this matter. . . . And uniformly was the matter so understood between successive comptrollers and myself. Also it is essential to the due administration of the department, that it should have been so understood.[13]

The Secretary of the Treasury was in no way responsible for the use of money issued from the Treasury for other departments. Disbursements, stated Representative Harrison Gray Otis in 1801, "are necessarily made under the immediate superintendence of the other departments, subject to a revision and final settlement by the Comptroller of the Treasury." The only responsibility of the Secretary of the Treasury was to refrain from making sums available in excess of those appropriated.

---

[11] Hamilton, *Works* (Hamilton ed.), IV, 271. For difficulties experienced in the collection of state taxes, see Allan Nevins, *The American States During and After the Revolution, 1775–1789* (New York: Macmillan, 1924), pp. 513–15.

[12] 1 Stat. 65 (Sept. 2, 1789). Treasury procedure during the Federalist period was described by three successive House investigating committees: Baldwin Report, May 22, 1794, in *American State Papers: Finance,* I, 281–301; Otis' Report, Jan. 28, 1801, *ibid.,* I, 690–93; Nicholson's Report, April 29, 1802, *ibid.,* I, 752–821.

[13] Nov. 11, 1795; Hamilton, *Works* (Lodge ed.), VIII, 150.

The routine of establishing accounts against which disbursements were made was simple. Immediately after Congress adjourned, a clerk in the office of the Secretary of the Treasury entered the various objects for which appropriations were made and credited each head with the whole amount of the sums appropriated to it. The Comptroller and the Register established similar accounts. The warrants were then charged against the proper accounts in each office. It was the responsibility of these offices to ensure that warrants were not issued above the amounts appropriated and made available; in 1801 the Otis Committee reported that in no instance did it appear expenditure had exceeded the legal appropriation.[14]

The warrants fell into two major categories, viz.: authorizations for payments for service rendered on the basis of an account certified by the Comptroller, and secondly, authorizations for advances to be subsequently accounted for. The greater part of payments relating to the civil list and to miscellaneous domestic expenses of a civil nature fell in the first class; in the second fell all foreign expenses and payments, advances to the War and Navy Departments, advances to the marshals for court expenses other than salaries, to the treasurer of the Mint for its expenses, and to some others, including payment on principal and interest of the public debt.[15]

During most of this period the advances to the State Department were made to the Secretary himself who became personally accountable. The individuals to whom he advanced money rendered their accounts to him. Advances to the War Department and Navy Department, both of which were relatively heavy spenders, were made on requisition of the respective Secretaries to the Treasurer of the United States, who then acted as the treasurer of these two departments. He made disbursements on warrants signed by the Secretaries of the War and Navy Departments, countersigned by the departmental accountant.[16] Individuals who received money from War and Navy then became responsible to the accountant in the first instance, and to the Treasury Auditor and Comptroller eventually.

The position of the departmental accountant in controlling disburse-

---

14 *American State Papers: Finance,* I, 691 (Jan. 28, 1801).

15 *Ibid.,* I, 756. Hamilton's explanation and defense of the system of advances is found in Hamilton, *Works* (Lodge ed.), VIII, 122–53, under date of Nov. 11, 1795.

16 For the statutory foundation of the office of accountant see, for the War Department, 1 Stat. 279 (May 8, 1792); for the Navy, 1 Stat. 610 (July 16, 1798).

ments gave rise to dispute and to a presidential determination in 1797. The accountants were charged by law with the settlement of all departmental accounts, subject to the inspection and revision of the Auditor and Comptroller in the Treasury Department. The War Department accountant, William Simmons, took it upon himself to decline to countersign a warrant for expenditures approved by the Secretary of War.[17] McHenry laid the matter before Adams, who secured the opinion of the Attorney General and the Secretary of State. Pickering's letter on the point at issue was characteristically forthright.

The accountant has fondly assumed an importance which does not belong to him. . . . The law has given him no discretionary or controuling power in such case: his duty is simply to *countersign them* [warrants]; unless he discovers an apparent error on the face of them; which of course he ought to point out to the secretary to be corrected.

The powers of the Comptroller of the Treasury are very different. He is explicitly directed to *controul* as well as *countersign* the warrants of the Secretary of the Treasury: for he is "to countersign all warrants drawn by the secretary of the treasury, *which shall be warranted by law.*" But when monies are once placed, with this precaution, at the disposal of the secretary of war, he alone is responsable for their particular application. To subject him to the controul of the accountant, would be to place an officer in a very subordinate station, to superintend the head of one of the great departments of government. If the Secretary of War directs, by warrant, a misapplication of the public money, He, and not the Accountant, is to be impeached for it. The accountant is to register the warrant, and to charge its amount to the person who is to account for its expenditure or delivery; and his countersignature is the evidence that he has so done.[18]

President Adams agreed with the advice he received from his Cabinet and the War Department accountant was put in his place. The terms of Adams' statement follow.

1. The Secretary of War is the sole judge of the time and manner of making disbursements. . . .

---

[17] This is the same Simmons of whom Pickering wrote McHenry in 1796 with reference to a pending claim, "I know how apt Mr. Simmons is to throw difficulties in the way of such settlements—& therefore I have advised the applicant to see you in person." *Virginia Magazine of History and Biography,* XII (1905), 266.

[18] Pickering to Adams, Dec. 7, 1797, Pickering Papers, VII, 523–24.

2. The Accountant of the War Department is, in no respect, comptroller of the disbursements ordered by the Secretary of War. The power of countersigning the warrants of the Secretary was given for the purpose of subjecting the said disbursements to a regular course of examination and settlement, and not for the purpose of restraining advances.

. . . .

5. The Accountant of the War Department is responsible, in the first instance, to the Auditor, and, finally, to the Comptroller of the Treasury, for observing proper rules and principles, in the settlement of accounts. . . .[19]

The system of accounts and disbursements which Hamilton established withstood successfully the critical examination of a suspicious opposition. It was well designed to safeguard the public moneys, given due diligence on the part of the several agents and the accountants and auditors.[20]

DISBURSEMENTS

There soon developed throughout the United States a considerable corps of disbursing officers, called into existence by administrative necessity rather than by act of Congress. They included, among others, the paymaster of the War Department, the navy agents who were paymasters at navy yards, the Purveyor, the collectors of customs and the supervisors of revenue, the deputy postmasters, the marshals of the federal courts, the procurement agents of the Treasury, War, and Navy Departments, the land agents, the recruiting officers, the invalid pension agents, and, overseas, the foreign representatives and agents. They performed an essential function without whose aid, it has been said, the Treasury system would have broken down. For twenty years they were unrecognized by law, until Gallatin regularized

---

[19] *American State Papers: Finance,* I, 816–17 (Dec. 28, 1797). Hamilton complained about Simmons' decisions repeatedly in connection with the expenses of the Provisional Army. Steiner, *James McHenry,* pp. 424–25.

[20] The influence of partisanship on judgments about administration is well illustrated by the Otis Report of 1801 (*American State Papers: Finance,* I, 690–93) and the Nicholson Report of 1802 (*ibid.,* I, 752–821). The former, controlled by the Federalists, declared, "the Department itself is so organized by law, and the mode of doing the business is so devised, as to afford the most perfect security to the nation" (p. 691). The latter, controlled by the Republicans, asserted that "considerable sums of public money have been greatly misapplied, and that much expense has been incurred without any legal authority. . ." (p. 754).

their status. "Their origin was illegitimate, their growth rapid and irregular, their fees enormous, their services indispensable." [21] These disbursing agents were only in part directly employed by the Treasury; many of them were field agents of other departments who were assigned this duty but who remained responsible to their usual superiors.

Nicholas Johnson, for example, a navy agent at Newburyport, Massachusetts, superintending the building of ships, became ex officio a disbursing officer. He received an advance of $2,000 with a notice to call for additional sums when needed. Later he was given an advance of $5,000 to supply "Captn Brown for recruiting his Crew," and a remittance to purchase clothing for sailors and marines: "if the Men are easily obtained, it will be best to have them measured. . . ." [22] He also supplied the ship's provisions, with the admonition from Stoddert that, "The Bread should be a quality equal to the very best furnished by the Merchants to their Ships, and with this the Sailors ought to be contented. . . ." [23] The form of the agent's accounts was prescribed by the navy accountant. [24] Johnson's commission was two per cent of his expenditures. [25]

THE AUDITING OF ACCOUNTS

The Continental Congress launched the process of auditing accounts on September 25, 1775, by means of a Committee of Accounts to "examine and report" upon all claims before payment. Frequent reorganizations growing out of perennial dissatisfaction finally eventuated in the creation of the office of Superintendent of Finance in 1781, in which were established the offices of Comptroller, Treasurer, Register, and Auditor.

These offices furnished the model of the auditing system written into the Treasury Department Act of 1789. In accordance with the views of Abraham Baldwin, who was "not an advocate for an unlimited

---

[21] E. I. Renick, "The Control of National Expenditures," *Political Science Quarterly,* VI (1891), 248–81 at 257–58; *American State Papers: Finance,* II, 335 (Feb. 4, 1809).

[22] "Letters of Benjamin Stoddert . . . to Nicholas Johnson," *Essex Institute Hist. Col.* LXXIV, 351, 352.

[23] *Ibid.,* LXXIV, 359.

[24] *Ibid.,* LXXIV, 353.

[25] John J. Currier, *History of Newburyport, Mass.,* I, 113.

authority in this officer [the Secretary of the Treasury]" and "hoped to see proper checks provided," [26] the function of settling accounts was vested in the Comptroller, not in the head of the Treasury.[27]

The initial examination of all public accounts was made by the Auditor, who received the accounts and supporting documents, examined them, and certified the balances to the Comptroller, sending him the vouchers for his review and decision. Any person dissatisfied with an adverse finding on a claim presented was given a right to appeal to the Comptroller.[28] His decision was conclusive.[29]

It was made the duty of the Comptroller to superintend the adjustment and preservation of the public accounts; to examine all accounts settled by the Auditor and to certify the balances to the Register; and to provide for the regular and punctual payment into the Treasury of all moneys collected. In addition to these duties directly connected with the audit, the Comptroller also was required to countersign all warrants drawn by the Treasury (thus ensuring that his decisions would be observed in payments to claimants); to devise and report accounting forms to the Secretary; and to direct prosecutions against delinquent collectors and for debts due the United States. The initial lodgment of this prosecuting function in the Comptroller throws light both on this office and on that of the Attorney General. The Register had no auditing duties but his office became the repository of the completed records.

The Secretaries of Treasury, War, and Navy were respectively held accountable for the sums appropriated to their departments. The officer held accountable for the expenses of the foreign service in the early days was the President himself. In the act authorizing these expenses forty thousand dollars was fixed as the maximum annual allowance,

---

[26] *Annals*, I, 392 (May 20, 1789). Madison also proposed unsuccessfully a fixed term for the Comptroller, in order to make him recurrently dependent upon the President and the Senate, *ibid.*, I, 612 (June 29).

[27] A brief account of the early history of auditing operations may be found in Darrell Hevenor Smith, *The General Accounting Office* (Baltimore: Johns Hopkins Press, 1927), ch. i. Some errors of fact and doubtful inferences were noted in this chapter.

[28] Thus was established the first quasi-judicial authority in the federal government; see Willard Eugene Hotchkiss, *The Judicial Work of the Comptroller of the Treasury* (Ithaca: Cornell University, 1911).

[29] Cf. an amusing note from Randolph to Hamilton, July 5, 1794: "E. Randolph begs the favor of Col. Hamilton to say to him . . . how he shall replace Fulwar Skipwith's money, so as to conform to the entries in the treasury department, and exonerate himself." State Dept., Domestic Letters, VII, 28.

and the maximum salary of each grade of minister was set. Congress recognized that secrecy might be essential in some cases and gave the President discretion to name the amount of such expenditures as he might think it advisable not to specify, while accounting in detail for the remainder.[30] The statements were, in fact, prepared by the Secretary of State.

The Nicholson Report of 1802 commented on the undisclosed sums for secret service in foreign intercourse, which by 1800 had been confined to the appropriation for contingent expenses. The committee noted "with considerable surprise" that the same principle of undisclosed expenditures had been adopted for the War Department and Navy and recommended that the practice cease.[31]

As nearly as can be ascertained Congress intended to adopt a plan of settlement of accounts which would require examination by the Auditor and revision by the Comptroller before actual payment should take place. This procedure was the one initiated in the fall of 1775 by the Continental Congress and carried on throughout the Confederation period. The organic acts of the departments conveyed no authority to them to settle their accounts, even tentatively.

Two lines of development caused an early abandonment of this simple system, with the exception of the Treasury Department itself. Hamilton quickly discovered that it was necessary to advance money to a variety of officials, especially those abroad, in order to provide essential services. Funds were actually paid out as occasion required by the persons to whom advances were made, not by the Treasury after each transaction had been examined and validated. The eventual settlement was made on the basis of quarterly accounts rendered by disbursing officers.

The second line of development began in 1792 when Congress authorized a quite different system of payment and audit in the War Department, involving the appointment of a departmental accountant. By this act the Treasurer was authorized to disburse money on the basis of the accountant's settlements, approved by the Secretary of War. Corresponding provisions were contained in the later law establishing the office of navy accountant. Examination by the Auditor and Comptroller occurred subsequently. In the act of 1792, therefore, Congress

---

[30] 1 Stat. 128 (July 1, 1790).
[31] *American State Papers: Finance,* I, 753–54.

specifically gave its approval to the settlement of accounts after payment of claims, that is to a post-audit.

Although the appointment of accountants in the War and Navy Departments was not designed to modify the legal responsibilities of the Auditor and Comptroller for settling accounts, the preliminary examination of claims tended to make the quarterly audit of the accountants' statements a merely formal matter.[32] This double audit, first in the department and second in the accounting offices, is the forerunner of the system of administrative examination of accounts prior to final audit. The same system prevailed also in the Post Office.[33]

The principles and practice of the Comptroller of the Treasury in settling accounts form a separate subject, too extensive and too technical for this study. The scrutiny of the Auditor and the review by the Comptroller were meticulous and exacting from the very beginning. Claims were required to be beyond criticism in form and substance. The Comptroller could rightly allege that he was the official watchdog of the Treasury, and John Steele, perhaps more than Oliver Wolcott, was ready to bark at the slightest provocation. One consequence was endless delay.[34] James O'Hara, an army contractor, was still trying to get a settlement of his 1796 contract in 1801.[35] A point

---

[32] The consequences were brought out quite flatly in 1816 in a report on the settlement of accounts submitted to the Senate jointly by James Monroe, Secretary of State, and the other Secretaries of the departments. *Annals*, XXX, 24 (Dec. 9, 1816). "The power of revision, both as to the accounts of the War and Navy Departments, was, and still is, reserved to the accounting officers of the Treasury. This power, however, from the period of the primary settlement of the accounts of the War and Navy Department, was withdrawn from the Treasury, ceased to be useful, and has been preserved merely for the sake of form." For confirming evidence, see *American State Papers: Finance,* III, 126, letter of the Comptroller (March 14, 1816).

[33] U. S. Treasury Department, Committee on Auditing, *The Accounting System of the United States from 1789 to 1910* (Washington: Govt. Printing Office, 1911), p. 9.

[34] Part of the delay was occasioned by failure to submit accounts promptly. Deputy postmasters were often negligent, and the accounts of foreign agents were necessarily slow in transmission. The Dutch firm of Willink, Van Staphorst, and Hubbard was the government's principal foreign fiscal agent. It opened an account with the Secretary of State for the expenses of the diplomatic officers. The latter were required to make annual statements on July 1. It was not until March 1792 that Jefferson received the first statement from the bankers, it having been four to five months in passage; and it did not provide the necessary detail for a settlement. State Dept., Domestic Letters, V, 9 (March 7, 1792).

[35] Wolcott Papers, XXII, 33.

of dispute was that an equivalent amount of each portion of the
soldier's ration had not been delivered as of the accounting date.
O'Hara maintained that he forwarded at one time large stores of rations
not subject to spoilage but made more frequent smaller shipments of
such items as meat. This reasonable explanation failed to satisfy the
Comptroller who apparently suspected failure to deliver. Arthur St.
Clair, Governor of the Northwest Territory, had endless difficulties
with the Comptroller, who "raised an infinity of objections [to payment of his accounts], and concluded, after much insolent altercation,
that an application must be made to Congress. . . . Misfortunes I can
bear with firmness, but the insolence of office throws me off my
center, and the hardest struggle I ever had was to keep my hands
off him." [36]

The Comptroller was an officer of great importance, perhaps the
most influential official *per officiis* in matters of administration. He was
considered second in rank in the Treasury Department, and Oliver
Wolcott went from the office of Comptroller to that of Secretary of
the Treasury. It would be easy, said Hamilton, "for the department to
run into disorder" if a mistake should be made in this post. He advised
Washington that, "It is of the greatest importance to the proper conducting the business of the Treasury Department that the Comptroller
should be a man of the following description: of strong sense, of clear
discernment, sound judgment, indefatigable industry, firmness, and
prompt decision of temper; possessing a comprehensive knowledge
of accounts, and of course good principles." [37]

The establishment of the offices of accountant in the War Department and the Navy, however, tended to diminish the Treasury capacity to control expenditures. Its review became more routine and per-
functory. John Steele was hardly justified, however, in complaining
that members of Congress were "in the habit of considering this an
office of mere detail & clerkship to which the real and efficacious
powers proposed ought not to be delegated." [38]

---

[36] *The Life and Public Services of Arthur St. Clair . . . with his Correspondence and
Other Papers* (William Henry Smith, ed., 2 vols., Cincinnati: Robert Clarke, 1882), II,
392–93; hereafter cited as *St. Clair Papers*. St. Clair had to borrow money from O'Hara,
and eventually was reduced to poverty.

[37] Hamilton, *Works* (Lodge ed.), X, 82.

[38] Wolcott Papers, XXII, 46.

That care on the part of the Treasury was warranted could not be doubted. The procedures of government business were in process of first establishment,[39] most operations were carried on at a distance, and business standards were not always satisfactory. Even in high quarters occasional problems arose. At the close of the session of Congress in July 1798, Speaker Dayton called for $33,000 for the compensation of members of the House. He neglected to settle his accounts and it was not until the winter of 1800 that the Treasury discovered he had retained $18,000. Wolcott called on him personally, wrote a very sharp letter, and eventually recovered the money, but the affair later got into the opposition newspapers.[40] Wolcott privately declared that Dayton's conduct had been indefensible.[41]

Smaller concerns may be illustrated by the case of Major Tousard who was engaged on construction at Fort Mifflin. It seems that the Major had employed "of his own property five Horses with Carts & one Yoke of Oxen," and that he drew pay for two drivers while employing only one. The matter, according to the War Department accountant, Simmons, was frequently mentioned to the Secretary of War but to no avail. Simmons, in pursuance of "a duty I owe to my Country," reported it to the Secretary of the Treasury.[42]

Fiscal authority sometimes affected the administrative decisions of the departments. Thus Wolcott, in a letter to the Secretary of War, while acknowledging that the head of the War Department could establish the pay of his clerks, went on to say, "it appears to me wrong and incongruous that the Accountant [of the War Department] should be allowed a Clerk with a higher salary than any now established, in the Offices of the Register of the Treasury or Commissioner of the Revenue." [43] On another occasion Steele, as Comptroller, wrote a peremptory letter to McHenry "recommending" three army procurement contracts instead of one. Probably recognizing he was on

[39] Postmaster General Osgood reported officially in 1790 that no man could be responsible (as he was) for the conduct of his deputies; "he must, to save himself, . . . keep the accounts in a manner that the treasury shall not be able to charge him with any more money than he chooses to be charged with; or he may endeavor to transact the business fairly, and hold the office until he finds he cannot preserve his reputation and credit, and then, if he is an honest man, he will resign." *American State Papers: Post Office*, p. 7.

[40] Wolcott Papers, VI, 91.

[41] *Ibid.*, XXI, 15.

[42] *Ibid.*, X, 34.

[43] *Ibid.*, X, 37.

dubious ground, Steele added, "these remarks being in some degree extra official it is expected that they will not be submitted to the perusal of any subordinate agent." [44] This is the same Steele who lost his temper over accounting instructions that McHenry had issued to his agents and contractors. "I am not an officer of the war department," Steele wrote indignantly to Wolcott, "and I will make no report to it; my duties are prescribed by law and I will not receive Mr McHenrys directions. Of all interferences that of attempting to impose duties, and to transfer responsibilities in a manner not authorized by law, is the most unreasonable and unjustifiable." [45]

The specific relation of Congress to the audit of accounts was barely explored. Madison proposed appointing a committee periodically to examine the books of the Treasury, on the model of the British committee on public accounts, and corresponding to the practice during the Confederation.[46] Ames had discussed the point in 1789, advocating an annual examination of public accounts but warning Congress not to depend on such an inquiry in lieu of reports from the Treasury.

It is, perhaps, a misfortune incident to public assemblies, that from their nature they are more incompetent to a complete investigation of accounts than a few individuals. . . . The science of accounts is at best but an abstruse and dry study; it is scarcely to be understood but by an unwearied assiduity for a long time; how then can a public body, elected annually, and in session for a few months, undertake the arduous task with a full prospect of success? . . . our knowledge will be far inferior to that of an individual, like the present officer. . . .[47]

Congress took no action to set up a select or standing committee on accounts, but from time to time the House appointed special committees to make investigations.[48]

---

[44] *Ibid.*, XXII, 29.

[45] *Ibid.*, XXII, 21.

[46] *Annals*, III, 226–27 (Dec. 2, 1791).

[47] *Ibid.*, I, 595–96 (June 25, 1789).

[48] Fred Wilbur Powell, compiler, *Control of Federal Expenditures: a Documentary History, 1775–1894* (Washington: Brookings Institution, 1939), *passim.*

Chapter Twenty-eight

DEBTS AND CLAIMS

T‌HE most crucial immediate problem of the new general government was to restore the public credit. The Confederation had been unable to meet payments of interest and principal on the foreign debt, and the arrearages on the domestic debt were so great that the value of securities had been greatly reduced. Both the internal economy and foreign credit were endangered, and the prospect of further financial support was slight unless order and confidence were restored.

The powers of the new government were ample to meet the problem. Congress at once earmarked the proceeds from the customs duties in excess of $600,000 for the payment of interest and principal on the debt. In January 1790, Hamilton presented his first report on the public credit, the recommendations of which were finally approved by Congress after a long and bitter struggle. The debt policy of the government included four major features: funding of the domestic debt; assumption of the debt incurred by the states in the prosecution of the war; new domestic loans to cover the funded and assumed debts; and a renewed pledge of the faith of the United States to meet its obligations, backed up by the assignment of specified revenue.[1] The same act authorized a loan of $12,000,000 to be applied to the foreign debt.

The long debate over the terms of payment to holders of depreciated securities, the speculation induced by the prospect of redemption at par, the bargain struck between Hamilton and Jefferson by which the federal capital was located on the bank of the Potomac in return for the scant margin of support for this fiscal program are not relevant to the history of administration. The net results of the act of 1790 were to restore the credit of the United States almost immediately but

---

[1] 1 Stat. 138 (Aug. 4, 1790).

not to reduce very much the amount of the debt; to estrange Hamilton and Jefferson; to start Madison on his way toward the emerging Republican party; and to increase the activities of the Treasury Department until they dwarfed all others.

MANAGEMENT OF THE PUBLIC DEBT

Before discussing the administrative organization necessary to manage the debt, it is useful to state briefly its form and amount. The foreign debt, including both principal and arrears of interest, amounted to $11,710,000; interest had been unpaid from four to six years, and installments on the principal due since 1787 had not been met. The domestic debt was estimated at $27,383,000 with an accrued interest of $13,030,000 and probably $2,000,000 additional unliquidated obligations. The state debts assumed by the federal government amounted in a first estimate to $21,500,000.[2] The total obligations of the new government were therefore well over $70,000,000, an amount which in 1790 seemed a truly colossal sum.

Loan commissioners. To handle the mass of detail that resulted from calling in a wide variety of former evidences of debt and replacing them with a uniform "stock" of the United States was a large undertaking involving thousands of individual transactions. For this purpose loan offices were established in each of the thirteen states to open books, receive and liquidate old certificates, issue new certificates, record transfers of ownership, pay interest due, and generally to perform related duties under the direction of the Secretary of the Treasury.[3]

Washington selected at least eight of the first thirteen loan commissioners from among persons who had held a corresponding office under the Confederation. Several men of considerable eminence served in this capacity. Jabez Bowen of Rhode Island was a Yale graduate, a lawyer who occupied a prominent place politically and socially, deputy governor of the state from 1778 to 1786, a trustee, and eventually chancellor of Brown University.[4] John Cochran of New York was an eminent physician and surgeon, appointed in 1780 as chief physician

---

[2] Davis Rich Dewey, *Financial History of the United States* (12th ed., New York: Longmans, Green, 1934), pp. 89–90, 93.

[3] 1 Stat. 138, secs. 6–7.

[4] *The National Cyclopaedia of American Biography* (32 vols., New York: James T. White, 1893–1945), VIII, 29.

and surgeon of the army and in 1781 as director general of military hospitals. He applied in 1789 for an appointment in the collection of revenue; disappointed there he became commissioner of loans, with an office in Federal Hall in New York.[5] Another physician who turned to finance was James Tilton of Delaware, a graduate of the medical department of the College of Philadelphia and an army surgeon from 1776 to the end of the war. His post as loan commissioner was not a lucrative one and in 1795 he sent in a letter of resignation upon the withdrawal of allowance for clerk hire.[6] From 1813 to 1815 he was physician and surgeon general of the U. S. Army.[7]

Commissioners to settle accounts with states. To settle the accounts arising out of the assumption of state debts a board of three commissioners was created.[8] Washington appointed William Irvine of Pennsylvania, John T. Gilman of New Hampshire, and John Kean of South Carolina. The task of this board was a difficult one, involving a wide range of discretionary judgment. Congress recognized its delicacy by directing a settlement according to the "principles of equity." The board eventually found that a number of states were indebted to the federal government, but the United States never succeeded in collecting the balances due from the debtor states.[9]

The commissioners were men of standing. William Irvine was a physician by training, a brigadier general in the Revolutionary Army, a delegate to the Continental Congress from 1786 to 1788, and from 1793 to 1795 a member of Congress. He was commanding officer of the Pennsylvania state troops quelling the Whiskey Rebellion.[10] John Taylor Gilman in his youth was a clerk in the office of his father, the state treasurer of New Hampshire; from 1783 to 1788, and again from 1791 to 1794, he was the treasurer, succeeding his father. In 1794 he became governor of the state, serving without a break to 1805, and subsequently from 1813 to 1816. He, too, was a member of the Continental Congress.[11] John Kean was a merchant; Washington had ap-

---

[5] *Dictionary of American Biography*, IV, 251–52.

[6] Hunt, *Calendar of Applications*, p. 128.

[7] *Dictionary of American Biography*, XVIII, 550.

[8] 1 Stat. 178 (Aug. 5, 1790).

[9] John Watts Kearny, *Sketch of American Finances, 1789–1835* (New York: G. P. Putnam's Sons, 1887), p. 28. As early as 1792 Hamilton recognized that the state debts to the United States might never be collected, Hamilton, *Works* (Hamilton ed.), IV, 250.

[10] *Dictionary of American Biography*, IX, 500.

[11] *Ibid.*, VII, 303–4.

pointed him a member of the commission to audit the accounts of the Revolutionary Army. He was a member of the Continental Congress from 1785 to 1787 and subsequently cashier of the Bank of the United States in Philadelphia.[12]

Sinking Fund Commission. To redeem the principal of the debt, Congress in 1790 established a board to purchase evidences of indebtedness.[13] It comprised the President of the Senate, the Chief Justice of the Supreme Court, the Secretary of State, the Secretary of the Treasury, and the Attorney General, a truly impressive body whose acts required the approval of the President. To this agency, which in 1795 became known as the Commission of the Sinking Fund, was given the customs and tonnage dues surplus; furthermore the President was authorized to borrow not over $2,000,000 for the redemption of the debt.

The Sinking Fund Commission naturally fell under the domination of Hamilton. It first met two weeks after its establishment; subsequent meetings occurred at intervals of from one to four months for the Commission to receive from Hamilton a statement of available surpluses and to direct the Treasurer of the United States to make purchases of specified evidences of debt.[14]

To float the loans authorized by Congress involved transactions on both the foreign and the domestic money markets. The President was empowered to make the loans, except in a few instances in which the Sinking Fund Commission became the direct agent of Congress. The President in turn delegated authority to Hamilton. Hamilton made William Short, minister at The Hague, his foreign financial agent. Most of the money borrowed abroad remained in Europe, and was used to meet debt payments in France and Holland. Domestic loans were arranged either through the Bank of the United States or by the sale of securities through the loan commissioners. The Bank became the ready source of funds throughout the decade, until its affairs were embarrassed by the amount of government securities it held.

---

[12] U. S. Congress, *Biographical Directory of the American Congress, 1774–1927* (Washington: Govt. Printing Office, 1928), p. 1168.

[13] 1 Stat. 186 (Aug. 12, 1790).

[14] The minutes of the Commission were transmitted to Congress in 1793 and are printed in *American State Papers: Finance,* I, 234–48.

The loan commissioners opened their books on October 1, 1790, for subscriptions to the loan to replace the outstanding domestic debt. The operation continued until December 31, 1797; the total amount of domestic debt thus funded was $41,963,561.98.[15] The loan commissioners completed the subscriptions to the funded debt assumed from the states on March 1, 1793, to the amount of over $18,000,000.[16]

The administrative machinery for dealing with debt problems thus centered in the Treasury, although involving a number of special agencies. Jefferson had some reason for concern as he watched the financial powers of his great rival expand into one region after another.

THE HOUSE INQUIRY INTO THE MANAGEMENT
OF THE PUBLIC DEBT, 1793–1794

The management of the public debt became one of the objects of the violent attack upon Hamilton by Republican members of the House of Representatives, led by Madison and Giles with the connivance of Jefferson.[17] Important relationships were raised, as well as technical problems of fiscal management.

Jefferson, viewing Hamilton's fiscal system as a whole, found it hostile to liberty and a danger to the Republic. In his letter of September 9, 1792, to the President, he referred to Hamilton as "the man who has the shuffling of millions backwards & forwards from paper into money & money into paper, from Europe to America, & America to Europe, the dealing out of Treasury-secrets among his friends in what time & measure he pleases, and who never slips an occasion of making friends with his means."[18] The scale of operations, the annoyance of the excise tax, popular suspicion of the moneyed class, the unrest of debtors, all combined to make the transactions of the Treasury an object of attention, quite irrespective of personal hostility to Hamilton.

The third, fourth, and sixth Giles resolutions (1793) specified alleged violations of law in disposing of the proceeds of loans authorized by Congress in acts of August 4 and August 12, 1790, and asserted that Hamilton had failed to keep the Sinking Fund Commission informed

---

[15] Kearny, *op. cit.*, pp. 18–19.

[16] *Ibid.*, p. 23.

[17] See above, ch. xix, for the setting of this affair.

[18] Jefferson, *Works* (Federal ed.), VII, 143; cf. Jefferson to Washington, May 23, 1792, *ibid.*, VI, 487–95.

of the sums available for the purchase of the public debt.[19] The presumed illegal action involved the use of part of the funds borrowed under the act of August 4,[20] and designed for foreign transactions, to buy a portion of the domestic debt and to meet interest charges on the domestic debt. Hamilton's defense was that the Dutch bankers preferred to loan on the joint foundation of the two acts of August 4 and August 12, and that the public interest dictated the use of the proceeds of these two loans indiscriminately. The House accepted Hamilton's defense by a large majority, but a new attack was launched in 1794.

One of the issues in 1794 was whether Hamilton had proper authority from the President for the various financial transactions involved in making provision for the public debt. Hamilton found himself on somewhat shaky ground. In 1793 he had informed Congress that the immediate superintendence of loans had been confided by the President to the Treasury Department, but that "a considerable latitude of discretion, nevertheless, from the very nature of the case, attended it." [21] Giles, however, accused him of acting beyond his delegation of authority. In writing to Washington to secure the President's confirmation of his authority Hamilton explained, "Before I made the disposition of any loan, I regularly communicated to the President my ideas of the proper disposition. . . . The communication and the sanction were verbal whenever the President was at the seat of government. In a case of absence, they were in writing." [22] Before the House Committee on April 1, 1794, he questioned the right of the committee to inquire into the relations existing between the President and the head of a department; the committee, however, persisted and on the same day Hamilton presented a full statement of his authority to act with regard to the disposition of money borrowed abroad.[23]

The authorities he claimed were (1) a general commission from the President to make the loans authorized by the acts of August 4 and 12, 1790; (2) an instruction with regard to the foreign agent to negotiate

---

[19] *Annals*, III, 900 (Feb. 28, 1793).

[20] 1 Stat. 138, sec. 2, provided that the proceeds of this loan of $12,000,000 "be appropriated solely" to the discharge of arrears and installments on the foreign debt. 1 Stat. 186, sec. 4, provided that the proceeds of this loan of $2,000,000, be applied to the purchase of the debt of the United States—by clear implication the domestic debt.

[21] *American State Papers: Finance*, I, 202.

[22] March 24, 1794, Hamilton, *Works* (Hamilton ed.), IV, 510.

[23] *Ibid.*, IV, 512–13.

the loans and the maximum amount; (3) from time to time specific approval of the disposition of each loan, either written or oral. The House Committee seized upon the weak link in the chain, the oral authorizations, and asked confirmation by the President.[24]

Washington's answer was far from satisfactory to Hamilton. He wrote:

I cannot charge my memory with all the particulars which have passed between us, relative to the disposition of the money borrowed. Your letters, however, and my answers, which you refer to in the foregoing statement, and have lately reminded me of, speak for themselves, and stand in need of no explanation.

As to verbal communications, I am satisfied, that many were made by you to me on this subject; and from my general recollection of the course of proceedings, I do not doubt, that it was substantially as you have stated it in the annexed paper, that I have approved of the measures, which you, from time to time, proposed to me for disposing of the Loans, upon the condition, that what was to be done by you, should be agreeable to the Laws.[25]

Hamilton construed this letter as entirely waiving the main point and asked the President either to "render the main fact unambiguous, or . . . record the doubt." In a rare outburst of complaint, he added:

The situation is indeed an unpleasant one. Having conducted an important piece of public business in a spirit of confidence; dictated by an unqualified reliance, on the one hand, upon the rectitude, candor, and delicacy of the person under whom I was acting; on the other, by a persuasion that the experience of years had secured to me a reciprocal sentiment . . . and by the belief, likewise, that however particular instances might be forgotten, the general course of proceeding in so important an affair could not but be remembered; I did not look for a difficulty like that which now seems to press me. . . .[26]

Despite this appeal there is no record that Washington gave a more explicit endorsement to the Treasury's fiscal operations. The House, however, exonerated Hamilton from any misuse of power.

---

[24] *Ibid.,* IV, 513–15.

[25] Washington to Hamilton, April 8, 1794, Washington, *Writings,* XXXIII, 318.

[26] April 9, 1794, Hamilton, *Works* (Hamilton ed.), IV, 518.

CLAIMS

One of the bothersome administrative tasks of the Federalist period was the settlement of claims arising out of the Revolutionary War. So far as claims developing from the activities of the new government were concerned, the Treasury Department, acting through the Auditor and the Comptroller, was the established agency for liquidation. The fiscal confusion of the war, however, gave rise to many other types of claims and much trouble in subsequent years. Almost every army officer at different stages of the war had power to contract debts binding upon the United States. The informality of the transactions, the loss of papers, and the scattering of witnesses made the proper proof of claims difficult and invited fraud. A special type of claim concerned invalid pensions due to former soldiers, originally provided by a resolution of Congress on August 26, 1776. During the Confederation period steps were taken to clear up claims against the United States, but with only partial success.[27] Ten more years of legislation and liquidation were required to complete the task.

Claims of all sorts and descriptions were presented directly to Congress. For example, on January 12, 1791, "Mr. Sedgwick presented petitions from a number of officers and soldiers in the Massachusetts line of the late army"; Mr. Fitzsimons presented "a petition from Joshua Barney, late a captain in the navy of the United States, praying to be reimbursed his expenses while a prisoner with the enemy," also a petition of sundry officers in the late American Navy.[28]

These claims were sometimes referred to the appropriate department, sometimes to a select committee. In 1794 the House of Representatives set up a standing Committee of Claims, "to take into consideration all such petitions . . . touching claims or demands on the United States as shall be . . . referred to them by the House, and to report their opinion thereupon, together with such propositions for relief therein, as to them shall seem expedient." [29] Uriah Tracy became chairman of the committee, but when he was proposed in 1795 for a second

---

[27] Act of June 7, 1785, concerning invalid pensions; act of November 2, 1785, concerning claims for services in the military department; act of July 23, 1787, concerning claims pertaining to the late commissaries, hospitals, clothier's, or marine departments. See *American State Papers: Claims*, pp. 202, 216.

[28] *Annals*, II 1861.

[29] *Ibid.*, IV, 880.

appointment, he begged to be excused: "He had been extremely hard employed last year, and had undergone much trouble about this business of claims." The House refused to give him relief but excused a second member, Gabriel Christie, who said that the state of his health required him to ride every morning, the time when the committee sat.[30]

The burden of hearing claims referred to it was particularly heavy on the War Department, and in 1791 Secretary Knox told Congress that "some general principles should be adopted in order to prevent unnecessary applications and waste of public time." [31] Congress responded in 1792 by pushing the load of claims for military pensions on the courts, or by trying to do so.

The responsibility for outstanding military pensions had been assumed by Congress in 1789, and $96,000 was appropriated for that year.[32] Payments were apparently made through the collectors of customs under the general direction and responsibility of the Secretary of War.[33] In 1792 two early statutes of limitations (1785, 1787) with reference to claims of officers' widows and orphans, and of officers and men, were suspended and the judges of the circuit court were directed to hear evidence thereon and report well-founded claims to the Secretary at War. He, however, was given authority to withhold names from the pension list if he suspected "imposition or mistake," and to report them to Congress.

The circuit court judges immediately rejected this delegation of nonjudicial authority, but agreed to sit as commissioners for the hearing of claims.[34] It was quickly discovered that they were poorly qualified

---

[30] *Ibid.*, V, 130.

[31] *American State Papers: Claims,* p. 28.

[32] 1 Stat. 95 (Sept. 29, 1789).

[33] On the subject of military pensions see William Henry Glasson, *History of Military Pension Legislation in the United States* (New York: Columbia University Press, 1900), and by the same author, *Federal Military Pensions in the United States* (David Kinley, ed., New York: Oxford University Press, 1918).

[34] 1 Stat. 243 (March 23, 1792); *American State Papers: Miscellaneous,* I, 49–53. The New York Circuit Court stated: "That neither the *legislative* nor the *executive* branch can constitutionally assign to the *judicial* any duties but such as are properly judicial, and to be performed in a judicial manner." They construed the act as referring to them as individuals, not as judges, and in the exercise of their individual choice decided to accept the duties of claims commissioners after adjournment of court. See the ensuing debate in the House, *Annals,* III, 556–57 (April 13, 1792), and Madison to Lee, April 15, 1792, Madison, *Letters* (Congressional ed.), I, 554.

to determine pension claims, and in 1793 the duty was transferred to the district judges, or "any three persons specially authorized by commission from said judge." [35] Even these claims commissioners made a poor record; in June 1794, Congress instructed the Secretary of War to return to the judges and commissioners incomplete records of claims sent in to him,[36] and in 1796 Congress was again forced to order the same procedure.[37] The process of screening claims through commissioners and judges lacked central direction and was apparently not well done.

The bulk of unliquidated claims carried over from the Revolutionary and Confederation periods was cleared up by 1795. The statutes of limitations of 1785 and 1787, although suspended for two years, 1792–94, covered most claims; the statute of limitations of 1795, effective January 1, 1797, covered claims represented by loan office certificates, final settlements, and indents of interest.[38] The final major report on these claims was made by the Committee on Claims, February 24, 1797. "It was essential," the committee said, "to the public administration that the extent of just demands upon the Government should be, within a reasonable period, definitely ascertained. It was essential to public safety and to right, in relation to the whole community, that all unsettled claims should be made known within a time when there were yet means of proper investigation, and after which the public responsibility should terminate, and the possibility of charging the Government by collusive and fictitious contracts should be at an end." [39]

The succession of claims, well and poorly founded, tells a good deal of what was taking place within and without the field of administration. Nathaniel Appleton, a commissioner of loans, saved the Treasury books while his personal possessions were consumed in a fire that burned down his house; he was refused reimbursement for loss of

---

[35] 1 Stat. 324 (Feb. 28, 1793).
[36] 1 Stat. 401 (June 9, 1794).
[37] 1 Stat. 495 (April 18, 1796).
[38] 1 Stat. 433, sec. 14 (March 3, 1795).
[39] *American State Papers: Claims*, p. 203. The liquidation of claims by the Auditor and Comptroller dragged interminably in some cases. Jefferson's accounts while minister at Paris, ending in 1789, were still unsettled in 1796, and he was expecting to have to go to Congress for relief. Jefferson to John Adams, Feb. 28, 1796, Jefferson, *Works* (Federal ed.), VIII, 220. The claim of Comfort Sands and others for damages suffered by loss of an army contract in 1782 was still before Congress in 1797. *Annals*, VII, 781 (Dec. 29, 1797).

property.[40] Andrew Jackson, a young Congressman from Tennessee, secured payment of claims covering an unauthorized expedition against the Indians under General Sevier.[41] Robert Harris was denied a claim to make good his losses suffered by receiving his army pay in depreciated currency.[42] George Smith asked Congress for his ransom money paid to escape from Algerine slavery, in the amount of $2,426.[43] The widow of a friendly Indian, Hanging Maw, petitioned for damages caused by an attack of the settlers.[44] General Kosciusko was granted $12,800 back pay.[45] Pierre Aupoix was forced to go to Congress to secure a drawback barred by an error of the collector of customs at New York.[46] John Vaughan was allowed a payment of $2,260 to cover losses caused by an error of the assayer of the Mint.[47] From the earliest days members of Congress tried to do justice to claimants whose cases before the Treasury were insufficient under the law but who, nevertheless, had good standing before the conscience of the country. But the line between their function and that of the Treasury puzzled them greatly. No one tried to state the two jurisdictions in general terms.

[40] *Annals*, IV, 1133–34 (Jan. 26, 1795).
[41] *Ibid.*, VI, 1737–38; 1741–46; 2155. This became a precedent to secure reimbursement for another such expedition, *ibid.*, VIII, 1522–24.
[42] *Ibid.*, VI, 1821–23 (Jan. 6, 1797).
[43] *Ibid.*, VI, 2326 (Feb. 28, 1797).
[44] *Ibid.*, VI, 2333–34 (March 1, 1797).
[45] *Ibid.*, VII, 761–63 (Dec. 22, 1797).
[46] *Ibid.*, VIII, 1414–15 (April 13, 1798).
[47] *Ibid.*, VIII, 1866 (June 1, 1798).

Chapter Twenty-nine

THE PURVEYOR OF THE UNITED STATES

O<small>N</small> J<small>ULY</small> 17, 1790, the *Gazette of the United States* carried the following communication from the Secretary of the Treasury.[1]

TREASURY DEPARTMENT

July 13, 1790.

Notice is hereby given, that Proposals will be received at the office of the Secretary of the Treasury, to the first day of October next inclusive, for the supply of all rations, which may be required for the use of the United States, from the first day of January to the thirty first day of December 1791, both days inclusive, at the places, and within the districts herein after mentioned, viz.

. . . .

The rations to be supplied are to consist of the following articles, viz.
One pound of bread or flour,
One pound of beef, or ¾ of a pound of pork,
Half a jill of rum, brandy or whisky,
One quart of salt,
Two quarts of vinegar,   } *per. 100 rations,*
Two pounds of soap,
One pound of candles,
The proposals must specify the lowest price per ration. No credit is required.

ALEXANDER HAMILTON,
Secretary of the Treasury.

Why Alexander Hamilton should have been purchasing army rations instead of the Secretary of War, who was put in charge of all "warlike stores," is a question that cannot be answered by reference to the

---

[1] Cf. *Gazette of the United States,* Sept. 29, 1790, for a notice inviting bids to build a lighthouse on Cape Henry.

statutes. The Treasury had no legal authority that has come to our attention to buy army supplies. Hamilton, drawn inevitably to vital points, had managed to convince Washington and overrule Knox so that Treasury secured the responsibility for some of the richest contracts of the decade. A long struggle for control of army contracts went on during the Federalist period, ending with the collapse of Treasury domination. This conclusion was not reached, however, until the first experiment in central purchasing had run its course.

CENTRAL PURCHASING

According to a subsequent congressional committee report in 1798, the Treasury had quietly assumed the authority to make all contracts for army rations, clothing, and magazine supplies. The War Department bought other supplies and military equipment.[2] The almost complete breakdown of army procurement in the Harmar campaign of 1790 and the St. Clair expedition in 1791 has already been noticed.[3] The contractors, one of whom was William Duer,[4] were extraordinarily negligent; but was the failure to control the contractors the fault of Treasury or the War Department? In fact, contracts once awarded—whether for purchase of army supplies, carriage of mail, or building of a naval vessel—were subject to almost no administrative supervision during these years.[5]

In any event, the supply failures of these two campaigns touched off a long contest for control of army purchasing. The victory went initially to Hamilton. The act of 1792, the first to deal specifically with

[2] Report of Committee on Expenditures of the Executive Departments, July 5, 1798, *American State Papers: Finance,* I, 590–92.

[3] See above, ch. xii.

[4] William Duer and Hamilton were close friends and their wives were cousins. Duer first came to America in 1768, buying timberland in New York and settling there permanently in 1773. He was active in civil affairs during the Revolution, and served from 1786 to 1789 as the secretary to the old Board of the Treasury. His appointment as Assistant to the Secretary of the Treasury had therefore some justification, but it was open to criticism, apart from the family connection. Duer was deeply interested in public securities and in business operations which were not above suspicion. Davis suggests that Duer took the position with the understanding that he need not drop his private affairs (Joseph Stancliffe Davis, "William Duer, Entrepreneur, 1747–99," *Essays in the Earlier History of American Corporations,* I, 176). He resigned after six months and engaged in land speculation and army contracts. His failure in 1792 caused a panic, losses being estimated at over $3,000,000. He died in 1799 in prison where he was committed for debt.

[5] Cf. above, ch. xiii, "The Navy Department"; and ch. xv, "The General Post Office."

government purchasing, provided that all purchases and contracts for supplying the army with provisions, clothing, quartermaster's department supplies, military stores, Indian goods, "and all other supplies or articles for the use of the department of War, be made by or under the direction of the treasury department." [6] This severe defeat for the War Department was not accomplished without a long debate in Congress, which was unfortunately not reported.[7] Knox resisted, even after Congress had spoken, but Hamilton (with Washington's aid) introduced the new system on September 1, 1792.

Hamilton assured Washington that "nothing shall be wanting in this department to furnish all requisite supplies for the army with efficiency and economy." [8] Thus ancient are these modern symbols! Provisions and clothing were handled as before by Treasury contract; the quartermaster was directed to continue the purchase of articles in his department under Treasury supervision; ordnance stores, Indian goods, and all contingent supplies were procured by a Treasury agent. The business fell into the hands of Tench Coxe. To concentrate the responsibility for receiving, holding, and distributing military stores, Congress provided in 1794 for a superintendent of military stores under the Secretary of War.[9]

The volume of business thus incumbent on the Treasury soon required a new organization. Tench Coxe complained of the overload of work and was relieved of his responsibility for purchasing at the close of 1794.[10] Hamilton told Washington that the business had gotten out of hand. "Including supplies for the navy, it is so extensive as, to be well executed, would occupy the whole time and attention of one person, possessing the requisite qualifications. This, with the growth of the country, must be every year more and more the case." [11]

Congress responded by creating the office of Purveyor of Public Supplies.[12] Hamilton now persuaded the legislative body to give the Treasury authority to make all purchases for the whole government,

---

[6] 1 Stat. 279, sec. 5 (May 8, 1792).

[7] *Annals*, III, 598 (May 7, 1792).

[8] Aug. 10, 1792, Hamilton, *Works* (Hamilton ed.), IV, 242.

[9] 1 Stat. 352, sec. 3 (April 2, 1794).

[10] Hamilton to Coxe, Dec. 29, 1794, Wolcott Papers, XXII, 58.

[11] Dec. 2, 1794, Hamilton, *Works* (Hamilton ed.), V, 56–57.

[12] 1 Stat. 419 (Feb. 23, 1795). The measure was favored by leading Federalists and opposed by Republicans. The final vote in the House was close, 40 to 35. *Annals*, IV, 1228.

centralized purchasing carried to its extreme. The Purveyor, under the direction of the Secretary of the Treasury, was authorized "to conduct the procuring and providing of all arms, military and naval stores, provisions, clothing, Indian goods, *and generally all articles of supply, requisite for the service of the United States.*" [13] The Purveyor was required to give bond in the amount of $20,000 and was strictly excluded from any personal business dealings. Hamilton's justification for Treasury intervention in War Department purchasing was stated in these terms. "The procuring of military supplies generally is, with great propriety, vested by law in the Department of the Treasury. That department, from situation, may be expected to feel a more habitual solicitude for economy than any other, and to possess more means of information respecting the best modes of obtaining supplies." [14]

So the matter stood during Washington's administration. The impending war with Great Britain had been averted before the new arrangements could be tested in a crisis. But in 1798 a second emergency arose, this time in relations with France; the Navy Department was established and a Provisional Army authorized; and the problem of responsibility for military supplies came again under discussion. A congressional committee, with Robert Goodloe Harper as chairman, brought in a report which condemned a "divided, and, consequently, an imperfect responsibility, and an incomplete interfering agency" in the purchase of military stores and supplies.

The Secretary of War, who uses them, does not know to what account they are charged; and the Secretary of the Treasury, who purchases and charges them, does not know for what purpose they are used. Hence must result an endless confusion and uncertainty in the accounts. . . . The Secretary of War cannot be responsible for the expenditure of the moneys appropriated for his Department. . . . the Secretary of the Treasury cannot be responsible for the due execution of the public service, since it does not depend upon him to cause the supplies which have been procured, to be properly used. [15]

Wolcott was unable to repel this attack upon the Treasury. Congress transferred the duty of purchasing military and naval supplies

[13] Italics are author's.
[14] Hamilton, *Works* (Hamilton ed.), V, 56.
[15] July 5, 1798, *American State Papers: Finance*, I, 591.

to the War and Navy Departments respectively.[16] Thus terminated the first attempt to establish central purchasing within the federal government.

ECONOMY AND EFFICIENCY

Under none of the various administrative arrangements was the procurement of army supplies either economical or efficient. The consequences of incompetence in getting and forwarding supplies to General St. Clair were disastrous. The system of central purchasing from 1792 to 1798 led to confusion and was abandoned. The purchase of supplies by the army after 1798 was the despair of Hamilton, then inspector general of the Provisional Army. In 1799 he wrote the Secretary of War:

the management of your Agents, as to the affair of supplies, is ridiculously bad. Besides the extreme delay, which attends every operation, articles go forward in the most incomplete manner. *Coats* without a corresponding number of *vests*. Cartouche boxes without belts &c &c nothing intire— nothing systematic. Tis the scene of the worst periods of our revolution war acted over again even with caricature.

. . . unless you immediately employ more competent Agents to procure and to forward supplies, the Service will deeply suffer and the head of the War Department will be completely discredited.[17]

McHenry agreed that Hamilton's complaints were well founded and said he would appoint an assistant to the incompetent Purveyor, Tench Francis. So far as the superintendent of supplies, Colonel Stevens, was concerned, the Secretary of War wrote that he had "so strong a supporter, that I dont see how to get rid of him." [18] To which Hamilton tersely replied, "Pray take a resolution adequate to the exigency & rescue the credit of your Department." [19]

The conditions of which Hamilton complained were exposed in a letter from Oliver Wolcott's home town, Litchfield, Connecticut.

Your favour of the 12th. relative the proposed Contract for officers shoes is duly recd. It furnishes me, too, with the knowledge of the Cause of the

---

[16] 1 Stat. 610 (July 16, 1798). An office of purveyor was then established in the War Department.

[17] Steiner, *James McHenry*, p. 390.

[18] *Ibid.*, p. 391.

[19] *Ibid.*, p. 398.

very miserable manner in which the soldiers are supplied with that article. Capt. Ramsey, who is stationed at this place, unites his protestation with those of his men against the scandalous frauds practiced on them. The shoes which have been dealt out to the men here, & I understand the same to be the fact at all the other stations, are of the very worst leather and, worst manufacture. A march of 20 miles would totally ruin the greater part of them—and the *heels* of many of them drop off immediately on handling them. The *hats* of the Soldiers are of the same quality, a rain or two has rendered several of them utterly useless—and the Cloaths are but little better, particularly in the *making*.

By these things the public service is discouraged, & the *Government* itself discreditted. Very many respectable people impute these defects to circumstances that should not be often named. . . .[20]

The purchase of materials and supplies for building and equipping naval vessels perplexed the War Department from 1794 to 1798. The Navy Department under Stoddert apparently had a much better record, possibly due in some measure to the administrative organization of the navy yards, and the provision for the appointment of an agent on the spot to purchase supplies and equipment and to supervise all matters incident to construction and outfitting.

DEPARTMENTAL SUPPLIES

Post office supplies were simple, and requisite only in relatively small quantities. Most of the office books, for accounts and records, were sent out from Philadelphia,[21] but portmanteaus and bags were secured by the deputy postmasters.[22] Locks for the portmanteaus were also sent out from headquarters. Stages and horses were supplied by the contractors, although late in the decade a government-owned line from Philadelphia to Baltimore required purchase of these essentials. Signs, where needed, were supplied by the postmaster.

Supplies for the territorial governments were perforce purchased in Philadelphia and sent out usually by an army wagon. They, too, were extremely simple: seals for the various officers, material for writing, and record books.

Lighthouse supplies, especially oil, were secured by the collectors of customs. They also bought supplies in the local markets for the revenue

---

[20] *Ibid.*, pp. 393–94.
[21] Postmaster General Letter Book A, p. 367.
[22] Letter Book A, pp. 250–51.

cutters. Court supplies were found by the marshals—firewood and candles, printed forms, ink and pens, and record books.

The only important supply problem was related to the armed forces and though the army and the navy were both maintained on a very modest scale, the business of procurement was poorly managed. With too little evidence at hand to warrant a firm conclusion, one suspects that favoritism in granting contracts in some cases, and lack of effective inspection and enforcement in most cases were responsible for an unimpressive record.

Chapter Thirty

GOVERNMENT IN THE WILDERNESS

On the morning of July 16, 1788, the inhabitants on the Muskingum gathered in the presence of Arthur St. Clair, first governor of the Northwest Territory. In an address to the first magistrate under the newly constituted government, they declared, "The taske is truly arduous and the undertaking great, to come to so remote a country as this, to reduce forests to proper cultivation and to rear towns and cities in places explored only by natives and wild beasts: but if we persevere as we have begun, we have but little to fear. . . ."[1] After five years in this remote country St. Clair wrote his friend, Alexander Hamilton, "In compassion to a poor Devil banished to another Planet, but like the Soul of some departed Sinner as they left us, still hovering about that he had left, tell me what is doing in Yours, if you can snatch a Moment from the weighty Cares of your Office."[2]

The establishment of civil authority and the rudiments of public administration was also a "taske truly arduous." For years St. Clair traveled by boat, on horseback, and on foot up and down the region north of the Ohio. In 1795 he said to the inhabitants of Cincinnati, "The vast Extent of the Territory and the Distance between the Settlements there is very little Connexion they have with each other which are nevertheless stretched out from one Extremity of it to the other render it scarce possible for the Governour to have a fixed residence any where at present and he is in Consequence of that Situation of things frequently exposed to Expense, much Fatigue and at Times to no little Danger."[3] Trouble of many kinds dogged his footsteps, but

---

[1] *The Territorial Papers of the United States* (Clarence Edwin Carter, ed., 12 vols., Washington: Government Printing Office, 1934–45), II, 133. Hereafter cited as *Territorial Papers.*

[2] Aug. 9, 1793, *ibid.,* II, 459.

[3] *Ibid.,* III, 435.

time was on his side. Slowly, little by little, counties were erected, local officials found, land patents confirmed and granted, Indians subdued, communications established, and the business of government put in motion among a pushing, adventuresome, boisterous, and not always law-abiding population.

The inhabitants were not disposed, however, to a state of anarchy. The magistrates of Kaskaskia welcomed the arrival of General Harmar in 1787, "to substitute order in the place of anarchy and confusion, under which we have groaned for a long time." [4] The authority of the magistrates, they said, "scarcely exists." The inhabitants of Illinois complained bitterly of their fate. From its first settlement to 1778 (when it was taken by the Americans), they said, Illinois Country was governed by Commandants, "was in a flourishing Situation and its Inhabitants rich and happy—That from that period to the year 1790 it was entirely neglected and left in a State of Anarchy. . . . That spirit of Industry which actuated them while under the immediate Care of officers appointed to govern them and which gave a spring to their Efforts, is no more, Agriculture is but feebly carried on and the Indian Trade may be said to be entirely decayed. . . . The Petitioners are fully persuaded that the Establishment of a Government to be administered among themselves would rescue them from their present miserable situation." [5] Man had been reduced nearly to the state of nature, and with Hobbes, found life "poor, nasty, brutish, and short."

THE TERRITORIAL GOVERNMENT

Congress began the improvement on nature by enacting the Northwest Ordinance in 1787 and by sending Arthur St. Clair to bring the blessings of order and liberty to a preponderantly French-speaking population.[6] In 1790 a second territorial government was established for the region south of the Ohio, from part of which in 1798 the Mississippi Territory was created. In 1800 the Indiana Territory was established. During these years two new states were admitted to the Union from territorial lands—Kentucky in 1792 and Tennessee in 1796. The course of government in the Northwest Territory and the

---

[4] Aug. 25, 1787, *ibid.*, II, 67.

[5] *Ibid.*, III, 76–77.

[6] In 1790 St. Clair commented on "their extreme Ignorance, and . . . their total want of the English language . . . not a fiftieth Man can either read or write any Language. . . ." *Ibid.*, II, 245.

Southwest Territory provided most of the substance of territorial affairs; that of the former was full of controversy and jarring personalities, but that of the latter was relatively quiet and peaceful.[7]

The form of government in all territories was alike. Until a population of at least 5,000 "free male inhabitants of full age" was attained, public authority consisted of the governor, the secretary, and three judges who also acted as a legislative body. Local governments were created by the governor as settlements were formed. In its second stage the government included an elected lower house and an upper house selected by the President from among names submitted by the territorial assembly. The governor retained an absolute veto, and St. Clair used it freely. This was government in a rudimentary form—the bare necessities of authority for the scattered and tiny settlements along the river banks. The benefits supplied to the people by this government were equally simple: protection from the Indians, a good title to land, and freedom to work out their destiny in the great struggle to subdue nature to their purposes.

As the single repository of the power to govern, the first magistrate of the territory performed a wide variety of duties, directly and personally. He erected counties and gave them officers. He examined claims to land and validated titles.[8] He granted licenses to marry, to keep a tavern, to operate a ferry, and to practice law. He received petitions from the people. He granted pardons. He fixed charges for the ferry—for "every single Person . . . Six Cents . . . And for Hogs Six Cents each."[9] As superintendent of Indians he licensed traders, secured and distributed gifts, issued passports to travelers, held conferences and in general acted for the Great White Father—but the army was a sharp competitor. These duties and his incessant travels more than filled his days.

The administrative authority of the territorial governor centered on the power to appoint and remove all officers civil and military, except the higher ranks in the militia, the judges, and the secretary, but including county and township officials.[10] He thus became the fountain-

---

[7] In 1794 Randolph told Washington that the Journal of Proceedings of the Executive in the Northwest Territory was very little more than a history of bickerings and discontent. *Ibid.*, II, 472.

[8] *Ibid.*, II, 245.

[9] *Ibid.*, III, 367.

[10] Governor Winthrop Sargent told the inhabitants of Mississippi Territory, "All appointments within the Territory, not specially provided for by the ordinance of the

head of official life, unchallenged by any competing authority, but at times greatly handicapped by lack of available qualified persons to serve in public capacity. His authority was so great that Judge David Campbell, instructing the grand jury in the Southwest Territory in 1792, thought it wise to tell his listeners that they "need not be alarmed at this very extensive Power confered on the Governor," since all his acts were subject to the control of the general government.[11]

St. Clair's establishment as governor apparently did not include even a single clerk, since the secretary of the territory was expected to keep the records. As Indian superintendent St. Clair presided over two deputies, two interpreters, a storekeeper, and occasional messengers.[12] Clerks indeed were unknown; Rufus Putnam hired one on his own authority in order to keep up with the task of surveying the western country, but officials were expected to do their own writing and record keeping. The governor's office was where he happened to be; his staff did not exist. Governor William Blount probably spoke for all incumbents of the office when he declared "the execution of its Duties very arduous & painful."[13]

The territorial secretary acted for the governor when he was absent. On leaving Kaskaskia by boat in 1790 St. Clair formally delegated authority to the secretary, Winthrop Sargent: "As soon then as I am gone on Board you will please to consider me as absent from the Territory, & that the Government has of Course devolved upon you."[14] Sargent in turn delegated powers to the United States attorney: "The Secretary in Governour St Clairs Absence intending to leave the County of Hamilton on public Business at Detroit Committed to the Care of Thomas Goudy Esquire United States Attorney in said County—twelve marriage Licenses—twelve Ferry Licenses and Ten Tavern Licenses—all Blanks to be filled up at his Discretion."[15]

Distance and separation combined to complicate the relationships of St. Clair and Sargent, although each retained the respect of the other.

---

honorable congress, are with the governor, and merit only can entitle a man to office. Strong and evident marks of attachment to the United States and good government, a disposition to preserve the peace and order of society, and harmonize contending sentiments" would be looked upon with favor. *The Mississippi Territorial Archives, 1798–1803* (Dunbar Rowland, ed., Nashville, Tenn.: Brandon Printing Co., 1905), I, 27.

[11] *Territorial Papers,* IV, 126.
[12] *Ibid.,* II, 195.
[13] *Ibid.,* IV, 422.
[14] *Ibid.,* III, 311.
[15] *Ibid.,* III, 446.

The secretary kept the seal and much inconvenience resulted in validating the governor's acts. In 1796 Sargent was in Detroit, laid out the county, and appointed officers, erroneously believing St. Clair absent. When the latter heard about the action he wrote, "two Governors at one and the same time in the same country (and perhaps counteracting each other) must impress the new subjects unfavorably, with respect to the government they have fallen under." [16] Sargent was innocent enough, and on his part asked protection against "Prosecution or Persecution for a public Act as Governour at Cincinnati when unluckily his Excellency had been at the Muskingum a few Days, but which I could not have known but by a Spirit of Divination." [17]

The difficulty of maintaining contact between the governor, the secretary, and the judges was great enough, assuming due diligence on their part. It was aggravated by the long absences from duty and from the territory of many of these officials, at times practically suspending the operation of government. St. Clair was the most serious offender, but Judge George Turner was also highly negligent. Hamilton asked Winthrop Sargent for an official report on St. Clair's absences up to January 1794, from which it appeared that the governor was away from the territory almost the whole year 1789, three months in 1790, most of the spring and summer, in making preparations for the expedition against the Indians, and, subsequent to his defeat, from December 8, 1791, to August 2, 1793—over a year and a half. [18]

These absences annoyed Washington, who began pressing Jefferson in the autumn of 1792 to force the territorial officials to their duty. [19] In March 1793 he told Jefferson that if St. Clair did not return, he would be "under the disagreeable necessity of issuing a peremptory order for that purpose," [20] and asked whether Judge Turner had set out for the west. After a delay of a couple of weeks Jefferson sent a very mild suggestion to Judge Turner, placing the initiative for his letter on Sargent. [21] Washington followed up with more pressure on Jefferson, expressing his surprise and mortification at Turner's conduct: "Such remissness . . . not only reflects upon the common rules of propriety

---

[16] *St. Clair Papers*, II, 410.
[17] *Territorial Papers*, III, 456.
[18] *Ibid.*, II, 471.
[19] *Ibid.*, II, 416.
[20] *Ibid.*, II, 444.
[21] *Ibid.*, II, 449.

but must implicate me in the shamefulness of their conduct. . . ." [22] Jefferson then told Judge Turner that the Attorney General had been directed to make an inquiry into his conduct.[23]

St. Clair failed to return until August 1793 and was again earning presidential reprimands in 1794. On this occasion both St. Clair and Sargent were absent, leaving no executive authority in the territory.[24] A subsequent compilation showed that St. Clair was away more than six months in 1794, three months in 1795, and continuously from May 1796 to May 1798.[25] Washington and Adams apparently gave up in despair.

This was an exceptional record, and in other territories officials generally paid proper attention to their duties. William Blount, governor of the Southwest Territory, formally asked for a short leave in 1791,[26] and when away in 1793 he apologized to the judges for the length of his absence.[27]

The judicial and legislative powers were vested in the hands of the territorial governors prior to eventual establishment of an assembly. The disputes of the judges in the Northwest Territory with St. Clair over their respective jurisdictions, the use of the veto, the sale of land, the control of local officers, and other matters were complicated by personal and political rivalry and do not concern this study.[28] The absences of the judges from the territory were excessive and were a constant theme of complaint by Sargent, at times the sole representative of the territorial government. "From various Causes there has been but Little Attention by the Gentlemen of the Bench to the important Business of their Commission." [29] "The long absence of two of the judges from the Government, has prevented the adoption of laws for more than the six months last past. . . ." [30] In 1793 Sargent reported to Jefferson that the absences of the judges were "virtually affecting a

---

[22] *Ibid.*, II, 450.

[23] *Ibid.*, II, 452.

[24] *Ibid.*, II, 479.

[25] *Ibid.*, II, 647–48.

[26] *Ibid.*, IV, 70–71.

[27] *Ibid.*, IV, 301.

[28] "If old Symmes [one of the judges] gets a private Interview with the President he will attempt to stab me in the Dark—unless your Excellency can guard me. . . ." Sargent to St. Clair (then in Philadelphia), Feb. 12, 1793, *ibid.*, II, 434.

[29] *Ibid.*, II, 224.

[30] *Ibid.*, II, 406.

total present Abdication upon the supreme Bench of this Territory."[31] Sargent was the more irritated because he could not get a leave of absence "and dared not to take it."[32] In the Northwest Territory he seemed alone to have had a sense of official duty.

To discover proper characters in the wilderness to fill public office was a perplexing problem. St. Clair told Washington in 1790 that he was "very much put to it to find proper Subjects to fill the different Offices";[33] in 1794 he commented on the same predicament;[34] in 1796 Acting Governor Sargent could not locate a qualified person in Wayne County for probate judge and appointed the prothonotary to the office;[35] and in 1797 he could recommend no one in the territory to fill a vacancy on the bench. For lesser offices of sheriff, straymaster, and the like, no difficulty existed.

Land speculation was an almost universal occupation and for some years officeholding and land operations were much intermixed.[36] Both Judge John Cleves Symmes and Judge Rufus Putnam were leading figures in the purchase of large tracts, and, as St. Clair pointed out, every land dispute could be traced to some transaction of one or the other, "and they are to sit in Judgement upon them." This, thought St. Clair, was "not a groundless cause of apprehension. . . . Interest hangs an insensible bias on the minds of the most upright men. . . ."[37] By 1798 the impropriety of combining land speculation with official posts was recognized in Philadelphia.[38]

No salary was provided for a legal adviser to the governor and there was much complaint until the omission was rectified.[39] In 1796 St. Clair induced his son to remove from Pittsburgh to Cincinnati, whereupon the younger St. Clair was appointed attorney general of the territory—an appointment that later subjected the governor to much criticism. Andrew Jackson was attorney for the Mero district of the Southwest Territory for a period.

---

[31] *Ibid.,* III, 407.

[32] *Ibid.,* II, 431.

[33] *Ibid.,* II, 247.

[34] *St. Clair Papers,* II, 330.

[35] *Territorial Papers,* III, 454.

[36] St. Clair had neither resources nor inclination to permit him "to engage largely" in land operations, but he asked Sargent to locate him a farm (Nov. 27, 1790). *Ibid.,* II, 312.

[37] *Ibid.,* II, 499.

[38] *Ibid.,* V, 31.

[39] *Ibid.,* II, 319–20.

One of the principal handicaps to effective government across the Alleghenies was the lack of means of communication. Travel was a laborious and time-consuming, occasionally a hazardous enterprise. On his way west in 1790 St. Clair was "more plagued and vexed than ever I was in the same time in my life." [40] During the last half of 1790 he traveled nearly five thousand miles either in an open boat or on horseback.[41] A boat provided for the use of the governor was commandeered by the army,[42] and Sargent was obliged to travel up and down the Ohio in an open canoe.[43] A military escort was essential to guard against the savages, but it was available only at the discretion of the local commandant.[44] For lack of an escort the judges "are obliged to be in a manner stationary." Even General James Wilkinson was obliged to confess the "Caprice and Contumacy sometimes found among military Gentlemen." [45]

The Northwest Territory was relatively close to Philadelphia and communications were fairly reliable. Governor William Blount in the Southwest Territory, with the seat of government at Knoxville, was less well situated. To communicate with Philadelphia in 1792 Blount could count on a period of from three to four weeks each way.[46] In July 1794 an express broke all records, traveling from Philadelphia to Knoxville in fourteen days and three hours, a distance of at least 650 miles.[47]

The governor of the Mississippi Territory, with headquarters at Natchez, was truly remote. To this post Winthrop Sargent had been promoted in 1798 and before many months had passed he was lamenting the "very Melancholy Consideration, that my Public and private Communications with the Atlantic States is so extreme difficult and tedious." [48] He was quite justified, for a letter from Natchez in 1799 could scarcely reach Philadelphia in less than sixty days in summer and more in the winter season. Pickering calculated that the passage of letters from Natchez was as tedious as from Europe, against a

[40] Ibid., II, 284.
[41] Ibid., II, 322.
[42] Ibid., III, 372.
[43] Ibid., III, 374.
[44] Ibid., III, 387.
[45] Ibid., III, 389.
[46] Ibid., IV, 162.
[47] Ibid., IV, 351.
[48] Miss. Territorial Archives, I, 117.

westerly wind.[49] How completely the governor of the Mississippi Territory was "on his own" is demonstrated by the fact that from May 12 to Christmas 1800 Sargent received only one letter from the Secretary of State.[50] This long silence may have been the fault of that office, which had changed hands from Pickering to John Marshall, for in early 1800 a "post road" was established from Natchez to Nashville, over "an Indian footpath very devious & narrow." [51]

The problem of communication from the seat of government to the territorial governors, and within the territories from one official to another remained a serious and insoluble handicap to good administration. Minor conflicts between army and civilian officials dragged on interminably while letters slowly passed back and forth to secure a solution from headquarters. Unity and energy, central to Hamilton's definition of good government, could hardly be conjured out of the state of the times.

THE INDIANS

The relations of the Indians to the white population, steadily pressing westward, were a constant source of concern to the federal authorities and state governments alike. Under the Constitution, responsibility for public policy was vested in the general government, but difficult problems of state-federal relations ensued.

The management of Indian affairs was complicated by the tension that surrounded the relations of the red men to the whites. Henry Knox, who was well informed on Indian affairs, told Congress in 1787 that "the deep rooted prejudices, and malignity of heart, and conduct, reciprocally entertained and practised on all occasions by the Whites and Savages will ever prevent their being good neighbours. The one side anxiously defend their lands which the other avariciously claim. With minds previously inflamed the slightest offence occasions death—revenge follows which knows no bounds. . . . Either one or the other party must remove to a greater distance, or Government must keep them both in awe by a strong hand, and compel them to be moderate and just." [52] Governor St. Clair said six months later,

---

[49] *Territorial Papers*, V, 57.
[50] *Miss. Territorial Archives*, I, 322–23.
[51] *Territorial Papers*, V, 118.
[52] *Ibid.*, II, 31.

"though we hear much of the Injuries and depredations that are committed by the Indians upon the Whites, there is too much reason to believe that at least equal if not greater Injuries are done to the Indians by the frontier settlers of which we hear very little." [53] From the edge of the Indian country, Major John F. Hamtramck reported, "But the worst evil of all is a number of Villains in this Village [Fort Knox] who keep the Indians continually drunk." [54] Nor was he optimistic about peace and order. "The people of Kentucky," he declared, "will carry on private expeditions against the Indians and kill them whenever they meet them, and I do not believe that there is a jury in all Kentucky who would punish a man for it. . . . as the thirst of war is the dearest inheritance an Indian receives from his parents, and vengeance that of the Kentuckians, hostility must then be the result on both sides." [55]

It was in such an atmosphere that the objects of public policy had to be pursued. They were to avoid war, to protect white settlers on the frontiers, to secure title to Indian land by treaty negotiation, to supervise trade, and to defend the tribes against wrongdoing by the whites. None of these objects could be fully secured, for government was not able to provide the strong hand that Knox thought essential.

Administrative responsibility. The War Department was the administrative agency through which the general government exercised its authority. The Ordinance of 1786 created two civilian superintendents of Indian affairs, one for the northern department above the Ohio, one for the southern department. [56] The first northern superintendent, Richard Butler, was an Indian trader as early as 1764, served in the Revolutionary Army, negotiated treaties with the Indians as a commissioner during the Confederation, and was active in Pennsylvania politics. He was killed by the Indians in 1791. James White, the first southern superintendent, was a captain in the Revolutionary Army who settled in Knoxville in 1786.

This simple and direct administrative arrangement was modified by the terms of the legislation establishing territorial governments under the Constitution. The governor became ex officio the superintendent of Indians. As governor he reported to the Secretary of State, but

---

[53] *Ibid.,* II, 89.
[54] *Ibid.,* II, 381.
[55] *St. Clair Papers,* II, 198.
[56] George D. Harmon, *Sixty Years of Indian Affairs,* p. 4.

as superintendent of Indians he reported to the Secretary of War. Thomas Jefferson tried to clear up the confusion by instructing St. Clair, "All the business of the Government is divided into 3. departments, to wit, of War, finance & State: to some one of the heads of these every possible matter belongs. as to whatever you have to do in your military Capacity, you refer yourself to the Secretary at War. I do not know that you can ever have anything to do in the line of Finance. every thing else falls into the department of State, to the head of which it should be addressed—to him the general report, given every Six Months, is referred, and if there are matters in it proper for the other departments he reports them to the President who sends the extracts to the proper department. . . ."[57] The problem was far from settled, however.[58]

St. Clair's relations with the War Department on Indian affairs were most unsatisfactory and in desperation he finally appealed privately to Washington.[59] Knox, doubtless smarting under the consequences to him of St. Clair's military defeat, apparently ignored the governor as superintendent of Indians; Indians were called to the seat of government without St. Clair's knowledge, official representatives came out to the Indians who were unknown to him and who failed to communicate with him; he was not informed of the name or residence of his deputy. Winthrop Sargent later told Pickering that St. Clair had been "a mere Cypher" as superintendent; "Military subaltern officers not unfrequently have exercised all his powers . . . thereby depriving him of almost all his consequence, *though* as the legitimate agent, all responsibility was *his*. . . ."[60] Washington took occasion to clear up the matter, involving a subordinate War Department official.[61]

The War Department, nevertheless, preferred to rely heavily upon its post commanders on the frontiers. This was natural. Even Governor Winthrop Sargent, a stout contender for preference in Indian affairs, wrote from the Mississippi Territory that the Indians were "taught by Education and habit, to look to the Sword as the source of power and Arbiter of Justice, a savages attention can not be diverted from Military

[57] *Territorial Papers*, II, 460. The rule of Jefferson's day was complicated later by attaching the office of surveyor general, and subsequently the land offices to the Treasury Department, *ibid.*, II, 588. All three departments consequently had a stake in the territories.

[58] *Ibid.*, II, 189–90, 629.

[59] *St. Clair Papers*, II, 390–94.

[60] *Miss. Territorial Archives*, I, 32.

[61] *St. Clair Papers*, I, 192.

Parades, and the display of the National Insignia, Standards, Arms, Embattled ranks, and Martial Musick impress the Inhabitants of our Forests, more forcibly than Argument." [62] The civil authority was hard put to it to find its place.

We have already noted Sargent's conviction that St. Clair had been only a cipher in the management of Indian affairs in the Northwest Territory. When Sargent became governor of the Mississippi Territory he determined to require the War Department to act through him rather than through the army commandants. "I trust," he wrote the Secretary of State of St. Clair's experience, "such conduct may not be attempted to be practiced upon me, for without the presidents express mandate in point, I shall not submit to it." [63] Circumstances were against him, however. A very able superintendent for the southern department, Colonel Benjamin Hawkins, was already well established and in the good graces of the Indians. Pickering told Sargent it would be expedient to leave Hawkins undisturbed.[64] Sargent continued, however, to complain that the Secretary of War had committed the whole business of Indian affairs to the military rather than to him.

Policy seems to dictate that the Officer who should preserve an Influence in Peace and War over the Indians should be Considered by them as the Fountain of all their Good, or at least the Channel through which Charity, the Donations of Government are to flow—but the reverse of this has been Observed—Subaltern—Noncommissioned Military Officers—in some instances, who were here to day and gone to morrow, whose Influence with Indians could nought avail Government have been supplied with the means of feeding and clothing them, whilst the legal Superintendent could not command for them a single Ration—That practice however it appears has of late been restrained, but some P R E S E N T S, I am informed are now ordered immediately to the Choctaw Indians to the disposal of the Agent, of *which* it seems to me, I should have been advised from the proper Department—Indeed sir I presume to believe that all affairs whatever of the Indians over whom I am to retain a Superintendency, should be managed through me, for otherwise in Justice, I ought not to be Responsible.— [65]

One of the principal points of controversy concerned the respon-

---

[62] *Miss. Territorial Archives*, I, 75.

[63] *Ibid.*, I, 32.

[64] *Territorial Papers*, V, 35, 46.

[65] *Miss. Territorial Archives*, I, 289–90; also *ibid.*, I, 54–55.

sibility for distributing presents to the Indians, a practice inherited from the British.[66] The appropriation for this purpose was to the War Department. Obviously it made much difference whether the Indians were to look to the military commanders or to the territorial governor for supplies and gifts. Sargent tried to seize the privilege on the ground of economy. As he left for Natchez he wrote Pickering:

very Subaltern Officers, (I know not under what authority) are instructed to speechify, and possessed of the endowments to "Conciliate" to render them important amongst the Indians, whilst the Superintendent is not capacitated to make unto them even the smallest present—May not the toleration of such proceedings open a door for monstrous abuses.—I have known at Detroit 1,000 Rations per day issued to the Indians, and at Advanced Posts, this Business submitted to Military, and very Subaltern officers discretionary, in whom I had no Confidence, at the same time that myself though the Legitimate Superintendent of Indian Affairs for the N. Western Territory, was cruelly forced to deny the Ottawa Indians from the Village of Arbirccooke hungry in the *extreme,* even a morsel of Bread; At a visit there made one year afterwards by General Wilkinson who was clothed with *the means* some handsome presents were made, and will not all this induce, Comparison unfavorable to your Superintendent, who for the interests of our Country, should Certainly be in high estimation with the red people? [67]

Pickering agreed that Sargent should supply provisions, at least during conferences with the Indians. "I cannot brook the idea, that every military commandant of a post should be authorized at discretion to issue provisions to the Indians, (and this it seems is the fact) while the Governor of a Territory erected, as I may say, in the Indian Country, and who is *ex officio, superintendant of Indian affairs,* should be denied a similar, or much larger authority." [68]

The issue was settled in principle by Alexander Hamilton in 1799 while he was inspector general of the Provisional Army and thus in a position to influence the Secretary of War. In a characteristically clean-cut letter to the army commander at Cincinnati he wrote:

You are aware that the Governors of the North Western Territory and of the Missisippi Territory are severally *ex officio* Superintendants of Indian

---

[66] Goods went to the Indians in part as a consequence of treaties in payment for lands, in part as gifts, and in part to relieve suffering from failure of crops.

[67] *Miss. Territorial Archives,* I, 23.

[68] *Territorial Papers,* V, 46.

Affairs. The management of those affairs under the direction of the Secretary of War appertains to them. The military in this respect are only to be auxiliary to their plans and measures. In saying this, it must not be understood that they are to direct military dispositions and operations; But they are to be the organs of all negociations and communications between the Indians and the Government; they are to determine when and where supplies are to be furnished to those people and what other accommodations they are to have. The military in regard to all such matters are only to aid as far as their Cooperation may be required by the superintendants; avoiding interferences without previous concert with them, or otherwise than in conformity with their views. This will exempt the military from a responsibility which had better rest elsewhere: And it will promote a regular and uniform system of Conduct towards the Indians, which Cannot exist if every Commandant of a Post is to intermeddle separately and independently in the management of the concerns which relate to them. This Communication is made in conformity with the instruction from the Secretary of War; who particularly desires that

"The military Officers may be required to refer the Indians in all matters relating to their national Affairs or grievances to the Governor of the North Western Territory and the Governor of the Missisippi Territory, or the temporary Indian agent nearest their posts as occasion may require; and that the Commandants of the Posts in the Missisippi Territory may be instructed to furnish on the order of Governor Sargeant when the same can be spared such rations for the Indians who may visit the said posts as he may from time to time direct." [69]

McHenry followed up this directive by making St. Clair the agent for the distribution of Indian goods.

Whether Abuses have or have not been committed in the issuing of Rations to Indians at military posts, the issues appear of such magnitude as to require a peremptory and general Regulation, to restrain within the most limited Bounds or to forbid them entirely. The provisions distributed to Indians at military posts far exceed in value the amount of their annual Stipends; encourage the Indians in idleness, and draw into and round our places of defence, those who had better be always kept at a distance, and in ignorance of their strength or weakness. I repeat it, the practice must be narrowed to acts of indispensable charity to travellers or individuals falling in the way of the Garrisons on their journies or by accident, or it must be absolutely terminated. I shall, therefore, unless most cogent

[69] *Ibid.*, III, 24–25.

Reasons occur to the contrary, cause the Commandants of Posts to be instructed accordingly.[70]

Regulation of Indian trade. The various arrangements for trading with the Indians were designed in part to counteract British and Spanish influence in the Mississippi Valley, in part to direct the flow of the fur trade through American hands, and in part to protect the Indians against sharp practices by unscrupulous traders and peddlers. Two different systems were used, the licensing of private traders and the maintenance of government "factories."

The initial plan favored private enterprise under public supervision. By an act of 1790 no person was allowed to carry on any trade or intercourse with the Indian tribes without a license issued by one of the superintendents of the Indian department.[71] The license was issued for a term of two years "to any proper person" and was thus discretionary, permitting the selection of trustworthy traders. It carried a bond of $1,000, which was conditioned upon observance "of such rules, regulations and restrictions, as now are, or hereafter shall be made for the government of trade and intercourse with the Indian tribes." The President was authorized to prescribe rules and regulations. The Indian superintendent was vested with "full power and authority to recall all such licenses" upon failure to observe the trading regulations. If on suit on the bond the trader was acquitted, he was, however, entitled to receive a new license.

In 1793 a provision was introduced requiring a special license for the purchase of a horse from an Indian, or from a white man in Indian territory. The purchaser was also required to make a particular return to the superintendent of the Indian department describing every horse purchased with a license. Any person knowingly purchasing an Indian horse from an unlicensed person forfeited the value of the horse.[72] In 1796 purchase from an Indian of a gun, any instrument of husbandry, cooking utensil, or article of clothing except skins or furs was prohibited, but no further administrative action was provided.[73]

In 1796 Congress authorized the establishment of government trading houses on the frontiers or in the Indian territories.[74] They were placed

---

[70] *Ibid.*, III, 82–83.
[71] 1 Stat. 137 (July 22, 1790).
[72] 1 Stat. 329, sec. 6 (March 1, 1793).
[73] 1 Stat. 469, sec. 9 (May 19, 1796).
[74] 1 Stat. 452 (April 18, 1796).

under the general supervision of the superintendents of Indian affairs, and in particular charge of an agent. He was required to give bond and to refrain from private transactions with the Indians. Congress appropriated $150,000 for the purchase of a stock of goods and directed prices to be fixed to avoid any diminution of investment.[75]

Two trading houses were established prior to 1801, one in Georgia among the Creeks and one in Tennessee among the Cherokees. A report early in Jefferson's administration showed that the business had been ably managed, that the original investment had increased slightly, and that the Indians had benefited.[76] The number of trading houses was increased under Jefferson, especially in the Northwest Territory.[77]

Protection of Indian lands. Successive efforts to protect Indian lands against encroachment involved relatively few administrative powers. The basic legal provision, introduced in 1790, forbade the sale of land by Indians except in consequence of a treaty under the authority of the United States; a penalty was added in 1793 for unlawful negotiation of sales but no administrative authority to prevent such sales was provided.[78]

In 1793 citizens and residents of the United States were forbidden to settle on Indian lands or to survey them or mark trees thereon; the President was empowered "to take such measures, as he may judge necessary" to remove offenders, and in 1796 was permitted to use the military for this purpose.[79]

---

[75] Wolcott's views on this experiment in public enterprise are of some interest because of his background and connections. He offered them to McHenry in these words:

". . . My opinion has, you know, been somewhat different from yours on the subject of Indian trade. I consider the public establishments, as in every respect, nuisances; the capital must, from the nature of things, be lost. Abuses will be committed by the public agents, sooner or later; and it is impossible that the Indians should be well supplied.

"The interest and policy of the government, in my opinion, requires that the Indian trade should rest principally in the hands of a few men of capital. The Indians require advances of certain articles on credit; the public cannot safely give this credit. The traders, if they be not mere pedlars, without capital or responsibility, will always be interested in preserving peace. War is destructive of trade. The government can always control real traders; though the pedlars will always be out of their power, and may frequently stimulate the Indians to mischief. My plan to keep the trade in few, but good hands, and to give up the public stores as soon as possible, without violating any public engagement." Gibbs, *Memoirs*, II, 247 (Aug. 17, 1799).

[76] *American State Papers: Indian Affairs*, p. 654.

[77] Harmon, *op. cit.*, p. 116, n. 78.

[78] 1 Stat. 137, sec. 4; 1 Stat. 329, sec. 8.

[79] 1 Stat. 329, sec. 5; 1 Stat. 469, sec. 5.

A new plan to prevent unauthorized settlement was introduced in 1796. A boundary line was established by law, and citizens and residents were forbidden to cross it to hunt or destroy game, or to drive stock on Indian lands. To enter Indian lands south of the Ohio, a passport was required, obtainable either from the governor of an adjoining state or from a military commander or other person delegated by the President.[80] Apart from the use of the military to dislodge squatters on Indian lands, the passport requirement was the principal administrative device to prevent trespass. Neither was effective.

The revision of 1799 added no provisions to protect Indian lands, apart from an injunction to the military to treat squatters "with all the humanity which the circumstances will possibly permit," with the added threat of a court-martial of officers responsible for maltreatment of whites.[81] It must be concluded, therefore, that Congress relied principally upon the deterrent effect of fines, forfeitures, and imprisonment after judicial conviction to protect the Indians in possession of their lands rather than upon administrative action, apart from the single requirement of a passport to enter Indian lands south of the Ohio.

SALE OF PUBLIC LANDS

By the treaty of peace and by cession from the states, the general government became the proprietor of a vast unsettled public domain west of the Alleghenies. During the Confederation period Congress took over the obligation to secure land bounties to Revolutionary soldiers, which were finally liquidated after 1789. To dispose of public lands in an orderly manner, the Ordinance of 1785 set up a land survey based on six-mile square townships, provided for sale by auction to the highest bidder, who received title in fee simple, set a minimum price of one dollar per acre, reserved four sections in each township and one-third of all precious metals, and set aside one section for the support of common schools.[82]

The general intent of this legislation was to secure the public lands to the people by direct sale from the government. Before 1789, however, this policy had been broken into by the competing policy of large sales

---

[80] 1 Stat. 469, secs. 1–3.

[81] 1 Stat. 743, sec. 16.

[82] On the history of land policy see Benjamin Horace Hibbard, *A History of the Public Land Policies* (New York: Macmillan, 1924); and Roy M. Robbins, *Our Landed Heritage: the Public Domain, 1776–1936* (Princeton: Princeton University Press, 1942).

to monied interests for speculative purposes; this program had the merit of promising quick and substantial revenue for a bankrupt government. Three huge sales, over a million acres each, were consummated to the Ohio Company, the Scioto Company, and to John Cleves Symmes, respectively. In 1790 Hamilton accepted the production of revenue as the first requirement of a land policy, but sales to land companies on a vast scale proved to be a fiscal snare and delusion.[83]

Despite much discussion of further plans for disposing of the public lands Congress marked time for years. In 1796 an important act combined the program of sales in large tracts of whole townships with smaller sales in lots of 640 acres to individuals.[84] The sale of land as a revenue measure, however, never came up to expectations; "as a regular source of income the receipts from the sale of public lands are about as bad as possible. They cannot be forced, limited, or predicted in any normal way corresponding with the needs of a well-ordered government."[85] In 1800, under the leadership of William Henry Harrison and Albert Gallatin, Congress moved decisively in the direction of sales to individual purchasers by reducing the minimum purchase and by granting time for payment.[86]

Little administrative machinery was required before 1801 to put into execution these land policies. A start was made under the Ordinance of 1785 by the appointment of a geographer (a reappointment in fact, since Thomas Hutchins had been serving since 1781 as geographer in the army). Under his direction the survey of the seven ranges, on the eastern boundary of Ohio bordering the river, was undertaken and completed after his death in 1789.

Thomas Hutchins, appointed "geographer to the United States" on July 11, 1781, is one of the earliest representatives of the impressive group of engineers and scientists who have followed their professions in the public service.[87] Left an orphan at an early age, he entered the

---

[83] Hamilton, "Plan for Disposing of the Public Lands," *American State Papers: Public Lands,* I, 8–9; Hamilton's interest in an adequate labor force for manufactures led him to seek to discourage the draining of the eastern labor supply into the open west.

[84] 1 Stat. 464.

[85] Hibbard, *op. cit.,* p. 6.

[86] 2 Stat. 73.

[87] From 1780 to 1783 the title of geographer to the United States was also held by Simeon De Witt. Hicks, "Biographical Sketch of Thomas Hutchins," in Thomas Hutchins, *A Topographical Description of Virginia, Pennsylvania, Maryland, and North*

British army and spent many years in the western country during which he acquired the foundations of his knowledge of surveying and engineering. The outbreak of the Revolution found him in London; he refused to serve against the colonists, and after loss of his British army commission made his way to the United States where he joined the southern army under General Greene. At the conclusion of the war he retained his office as civil geographer and under the Ordinance of 1785 started the survey of the seven ranges. He also did important surveys for Pennsylvania, and ran the boundary line between New York and Massachusetts. A contemporary, Ebenezer Hazard, described him as "a man of good character, of polite manners, of great integrity, who made a regular profession of religion." [88] Whether or not he invented the township and section plan of survey is disputed, but he was certainly the first to apply it. [89]

In 1796 Congress adopted the basic administrative pattern which Hamilton had proposed in 1790. To continue the survey the office of Surveyor General was established, and its incumbent authorized to appoint a "sufficient number of skilful surveyors," to make rules and regulations for their conduct, and to remove them for negligence or misconduct. Sales of whole townships (which never materialized) were to take place at Philadelphia; sales of sections at Pittsburgh and Cincinnati under the direction of the governor or secretary of the western territory and the Surveyor General. In the latter case payments were made to an agent appointed by the President to attend the sales, [90] the first instance of local land receivers.

The Land Act of 1800 laid the foundation for the local land offices, which were first set up in Cincinnati, Chilicothe, Marietta, and Steubenville. [91] Each office was placed under the direction of a register of the land office; his importance was attested to by the requirement of Senate confirmation and by the prescribed bond of $10,000. In each office was also appointed a receiver of public monies for lands, subject to confirmation by the Senate and a similar bond. The essential duties of the register were to receive applications for purchase, keep records

Carolina (reprinted from the original ed. of 1778; Frederick Charles Hicks, ed., Cleveland: Burrows Brothers, 1904), p. 28.

[88] *Ibid.*, p. 7.

[89] *Ibid.*, p. 40; *Dictionary of American Biography*, IX, 435–36.

[90] 1 Stat. 464 (May 18, 1796). Until 1796 all sales of land were made in Philadelphia at the office of the Treasury.

[91] 2 Stat. 73.

of payments, and upon final payment to grant a certificate to be presented to the Secretary of the Treasury, on the basis of which the patent was issued by the President to the purchaser. The act of 1800 also recognized the superintendents of public sales, who had apparently emerged under the act of 1796 in connection with sales at Pittsburgh.

Rufus Putnam, the first Surveyor General, succeeded to the duties of Thomas Hutchins. He was a "man to delight the soul of a historian. He not only made history, he also recorded it." [92] Born in Sutton, Massachusetts, in 1738, at the age of seven he was left upon the death of his father to the care of different relatives. His education was largely self-acquired, and did not extend to a full command of spelling. At the age of nineteen he enlisted for the French and Indian Wars, after an apprenticeship as a millwright, and from 1760 to 1775 was busy on his farm, surveying, and building mills. He was commissioned lieutenant colonel at the outbreak of the Revolutionary War and served with success as an engineer and builder of fortifications.

On April 7, 1788, he arrived in Marietta, Ohio, superintendent of the first settlement of the Ohio Company, and for many years was one of the leading figures in the Territory. In 1796 he became Surveyor General of the United States. To have acquired the confidence of General Washington was one of his great satisfactions. "To be able," he wrote, "to leve behind me such indubitable evidence of the esteam, frindship, & patronage of so great & good a man as General Washington (continued for more than twenty years) *is no small Source* of consolation, under the persecution I have suffered from the Arch enemy, of Washingtons Administration." [93] Washington characterized him as possessed of a strong mind, discreet and firm, but with nothing conspicuous in his character.[94]

As Surveyor, General Putnam was diligent but his deficiencies in mathematics, self-taught, left much to be desired in his survey of the military tract. He had to an exceptional degree the qualities of common sense and sound judgment, most useful in the wilderness. He was also an independent spirit, yielding to no man. He asserted indignantly that he was removed by Jefferson not for want of ability, integrity, or industry, but because he did not subscribe to Jefferson's measures—"Because I did not die nor resigne." When he carefully

[92] Putnam, *Memoirs,* p. vii.
[93] *Ibid.,* p. 100.
[94] Washington, *Writings,* XXXI, 512.

and promptly turned over his papers to his successor, he wrote the
Secretary of the Treasury, Albert Gallatin, "prehaps you may imagine
this conduct looks like passive obedience and nonresistence, or that I
am courting favor. mistake me not I have don no more then what I
concive to be the duty of every public officer in like circumstances,
and I am too independent to be influenced by the prejudices of the
times—" [95]

Affairs on the distant frontiers tended to get attention at the seat
of government only when foreign or domestic crises demanded. The
danger of losing the Mississippi Valley to Spain was ominously in
men's minds; the possibility of a cruel and devastating Indian war was
never remote; the likelihood of a collision between the authority of
the border states and of the general government was ever present.
These were the issues that the territories presented, rather than the less
urgent problems of their civil administration. It was fortunate, as
Governor Blount noted in 1793, that "no man on Earth has a more
just idea of the Indian business than the President." [96] It was less fortunate that Secretaries of State could spare little time to the distant and
tiny islands of white population lost amidst the forests and prairies
of the west. Something would certainly have been gained if the
dynamic energy of Alexander Hamilton had been put to work to
organize and direct the civil authority. The frustrating conflict over
responsibility for dealing with the Indians could have been terminated
when it first arose rather than years later. The annoying feud between
the judges of the Northwest Territory and Governor St. Clair could
have been subdued. The energy and effectiveness of the territorial government could have been increased by decisive directions to the principal officers to remain at their posts.

But the conditions of good administration were largely lacking. The
population was unprepared and probably unwilling for much government. The means of communication were almost wholly lacking. The
financial resources of local and territorial governments were meager.
The skills of administration were wanting and in any event would
have found small opportunity for their exercise. Life was rough and
simple in the wilderness; so was government and administration.

---

[95] Putnam, *Memoirs,* pp. 125, 441.
[96] *Territorial Papers,* IV, 302.

Chapter Thirty-one

FEDERAL-STATE ADMINISTRATIVE
RELATIONS

W HETHER or not the new general government inaugurated in 1789 would endure was much in men's minds in the early years of the great experiment. Never before had so many people spread over so great an area tried to govern themselves as a federation. Fortunately the institutions of government, the quality of its leadership, and the prosperity of its people combined to give an early answer; the general government *was* capable of holding different interests, areas, and personalities in a successful equilibrium. An undercurrent of doubt never ceased to run, however, and before Adams left the White House an alarming challenge had been issued from across the Alleghenies. The Federalists, who represented the interests that stood most obviously to gain from the new regime, were most concerned about its future. When Virginia protested against the assumption of state debts in 1790, Hamilton wrote Jay, "This is the first symptom of a spirit which must either be killed or will kill the Constitution of the United States." [1] Jay urged restraint upon his younger friend: "Every indecent interference of State assemblies will diminish their influence; the national government has only to do what is right and, if possible, be silent." [2] Within a couple of months Adams was writing John Trumbull, "The rivalry between the State governments and the National government, is growing daily more active and ardent." [3] Oliver Wolcott wrote his father in Connecticut, "The indications of the public sentiment with respect to the new government, are very equivocal. The northern States, and the commercial and monied people, are

---

[1] Jay, *Correspondence*, III, 405.
[2] Nov. 28, 1790, *ibid.*, III, 410.
[3] Jan. 23, 1791, Adams, *Works*, IX, 573.

zealously attached to it. The state executives and officers cannot be considered as good friends; many of them are designing enemies." [4]

The broad separation of the country into three sections, eastern, middle, and southern, was generally recognized, and when an executive council was under discussion in the Convention it was suggested as a good geographical foundation. The division between north and south, commerce and agriculture, free and slave areas, however, crowded the threefold distinction out of men's minds. Before long the rise of a restless and ambitious West caused many to expect that the territory across the Alleghenies would go its own way. The forces of division were not weak.

Feelings were greatly embittered by the impact of foreign relations on the domestic scene. A strong anti-British sentiment, the natural residue of the war for independence, was strengthened by impressment of American seamen; the common people suffered while the merchant class prospered. The Jay Treaty proposals brought anti-British sentiment to a climax. Meanwhile strong pro-French sympathies, founded on aid to the colonies and warmed by the French Revolution, swept over the country as Great Britain and France took up arms against each other.

The viability of the new order was also threatened by alarm over national encroachment on states' rights. The tenth amendment did much to quiet early apprehensions, but Hamilton's bold plans for a bank and for aid to manufactures involved a theory of liberal construction against which Jefferson and his friends instantly set themselves. The passage of the Alien and Sedition Acts deeply disturbed the states' rights advocates; the Kentucky Resolutions of 1798 and 1799 declared the union was a compact among states, the use of delegated powers was subject to review by the states, and the remedy for an attempt to pass beyond the delegated powers was nullification.

These great constitutional and political issues are beyond the subject matter of this study. While spirits ran high on such problems, the day-by-day business of government had to be carried on within the framework of a dual system, each part of which in considerable measure paralleled the other. How to fit together—or keep effectively apart—the two systems was the great administrative problem inherent in the first large-scale federal government.

---

[4] Feb. 12, 1791, Gibbs, *Memoirs,* I, 62.

The Constitution of the United States assumed the coordination and cooperation of the general and the state governments. The election of presidents, senators, and representatives depended upon provisions of state laws; the states were entitled to call upon the federal power to repel invasion or suppress insurrection; and state officials of all descriptions were required to take an oath to support the Constitution of the United States. The range of potential relationships at the administrative level, however, could hardly have been foreseen. Neither the debates in the Convention nor the terms of the Constitution suggested the variety of contacts that developed under the Federalists.

The adjustment of state and federal structures of government came up in the first session of Congress. The principle of a separate and independent administrative organization for the new government was then established. Almost from the beginning, however, the general government relied upon state agencies for help in some matters, and the idea of federal-state administrative cooperation was accepted in others. In broad outline two administrative worlds appeared, but the forces of attraction brought each of them within the sphere of influence of the other.

There was occasional administrative competition as well as cooperation. On the whole the states withdrew quickly and without ill feeling from activities which were assumed by the general government in 1789. Several years were required, however, to complete the transition. By the time the change had been worked out, new forms of cooperation had begun to appear.

STATE OR FEDERAL ADMINISTRATION OF FEDERAL BUSINESS

When Congress convened in April 1789, it faced the task of enacting organic laws and providing the means of their enforcement. What should these means be? Some believed that most of the business of the new government could and should be turned over to the states and their officials.

The states were going concerns with a long and uninterrupted administrative experience. The transition from colony to state hardly affected their administrative organization, which in some cases stretched backward more than one hundred and fifty years. This organization was complete; every state in 1789 had a complement of officials sufficient to maintain itself as a self-contained unit, and the states could readily have absorbed at least a considerable part of the internal administrative activities of the Union.

In May 1789 the balance might well have seemed to tip in the direction of extensive use of state officials for federal purposes. The jealousy of the states and the hostility of many persons to a strong central government, which had been barely overcome in the ratification of the Constitution, were deep-seated. Moreover, the states still occupied first place in the affections of the people. This was admitted by the friends of a stronger government, with concern, but nevertheless without question. The reasons were set out by Madison in *The Federalist*.

Many considerations, besides those suggested on a former occasion, seem to place it beyond doubt that the first and most natural attachment of the people will be to the governments of their respective States. Into the administration of these a greater number of individuals will expect to rise. From the gift of these a greater number of offices and emoluments will flow. By the superintending care of these, all the more domestic and personal interests of the people will be regulated and provided for. With the affairs of these, the people will be more familiarly and minutely conversant. And with the members of these, will a greater proportion of the people have the ties of personal acquaintance and friendship, and of family and party attachments; on the side of these, therefore, the popular bias may well be expected most strongly to incline.[5]

Madison also made it clear that he expected the federal revenue would be collected by state officials and that the state courts would carry "the correspondent authority of the Union." [6] The empty federal treasury and democratic fears about impending danger to liberty strongly supported Madison's ideas.

On the other hand, the friends of the new order intended to safeguard the position of the central government. The assumption of the state debts, the early provision of adequate revenues to pay the interest on state and federal debts and gradually to liquidate them, the formation of the Bank of the United States were major policy decisions looking in this direction. In the realm of administration, these same

---

[5] *Federalist Papers*, No. 46. Cf. his remarks in the Virginia Convention to ratify the Constitution, Madison, *Writings* (Hunt ed.), V, 161.

[6] *Federalist Papers*, No. 45.

leaders, recalling the feebleness of the Confederation in its relations with the states, did not look with favor upon further reliance on state officers.

The division of responsibility between the federal and state authorities—i.e., *responsibility for federal business*—was not worked out, however, without extended debate. The first solutions, moreover, were not all of one pattern; in some instances, as the militia, joint responsibility was required by the Constitution; in others, joint operations were provided by Congress. The major policy was, however, federal agents for federal business. This guiding rule was developed with respect to the collection of customs, the trial of federal causes, the naturalization of aliens, and the collection of the excise tax.

The collection of customs. Before the Treasury Department was established on September 2, 1789, Congress had already enacted laws imposing duties on imports and a tonnage tax, and providing machinery for the collection of these revenues. In connection with the latter, Congress was faced squarely with the issue whether to use state revenue officers to collect federal customs duties and the tonnage tax, or whether to organize a separate and independent customs service.

First expressions of opinion favored reliance on the states. Elias Boudinot, who was to become a convinced Federalist, took this position;[7] and John Laurance expressed his distaste for "a mode of collection odious to all, on account of the numerous train of officers it would require in its execution."[8] A collection bill was introduced in May 1789 by Elbridge Gerry. Lacking a copy of the bill (of which one hundred copies were ordered printed for the use of the House) we can only deduce its provisions from the adverse remarks made by its opponents. These are, however, sufficiently well reported to permit some deductions.[9]

1. The bill was founded upon the laws of the several states.
2. Collection was provided for according to the systems of the several states.

---

[7] *Annals,* I, 119 (April 11, 1789).

[8] *Ibid.,* I, 128 (April 14, 1789). State collection had been proposed in 1783 by the Continental Congress.

[9] *Ibid.,* I, 291 (May 8); 367–68 (May 18, 1789). Boudinot suggested a similar plan as a temporary measure in terms which indicate that he and Gerry were in touch with each other, *ibid.,* I, 119 (April 11, 1789). The proposal was again made in 1796, without support, *ibid.,* V, 293 (Feb. 4, 1796) and 349 (Feb. 19, 1796).

3. Collections in a state which had no customs service
(Connecticut, New Jersey, and Delaware) were to be governed
by the laws of the adjoining states.

In his plan, Gerry would have had no federal customs officers. The
states would have become the agents of the new government, and
would have added the collection of federal customs and the tonnage tax
to the duties of their tax officials.

Gerry apparently did not speak in support of his bill nor did
Madison.[10] Laurance pointed out that the diversity of state valuation
and collection systems contradicted the constitutional requirement that
all duties, imposts, and excises shall be uniform; Benjamin Huntington observed collections would be enforced with a greater or less degree
of energy according to the systems of the several states, and asked,
"How would one State like to be regulated by the laws of another?";
John Vining saw "insuperable difficulties" for Delaware and Jersey
which stood in the same predicament as Connecticut, having no impost
law.

Congress agreed "to have nothing more to do with the bill." Eventually a new bill was brought in that provided for a full complement of
federal customs officers; it became law on July 31, 1789, without
further discussion of the possibility of reliance upon state tax officials.

Trial of federal causes. The issue implicit in Gerry's collection bill
promptly reappeared in the House debates on the judiciary bill in
August 1789. A sharp division of opinion developed on the establishment of federal district courts for any other than admiralty cases; the
debate ranged over a wide area of constitutional, political, and administrative considerations.[11] The problem now was whether federal
judicial business would be assigned for original hearing to the state
courts (excepting the original jurisdiction of the Supreme Court and
its jurisdiction over admiralty cases) or whether a comprehensive set of
federal district courts should be established, with concurrent jurisdiction
in the state courts for lesser cases involving federal law.

The most impressive argument for reliance on state courts was made
by Judge Samuel Livermore, who had been chief justice of the New
Hampshire Supreme Court from 1782 until his election to Congress.

---

[10] Gerry's biographer does not mention the subject; see James T. Austin, *The Life of
Elbridge Gerry* (2 vols., Boston: Wells and Lilly, 1828–29).

[11] *Annals,* I, 782–84 (Aug. 24, 1789); 796–834 (Aug. 29, 31, 1789).

He pointed out that the state courts had hitherto decided all cases "of a national or local import" without any charge of partiality. There could be no danger of erroneous decisions in the state courts, since an appeal lay to the United States Supreme Court. A separate set of district courts would be burdensome and occasion unnecessary expense. Confusion would ensue from a system of concurrent jurisdiction; every state would have two kinds of courts for many causes, and conflict would arise for precedence, for the custody of offenders, and for the issue of process. This "new fangled system" would swallow up the state courts, the plan would establish a government within a government, and one "must prevail on the ruin of the other." [12]

Others counseled inaction until experience had clearly demonstrated the failure of state courts to handle federal business adequately. Thus Michael Jenifer Stone argued that the case for district courts rested on mere suspicion of the want of judgment or integrity of state courts. He continued, "I declare I can contemplate a time, with great pain, when one of those cases may happen; but I believe the time is not yet arrived, and we ought not to adopt a system which presupposes it." [13] "I am, sir, for this Government moving as silently as death, that the people should not perceive the least alteration for the worse in their situation. . . ." [14] Thomas Sumter "knew too sensibly the situation of his constituents, to suppose that such an expensive and distrustful system could be agreeable to them. It would be cruel in their present distressed situation. . . . It was hostile to their liberties, and dangerous in the extreme; . . . it was a system of oppression which the people neither desired, nor were prepared to receive." [15]

For the most part, however, opposition to the federal district courts was based on concern for the predominance of the state governments and the independence of the state judiciary, for the convenience of suitors, and for economy; and on confidence in the capacity of the state courts to handle effectively and impartially most causes involving federal jurisdiction.

---

[12] *Ibid.*, I, 783–85, 820. James Jackson opposed any system of federal district courts (except for admiralty and revenue cases) because offenders might be "dragged" to a distant spot, thus denying the right of trial by a jury of the vicinage, a view which was echoed by Ædanus Burke.

[13] *Ibid.*, I, 811.

[14] *Ibid.*, I, 827.

[15] *Ibid.*, I, 832.

On the other side William Smith[16] frankly asserted his unwillingness to trust the state judiciary for federal business. "It would," he said, "be *felo de se* to trust the collection of the revenue of the United States to the State judicatures. The disinclination of the judges to carry the law into effect, their disapprobation of a certain duty [i.e., a tax measure], the rules of the court, or other obvious causes, might delay or frustrate the collection of the revenue, and embarrass the National Government."[17]

On constitutional grounds it was argued that since state judges often held office for a specified term, and were not always protected against a reduction of their salary, they could not qualify as members of the federal system. Gerry now flatly asserted, "You cannot make Federal courts of the State courts, because the Constitution is an insuperable bar; besides, the laws and constitutions of some States expressly prohibit the State Judges from administering or taking cognizance of foreign matters."[18] Madison summed up the argument by saying, "On the whole . . . he did not see how it could be made compatible with the Constitution, or safe to the Federal interests, to make a transfer of the Federal jurisdiction to the State courts."[19] A complete set of federal courts was established by the Judiciary Act of 1789.

Naturalization. The question of the use of state officials for federal business was raised again in the early days of the second session in connection with naturalization. Two issues relevant to federal-state relations came up in the course of debate. The first was primarily a constitutional problem—whether Congress, in providing the terms and conditions of naturalization, was empowered to prescribe the conditions on which a naturalized citizen could participate in state

---

[16] In a letter to C. C. Pinckney, Oct. 10, 1792, Hamilton observed of Smith, "He is truly an excellent member—a ready, clear speaker, of a sound analytic head, and the justest views." Hamilton, *Works* (Lodge ed.), X, 24.

[17] *Annals,* I, 799–800. Note also the argument of Fisher Ames: "We live in a time of innovation; but until miracles shall become more common than ordinary events, and surprise us less than the usual course of nature, he should think it a wonderful felicity of invention to propose the expedient of hiring out our judicial power, and employing courts not amenable to our laws. . . ." *Ibid.,* I, 806–7.

[18] *Ibid.,* I, 828.

[19] *Ibid.,* I, 813. On the motion to strike out the clause of the judiciary bill creating the district courts, the House divided; eleven voted for and thirty-one against the motion. Late in the decade Hamilton complained about the indifference of state courts to federal rights: "the cold and reluctant protection of State courts, always temporizing and sometimes disaffected." Hamilton, *Works* (Hamilton ed.), VI, 387–88.

elections and become a candidate for state elective offices. The pro-visions in the bill on this point were eliminated in deference to the general opinion that they were beyond the powers of Congress.[20]

On the second point, i.e., where the function should be placed, two distinct alternatives were involved. George Clymer and Benjamin Huntington apparently would have declined to enact a uniform rule of naturalization at all, leaving to the states the full powers which they had hitherto exercised to admit to state citizenship, presumably recog-nizing such citizenship as carrying with it the rights of federal citizen-ship. For many years there was a difference of opinion as to which was primary. The other alternative, and the one eventually adopted by Congress, was to enact a uniform rule of naturalization, leaving its administration to the state courts. A third possibility—a uniform rule administered by the federal courts—was not apparently favored by any substantial number, and was to become the normal method of naturalization only after more than a hundred years, in 1906.

The debates give no clue concerning the reasoning of members of Congress on the location of authority to naturalize, and there was no roll call. Two or three guesses may be made. As already indicated, there was uncertainty whether citizenship had basically a state or federal quality. If the former, the use of the state courts, applying a uniform rule, was logical. Furthermore, the state courts in several states already had jurisdiction over the subject matter. In addition, there was a strong sentiment favoring a simple and easy naturalization procedure in order to accelerate immigration and thereby the acquisi-tion and opening up of the western lands. This objective also sug-gested the state courts, more numerous and more conveniently situated throughout the country. The authority clearly was not one which the Federalists feared to place in the hands of the states. They were content with a uniform rule, enforced by the respective states.[21]

The excise tax. In the third session of the first Congress, the problem of federal-state administrative relations recurred in the debate on the excise tax on spirits distilled in the United States. The issue was closely parallel to that put by the collection bill of the first session. The case for state collection of the excise on spirits was much stronger: the excise was an internal revenue; the stills were scattered up and down the country within the jurisdiction and knowledge of county revenue

---

[20] See, for example, remarks of Alexander White, *Annals,* I, 1113–14 (Feb. 3, 1790).
[21] 1 Stat. 103 (March 26, 1790).

officials; the expense of setting up a parallel set of revenue officers was great; and the affront to republican suspicions distinctly more serious.

It could be argued also that this was a dangerous trial of strength by the federal authorities. Senator William Maclay, who was well acquainted with the hostility of western Pennsylvanians to payment of the state excise laws, noted in his diary on February 9, 1791, "I . . . told them plainly of the precipice which I considered them as having approached; that the Legislature of Pennsylvania had been obliged to wink at the violation of her excise laws in the western parts of the State ever since the Revolution; that, in my opinion, it could not be enforced by collectors or civil officers of any kind, be they ever so numerous; and that nothing short of a permanent military force could effect it; that this, for aught I knew, might be acceptable to some characters." [22] In the House, Josiah Parker, while granting that "the Government has proceeded with a degree of prosperity and success beyond the most sanguine expectations, yet he very much doubted the policy of trying its strength by an experiment of this nature." [23]

The first bill to impose an excise on spirits distilled in the United States was defeated on June 21, 1790. A second bill was passed by the House on January 27, 1791. The debates are not reported sufficiently to disclose how widely there was objection to the formation of a new set of federal officers, but Parker opposed them vehemently. He "reprobated" the bill as hostile to the liberties of the people, "particularly on account of the mode of collecting the tax. It will, said he, convulse the Government; it will let loose a swarm of harpies, who, under the denomination of revenue officers, will range through the country, prying into every man's house and affairs, and like a Macedonian phalanx bear down all before them." [24] Boudinot moved to limit the number of revenue officers but the motion was defeated.[25] A vote to recommit was lost by the narrow margin of three, 27 to 30,[26] and after an unsuccessful effort to prevent revenue officers from interfering in elections, the bill finally became law on the last day of the

---

[22] Maclay, *Journal,* pp. 387–88.

[23] *Annals,* II, 1844 (Jan. 5, 1791).

[24] *Ibid.,* II, 1844; so also Maclay in the Senate, Maclay, *Journal,* pp. 386–88, 389–90, 398–99.

[25] *Annals,* II, 1872 (Jan. 18).

[26] *Ibid.,* II, 1875 (Jan. 19).

session.[27] The collection was placed in the exclusive hands of federal revenue officers.

Hamilton's influence was thrown strongly in favor of an independent federal revenue organization; he was almost certainly consulted on the customs collection act of 1789 and he helped prepare the excise act of 1791. Madison shifted from his early position to favor a federal system of administration independent of the states. Members of Congress who later became Jeffersonian Republicans were strongest in their claims for state performance of federal business.

The militia. Both the states and the general government had constitutional standing with respect to the militia: the latter to lay down the general rules, the former to maintain the militia in accordance therewith. Washington proposed a plan for the regulation of the militia which would have reserved important federal control over discipline and inspection.[28] The militia was a tender point, however, and Congress faithfully reflected local pride and civic jealousy in refusing to allow effective federal direction of the power to bear arms.[29] The militia bill of 1792 was a deep disappointment to the President, who signed it hoping for subsequent improvement. The states, however, stood fast; the militia law recognized the essentially local responsibility for an armed citizenry.

The states, when called upon in 1794 to provide 15,000 militiamen to advance against the western Pennsylvania distillers, promptly responded, although Governor Mifflin of Pennsylvania (who was in a difficult position) showed some hesitation. Hamilton was well justified in writing later that, "The idea of the late President's administration of considering the Governor of each State as the first general of the militia, and its immediate organ in acting upon the militia, was wisely considered, and in my opinion, wisely adopted, and well to be adhered to. In its final operation, it will obviate many difficulties and collisions, and by enhancing their importance, tend to draw the State Executives to the general government." [30]

---

[27] 1 Stat. 199 (March 3, 1791).

[28] Cf. remarks of Boudinot, *Annals*, II, 1819 (Dec. 21, 1790).

[29] *Ibid.*, III, 422–23 (Feb. 21, 1792).

[30] Hamilton, *Works* (Hamilton ed.), VI, 405. The governors became the regular channels of communication with the federal government; the Domestic Letters of the Department of State contain many examples. James Monroe thought the dignity of the states was compromised by the fact that governors corresponded with federal Secretaries

Cities. Throughout the Federalist era there were no direct relations between the general government and cities, except for the new seat of government on the Potomac.[31] No act of Congress bore on city problems as such, and no federal agent had official relations with cities. The states retained unimpaired their full responsibility for municipal corporations and local government. Despite the recurrent epidemics which forced Congress and the executive departments out of Philadelphia, no one thought of seeking national aid in removing the menace to health and to the uninterrupted conduct of public affairs. Only in the "federal city" did Congress and the President have an interest; here the whole responsibility was in their hands. The unique duty of making a city was almost beyond their technical capacity.

ADMINISTRATIVE ADJUSTMENTS OF THE STATES
AND THE GENERAL GOVERNMENT

The establishment of the new government set in motion a long train of readjustments between it and the several states. Most federal laws implementing the Constitution required either local cooperation or the curtailment or abandonment of a state activity.[32] The adjustments took place over a considerable period of time, even in cases in which the constitutional authority of the state seemed to have been terminated in 1789. In some instances, however, the changes occurred at once.[33]

The collection of state customs presumably became outlawed on

---

of State rather than the President, but his complaint to Jefferson did not alter the practice. *The Writings of James Monroe* (Stanislaus Murray Hamilton, ed., 7 vols., New York: G. P. Putnam's Sons, 1898–1903), III, 282–84. Washington wrote directly to governors from time to time.

[31] An occasional letter from Pickering, Secretary of State, to mayors has been noticed. In 1797 he wrote the mayor of Norfolk in response to the latter's inquiry about provision for certain Portuguese sailors who were stranded there (Pickering Papers, VII, 90); and in 1798 he sent the mayor of Augusta, Georgia, copies of a pamphlet for distribution (*ibid.*, IX, 166).

[32] In this section I have relied upon a valuable unpublished doctoral dissertation by Frank L. Esterquest, "State Adjustments to the Federal Constitution, 1789–1800" (University of Chicago, 1940).

[33] One such immediate innovation was a modification of the oath taken by state officials; they were required to swear to support the Constitution of the United States, as well as of their own state (1 Stat. 23, June 1, 1789). The form of authentication of acts of state legislatures and state courts for federal purposes was fixed in 1790 (1 Stat. 122, May 26, 1790), but no notice was taken of administrative acts or of the records of county or municipal bodies.

March 4, 1789. Actually, no state ceased collecting dues on that date, although some believed they could collect only on federal account. As soon as the federal collectors took office, during August and September 1789, the states withdrew from this field of administration. The collection of state tonnage dues ceased with equal promptness.

The relinquishment of the state lighthouses dragged over several years, due chiefly to a dispute about the service of state writs of a civil or criminal nature in territory ceded for lighthouse purposes. A number of states acted within the original time limit of one year, but it was not until 1795 that all the states gave up control of their lighthouses to the general government.[34]

Patents and copyrights had been granted in all the states before 1789, patents usually by private act. The laws continued in force, many believing that these were concurrent powers. The preference of inventors and authors for national protection for their work quickly solved the problem. The federal laws of 1790 substantially destroyed the patent and copyright business of the states, although four states enacted patent laws after 1800.

The emission of paper money by the states was forbidden by the federal Constitution. Only Virginia and Delaware observed the deadline of 1789. State paper money continued to circulate throughout the eighteenth century, due in part to the tardiness of the federal government in supplying a substitute. No one raised the constitutional issue, and circumstances gradually brought practice into conformity with the Constitution.

Whether or not the states were allowed to continue to maintain forts was uncertain. New Hampshire ceded Fort William and Mary in 1791, but South Carolina did not cede Fort Johnston until 1805. The threat of war with Great Britain in 1794 went far to settle the question: the federal government built forts at various points and the desire to maintain state fortifications waned. The general government finally took control of all fortifications.

Whether the post office was a federal monopoly or merely a competitor with the states was also disputed by some. Congress gave an answer in 1792 but New Hampshire apparently continued a supplementary postal service for several years. With this exception the states did not participate in the carriage of the mails after 1789.

---

[34] Esterquest, *op. cit.,* p. 69.

These examples illustrate the process of adjustment to the new regime. It involved a considerable area of governmental activity; Esterquest suggests that "a by no means exhaustive list would include . . . paper money, coinage, legal tender, admiralty jurisdiction, Indian affairs, customs, inspection, foreign affairs, copyright, patent, and naturalization." The change-over was facilitated both by the indulgence of the federal government and the generous compliance of the states to the spirit of the Constitution. By 1800 the transition from the Confederation to the new government was practically complete.

What happened to state officeholders whose jobs disappeared under the new order? And what provision was made for the officials and employees of the Confederation government? Washington held the opinion that a state official whose duties were transferred to the federal government and whose services had been satisfactory was entitled to prior consideration. He reserved freedom of judgment, nevertheless, and many failed to secure new appointments. In the customs service, he made 153 appointments from August 1789 to August 2, 1790: of these 63 had been former state customs officials, while 90 had not. But the principal state collectors, numbering 63, were usually transferred to the new service; 46 were appointed and 17 failed to secure office. The minor customs officials (inspectors, weighers, gaugers, and measurers) were almost all continued in office. Those holding intermediate rank suffered most.[35] In the state admiralty courts there were fifteen judges. Two were appointed to the federal bench, three were made state judges, but two-thirds lost office. The marshals and clerks of the courts also lost heavily; only four of twenty secured federal places, and none got state jobs. Apparently all the state lighthouse keepers stayed on.

New appointments under the federal government were normally forthcoming for the officials and employees of the Confederation. All the territorial officers were continued; the judges of the single Confederation court were absorbed on the federal bench. Almost all the postmasters were kept on without a break. The few clerks in the Treasury Board, the Foreign Office, and the War Department were also carried over. A large proportion of the members of the last Confederation Congress also found immediate federal employment. Out of

---

[35] Esterquest, *op. cit.,* pp. 273–75. There was some tendency on the part of states to make state and federal office incompatible.

a total of forty-nine, twenty-five were in the federal government from 1789 to 1791, of whom twenty were either representatives or senators in the new Congress. Five others secured state posts.

MUTUAL SERVICES

Mutual convenience quickly induced cooperative relations between the two separate systems of administration. The foundations for these mutual services were laid by act of Congress, and by formal or informal acceptance by the states. In some instances the general government was the beneficiary; in others, the states.

Federal services to states. Systematic federal services to the state governments began in 1790 when the collectors were authorized to assist in enforcing the state quarantine laws.[36] In 1796 the President was empowered to direct the revenue officers and the officers commanding forts and revenue cutters to aid in the execution of quarantine and other state health laws.[37] Three years later federal officials generally were enjoined to observe these laws, and the Secretary of the Treasury was authorized to "vary or dispense with" Treasury regulations to conform to state health law requirements.[38]

State licenses to auctioneers were accepted in lieu of a federal license in connection with the tax on property sold by auctioneers in 1794, and state and municipal policy in regulating them was protected by the same act.[39] The federal purpose was to tax, not to regulate. The federal land tax of 1798 exempted state property.[40] The federal bankruptcy act of 1800 specifically safeguarded state bankruptcy laws and debts due to the states.[41] State interests were thus recognized and protected from impairment in this type of legislation.

---

[36] 1 Stat. 106 (April 2, 1790). Livermore objected, claiming this was an unconstitutional interference with the powers of the states. The Constitution expressly reserved to the states the power to make inspection laws, and by implication the power to enforce them. "Those laws will doubtless be executed without an interference on our part." But others spoke on the great importance of their punctual execution. *Annals,* II, 1476–77 (March 26, 1790).

[37] 1 Stat. 474 (May 27, 1796); in 1790 Rhode Island was permitted to continue the collection of tonnage dues to pay for dredging a harbor; Maryland, for meeting the expenses of the warden of Baltimore port; and Georgia, for clearing the Savannah River, 1 Stat. 184 (Aug. 11, 1790).

[38] 1 Stat. 619 (Feb. 25, 1799).

[39] 1 Stat. 397, secs. 2, 4 (June 9, 1794).

[40] 1 Stat. 580, sec. 8 (July 9, 1798).

[41] 2 Stat. 19, secs. 61, 62 (April 4, 1800).

But not all aid requested could be given. Governor Mifflin of Pennsylvania desired John Adams to ask Congress for a remission of duty on ten thousand stand of arms to be imported for the militia. President Adams politely declined.[42]

State services to the federal government. State assistance to the general government was also quickly forthcoming. In 1789 it had courts and marshals but no jails wherein to lodge prisoners. The states were consequently invited to pass laws making it the duty of state jailers to receive federal prisoners, a service for which the United States offered fifty cents a month for each prisoner.[43] No jailer grew rich on this expense account, but all the states except Georgia complied with the request at once.[44]

The states also helped the federal government materially by permitting the use of state courts for suits by federal officials to collect fines or forfeitures. The issue first arose in the enforcement of the tax on stills; delinquent farmers in western Pennsylvania were required to cross the length of the state to appear in the district court at York, a journey which was a time-consuming and irritating experience in itself. In the face of near revolution, Congress authorized the state courts to hear suits arising out of the liquor excise laws when the offense occurred more than fifty miles from a federal district court.[45] The fifty-mile rule was also established for the enforcement of the license on sellers of wine and foreign liquor,[46] and the tax on property sold by auctioneers.[47] In 1798 the state criminal courts became federal agencies for the enforcement of the Aliens Act.[48] In 1799 the state courts and magistrates were given full jurisdiction to determine causes under the postal laws.[49] The convenience of citizens was the moving influence which induced Congress to turn to the states for help; the alternative would have been an extensive, costly, and un-

---

[42] Mifflin to Adams, May 12, 1797, Adams, *Works,* VIII, 542; Adams to Mifflin, May 22, 1797, *ibid.,* VIII, 544.

[43] 1 Stat. 96, Res. 2 (Sept. 23, 1789).

[44] Esterquest, *op. cit.,* p. 96, gives a list of these state laws. The naturalization of aliens, as already noted, was turned over to the state courts in 1790, any common law court of record being qualified to act.

[45] 1 Stat. 378, sec. 9 (June 5, 1794).

[46] 1 Stat. 377, sec. 5 (June 5, 1794).

[47] 1 Stat. 397, sec. 12 (June 9, 1794).

[48] 1 Stat. 577 (July 6, 1798).

[49] 1 Stat. 733, sec. 28 (March 2, 1799).

popular increase in the number of federal judges and court officials.

At another point the state courts also came to the help of the federal government. At an early date Congress provided for the discretionary remission of fines and penalties by the Secretary of the Treasury, on the basis of a hearing before a federal district judge. Originally designed for relief from customs fines and seizures, the federal district judges were well stationed and reasonably adequate. The excise tax scattered pleas for remission throughout the country; the few district courts became inadequate and inconvenient; and in 1794 Congress vested state courts with federal hearing powers.[50]

The federal government occasionally incorporated administrative arrangements of the states into its own system. The powers of United States marshals were defined in 1792 to include the same powers in executing federal laws as state sheriffs possessed in executing state laws.[51] The privileges of certain federal prisoners were defined by reference to state practice.[52] Fees for state agents serving federal warrants were fixed to conform with local scales.[53] Federal jurors were selected in accordance with state practice, and state qualifications were accepted for federal juries.[54] State rules in apprehending offenders were extended to federal cases.[55] The forms of writs and executions in federal courts, and the standards of fees were first established on state models.[56] The Judiciary Act of 1789 accepted the laws of the several commonwealths as rules of decision in trials at common law in the courts of the United States.[57] In short the general government borrowed at a number of points from the states. This implied that federal forms and procedures would not always be uniform, but it meant also that they would be familiar and consistent with established custom in the various localities.

These examples of mutual service suggest the great force of administrative convenience (both to citizens and officials) in the coordination of two separate but related official organizations. The theory

---

[50] 1 Stat. 378, sec. 18 (June 5, 1794); extended by 1 Stat. 506 (March 3, 1797).
[51] 1 Stat. 264, sec. 9 (May 2, 1792).
[52] 1 Stat. 265 (May 5, 1792).
[53] 1 Stat. 537, sec. 9 (Jan. 23, 1798).
[54] 1 Stat. 73, sec. 29 (Sept. 24, 1789).
[55] 1 Stat. 73, sec. 33.
[56] 1 Stat. 93, sec. 2 (Sept. 29, 1789).
[57] 1 Stat. 73, sec. 34.

of states' rights combined with some jealousy and suspicion did not foreclose such common-sense and useful arrangements.

FEDERAL-STATE COMPETITION

During the Federalist period the potential competition between state and federal governments which Judge Livermore feared so deeply failed to materialize. The range of federal activities was small; encroachments on the states were few and relatively incidental; federal aggressions were unknown. The dual system of administration started under favorable circumstances. In one area only the shadow of competition fell across a generally bright landscape.

Common sources of revenue were certain sooner or later to bring about rivalry for their control.[58] Hamilton clearly foresaw this prospect and took timely steps to ensure sound federal footing in the field of internal revenue. In his defense of the funding system he frankly declared that the solution was "to leave the States under as little necessity as possible of exercising the power of taxation." [59] With reference to the federal excise tax introduced in 1791 he "thought it well to lay hold of so valuable a resource of revenue before it was generally preoccupied by the State governments"; he feared that failure to exert national authority over internal revenue might "beget an impression that it was never to be exercised, and next, that it ought not to be exercised." [60] Jefferson and his party promptly repealed the excise taxes, but the precedent had been set.

James Madison, writing a few days after the final adjournment of the Constitutional Convention observed, "The double object of blending a proper stability & energy in the Government with the essential characters of the republican Form, and of tracing a proper line of

---

[58] Washington's first forecast of federal sources of revenue left little to the states and revealed his basic nationalism. He proposed to assume the value of all contributions in money, provisions, etc., made by the states, and pay them six per cent. "With that interest each state may pay annually the interest of the debts they owe, and the annual expences of their Government. They will then have no occasion for Taxes and consequently may abandon all the subjects of taxation to the Union" (October? 1789). Washington, *Writings*, XXX, 454.

[59] Hamilton, *Works* (Lodge ed.), IX, 5.

[60] Hamilton, *Works* (Hamilton ed.), IV, 256. In this same passage he wrote of the desirability of "avoiding the collision of thirteen different and independent systems of finance under concurrent and coequal authorities, and the scramblings for revenue which would have been incident to so many different systems." *Ibid.*, IV, 255.

demarkation between the national and State authorities, was necessarily found to be as difficult as it was desirable, and to admit of an infinite diversity concerning the means among those who were unanimously agreed concerning the end." [61] Twelve years of experience under the Constitution sufficed to reveal much difference of opinion and considerable variation in practice on the administrative arrangements implementing the constitutional decisions. But good will and restraint on both sides marked the initiation of the new order.

[61] Madison, *Writings* (Hunt ed.), V, 1–2.

Chapter Thirty-two

THE LAW ENFORCEMENT MACHINERY

THE new government instituted in 1789 rested immediately upon the citizens of the United States, differing fundamentally in this respect from the government under the Articles of Confederation. Laws made by Congress became direct obligations of persons; Congress was empowered to see to their enforcement in its own courts and by means of its own officials. By 1801 the various branches of the law enforcement machinery were established: the United States attorneys, the federal marshals, and in a lesser vein, informers. Back of all these stood the army and the militia.

THE UNITED STATES ATTORNEYS

The Judiciary Act of 1789 designated each of the eleven states which had then ratified the Constitution a judicial district and added Maine and Kentucky. In each district the act required the appointment of "a meet person learned in the law" to act as attorney for the United States. He was empowered to prosecute all delinquents for crimes and offenses under the jurisdiction of the United States and all civil actions in which the United States was concerned, except before the Supreme Court. He had no salary but derived his official income from fees.[1] Immediately after the passage of the Judiciary Act, Washington appointed thirteen attorneys. Their supervision came, as has already been noted, not from the Attorney General, but from the Secretary of State, and there it remained throughout the Federalist period.

Probably the largest group of cases requiring the services of the United States attorneys arose from customs and internal revenue. Offenses against the revenue laws occurred in the field, and were

---

[1] 1 Stat. 73, secs. 2, 35 (Sept. 24, 1789).

brought to the attention of the attorney directly by the local revenue officers. Actions against shipowners and captains who ran afoul of the navigation acts were related to these derelictions.

The division of responsibility between collectors and district attorneys for enforcement proceedings apparently gave no trouble. The letters of Jeremiah Olney, collector of the port of Providence, Rhode Island, illustrate the actual practice. Thus when Welcome Arnold failed to discharge his bond due June 13, 1791, for upward of $1,000, Olney promptly transmitted it to the district attorney, who put it in suit.[2] On September 13, 1791, the brigantine *Betsey* hove to in Providence harbor bringing ten kegs of brandy from Bordeaux in contravention of the law; although Olney stated to the Secretary of the Treasury that he thought the master had not the least intention of defrauding the revenue, he seized ship and cargo and requested the district attorney to proceed against the owners and master.[3] In at least one recorded instance, Olney applied for and received permission to employ special counsel; after failing to retain Judge Sullivan he secured the services of one of the leading Federalist lawyers, Harrison Gray Otis—"a Gentleman of approved abilities and talents, in the Law," as Olney put it.[4] In 1796 a House committee stated that the district attorneys were always consulted by the revenue officers "in every difficult case." [5]

Another type of case of considerable importance which often came to the attention of the Secretary of State involved actions against ships, especially prizes, privateers, and foreign vessels. The embargo of 1794 and the Nonintercourse Act of 1798 gave much work to the law officers, central and local; the issues were such as to require direction from the State Department.

Prosecutions under the Sedition Act of 1798 were not numerous, but they were especially important.[6] In this group of cases Timothy Pickering, as Secretary of State, was an active intervener. For some time he apparently read the leading opposition newspapers systematically, on the lookout for seditious utterances. Thus we find him writing to Richard Harison, U. S. attorney for New York, requesting the

---

[2] Letters from the Collector at Providence, Vol. I, Olney to the Secretary of the Treasury, June 21, 1791.

[3] *Ibid.*, Sept. 15, 1791.

[4] *Ibid.*, March 31, 1794.

[5] *American State Papers: Miscellaneous*, I, 152.

[6] Frank Maloy Anderson, "The Enforcement of the Alien and Sedition Laws," Am. Hist. Assoc., *Annual Report, 1912,* pp. 113–26.

prosecution of John D. Burke; and to William Rawle, U. S. attorney for Pennsylvania, concerning prosecutions of William Cobbett, Schneider, and Duane of the *Aurora*. Adams pushed on Pickering in the matter of the *Aurora,* writing from Quincy, "If Mr. Rawle does not think this paper [i.e., the *Aurora*] libellous, he is not fit for his office; and if he does not prosecute it, he will not do his duty. The matchless effrontery of this Duane merits the execution of the alien law. I am very willing to try its strength upon him." [7] The suit had already been instituted.

Contacts between the district attorneys and the Department of State were apparently largely fortuitous. Unlike the consuls, for example, the district attorneys apparently received no standard instructions, nor did they render annual or other regular reports. Apart from cases of exceptional importance and difficulty, they operated largely on their own responsibility as matters developed within their respective districts. The general tenor of central direction is revealed in the following excerpt from a letter of the Secretary of State to the district attorney in Virginia: "I transmit the enclosed complaint from the Minister of his Britannic Majesty, in order that you may proceed therein according to law and right." [8] Pickering was more ready than Randolph to urge on the district attorneys in particular cases, but his letters were not put in terms of orders. [9] Discontinuance of a prosecution was occasionally directed from Philadelphia, especially where foreign relations were involved. [10]

During Washington's administration there was some difficulty in keeping attorneys in a few states. Washington's first appointment in Virginia, John Marshall, resigned almost at once, and there were three other incumbents before Adams took over. [11] Kentucky (a territory

---

[7] Aug. 1, 1799, Adams, *Works,* IX, 5.

[8] State Dept., Domestic Letters, VII, 50.

[9] For example, *ibid.,* VIII, 398, 420.

[10] Thus Randolph requested Gore to discontinue the prosecution of a French consular officer accused of arming a frigate in Boston harbor. *Ibid.,* VI, 298.

[11] In 1796 two prominent Virginians, Edward Carrington and William Heth, wrote Wolcott strongly recommending Bushrod Washington for the vacant office in Virginia. "We are well aware of the Presidents delicate Scruples in such cases. . . . The object therefore of this address is to request, that if you should find the President . . . will not consent . . . that you will be good enough to communicate this address to that body [the Senate]—if you should feel no impropriety in so doing. . . ." This ingenious plan to circumvent Washington in favor of his nephew was not pursued. Wolcott Papers, X, 17.

until 1792) was the most troublesome; Washington nominated no less than six men as United States attorney during his eight years, and Adams one. The difficulty in Kentucky was given away in a letter from Randolph to the President. "William McClung has refused to accept his commission as Attorney for the District of Kentucky. I suspect that we must see some turn in the minds of the people there, before any body will venture upon an office, which will be chiefly conversant in the excise penalties." [12] Randolph advised Tench Coxe, Commissioner of Revenue, to depend on special counsel in Kentucky.[13]

In general, however, the record of tenure is a stable one. In the Maine district, William Lithgow served from 1789 to 1796, and his successor through Adams' term. In Massachusetts, Christopher Gore and the distinguished Judge Davis covered the Federalist period, except for a brief interval occupied by Harrison Gray Otis. In Connecticut, Pierpont Edwards was the only incumbent, a record equaled by Richard Harison of New York and George Read, Jr., of Delaware. Most states had two, or at the most three, United States attorneys from 1789 to 1801.

The incumbents were men of substantial ability and prominence, measuring up well to Washington's high standards. In 1796 a House committee reported that the "attorneys are men of the first reputation for talents and integrity." [14] Of the forty-four persons who held the office during Washington's and Adams' administrations, thirteen were recognized over a century later in the *Dictionary of American Biography*. The bearers of the most distinguished names, such as John Marshall and Harrison Gray Otis, held the office of attorney for so brief a period that it can hardly be argued they were characteristic of the group. But at a somewhat lesser level, men of distinction held the post over long periods.[15]

Among them was William Rawle, United States attorney for Pennsylvania from 1791 to 1800. Of Quaker stock, he belonged to a Loyalist family and after reading law in New York continued his studies in England during 1781 and 1782. Returning to Philadelphia, he became

---

[12] State Dept., Domestic Letters, VII, 357.
[13] *Ibid.*, VIII, 206.
[14] *American State Papers: Miscellaneous*, I, 152.
[15] For a brief sketch of Richard Harison, sometimes spelled Harrison, district attorney in New York, see Dixon Ryan Fox, *The Decline of Aristocracy in the Politics of New York*, pp. 12–13.

a friend of Franklin and was elected to the American Philosophical Society and to the Society for Political Inquiries, of which both Franklin and Washington were members. He served for a year in the Pennsylvania legislature (1789) and in 1791 was confirmed as United States attorney for Pennsylvania. His most important task was to prosecute the culprits who were seized in connection with the Whiskey Rebellion. In politics he was a Federalist. He had wide intellectual interests. In 1795 he was elected a trustee of the University of Pennsylvania and late in life he became the first president of the Historical Society of Pennsylvania.[16]

His predecessor as United States attorney (1789–91), William Lewis, was also a Quaker. A thorough Federalist, he served as a member of the Pennsylvania legislature in 1787 and 1789 and as a member of the state constitutional convention of 1789. He left the office of attorney to accept Washington's appointment as district court judge. In 1792 he returned to private practice and was widely known as one of the leading Quaker lawyers of Pennsylvania.[17]

Pierpont Edwards, United States attorney for Connecticut from 1789 throughout the Federalist period, was the youngest child of the celebrated divine, Jonathan Edwards. He graduated from the College of New Jersey, read law, and began practice in New Haven in 1771. He served repeated terms in the Connecticut House of Representatives, was three times speaker, and a member of the convention to ratify the Constitution. He was the first United States attorney for Connecticut. His liberal views in both politics and religion induced his affiliation with the Jeffersonian Republicans, and after 1800 he was the Connecticut party leader. In 1806 Jefferson appointed him judge of the district court for Connecticut. One of his last and most important public services was to draft the state constitution, as a member of the Constitutional Convention of 1818.[18]

Christopher Gore graduated from Harvard in 1776, read law with Judge Lowell, and later became the law tutor of Daniel Webster. He corresponded freely with Wolcott and King regarding federal appointments in Massachusetts in 1789 and solicited the office of district attorney, in which he served with distinction from 1789 to 1796. In this year he was appointed one of three commissioners to settle American

---

[16] *Dictionary of American Biography,* XV, 400–1.

[17] *Ibid.,* XI, 225.

[18] *Ibid.,* VI, 43–44.

spoliation claims against Great Britain and remained abroad until 1804. He was governor of Massachusetts in 1809 and United States senator from 1813 to 1816.[19]

These were men of ability and standing in their communities.

THE MARSHALS

The Judiciary Act of 1789 also created the office of marshal, one in each district. The appointment required confirmation by the Senate; contrary to the usual federal practice, tenure was for four years, and the incumbent was specifically made removable at pleasure. Reappointment was customary.[20] Each marshal was authorized to appoint one or more deputies who were subject to removal at the pleasure of either the district or circuit court judges; he was also empowered "to command all necessary assistance in the execution of his duty," a statutory equivalent of the common law *posse comitatus*. Official duties were simply and broadly described: to attend the district and circuit courts, and the Supreme Court, and to execute all lawful precepts directed to him.[21]

The marshals, along with the collectors, quickly became the handy men of the federal administration. They were instructed to take the first and second censuses.[22] In 1791 they were authorized to hire jails for federal prisoners where states had not agreed to provide this service, and to supervise jails and prisoners.[23] They were designated the competent executive officers to receive and execute precepts from French consuls and vice consuls.[24] They, rather than the state sheriffs, were instructed to collect fines and enforce jail sentences imposed by militia courts-martial; the courts-martial were composed of militia officers only, but the execution of sentence was taken in hand by a federal agent.[25] In 1792, the marshals were given custody of all vessels and goods seized by any officer of the revenue—an authority hitherto in the Treasury

---

[19] *National Cyclopaedia of American Biography,* I, 112.

[20] In 1793 Jefferson sent out reappointment notices in batches. State Dept., Domestic Letters, V, 247–48.

[21] 1 Stat. 73, sec. 27 (Sept. 24, 1789).

[22] 1 Stat. 101 (March 1, 1790); 2 Stat. 11 (Feb. 28, 1800).

[23] 1 Stat. 225, Res. V (March 3, 1791).

[24] 1 Stat. 254 (April 14, 1792).

[25] 1 Stat. 264, secs. 6–7 (May 2, 1792).

Department;[26] and later they became responsible for summoning appraisers to value goods taken in execution of judgment.[27] The marshals also became the local agents of the Comptroller of the United States in serving notice upon delinquent officers accountable.[28]

By an act of 1792, the marshals became the fiscal agents of the courts. They bought fuel, candles, and other "reasonable contingencies," and became paymasters, handling jurors and witnesses fees, fees to clerks of courts, and other such payments.[29] By the Alien Acts of 1798 the marshals become direct agents of the President. The first Alien Act

TABLE V

MARSHALS' FEES, 1799

Duty	Fee
Service of a writ	$2.00 for each person served
Travel	five cents per mile
Travel to attend court	ten cents per mile
Issuance of bail bond	fifty cents
Summoning witnesses or appraisers	fifty cents
Commitment or discharge of a prisoner	fifty cents
Proclamation in admiralty	thirty cents
Sales of vessels or property	2½ per cent of value up to $500; thereafter 1¼ per cent
Summoning of jury	$4.00, with a maximum of $50.00 for any one court
For attending Supreme or Circuit Court	$5.00 per day
For attending District Court	$4.00 per day
For taking census	from $100 to $500, depending on population of the state
For all other services	fees as established by the state Supreme Court

---

[26] 1 Stat. 275, sec. 4 (May 8, 1792).

[27] 1 Stat. 333, sec. 8 (March 2, 1793); the marshals were authorized in 1800 to sell lands possessed by the United States in satisfaction of judgments. 2 Stat. 61 (May 7, 1800).

[28] 1 Stat. 441, secs. 1–2 (March 3, 1795).

[29] 1 Stat. 275, sec. 4 (May 8, 1792).

directed them to execute all precepts and orders issued by the President;[30] the second made it their duty to deport an enemy alien on the order of the President or of any court or judge.[31]

Apart from these various and sundry duties and powers, the authority of the marshals was broadly enlarged in 1792 by granting them the same powers in executing the laws of the United States in their respective districts as the sheriffs had in executing the laws of the respective states.[32] This grant of power vested them with common law authority in the discharge of their duties.

Marshals, like many other federal officers, were paid by fees. The table of fees settled in 1799 gives a good summary of the various types of work which they had to perform, and the value set upon each.[33] In the smaller (or more peaceful) districts the amount of business was insufficient to make the office attractive. It was one which carried less prestige than that of the principal revenue offices, and certainly less than that of United States attorney.[34] Pickering described the office of marshal of Delaware as "an office of more burden than profit," and recommended him for loan commissioner.[35]

In the performance of their duties the marshals were subject to the immediate direction and orders of the court, and reported their actions to the judge from day to day. The Secretary of State also could issue instructions of a general nature; Randolph advised the marshal of New York, against whom complaint had been made by the French minister, to consult with the district attorney as to his line of conduct.[36]

The life of a marshal was usually not a hazardous one, despite his preoccupation with that part of the population which filtered through courts and into jails. But in such crises as the Whiskey Rebellion, the marshal's job became troublesome enough. After an assault on the collector of the revenue in western Pennsylvania (1791), process was issued by the federal district court in Philadelphia. The marshal confided it to a deputy who, deterred by threats, sent the writ by a private messenger. He was seized, whipped, tarred and feathered, and tied

[30] 1 Stat. 570, sec. 4 (June 25, 1798).

[31] 1 Stat. 577, sec. 3 (July 6, 1798).

[32] 1 Stat. 264, sec. 9 (May 2, 1792).

[33] 1 Stat. 624 (Feb. 28, 1799); for census fee, see 1 Stat. 101, sec. 4 (March 1, 1790).

[34] Note Nathaniel Rogers, marshal of New Hampshire, appointed supervisor of revenue, Feb. 19, 1798, *Senate Executive Journal*, I, 262.

[35] Pickering to Washington, Feb. 22, 1797, Pickering Papers, XXXVII, 53.

[36] Jan. 31, 1794, State Dept., Domestic Letters, VI, 49.

in the woods.[37] On May 13, 1794, writs were issued from Philadelphia against 175 distillers, which it became the duty of the marshal to serve. Those who were first encountered pursued him, one of thirty or forty men discharged his rifle, and the next morning the marshal was taken prisoner. He escaped, however, and returned to Philadelphia by a circuitous route, descending the Ohio River.[38] For a short time the life of the marshal was in jeopardy during the Fries Rebellion, when an armed mob forced the release of prisoners.[39] These, however, were highly exceptional circumstances.

An able group of men served as marshals during the Federalist period, representing on the whole a type that was politically active. Forty-five appointments were made in the twenty-two districts, ten of whom are listed in the *Dictionary of American Biography*. A very large proportion had served in the Revolutionary Army.

Henry Dearborn, marshal of the district of Maine from 1789 to 1793, was a practicing physician who had been on Washington's staff during the war with the rank of colonel. He resigned the office of marshal to be elected as a Republican to Congress (1793–97), became Secretary of War under Jefferson and in 1809 was appointed collector of the port of Boston. He took up active service in the army again from 1812 to 1815, without adding to his reputation, and closed his public life by serving as minister to Portugal from 1822 to 1824.[40]

Edward Carrington, marshal of Virginia, was a close friend and political correspondent of both Washington and Hamilton. His father was a wealthy and influential planter and John Marshall was his brother-in-law. He was an officer of the Revolutionary Army and in 1785 and 1786 a member of the Continental Congress. He also held the office of supervisor of revenue for the district of Virginia. His influence far outran the public offices he held.[41]

The first marshal of Massachusetts, 1789–91, Jonathan Jackson, led an active public life in his native state. A Harvard graduate, he engaged in mercantile pursuits in Newburyport and was once a partner

---

[37] Townsend Ward, "The Insurrection of the Year 1794, in the Western Counties of Pennsylvania," *Memoirs of the Historical Society of Pennsylvania*, VI (1858), 130–31.
[38] *Ibid.*, 156, 170–72.
[39] William W. H. Davis, *The Fries Rebellion, 1798–99* (Doylestown, Pa., 1899), pp. 63–66.
[40] *Dictionary of American Biography*, V, 174–76.
[41] *National Cyclopaedia of American Biography*, V, 54–55.

of Stephen Higginson. He quickly turned to politics, however, became a member of the provincial Congress of 1775, of the state House of Representatives in 1777, of the Continental Congress in 1782, and of the state Senate in 1789. He aspired to the position of collector of the port of Boston, but learning that his friend, Benjamin Lincoln, was also a candidate he urged the latter upon Washington. Lincoln was appointed. The President later heard of this act of friendship and made Jackson marshal, where he served for two years, then offered him the post of Comptroller of the Treasury in 1795, and appointed him supervisor of revenue for the Massachusetts district in 1796. From 1802 to 1806 he was treasurer of the Commonwealth. His connection with Harvard was close, and he served as president of the Harvard corporation.[42]

These were among the best known of the first marshals, but others were prominent in their communities: Clement Biddle of Pennsylvania, Matthew Clarkson of New York, Isaac Huger of South Carolina, Allan McLean of Delaware, and Nathaniel Ramsay of Maryland. Jacob Graybell, successor to Ramsay, made a career of the post; he was marshal of the state admiralty court and deputy marshal of the district court before he became marshal in 1794.

INFORMERS

Reliance upon private informers to bring law violations to the attention of prosecutors or courts was a part of English procedure in the eighteenth century and was widely adopted by Congress. Its history in England indeed goes back to times medieval. A statute of Richard II provided a third part of certain shipping forfeitures to the informer, "the person who *duly espieth and duly proveth* any offence against that statute." [43]

From 1789 to 1801 Congress made provision for rewards to informers in over twenty instances. The object most frequently safeguarded was the revenue. Informers, however, were invited in several statutes to report on offenses against the various acts governing trade and intercourse with the Indians. Other offenses thought suitable for their eye

---

[42] *Biographical Directory of the American Congress, 1774–1927*, p. 1143; Thomas C. Amory, *James Sullivan*, I, 249.

[43] John Reeves, *A History of the Law of Shipping and Navigation* (London: E. and R. Brooke and J. Sewell, 1792), p. 12.

included violations of the postal law, stealing goods belonging to or under the jurisdiction of the United States, engaging in the slave trade, violating the Embargo and Nonintercourse Acts, fitting out privateers, and neglect on the part of aliens to register.

The amount of the potential reward to informers varied greatly, from one half the small penalties of two dollars on aliens to a "moiety" of the value of ships and stores illegally fitted out as privateers. In the revenue laws, the customary provision reserved one half of all fines, forfeitures, and penalties to the United States; the other half was divided among the collector, naval officer, and surveyor in equal parts. But if an informer produced the proof, he secured one half the share of the customs officers.

The object in view was principally to induce *private citizens* to observe the law. In a few cases, however, informers were put on the trail of delinquent *officials*. Thus informers were invited to see to it that collectors kept in some public place a table of the rates of all fees and duties. The fine of $100 went to the informer.[44] All Treasury officials were forbidden to engage in trade or commerce by the organic act setting up the Department; one half of the penalties up to $3,000 went to the informer.[45] The first census act required marshals to submit returns on specified dates, subject to a fine of $800, of which one half went to the informer if he started the suit.[46] Finally we note that Indian agents and clerks were forbidden under penalty of not over $1,000 to engage in private trade; the informer was entitled to one half.[47] Usually, however, he was put on the trail of private citizens.

An important procedural point turned on whether the informer was required to prosecute on his own initiative and secure judgment, or whether he need merely offer the information on which the public prosecutor acted. Both cases occurred, and in about equal numbers. In customs and internal revenue cases, privateering, and offenses by officials (with one exception), the informer was not held to prosecute; in other cases he must initiate the action as, for example, offenses against the post office, trading with Indians, the slave trade, trading with France, persons stealing certain goods, and neglect of aliens to register. While the line is not clear, it appears that where the more

---

[44] 1 Stat. 29, sec. 29 (July 31, 1789).

[45] 1 Stat. 65, sec. 8 (Sept. 2, 1789).

[46] 1 Stat. 101, sec. 3 (March 1, 1790).

[47] 1 Stat. 452, sec. 3 (April 18, 1796).

urgent necessities of law enforcement were involved, the informer was encouraged to come forward with evidence, the suit being pressed by the district attorney.

By 1799 the tide had begun to turn against informers, although there was yet no repeal of legislation offering them inducements. In the revised collection act of 1799, rewards were henceforth barred to informers whose testimony was necessary to prove guilt; [48] the same precaution had been taken as early as 1792 and 1793 with respect to customs officials concerned with the registration and clearance of vessels.[49] Congress further took occasion to hold informers for costs and fees of prosecution in cases where the prosecution was non-suited or the defendant acquitted.[50] The possibility of having to stand costs was a deterrent at least to any speculative enterprise.

Experience with informers had not been such as to warrant the reliance which Congress placed in their activities. In the old country they were a despised and hated tribe; in 1733 the collector at Inverness reported to his superiors that "a Person under suspicion of being an Informer dreg'd across the Firth and his ears cut out." [51] In 1769 informers to the king's customs in Philadelphia were seized, pilloried, and tarred and feathered.[52] Both in the home country and the colonies informers brought scant direct support to the customs officers, although it is of course impossible to estimate what restraining effect they may have indirectly induced. Of seventy cases in which it was possible to determine who lodged the information, only three were initiated by informers, and only one with intent to recover the informer's moiety.[53]

THE ARMY AND THE MILITIA

In every government the ultimate power of enforcement is armed power. The United States Army during the Federalist period was not used for the purpose of internal law enforcement, except for a brief

---

[48] 1 Stat. 627, sec. 91 (March 2, 1799).

[49] 1 Stat. 287, sec. 29 (Dec. 31, 1792); 1 Stat. 305, sec. 35 (Feb. 18, 1793).

[50] 1 Stat. 624, sec. 8 (Feb. 28, 1799).

[51] Henry Atton and Henry Hurst Holland, *The King's Customs* (2 vols., London: J. Murray, 1908–10), I, 231.

[52] William Smith McClellan, *Smuggling in the American Colonies at the Outbreak of the Revolution* (New York: printed for Williams College, 1912), p. 87.

[53] Lawrence A. Harper, *The English Navigation Laws* (New York: Columbia University Press, 1939), p. 170.

show of force in connection with the Fries Rebellion. The only statutory reference to its duties other than defense against foreign enemies and Indians occurred in connection with the Indian Trading Act of 1796, wherein the army (not the militia) was authorized to apprehend persons unlawfully within Indian territory and to convey them, within ten days, to a neighboring civil authority.[54]

The ancient English institution of the militia was promptly transferred to Massachusetts, where the Military Company of the Massachusetts Bay was formed in 1638. As the Ancient and Honorable Artillery Company of Massachusetts, its annual parades past Boston Common in traditional eighteenth century uniform may still be enjoyed. The military value of the militia during the Revolution proved only moderate, but the tradition of a volunteer citizen army was deep. Independence won, the states regularized their militia; and for many years popular distrust of a professional army shed a reflected confidence upon these citizen forces.[55]

The possibility of the use of the militia to enforce federal laws was foreseen at an early date. The first Militia Act (1792) authorized the President to call out the militia in the following cases: invasion from any foreign nation or Indian tribe; insurrection within a state, on request of the legislature (or of the governor, if the legislature were not in session); and opposition to or obstruction of the execution of the laws of the United States by combinations too powerful to be suppressed by the ordinary course of judicial proceedings or by powers vested in marshals. Two conditions were imposed in the latter case: a notification of the existence of the obstruction of the law by a federal judge, and a prior proclamation of the President commanding the insurgents to disperse and "retire peaceably to their respective abodes."[56] In a subsequent statute Congress authorized the President to employ the militia to enforce the neutrality of the United States.[57]

The first, and for many years the most dramatic, occasion for the use of the militia to support the enforcement of the federal laws was

---

[54] 1 Stat. 469, sec. 16 (May 19, 1796).

[55] A valuable historical record is by James Brown Scott, *The Militia,* Sen. Doc. No. 695, 64th Cong., 2d sess. (Jan. 12, 1917). There is no adequate history of the militia.

[56] 1 Stat. 264 (May 2, 1792).

[57] 1 Stat. 381, sec. 7 (June 5, 1794). Washington did not favor a standing army but neither would he accept a "milk and water" militia. Washington, *Writings,* XXXI, 494, Feb. 1792.

the refusal of farmers in western Pennsylvania to pay the tax on stills and distilled spirits, culminating in the Whiskey Rebellion.[58] The tax on distilled liquors was approved by Washington on March 3, 1791; [59] the rates were lowered and the administration of the tax alleviated in a further act of May 8, 1792.[60]

Opposition to the payment of the federal tax appeared without delay. That the excise caused genuine hardship and inequality of burden cannot be doubted. Aroused by a sense of wrong and by determination to defeat the federal excise as they had caused repeal of the state tax, the inhabitants of the western counties organized to resist. At a meeting held in Pittsburgh, August 21, 1792, steps were taken to petition Congress for repeal and "to persist . . . in every other legal measure that may obstruct the operation of the Law until we are able to obtain its total repeal." The sting in this resolution appeared in the pronouncement against the revenue officers: "*Resolved, therefore,* That in future we will consider such persons as unworthy of our friendship; have no intercourse or dealings with them; withdraw from them every assistance, and withhold all the comforts of life which depend upon those duties that as men and fellow citizens we owe to each other; and upon all occasions treat them with that contempt which they deserve. . . ." [61] The President replied with a proclamation on September 15, 1792, exhorting the obstructionists to cease and desist.

Discontent slowly gathered strength during 1793, and came to a head in the latter half of 1794. The collector at Pittsburgh resigned his office July 20, 1794, and a number of revenue officers were seized, tarred and feathered, and otherwise maltreated. On August 4, federal Judge James Wilson notified the President that the laws of the United States were opposed by "combinations too powerful to be suppressed by the ordinary course of judicial proceedings or by the powers vested in

---

[58] The principal references to the events of the Whiskey Rebellion are *American State Papers: Miscellaneous,* I, 83–113; "Papers Relating to What is Known as the Whiskey Insurrection in Western Pennsylvania, 1794," John B. Linn and Wm. H. Egle, eds., *Pennsylvania Archives,* 2d Series, Vol. IV (1896), 1–462, cited herein as "Papers"; Townsend Ward, "The Insurrection of the Year 1794, in the Western Counties of Pennsylvania," *Memoirs of the Historical Society of Pennsylvania,* VI (1858), 117–82; Leland D. Baldwin, *Whiskey Rebels* (Pittsburgh: University of Pittsburgh Press, 1939). For Gallatin's connection with the affair, see Henry Adams, *The Life of Albert Gallatin,* pp. 87 ff.

[59] 1 Stat. 199.

[60] 1 Stat. 267.

[61] "Papers," pp. 25–26.

the Marshall." [62] Three days later Washington issued the proclamation required by law, and called upon the governors of Pennsylvania, New Jersey, Maryland, and Virginia for contingents of militia, eventually fixed at 15,000. Before putting them in the field he dispatched commissioners to persuade the belligerent frontiersmen to yield; but on September 24, the commissioners reported, after negotiations on the spot, that some more competent force than the civil authority was necessary to cause the laws to be duly executed. [63] After a second proclamation, the militia was put in motion and eventually reached Pittsburgh. All organized opposition had evaporated. On November 20, the office of inspection was again open to receive the entry of stills and the payment of duties. [64]

The appearance of armed forces on the scene achieved the purpose in view, the submission of the rebellious whiskey distilling farmers. What can be said of the record of the militia? At the outset there was reluctance to embark upon a campaign against fellow citizens, and despite Governor Mifflin's schedule of a dozen addresses, it was necessary to resort to the draft to fill up the Pennsylvania quota. [65] This sentiment was balanced by a crusading spirit among others who were determined to support the government.

The record of the Pennsylvania militia was not reassuring. Supplies and stores were seriously lacking. Mifflin issued the call for militia on August 7, 1794; on September 6, Colonel Russell informed General Harmar that no dependence could be placed on the state arms or equipment. He had received fifty muskets, all unfit for service. [66] On September 22, writing en route from Buck Tavern, Major Rees implored General Harmar for knapsacks: "Cusack's Company are determined not to march in the morning without. For God sake have this thing attended to, for one revolt will I fear encourage others." [67] On September 26, Colonel Russell wrote Governor Mifflin from Yorktown, "notwithstanding . . . we expected the Arms & Equipments, Tents &

---

[62] *Ibid.*, p. 70.

[63] *Ibid.*, pp. 293 ff.

[64] *Ibid.*, p. 378.

[65] *Ibid.*, p. 237; the militia in the western counties, as might have been suspected, were quite unreliable; many of them were members of the Mingo Creek Society which was deeply implicated in the insurrection; see Townsend Ward, *op. cit.*, pp. 139–40.

[66] "Papers," p. 223.

[67] *Ibid.*, pp. 285–86.

Camp Equippage before this time, none have yet arrived." [68] And from Carlisle, the rendezvous, the commanding general, Irvine, wrote the Governor his fear of a great deficiency of arms.[69]

General Irvine could hardly be blamed for these breakdowns; he wrote Mifflin on September 18 that while he had read in the newspapers that he had been appointed to command the militia, he had had no official notice of his authority.[70] The adjutant general had neglected to transmit to the commanding officer the Governor's appointment and instructions.[71]

Not only were there deficiencies of arms and equipment. The civil authority was worried concerning the discipline of the militia and its relations with the population. The adjutant general issued a general order on September 20, containing this passage: "The Governor being solicitous for the reputation of the militia that the utmost order should be observed on the march, he trusts that he shall be excused in repeating his earnest desire that the strictest attention may be paid to sobriety and regularity of conduct." [72] Two citizens having been killed by the militia en route, Hamilton wrote Governor Mifflin on October 10, conveying President Washington's "poignant regret": "It is a very precious & important idea that those who are called out in support & defence of the Laws, should not give occasion, or even protect [pretense] to impute to them infraction of the laws. They cannot render a more important service to the cause of government & order, than by a conduct scrupulously regardful of the rights of their fellow citizens and exemplary for decorum, regularity & moderation." [73] While there was a general indifference to the call to sobriety, the discipline of the militia was maintained at a point where no widespread difficulties with the civil population developed.

The difficulties of transportation across the Pennsylvania mountains were doubled by heavy rains. Wagons broke down, horses became lame, "food, tents, and baggage struggled in the mud miles behind" the militiamen. "The beef was bad, there was no way to bake bread most of the time, the whiskey was weak, and the straw for bedding was

---

[68] *Ibid.*, p. 316.
[69] *Ibid.*, p. 326.
[70] *Ibid.*, p. 273.
[71] *Ibid.*, p. 285.
[72] *Ibid.*, p. 278.
[73] *Ibid.*, p. 341.

insufficient or soaked." [74] The militia, nevertheless, finally won its way —against nature, not the rebel farmers—to Pittsburgh. The authority of the general government was triumphantly vindicated, and by the people themselves.

This fortunate outcome, however, did not conceal the shortcomings of the militia as an enforcement agency. In his annual message to Congress in November 1794, Washington declared that "the militia laws have exhibited such striking defects as could not have been supplied but by the zeal of our citizens. Besides the extraordinary expense and waste, which are not the least of the defects, every appeal to those laws is attended with a doubt on its success." [75]

The reenactment of the Militia Act in 1795 with only two minor changes failed to strengthen the system.[76] The militia continued as a semisocial, semimilitary organization, far from General Knox's ideal of "an energetic national militia." [77] Its character is suggested by such individual designations as the Macpherson Blues, the City Greens, etc. The annual muster and parades became a popular holiday. "These fall parades became famous for their varied attractions, the public flocking from far and near to see the many sights incident to a general muster, and to feast on the popular rations of gingerbread and cider." [78]

Recourse to military force to secure observance of the law occurred once more under the Federalists, in connection with the Fries Rebellion. Resistance to the assessment of land and buildings in accordance with the act of 1798 broke out in eastern Pennsylvania. The federal marshal ordered the arrest of the ringleaders, whereupon a body of men stormed the tavern in which they were temporarily held and forced the marshal to release them. Members of a militia company of light horse were involved in the rescue of the troublemakers. John Adams promptly called upon the Pennsylvania militia and sent about five hundred men in the United States Army to proceed against the rebels. They and

---

[74] Baldwin, op. cit., pp. 231–32.

[75] Richardson, Messages, I, 166–67.

[76] Cf. 1 Stat. 264 and 1 Stat. 424.

[77] In 1799 the Frederick Town barracks were found so much out of repair as to make them useless for the Provisional Army. Washington, Writings, XXXVII, 423.

[78] Ellery B. Crane, "The Early Militia System of Massachusetts," Collections of the Worcester Society of Antiquity, IX (1891), 122. A function of the Second Troop Philadelphia City Cavalry during the 1790's was to escort the President upon his return to the seat of government. See W. A. Newman Dorland, "The Second Troop Philadelphia City Cavalry," Pennsylvania Magazine of History and Biography, XLVII (1923), 357; and XLVIII (1924), 270.

their leader, John Fries, were seized without resistance. In a subsequent trial for treason, Fries was convicted and sentenced to death. Against the advice of his Cabinet, Adams eventually pardoned Fries and his accomplices.[79]

---

[79] For an account of the Fries affair, see W. W. H. Davis, *The Fries Rebellion, 1798–99;* Francis Wharton, *State Trials;* and *American State Papers: Miscellaneous,* I, 185–89.

Chapter Thirty-three

THE STATUTORY LAW OF OFFICERS

A T THE time of the Revolution, the common law contained a well-developed system of duties, rights, and liabilities of public officers which with various modifications had been recognized in the colonies and the states. Whether or not the common law (including the law of officers) became a part of the legal system of the general government in 1789 was a point disputed both by lawyers and statesmen. Jefferson and his fellow Republicans resisted such claims, since their acceptance would magnify the power and importance of the federal authorities and diminish correspondingly the position of the states. Pickering took it for granted that federal officials were subject to the provisions of the common law of England.

The issue came to judicial notice in the circuit court of Pennsylvania in a case involving the attempted bribery of Tench Coxe, Commissioner of Revenue, by a contractor, Worrall, to secure the contract for building a lighthouse. His defense was that he had committed no crime, since the common law did not obtain and since Congress had not created the offense of seeking to bribe the Commissioner. The two judges of the court divided. Chase held that the indictment could not be maintained in the federal courts if supported solely by the common law; Peters asserted that the United States was constitutionally possessed of at least the common law power to punish misdemeanors. "Whenever," he said, "an offence aims at the subversion of any Federal institution, or at the corruption of its public officers, it is an offence against the well-being of the *United States;* from its very nature, it is cognizable under their authority. . . ."[1] After consultation the judges imposed sentence upon the defendant.

The matter remained in dispute, but Congress at once began to build a superstructure of official rights and obligations. The provisions

---

[1] 2 Dallas 384, at 395 (1798).

of this branch of the law fell into four principal classes: (1) securing of effectual performance of duties; (2) prevention of bribery, fraud, extortion, and oppression; (3) safeguarding against collusion between officials and citizens to evade the laws; and (4) protection of officers in the performance of their duties.

PERFORMANCE OF DUTIES

Oath. The first enactment of Congress prescribed an oath of allegiance to be taken by its own members, by all state officials, and by all officers appointed under the authority of the United States.[2] The terms of the oath were simple: "I, A.B. do solemnly swear or affirm (as the case may be) that I will support the Constitution of the United States." The collection act, a few weeks later, introduced the first of a long series of special oaths taken by particular groups of officials to execute faithfully the law with which they were concerned. The collectors, naval officers, and surveyors, as well as their subordinates, each were required to swear, "I, ——— ———, do solemnly swear . . . that I will truly and faithfully execute and perform all the duties of a ——— of the port or district of ——— according to law, and the best of my skill and ability."[3] Officers and persons collecting the tax on distilled spirits were required to swear "diligently and faithfully" to execute the duties of their offices and "to use their best endeavours to prevent and detect frauds."[4] The basic oath of allegiance was thus supplemented by a second oath to perform well the duties of the office in question.

Neglect or refusal to perform duty. The principal classes of officers specifically subjected to penalty for neglect or refusal to perform their duties were the customs officials and the internal revenue officers. By the terms of the ship registration act, any person wilfully neglecting or refusing to perform duties required by law forfeited $500 for the first and second offenses and thereafter was excluded from office.[5] These provisions were supplemented from time to time by others which probably arose from particular evils. Thus a boarding officer who refused to certify the delivery of manifests by the master forfeited

---

[2] 1 Stat. 23 (June 1, 1789).

[3] 1 Stat. 29, sec. 8 (July 31, 1789); see 1 Stat. 627, sec. 20 for a later version (March 2, 1799).

[4] 1 Stat. 199, sec. 6 (March 3, 1791).

[5] 1 Stat. 55, sec. 34 (Sept. 1, 1789).

$500;[6] and an inspector placed on board a vessel was penalized $50 for neglect of duty or any act contrary to law; for the second offense he was "displaced" and disqualified for any employment in the revenue service for seven years. Furthermore for performing any duties other than those of an inspector, he was disqualified from acting as such.[7]

In the internal revenue service, an officer of inspection who caused damage by neglect to perform his duties was subjected to suit by the injured party who was entitled to recover full damages and costs.[8] The assessors concerned with the land tax of 1798 were subject to a fine of $200 and costs and discharge from office for failure to perform their duties without cause.[9]

One or two other examples may be noted. The Bankruptcy Act of 1800 imposed a penalty of not over $3,000 for wilfully and negligently allowing a bankrupt to escape or to go without the walls of the prison.[10] An interesting variant was developed in the land tax act of 1798, fining tax commissioners $10 for failure to attend general meetings held in each state without cause acceptable to the board of land tax commissioners.[11] There were also occasional examples penalizing neglect of duty of an official to his departmental superiors.[12]

Prohibition against engaging in private business. Congress was sensitive from the beginning to the danger of official enrichment by means of private transactions aided by official knowledge. This still perplexing problem was met in dealing with three principal groups of officials; customs, internal revenue, and Indian agents. The act establishing the Treasury Department forbade persons holding office under it to be concerned directly or indirectly in carrying on any trade or commerce, to own in whole or in part any "sea-vessel," to purchase any public lands or other public property, or to be concerned in the purchase or disposal of any public securities.[13] The penalty was severe:

---

[6] 1 Stat. 145, sec. 12 (Aug. 4, 1790).

[7] 1 Stat. 627, sec. 53 (March 2, 1799).

[8] 1 Stat. 199, sec. 41 (March 3, 1791).

[9] 1 Stat. 580, sec. 17 (July 9, 1798).

[10] 2 Stat. 19, sec. 40 (April 4, 1800).

[11] 1 Stat. 580, sec. 6 (July 9, 1798).

[12] Marshals, for failure to make census returns, 1 Stat. 101, sec. 3; inspectors, for failing to inspect, 1 Stat. 627, sec. 73.

[13] 1 Stat. 65, sec. 8 (Sept. 2, 1789). The same prohibition was imposed upon Treasury clerks in 1791 (1 Stat. 215) but was partially lifted, for the clerks, in 1792 (1 Stat. 279, sec. 12). Officials of the U. S. Bank were forbidden to buy or sell goods (1 Stat. 191, sec. 8).

the offense was deemed a high misdemeanor, subject to forfeiture of $3,000, removal from office, and disqualification forever from holding any office under the United States. In 1792 the Commissioner of Revenue, the commissioners of loans, and all persons employed in their offices, as well as all persons concerned in the collection or disbursement of the revenue were forbidden to deal in the funds or debts of the United States or any state, or any public property of either.[14]

Customs officers were forbidden in 1793 to own in whole or in part any vessel, or to act as agent for the owner of a vessel or of its cargo, or to be concerned in the importation of merchandise.[15] Corresponding restrictions were laid upon supervisors and inspectors of the revenue (subordinate internal revenue officers) in 1794. They were barred from any foreign trade or commerce relating to the duties of their office, and from the sale of wines, spirits, or tea.[16]

The Purveyor of Public Supplies was forbidden to be interested, directly or indirectly, in trade or commerce, or to own any share in a sea-vessel, or to purchase public lands, or the public securities of any state or the United States.[17] His clerks were not subject to this rule.

Indian agents in charge of trading houses, their employees and clerks, were forbidden to be interested in any trade or commerce other than on the public account; the agents were held to an oath not to be concerned with private trade with the Indians; and were subject to a particular prohibition against purchasing an Indian gun, instrument of husbandry, or article of clothing, except skins and furs. Upon the superintendent of Indian affairs was imposed the duty of collecting evidence of infraction of the law and of prosecuting offenders.[18]

Congress thus emphatically rejected the theory of "honest graft," i.e., private benefits that might be derived from official station. A sharp separation between official duties and personal advantage was required, establishing a standard of official ethics that was well in advance of that of the mother country.

Bond. Most federal officials, and especially those responsible for

---

[14] 1 Stat. 279, sec. 12 (May 8, 1792).

[15] 1 Stat. 336, sec. 5 (March 2, 1793); see also 1 Stat. 627, sec. 86 (March 2, 1799), for reaffirmation.

[16] 1 Stat. 378, sec. 14 (June 5, 1794).

[17] 1 Stat. 419, sec. 2 (Feb. 23, 1795).

[18] 1 Stat. 452, secs. 2, 3, 7 (April 18, 1796); similar prohibitions in 1 Stat. 743, sec. 11 (March 3, 1799).

money, were subject to bond in amounts specified by statute. The first example, in the collection act of 1789, set the pattern: "every collector, naval officer and surveyor, shall . . . give bond with one or more sufficient sureties, to be approved of by the comptroller of the treasury . . . conditioned for the true and faithful discharge of the duties of his office according to law." [19] The sums varied with the amount of business expected; Philadelphia ranked first with a bond of $60,000, New York followed with $50,000, and so on down to a bond of $1,000 for the surveyors in the smaller ports. The bonds were filed with the Comptroller and it was his responsibility to put them in suit upon breach of duty. The bond of $10,000 required of Mint officials needed sureties approved by the Secretary of the Treasury.[20] Deputy postmasters and contractors for carrying the mails, contractors to furnish public supplies, and others were likewise bonded.

Penalties. The sums represented by bonds were an assurance that fines and forfeitures incurred by officials for dereliction of duty would be collected—assuming the solvency of the surety. Furthermore Congress did not hesitate to impose fines, forfeitures, imprisonment, and occasionally public whipping or death for infraction of duty. The penalties that hung over the heads of importers and shipmasters in the navigation and collection acts were severe; they were paralleled by those directed against collectors and their subordinate customs officers. The harshest penalty (attending what must have been reckoned a major crime) was death to any postal agent who embezzled or destroyed a letter containing money or evidence thereof.[21]

Incentives. The foregoing statutory provisions were negative in character. They were penalties against failure to perform official duties according to the letter and spirit of the law. The ingenuity of Congress in predisposing officers to do their work well and faithfully was not exhausted by such means. Congress also provided rewards for energetic enforcement of the law, especially in the customs and revenue services.

Most field agents were paid on the basis of fees. This arrangement obviously engaged the interest of the official in exacting compliance of citizens—no business, no fees. But the principal incentive (on a large scale) arose from the right to share in the proceeds of seizures—of

---

[19] 1 Stat. 29, sec. 28 (July 31, 1789).
[20] 1 Stat. 246, sec. 5 (April 2, 1792).
[21] 1 Stat. 232, sec. 16 (Feb. 20, 1792).

vessels violating the navigation act, of forfeited imports whose owners tried to escape the payment of duties, of distilled spirits offered for sale without the certificate of the supervisor of revenue. Officials and informers were protected in case the Treasury remitted the penalties on an appeal; the court was authorized to require such payment to them as it deemed just. Congress thus tried to secure the faithful performance of duty both by discouraging officials from unlawful acts or omissions and by encouraging them to energy and care.

PREVENTION OF BRIBERY, FRAUD, EXTORTION, AND OPPRESSION

The offenses of bribery and accepting greater fees than allowed by law were widely recognized in the statutes and severely repressed. In the customs service, each official was required to post in a conspicuous place the table of fees and rates of duty; receiving or demanding a greater fee incurred a fine of $200 to the use of the injured party.[22]

The first collection act furthermore provided a heavy penalty for taking a bribe—a fine ranging from $200 to $2,000 and exclusion from office. Corresponding fines fell upon the giver of the bribe. The first act specifying federal crimes included bribery of a judge who, upon conviction, became subject to fine and imprisonment and to exclusion from office.[23] The act imposing a tax on distilled spirits punished the giver of a bribe, and also punished officers guilty of fraud or collusion, bribery not being specifically mentioned.[24] The Post Office Act of 1792 imposed penalties upon a deputy postmaster who fraudulently demanded or received any rate of postage or any gratuity or reward other than provided by law—a fine of $100 and disqualification for any office under the United States.[25] In short, the common law offense of bribery was buttressed at the danger points by specific statutory penalties of substantial magnitude.

Early in the Federalist period legislative notice was taken of the offense of extortion or oppression, in connection with the tax on dis-

---

[22] 1 Stat. 29, sec. 29 (July 31, 1789).
[23] 1 Stat. 112, sec. 21 (April 30, 1790).
[24] 1 Stat. 199, secs. 47, 49 (March 3, 1791).
[25] 1 Stat. 232, sec. 11 (Feb. 20, 1792); see also 1 Stat. 275, sec. 7 (clerks, marshals, and attorneys).

tilled spirits.[26] The same offense was again recognized in the tax on land in 1798. This tax, which required a valuation of all land and buildings, necessitated the appointment of thousands of local assessors and collectors and offered widespread opportunities for political or personal vengeance. The act consequently imposed upon the local collectors (one in each assessment district) liability to suit by any party injured by extortion or oppression and to damages not exceeding $300 and costs.[27]

Falsification of records was singled out in some instances for condemnation. Thus making a false record in the registration of a ship was penalized.[28] Falsifying court records whereby a judgment was reversed or voided was condemned with the exceptional penalty of a fine of not over $5,000 or imprisonment for not over seven years, and not over thirty-nine stripes.[29] A unique arrangement was invented in the second census act to ensure accurate returns from the marshals; the judges of the district courts were directed to "give this act in charge to the grand juries" and cause the returns to be laid before them for inspection.[30]

The ill reputation of the post office for failure to safeguard the secrecy of the mails and the necessity for protecting the mercantile interest in the carriage of money and securities combined to put upon postal employees heavy penalties for violating their duty. The postal act of 1792 imposed a fine of not over $300 or imprisonment for not over six months or both "according to the circumstances and aggravations of the offence" upon any employee of the General Post Office who unlawfully detained, delayed, or opened a letter or packet, or who secreted, embezzled, or destroyed any letter or packet not containing money or securities; but if the letter or packet contained money or securities, the penalty was death. A carrier who quit or deserted the mail before arriving at the next post office forfeited not over $500 for each offense. Any violation of the act concerning carriage of mail was subject to forfeiture of not over $50.[31] These provisions against

---

[26] 1 Stat. 199, sec. 39 (March 3, 1791).

[27] 1 Stat. 597, sec. 18 (July 14, 1798).

[28] 1 Stat. 55, sec. 34 (Sept. 1, 1789); 1 Stat. 287, sec. 26 (Dec. 31, 1792); 1 Stat. 305, sec. 29 (Feb. 18, 1793).

[29] 1 Stat. 112, sec. 15 (April 30, 1790).

[30] 2 Stat. 11, sec. 3 (Feb. 28, 1800).

[31] 1 Stat. 232, sec. 16 (Feb. 20, 1792).

tampering with the mail were repeated in subsequent legislation, but the death penalty against carriers for stealing money from the mail was reduced to forty stripes and imprisonment for not over ten years—a sufficient deterrent!

Officers of the Mint were subject to the penalty of death for wilful debasement of the coinage or for embezzling metals or coins.[32]

PREVENTION OF COLLUSION
TO EVADE THE LAW

The long history of collusion to evade payment of imperial customs and port dues during the colonial period forewarned the drafters of the collection and customs acts. The first collection act penalized customs officers for conniving at a false entry;[33] the first ship registration act, for conniving at a false register.[34] The law imposing a tax on distilled spirits was also emphatic in penalizing collusion to violate or evade the act or fraudulently concur in the delivery of spirits.[35]

PROTECTION OF OFFICERS IN THE
PERFORMANCE OF THEIR DUTY

Two sets of circumstances prompted Congress to provide protection to public officers in the execution of their duty—one, forcible resistance; the other, suit against them arising in course of duty.

The first collection act provided a fine of not over $400 for forcible resistance to a customs officer.[36] This offense was extended in the act for the punishment of crimes against the United States, which established a fine of not over $300 and imprisonment for not more than twelve months for wilful obstruction of any officer serving a writ or executing an order of a United States court, or for assaulting an officer serving a writ.[37] In the same act severe penalties were levied against persons rescuing prisoners convicted of treason, murder, or other capital crime (death penalty) or persons charged with these or other

---

[32] 1 Stat. 246, sec. 19 (April 2, 1792).
[33] 1 Stat. 29, sec. 35 (July 31, 1789).
[34] 1 Stat. 55, sec. 34 (Sept. 1, 1789).
[35] 1 Stat. 199, sec. 49 (March 3, 1791).
[36] 1 Stat. 29, sec. 27 (July 31, 1789).
[37] 1 Stat. 112, sec. 22 (April 30, 1790).

crimes.[38] The act putting a tax on distilled liquors included penalties for obstructing an officer or for forcibly rescuing any spirits subjected to seizure.[39] Despite the provisions of the first collection act, shipmasters apparently continued to give trouble, for an act of 1795 specifically told them to cease obstructing boarding officers or run the risk of fines ranging from $50 to $500.[40]

Energetic performance of duty was obviously conditioned upon protection to officials against suit instigated by persons whose interests had been wounded. The law sought to give such protection, but at the same time tried to guarantee citizens against arbitrary or illegal action by officials: a delicate balance of public and private interests.

The first example occurred in the collection act of 1789, providing that any officer or person sued or molested in the seizure of goods might "plead the general issue" and give the collection act in evidence as his authority. The act also discouraged ill-founded suits against officials by providing that if the plaintiff lost, the defendant official recovered double costs. In addition the burden of proof was put on the person claiming seized goods.[41] Where, moreover, judgment passed in favor of the claimants, the official was protected against paying costs and against liability to any action, judgment, or suit on account of the seizure if the court certified reasonable cause for his action.[42]

In the second instance, with reference to seizures under the act imposing a duty on distilled liquors, greater deference was paid to the citizen. In any prosecution against an officer arising out of a seizure, the revenue agent was required to show probable cause, upon which the verdict passed in his favor. But in any action alleging "irregular or improper" conduct by a revenue officer, the trial was by jury—a requirement certainly favoring the citizen distiller. Moreover, if the verdict in an action for seizure was rendered in favor of the officer, the jury could nevertheless assess damages against him for any "prejudice or waste" and for the loss caused by detention at the rate of six per cent on the value of the property. These damages were paid by the government, unless caused by negligence of the officer, in which case he became responsible to the United States.[43] This

---

38 *Ibid.*, sec. 23.
39 1 Stat. 199, sec. 48 (March 3, 1791).
40 1 Stat. 420, sec. 1 (Feb. 26, 1795).
41 1 Stat. 29, sec. 27 (July 31, 1789).
42 *Ibid.*, sec. 36.
43 1 Stat. 199, sec. 38 (March 3, 1791).

formula is distinctly different from that employed in customs seizures.

In a third enactment Congress undertook to protect all prosecuting officers against liability for costs in cases which went against them. They were relieved from liability if the court certified upon the record, at the trial in open court, that there was reasonable cause for commencing the action.[44] Congress was obviously experimenting to find a formula which would protect officials against vexatious suits having for their consequence a reluctance to enforce the law energetically but which would at the same time protect citizens against ill-tempered or rapacious officials. The experiment was left at this point.

[44] 1 Stat. 275, sec. 5 (May 8, 1792).

Chapter Thirty-four

ADMINISTRATIVE POWERS AND SANCTIONS

The law of officers is largely protective in nature. It gives no indication of the powers vested in officials, being devoted to the safeguards against abuses. The effectiveness of administration is secured, however, by the exercise of legal authority and is conditioned by the quality of such authority as surely as by the availability of administrative skills and the pattern of official relationships. Authority must be adequate to the end in view. Good administration, moreover, requires means of action wisely proportioned to the objective, and to the temper of those upon whom public power must operate.

Administrative powers in the present sense are those which bear upon persons outside the official organization. They are designed to gain compliance with law, not to order internal official relationships. In the 1790's they were the means by which importers were constrained to pay customs dues, manufacturers of snuff to pay the excise tax, masters of vessels to register and clear their ships, Indian traders to deal honestly with the red men, and owners of ferries to expedite the passage of stages carrying the mails.

Since such powers affect the private citizen, they have always been the subject of solicitude by representative bodies and courts. The opposition of the colonists to imperial officials and the great debates that led to armed resistance and independence had caused Americans to cherish personal freedom and liberty, and to look with suspicion upon official authority. Personal rights, not public power, were consequently the principal concern of legislative bodies and courts.

Power had nevertheless to be placed in executive hands, for it was impossible to rely entirely upon judicial action to implement the public interest. Especially was this the case in matters of revenue and in the control of shipping, closely allied with the collection of customs. Here large powers and wide discretion were bestowed upon officials, but so limited were federal activities that administrative authority over persons or property was otherwise exceptional. The Alien and Sedition Acts provided the principal case, and the difference in treatment of the rights of aliens under the former and the rights of citizens under the latter was instructive.

ADMINISTRATIVE POWERS IN THE COLLECTION OF THE CUSTOMS

One of the first cares of Congress was to provide a sorely needed revenue. A complex network of official powers and private obligations was created by the collection act of 1789.[1]

The first major problem of customs collection was to guarantee that imported goods would come under the control of the customs officers. The initial step taken by Congress was, therefore, to limit the number of places where goods might be imported; this was done by specifying ports of entry and prohibiting the introduction of goods from abroad at any other place.

The second major problem was to ensure payment of dues. Goods once unloaded fell under the jurisdiction of the collector who determined the amount of duties on imports and of tonnage dues on the ship. Removal of goods from the wharf or building for delivery to their owner also required a permit, conditioned on the immediate payment of duties or on furnishing a bond with sufficient sureties for payment of duties within a specified period. The permit was the basic form of administrative action, the essential center of control. It had the legal effect of removing a legislative prohibition, in this case allowing the landing and delivery of goods.

Other administrative powers were also vested by the collection act to enforce these procedures, especially the power to inspect. The collector was authorized to put on board a vessel seeking entry one or more inspectors, to prevent any unloading without a permit, and to keep a record of goods unladen.[2] In case of suspicion of concealment, the

---

[1] 1 Stat. 29 (July 31, 1789). Early American customs laws and administrative practice were based on English precedents. See George Louis Beer, *The Old Colonial System, 1660–1754* (2 vols., New York: Macmillan, 1912), especially ch. iv. For a technical analysis of customs authorities see Ernst Freund, *Administrative Powers over Persons and Property* (Chicago: University of Chicago Press, 1928), secs. 260–62, pp. 553–60.

[2] 1 Stat. 29, sec. 15.

inspector was authorized to enter a ship and search it; but to enter a house, store, or other place to search for concealed goods a warrant issued by a justice of the peace was required.[3]

These administrative powers were balanced by a long list of duties and prohibitions imposed upon shipmasters, importers, and others, the violation of which became the subject of fines, forfeitures, and other penalties. One group of these duties and prohibitions was designed to discourage smuggling.[4] Another was intended to promote honest declarations by shippers and importers. Penalties were invoked against fraudulent invoices and manifests, against describing goods incorrectly with intent to defraud the revenue, and against concealing goods. At various stages in the process of entry, oaths were required of shipmasters, importers, and others, and severe penalties for perjury were written into the law.

The collection act of 1799 was much more explicit than the first statute of 1789, but the pattern of administrative powers, private duties, and forms of recovery remained unchanged. To repeat, the basic administrative act was the granting of a permit to "unlade and deliver"; the impressive penalties, fines, and forfeitures were judicially administered on complaint of the collector, spurred on to his duties as complainant by promise of a share in the recoveries.

The act imposing a duty on distilled spirits created a corresponding pattern of administrative powers and private obligations. The central official authority was the issuance of a permit to remove spirits from the distillery; it was conditioned on payment of the duty. Elaborate obligations were put upon the owner of the still, for violation of which various penalties were established. The power to issue the permit to remove spirits was supplemented by the power to inspect the premises and records of production.[5]

ADMINISTRATIVE POWERS CONCERNED WITH THE REGISTRATION OF VESSELS

The registration, enrollment, and licensing of vessels was an important duty of the collectors of customs. The basic procedure was

---

[3] *Ibid.,* sec. 24.
[4] See below, ch. xxxvi.
[5] 1 Stat. 199 (March 3, 1791).

laid down in the act of 1789.[6] This legislation was founded on long British experience in the registration of vessels, and followed closely the parliamentary revision of 1786.[7] The broad purposes sought by the British registration laws were to encourage the home shipbuilding industry, to provide a training school for the British navy, to prevent smuggling and to protect the revenue, and to give aid to underwriters against fraud.[8] The language of the American registration act of 1789 shows clearly the influence of the British model.

The objectives of early American registration laws, apart from identifying vessels entitled to the protection of the United States, were principally to safeguard the customs dues and to restrict the coastwise trade to American vessels.[9] These objects were legally encompassed by the provisions of the registration laws themselves, without the support of discretionary acts by customs officials; the latter were, however, the functionaries through whom the formalities of registration took place and who had to be satisfied with the facts upon which registration occurred.

In terms of the law, registration of vessels was optional at the discretion of the owners. Only a registered ship, however, was deemed a vessel of the United States and entitled to the benefits of such ships. They were so substantial that registration took place as a matter of self-interest. They included (1) the customary basis for entry in a foreign port; (2) the protection of the United States upon the high seas or in foreign ports; (3) more immediately, a discount of ten per cent on the customs dues on all imports, and special rates on imports of tea;[10] and in the coastwise trade, privileges which by the act of 1793 became to all intents and purposes a monopoly. The registration act of 1789 was the first American example, in clear terms, of the pur-

---

[6] 1 Stat. 55 (Sept. 1, 1789), amended by 1 Stat. 287 (Dec. 31, 1792); 1 Stat. 305 (Feb. 18, 1793).

[7] 26 Geo. III, c. 60; for earlier acts see 7 & 8 Will. III, c. 22, and the famous Navigation Act of 1651.

[8] A valuable and illuminating contemporary account is available in John Reeves, *A History of the Law of Shipping and Navigation* (London, 1792). In appendices are found early forms of certificates of registry and of oaths required to establish British ownership.

[9] Unfortunately the debates on the act of 1789 were not reported; the bill was introduced by Gerry, and debated for three days in Committee of the Whole. There is only a brief and unimportant reference in the *Annals* to the debates in 1792. *Annals*, I, 670, 673 (July 1789); III, 724–25 (Nov. 22, 1792).

[10] 1 Stat. 24 (July 4, 1789).

chase of consent by the grant of benefits rather than by the weight of sanctions. There was no penalty for failure to register a vessel, apart from exclusion from the benefits granted to American vessels, although there were fines and forfeitures for fraud in securing or using the register.

Four different but analogous administrative procedures were established for the various categories of ships. Any vessel built within the United States and owned wholly by American citizens, of which the master was a citizen of the United States, was entitled to be *registered* (these were primarily engaged in the foreign trade); vessels built within the United States, owned wholly or in part by foreigners, were required to be *recorded;* vessels over 20 tons burden built within the United States and owned by American citizens, not registered, and destined for the coastwise trade or the bank and whale fisheries, were entitled to be *enrolled;* vessels over 5 tons and under 20 were required. to secure an annual *license,* exempting such vessels from clearance and entry. In addition, ships over 20 tons engaged in the coastwise trade or bank or whale fisheries were required to have an annual license, conditioned on payment of tonnage dues and subject to a bond of $1,000 against "any illicit trade or commerce"; lack of a license subjected the vessel to payment of the heavier tonnage dues required of foreign vessels.

Power to inspect ship's papers was first specifically granted in the act of 1793, which provided that an officer concerned in the collection of revenue could inspect the enrollment or license of any ship.[11] A broader inspection power in the same act authorized revenue officers to go on board a ship "and the same to inspect, search and examine";[12] the context implies that these powers related to the collection of customs dues rather than to verification of registers, enrollments, or licenses. Registers were required to be deposited with the collector upon entry, and were thus automatically subject to scrutiny.

The basic administrative powers established by the ship registration acts were, therefore, three: to register and enroll; to license; and to inspect. No power to cancel or revoke a license was expressly granted, although as a ministerial act the collectors were authorized to cancel a license when delivered up by the master in certain circumstances.

---

[11] 1 Stat. 305, sec. 13 (Feb. 18, 1793).
[12] *Ibid.,* sec. 27.

The penalties for violating the terms of a license were suit on a bond, or seizure and forfeiture after judicial action, not revocation by the collector.

ADMINISTRATIVE POWERS CONCERNED WITH THE CLEARANCE OF VESSELS

The objects sought by the clearance of vessels engaged in *foreign trade* were: to provide the necessary papers to permit a ship to enter a foreign port, especially the manifest; and to secure information concerning the character, amount, and destination of American exports. Clearance of vessels in the *coastwise trade* was designed to ensure the exclusion of foreign vessels, to suppress smuggling, to enforce the annual payment of the tonnage dues, and to help secure the payment of excise taxes on distilled liquors of domestic origin. The essential administrative act was the grant of a permit to proceed on a specified voyage, i.e., a clearance.

The registration and clearance act of 1789 authorized and directed the collector to grant a clearance for a *foreign* voyage subject to one condition: the master of the vessel must deliver to the collector a manifest and make an oath to the truth thereof. No further discretion to withhold a clearance lay in the collector. Departure for a foreign port without a clearance made the master liable to a fine of $200 for each offense.[13]

The grant of a permit to proceed on certain voyages in the *coastwise trade* was subject to the same type of condition. The master of a ship, possessing a license to engage in the coastwise trade, having on board goods of foreign growth or manufacture of the value of $200, or rum or other ardent spirits exceeding $400 in value, was required to deliver manifests of the whole cargo, to swear to the truth thereof, and also to swear that he had no reason to believe that the revenue had been defrauded in respect to his cargo.[14] Upon these formalities, it became the duty of the collector to grant a permit to proceed to the ship's destination. Coasting vessels not carrying the goods enumerated were not required to secure a permit.

In the coastwise trade as in the foreign trade, a permit to unload was necessary. The collector was directed to grant such permit upon

---

[13] 1 Stat. 55, sec. 24 (Sept. 1, 1789).
[14] *Ibid.,* sec. 25.

delivery of the manifest and the permit to depart from the place of loading (if required), and upon taking an oath by the master (if not required as a condition of clearance) as to the truth of the manifest.[15]

The general pattern of administrative control of the coastwise trade was thus the same as that imposed upon the foreign trade, although the formalities were somewhat less involved. It turned in both cases on the administrative act of granting clearances or permits to proceed on a voyage, and a permit to unload at its termination.

The coastwise shipping act of 1793 tightened up the provisions designed to prevent coasters from engaging surreptitiously in the foreign trade. The act of 1789 merely imposed a fine of $100 upon the master of a vessel licensed to trade or fish who failed to surrender his license when sailing to a foreign port.[16] By the act of 1793 the master of a vessel engaged in the fisheries intending to touch and trade at a foreign port was required to obtain a permit from the collector, and to deliver manifests and make entry as in the case of any other vessel arriving from a foreign port. Penalties for failure to secure a permit, however, were imposed only for possession of foreign goods of over $500 value.[17] The object was to protect the revenue, not to regulate the foreign sale of fish.

ADMINISTRATIVE POWERS ASSOCIATED WITH
THE ALIEN AND SEDITION ACTS

The naturalization act of 1798 required registration of all white aliens who continued to reside in the United States or who subsequently arrived in this country. Registration took place before either a collector or the clerk of a district court, who delivered a certificate of registration to the alien. Failure to register and possess a certificate made the alien liable to be summoned before any justice of peace to give surety for good behavior, or in default thereof to be committed to jail. The administrative phase of this type of alien control was purely ministerial, i.e., registration, and was shared with the clerk of the district court.[18]

The second act of 1798 concerning aliens offered more room for administrative action. This law empowered the President to order

---

[15] *Ibid.*, secs. 27–28.
[16] *Ibid.*, sec. 30.
[17] 1 Stat. 305, sec. 21.
[18] 1 Stat. 566 (June 18, 1798).

aliens dangerous to the peace and safety of the United States to depart, and to grant licenses to aliens permitting them to remain. The President was also authorized to revoke such a license at his discretion. He could furthermore order the deportation of any alien imprisoned under the act; and in case of voluntary return, he could order imprisonment for such term as in his opinion the public safety might require. These were extraordinary powers, especially the authority to commit to prison at executive discretion; they were, of course, applied only to aliens, and presumably only to those who were "dangerous to the peace and safety of the United States." [19]

The third act of 1798, effective in case of a declared war and after a presidential proclamation, subjected alien enemies to detention and deportation. The President was authorized to direct the conduct of the United States toward enemy aliens, the manner and degree of restraint, the cases where residence was permissible, and the procedure for removal; "and to establish any other regulations which shall be found necessary in the premises and for the public safety." [20] Even in the face of the great alarm over a threatening French invasion Congress wrote into this statute the requirement that full time should be allowed aliens for the disposal of their goods and their departure, according to treaty or "the dictates of humanity and national hospitality." As already noted, the marshals became the immediate agents of the President for the enforcement of his orders.

The Sedition Act, which was aimed against citizens, authorized no administrative enforcement procedures whatever. To the contrary, a jury was vested with the right to determine the law and the fact, and the defendant was allowed to plead the truth of the matter whose publication was charged as a libel. [21] The contrast between the Alien Acts and the Sedition Act is striking and well illustrates the settled determination of federal lawmakers to leave to courts the enforcement of penalties against the person of citizens.

LABOR CONTRACTS IN THE SHIPPING INDUSTRY

The regulation of contracts of employment was a subject matter which in general lay with the states and was destined to receive atten-

---

[19] 1 Stat. 570 (June 25, 1798).
[20] 1 Stat. 577 (July 6, 1798).
[21] 1 Stat. 596 (July 14, 1798).

tion from the federal government only much later in American history. The commerce power, however, gave the general government standing to regulate the wage contracts of seamen, and here is to be found the beginning of its intervention in the field of labor.

The act for the government and regulation of seamen in the merchant service depended entirely upon courts for implementation.[22] It was designed partly to protect seamen, partly to afford guarantees against desertion. A written contract between master and men was required before sailing, failing which the seamen became entitled to the highest rate of pay from the port of departure and the master fell subject to a forfeiture of $20 for each seaman. In case the vessel appeared to a majority of the crew and the first mate to be unseaworthy, the master was required to put in at the nearest port; the local justice was directed to secure the opinion of "three persons in the neighbourhood, the most skilful in maritime affairs that can be procured," and to order any necessary repairs or further equipment. Provision was made for the recovery of wages at the end of a voyage, either by action at common law or by recourse to admiralty procedures. Finally the act required every outward bound vessel to have on board a medicine chest, examined annually by an apothecary; and the amount of water and provisions was specified. In all this no federal official intervened.

On the other side of the ledger were the provisions against desertion. If a seaman refused to proceed on a voyage after inspection and approval of a ship alleged to be unseaworthy, he was clapped in jail "there to remain without bail or main prize" until he paid double the sum of his wage advances and costs. For harboring a deserter a penalty of $10 a day was established. For delay of more than forty-eight hours in returning to duty, a seaman forfeited all wages due him and all his goods and chattels on board ship; furthermore he became liable to the owners in a civil suit for damages caused by being obliged to hire other seamen. For desertion in any American port, the master could cause the errant mariner to be held in the common jail until the ship was ready to depart. None of these procedures required the aid of any administrative officers.

Corresponding provisions governing employment contracts in the cod fisheries were introduced in the act of 1792 granting bounties.

---

[22] 1 Stat. 131 (July 20, 1790).

Written agreements were required specifying how the bounty would be divided between owners and men; failure on the part of a seaman to perform "his proper duty" was penalized by loss of his share of the allowance and by civil responsibility for damages; and the seamen were given judicial protection to secure payment of their wages and shares.[23] No administrative agency was involved in the enforcement of these requirements.[24]

SANCTIONS

The preceding pages suggest that sanctions were principally judicial, not administrative in character. They were specified in each case by Congress, and duly weighed to ensure that citizens would perform their respective duties toward government. Sanctions tended to remain stable during the short period under review, although they were mitigated somewhat for the offense of robbing the mail, and conversely increased in some instances connected with the revenue and with securing protection for Indian lands against white encroachment. The penalties from among which Congress selected the appropriate sanction in particular cases included the deprivation of benefit or privilege; the loss of capacity to hold an office of trust or profit; fines and forfeitures; imprisonment, lashes, and death.

Loss of benefit or privilege occurred principally in case of refusal or revocation of license or permit, such as to trade with Indians, to register a vessel, or to clear a vessel for a voyage. The loss of the right to hold an office of trust or profit under the United States was imposed, for example, for unloading a vessel without a permit or except in

---

[23] 1 Stat. 229 (Feb. 16, 1792).

[24] There are many examples of the enforcement of statutory rights of persons through the courts alone. In some of these cases the courts still remain the principal, or exclusive, enforcement agency; in others complementary administrative action gradually emerged.

Patents. The first patent act authorized the Secretary of State, Secretary of War, and the Attorney General (or any two of them) to issue letters patent, with due provision for public notice and authentication (1 Stat. 109). The sole recourse of the patentee for infringement was to a court; the penalties were such as were assessed by a jury, and the forfeiture of things devised and sold. No public interest in the enforcement of patent rights was otherwise recognized.

Copyright. The first copyright act vested exclusive privileges in the author of a map, chart, or book upon recording the title with a clerk of any district court (1 Stat. 124). Infringement of a copyright became the basis of a private action for debt, but no other official was involved in any aspect of the grant or enforcement of copyright.

open day, and in this instance was directed against the master of the ship for a term not exceeding seven years.[25] The penalty was also, and more commonly, directed against officials for dereliction of duty, as for taking a bribe,[26] for entering into collusion to evade the tax on distilled spirits,[27] or for taking a false oath in connection with the tax on carriages.[28] It was not imposed for violating the various embargo and nonintercourse acts, or for unlawful negotiation with foreign powers.

The customary penalty was a fine. The statute book is full of examples, ranging from two dollars imposed upon an alien for failure to register (1798) to $10,000 for engaging in foreign privateering (1797). Some cases will suggest the variety of offenses and the amount of fine which Congress thought adequate to prevent their occurrence. *In the customs laws:* neglect to enter a ship, $500; forcible resistance to a customs officer, $400; giving a bribe to a customs officer, from $200 to $2,000; violating regulations governing coastwise traffic in arms, not over $1,000. *In the shipping laws:* alteration or forgery of a certificate of registry, $500; clearance without permission, $200. *In the excise tax laws:* failure to enter a distillery or a snuff mill, $500; counterfeiting certificates showing payment of tax, $500; failure of an auctioneer to keep books, $500; selling at an auction without a license, $400; the retail sale of liquor without a license, $50. *In the postal laws:* obstructing the mail, $100; carrying the mail by an unauthorized person, $200; wilful delay of the mail by a ferryman, $10 for each half hour; counterfeiting a frank, $100. Penalties for robbing the mails were more severe and are noted below. *In the laws regulating seamen:* failure of a master to execute a contract with seamen, $20 for each seaman; harboring a deserting seaman, $10 a day; failure to pay to the collector deductions from seamen's pay to provide hospital expenses, $100; failure of a seaman to perform his duties, loss of share in proceeds of the voyage and civil liability for damages. *In the Indian trade:* unauthorized purchase of a horse from an Indian, from $30 to $100.

Forfeiture is a term usually employed to denote the surrender of a particular thing, by way of a penalty for violating the law. There

---

[25] 1 Stat. 29, sec. 12.
[26] *Ibid.,* sec. 35.
[27] 1 Stat. 199, sec. 49.
[28] 1 Stat. 373, sec. 9.

were many examples of such penalties, but the use of the term was far from consistent. In some cases the law declared that a delinquent should forfeit a particular sum of money, using the term in the sense of a fine. Forfeiture in the strict sense of the term was a penalty chiefly confined to the revenue laws, where it was common. Thus for unloading imported goods without a permit or except in open day (in addition to a fine upon the master), the law imposed forfeiture of all goods unlawfully landed, and if their value exceeded $400, the forfeiture of the vessel with her tackle, apparel, and furniture;[29] for presenting an incorrect invoice with intent to defraud the revenue, forfeiture of the goods involved;[30] for failure to enter with the supervisor of revenue, forfeiture of a snuff mill and utensils, in addition to a fine;[31] for removing spirits from a distillery without a certificate, forfeiture of the spirits, containers, and means of removing them;[32] for violating the embargo on export of arms and ammunition, forfeiture of vessel and apparel.[33] The penalty of forfeiture was, or might be, a severe one, and a proportionately effective deterrent.

Threat of imprisonment was often combined with fines. A few examples will suggest the degree of confinement which Congress thought appropriate. For landing goods in the United States for which a drawback had been collected, not more than six months' imprisonment; for a false oath to the collector, the same; for unauthorized purchase of land from an Indian, not more than one year; for carrying on unauthorized negotiations with Indians, not over two years; for serving on a foreign slave trader, not over two years; for violation of the Sedition Act, from six months to five years; for accepting a commission or enlisting in a foreign armed force, not over three years.

Offenses thought deserving heavier punishment were met with the lash or with death. Both of these penalties were exceptional. The first Post Office Act provided the death penalty for robbing the mail.[34] The revision of 1799 ameliorated the punishment by fixing the penalty for the first offense at not over ten years' imprisonment or not over forty lashes, or both; but a second offense was met by a death sentence; and if life were put in jeopardy in any attempt to rob the mail, the

---

[29] 1 Stat. 29, sec. 12.
[30] Ibid., sec. 22.
[31] 1 Stat. 384, sec. 4.
[32] 1 Stat. 199, sec. 19.
[33] 1 Stat. 369.
[34] 1 Stat. 232, sec. 17 (Feb. 20, 1792).

death penalty was exacted. For taking mail from a post office or
securing mail by fraud, the sentence was not over two years' imprisonment or not over thirty lashes, or both.[35] The social stigma attached to
whipping was considerable, and we find President Adams directing
a remission of lashes in the case of one Scotchler. The only other offense
of the type under review which was punishable by death was the
murder of an Indian.[36]

Except for the withholding or revocation of a privilege none of these
sanctions were at the disposal of administrative officials, whether heads
of departments, collectors of customs, supervisors of revenue, postal
officials, or superintendents of Indian affairs. "All penalties . . . shall
be sued for and recovered . . . in any court proper to try the same,
by the collector of the district. . . ."[37] The collector (with the district
attorney) appeared in the role of prosecutor; the importer, shipmaster,
or owner, in the role of defendant; the penalties and forfeitures were
imposed by the judge. The proceeding gave the court opportunity
to decide upon the legality and correctness of official action.

One sanction, however, peculiar to sea-borne shipping, was purely
administrative in its application: the retention of the ship's register and
papers. The tonnage dues were required to be paid, or sureties given,
within ten days after entry and before clearance, to ensure which the
ship's register was required to be deposited with the collector, "and
there remain until such clearance." Since no ship could sail without
its papers, this requirement was extremely effective. By 1799 control
of the register had become a means of enforcing compliance with all
formalities of entry, payment of dues, making of sundry reports (as on
impressed seamen), delivery of mail, and other requirements imposed
upon shipmasters and shipowners. In its generalized form, the act of
1799 provided, "And the register, or other document in lieu thereof,
together with the clearance and other papers [granted by customs
officers at the place of departure] shall previous to such entry be produced to the collector . . . and shall remain in his office; and on the
clearance of such ship or vessel the register and other documents shall
be returned to the master. . . ."[38] This was a purely administrative
means of enforcement not requiring aid from any court.

---

[35] 1 Stat. 733, sec. 15 (March 2, 1799).
[36] 1 Stat. 469, sec. 6 (May 19, 1796).
[37] 1 Stat. 29, sec. 36 (July 31, 1789).
[38] 1 Stat. 627, sec. 63 (March 2, 1799).

A general view of these administrative powers suggests that where revenue was concerned the federal government was determined to give its agents sufficient authority to secure collection and to establish penalties for noncompliance adequate to impress a hesitant taxpayer. At the same time, the courts were recognized as the ready means of redress in case of error, excess of zeal, or abuse of power on the part of officials. The fate of the Republic rested upon the collection of revenue and the Federalists were not inclined to trifle with the issue. Success depended in large part upon energy and competence in the revenue system; Hamilton provided these. It also depended on adequate legal means of action; Congress put them in the hands of the revenue officers and the courts.

Chapter Thirty-five

ADMINISTRATIVE DISCRETION

Official acts may be either exactly prescribed or discretionary. Official authority is obviously enlarged by extension of discretionary power. The danger of encroachment on private rights also becomes greater. Among a people as devoted to liberty as were eighteenth century Americans, we would expect official discretion to be looked upon with concern and to be strictly limited. So far as subordinate officials were concerned, there is much evidence to show that they were intended to possess not more than a minimum, although in revenue this was substantial. The Chief Executive, however, stood in a different position; and the great officers of state, especially heads of departments, the Comptroller, and the collectors of customs had discretionary authority of considerable magnitude.

Hamilton clearly understood the nature of administrative discretion. In principle he opposed any discretionary powers in the subordinate tax officers. He favored a revenue system in which "the passions and prejudices of the revenue officers" would be confined to the narrowest limits.[1] He declared that "all revenue laws which are so constructed as to involve a lax and defective execution, are instruments of oppression to the most meritorious."[2] He praised the English system of taxation "because little or nothing is left to the discretion of the officers of the revenue."[3]

Hamilton knew that discretion had to be vested somewhere, since no statute could foresee all contingencies. He sought to place it high in the official ranks. In the customs service he drew into his own hands the power to make rulings on disputed points of general importance. In his Report on Public Lands he proposed that the land commissioners

---

[1] Hamilton, *Works* (Lodge ed.), IV, 162.

[2] *Ibid.*, II, 342.

[3] *Ibid.*, VIII, 34; L. K. Caldwell, *Administrative Theories of Hamilton and Jefferson*, p. 58.

make all the rules and regulations to "define and fix the most essential particulars . . . and where they leave any thing to discretion . . . indicate the general principles or policy intended by the Legislature to be observed: for a conformity to which the Commissioners will, of course, be responsible. They will, at the same time, leave room for accommodating to circumstances, which cannot, beforehand, be accurately appreciated, and for varying the course of proceeding, as experience shall suggest to be proper, and will avoid the danger of those obstructions and embarrassments in the execution, which would be to be apprehended from an endeavor at greater precision and more exact detail." [4] Hamilton thought discretion was safest when in the most responsible hands.

Congress agreed. It gave great discretionary powers to the President. It distrusted discretion in the hands of subordinates. In 1796 William Smith proposed a subsidy to every citizen owner of a ship so constructed as to be readily convertible into a vessel of war, the determination to be made by the collector of customs. Madison immediately objected "to the immense discretion proposed to be vested in customhouse officers; it would be a great discretion to be placed any where." [5] The plan was promptly withdrawn. In 1800 objection was successfully raised to giving surveyors of the revenue power to alter assessment rates in certain instances: "it gave too unlimited power to an individual." [6]

DISCRETIONARY POWERS OF THE PRESIDENT, THE HEADS OF DEPARTMENTS, AND THE COMPTROLLER

As the head of the state and holder of the executive power, the President performed many acts and made many decisions of high policy that were essentially discretionary. As commander in chief Washington disposed of the armed forces from time to time, and Adams directed the movements of naval vessels. The President received ambassadors, thus according recognition to a foreign state, and determined the course and direction of negotiations with them. In its

---

[4] *American State Papers: Public Lands,* I, 9.

[5] *Annals,* V, 889 (April 8, 1796).

[6] *Ibid.,* X, 701 (May 5, 1800). Cf. remarks of Fitzsimons: "He did not like to leave it to the discretion of collectors [of internal revenue], who, perhaps, never saw a carriage before, to put a value upon one." *Ibid.,* IV, 1276 (March 2, 1795).

legislation Congress vested the widest discretion in the Chief Executive, notably in such matters as calling out the militia, concluding transactions with respect to the public debt, raising additional regiments in the regular army, removing whites from Indian lands by force, fortifying ports, laying, raising, and making exceptions to an embargo, detaining vessels, seizing foreign vessels on the high seas, controlling the movements of aliens and, exceptionally, holding them in jail at his pleasure, and selling naval vessels or laying them up on land.

These are matters of policy in which Congress usually indicated the course of action which it thought should be followed but sometimes merely authorized the President to take such steps as he deemed expedient. In other cases the duties of the President were on a lower level of operations, but still discretionary. These may be illustrated by the determination of the number of revenue cutters—up to ten—the location of the arsenals, and the designation of boundary lines of some administrative districts. Only in rare instances did acts of the President affect personal or property rights immediately. The actual decision in these infrequent cases had already been made in the departments; his signature was usually formal.

The discretion of heads of departments, like that of the President, had to be considered from the double point of view of public policy and of private rights. In most matters of policy their discretion was subordinated to that of the President, except in so far as he delegated to them authority to act in his name. These delegations were frequent and were foreseen by the organic acts, which instructed the Secretaries of departments to follow the directions of the President.

The discretion granted the Comptroller in settling accounts was great. The organic Treasury act and later amendments contained no instructions as to the manner in which and the rules by which he performed his duty of seeing that no money was drawn from the Treasury except in pursuance of law. This duty compelled him to state for what purposes and according to what restrictions the law permitted money to be drawn, and to establish the forms of proof that money had been properly used. These were matters of the widest discretion, taking a quasi-judicial form.

DISCRETION IN SUBORDINATE OFFICIALS

Two major problems arose with respect to the discretion of subordinate officials, especially in the revenue service: to what extent should any discretion be permitted; and to what extent should it be directed and controlled by superior officers? Considerable discretion had to be put in the various revenue agents, especially with reference to valuations, security, sufficiency of proof, substantial compliance, intent to defraud, and "unavoidable violations." The tendency between 1789 and 1801 was to reduce the scope of their discretion, both by law and administrative action. One important trend was to give the Secretary of the Treasury an expanding authority to remit fines and forfeitures for violations of the revenue laws.

Valuation. Discretion in the valuation of goods and property for purposes of taxation was a ticklish problem. The people were tax conscious, had fought the War of Independence to be free of imperial taxation (among other reasons), in many quarters were suspicious of the new government, and in others were disposed to pay taxes to no government. Revenue had to be secured, nevertheless, but to the extent that inquisitorial methods and personal judgment could be avoided, political wisdom suggested strongly such a course of action.

Congress responded to these considerations by setting up a revenue system which for some years avoided the necessity of discretionary valuation of property. It withdrew immediately the element of discretion involved in ad valorem duties by directing (in the collection act of 1789) that they should be estimated by adding twenty per cent to the actual cost of imports from the Cape of Good Hope or beyond, and ten per cent otherwise. Discretion was thus replaced by the bill of sale.[7]

The act imposing the duty on spirits distilled in the United States conformed closely to Hamilton's ideal.[8] The operation of the act was almost automatic. The rate of duty upon spirits was fixed in the law; no valuation was required of revenue officers. No spirits could be withdrawn from the distillery except upon payment of or security for the duties; the function of the revenue officer was to grant a certificate upon payment—a purely ministerial act.

Discretionary authority of local revenue officials in four other cases was also wholly avoided. The tax on licenses to sell spirits and wines vested no discretion in the supervisors of revenue; the license "shall be granted to any person, who shall desire the same," who applied in

---

[7] 1 Stat. 29, sec. 17 (July 31, 1789).
[8] 1 Stat. 199 (March 3, 1791).

writing and paid the tax.[9] The tax on property sold by auctioneers involved the grant of a license by the supervisors of revenue; it, too, was purely ministerial: "the several supervisors . . . upon request of any person . . . shall grant licenses, without fee or reward." [10] The tax on snuff and sugar was set at eight and two cents per pound; the manufacturers were required to report the amount of production; and the revenue officers were merely agents to receive payments due.[11] The sale of stamped paper in connection with the stamp tax also involved no official discretion.[12]

The duty on carriages proved administratively troublesome, and the first enactment, vesting substantially no discretion, had to be worked over a couple of years later to recognize a substantial degree of administrative leeway.[13] How to differentiate chariots, coaches, four-wheeled carriages "having framed posts and tops, and hanging on steel springs," curricles, chaises, and chairs baffled the members of Congress; they did what they could but added that in cases of doubt any carriage should be deemed to belong to that class to which it bore the greatest resemblance. Here was a classification problem analogous to that of the customs officers.[14]

The tax on land, dwellings, and slaves (1798) also involved a wide area of official discretion. It required a valuation of property (excluding slaves) for which Congress formulated some general rules that left the assessment largely to the judgment of the local assessors—but subject to an administrative review. Thus every dwelling house "shall be valued" at the rate it was "worth in money with a due regard to situation." Lands and town lots were valued "in a due relation to other lands and lots, and with reference to all advantages, either of soil or situation." [15] These statutory rules hardly diminished official judgment.

Security. Although discretion in valuation was avoided so far as

[9] 1 Stat. 376, sec. 3 (June 5, 1794).

[10] 1 Stat. 397, sec. 4 (June 9, 1794).

[11] 1 Stat. 384 (June 5, 1794).

[12] 1 Stat. 527 (July 6, 1797).

[13] 1 Stat. 373 (June 5, 1794); 1 Stat. 478 (May 28, 1796). The New Jersey collector applied the tax to wagons of farmers going to market. *Annals,* IV, 1204 (Feb. 6, 1795).

[14] 1 Stat. 478, secs. 1–2. The tax on carriages gave rise to the leading case of *Hylton* vs. *United States* argued by Alexander Hamilton for the government. On the issue whether the tax was direct and thus required to be apportioned according to population, the court took Hamilton's view in the negative. 3 Dallas 171 (1796).

[15] 1 Stat. 580, sec. 8 (July 9, 1798).

possible, discretion at other points of the process of collecting the revenue was inevitable. In both customs and excise the judgment of local officials was relied upon to ensure the sufficiency of bonds. The collection act of 1799 indicated the standard provisions. An importer was allowed to postpone payment of duties for specified periods and to remove his goods for sale by giving bond for payment of amounts due. In this and other contingencies, the law required the bond to have "one or more sureties, to the satisfaction of the collector." [16] The excise act of 1791 provided analogously that payment of the duties on distilled spirits could be postponed by filing bond "with one or more sureties, to the satisfaction of the chief officer of inspection." [17] These were discretionary powers.

Sufficiency of proof. Provision for payment of drawbacks due merchants on imports subsequently exported of necessity included proof of exportation. The collection act of 1799 vested discretion in the collector as to the adequacy of proof where the normal evidence was not available and where the amount involved was less than $200, pursuant to rules prescribed by the Comptroller; in other cases, the discretion was put in the hands of the Comptroller.[18]

Substantial compliance. The collection act of 1799 made formal recognition of wide discretion as to imposition of fines or forfeitures in case of substantial compliance: "in cases where the forms of official documents . . . shall be substantially complied with and observed, according to the true spirit, meaning and intent thereof, no penalty or forfeiture shall be incurred by a deviation therefrom. . . ." [19] This injunction was not specifically directed to any officer, but was a guide to the collectors, the Comptroller, the Secretary of the Treasury, and the courts. The collection act of 1790 had already recognized the principle, by authorizing omission of a forfeiture of $500 caused by variation between the cargo and manifest if occasioned "by accident or mistake." [20]

Intent to defraud. At a number of points collectors were required to determine intent to defraud, an elusive element of conduct, the judg-

[16] 1 Stat. 627, sec. 62 and *passim* (March 2, 1799).
[17] 1 Stat. 199, sec. 17.
[18] 1 Stat. 627, sec. 81.
[19] *Ibid.,* sec. 111.
[20] 1 Stat. 145, sec. 34 (Aug. 4, 1790).

THE FEDERALISTS

ment of which is essentially discretionary in nature. Thus shipmasters whose manifests were irregular or missing were subject to a heavy fine unless the customs officers or the court were satisfied that the manifest had been lost "without fraud or collusion" or had been defaced by accident or was incorrect by mistake.[21] Forfeiture of goods, the nature of which failed to agree with the entry, was the rule unless the collector, or the court in which the prosecution took place, were satisfied that the variation did not arise from "an intention to defraud the revenue." [22]

Unavoidable violations. The shipping law recognized the unpredictable element of storm and distress and authorized customs officers to use discretion in such cases. Thus if a master could prove "unavoidable accident, necessity or distress of weather," he was released from the penalties attached to unloading a cargo before entry.[23] Departure of a vessel without having made an entry was excused if the collector were satisfied that it was caused by "distress of weather, pursuit or duress of enemies, or other necessity"—the last certainly a very elastic phrase.[24]

Each of the foregoing situations, excepting claims for drawbacks of value of over $200, resulted in the lodgment of wide discretion in the hands of local revenue agents. The facts on which a determination was to be made were such that the findings could best be reached on the spot, if indeed they could have been made at all elsewhere, in the first instance.

Hamilton did not pretend to review individual decisions of collectors in these discretionary determinations. He guided collectors by instructions and by rules, and responded to collectors' requests for advice in particular cases. Their determinations were, therefore, channeled by central direction but they were not foreclosed. The exercise of discretion was by law and in fact placed in their hands.

With respect to the other principal field agents, the range of discretion was closely governed by the nature of their duties. The powers of

---

[21] *Ibid.,* sec. 10.

[22] *Ibid.,* sec. 47; same provision in 1 Stat. 627, sec. 84.

[23] 1 Stat. 145, secs. 13, 14.

[24] *Ibid.,* sec. 15; see also *ibid.,* sec. 20. Other examples of discretionary decisions by collectors included determination of "necessary costs and charges" in suits for recovery of penalties (1 Stat. 29, sec. 36); the public character of a foreign vessel (1 Stat. 145, sec. 17); excessive sea stores (*ibid.,* sec. 22); refuge in harbor by distress of weather or necessity (*ibid.,* sec. 38).

the attorneys of the United States were barely mentioned in the statutes and were chiefly drawn from English precedents. They were highly discretionary; even when Timothy Pickering asked the attorney for Pennsylvania to commence a prosecution under the Sedition Act, he added, "if you think an offense has been committed." The marshals, on the other hand, were ministerial officers. They were required "to execute . . . all lawful precepts" directed to them. These precepts dealt normally with a particular person or persons and required a specific action to be performed at the direction of a court.

The authority of the Indian superintendents to license Indian traders was a delicate one, far different in its bearings from the authority to license auctioneers. The purpose of the Indian license was to bar untrustworthy traders; the law consequently directed the superintendents to issue licenses "to any proper person." [25] No criteria of judgment were laid down in the statute, but qualifications of character were clearly implied. The superintendent, moreover, was given full power to "recall" all licenses for violation of any of the regulations governing trade and intercourse with the Indians. Congress clearly intended to vest wide discretion in the licensing of Indian traders, in the hope of stabilizing relations with the Indian tribes.

ADMINISTRATIVE REVIEW

Congress was not willing, however, to permit officials finality of judgment. No penalty, fine, or forfeiture was collectible except by judgment of a court. Judicial review was therefore an ultimate protection against error, bad judgment, partiality, or venality of the customs officers.

A more immediate remedy in certain cases was provided by laws establishing a higher administrative review. An aggrieved owner of a carriage who asserted an incorrect classification of his pleasure vehicle by the internal revenue agent was entitled to an appeal to the supervisor of revenue and a subsequent appeal to the Secretary of the Treasury, as well as a statutory right to sue for recovery of the allegedly erroneous tax.[26] An analogous double administrative appeal was established in connection with the tax on land and dwellings, where wide variation in standards was probable. The owner was entitled to appeal

---

[25] 1 Stat. 137 (July 22, 1790).
[26] 1 Stat. 478, sec. 9 (May 28, 1796).

from the assessor to the principal assessor and then to the board of
land tax commissioners in each state. There was no further appeal to
the Treasury.[27]

Remission of fines and forfeitures. While Congress intended revenue
officials to be firm, it did not intend to penalize shipowners and merchants for inadvertent errors committed with no intent to defraud the
revenue. To meet such cases by introducing an element of elasticity into
the enforcement of the law, a procedure for the administrative remission of fines and forfeitures was devised which well illustrates
Federalist views on the problem of discretion.

In January 1790 the petition of Christopher Saddler for relief from
a forfeiture came to the House and was referred to Hamilton. He
took the occasion to recommend a general procedure for the mitigation
or remission of fines and forfeitures which would place the final decision in the Secretary of the Treasury. Noting other cases in which forfeitures had been incurred, manifestly through inadvertence and want
of information, he told Congress that there was a necessity, in conformity with the usual policy of commercial nations, of vesting somewhere a discretionary power of granting relief—"a power," he added,
"of too much delicacy and importance to be determined otherwise
than upon mature deliberation."[28]

In response to this request, Congress passed an act combining executive remission with a preliminary summary judicial hearing. A person
liable to a fine, penalty, or forfeiture, or interested in a vessel or goods
subject to seizure and forfeiture was allowed to petition the judge of
the district court in which the penalty accrued for mitigation or remission. The judge held a summary hearing, with notice to parties, and
prepared a statement of facts for transmission, with the petition, to the
Secretary of the Treasury. The Secretary "shall thereupon have power
to mitigate or remit such fine, penalty or forfeiture, or any part thereof,
if in his opinion the same was incurred without wilful negligence or
any intention of fraud." He could also direct the discontinuance of
prosecution, "upon such terms or conditions as he may deem reasonable and just."[29] The power to remit was granted only until the

[27] 1 Stat. 580, secs. 19–22 (July 9, 1798).

[28] *American State Papers: Finance,* I, 37; also in *Annals,* I, 1066–67 (Jan. 19, 1790).

[29] 1 Stat. 122 (May 26, 1790). The Senate was unwilling to put this discretion in the
hands of one person, and tried, without success, to set up a board comprising the Secretaries of Treasury and State and the Attorney General. *Annals,* II, 1474 (March 24,
1790).

expiration of the next Congress, but was regularly renewed, was extended to the excise taxes, and in 1797 was amended to include remission of "disabilities." [30] In 1800 the House declined to extend the practice to the remission of forfeitures under laws prohibiting the export of arms or ammunition. A committee declared, "It must pertain [to the President] to judge of the extent of the mischiefs flowing from the violations of such political measures and regulations." [31]

Hamilton kept in his own hands the duty of acting upon petitions for remission of fines and forfeitures. Unfortunately we have found it impossible to reconstruct the record of his decisions [32] and the policy that he developed. When about to leave Philadelphia in 1794 to accompany the militia to western Pennsylvania, he delegated his authority as Secretary of the Treasury to the Comptroller, Oliver Wolcott, but asked Wolcott to refrain, if possible, from dealing with remission cases.

Being about to leave the seat of government for a few weeks, to accompany the army in its march against the western insurgents of Pennsylvania, I commit to you during my absence the management of those matters which are reserved to my superintendence, under the constitution and regulations of the department, especially the receipts and expenditures of money, and I rely upon your diligence and zeal that nothing will suffer during my absence. With regard to remissions and mitigations of penalties and forfeitures, it will be best to avoid acting in any case in which particular inconvenience will not arise from delay, as there is not time to explain the principles which have governed in the past, and the course of policy may, without such explanation, be innovated upon so as to occasion something like inconsistency. But in urgent cases you will act, consulting the most recent precedents in similar cases. To preserve the usual forms, I have signed and left in my office a large number of blank warrants of the different kinds which issue. . . . [33]

From this letter it is safe to deduce that Hamilton, in these discretion-

---

[30] Occasional appeals for relief found their way into Congress after this legislation was in force, but they were usually rejected. Thus a motion to refer to a committee the petitions of two Philadelphians for having sold a small quantity of wines and spirits without a license was denied "by a great majority." *Annals,* VI, 1788–89 (Jan. 4, 1797). Cf. *ibid.,* IV, 673 (May 10, 1794), where a favorable resolution was reported.

[31] *Annals,* X, 643, 1322–23 (March 25, 1800).

[32] They have not been brought into a single file in the Treasury archives and probably many if not most have been destroyed. Two or three have been noted in early Treasury papers but they are insufficient to draw any conclusions.

[33] Hamilton to Wolcott, Sept. 29, 1794, Hamilton, *Works* (Lodge ed.), X, 76.

ary determinations, had a policy, that it was based on principle, and that it was applied consistently. Principle and practice were not, however, committed to writing.

Wolcott's letters while Secretary of the Treasury give a few clues. To Collector William Lindsay he wrote, "The Collectors are to execute strictly; & the power of mitigation is to be exercised only upon a statement of facts found by the District Judge." [34] To the collector at Perth Amboy he sent a strong admonition:

the business of your Office has been conducted in a Manner highly objectionable & calculated to render the Laws burdensome & odious to the people. . . . You ought to remember that the object of the Government is to secure a strict and correct observance of the Laws, not to exact Penalties from the People. . . .

I have to request that hereafter . . . care may be taken by a steady course of conduct to prevent the necessity of instituting a great number of prosecutions at one time; that when as will sometimes happen with the best disposed men, penalties are accidentally incurred the Comptroller of the Treasy may be consulted or the applications of the parties to the District Judge may be facilitated, & generally that the execution of the Laws be rendered as little burdensome to individuals as possible.[35]

Joseph Agnew was convicted of smuggling coffee, and petitioned for remission of penalties. Wolcott wrote Washington, "It however appears to the Secy that the petitioner, was not the principal actor in the said violation of Law, & that he is a poor man & utterly unable to pay the penalty imposed, & that an aged mother depends upon his assistance for support & moreover that his testimony may be necessary to the conviction of the principal offender." Since Agnew clearly was guilty of intent to defraud he was not eligible for remission of penalty, but Wolcott suggested instead a pardon.[36]

It was not until 1797 that discussion of these important powers arose in Congress. The proposal to extend the remission to "disabilities" touched off a debate and resulted in a roll call.[37] Edward Livingston claimed that the power to mitigate or remit penalties was legislative in nature and could not be delegated, and declared the power was too

---

[34] Wolcott Papers, XLIII, Jan. 5, 1796.
[35] Ibid., XLIII, Feb. 5, 1799.
[36] Ibid., XLII, 4, Dec. 22, 1796.
[37] Annals, VI, 2284 ff.

extensive to be placed in the hands of any one man—"What an influence it gave him!" Ames analyzed the situation with his customary ability, pointing out that the House must either make the revenue laws "loosely, and give considerable discretion to the officers in the execution of them, or make the rules so strict as to be in some degree rigid. If this latter plan were adopted, it would be necessary for them to provide some relaxation in cases which might bear hard upon individuals. He thought the latter the best mode." [38] He agreed that "this was a delicate power," but argued it was better placed in executive than in legislative hands. The vote to continue and extend the power was carried 50 to 34; on one side were such good Federalists as Ames, Dana, Harper, and Murray and on the other such staunch Republicans as Blount, Claiborne, Gallatin, Andrew Jackson, Livingston, and Nicholas.[39]

Congress thus recognized that government could not proceed in its day-by-day business without some margin of official discretion in the application of the laws. Although the Federalists intended to establish a government of law, they insisted also upon admitting the judgment of men.

---

[38] *Ibid.,* VI, 2286.

[39] *Ibid.,* VI, 2292. The revised act is 1 Stat. 506 (March 3, 1797). In a somewhat related instance no discretion was allowed the executive branch, i.e., the repayment of duties to an importer in certain exceptional cases. A common example was a claim for repayment of duties on goods destroyed by fire after release from customs but before sale. Such claims were often presented to the House. Its policy was stated in 1797 in these terms: "the House had of late years rejected all such applications, not only as inequitable, but on the ground of its being impossible to guard against imposition." *Annals,* VII, 671 (Dec. 4, 1797). The records of a number of such cases are found in *American State Papers: Finance,* I, *passim.* See also Hamilton's memorandum on remission of duties, April 20, 1792, Hamilton, *Works* (Hamilton ed.), III, 337–38.

Chapter Thirty-six

THE PROBLEM OF SMUGGLING

The powers and duties vested in customs officers had to be sufficient to wage successful war on an active and enterprising population of smugglers. Smuggling was a custom well established during the colonial period; as Fisher Ames declared in 1789, "The habit of smuggling pervades our country. We were taught it when it was considered rather as meritorious than criminal. . . ." [1]

Many tricks and stratagems had been perfected to outwit the King's customs officers. Goods from abroad were unloaded on near-by islands and then brought ashore in small boats at night while inspectors slept. False statements of quantity of goods imported were made, or their nature, grade, and quality falsified—brandy became rum and the grade of tea was low. There was collusion between customs officers and shipowners, by which goods on ships were seized, condemned, and sold at a nominal figure less than the duties. Sailors smuggled in small quantities unknown to the master of the ship.

Sometimes there was even resort to force. The sloop *Liberty,* belonging to the distinguished patriot, John Hancock, arrived in Boston harbor in May 1768 with a cargo of Madeira wines. "The tide-waiter, who was put on board, refusing to retire to the cabin, as had been usual heretofore, was seized by force and confined there, while the greatest part of the cargo was unladen in the night, and put into stores; and the next day the sloop was entered at the custom house, with a few pipes of wine only. These facts were not disclosed until about the 10th of June following, when the sloop was seized, for a false entry. The vessel was soon after, taken and removed from the wharf, by armed boats, and placed under the protection of the guns of the

---

[1] *Annals,* I, 299 (May 9, 1789).

Romney, a ship of war, then in the harbor. This novel mode of procedure, excited the indignation of the people of Boston, who collected on this occasion, and not only attempted to prevent the removal of the vessel, but proceeded to acts of personal violence and outrage against some of the custom house officers. Their houses were, also, attacked and injured; and the boat of the collector was seized, carried to the commons and burnt." [2]

The state customs laws during the Confederation had not been well enforced, the colonial tradition carrying on during a period of commercial rivalry. The new federal collector at Penobscot wrote Hamilton at the close of 1789, "Under the State government by far the greatest part of these Vessels [i.e., coasting ships] found means to avoid the regulation then prescribed. . . . Coasters have so long trampled upon the Revenue Laws of this State with impunity that they now think they are bound by no Laws. . . ." [3]

Discussion of the first tariff act in the House brought forth apprehensive remarks about smuggling and the forbidding problem of guarding the coasts. Elias Boudinot almost gave up hope. "When I recollect," he said, "the numerous volumes of laws made to secure and regulate this point, the inefficacy of them all, though accompanied with the most terrible denunciations and penalties, and the careful observing eye of long experienced officers—I say, when I recollect all this, and consider it may be necessary for the United States to adopt a similar plan, I own that I almost shrink from the task as an extraordinary work, requiring the most superior abilities." [4]

The task was certainly formidable. The Americans lived on a seaboard abounding in harbors, rivers, inlets, and in some sections great numbers of off-lying islands that made an ideal refuge for smugglers. "The State of Massachusetts," said Ames, "has a prodigious extent of seacoast, of near one thousand miles in length, indented with innumerable bays and rivers, forming the finest, most accessible, and securest harbors in the world. It must be impossible to guard them all . . . add to this, that there are two thousand sail of vessels, large and small, coming in and going out constantly." [5]

[2] Timothy Pitkin, *A Political and Civil History of the United States of America, from . . . 1763 to . . . March, 1797* (2 vols., New Haven: H. Howe and Durrie and Peck, 1828), I, 228.

[3] Wolcott Papers, XXV, 1.

[4] *Annals,* I, 118 (April 11, 1789).

[5] *Ibid.,* I, 299 (May 9, 1789).

At the outset the revenue officers had nothing more than small open boats with which to inspect and guard their ports; ten revenue cutters were quickly authorized but naval vessels were lacking to supplement their necessarily restricted patrols. The West Indies, long a haven for smugglers and pirates and a center of trade, lay at an easy distance.

These circumstances weighed heavily on tariff legislation. Thomas T. Tucker declared in 1789, "if we lay high duties on the importation of goods, a system of smuggling will be adopted before we can possibly make the necessary provision to prevent it. . . . the higher the duty, the greater the advantage the smuggler has over the fair trader."[6] Nearly ten years later the advocates of a low tariff were repeating the same argument. ". . . the moment the duties were so high as to offer a sufficient temptation, smuggling would be entered into, upon trade calculations, with respect to the advantages to be derived from it."[7]

The due collection of the revenue and the suppression of smuggling were promoted by several factors. Prominent among them was Hamilton's administrative capacity. The attitude of the merchants was also very important; they were the friends of the new government and were willing to support it by paying the customs dues. The Philadelphia merchants entered a compact to this end by forming an association to prevent smuggling.

We the subscribers, Merchants and Traders of the city of Philadelphia, do hereby pledge ourselves to each other, and to our fellow citizens at large, that we will not be concerned directly or indirectly in any trade contrary to the revenue laws of the United States; but will, by every effort in our power, discourage such illicit practices, by not employing, or by dismissing from our service, any Master or Mate of a vessel, or any Pilot, who shall be engaged in a contraband trade, or in aiding or abeting others in such collusive employments.[8]

The *Gazette of the United States* declared that under a free government "every good and honest man will think it HONORABLE and PRAISEWORTHY" to detect frauds and impositions.[9]

The attitude of the courts was also beyond criticism. The judges supported the customs officers in cases that came before them. The

[6] *Ibid.*, I, 291, 292 (May 8, 1789).
[7] Samuel Smith, *ibid.*, VI, 2265 (Feb. 23, 1797).
[8] *Gazette of the United States,* Sept. 19, 1789.
[9] *Ibid.*, Oct. 7, 1789.

Supreme Court declared in 1800, "Public policy, national purposes, and the regular operations of government, require, that the revenue system should be faithfully observed, and strictly executed." [10]

The administration of the collection act, as noted in the previous chapters, was both vigorous and exact. The effect was not lost upon the public. "Smugglers, too, soon came to realize the energetic character of the new administration. Accustomed to ply their trade almost with impunity, they now found that infractions of the law were followed by vigorous prosecution. Before the first month of the new regime had gone by several of these offenders were caught and heavily fined." [11]

Successful administration was handicapped by the force of tradition and the hope of gain. A leading merchant of Savannah wrote, "foreigners will embrace every opening, and too many of our own citizen's may be found too prone to assist them in their attempts, and not a few of them also may be as willing to take advantages of that kind. . . ." [12] No general estimate of the frequency of evasion of the customs officers can be made, but examples from two ports of entry, Portsmouth, New Hampshire, and Philadelphia, give some clues.

From Portsmouth was reported a small seizure in 1791—one barrel, one half barrel, and three small bags of coffee were abandoned by persons in a small boat upon the approach of an inspector. [13] In 1793 the sailors of the brigantine *Rising Sun* were caught smuggling cocoa and coffee: "in the night following [its arrival] an Officer of the Cutter Scammell laying not far from the Brig, discovered people on board the latter, who appeared with silence to be delivering goods over the side of the Vessel into a boat, on the approach of the Officer, the Boat put off with the people in her. . . ." [14] The letters of the collector disclosed only a few such petty cases.

The records of the district court of Pennsylvania reveal a somewhat larger number of seizures than in Portsmouth and a few instances involving considerable amounts and values. The first case that came to

---

[10] *Priestman* vs. *United States,* 4 Dallas 28, at 33.

[11] Frank Fletcher Stephens, *The Transitional Period, 1788–1789, in the Government of the United States* (Columbia, Mo.: E. W. Stephens, 1909), p. 97.

[12] "Letters of Joseph Clay, Merchant of Savannah, 1776–1793," *Collections of the Georgia Historical Society,* VIII (1913), 215.

[13] Letters from the Collector, Portsmouth, N. H., Feb. 9, 1791.

[14] *Ibid.,* April 13, 1793.

the attention of the court occurred in July 1793, *United States* vs. *Twelve Bags of Coffee*. One or two cases of presumed smuggling were brought before Judge Peters each year. A seizure in 1795 included 121 cases of wine, 4 bags of coffee, and 1 hogshead of rum. These were the usual commodities sought to be introduced, with an occasional piece of silk. Later in the decade, watches were smuggled. In 1797 appeared on the court docket the case of *United States* vs. *354 silver watches, 30 gold watches, and 500 watch keys*. They were sold by order of the court and the proceeds, $4,670.66, turned over to Sharp Delany, the collector, to be distributed—one half to the United States and one half to the customs officers.[15]

A Boston merchant wrote Nicholas Gilman in 1798:

At Gloucester last Summer *Smuggling* was several times the subject of conversation among men of business; each in good humour accusing others of smuggling, and it seemed generally agreed that the Salem merchants beat them and did more than their share.

By their conversation I understood that they defrauded the Revenue in this way . . . in the night or at a busy time they put on board of the Coaster that part of the Cargo which is not entered. . . . From their conversation I have no doubt that many goods are smuggled in this way. . . .

In all the small Towns I suspect there is more smuggling than in the larger—The Officers of Government are the friends and acquaintances of the Merchants & are not so critical as in the populous Citys.[16]

Contemporary testimony suggests that the amount of smuggling was relatively small. In 1791 Samuel Livermore said in the House of Representatives, "It is acknowledged . . . on all hands, that the patriotism and punctuality of the importers has been such as to produce a very strict compliance with the revenue laws." [17] In his second annual message to Congress, Washington told the country that the productive revenue of 1790 "bears an honorable testimony to the patriotism and integrity of the mercantile and marine part of our citizens." [18]

The contrast between substantial compliance within shipping and mercantile circles and the open defiance of the whiskey distillers of

---

[15] These references are to the original manuscript Minute Book, U. S. Federal Court, Pennsylvania District, in the office of the present Clerk of Court, Philadelphia.

[16] Wolcott Papers, X, 32.

[17] *Annals,* II, 1875 (Jan. 20, 1791).

[18] Richardson, *Messages,* I, 81 (Dec. 8, 1790).

Pennsylvania to the excise tax is marked. "It must ever be very prejudicial," wrote Collector John Lee to Hamilton, "for Government to Enact Laws and not have them carried into effect . . ."[19] This prejudice the Federalists avoided in customs and overcame in excise.

---

[19] Wolcott Papers, XXV, 1.

Chapter Thirty-seven

THE STATE OF THE ADMINISTRATIVE ART

A CERTAIN level of administrative capacity is characteristic of each generation. It is the product of community experience and fixes the dimensions of community operations. It is affected by the extent of technical development, the degree of personal and social discipline, the quality of leadership, and the possession of management skills. One generation is able to organize only simple forms of business partnership, another can create a complex fiscal-managerial-technical corporation capable of combining a hundred thousand persons into a single coordinated structure. Carrying the mails quickly and intact over two thousand miles of post road strained the managerial abilities of one generation; later the task, multiplied a hundredfold, became routine. The difference lies in the technical proficiency and administrative capacity of the same community at successive periods of its evolution.

The stage in the development of administrative and technical skills reached by the American people in the years 1790–1800 was still relatively rudimentary. The business of local government and of private enterprise with which they were familiar was simple in character. The level of administrative competence the world over was not high and had reached its greatest perfection at the hands of one of the most notable absolute monarchs, Frederick the Great. The capacity of the Americans to forge a nation was untested and problematical; their attention had been focused on liberty and rights, not on organization and discipline. That so much was done so rapidly was more than could have been anticipated when the members of the Federal Convention set their signatures to the new Constitution in Philadelphia.

The great issue of the time was liberty—political, economic, and personal. "The revolutionists had unlimited time to talk vaguely on abstract matters of freedom, representation and government; they delighted to get together and discuss their wrongs and rights; but their knowledge of good administrative methods was slight, while their interest in governmental efficiency was not apparent. All their ideas were colored with extravagant notions of individual liberty." [1] Some years after the Constitution had been adopted, an English traveler, Isaac Weld, observed: "The Americans, however, are for ever cavilling at some of the public measures; something or other is always wrong, and they never appear perfectly satisfied. If any great measure is before congress for discussion, seemingly distrustful of the abilities or the integrity of the men they have elected, they meet together in their towns or districts, canvass the matter themselves, and then send forward instructions to their representatives how to act. . . . Party spirit is for ever creating dissensions amongst them, and one man is continually endeavouring to obtrude his political creed upon another." [2] This restless sense of liberty, combined with the lure of new land on the frontier, was not conducive to administrative discipline.

RURAL LIFE AND THE ADMINISTRATIVE ART

The administrative art develops in group activities. It is favored by an urban and industrial community rather than by a rural society. In the late eighteenth century the prestige of rural life, of farm and country, was high in America. Jefferson placed the farmer in the very center of his social and economic system. Washington and Adams hurried to their country homes at every break in their official duties. Timothy Pickering set out for the west in 1800 to reestablish himself on the soil after nearly ten years in the Cabinets of two Presidents. The virtues of rural life were put eloquently by Jeremy Belknap at the close of his great work on New Hampshire.

Were I to form a picture of happy society, it would be a town consisting of a due mixture of hills, valleys and streams of water: The land well fenced and cultivated; the roads and bridges in good repair; a decent inn for the refreshment of travellers, and for public entertainments: The inhabitants mostly husbandmen; their wives and daughters domestic manu-

---

[1] John Dean Goss, *The History of Tariff Administration in the United States from Colonial Times to the McKinley Administrative Bill* (2d ed., New York: Columbia University, 1897), p. 11.

[2] Isaac Weld, Jun., *Travels through the States of North America . . . during the Years 1795, 1796, and 1797* (4th ed., 2 vols., London: John Stockdale, 1807), I, 124–25.

facturers; a suitable proportion of handicraft workmen and two or three traders; a physician and lawyer, each of whom should have a farm for his support. A clergyman of any denomination, which should be agreeable to the majority, a man of good understanding, of a candid disposition and exemplary morals; not a metaphysical, nor a polemic, but a serious and practical preacher. A school master who should understand his business and teach his pupils to govern themselves. A social library, annually increasing, and under good regulation. A club of sensible men, seeking mutual improvement. A decent musical society. No intriguing politician, horse jockey, gambler or sot; but all such characters treated with contempt. Such a situation may be considered as the most favourable to social happiness of any which this world can afford.[3]

This ideal was hardly favorable to the formation of the managerial skills needed to carry on the affairs of a nation. The sources of the administrative art in the Federalist era must be sought elsewhere.

THE BRITISH TRADITION

What the Americans could learn from the mother country to guide them in the management of their own was not reassuring. The administration of the United Kingdom during the last half of the eighteenth century was in disrepute and after 1780 was under constant investigation as a consequence of Edmund Burke's demand for "economical reform." Reform came too slowly to be of use to the one-time colonists.

The British civil service with which the Americans of 1780–1800 were familiar was almost the antithesis of the model held up to them a century later. The appointing power, wrested from the King in 1688, was in the hands of the landed gentry. The civil list "was a roster of the politically active aristocracy, together with their illegitimate children, cast-off employees, mistresses, and poor relations."[4] Persons so bereft of qualifications that they were useless in the conduct of public business were nominated to offices by the great families. The sale of office was so enshrined in custom that the comptroller of the Navy did not hesitate to assert in 1786 that his average annual income of 300

[3] Jeremy Belknap, *The History of New Hampshire* (3 vols., Boston, 1784–92), III, 333–34.

[4] J. Donald Kingsley, *Representative Bureaucracy: An Interpretation of the British Civil Service* (Yellow Springs, O.: Antioch Press, 1944), p. 28.

guineas from this source was nothing but a part of his official income.[5] Sinecures abounded, and the practice of hiring a deputy to perform official duties was widespread in positions high and low.

Standards of performance were mediocre and remained indifferent throughout the first half of the nineteenth century. The collection of the revenue was in arrears to the amount of nearly £400,000 in 1780.[6] The exchequer clung obstinately to the use of the Latin language and Roman numerals; to add them it was necessary to transcribe the columns into Arabic numerals and then translate back again to Latin.[7] Lord Nelson asserted that the Navy had been defrauded by the official victualers "in a most scandalous and infamous manner."[8] So great, however, was the traditional respect for the governing landed aristocracy that their patronage was unquestioned—even defended by such reformers as Burke and later by Cobbett, who upheld sinecures as a means of supporting those among "the ancient nobility and gentry, who otherwise might fall into a state that would inevitably bring disgrace upon rank."

These were the drab public service traditions of the mother country when American standards were in the process of formation. Lax, corrupt, and class-ridden, they were characteristic of their age.

They were the only external standards that were well known to the Americans of 1780–1800. Jefferson was acquainted with France and was to warn his fellow countrymen against the excess of government, the oppression, and the class domination of the public service of the old regime; but few Americans knew the French system of administration. Its formalism, excessive centralization, and great powers would have caused a revulsion, had they been understood. Most Americans were also unaware of the able, disinterested, intelligent, but undemocratic public service of Prussia which Frederick the Great had brought to a high pitch of excellence by 1780. It was nearly as remote from American thought and comprehension as the classical Chinese civil service already many centuries old. If a model from across the seas were to guide the new government on the Atlantic seaboard, it could only have been the English.

---

[5] Emmeline W. Cohen, *The Growth of the British Civil Service, 1780–1939* (London: George Allen and Unwin, 1941), p. 25; and official documents cited at this point.

[6] *Ibid.*, p. 32.

[7] *Ibid.*, pp. 31, 50.

[8] *Ibid.*, p. 37.

COLONIAL EXPERIENCE

The colonists were primarily concerned with self-government. Colonial attitudes were unfriendly to executive power, to governmental activity, and to an official class. This point of view was not merely critical of the mother country. It was based on general distrust of authority, the lack of fiscal resources to support an active government, a strong sense of individualism, and a jealous regard for personal rights and political freedom. It also reflected a relatively low scale of community needs, and aspirations which could be met by personal effort.

As colonists the Americans had learned little of the art of administration other than in local affairs. With a few exceptions they had been excluded from the principal administrative office, the governorship. But they often sat close to the governor in executive council or in such offices as the treasurer and receiver-general. In the legislatures, too, they fought a long battle, on the whole successful, to restrict the powers of the executive.

In county and town affairs, however, the people found a congenial school of self-government. Their institutions were autonomous to a large degree and the number of small positions was considerable. Local officials carried on most of the government of the time. Officeholders were elected, whether in the northern, middle, or southern colonies, and for short terms. The scale of operations was small. Their duties were simple and called for no special skill or competence. Popular election, moreover, prevented the establishment of a hierarchy; each elected official stood on his own feet, responsible to no superior but the community.

The art of *self-government* was thus in a flourishing state. The art of *management,* however, hardly existed in the length and breadth of colonial government except in the imperial customs service. Here was an extensive network of offices, forming a hierarchy centered in London, subject to common instructions and to administrative direction. It was not a hierarchy in which Americans participated except in humble capacities. Although it formed a model for the Treasury Department in 1789, it was not a school for the native population.[9]

The generation which had to establish a nation-wide system of

[9] Experience under the Confederation was too brief and too limited to have produced a trained body of government officials and employees. The public service of the states before and after 1789 was, on the other hand, a good recruiting ground for men

customs and excise offices and operate the post office had therefore learned little of the art of administration in the colonial era. It had learned much about the art of evading government, and had become sensitive to the rights of citizens.

BUSINESS EXPERIENCE

The country possessed a substantial body of men experienced in business management, some of whom dealt in large affairs. As a class it was they who carried the wisdom and lore of the management art; it was their methods which provided the foundation for the business operations of government. They were, moreover, the patrons of the lawyers who furnished many public officials from the outset.

American business, important though it was as a source of knowledge about the managerial art, was still in its infancy. No firm or enterprise operated on so extensive a scale as either the contemporary Treasury, Post Office, or War Department. A southern plantation, with a hundred or more slaves and overseers, would rank high in terms of size in the eighteenth century. An important northern shipyard would employ not more than fifty workmen.[10] A Connecticut button manufacturer was considered to have a large establishment in 1791 when twelve workmen were employed.[11] The Massachusetts Bank had only three employees in 1789 with a pay roll amounting to $2,100; by 1809 there were only nine employees.[12] But the Aera and Aetna Iron Works of North Carolina, with four gristmills and two sawmills, had attached to it about ninety workmen.[13] And Washington reported a visit to a northern carding mill which employed 900 hands.[14] Such a massing of manpower was, however, exceptional.[15]

Many business practices and experiences illustrate how definite a handicap was the absence of habit and skill in coordinating the work

who were familiar with government forms and ways of conducting affairs. As noted above, many of them made their way into the customs service, and presumably into other branches of administration.

[10] John G. B. Hutchins, *The American Maritime Industries and Public Policy, 1789–1914* (Cambridge: Harvard University Press, 1941), pp. 103–4.

[11] Joseph S. Davis, *Essays in the Earlier History of American Corporations*, II, 256–57.

[12] Margaret Hadley Foulds, "The Massachusetts Bank, 1784–1865," *Journal of Economic and Business History*, II (1930), 256–70 at 264.

[13] Davis, *op. cit.*, II, 257.

[14] Oct. 28, 1789, Washington, *Diaries*, IV, 38.

[15] Business was small also in the light of the capital employed. Phineas Bond, British consul at Philadelphia, reported in 1790 that the ordinary capital of paper mills in

of groups, and how anxiously pioneers followed the few examples to which they could turn. The problem of management "was so troublesome that it set very narrow limits to the profitable scale of operations." [16] Business was taking hesitant steps guided by men who knew little of either the technical or managerial requirements of success. Archibald Mercer, a director of the Society for Useful Manufactures, urged Hamilton in 1792 to attend a meeting of the board of directors: "for my part I confess myself perfectly ignorant of every duty relating to the Manufactoring business. . . ." [17] Hamilton, searching everywhere for a superintendent, concluded, "it is far from easy to find a choice of proper characters." [18] A potential British investor in the S. U. M. expressed his fears of failure: "I repeat it, Sir, unless God should send us saints for workmen and angels to conduct them, there is the greatest reason to fear for the success of the plan." [19] Neither saints nor angels appeared at Paterson, New Jersey, the site of the Society's operations.

Symbolic of the state of the administrative art in early American business was the preference for committees rather than single executives. The directors of the Massachusetts Bank confided even the smallest matters to committees of the board—the alteration and repair of the building into which they were to move, "the form and the situation of the Desks and Counters," the procurement of a bell in case of fire or robbery, erecting another "Iron Rod . . . to guard against Lightning," and "paving the yard before the bank." [20] A committee

---

that vicinity was about £1,500 to £1,600, four fifths invested in mills and buildings ("Letters of Phineas Bond," Am. Hist. Assoc., *Annual Report, 1896,* I, 633–34). The Hartford woollen manufactory had a stock of about £2,800; the Boston sailcloth manufactory, a capital investment of $6,200; and a Boston glass factory, $11,000 (Davis, *op. cit.,* I, 369). In 1790 the largest financial enterprises were the three banks, two with capital of a half million, and the Bank of the United States with a million; the big canal and navigation companies, none of which were authorized to raise more than $400,000; and a few insurance companies. Most corporations in existence before 1800 had capital of less than $50,000 (*ibid.,* II, 291). The Society for Useful Manufactures, set up in 1791 with Hamilton's assistance, was an industrial giant with a capital of $1,000,000. It came to an untimely and, in the minds of many small enterprisers, a not unwelcome end (*ibid.,* I, 349–522).

[16] *Ibid.,* II, 282; the quotations in this paragraph are reprinted with the permission of the Harvard University Press.

[17] *Ibid.,* I, 416.

[18] *Ibid.,* I, 417.

[19] *Ibid.,* I, 483.

[20] N. S. B. Gras, *The Massachusetts First National Bank of Boston, 1784–1934* (Cambridge: Harvard University Press, 1937), pp. 231 ff.

determined which bank officers should reside in the bank with their families and what parts of the house they should occupy. The direct supervision of banking transactions was the duty of a "sitting director," selected in turn by the alphabet, to be in charge for a week—a kind of rotating chief executive.[21]

So difficult, indeed, appeared the task of organizing an enterprise on a national scale that intelligent men despaired of its possibility. Pelatiah Webster expressed this sentiment in discussing the establishment of a central bank with branches in different cities. "Indeed," he said, "it appears to me *morally impossible* that any institution of such delicacy, variety and importance, as is that of the Bank, should ever be managed in *different departments* ramified *thro' a continent of 1,500 miles extent,* with that *uniformity, prudence,* or even *integrity,* which the *safety and success* of it would absolutely require."[22] Alexander Hamilton believed that the prospect of a safe and orderly administration of branches of the first Bank of the United States was so desperate as to forbid the experiment.[23]

The business tradition was one, in short, which cultivated the virtues of individual enterprise and personal responsibility in the management of small undertakings rather than the skills of large affairs. Corporations were few, and where difficult management problems were involved they were hampered by lack of experience. The art of organizing, coordinating, and directing the work of many individuals toward a single end was in fact a "mystery." With all its limitations business was, nevertheless, a principal source of the kind of experience required in the conduct of public affairs.

ARMY EXPERIENCE

Americans acquired much experience in organization and management during the Revolution. Despite the fact that the army was tiny,

---

[21] *Ibid.,* pp. 26–27. Other ideas of management were stirring. The directors of a canal company in New York recommended that the business should be committed "to a single directing head, to a man of known and acknowledged abilities, of a mind so comprehensive, as to combine and form all the arrangements, with a minute detail of each part; capable of foreseeing what will be wanting in future. . . . In short, a man, who if he has not had practical experience, has activity, ingenuity and judgment sufficient to compensate in a degree for that defect. . . ." Davis, *op. cit.,* II, 162–63.

[22] Quoted in James O. Wettereau, "The Branches of the First Bank of the United States," *The Tasks of Economic History* (1942), p. 72.

[23] *Ibid.,* p. 70.

on a modern view, and was divided into substantially independent units operating in different parts of the country, it familiarized the people with the ideas of organization, hierarchy, discipline, leadership, and control. Here, too, the engineer made his early contributions to the government. Moreover, the task of supplying the army exceeded any contemporary private ventures and gave experience which was to be put to use after the war by many of the most active businessmen of the Federalist era.

Former army men went into the public service of the new government in considerable numbers, bringing with them a background in handling men and affairs. Many prominent businessmen of the time had been employed in the army commissariat. Continental purchasing agents and prize agents stationed at home included a number of outstanding merchants. Deputy commissary generals and quartermaster generals had wide experience in purchasing and transporting goods. "All were learning the importance of national business organization and cooperation." [24] All were acquiring a national point of view gradually overgrowing deep-seated provincial sentiments. The knowledge and experience which the merchants acquired were a community gain, available for the business transactions of the federal government.

THE ADMINISTRATIVE SKILLS

Despite the absence of widespread experience in large affairs, most of the special skills necessary for their conduct were available in 1789. They could not always be secured, and in most cases they were never abundant; but on the other hand the need was not for large numbers, and most subordinate tasks were simple enough so that special preparation was unnecessary.

The skills of the lawyer were essential and were well supplied. The federal bench required men of sound legal training, high ability, and public standing. The Attorney General and the district attorneys were perforce lawyers. A legal training was also valuable to the heads of departments and the principal fiscal officers, diplomats, and special agents, such as those settling claims against the British. A large proportion of leading federal officials were either practicing lawyers or

---

[24] Robert Abraham East, *Business Enterprise in the American Revolutionary Era* (New York: Columbia University Press, 1938), p. 47.

initially trained in the law. By way of example we note Hamilton, perhaps the leading lawyer of his time, Jefferson, Jay, John Adams, Pickering, Edmund Randolph, John Marshall, and Charles Lee. Many members of Congress were also lawyers.

The study of law was recognized as one of the best foundations for success in public life, whether political or official. Jefferson told his son-in-law, "The study of the law is useful in a variety of points of view. . . . It is the most certain stepping stone to preferment in the political line." [25] Pickering, who had a prudent eye to success, said, "But for public employments, a previous study of the law is highly useful— I had almost said essential." [26] And James McHenry advised his nephew, "Let me entreat you to pursue with unremitted attention, your legal studies. You must rely upon the law, not only as a profession, but if you are desirous of assisting your country at any crisis, or at any time, upon its being the best ladder to public notice or official station." [27]

Able top executives were much less abundant than competent lawyers in the public service. The twelve years of Federalist rule turned up one genius (Hamilton), several well able to keep an organization in good working order (Wolcott, Pickering, Stoddert, for example), and a number who were indifferent or failures (McHenry, St. Clair, Tench Francis). The Treasury Department, the War Department, the Post Office, and the office of Purveyor had the greatest need for executive talent. The Treasury found superior capacity in a lawyer-soldier, and in an accountant. The Post Office found moderate talent in a former army officer with legal training but no legal experience, and in a merchant. The Purveyor was incompetent; the War Department was badly served. Nor did the state governors contribute executive skill to the new federation; they tended to pursue political rather than official careers. Their administrative experience (except in New York and Massachusetts) would have been modest, in any event.

While experience in large-scale management was perforce uncommon, Americans had acquired capacity to handle effectively particular tasks. The job of middle management, especially in the customs and internal revenue offices, was on the whole well done, and despite trouble

---

[25] Jefferson to Thomas Mann Randolph, May 30, 1790, Jefferson, *Works* (Federal ed.), VI, 62.

[26] Pickering to Rufus King, Jan. 20, 1799, Pickering Papers, X, 250.

[27] James McHenry to John McHenry, May 20, 1800, Gibbs, *Memoirs*, II, 348.

in the post office at some points most postmasters were conscientious public servants. The daily routine of public business moved forward adequately.

Skill in fiscal management was more highly developed. Every state government had its treasurer and comptroller, the handful of banks had a small group of officials who were familiar with financial trans- actions, and every large mercantile establishment had its accountants. The secretaries to large southern plantation owners had similar duties and experience. The offices of Auditor and Comptroller in the Treasury Department, of the accountants in War and Navy, and the principal fiscal offices in the field could and did draw upon this reservoir of skill for their staffs.

The other skill universally required was that of the clerk. Here the supply was none too adequate. So far as experience was demanded, applicants had to be found in the mercantile establishments. Many men became clerks, however, merely because they could write legibly and spell correctly. Occasionally literary talent was rewarded but the literati ranked low as a source of clerical skill.

In purchasing its supplies the government had to call upon the skill of the merchant and trader. Here experience and talent were abundant. Another specialty needed for government purposes was marine insur- ance; there were a considerable number of insurers in the principal ports, notably Boston, New York, and Philadelphia.

THE LITERATURE OF ADMINISTRATION

The men who had to organize the state and federal governments from 1780 to 1790 found nothing in the books of their time to guide them. The great classics on government with which they were familiar —Locke, Sidney, Montesquieu—were unconcerned with the business of administration. Blackstone in his *Commentaries on the Laws of England,* of which an American edition had been published in Phila- delphia in 1771–72, did no more than warn his readers in a single paragraph against the "influence most amazingly extensive" arising from the royal patronage.

Political writing by Americans, before the *Federalist Papers,* was equally barren of help to officials who had to carry on the daily routine of government. The library of George Washington contained many books on agriculture, the military art, and religion, but few on government, and of these none which could have been the slightest use to him as the head of the new administrative system.[28] Jefferson's *Notes on the State of Virginia* informed his readers about the history of colonial charters and the principal elements of the state constitution, but left untouched the way in which the government was actually carried on by its officers.

One of the important libraries of the time was the Boston Athenaeum. Its holdings in 1800 revealed almost nothing serviceable to the men who set up the administrative system of states and nation. Necker's two-volume work, *Du Pouvoir Exécutif,* was published in 1792, and in the same year appeared an English translation. At best it would have been of slight influence, and it came too late to affect American thought during the formative period. Adam Smith's *Wealth of Nations* was available, but taught little of public administration. The *Annual Register,* from 1758, gave a yearly account of events, political, military, and international, but not administrative. The collected works of Bolingbroke, Burke, and other public figures were hardly helpful to officials, nor were the books dealing with business and commerce. There was no account of the greatest quasi-public corporation of the time, the East India Company. As the first president of the Bank of North America complained in 1784, "no Book then spoke of the Interior Arrangements or Rules observ'd in Europe." [29] The work by Wyndham Beawes was mercantile law, not practice.[30] Shipowners' manuals came nearer to business needs, but were chiefly reprints of shipping laws, tables of duties, and explanations of shipping procedure in formal terms.[31]

---

[28] The incomplete inventory of Washington's books by the executors of his estate is printed in Edward Everett, *The Life of George Washington* (New York: Sheldon and Co., 1860), Appendix No. II, and in Benson J. Lossing, *The Home of Washington* (Hartford, Conn.: A. S. Hale and Co., 1870), pp. 376 ff; see also J. M. Toner, "Some Account of George Washington's Library and Manuscript Records . . . ," Am. Hist. Assoc., *Annual Report, 1892,* pp. 71–111. The Athenaeum collection of Washington's books is catalogued by Appleton P. C. Griffin, *A Catalogue of the Washington Collection in the Boston Athenaeum* (Cambridge: University Press, 1897).

[29] Gras, *op. cit.,* p. 210.

[30] *Lex Mercatoria Rediviva* (London, 1752).

[31] See for example the volume, *The Ship-Owner's Manual:* or, Sea-Faring-Man's Assistant, containing A General System of the Maritime Laws, on the Most Interesting Subjects: viz. Fraught, Charter-Parties, Demurrage, Insurance, Salvage, Average, Quarantine, Disbursements, and other Ship-Accompts, with New Adjudged Cases, useful Tables, and other Articles. Particularly, correct Tables of the Net Consolidated Duties.

Writing in the field of public administration, in fact, began in the United States. It was Alexander Hamilton who first defined the term in its modern usage and who first worked out a philosophy of public administration.[32] His contribution was original, although his ideas were not congenial to many of his fellow countrymen.

At a later stage of the development of the administrative art, the scanty resources of the 1790's would have seemed an insuperable handicap to good administration. Future managerial assets were not missed because their advantages had never been experienced. In their own way, and with their own administrative tools and experience, such as they were, the first federal officials achieved a respectable measure of the uniformity, prudence, and integrity that Pelatiah Webster rightly thought essential. Many, indeed, believed the new federal government was reaching too far, both because it might encounter public resistance and because it could not produce the results at which it aimed for mere lack of capacity to govern. The state of the administrative art from 1789 to 1801 was such as to set limits to what was administratively feasible, but manpower and skills proved sufficient for the measures that were undertaken. Fortunately much of the administrative art is synonymous with common sense, sound judgment, initiative, and courage—homely virtues that were doubtless as readily at hand then as now. The art was practiced, but we cannot say that it was cultivated for yet a hundred years.

Revised by a Gentleman of the Customs. Also, The Navigation Act, Register Act, Manifest Act, Ship-Owner's Act, Whale Fishery Act, Smuggling Acts, &c. The Sixth Edition, carefully revised. Newcastle upon Tyne: printed by D. Akenhead, on the Sandhill. MDCCXC.

[32] The development of the use of the term, public administration, is traced by John A. Fairlie, "Public Administration and Administrative Law," *Essays on the Law and Practice of Governmental Administration* (Charles G. Haines and Marshall E. Dimock, eds., Baltimore: Johns Hopkins Press, 1935), pp. 1–43. Toward the end of the seventeenth century it was being used for the management of public affairs and early in the eighteenth for the work of the executive branch. Fairlie notes that it was only since the last decade of the nineteenth century that the term received extended recognition in English-speaking countries. One of the earliest French titles using the term is Charles-Jean Bonnin, *Principes d'administration publique* (1st ed., 1809; 3d ed., 3 vols., Paris: Chez Renaudière, 1812).

Chapter Thirty-eight

THE PROBLEM OF COMMUNICATIONS

THE need for a quick and reliable system of communication is universal in any widespread organization. While the federal government was small, on present standards, it was large in the setting of its time. Its means of communication were elementary and often uncertain.[1] Such as they were, they had to suffice to maintain as effective connection as was then technically feasible between the center and its outlying agents, including foreign representatives. The slowness and unreliability of the means of communication were, however, serious handicaps to the conduct of administration in these early years.

The conditions of travel are well illustrated by the experiences of six members of Congress when journeying to Philadelphia in 1790. "Burke was shipwrecked off the Capes; Jackson and Mathews with great difficulty landed at Cape May and traveled one hundred and sixty miles in a wagon to the city; Burke got here in the same way. Gerry and Partridge were overset in the stage; the first had his head broke . . . and the other had his ribs sadly bruised. . . . Tucker had a dreadful passage of sixteen days with perpetual storms."[2]

At the seat of government in Philadelphia official contacts were easily maintained. The President, the heads of departments, and members of Congress lived within comfortable walking distance of each other; Secretaries, Congressmen, and members of the diplomatic corps who did not live with their families often stayed at the same boardinghouse. A single messenger employed by each of the principal offices sufficed to transport papers and messages from one to the other. In

---

[1] Seymour Dunbar, *A History of Travel in America* (4 vols., Indianapolis: Bobbs-Merrill, 1915).

[2] Allen Johnson, *Union and Democracy* (Boston, New York: Houghton Mifflin, 1915), pp. 105–6.

the early days, the President's private secretary, Tobias Lear, some-times carried documents from Washington to Congress; and General Knox served as such a messenger on at least one occasion. Beyond Philadelphia, however, difficulties of communication mounted pro-gressively toward the periphery of the new Republic.

The available methods of communication from Philadelphia to federal officials stationed in different parts of the country were (1) the post office; (2) an express, i.e., a special messenger hired to execute a special mission; (3) conveyance privately by the hand of a friend or some trustworthy person who happened to be traveling to a given point,[3] including merchants voyaging abroad; (4) coastwise vessels whose masters accommodated official requests, especially for the car-riage of packages. To communicate with our diplomatic and consular agents abroad, the British packets were preferred for their regularity, but much use was made of American and other ships.

POST OFFICE TIME SCHEDULES

The post office provided the principal lines of communication between the seat of government and the rest of the country. Its unreliability has already been noted.[4] The time consumed in transmission was con-siderable and improved little under the Federalists. The first land conveyance of letters between Boston and New York had been estab-lished in 1673, the trip taking three weeks. By 1717 mail was carried from Boston to Virginia in one month during the summer; two months in the winter. Regular mail from New York to Philadelphia, which took three days in 1720, required only one and a half days in 1754; and ten years later, one day, proceeding by relays. From Boston to New York the mail took five days in 1790; in 1793 the time was reduced by a new line to three and one half. The proprietor advertised to the public that his stage carriages would be "small, genteel and easy," in which but four inside passengers would be admitted, "with smart, good horses, and experienced and careful drivers." [5] By 1802 an unbroken line of stagecoaches was opened from Boston to Savannah, requiring

---

[3] For example, Pickering to Washington, April 27, 1797: "Not meeting myself with any private conveyance, I have committed to the Atty General the care of forwarding the packet with your buckles. . . ." Pickering Papers, XXXVII, 130.

[4] See above, ch. xvi. This was nothing new; Jay frequently complained during the ten years before 1789. Jay, Correspondence, I, 193, 355, 440.

[5] Dunbar, op. cit., I, 177, n. 2; and I, 188.

twenty-two and one half days for the journey, at a cost of $70.00. To send a notice from Philadelphia to Georgia in 1794 required thirteen days;[6] it was as distant in point of time as Pittsburgh. It was not surprising that Jefferson found himself almost cut off from knowledge of public affairs when he returned to Monticello in 1794. In February he wrote Madison, "I could not have supposed, when at Philadelphia, that so little of what was passing there could be known even at Kentucky, as is the case here. Judging from this of the rest of the Union, it is evident to me that the people are not in a condition either to approve or disapprove of their government, nor consequently to influence it."[7]

Inspection of the correspondence of Washington, Jefferson, and other statesmen gave evidence as to the time actually consumed in forwarding letters from place to place. For example, *from Boston to New York*, in 1790, four to seven days;[8] *from Philadelphia to Mount Vernon,* four or five days;[9] but letters to Jefferson from Virginia were noted which required eighteen days for transmittal.[10] From time to time extraordinary delays occurred. Thus Governor Telfair of Georgia wrote to Jefferson on January 2, 1791; the letter reached Jefferson on March 4, 1791, an interval of 61 days.[11] Washington wrote to Governor Beverly Randolph of Virginia from New York on October 3, 1789; the letter was delivered 58 days later, November 30.[12]

Communication to the westward was uncertain throughout the period, although gradually improving by 1800. In 1798 the scheduled time of the mails from Philadelphia to Lexington, Kentucky, was 19 days, but bad roads and poor connections accounted for delays up to 31 days.[13] The army had its own courier service, but the State Department lacked quick contact with territorial officers in the northwest and the southwest. In a period when so much turbulence prevailed across the Alleghenies, with a strong inclination toward alliance with Spain, the problem of communication was a serious one.[14]

---

[6] *Annals,* IV, 658 (May 8, 1794).

[7] Feb. 15, 1794, Jefferson, *Works* (Federal ed.), VIII, 139.

[8] Washington, *Writings,* XXX, 317, 384; XXXI, 12, 13.

[9] *Ibid.,* XXXI, 252, 259; XXXII, 49, 115.

[10] Jefferson, *Works* (Federal ed.), VI, 234, 241.

[11] *Ibid.,* VI, 226.

[12] Washington, *Writings,* XXX, 477.

[13] Wesley E. Rich, *History of the United States Post Office to the Year 1829,* p. 74, citing Postmaster General Letterbook H, pp. 242 ff.

[14] Communication with the Mississippi Territory has already been noted, see above, pp. 373–74.

DISTRIBUTION OF LAWS AND PUBLIC PAPERS

The distribution of laws and other public documents to the states and the people occasioned some interesting arrangements. Copies of laws were usually sent to the governor of each state. In Georgia this was apparently unsatisfactory; Congressman Baldwin declared that "rather than see the heartburning which had existed among the people of Georgia for the last six years, from ignorance of the laws, he would pay a part of the expense of distributing them himself."[15] The carriage of such heavy packages was apparently usually by boat. To get them to the seat of government in Bennington, Vermont, in 1797 they were sent by sloop from Philadelphia to New York in care of the collector, who was requested "to embrace the first good opportunity of forwarding them to some Gentleman in Albany on whom you can rely to have them safely conveyed to the Governor."[16] To Baltimore in 1798 went by "water stage" five boxes of the laws of the United States addressed to the governor of Maryland at Annapolis, the Baltimore collector being responsible for the last lap.[17]

At the height of the French crisis in the summer of 1798 Congress ordered 10,000 copies of the instructions and dispatches to and from the American envoys in Paris to be printed and distributed. Pickering's directions for their distribution tell us a good deal both about the condition of communications and the political aspects of the enterprise.

In general large consignments of these documents were forwarded to one trustworthy person in each state, who then sent them in bundles of 5, 10, or 15 (already packed by Pickering's clerks and franked) to one or more individuals in each county who could be depended on "for their most useful dissemination among the people."[18] To Winchester, Virginia, were sent 645 copies by means of "a waggon . . . loading with cloathing for a recruiting party."[19] To Tennessee (by the same wagon as far as Winchester) went a barrel with 300 copies.[20] To Pittsburgh 300 copies were transmitted for western Penn-

---

[15] *Annals,* IV, 1082 (Jan. 13, 1795).
[16] Pickering to Joshua Sands, Dec. 1, 1797, Pickering Papers, VII, 487.
[17] Pickering to Robert Purviance, Dec. 1, 1798, *ibid.,* X, 2.
[18] Pickering to Edward Carrington, July 24, 1798, *ibid.,* IX, 97.
[19] Pickering to William McGuire, Aug. 3, 1798, *ibid.,* IX, 143.
[20] *Ibid.,* IX, 144.

sylvania, in care of the commandant, for distribution by Senator James Ross.[21] The collector in New York received 800 copies to be distributed as directed by Governor Jay.[22] To the mayor of Augusta, Georgia, via the collector at Savannah, went a barrel containing 310 copies aboard the schooner *Sally*.[23] Those destined for New Hampshire traveled to Boston, thence to Portsmouth, en route to Governor Gilman.[24]

Not all governors were entrusted with the distribution of this official literature and Pickering's cautions to Governor Jay gave away the political implications of this effort to enlighten the people. In a postscript he wrote, "I thought I should hazard a proper distribution of the dispatches, if I committed them to the governors of *some* of the States . . . for this reason it will be necessary that the Governors whom I do address on the subject, should *not* notice it in any of their public acts." [25]

TRAVEL AND JUDICIAL BUSINESS

The conduct of the judicial business of the United States suffered from poor roads—or none. Judge Samuel H. Parsons, traveling in the Northwest Territory, lost his life when his canoe was dashed to pieces passing over falls in Big Beaver Creek.[26] Another judge nearly lost his life when passing over a high bridge. "His horse starting a little and there being no kind of railing or guard on the sides of the bridge, the wheels of his carriage were carried over, and nothing but a very sudden exertion saved him from utter destruction." [27]

In 1792 the judges of the Supreme Court respectfully complained about their duty to attend the circuit courts. The task of holding twenty-seven circuit courts they found "too burdensome." ". . . to require of the judges to pass the greater part of their days on the road, and at inns, and at a distance from their families," they thought unnecessary. They declared that some of the judges were unable to undergo the "toilsome journeys through different climates and

---

[21] Pickering to Ross, Aug. 6, 1798, *ibid.*, IX, 148.
[22] Pickering to Jay, Aug. 6, 1798, *ibid.*, IX, 149.
[23] Pickering to Thomas Cumming, Aug. 8, 1798, *ibid.*, IX, 166.
[24] Pickering to Gilman, Aug. 13, 1798, *ibid.*, IX, 192.
[25] Pickering to Jay, *ibid.*, IX, 151.
[26] *Gazette of the United States,* Dec. 23, 1789.
[27] *Ibid.,* July 30, 1791.

seasons," and asserted that no set of judges, however robust, would be able to endure such severe duties for any length of time.[28] Congress modified the arrangements to reduce the amount of travel.

Suitors before the courts were also hard pressed by the poor means of communication. We have already seen that the intent of Congress to try offenses against the federal law only in federal courts broke down in face of the extreme inconvenience to parties, and that Congress had to endow the state courts in 1792 with certain types of federal business.[29] The trouble was not easily cured, however. In 1794 the hardships to litigants were discussed in the House; members brought up a number of distressing cases and it was agreed "that considerable grievances of this kind existed, but to point out an effectual remedy seemed very difficult." [30] In 1800 a southern member told the House of the troubles of his constituents who for crimes against Indians on the frontiers had to be conveyed 150 miles "under an escort of United States troops, however trivial and harmless the offence may be." [31] The House was not willing, however, to extend the federal jurisdiction of inferior Georgia courts.

FOREIGN COMMUNICATION

The greatest difficulty arose in keeping in touch with American representatives abroad. They were not numerous, since our diplomats were found only at Paris, London, The Hague, Madrid, Lisbon, and Berlin. To communicate with them, the single recourse was a sailing vessel. The collectors notified the Secretary of State of ships bound for Europe from New York, Philadelphia, and Baltimore.[32] Standard practice under Jefferson is disclosed in his letter of instructions to Short. He requested, once or twice monthly, news of events in Holland and of the general affairs of Europe; transmission "of the Leyden gazette by every British packet . . . which proves to be very regular"; and other publications on important matters. "The English packet," Jefferson continued, "is the most certain channel for such epistolary communications as are not very secret. . . . Intermediate letters, secret

---

[28] *American State Papers: Miscellaneous,* I, 52.
[29] See above, ch. xxxi.
[30] *Annals,* IV, 609 (April 28, 1794).
[31] *Ibid.,* X, 627 (March 14, 1800).
[32] State Dept., Domestic Letters, VI, 37.

communications, gazettes and other printed papers had better come
by private vessels from Amsterdam, which channel I shall use generally
for my letters, and always for gazettes and other printed papers." [33]

The case of the packet *Chesterfield* was certainly an extraordinary
example of the hazards of diplomatic mail. The story can best be
told in the words of the Secretary of State, Timothy Pickering.

In the British Packet Chesterfield, Capt. Robert Jones, which was to have
sailed last week from New-York, I had lodged some letters for you from
your friends at Charleston and from myself: but they are lost. The steward
of the packet was indebted to a porter or carman a few shillings (less than
a dollar) for bringing some articles on board; but one (a lump of beeswax)
being missing, the steward refused to pay the porterage. The porter obtained a *capias:* a constable went on board to serve it: he was resisted and
threatened by Captain Jones: He then obtained a warrant against the captain for a breach of the peace: the report brought together a collection of
citizens, some from curiosity, others to aid the peace officers if necessary.
Capt. Jones defended himself but was overpowered and arrested. In this
situation he rashly ordered the packet's colours to be struck, and the mail
to be sunk! both orders were executed, to the great disappointment & injury
of many of our mercantile citizens & of those who had public letters on
board.[34]

The mail was subsequently raised from the bottom of New York
harbor without suffering any considerable damage, but the matter
became an international incident. The British packet was considered
by His Majesty's Government as on the footing of ships of war and
Pickering was forced to write Richard Harison, the United States
attorney in New York, to restore the captain of the packet to his
liberty, and to punish any aggressors against the law of nations.

The Department of State was without any regular channels of
communication. In 1795 the minister of Portugal accommodated some
American dispatches with his own.[35] In 1797 Pickering wrote our envoy
in Portugal, "I have had by me for some time letters addressed to you:
but no conveyance has presented; and I now write in a state of uncertainty when my letter may leave America." [36] To the American consul

---

[33] Jefferson to Short, Jan. 23, 1792, *Works* (Federal ed.), VI, 371–72.

[34] Pickering Papers, X, 442, 455; XXXVII, 401. The incident took place about March
1, 1799.

[35] State Dept., Domestic Letters, VIII, 413.

[36] Pickering to William Smith, Sept. 23, 1797, Pickering Papers, VII, 222.

in London he sent a letter and packet, the packet "given to the Captain's charge to be delivered to M.r Bayard personally or left for him at one of the American Coffee houses in London, where his address is known." [37] The mercantile house of Thomas and Peter Mackie notified the Secretary of State of the departure of any of their vessels overseas. [38] An important box of papers dealing with claims of American shipowners against Great Britain was forwarded in the care of John Shallcross, a Philadelphia merchant: "it will be a fortunate conveyance," said Pickering. [39] A Danish vessel took letters and packages for John Quincy Adams at Berlin, by way of the United States consul at Hamburg. [40]

The lines of communication were, in short, fortuitous. The exchange of dispatches was a tedious process. In the summer of 1790, Jefferson recorded that the transmission of dispatches from William Short (then at The Hague) required on the average eleven weeks and a half; "the longest are of near eighteen weeks coming. Our information through the English papers, is of about five or six weeks, and we generally remain as long afterwards in anxious suspense, till the receipt of your letters may enable us to decide what articles of those papers have been true." [41] To complete an exchange of correspondence between America and Europe in 1790 thus required on the average about six months, not counting additional time necessary to prepare the documents. In considerable measure Washington and Adams were forced to conduct their foreign policy on the basis of conjecture or probability rather than solid fact.

To make matters worse dispatches were often lost en route, sometimes by being intercepted, sometimes by the capture of a vessel or its loss at sea. [42] Such interruptions caused annoyance on both sides. Early in 1790 Jefferson wrote Short, "I now, therefore, am at about the 7th of October, 1789, as to what has been passing in Europe; that is to say, I know no one circumstance later than the King's removal

---

[37] Pickering to the collector of New York, Sept. 26, 1797, *ibid.*, VII, 230.

[38] Pickering to Thomas and Peter Mackie, Oct. 4, 1797, *ibid.*, VII, 259.

[39] Pickering to Sands, Jan. 13, 1798, *ibid.*, VIII, 55.

[40] Pickering to Joseph Pitcairn, July 28, 1798, *ibid.*, IX, 102.

[41] Jefferson, *Writings* (Memorial ed.), VIII, 65–66.

[42] For example, the commission of the consul at Essequibo and Demerara had to be replaced, the ship carrying the original having been captured. Pickering to Nicholas Rousselet, Aug. 7, 1798, Pickering Papers, VIII, 415.

to Paris. I will complain not only of your not writing, but of your writing so illegibly, that I am half a day decyphering one page, and then guess at much of it." [43] On the other hand Morris and other ministers abroad were "continually repeating and complaining of their want of information from the Department of State." [44] Early in 1799, Murray, minister at The Hague, reported that he had received no letters from the Department of State since July 1798 nor any newspapers since those of July 16. Pickering had sent some, and replied, "The spring I trust will have admitted the vessels carrying them to your coast." [45] In 1792 Washington took Jefferson to task for failure to send Short his commission and instructions. It appeared finally that the vessel carrying these papers was wrecked. [46]

To avoid the loss of papers Washington directed that duplicates always be forwarded and in some cases triplicates. [47] By 1797 the losses were so great that Pickering and Pinckney, in Paris, sent quadruplicates. [48] But to cure the uncertainty arising from tardy or imperfect information was impossible.

RESPONSIBILITY—NATIONAL OR LOCAL

The improvement of roads and bridges was within the grasp of the technical knowledge of the period. Time and money and resolution were required, and all were potentially available. But the Federalist years ran their course with no action on a matter that some saw already to be a national problem. The conflict of opinion concerning the advisability of expenditure by the general government on what was then a county responsibility was deep-seated, apart from the problem of constitutional power.

In 1796 Madison took the lead in proposing a survey of the best route for the post roads between Maine and Georgia. The plan was warmly endorsed by a Georgia representative, Abraham Baldwin. "It was properly the business of the General Government, he said, to un-

---

[43] Jefferson to Short, March 12, 1790, *Works* (Federal ed.), VI, 35.

[44] Washington to Randolph, June 30, 1794, Washington, *Writings*, XXXIII, 419.

[45] Pickering to Murray, June 14, 1799, Pickering Papers, XI, 278.

[46] Washington to Jefferson, June 29, 1792, Washington, *Writings*, XXXII, 74, and n. 46.

[47] Washington to Randolph, June 30, 1794, *ibid.*, XXXIII, 419.

[48] Pickering to C. C. Pinckney, October 17, 1797, Pickering Papers, VII, 317.

dertake the improvement of the roads, for the different States are incompetent to the business, their different designs clashing with each other. . . . There was nothing in this country, he said, of which we ought to be more ashamed than our public roads." [49]

Jefferson, in seclusion at Monticello, took alarm at such an extension of federal activity. He spoke plainly to Madison.

Have you considered all the consequences of your proposition concerning post roads? I view it as a source of boundless patronage to the executive, jobbing to members of Congress & their friends, and a bottomless abyss of public money. . . . it will be a scene of eternal scramble among the members, who can get the most money wasted in their State; and they will always get most who are meanest. We have thought, hitherto, that the roads of a State could not be so well administered even by the State legislature as by the magistracy of the county, on the spot. What will it be when a member of N H is to mark out a road for Georgia? Does the power to *establish* post roads, given you by Congress, mean that you shall *make* the roads, or only *select* from those already made, those on which there shall be a post? If the term be equivocal, (& I really do not think it so,) which is the safest construction? That which permits a majority of Congress to go to cutting down mountains & bridging of rivers, or the other. . . . The roads of America are the best in the world except those of France & England. . . .[50]

Madison replied in a conciliatory vein, suggesting that when the post roads had been determined, the local authorities would probably undertake their improvement.[51] The proposal came to nothing. The roads remained wretched.

---

[49] *Annals,* V, 314 (Feb. 11, 1796).
[50] March 6, 1796, Jefferson, *Works* (Federal ed.), VIII, 226–27.
[51] April 4, 1796, Madison, *Letters* (Congressional ed.), II, 89.

Chapter Thirty-nine

ADMINISTRATIVE HOUSEKEEPING

Every age has its ways of life, conditioned by the progress of the arts and the pull and tug of change and habit. The administrative business of the infant republic was carried on in a generation when the sailing vessel and the stagecoach were the chief means of transportation, when quill pens were the usual implements of writing, and when commercial enterprise was a personal, not a corporate venture. All the elaborate present-day means of expediting and facilitating personal intercourse and the mass performance of business were absent.

The affairs of the new general government nevertheless required men, equipment, space, and system in work. In one way or another, with the materials at hand and the methods of management that were known, the business of collecting revenue, transporting mails, buying army supplies, trading with the Indians, building ships, and taking a census was put in motion. In the pages that follow are notes on some of the commonplaces of administrative life: offices, letter writing, the filing and care of papers, departmental libraries, and the publication of official papers.

OFFICES

The general government sat in New York for a little over a year, moving to Philadelphia in 1790. Shortly afterward the decision was reached to establish the permanent seat of government on the Potomac, near Georgetown. Not until 1800, when John Adams led the exodus to the open spaces and muddy paths of Washington, did the departments acquire office space built for their use. The relatively small amount of business transacted in the departments and agencies permitted makeshift arrangements which usually combined living quar-

ters and public offices in a single building. The White House, and
fourth-class post offices, even today follow this plan.

The accommodation of the President was a matter of more than
personal importance. When the Pennsylvania legislature resolved in
1791 to construct an official residence for the Chief Magistrate, a correspondent in the *Gazette of the United States* observed, "every dictate
of sound policy is in favor of making such provision as may impress
the minds of foreigners with proper sentiments of respect toward us,
and evidence the veneration of the people for their own government." [1]

Before Washington arrived in New York he was invited to be the
guest of Governor George Clinton. He declined, expressing a dislike
to be a burden to any private family and indicating his intention of
taking "hired lodgings, or Rooms in a Tavern until some House can
be provided." [2] On his arrival he took up his abode in the house of
Samuel Osgood, so small that three of his secretaries had to share one
room.[3] Later he moved into the more commodious house of Alexander
Macomb with his office "in a front room below" where persons on
business were admitted.[4]

In Philadelphia he occupied the house of Robert Morris, of which
he has left an interesting description in a letter to his secretary, Tobias
Lear.

The House of Mrs. R. Morris had, previous to my arrival, been taken
by the Corporation for my residence. It is the best they could get. It is,
I believe, the best *single House* in the City; yet, without additions it is
inadequate to the *commodious* accomodation of my family. These, I believe
will be made.

The first floor contains only too public Rooms (except one for the *upper*
Servants). The second floor will have two public (drawing) Rooms, and
with the aid of one room with the partition in it in the back building will
be Sufficient for the accomodation of Mrs. Washington and the Children,
and their Maids; besides affording me a small place for a private Study
and dressing Room. The third Story will furnish you and Mrs. Lear with
a good lodging room,—a public Office (for there is no place below for

---

[1] *Gazette of the United States,* March 30, 1791. New York also proposed to build a
residence for Washington, *ibid.,* March 6, 1790.

[2] Washington, *Writings,* XXX, 251.

[3] Homer Carey Hockett, *Political and Social Growth of the United States, 1492–1852*
(rev. ed., New York: Macmillan, 1933), p. 308.

[4] Washington, *Writings,* XXXI, 153; *Diaries,* IV, 83.

one) and two Rooms for the Gentlemen of the family. The Garret has four good Rooms which must serve Mr. and Mrs. Hyde [5] (unless they should prefer the room over the wash House); William, and such Servants as it may not be better to place in the addition (as proposed) to the Back Building. There is a room over the Stable (without a fire place, but by means of a Stove) may serve the Coachman and Postilions; and there is a smoke House, which, possibly, may be more useful to me for the accomodation of Servants than for Smoking of meat. The intention of the addition to the Back building is to provide a Servants Hall, and one or two (as it will afford) lodging rooms for the Servants; especially those who are coupled. There is a very good Wash House adjoining to the Kitchen (under one of the rooms already mentioned). There are good Stables, but for 12 Horses only, and a Coach House which will hold all my Carriages.[6]

The Pennsylvania legislature appropriated £20,000 for an official residence, a sum that later was nearly doubled; even so the house was not finished until John Adams became the Chief Executive. Governor Mifflin offered it to Adams, who, however, declined, lacking authority from Congress to accept.[7] By 1796 the Republicans were complaining about the house then being built near the Potomac for the President, as "much too magnificent." [8]

Office buildings, in the present sense of the word, were unknown in Philadelphia during these years. Commercial and exporting concerns had their countinghouses, often on the waterfront, but they were for the use of the firms which owned them. The state of Pennsylvania had its famous capital building, Independence Hall, but the new general government, pending its removal to the Federal City, was forced to do its best in rented houses remodeled to become public offices.

The provision of office space for the departments was a simple matter, except for the numerous Treasury clerks. Jefferson indulged himself in ample quarters for his personal convenience and his official duties.

---

[5] John Hyde, the steward, and his wife.

[6] Sept. 5, 1790, Washington, *Writings*, XXXI, 110–11. Washington paid £500 a year for this house, *ibid.*, XXXI, 377. A sum was appropriated for furnishing; when Adams' term expired, Congress provided that such articles of furniture "as may be decayed, out of repair, or unfit for use" should be sold under the direction of the heads of State, Treasury, War, and Navy. These dignitaries became vendue masters. 2 Stat. 121.

[7] Mifflin to Adams, March 3, 1797, Adams, *Works*, VIII, 530; Adams to Mifflin, March 3, 1797, *ibid.*, VIII, 531; *Annals*, V, 836 (March 31, 1796).

[8] William B. Giles, *ibid.*, V, 367 (Feb. 24, 1796); *ibid.*, V, 374, 827.

When the move from New York to Philadelphia was imminent, he corresponded with William Temple Franklin and in the exchange of letters described the accommodations he desired.

On further reflection it appears to me that the houses you mentioned of Mrs. Buddin', would suit me so perfectly that I must beg the favor of you to insure me the refusal of two of them adjoining to each other, on the best terms you can. . . . My object in taking two houses is to assign the lower floor of both to my public offices, and the first floor and both gardens entirely to my own use. Perhaps the third floor of one of them might also be necessary for dead office papers, machines, &c. I should wish for such a gallery on the back of the building as I have had erected here. . . . A good neighbor is a very desirable thing. Mr. Randolph the Attorney Genl. is probably now in Philadelphia, & I think would like the same part of the town. I wish the 3d. house (my two being secured) could be proposed to him. . . .[9]

The office of the State Department was in various places from 1790 to 1800; first on Market Street, then on the southeast corner of Arch and Sixth Streets, then in North Alley, and finally at the northeast corner of Fifth and Chestnut Streets, where it remained until moved to Washington, except for an interval of three months in 1798 when it occupied the State House at Trenton, New Jersey.[10] By Randolph's time (1794-95) the residence and the office of the Secretary of State were separate.[11]

When Timothy Pickering became Postmaster General in 1791, he was faced with a housing problem induced by a large family and the need for space in which to transact his official business. He found a house adequate for both purposes, but prudently asked Hamilton for his approval. His letter described his official and domestic arrangements.

After much inquiry, I have found a house which would accommodate my numerous family, and at the same time give me office room. The *greatly extended* business of the department, I think, may be accomplished with the *same help* which has been used since the time of Mr. Osgood's appoint-

---

[9] Jefferson to Franklin, July 16, 1790, Jefferson, *Works* (Federal ed.), VI, 105-6. A picture of the first house occupied by the Department of Foreign Affairs, 1781-83, is found in U. S. Dept. of State, *History of the Department of State of the United States* (Washington: Govt. Printing Office, 1901), p. 8.

[10] Gaillard Hunt, *Department of State,* p. 428.

[11] State Dept., Domestic Letters, VI, 27; VII, 374.

ment; to wit, an assistant and a clerk. For these, with their necessary writing-desk, table, boxes, cases, and shelves, for a considerable bulk of books and papers, would sufficiently occupy one room; and another room would be convenient for myself. A servant also will be wanted to keep the rooms in order, make fires, and perform other services. These services, however, not being constant, I could employ a *domestic* servant, but one selected with a reference to such public service. If, for the two rooms for the General Post-office, a cellar for wood, and the necessary attendance of my domestic servant, I might make a charge of about three hundred dollars, I would then engage the house referred to; but, previous to such engagement, I wish to obtain your opinion of the propriety of the charge.[12]

That all the problems of official housing were not readily solved in Philadelphia appears from a complaint made by Pickering, then Secretary of State, in 1797. At that time the State Department and the Post Office were accommodated in the same house, which also served as lodgings for the doorkeeper and messenger. Pickering's indignant letter to his landlord, with a bill of particulars, tells its own story.

I inclose Mr Taylor's memorandum of many deficiencies in your house now occupied for my office and that of the postmaster general. It is plain that these defects expose both offices to access by bad men, and especially to incendiaries, and ought long since to have been remedied. I wish also that no further injuries may happen from the want of railing round the steps at the door. You cannot justly expect the stipulated rent for the house in the situation described in the memorandum: this, however, is of the least moment to the public; to whom it is of the highest importance to have the public offices secure. . . .

Memorandum of the fastening
necessary for the security of the office.

The window leading to the Piazza requires out side shutters with bolts.
The two cellar windows front have neither sashes nor shutters.
The Porch and steps require railing. a member of Congress has already fallen off the porch and received some injury.
The entrance under the porch is also open.
The cellar windows opening into the alley have neither sashes nor shutters.

---

[12] Pickering to Hamilton, March 9, 1792, in Charles W. Upham, *Timothy Pickering,* III, 3.

All the sash windows in the upper part of the house require to be fitted and hung with leads or weights

In fact such is the situation of the lower part of the house, that any incendiary might enter and set fire to it, during the night in spite of the watchfulness of the doorkeeper and messenger. He is under the necessity of lodging in the 3rd Story front room. He says he regularly examines the office fires every night about eleven or twelve oclock. Hence it is conceived that the only danger to be apprehended, is from the want of proper fastenings to the House.

In front of the house there is no foot pavement, which will make the passage to and from the office, especially in time [of] thaw, very uncomfortable.[13]

The private establishment of Oliver Wolcott, when Secretary of the Treasury, was modest. William Vans Murray described it to James McHenry in these words, "a neat house of two rooms, one small, on a floor." [14] Accommodations for statesmen were usually simple, a room in a tavern being the common lot. Oeller's Hotel on Chestnut Street was preferred, both on account of its central location and its excellent table and comfortable beds.[15] In an emergency, such as the congressional meetings in Germantown to avoid the Philadelphia plague, quarters were sometimes precarious. Jefferson hunted rooms for his friends Madison and Monroe: "I have got good lodgings for Monroe & yourself, that is to say, a good room with a fireplace & two beds, in a pleasant & convenient position, with a quiet family. They will breakfast you, but you must mess in a tavern; there is a good one across the street. This is the way in which all must do, and all I think will not be able to get even half beds. . . ." [16]

LETTER WRITING

Official correspondence in the eighteenth century was laborious and time consuming. None of the present-day mechanical aids existed; the only way to secure many copies was to print them; the legibility of handwritten manuscripts was often dubious. John Adams was not the

---

[13] Dec. 1, 1797, Pickering Papers, VII, 495–96.
[14] Steiner, McHenry, p. 167.
[15] Leary, That Rascal Freneau, p. 195.
[16] Jefferson to Madison, Nov. 17, 1793, Jefferson, Works (Federal ed.), VIII, 72.

only one to complain of spending irritating hours in deciphering almost unreadable scrawls.[17]

Washington had become accustomed to secretarial help while commander in chief, his young military aides serving him in this capacity.[18] By 1785 he was in despair over his correspondence, and like other wealthy planters in the south he sought out a personal secretary. He was fortunate in discovering Tobias Lear, the great secretary of the period, who served him loyally from 1786 to 1793 and again from 1798 to Washington's death. Congress, however, made no appropriation for an official secretary to the Chief Executive or the heads of departments.

Lear was born in Portsmouth, New Hampshire, in 1762, of well-to-do parents who sent him to Harvard. After graduating in 1783 he traveled and studied abroad for a year. In 1785 Washington wrote his friend, David Humphreys, of his urgent need for a secretary.

What with letters (often of an unmeaning nature) from foreigners. Enquiries after Dick, Tom, and Harry who *may have been* in some part, or at *sometime,* in the Continental service. Letters, or certificates of service for those who want to go out of their own State, Introductions; applications for copies of Papers; references of a thousand old matters with which I *ought* not to be troubled, more than the Great Mogul, but which must receive an answer of some kind, deprive me of my usual exercise; and without relief, may be injurious to me as I already begin to feel the weight, and oppression of it in my head, and am assured by the *faculty,* if I do not change my course, I shall certainly sink under it.[19]

Relief arrived in June 1786 when the young Harvard graduate walked across the Mount Vernon lawn for the first time. He instantly made himself acceptable; within a few days Washington wrote his former comrade-in-arms, General Lincoln, that Lear "appears to be a genteel,

---

[17] Pickering to Joshua Sands, Nov. 3, 1798, "It is of some importance that proper names should be *fairly written;* for there is nothing to lead to the knowledge of them but the clearness of the letters composing them. In the reports of alien passengers many names are utterly illegible, especially names not English. Good writers are as apt to confound many letters, as the worst." Pickering Papers, IX, 556.

[18] McHenry, one of these aides, told how the Commander in Chief proceeded with his correspondence. He gave notes to his aide who then wrote a letter that was submitted for correction and approval, "afterwards copied fair, when it was again copied and signed by him." Steiner, *McHenry,* p. 27, n. 1.

[19] Feb. 7, 1785, Washington, *Writings,* XXVIII, 65–66.

well-behaved young man." [20] After taking time to form his judgment, Washington wrote President Joseph Willard of Harvard that Lear's deportment had been such "as to obtain the esteem, confidence, and love of every individual" in his family.[21] Lear's second and third wives were nieces of Martha Washington.

Lear was discreet and trustworthy. The whole of Washington's correspondence, official and private, went through his hands. He carried messages to Congress, conveyed papers to the heads of departments, and was informally consulted by them on matters which were to come before the President. There is no evidence that he became a power in his own right, that he ever sought for influence, or that he expressed his views on issues of public policy. He worked with a "passion for anonymity." As a mark of respect, Jefferson appointed him consul in Santo Domingo in 1801 and subsequently in Algiers, where he remained until 1812. Returning to Washington, he became the accountant in the War Department; in 1816 he committed suicide.[22]

When it became known in 1789 that Washington would be the first President, his correspondence grew by leaps and bounds. Despite Lear's aid, the number of answers which Washington felt obliged to give in his own hand became "an almost insupportable burden." [23] In March 1789, he invited his nephew, Robert Lewis, to work in his household as a copyist: "I may have occasion for a young person in my family of a good disposition, who writes a good hand, and who can confine himself [to] a certain reasonable number of hours in the 24 to the recording of letters in books. . . ." [24] In 1792 he employed Robert's brother, Howell, in the same capacity, allowing him "at the rate of Three hundred dollars a year, provided he is diligent in discharging the duties of it from breakfast until dinner, Sundays excepted. . . . it

[20] June 7, 1786, *ibid.*, XXVIII, 455.

[21] Washington to Willard, March 10, 1787, *ibid.*, XXIX, 174.

[22] *Dictionary of American Biography*, XI, 76–77.

[23] Washington to Vaughan, March 21, 1789, Washington, *Writings*, XXX, 238.

[24] Washington to Elizabeth Washington Lewis, March 15, 1789, *ibid.*, XXX, 228. Washington's preference for a young member of his family was justified in a letter to David Stuart on July 26, 1789, in which he said, "there are few persons of whom I have *no* personal knowledge, or good information, that I would take into my family, qualified for the duties of which; many things are requisite, to wit, a good address, abilities above mediocrity, secresy and prudence, attention and industry, good temper, and a capacity and disposition to write correctly and well, and to do it obligingly." *Ibid.*, XXX, 365.

is for recording letters, and other papers I want him." [25] An excerpt from Washington's diary suggests that in his early days as Chief Executive, the heads of departments did some writing for him. On December 15, 1789, he noted that he called on Henry Knox, the Secretary of War, and "gave him the heads of many letters." [26] The picture of the President dictating correspondence to the Secretary of War in the latter's office provides a charming commentary on the state of the administrative art in 1789. Clerks did some writing for the heads of departments. But the Secretaries toiled long hours over their letters, and their private correspondence with leading men was usually written in their own hands. Under the circumstances the amount of correspondence carried on by the statesmen of the time was stupendous. After Jefferson retired from the State Department and while enjoying the luxury of rural freedom, he wrote John Adams, "Instead of writing 10. or 12. letters a day, which I have been in the habit of doing as a thing of course, I put off answering my letters now, farmerlike, till a rainy day. . . ." [27]

Timothy Pickering was a voluminous letter writer.[28] His biographer noted that "a very large part, in fact, nearly the whole, of the papers and letters that proceeded from the Secretary, were written and rewritten by his own hand. He made a first draught, and, after reflection, amended it by interlineation and erasure. He then made a fair copy, which was sent to its destination after a press copy of it had been taken. Those press copies show that they were from pages in his own handwriting." [29]

This was the common procedure, supplemented by the final step of copying the letters in bound letterbooks, in chronological order. A large amount of outgoing correspondence has been well preserved in such letterbooks, but the incoming correspondence received no such careful treatment and much of it has disappeared. The letterbooks are in the National Archives, the Library of Congress, and the departments. The writings of some of the principal men have been collected and printed; they range over a much wider ground than the official correspondence.

---

[25] Washington to Elizabeth Washington Lewis, April 8, 1792, *ibid.*, XXXII, 17.

[26] Washington, *Diaries*, IV, 58.

[27] Jefferson, *Works* (Federal ed.), VIII, 144–45.

[28] The bulk of the Pickering manuscript is in the library of the Massachusetts Historical Society.

[29] Upham, *Timothy Pickering*, III, 330–31.

The equipment of a public office for purposes of writing is disclosed in a requisition drawn August 31, 1798, by Timothy Pickering in favor of Winthrop Sargent, the governor of the Mississippi Territory.[30]

Memorandum of Stationary to be procured for Winthrop Sargeant Esqr Governor of the Mississipi Territory, for the use of that Government.

Folio writing paper of the ordinary size	6 reams
Letter paper	4 do
Quills	500
Penknives	6
Wafers of the common size for letters	1 lb
do—of the diameter of 1¼ inch	1500
Black sand	2 quarts
Wrapping or cartridge paper for covering packets of the large folio size	2 reams
Ivory Paper folders	2
Pounce	½ pint
Black lead pencils	2 doz.
Blank books of the good demipaper for records	6.
do .... of the smaller (foolscap)	6.
Papers of Ink-powder	12.
Tape—red—for tying papers	20 pieces.
Sealing wax	2 lb.

Red tape had already become an indispensable article! Candles for dark days, wood for the office fireplace on cold days, tables and desks with pigeonholes completed the essentials.

Paper and ink were of excellent quality. Original manuscripts of the period are usually well preserved; in many cases the ink seems hardly to have faded.[31] Copies made by letter press were on thin porous paper and are much less legible than the originals. Some of the Pickering letter-press copies are indeed faded beyond recognition.

The art of shorthand was known to a few but was not used in the

---

[30] Pickering Papers, IX, 241–42.

[31] The paper and ink were not always satisfactory, however, as an excerpt from a letter of the collector of the port at Portsmouth, N. H., to Oliver Wolcott will testify: "I have to remark for your information that one or more of the last Passports [for vessels], which were received, from the ill quality of the Ink, or the imperfection in the Manufacture of the Parchment were subject to obliteration by the smallest friction & when in moist situations, as at sea, will probably be defaced with the slightest touch." Letters from the Collector, Portsmouth, N. H., July 14, 1797.

course of departmental business. David Robertson of Petersburg, Virginia, reported the debates of the Virginia Constitutional Convention of 1788, and Thomas Lloyd, "the father of American shorthand reporting," was the official reporter of the House of Representatives at the first session of the first Congress. But neither Washington nor any department head had the services of a stenographer; everything was done in long hand.[32] To employ stenographers as an aid to letterwriting was apparently not a contemporary idea; they were used only for public assemblies, and rarely there.

The stenographic reports of the proceedings of the House were far from satisfactory and it was darkly hinted that the note-takers, who were retained privately by the printers, were politically inspired. William Smith defended the integrity of the stenographers but made sport of their reports. In the publication of the debates he discovered that the House had set up a committee to consider the regulation of the *barbers* of the United States: "this struck me," he said, "as a very gross misrepresentation, for I could hardly believe that the Legislature of the Union would, at so early a day, attempt to usurp an authority not vested in them by the Constitution, and that, too, over a body of men, who could at any time put an end to the tyranny with the edge of the razor. . . ." The bill was designed to regulate the *harbors* of the United States.[33] In 1795 and 1796 the House considered the appointment of an official stenographer, but after further acrid comments on the quality of shorthand notes, the idea was abandoned.[34]

---

[32] James Henry Lewis, *An Historical Account of the Rise and Progress of Stenography* (London, 1816).

[33] *Annals*, I, 1061 (Jan. 15, 1790).

[34] *Ibid.*, V, 274, 286. Randolph was requested to make recommendations for a stenographer and on June 5, 1795, wrote a long letter to David Robertson setting out the specifications, from which the following excerpts are taken. "Fidelity and skill constitute the leading features of his character; whether we regard the influence, which his work may have upon the public mind, or the justice, due to those, whose speeches he details.

"To execute his functions with *fidelity*, the reporter ought, in my judgment, to possess the following qualifications. 1. He ought to be an adherent *to no party*. He, like other men, will undoubtedly have his political predilections; but they ought to be predilections for truth alone, untainted by antipathies to individuals. 2. His temper ought to be equal. 3. His industry ought to be unremitted, and his abhorrence of dissipation unquestionable. 4. He should be free from the insincerity and vanity of attempting to make better speeches, than are delivered; and should possess firmness to resist every effort to seduce him into misrepresentations, favorable or unfavorable to the speaker.

"The next cardinal quality is skill in his art.

"1. The foundation of this skill is a general knowledge of the subjects in discussion,

THE PUBLIC PAPERS

The care of papers was in an embryonic state. As John Jay observed to John Adams (then envoy abroad), "It is common, you know, in the course of time, for loose and detached papers to be lost, or mislaid, or misplaced." Jay informed Adams that he had collected the latter's public letters and dispatches, "and a good clerk has already recorded a large volume of them. . . . It is to papers in this office that future historians must recur for accurate accounts of many interesting affairs respecting the late revolution; it is best, therefore, that they should be recorded regularly in books; and, although it will take much time and labor, which some may think unnecessary, I shall nevertheless persevere in the work." Adams agreed that despite the "very negligent

---

and the faculty of quickly entering into those particular details to which the situation of a legislator may afford a superior access. Unless the logographic experiment in France has succeeded in taking down *every* word, which is uttered, I doubt whether such a thing has ever been accomplished. In stenography the ellipses of words, syllables and letters are innumerable. So that the filling up of the notes depends much on the supply of matter, which will always be best recollected by him, who has provided, as it were, an apartment for it by kinderd [*sic*] studies and kindred reflection.

"2. A proficiency in literary composition is also requisite, to catch the different styles, to be a mirror of the various speakers, and to correct unessential inaccuracies of language, so natural to the warmth of debate.

"3. With the foregoing talents, I really believe that a man, wholly ignorant of what are technically called *stenographic characters,* may form, from the characters of his ordinary writing abbreviations, almost equally fitted for expedition. I do not deny the advantage of Stenography; but unless the artist be *practically* conversant with the business, the difficulty of execution must be immense. Therefore, the acquaintance with the characters in stenography, unless practice be combined with it, will fall very far short of the expectation of the House of Representatives.

"The plan, which in my view is most eligible is the following.

"1. As it requires eight hours to copy and enlarge the minutes of one, the labour and delay must be excessive. Sickness may add to the procrastination so much, that the public could be certain of no reasonable time, within which they could obtain a knowledge of the debates. I disapprove therefore the appointment of *one* stenographer only.

"2. Three would be preferable; one of whom should be the principal; the other two subordinate to him. The two subordinates should be placed on opposite sides of the House, and both take notes of all the debates. The principal should be stationed in another convenient position, or move as he pleases; with liberty to take notes or not, as he should find most convenient for his attention to the discussions. From the notes of the assistants and his own collection of matter, he should draw off the debates at, full length, without any unnecessary loss of time." State Dept., Domestic Letters, VIII, 246–48.

dress and disordered air" of his dispatches the plan was "indispensable."[35]

One of the greatest collections of public papers was that accumulated by George Washington. Copies of his military documents had been made by his recording secretary, Richard Varick, toward the close of the Revolutionary War and deposited at Mount Vernon. Upon leaving Philadelphia and the presidency in 1797, another mass of public papers was taken to Mount Vernon.[36] Washington began their arrangement in the winter of 1797–98, a task interrupted by his appointment to the command of the Provisional Army in 1798 and never completed.

The Treasury Department records had become so voluminous by 1796 that Wolcott recommended using "a few rooms" in the new Washington headquarters for their disposition.[37] This suggestion was probably the first of many that led eventually to the establishment of the National Archives.

What part of an official's papers are private and what part public is a perplexing problem. Washington established the precedent by which presidents take with them the bulk of their public papers, but we know from one of his letters that he left some for his successor.[38] When Wolcott resigned in 1800, fearing a subsequent attack from Adams, he took away press copies and rough drafts of Timothy Pickering's official correspondence as Secretary of State, with the permission of John Marshall, Pickering's successor.[39] Notified of this, Pickering told Wolcott, "I am glad you have obtained the draughts and press copies of my letters in the department of State. I never had thought it necessary or proper to do this, although Mr. Jefferson and Mr. Randolph respectively had withdrawn theirs; but these are uncommon times and justify the measure."[40] Practice concerning possession of such papers was clearly not fixed.

The rules of access to public papers were apparently very loose. Some appear from casual comments in contemporary correspondence. Dispatches from foreign ministers to the State Department were open for

---

[35] July 25, 1787, Adams, *Works*, VIII, 446, 451.

[36] Washington, *Writings*, I, xlvi–xlviii.

[37] Wolcott Papers, XLIII, Feb. 1, 1796.

[38] Washington, *Writings*, XXXVI, 2.

[39] Gibbs, *Memoirs*, II, 461.

[40] *Ibid.*, II, 462. These press copies are still among the Wolcott Papers in the archives of the Connecticut Historical Society.

inspection to members of Congress to read but not to copy.[41] Abraham Baldwin took papers from the Register's office, "making himself personally responsible for their safety."[42] Papers in the State Department necessary to establish private claims of merchants were made freely available; if they were confidential they had to be examined in the office, "but as to the residue which probably constitute the great mass . . . they shall be delivered to your clerk on his leaving a receipt for them at the office."[43] Randolph offered to procure for Jeremy Belknap any document in the archives he would specify.[44]

The greatest losses came not from laxness but from fires. One of the customs officers told Wolcott that the large ports should have vaults to protect against fire or theft. In New York the collector held bonds worth about two million dollars. Wolcott ordered vaults in seven of the larger ports but in others no special precautions were directed.[45]

There was gross inattention to the security of papers in the central offices, however. Some Treasury papers were destroyed by fire in 1794,[46] and early in November 1800 all the War Department papers except the accountant's were lost by fire.[47] Prophetically McHenry wrote Wolcott, "The conflagration of the papers and records of the office of the Secretary of War is indeed a great public misfortune, and must be productive of long and positive evils. I lament it in a national and individual point of view. What will it not enable the calumniators to say & insinuate and how shall the innocent man find his justification?"[48]

Within two months another fire broke out in the Treasury office and Wolcott was accused of being implicated, as a means of preventing full disclosure of his Treasury transactions.[49] It appeared that after his resignation he had spent some weeks in the Treasury build-

---

[41] Wolcott Papers, VI, 33.

[42] Annals, III, 225.

[43] Jefferson to William Irvine and John Kean, commissioners for settling accounts between the United States and individual states, State Dept., Domestic Letters, IV, 256–57.

[44] Ibid., VI, 417.

[45] Wolcott Papers, X, 26.

[46] American State Papers: Claims, p. 77.

[47] American State Papers: Miscellaneous, I, 232; Steiner, McHenry, pp. 476–77, n. 1, has a short account of the fire.

[48] Wolcott Papers, VI, 33.

[49] Gibbs, Memoirs, II, 478–83.

ing collecting copies of official reports and supervising the transcript of official papers. They were almost ready for removal when the fire broke out. Wolcott hurried to the scene and met a Treasury clerk, John Coyle, to whom he said he must save his private papers, as the justification of all his official transactions depended on this. He sent Coyle to get a cart, and carried off a chest, a trunk, two boxes, and a small writing desk. There was a House investigation in which Wolcott was cleared of the charge of taking away public papers, but as to the cause of the fire the committee refrained from expressing an opinion.[50]

The method of filing and keeping papers was simple. When Henry Remsen, Jr. resigned his post of chief clerk in the State Department in 1792 he left for his successor an account of his filing system.

Such of the *Foreign letters* as are not filed away in the cases, are for the present put on my desk in the two pigeon holes at the right hand side. The *Consular returns* are at the bottom of said desk right hand side; and so are the *Letters from the Attornies of districts,* which are tied together. The drafts of foreign proceedings, such as ratifications, exequaturs on foreign consular commissions, letters to European powers, are filed in said desk left hand pigeon hole. The letters from our ministers & chargé des affaires now in commission Mr. Jefferson keeps. . . .

Petitions for patents are to be endorsed according to the present mode, the day of their receipt, and noted in the minute book, which petitions are filed together in the desk up stairs in one of the pigeon holes. In the said desk are filed in another pigeon hole, the petitions decided on; and also the drafts of the patents issued. . . . Some of the specifications are in said desk, and others in the closet. . . .

a little attention will be necessary in separating the foreign from the domestic letters, as they are sent to the Office by Mr. Jefferson to be filed. My rule in making the separation was by reading them. The *domestic* letters to be filed in the Office down stairs, the foreign Letters in the Office up stairs.[51]

Order and care doubtless varied with the habits of the paper-keepers. The War Department was apparently none too methodical, for one of its clerks testified, with respect to the fire, that many pamphlets

---

[50] *American State Papers: Miscellaneous,* I, 247, 251–52.
[51] State Dept., Reports of Bureau Officers, Vol. 1A, 1790–1834.

and loose papers had been thrown behind a number of large volumes on the lower shelf of the library.[52] There are occasional references to papers mislaid, but on the whole surprisingly few. The chief clerks apparently had good control of their papers, even though their filing system and equipment were rudimentary.

LIBRARIES

The need for library collections as an aid to administrators was discovered at the outset, and the State Department tended to become the central depository.[53] Jefferson directed Remsen to secure newspapers published from New Hampshire to Georgia.[54] A few months after his accession to office, Jefferson wrote Rittenhouse from New York, "this place yields fewer resources in the way of books than could have been imagined." [55] He set to work to secure the essentials: "I have it much at heart to have one complete set of the laws of all the States in a deposit where they will be tolerably sure of being preserved." [56] Christopher Gore became his agent to collect the Massachusetts laws. How poorly the Department was equipped is revealed in Jefferson's request of the governor of New York to supply him with copies of Indian treaties.[57]

John Adams was interested both in the Navy and in the collection of books for its officers. In 1800 he wrote the Secretary of the Navy, requesting the preparation of a catalogue of books for navy use. "It ought to consist of all the best writings in Dutch, Spanish, French, and especially in English, upon the theory and practice of naval architecture, navigation, gunnery, hydraulics, hydrostatics, and all branches of mathematics subservient to the profession of the sea. The lives of all the admirals, English, French, Dutch, or any other nation, who have distinguished themselves by the boldness and success of their naviga-

---

[52] *American State Papers: Miscellaneous*, I, 247. Absence of card files reduced attention to alphabetizing. It was not until 1792 that Hamilton directed the collectors to alphabetize the articles of export, and sent them a standard list. Hamilton, *Works* (Hamilton ed.), III, 570.

[53] State Dept., Domestic Letters, VI, 35.

[54] *Ibid.*, IV, 187.

[55] June 12, 1790, Jefferson, *Writings* (Memorial ed.), XIX, 73.

[56] State Dept., Domestic Letters, IV, 254.

[57] *Ibid.*, V, 55.

tion, or their gallantry and skill in naval combats." [58] Here was the foundation of the library of the Navy Department.

The library of the Attorney General was not begun until 1831.[59] The origin of the Post Office library is unknown. A small collection of postal reference volumes was maintained in the office of the chief clerk but it was late in achieving the dignity of a library.

THE PUBLIC PRINTING

The bulk of public printing in the 1790's came from Congress, which in 1789 directed the publication of 600 copies of the laws and 700 copies of the journal. These were distributed to members, to the President and executive departments, to the courts, and to the governors of the states. John Fenno, publisher of the *Gazette of the United States,* had been well recommended to Senator King by Christopher Gore,[60] and was to give sturdy support to the Federalists. In 1793 he was selected as printer to the Senate, Child and Swaine to the House.[61]

The debates of Congress were not officially printed, but enterprising reporters, notably Joseph Gales, made extensive summaries for the press. Gales had been forced to flee England on account of his radical views and after a brief sojourn in Schleswig-Holstein arrived in Philadelphia in 1795. A master printer by trade and a skillful stenographer, he became a reporter for the *American Daily Advertiser* and "startled the Americans by making the first verbatim report of proceedings in Congress." [62] His reporting failed to satisfy Harrison Gray Otis, who gave him five dollars as a douceur. Overnight he returned the money. "It was the first time I had ever been offered any money for any thing which I had done in the business of debate taking." [63] Gales' editor had required him to put every day's proceedings into one paper, which forced much abbreviation and Otis' dissatisfaction. Late in life Gales edited the first two volumes of the *Annals of Congress,* taking the debates from contemporary newspaper columns.

---

[58] Adams, *Works,* IX, 47.

[59] James S. Easby-Smith, *The Department of Justice* (Washington: Lowdermilk, 1904), p. 42.

[60] King, *Correspondence,* I, 357.

[61] Laurence F. Schmeckebier, *The Government Printing Office* (Baltimore: Johns Hopkins Press, 1925), pp. 2–3.

[62] *Dictionary of American Biography,* VII, 99–100.

[63] Samuel Eliot Morison, *Harrison Gray Otis,* I, 63–64, n. 5.

The publication of the laws was far from satisfactory. They were printed under the direction of the Secretary of State in five newspapers of general circulation,[64] but Jefferson thought this quite inadequate and "altogether too partial and too perishable." [65] Pickering appointed Philip Freneau's brother, a prominent Republican, and his partner to publish the laws in South Carolina, but as time passed the selection of printers became a partisan act. Pickering asked a Kentucky correspondent to nominate a printer suitable "for correctness in typography, intelligence, and *real,* not boasting & *professing,* patriotism." [66]

Departmental printing was concerned chiefly with circulars, instructions, and forms. There were no printed annual reports; special reports, being made usually to Congress, were published under its authority. The reports of judicial decisions were privately printed.

John Adams, familiar with European practice and sensitive to the importance of timely printing of public documents, proposed an official gazette in 1800. "The President," he said, "must issue proclamations, articles of war, articles of the navy, and must make appointments in the army, navy, revenue, and other branches of public service; and these ought all to be announced by authority in some acknowledged gazette. The laws ought to be published in the same. . . . It is certain that the present desultory manner of publishing the laws, acts of the President, and proceedings of the Executive departments, is infinitely disgraceful to the government and nation, and in all events must be altered." [67] In thus projecting the *Federal Register,* Adams was over 130 years ahead of his time.

---

[64] Pickering Papers, VI, 366.
[65] State Dept., Domestic Letters, V, 103.
[66] Pickering Papers, X, 564.
[67] Adams, *Works,* IX, 51.

Chapter Forty

THE ADMINISTRATIVE THEORY AND ACHIEVEMENTS OF THE FEDERALISTS

THE Federalists developed a body of doctrine which was clear-cut, well considered, consistent in its several parts, and which as a whole formed an intelligent system of theory and practice of public administration. Hamilton was both its foremost expounder and its greatest practitioner, but many others in the legislative and executive branches had a part in its formulation and growth. The theory of administration and the achievements of the Federalists may be brought into focus by reviewing the ends which they sought and the means that they adopted.

PUBLIC POLICY

The Federalists had four cardinal planks in their national policy. First they planned to reestablish public credit. In this they were eminently successful, funding the national debt, assuming the state debts, creating a bank, and providing adequate revenue for payment of interest and principal. Next they proposed to develop the national estate. Their leaders intended to encourage manufactures, aid the shipbuilding industry and sea-borne commerce, support the fisheries, build roads, bridges, and canals, protect the rights of inventors, give bounties on certain agricultural products, and open up the western lands. Except for genuine success in restoring prosperity in the shipbuilding industry, sea-borne commerce, and the fisheries (with the accidental but powerful aid of a European war market), the Federalists failed to achieve their economic program.[1] Third, they undertook to protect

---

[1] In common with all Americans in the 1790's, the Federalists relied principally upon private endeavor in building up the national estate. They were not unwilling, however, to undertake public enterprises, and before 1801 had expended funds for forts and

507

the frontiers. With a small standing army and the state militia, this task was performed tolerably well. Finally they endeavored to keep the country out of foreign war, and although twice on the edge of hostilities, they succeeded. On the issue of peace and war, however, the country was so deeply involved—financially and otherwise—that programs of internal improvement were paralyzed. The Federalists planned more than they could bring to pass.

To attain these great objectives the Federalists were led to advocate certain definite ideas about the role of government in the economic life of the community, the predominance of the nation over the states, executive leadership and administrative energy, the nature of executive power, and the quality of the public service. These views identified them as a group and separated them from others who rallied around Jefferson, Gallatin, and their friends to form an active and powerful opposition. The leaders of both parties looked far ahead. They were fighting to control the future pattern of economic life, of governmental organization, and, as the Jeffersonians believed, of human liberty.

THE ROLE AND STRUCTURE OF GOVERNMENT

The Federalist concept of public administration was firmly based on a political theory which, although antimonarchical, was not warmly democratic. Federalists accepted the philosophy of government for the people, but not government by the people. In their view, government could only be well conducted if it was in the hands of the superior part of mankind—superior in education, in economic standing, and in native ability.

The Federalist view of government and public administration was most systematically set forth by Hamilton in the *Federalist Papers*, and by Washington and Hamilton in their letters and public documents. It was also implicit in the writings of John Adams, Oliver Wolcott, and Timothy Pickering, and in the speeches of statesmen such as Ames, William Smith, Boudinot, and Harper in the House, King, Ellsworth, and Cabot in the Senate. All these men shared the same general point of view, reflecting the interests and ideals of the commercial world of their time.

---

arsenals, warships and cutters, lighthouses and beacons, piers for commercial use, hospitals, storehouses, Indian trading houses, post coaches, office buildings in Washington, and tracts of land bearing live oak suitable for naval construction.

The Federalists were not prepared to leave the development of the country to chance, nor did they want to perpetuate the dominant agricultural type of economy which had prevailed in the colonies. They thought it a duty of government to decide on the kind of a society that should be preferred, and then to guide human energy in that direction. The type of public economy which seemed to them prudent was a balanced agricultural-manufacturing-trading society with a solid financial foundation. Since agriculture was well established and sea-borne commerce was well protected by the tariff and navigation laws, they pushed hard to encourage manufactures. Time and circumstances were against them.

The Federalists clearly understood that their program of governmental action to foster a balanced economy could not be achieved by thirteen independent states. A single direction of an integrated policy was essential, so far as the Constitution permitted. They consequently became the supporters of the general government and of a liberal interpretation of its powers. As they shaped the governmental and administrative structure in 1789 and 1790, they took care to provide leadership in national rather than state agencies at the crucial points. On the other hand, Americans who preferred the agricultural economy which had prevailed for over a century and a half needed little governmental aid, and feared that a strong government might endanger their liberty. They therefore tried to restrict the powers of the national government and to establish a federal organization that would depend upon the administrative agencies of the states.

As Robert Goodloe Harper left the national scene, he wrote on March 5, 1801, a letter to his constituents, "this last and concluding act of my public life," stating the political principles and system of the Federalists.[2] In this able and at times moving document, Harper declared, "the federalists considered it as a principle of the utmost importance for the preservation of the federal government, to render it as independent as possible of state influence; to give it a movement of its own, and complete power to enforce its own laws; to resist state encroachments; and to restrain the state governments within their just and proper bounds."[3]

The Federalists were steady supporters of a strong executive branch,

---

[2] *Select Works of Robert Goodloe Harper,* pp. 324–50.
[3] *Ibid.,* p. 332.

believing it essential to the vigor of government and fearing it would be overborne by Congress. "If we are not sound and able in the executive, our chance of an orderly government, that can protect the liberties of the citizens, will be desperate," wrote Christopher Gore.[4] These views were repeated by Harper in his summary of Federalist principles and achievements: "As to the federal government itself, their second great maxim was to support the executive power, against the encroachments of ambition and the superior strength of the popular branch."[5] Oliver Wolcott's father wrote him in 1794 that men of information in Connecticut never rated Congress so low as then and wished "not to see the least cession" of the President's constitutional powers.[6]

With these ideas, the Federalists were not content to leave Congress to find its own way either in great matters of state or in such relatively lesser matters as the organization of the public service. The department heads not only responded to congressional requests for plans and proposals but fought to retain the initiative. So far as personalities were concerned, this meant the decline of Madison and the rise of Alexander Hamilton. Within two years the relations of these collaborators in writing *The Federalist* were broken irrevocably.

The Federalist preference for the executive branch was a faithful reflection of their distrust of the people. An intelligent perception of sound public policy, in their view, could come only from well-educated men of affairs, men with trained minds and broad experience—in short from the upper classes. Decisions on programs thought out by these national leaders might be subject to the vote of popular assemblies, but the latter, in the opinion of the Federalists, had neither the capacity, nor the unity, to work out the plans themselves.

The Federalists did not fear executive power. To the contrary, they had a deep fear of governmental impotence. The interests which they cherished had suffered deeply from the lack of a government which could govern, and the need for power was not subject to debate. The Federalists were not, however, in favor of irresponsible power; they did not propose an American copy of an arbitrary king from whose control they had recently won independence.

The Federalist philosopher on the role of power was Alexander

---

[4] King, *Correspondence,* II, 31.
[5] Harper, *op. cit.,* p. 333.
[6] Gibbs, *Memoirs,* I, 132.

Hamilton. His theoretical views were cogently set out in the *Federalist Papers,* and his practical applications in the management of the Treasury. In number 70 of *The Federalist* he praised energy as the leading feature of good government and declared that all men of sense must agree in the necessity of an energetic executive. Although he also advocated a due dependence on the people and a due responsibility, his emphasis was on action—and decisive action. "Whenever the government appears in arms, it ought to appear like a *Hercules,* and inspire respect by the display of strength," he wrote to McHenry. "The consideration of expense is of no moment compared with the advantages of energy." [7]

Hamilton was only the most precise of the Federalist exponents of executive power and energy. Harper told his constituents as he bade them farewell; "To enforce the execution of the laws with vigour, and yet with mildness, was also a principle adopted and pursued by the federalists: for they knew that force displayed in due season, and with energy and promptness, will often put an end to opposition, and preclude the necessity of rigour. When you are known to be strong you may pardon; if thought to be weak you are compelled to punish." [8]

The sense of power eventually overreached the Federalists, however, and helped to cause their downfall. Faced with a "fifth column" in the shape of numerous Frenchmen, many actively combating the Federalist foreign policy, in 1798 Congress passed the Alien and Sedition Acts. The former caused little commotion except that created by departing French agitators. The latter was directed against citizens, and, although enforced on the whole with discretion, caused a popular revulsion. The terms of the Sedition Act were certainly severe. They forbade writing or speaking with intent to defame the government, Congress, or the President, or to bring any of them into disrepute, or to excite against them the hatred of the "good people" of the United States. The Republicans saw in these measures the "racks and thumbscrews of a political inquisition." Good Federalists like Harrison Gray Otis defended them to the end; but they helped materially to end the Federalists.

Many substantial contributions to American government were achieved before leadership passed from the Federalists. They spelled

---

[7] Hamilton, *Works* (Hamilton ed.), V, 235–36.
[8] Harper, *op. cit.,* p. 338.

out the scanty sections of the Constitution and created from almost nothing an administrative system. Their handiwork included:

1. The establishment of an independent chief executive vested with substantially all administrative authority and responsible for the conduct of the official business of the new government.

2. The working out of relations between the executive branch and Congress which left substantial freedom of action to high officials and kept Congress out of most administrative details, but which recognized the responsibility of the executive to the legislative branch.

3. The effective delegation of authority by the President to heads of departments and by them to their immediate subordinates and representatives in the field, while at the same time retaining controls over performance.

4. The creation of an administrative organization separate from and independent of the states, complete in itself, but with acceptance of state agencies for federal business in certain cases; and the beginning of cooperation between the two sets of officials.

5. Orderly and stable relationships among officials, based on law, instructions, and precedents.

6. The formation of a fiscal system that ensured the proper use of and accounting for public funds.

7. The maintenance of good standards, especially canons of integrity and levels of competence.

8. The acceptance of responsibility by the dominant party to determine the policy of government and to conduct the administration of its affairs.

9. The approval of the right of public criticism of policy and administration, marred by the passage of the Sedition Act.

10. The recognition of the claims of locality in the sense of preference for local and state residents for federal offices with local and state jurisdictions.

11. The recognition of the moral authority of the general government, a victory won by the character of Washington, the integrity of the public services, and the decisiveness with which the challenge to federal authority in western Pennsylvania was met.

SUCCESS AND FAILURE

The Federalists could not escape the necessity of organizing the new government. They did it well. For twelve years they had the responsibility of managing national affairs. Here they had both impressive success and relative failure. Their ideals, combined with an intuitive grasp of the administrative art, marked them as fit for their duties. They set new levels of achievement before a people still close to colonial dependence.

Washington and his assistants had a keen sense of good organization. They gathered all the activities of government into three departments so that nothing was left at loose ends. They insisted that single officials bear the responsibility for administration rather than boards. They provided everywhere for due subordination and for authority commensurate with responsibility. They valued competence at all levels. They were alert to the importance of a favorable public opinion. The principal officials were conscientious and hard-working.

It is not difficult, nevertheless, to find examples of tasks that were bungled. The Post Office was slow and unreliable and its direction was unimaginative. The purchase of army supplies was badly done whether by the Treasury or by the War Department. The Mint was such a disappointment that Congress nearly abolished it, and left it, a humiliated orphan, in Philadelphia when every one else went off to Washington. The building of the new capital was a succession of troubles, mostly plain deficiencies in administration.

Particular matters often dragged interminably. The granting of patents by the original ex officio board (Secretaries of State, War, and the Attorney General) was attended with "great delay and expense"; inventors had to wait until the department heads could find leisure from the special duties of their offices. The erection of an arsenal at the mouth of the Shenandoah was so *shamefully* neglected" that Washington suspected deliberate sabotage of his directions.[9] Delay in beginning the construction of a frigate for the Dey of Algiers forced him to write a sharp letter to the Secretary of War.[10] The Attorney General left the seat of government with all his official papers locked up in his house, where they could not be reached; business stopped until he chose to return.[11] Our minister at London wrote to the State Department in a cipher of which there was no copy in Philadelphia; the message was completely unintelligible.[12] A whole section of an act

[9] Washington to Tobias Lear, Feb. 15, 1796, Washington, *Writings,* XXXIV, 465.
[10] July 13, 1796, *ibid.,* XXXV, 136.
[11] Pickering to John Davis, Oct. 5, 1797, Pickering Papers, VII, 262.
[12] Washington to the Acting Secretary of State, Oct. 12, 1795, Washington, *Writings,* XXXIV, 336.

for the relief of seamen was omitted in copying and the act was un-
wittingly approved in this form by Washington, much to his annoyance.[13] Such errors and omissions are bound to occur in any organization, and the Federalists had their share.

The moral standards of the Federalist public service were extraordinarily high—higher by far than those prevailing in the British public
service or the French and approaching the austerity of the administrative system perfected by Frederick the Great in Prussia. The sale of
office was unknown and would have been intolerable. Fraud in the
financial transactions of the general government could not be discovered even in repeated investigations by Hamilton's opponents.
The number of revenue officers who had to be removed for delinquency
was exceedingly small. Probably never in the history of the United
States has the standard of integrity of the federal civil service been at
a higher level, even though the Federalists were sometimes unable to
maintain their ideals.

The public standing of the civil service was also high. Washington
insisted that everyone who held a federal post should have the confidence of the community in which he lived. Men who had been rejected for local office by their neighbors were under a heavy handicap;
men whose character was open to doubt were never knowingly appointed. The Federalists took for granted permanence of tenure and
were sensitive to the claims of officeholders except where they proved
untrustworthy. They believed that only by a good public service
could the interests of the mercantile classes be properly served; and to
these interests they were well attuned. The country, as well as the
merchants, was well served by its officials.

The literary standards of the public service were notably good. The
public documents and reports coming from the pens of Hamilton
and Jefferson were models of clarity and incisiveness. Washington's
public papers, to which a number of his advisers contributed, were
restrained and correct; despite his addiction to the involved construction which was the style of the time, he was never confused and at
times was genuinely eloquent. The letters of Pickering and Wolcott,
Jay and King, Ellsworth and Adams were of a high order of literary
merit. John Adams was a political scientist of repute; Freneau was a

[13] Washington to the Secretary of the Treasury, July 4, 1796, *ibid.,* XXXV, 116.

poet of distinction, although not for long a government clerk; the letters from collectors of customs were usually admirably composed. The federal officeholders were a literate tribe.

But these eminent qualities of character and taste did not merge automatically into an effective administrative organization. Talents of another order were also required. In different combinations, Washington and Hamilton possessed these qualities to an eminent degree. The administrative record of the Federalists was superlative at its best, but its best was concentrated in the Treasury Department. Elsewhere the record corresponds more closely to the national levels of management skill that a relatively unadministered society could provide.

The customs service under Hamilton was the best example of the administrative ideal of the Federalist party. The new government started with an old tradition of tax evasion. Washington and Hamilton agreed on the necessity of setting a better administrative pattern quickly and firmly. Not only was the need for revenue pressing; the need to fix the temper of the new government in the mind of the people was even more urgent. Hamilton directed the collectors to start suit on delinquent importers' bonds the very day they became overdue. He exacted a weekly report of collections and regular settlements with the Treasury. Without hesitation he removed an occasional delinquent or dilatory collector. He sharply reprimanded one who had initiated an unauthorized expenditure for a local customs building. He denied the collectors any right to make their own interpretations of the revenue laws, and required all of them to observe the interpretations which came in a steady stream from his pen. At the same time he enjoined strict fairness and impartiality toward all importers and shipowners, encouraged the collectors by commendation, and sought to improve their scales of pay. The early customs service was in a special sense the shadow of a man.

With the proper pride of those who believed they had builded well, the Federalists looked with anxious concern upon the fate of their handiwork as the day approached for Jefferson to enter the White House. The more extreme partisans predicted calamity and the subversion of all they had wrought. But others spoke in more hopeful terms.

Thus Harper wrote, "the men who have hitherto conducted the affairs of this government, have left an easy task to their successors. Every thing has been done to their hands. . . . All that is required of them is to preserve things in their present state, to keep up the fences which have been made on the farm, to prevent the buildings which have been erected from falling down through want of repair, to keep the fields from being over-run by briars and weeds." [14] "Should Mr. Jefferson conduct the government on rational principles, and with steadiness vigour and prudence, his elevation will prove a public blessing." [15] And from far across the seas, with the perspective of distance and with a serene mind, Rufus King had said, before the event was certain:

But I have no notion that our Government, or the security of our property can or will be, in any material degree, affected by any changes that have happened or that in my opinion are likely to happen. I should be sorry for the important change that you mention but which I do not think will take place; should your conjecture however prove true it would doubtless be followed by the removal of several persons whose continuance in office might be agreeable to the impartial public as well as themselves, and likewise by variations more or less considerable in the measures of administration. But I should not from thence conclude that the Government was lost, that the public faith and character were destroyed, and that property would be thrown off its foundation. . . . Presidents, Secretaries, Generals and Ministers—myself among them—may be removed, still the machine will move on! . . .[16]

King's words were prophetic. Under different leadership the machinery of government did move forward without a break. The Federalists were never again to resume national power. Still they might have recalled in after years, even if with melancholy satisfaction, the words of their leader, Alexander Hamilton, addressed to King: "I anticipate with you that this country will, erelong, assume an attitude correspondent with its great destinies—majestic, efficient, and operative of great things. A noble career lies before it."

---

[14] Harper, *op. cit.*, p. 349.
[15] *Ibid.*, pp. 324–25.
[16] King, *Correspondence*, III, 269.

Appendix I

PRINCIPAL EXECUTIVE OFFICERS, 1789–1801

Office	Incumbent	Term of Office	Notes
President	George Washington	April 30, 1789–March 3, 1797	
	John Adams	March 4, 1797–March 3, 1801	
Vice President	John Adams	April 30, 1789–March 3, 1797	
	Thomas Jefferson	March 4, 1797–March 3, 1801	
Secretary of State	Thomas Jefferson	March 22, 1790–December 31, 1793	Commissioned Secretary of State, September 26, 1789; assumed office March 22, 1790; John Jay acting *ad interim*
	Edmund Randolph	January 2, 1794–August 20, 1795	Acting Secretary of State from August 20 until commissioned, December 10, 1795
	Timothy Pickering	August 20, 1795–May 12, 1800	
	Charles Lee	May 13, 1800–June 6, 1800	Acting *ad interim*
	John Marshall	June 6, 1800–March 4, 1801	Commissioned Secretary of State, May 13, 1800; assumed office June 6; commissioned Chief Justice, January 31, 1801
Secretary of the Treasury	Alexander Hamilton	September 11, 1789–January 31, 1795	
	Oliver Wolcott, Jr.	February 2, 1795–December 31, 1800	
	Samuel Dexter	January 1, 1801—May 6, 1801	
Secretary of War	Henry Knox	September 12, 1789–December 31, 1794	
	Timothy Pickering	January 2, 1795–February 5, 1796	
	James McHenry	February 6, 1796–May 31, 1800	Commissioned Secretary of War, January 27, 1796; assumed office February 6

Appendix I

(Continued)

Office	Incumbent	Term of Office	Notes
Secretary of War	Benjamin Stoddert	June 1, 1800–June 12, 1800	Acting *ad interim*
	Samuel Dexter	June 12, 1800–March 3, 1801	Commissioned Secretary of War, May 13, 1800, assumed office June 12; commissioned Secretary of the Treasury, January 1, 1801, and headed both departments for two months
Attorney General	Edmund Randolph	February 2, 1790–January 2, 1794	Commissioned September 26, 1789; assumed office February 2, 1790
	William Bradford	January 27, 1794–August 23, 1795	
	Charles Lee	December 10, 1795–March 3, 1801	No incumbent from death of Bradford to appointment of Lee
Postmaster General	Samuel Osgood	September 26, 1789–August 19, 1791	
	Timothy Pickering	August 19, 1791–January 2, 1795	Commissioned August 12, 1791; assumed office August 19
	Joseph Habersham	February 25, 1795–November 2, 1801	
Secretary of the Navy	Benjamin Stoddert	June 18, 1798–March 31, 1801	Commissioned May 21, 1798; assumed office June 18, 1798

518

Appendix II

Principal Public Functions under the Federalists

Function or Activity	Agency	Date of Origin	Citation
Conduct of foreign affairs	State Department	1789	1 Stat. 28
Collection of customs revenue	Treasury Department	1789	1 Stat. 29
Collection of tonnage dues	Treasury Department	1789	1 Stat. 29
Settlement of accounts between states and United States	Board of Commissioners	1789	1 Stat. 49
Organization and management of army	War Department	1789	1 Stat. 49
Government of Northwest Territory	Territorial Governor	1789	1 Stat. 50
Establishment of lighthouses, beacons, buoys, and public piers	Treasury Department	1789	1 Stat. 53
Negotiations with Indians	Commissioners (*ad hoc*)	1789	1 Stat. 54
Registration and clearance of vessels	Treasury Department	1789	1 Stat. 55
Conduct of fiscal affairs	Treasury Department	1789	1 Stat. 65
Safekeeping of acts, records, and seal of the United States	State Department	1789	1 Stat. 68
Carrying of mails	Post Office	1789	1 Stat. 70
Conduct of judicial business	Courts	1789	1 Stat. 73
Prosecution of suits	Attorney General and District Attorneys	1789	1 Stat. 73
Legal advice to President and heads of departments	Attorney General	1789	1 Stat. 73
Payment of pensions to disabled veterans	War Department	1789	1 Stat. 95
Custody of prisoners	State Governments	1789	1 Stat. 96
Taking of census	Marshals	1790	1 Stat. 101
Naturalization of citizens	State or Federal Courts	1790	1 Stat. 103
Supporting state inspection laws	Treasury Department	1790	1 Stat. 106
Grant of patent	Ex officio Board (Secretaries of State and War and Attorney General)	1790	1 Stat. 109
Government of territory south of the Ohio River	Territorial Governor	1790	1 Stat. 123
Grant of copyright	Clerk of District Court	1790	1 Stat. 124
Purchase of land and construction of buildings in national capital	Commissioners	1790	1 Stat. 130
Regulation of seamen	Admiralty Courts and Justices of the Peace	1790	1 Stat. 131

519

Appendix II

(Continued)

Function or Activity	Agency	Date of Origin	Citation
Regulation of trade with Indians	War Department (Superintendents of Indian Affairs)	1790	1 Stat. 137
Payment of debt of United States, and assumption of state debts	Treasury Department and Commissioners	1790	1 Stat. 138
Grant of land to veterans	War Department	1790	1 Stat. 182
Survey of lands in western territory	Treasury Department	1790	1 Stat. 187
Supervision of Bank of United States	Treasury Department	1791	1 Stat. 191
Collection of excise taxes	Treasury Department	1791	1 Stat. 199
Grant of bounties on fish	Treasury Department	1792	1 Stat. 229
Coinage of money	Mint	1792	1 Stat. 246
Regulating militia	War Department	1792	1 Stat. 271
Purchase of debt of United States	Sinking Fund Commission (President of Senate, Chief Justice, Secretaries of State and Treasury, and Attorney General)	1792	1 Stat. 281
Fortification of ports and harbors	President	1794	1 Stat. 345
Provision and use of naval vessels	President	1794	1 Stat. 350
Provision of arsenals	War Department	1794	1 Stat. 352
Embargo on exportation of arms and ammunition	Treasury Department	1794	1 Stat. 369
Laying, regulation, and revoking of embargoes	President	1794	1 Stat. 372
Purchase of public supplies	Treasury Department (Purveyor of Public Supplies)	1795	1 Stat. 419
Sale of lands in Northwest Territory	Treasury Department	1796	1 Stat. 464
Aid in execution of state quarantine laws	Treasury Department	1796	1 Stat. 474
Aid to impressed seamen	President (Agents)	1796	1 Stat. 477
Grant of passports to American vessels	State Department	1796	1 Stat. 489
Settlement of claims with Great Britain	Attorney General (Claims Agent)	1797	1 Stat. 523
Management of naval affairs	Navy Department	1798	1 Stat. 553

Appendix II

(Continued)

Function or Activity	Agency	Date of Origin	Citation
Manufacture of cannon, arms, ammunition	President (War Department)	1798	1 Stat. 555
Regulation of aliens	President	1798	1 Stat. 570
Regulation of alien enemies	President (Marshals)	1798	1 Stat. 577
Valuation of lands and enumeration of slaves	Commissioners	1798	1 Stat. 580
Establishment of a marine corps	Navy Department	1798	1 Stat. 594
Relief of sick and disabled seamen in marine hospitals	Treasury Department	1798	1 Stat. 605
Erection of docks for repairing public ships	President (Navy Department)	1799	1 Stat. 622
Purchase of timber or timber lands	President (Navy Department)	1799	1 Stat. 622
Examination of hospital personnel	War Department (Medical Board)	1799	1 Stat. 721
Medical service for army and navy personnel	Medical Establishment	1799	1 Stat. 721
Discharging debts of bankrupts	District Courts	1800	2 Stat. 19
Selling stamps for revenue	Treasury Department (General Stamp Office)	1800	2 Stat. 40
Sale of lands obtained by United States in civil cases	Marshals	1800	2 Stat. 61

INDEX

Absences from office, of Washington, 42; of John Adams, 42–43, 241; of Charles Lee, 165; of territorial officers, 370–72

Accountant, departmental, duties and responsibility, 338–40, 343–44

Accounts, form of, 338

Adams, Abigail, influence on appointments, 273 n

Adams, John, on Washington's retirement, 10; on a divided executive, 29; on the Treasury, 30; and press of business, 32; and Cabinet, 41 ff.; absences from seat of government, 42–43 and footnotes; consultation with Cabinet, 43; on President and Cabinet, 44; on legislative and executive powers, 51; executive leadership, 59; and appointments, 85–86; on Senate confirmation of appointments, 82–83; on executive power, 92–93; on diplomatic discretion, 130; on Rittenhouse, 143; attitude toward Hamilton, 240, 243 n; absences, 241; transacts business by post, 241; first mission to France, 242 ff.; and Hamilton's military rank, 244 ff.; appoints staff officers, 245; on relations to Cabinet, 248, 250 ff.; on vice-presidency, 265; on nepotism, 267, 278–80; on merit, 267; on partisanship, 272; on Jacobins under Washington, 273; on partisanship as a test for office-holding, 273, 274; and Col. William S. Smith, 279–80; and Joshua Johnson, 280; on removal of Gardner and Whipple, 288; removes Tench Coxe, 289; on salaries, 294 n; on estimates, 324; on duties of War Department accountant, 339; on federal-state relations, 387; urges prosecution under Seditions Act, 408; pardons Fries, 423; Scotchler, 446; declines house built by Pennsylvania, 491; on naval library, 504; and an official gazette, 506

Adams, John and Alexander Hamilton, see Hamilton–Adams conflict

Adams, John Quincy, 265; on nepotism, 278

Administration, and the Constitution, 15–16; defined by Hamilton, 28; see also public administration

Administrative art, and rural life, 467; and the British tradition, 468–69; and colonial experience, 470–71; and business experience, 471–73; and army experience, 473–74; and the administrative skills, 474–76; and the literature of public administration, 477–78

Administrative housekeeping, offices, 489–94; letter writing, 494–500; public papers, 500–4; libraries, departmental, 504–5; public printing, 505–6

Administrative powers, in customs, 435–36; in excise, 436; in registration of vessels, 436–39; in clearance of vessels, 439–40

Administrative review, 455–56

Administrative rules, Giles on, 53

Administrators, sketches of, Oliver Wolcott, 123–25; Alexander Hamilton, 125–27; David Rittenhouse, 142–43; Thomas Jefferson, 143–44; Henry Knox, 152–53; James McHenry, 153–54; Benjamin Stoddert, 162–63; Edmund Randolph, 169–71; Sebastian Bauman, 181–82; Levi Pease, 185–86; Joseph Habersham, 193–94; Timothy Pickering, 194–98; William S. Smith, 278–80; Tench Coxe, 288–90; Benjamin Lincoln, 304–5; John Lamb, 305; Jeremiah Olney, 305–8; John Steele, 308–9; Joseph Nourse, 309; Thomas Hutchins, 383–84; Rufus Putnam, 385–86; William Rawle, 409–10; Pierpont Edwards, 410; see also clerks

Advances of funds, 338, 343; to navy agent, 341; to Dayton, Speaker of the House, 346

Aliens, required to register, 440; control over, 440–41

528   INDEX

INDEX

529

Hamilton–Jefferson conflict (*Cont.*):
ton, 228–29; statement of Jefferson's charges, 228–29; attack in the press, 229–30, 231; succession to the presidency, 230–31; Washington intervenes, 232–34; resignations, 234–36

Hamilton, John, asks for office, 269

Hammond, George, communicates with Hamilton, 213

Hamtramck, Major John F., on Indians, 375

Hancock, John, and George Washington, 108; and smuggling, 460–61

Handwriting, Adams on, 32

Harison, Richard, 407

Harper, Robert Goodloe, on Washington, 11; on unity in the Cabinet, 47; on Jefferson, 143; on Navy Department, 157; on salaries, 292; on officeholding, 317; on central purchasing, 362; on Federalist policy, 509, 511, 515–16

Hawkins, Col. Benjamin, on civil-military relations, 151–52; superintendent of Indians, 377

Haywood, John, on unity in the Cabinet, 48 n

Hayburn's Case, 168

Hazard, Ebenezer, on congressional investigations, 81 n; Postmaster General, 193

Henry, Patrick, on excessive ceremony, 109; offered State Department, 264

Higginson, Stephen, quoted, 4; on public relations, 88; adviser on Navy, 160–61; on Hamilton's control of customs, 208; asks for appointment, 269; on partisanship, 275 n; on removal of Gardner and Whipple, 288

Home Department, proposed by Vining, 132

Hoomes, John, post office contractor, 183, 184, 185

Hopkinson, Joseph, on Wolcott, 125

Hours of work, in post office, 190; of clerks, 311; Dennie on, 315

House of Representatives, and heads of departments, 67 ff.; on references to heads of departments, 68 ff.; and finance, 71–74; and administration, 77 ff.; and power to call for papers, 80 ff.; and power to investigate, 80 ff.; and appointing power, 84 ff.; investigates Hamilton's

House of Representatives (*Cont.*):
debt operations, 352–54; Committee on Claims, 355–56; shorthand reporting of debates, 499–500

Howard, John E., 264

Huger, Isaac, 415

Humphreys, David, 265

Humphreys, Joshua, naval constructor, 159

Huntington, Benjamin, on customs collection, 392

Hutchins, Thomas, geographer of the United States, 383–84

Impeachment, 15

Impressment, 134–35

Importers, and collectors of customs, 305 ff.

Incentives, for official performance of duty, 428–29

Indians, subject to War Department, 146; Henry Knox on, 374; St. Clair on, 375; Hamtramck on, 375; administrative responsibility for, 375–80; presents to, 377–78; regulation of Indian trade, 380–81; protection of Indian lands, 381–82

Informers, use of, 415–16; rewards to, 416; procedure, 416

Inspection, of deputy postmasters, 180; of goods on ships, 435; of ship's papers, 438

Instructions, 132; Adams on, 130; Jefferson to Randolph, 167 n; in management of debt, 353–54; in territorial government, 369, 378–79

Intent to defraud, discretion in determining, 453–54

Interdepartmental relations, 210 ff.; War and Navy, 324

Interdepartmental services, 211–12

Internal revenue service, established, 200

Investigation, power of, 80–81

Irvine, William, commissioner to settle accounts with states, 350, 421

Itemization of appropriations, 328 ff.

Izard, Ralph, 57

Jackson, Andrew, attorney, Southwest Territory, 372

Jackson, James, on removal power, 22; on legislative-executive relations, 67

Jackson, Jonathan, marshal, 414–15

Jay, John, quoted, 14; Secretary of Foreign